THE
POETIC HOME

DESIGNING THE 19th-CENTURY DOMESTIC INTERIOR

Fire Places

Pl. 1.

Stefan Muthesius

THE
POETIC HOME

DESIGNING THE 19th-CENTURY DOMESTIC INTERIOR

with 396 illustrations, 120 in color

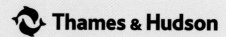
Thames & Hudson

For Kasia

on the half-title page Charles James Richardson,
'various articles of furniture' from the Great
Exhibition, London, 1851.

on the title page Details of fireplaces from
16th- and 17th-century houses in London and
Norwich, illustrated by Charles James Richardson,
1840 (see p. 214).

*opposite Consult me … on household management …
I will tell you how to wash, get up linen, polish furniture –
to keep the house clean and sweet, to beautify the person.*
Frontispiece of an anonymous English household
book of 1866.

overleaf A 19th-century view of 18th-century
restraint: the Petit Trianon, Versailles, from Henry
Havard's *Dictionnaire de l'ameublement et de la décoration
depuis le XIIIe siècle* (1887–89) (see p. 284).

First published in 2009 in hardcover in the United States of America by Thames & Hudson Inc.,
500 Fifth Avenue, New York, New York 10110

thamesandhudsonusa.com

Library of Congress Catalog Card Number 2007910202

ISBN 978-0-500-51419-1

Printed and bound in China by C&C Offset Printing Co. Ltd

Contents

Acknowledgments

I am greatly indebted to the University of East Anglia for its continuous research support and in particular to the successive deans of the School of World Art Studies – Richard Cocke, Ludmilla Jordanova, Sandy Heslop and Simon Dell – and to my other colleagues of long standing – Jane Beckett, Joanne Clarke, Alastair Grieve, Ferdinand de Jong, John Mack, John Mitchell, John Onians, Margit Thøfner and David Thomson. My thanks also go to the School's reprographers: Michael Brandon-Jones, Maxine Adcock, Marjorie Rhodes, and most especially to Nick Warr, for his continuous patient help with all computer work, as well as to Gyöngyvér Horvath and Beverley Youngman.

I am much indebted to the Centre for the Study of the Domestic Interior of the Royal College of Art/Victoria & Albert Museum, London (until 2006), and its director, Jeremy Aynsley; to the Zentralinstitut für Kunstgeschichte in Munich, its director, Wolf Tegethoff, and his colleagues Peter Diemer and Christoph Hölz (now Innsbruck), for support; and to Wolfgang Brönner (Mainz), for stimulating discussions. Jean-Michel Leniaud greatly facilitated my contacts in France, Vivian Constantinopoulos, Philippa Hurd and Sally Salvesen provided early encouragement. It took the superb team at Thames & Hudson to knock it all into final shape.

I also wish to thank Anne Anderson, Robert Bage, Arnold Bartetzky, Barry Bergdoll, Dominique Blaser, Hans-Olof Boström, Elisabeth de Bièvre, Paul Bissegger, Adrian von Buttlar, Louise Campbell, Deborah Cohen, Alan Crawford, Elisabeth Crettaz-Stürzel, David Crowley, Sophie De Caigny, Jan De Maeyer, Anne Dion-Tenenbaum, Janusz Dobesz, Martina Droth, Ian Dungavell, Steven van Dyck, Jens Christian Eldal, Sigrid Epp, Thomas Eser, Daphne Fordham, Gunilla Frick, Brigitte Gedon, E. Gerum, Marc Girouard, Inger Johanne Glasø Røkke, Miles Glendinning, Anna Green, Heidi Grieve, Géza Hajos, Tanya Harrod, Wolfgang Hase, Uta Hassler, Mircea Hortopan, Ken Ireland, Teresa Jabłońska, Alena Janatková, Shona Kallestrup, N. Kardinar, Pat Kirkham, Gabriele Klempert, Michael Koch, Hans-Curt Köster, Stéphane Laurent, Sophie le Couedic, Cecilia Lengefeld, Sarah Lichtman, Robin Lucas, John Maciuka, Peter Mandler, Sergiusz Michalski, Benoît Mihaïl, Józef Mrozek, Manfred Mückstein, Michael Müller, Michał Murawski, Bianca Muthesius, Gillian Naylor, Eva Ottillinger, E. Palmér, Carmen Popescu, Anders Poulsen, Helmut Proff, Jacek Purchla, Mara Reissberger, Charles Rice, Eva Riemann, Julia Rosenbaum, Joseph Rykwert, Andrew Saint, Gabriele Schickel, Michael Schlaefer, W. G. Sebald, József Sisa, Penny Sparke, Stephan Strauss, John Styles, Andrzej Szczerski, Alice Thomine, Paul Thompson, Leslie Topp, Dell Upton, Irène Vogel-Chevrolet, Jindřich Vybíral, Clive Wainwright, Jane Wainwright, Chris Wakeling, Toshio Watanabe, Mark Westgarth, Sabine Wieber, Arthur Willis, Richard Wilson, Susan Wilson and many others.

The work for this book could not have been undertaken without the holdings of the British Library and the National Art Library (Victoria & Albert Museum, London). Of vital help were also the libraries of the Royal Institute of British Architects, London, and of the School of Architecture at Cambridge University (thanking Madeleine Brown), as well as Cambridge University Library; Bayerische Staatsbibliothek, Munich; Stadtbibliothek Trier; Kunstbibliothek Berlin; Deutsche Bibliothek in Frankfurt am Main; Zentralinstitut für Kunstgeschichte in Munich; Germanisches Nationalmuseum, Nuremberg (thanks to A. Kollinger, Erna White-Missbach); Kunsthistorisches Institut der Universität Bonn; Technische Universität Hannover; the Bibliothèque Fornay and the library of the Musée des Arts Décoratifs in Paris; Avery Library, Columbia University, New York; Winterthur Museum in Wilmington, Delaware; and the Rijksmuseum, Amsterdam. Other libraries were: Augsburg; Berlin (Staatliche Museen, Preussische Staatsbibliothek, Humboldt Universität, Technische Universität, Gründerzeit Museum Mahlsdorf); Braunschweig; Brussels (Bibliothèque Royale); Museumsdorf Cloppenburg; Cologne (Universität, Volkshochschule); Darmstadt; Detmold (Fachhochschule, thanks to Frau Lux); Dortmund (Museum für Kunst- und Kulturgeschichte); The Hague (Koninklijke Bibliotek); Innsbruck (Universität, Tiroler Volkskunstmseum); Kiel (Kunsthistorisches Seminar, Universität); Krakow (Instytut Sztuki, Jagiellonian University, thanks to A. Siemaszko); Leipzig (Grassimuseum, Herr Patzig; Deutsche Bibliothek, Universität); London (Courtauld Institute, Geffrye Museum, Institute of Germanic Studies, School of Slavonic and East European Studies, University of London Senate House, Warburg Institute); Mainz; Munich (Bayerisches Nationalmuseum, Haus der Bayerischen Geschichte, Ludwig-Maximilans-Universität and its Institut für Volkskunde, Technische Universität, Monacensia Bibliothek, Stadtmuseum [thanks to Norbert Götz]); New York (Cooper-Hewitt, National Design Museum, Metropolitan Museum, Public Library); Norwich (Public Library, Norwich School of Art [thanks to Kitty Guiver], Sainsbury Research Unit [thanks to Pat Hewitt]); Oxford (Bodleian, Sackler); Paris (Bibliothèque Nationale de France, Institut National de l'Histoire de l'Art [INHA], Musée Carnevalet); Salzburg (Museum, thanks to Dr Karl Ehrenfellner); Schwerin; Vienna (MAK); Warsaw (University, Instytut Sztuki PAN, Stowarzyszenie Historyków Sztuki [SHS]); and Washington (Library of Congress). The library of the University of East Anglia helped unfailingly.

Finally, I am much indebted to many for the hospitality of their comfortable homes: Bianca and Paul Lee, Elke and Peter Muthesius, Dorothea Muthesius and Manfred Mückstein, Jill and Bob Bage, Ursula and Jan Gehlsen, Gela Mangold, Heide and Massa Stärk, Elisabeth de Bièvre, and Kazimiera and Józef Zabroccy. Today's homes may differ considerably from the 19th-century ideal. But they can still serve as places of peace as well as of intellectual stimulation – provided, if one is lucky, by one's spouse or partner. For all this I am deeply thankful to my wife, Kasia Murawska-Muthesius.

Stefan Muthesius
Norwich, August 2008

Preface

The Poetic Home is devoted to the design and décor of the Western domestic interior from the 1800s to the mid-1890s, in all the trendsetting centres of Europe – France, England, the German-speaking countries, Belgium, the Netherlands and several others – as well as in the United States.

'Poetic home' was a 19th-century catchphrase that posed a new challenge for the designer: to create atmosphere and character in the ordinary living room. Until now, the interior furnishings of the 19th century have been explained in two ways: either by concentrating on the individual artefact – wallpapers, clocks, chairs or carpets – or by studying them all together under a succession of period headings, from Regency or Biedermeier, via historicism or Victorian, to Arts and Crafts and proto-Modern. More recently, scholars have traced some of the psychological, gender and social and economic meanings of these furnishings, but have thereby sidelined the visual aspects of design and craft, if not left them out altogether.

This book departs from these essentially 20th-century approaches. It concentrates on the design of the interior as a whole, and deals with what the designers, the makers and their spokespersons postulated themselves during the 19th century. They placed a new emphasis on the textural and colour effects of fabrics, wood or metal objects as attractive in themselves, and they evolved a new, more abstract terminology of form and colour, light and dark. A new notion of intense interiority had arisen, which stressed the 'mood' of each room. In addition,

M. H. Baillie Scott, design for a hall, 1895. This interior is marked by an intense 'medieval' fairytale atmosphere, and in this way sums up the efforts of many 19th-century artists and designers. Yet it also points forward to the 20th-century fascination with 'old Tudor beams'.

many designers joined in the fervent new concern for, and the construction of, nationalities or ethnicities and their bygone worlds. The style of a house or an interior should express an Old English, *Altdeutsch*, *Oud Hollandsch*, *ancien régime* or Old Colonial character. By the later 19th century, a poeticized ethnicity appeared the ultimate guarantee of comfort – a formula that has stayed alive ever since.

In order to communicate these heightened expectations to a rapidly widening audience, a whole new infrastructure was put into place: large-scale manufacture, meticulously organized shops, handbooks, journals, and a new understanding of the client's role – all of which employed a completely new verbal and visual language. A mass of illustrations became widely available for the first time. Essentially, this discourse is with us still, and most of us take it entirely for granted: we would all claim to know a good interior – a home that conveys atmosphere and character – when we see one, either in person or strikingly illustrated in a book or magazine. While some of the 19th century's beloved 'poetic' homes may now look a little faded, the way in which the design of a room was visualized and discussed in the 19th century still informs our understanding of the domestic interior today.

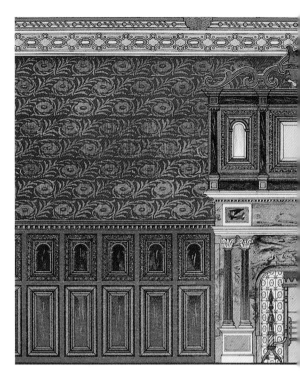

Sources and methods

For the history of art, design or material culture generally, the obvious source is the actual artefact. It is unfortunate, therefore, that few interiors of the kind explored here have been preserved, and that even fewer are easily accessible. Instead, the historian has to rely heavily on another source: illustrations. This poses fundamental problems, however, since there are always many different ways in which one can represent an artefact.

While it seems to go without saying that any image will show how an object is or was shaped, there have been disagreements regarding the most suitable kind of illustration for those considering the history of interior design. Mario Praz and Peter Thornton put together their exhaustive books – *An Illustrated History of Interior Decoration* (1964) and *Authentic Décor: The Domestic Interior 1620–1920* (1984), respectively – using exclusively old, 'original' pictures, but others have insisted on studying rooms in recent photographs wherever possible.[1] This book sides rather with Thornton, but it does not share his exclusive aim of establishing factual truth and documentary breadth.

Any illustration of an interior, whether an old view or a modern photograph, will also be an interpretation.[2] Moreover, modes of pictorial representation go through complex developments. It should be noted at the outset that early in the 19th century competent and attractive views of whole interiors were still very hard to obtain, while by the century's end the supply of striking images of very diverse kinds had vastly increased. Chapter II includes an overview of the development and the diversity of illustrations of the domestic interior. Furthermore, this book shows not only the 19th century's views of, or designs for, its interiors, but also many 19th-century images of older rooms, since these, in turn, throw light on the period's own preconceptions. There are, lastly, many purely imaginary views that served the newly developed theories of interior design, some of which even aimed to demonstrate how not to design a room.

Apart from images, this book relies heavily on texts. As with illustrations, one should be aware that it was only in the later 19th century that focused treatises on interior design – and a great number of them – appeared. The main rationale of this novel kind of book, as it is with today's primers on interior design, was to show, in non-technical language, how one could create unified furnishings and judge what was aesthetically good or bad. Like illustrations, all texts present facts, judgments and interpretations. While one may argue that the exterior of a building, or for that matter a piece of furniture, can be scientifically, concretely measured, and its data conveyed without images or even words, an interior,

A design for an interior demonstrating a diversity of materials, likely to have originated in many countries, if not continents. Drawing by John Dando Sedding, published by the decorating firm T. Knight & Son in 1880.

especially a living room, lacks any real solid existence and is without exact and permanent borders. Just as a long tradition in art and literature allows us to visualize and to interpret trees, fields and clouds together as a 'landscape', so the way in which walls, windows, chairs or cushions are painted, photographed or written about makes us see them as 'roomscapes', as 'interiors'. Any history of an artefact, and especially of such a complex one as the domestic interior, is thus both a history of its shaping and making, *and* a history of its interpretation – as a 'poetic' interior, for instance.

Much recent research on the history of the domestic interior undertaken in the areas of visual culture and material culture studies has also stressed the interpretative functions of 'representation'.[3] Furthermore, representation – in its broadest sense the creation of meaning – is closely allied to consumption: meaning is created by both producers and beholders. During the last forty or so years in the sphere of planning and design, interest has shifted from production, or from the designers' intentions, to the use or consumption of an object. It is held that there is a world of users that exists – has a right to exist – quite independently of the producers. Recent historians have employed a whole spectrum of new theories from a wide range of disciplines to investigate these 'users' – research that seemingly goes well beyond the immediate sphere of the domestic interior.[4]

The subject of the dwelling, which incorporates the 19th-century ideal of the home and its 20th-century progeny, 'interiority', is undoubtedly one of the most multifaceted topics in the humanities, reaching into a great diversity of disciplines. The focus of investigations has thus varied widely, from quite abstract analyses of the psyche or the society of the users, to the connoisseurs' description of material or visual detail, to the line taken by modernist art historians who construct a story of 19th-century design largely around the great artists and gurus of the British Arts and Crafts movement. Ideally, a multidisciplinary or interdisciplinary approach would synthesize a great number of factors and might even make a claim to a completeness of understanding. In practice, however, these methods often lead to the foregrounding of one or two disciplines at the expense of others. With regard to art, design and craft, one is often left with a lack of reflection. The connoisseurs' and collectors' approaches, as well as those of modernist art historians, take the concept of 'art' as read. The cultural theorist, on the other hand, is deeply suspicious of all art historical approaches. Art, artistic intention and creation are now widely seen as deeply problematic and, with the receiver or consumer occupying centre stage, the world of production is neglected. The term 'design' appears relegated to the collector's sphere. The art aspect is never completely excluded, however. In most analyses of the interior, it lives on, seemingly unchanged in its meaning, under the term 'aesthetic', or even under that age-old expression 'taste';[5] and it usually appears as a kind of appended element, or as one quasi-independent factor among many.

This book will once again foreground the terms 'art' and 'design'. It will thereby also shift the emphasis back to production and intention, including the devising of languages, modes of illustration and, to a somewhat lesser extent, the processes of manufacture. As has already been emphasized, this book's argument is based around the texts and images of the period. The emergence of great numbers of books and a huge mass of illustrations in the 19th century constitutes a major historical fact in itself. In addition, more recently formulated issues of psychology, anthropology, sociology, economics, consumption and gender studies, whether they concern production or consumption, will be discussed as and when they relate to design.

However, concentrating on the central 19th-century concerns of art and design does not mean taking them as absolutes. This book may be called a history of ideas and of artistic preferences, but it does not involve simply a citing of ideals, as so often was the case in earlier art histories of design and in all modernist hagiographies; rather, it is an analysis of the context in which pronouncements about art were uttered, different media were used and audiences were envisaged. The discussion of ideas will then focus on frequent changes of direction, fundamental disagreements and contradictions. The designer's intentions appeared crucial, but they were understood in widely different ways, ranging from a belief that art arises from the artist's deepest subjectivity, to demands that one should follow narrow sets of stylistic rules. There was likewise a vast and multifarious debate surrounding the meaning of art, in which some demanded art for its own sake (or 'form without content'), while others saw it as an instrument for the benefit of society. The domestic interior was a case in point: there was a new stress on purely visual effects – shapes, lighting, colours and textures – but also a deepening holistic sense of all cultural concepts being interconnected. All this was summed up in a demand for a psychologically, socially, artistically and even politically satisfying home. The main emphasis here is on the designers' vociferous claims for the beneficial effects of *their* work on all the uses of the home.

This account thus differs from many art historical or collector-oriented works on 19th-century design. The way in which artistic intention is mainly taken as generic, even as following the rules of fashion, means that the present book does not, yet again, deal principally with a small number of great independent originators. It also turns away from the well-rehearsed 20th-century narrative of a progression of styles from Regency to early modern. That grand narrative is crucial for understanding modernism from the 1890s to the 1950s, but it ought to be given a rest for the 19th century, just as today we would reject most of what the 19th century held to be true of its preceding periods.

Finally, the reader should bear in mind the circularity of all debates surrounding the methods of history writing. On the one hand, the historian chooses the facts, events, people and concepts of the past on which he or she will focus, and this, in turn, determines the choice of sources. On the other hand, it may be the kinds of sources that are most readily available that direct the historian's selection of a topic and the angle to be taken.

Scope

One particular aspect of consumers of the poetic home should be clear from the start: their economic status. The happy, ordinary home was, first and foremost, a vast project, a fervent hope of the 19th century. By the end of that period, most housing reformers were demanding a small detached house with a garden for the whole of the population, including all working-class families. Very few could yet afford such a dream, and a 'poetic' working-class home could hardly yet exist. On the other hand, within the context of this book, the terms 'ordinary' and 'everyday' also avoid a foregrounding of the highest levels of society, with their unlimited funds – outstandingly individualistic patrons of design such as King Ludwig II of Bavaria or the wealthiest of the American entrepreneurs – or wholly exceptional designers like William Burges. Neither should the patrons of the interiors shown within these pages be defined primarily as an 'elite', since this term covers a number of different groups: early in the century it would have meant the social elite, but later on would be synonymous with small groups of artists and critics.

The social elite comes up in Chapter III, while the design elite will dominate parts of Chapter V. Yet the chief figures of this book are not those who commission or create the most individualized interiors, but the wider band of producers and users of the well-appointed house. One can estimate (admittedly with some difficulty) that those who could afford to have at least one room fitted out professionally – that is to say, designed as a whole – amounted to 10 to 20 per cent of the population by the end of the 19th century.[6] The problems of labelling this income group as the bourgeoisie will be taken up in the Introduction. By the end of the century, some texts aimed their proposals also at smaller purses. But this growing rhetoric of modesty must be treated with caution. A case in point was the fashion for complete wooden

A 'wall decoration' designed by Professor Josef Storck, 1875. It exhibits tight stylistic control and symmetrical coordination, as demanded by the Vienna applied arts reformers.

panelling and ceilings, often meant to convey a low, even a peasant image, while in reality such fittings were usually rather expensive. On the other hand, with the cheapening of certain materials, techniques and colours it had become harder to tell the cheaper and the more costly furnishings apart.

It should be stressed at the outset that this book deals with interiors in both apartments and houses, and very rarely differentiates between them – hence the frequent use of the neutral but awkward and officious-sounding 'dwelling'.

The West

It remains to outline the book's geographical remit, since today globalization demands an ever greater geographical explicitness. What cannot be done here is to place the 'Western' interior in a context of world domestic interior design. Nothing will be said about any presumed 'poetic homes' elsewhere, except when the argument touches on the Western Orientalist notion of Eastern homes. Furthermore, for reasons of manageability, 'Western' here has been restricted largely to central and north-western European countries and to aspects of design in the United States.

Virtually all works on the history of the domestic interior so far have dealt with countries separately.[7] This book, however, holds that much common ground is shared by the whole of the West. A common European and world market for luxury goods had existed for several centuries, and certain commodities – such as tropical woods, for instance, or expensive colour substances – should be studied only in a Western or a global context. Furthermore, the Western world had also been relatively centralized for some centuries, in that one country,[8] France, had dominated in most matters relating to luxury fashions and décor. England grew gradually stronger throughout the 19th century and by the mid-1880s had eclipsed France in terms of international influence. By then, the United States had also quite suddenly begun to gain an international reputation. The German-speaking countries and regions, which had allied themselves to Western Europe in all matters of fashion and dwelling at least since the 18th century, chiefly formed a large internal market, and only occasionally succeeded in being noticed by the two dominant players. By about 1880, however, work from Vienna and Munich was seen as innovative in Northern and parts of Southern Europe.[9]

Although it cannot be assumed that everybody in the West knew what everybody else was doing, there was a widespread, albeit partial, knowledge of developments. Certainly, most top producers, their spokespersons and their patrons were also aware of some trends beyond their own borders. Thus the book mostly stresses what countries shared; attention is then given to situations in which one country served as a model for others; and lastly, some of the more obvious differences between countries are discussed. It has not, however, been possible to give a complete and systematic treatment to all geographical issues.

A new situation arose from the 1860s, when almost all European nations, as well as some regions such as New England, began to insist on their stylistic distinctiveness. Smaller countries, and even smaller regions, could now also make their mark. Paradoxically, even these movements – played out frequently at World Fairs – constitute an international phenomenon. By the later 1890s, it was fully accepted that all design (within the West, at least) was international in scope.[10]

Introduction

Modernity, Anti-Modernity, Comfort and Décor since 1800

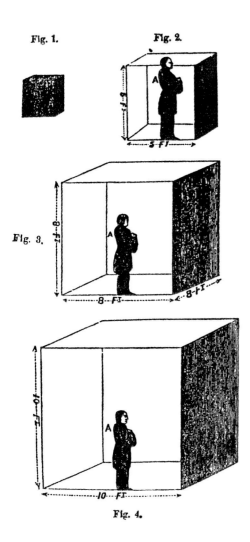

Fig. 1.   Fig. 2.

Fig. 3.

Fig. 4.

above Modern science and the dwelling: diagrams measuring breathing space. The small box top left represents the amount of air breathed by one person in an hour. From a report on New York's sanitary problems, 1865.

opposite A satirical peep into private worlds: this section through a Paris block of flats in 1852 reveals vast differences in class and lifestyle.

Modernity

'The improvements in comfort and convenience enjoyed in modern society …'[1] When one of Britain's most influential landscape designers, Humphry Repton, wrote these words in 1816, they probably sounded quite fresh. But before long, no statement on the subject of housing could have been more commonplace. The story of the dwelling over the last two hundred years has been one of constant advances in comfort and convenience – one may recall the great leap made in Europe in the decades following the Second World War. Probably the most decisive changes took place in the later 19th century. Virtually everyone in the major Western countries, at all levels except for the very highest and lowest, could – and did – move to a 'better', a more 'modern' dwelling. Broad expectations of comfort and convenience entertained in that period remained valid at least until the 1970s.

Of Repton's two terms, the second, 'convenience' (in the sense of the now old-fashioned term 'mod cons'), is taken entirely for granted in this book. The new and – to use a 20th-century modernist term – purely functional parts of the dwelling, such as the lavatory, the bathroom and the kitchen, are important here only in one sense: they serve as a backdrop against which the sphere of the living room is all the more clearly marked out. Another part of the house that first separated itself from the rest of the dwelling during the 19th century – the bedrooms – is likewise not dealt with here.[2]

'Comfort', however, can be understood as a much bigger concept, comprising both physical and psychological qualities (the latter will be of special interest in Chapter IV). Some of the most straightforward modern comforts were greater size and space, both outside and inside the dwelling: wide streets and tall ceilings ('high, free rooms'[3]). Although it was increasingly argued that the best kinds of dwelling were those situated in the country, or at least in the outer suburbs, such a view disregarded the fact that a 'modern apartment' (Henry Havard)[4] could equally be found in the inner areas of towns. A strong proviso has to be made, however, with regard to this new spaciousness: homes were usually far more crowded than they are today, since the average household was at least twice the size.[5]

One of the most deceptive terms of the 20th century was 'functionalism'. It implied that the types of buildings serving their practical function with the greatest precision were created by modernism, and that the 19th century did nothing more than decorate. In fact, it was during the 19th century that most of types of building common today were conceived; some, such as railway stations, served entirely new purposes, but radical changes also occurred in existing building types, such as hospitals or prisons. For the dwelling, too, entirely fresh plans were devised. Greater size and height of all rooms was one novel element, but the desire for more space was nothing new as such. The new principle of planning was, rather, the subdivision of functions. First, habitation had to be separated decisively from work and from communal life. The overall principles for this plan, first formulated in 18th-century French architectural theory,

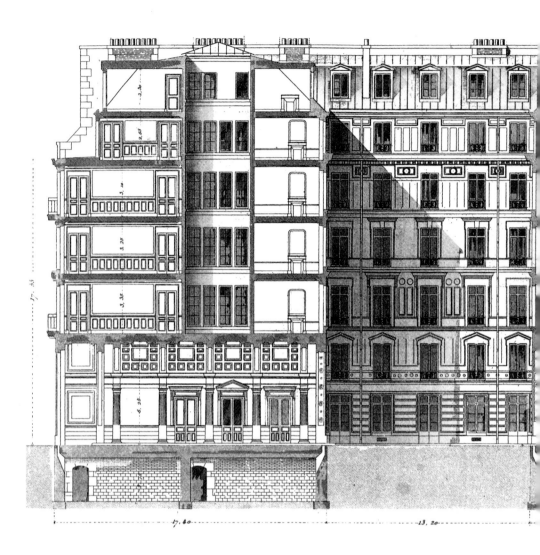

Standardization in domestic architecture: a block of flats in Paris, 1861. Unlike the satirist on p. 14, the architects and the building industry promised an almost complete equality of provision.

were *distribution* and the key quality *commodité*. Each room should be shaped and located according to its specific purpose, even according to its user's mental disposition. The idea of a minute separation of all human activities reached its height around 1860–80, when, for instance, the German architect Oskar Mothes proposed thirteen different kinds of living room.[6]

Much discussion concerned the carefully circumscribed character of the most common rooms: the 'formal' dining room, introduced in the late 17th century,[7] and the *salon*. This French term was derived from the much older Italian *sala* and *salone*, and continues to be used in many countries. Its British equivalent, 'drawing room', and the preferred American 'parlour' sounded slightly less formal.[8] In addition, there were two further kinds of room in which the man and woman of the house could be by themselves: the study and the boudoir, respectively. Collectively, these room characterizations also indicate one further division in the home, that between private family life and, to use the French term, *société* ('those parts which are in some sense exterior, the salon, the dining room'[9]). Lower down the social scale, the division became stronger during the 19th century, often leading to the lower middle classes demonstratively avoiding daily use of the parlour or the *gute Stube* ('room for best').

Throughout the period in question, it was believed that the benefits of comfort were spreading downwards.[10] An old analysis, maintained long into the 19th century, allowed for luxury for the aristocracy, comfort for the bourgeoisie and mere necessity for the working class.[11] However, already from the later 18th century Adam Smith's enlightened capitalism, as well as Jeremy Bentham's utilitarianism, were claiming that all members of society were entitled to increased consumption. It was only then that the English word 'comfort' acquired the meaning that is relevant here, distinct from the original meaning of 'comforting' somebody; and with its new

meaning the term soon entered many other languages. By the end of the 19th century 'comfort' seemed to have trickled downwards to the extent that the *petits bourgeois* – in an exaggeration that was itself typical of the discourse of the day – could live like the *plus grand seigneurs* of the past.[12]

To designate a function for a room is of course not yet entirely synonymous with assuring 'comfort'. From the later 18th century, a climate of comprehensive 'scientificness' also reigned – a belief in the natural sciences and in mechanics that was aimed also at everyday surroundings. A German comment written in 1842 even applied a novel analogy to the home: 'the private dwelling ... [is] in a way an artificially put-together machine for all fittings of domestic life'.[13] Americans in particular maintained that they had invented it all: 'American architecture ... the most comfortable, convenient and healthful in the world'.[14]

The most universally accepted aspect of comfort was warmth. And yet heating, which was required even in France 'at least six months in the year',[15] remained essentially a problem, at least in the context of Anglo-American attitudes towards the open fire, to which we shall return later. As far as artificial light is concerned, technical and economic progress is more straightforwardly reported, moving from the miserable oil lamp to the efficient and relatively versatile gaslight.[16] Seemingly lesser items, such as new kinds of lock embedded in the door – among them, from 1865 onwards, the Yale lock – created a feeling of greater safety, especially in crowded towns. The epitome of physical comfort was of course the upholstered seat, steel sprung from the 1830s onwards, being the item of furniture that comes closest to the body.[17]

Of equal importance in the demonstration of 'progress' was décor. The methods by which it was produced grew ever more effective. 'The further civilization advances, the more sumptuous the furniture', thus lifting it above earlier 'poverty-stricken sobriety and ugly

Diversity of room use: the main living rooms of the house as presented in *Unser Heim im Schmucke der Kunst* ('Our Home as Beautified by Art', 1879), a book on interior decoration by Oskar Mothes. The author and the artist take great pains to distinguish between the rooms – not so much through varying styles of décor, as might have been expected at this date, but by showing differences in the users' behaviour. More of Mothes's interiors are on pp. 156, 157 and 168.

The anteroom.

The dining room.

The salon.

The music room.

The 'ladies' room'.

The 'gentlemen's room'.

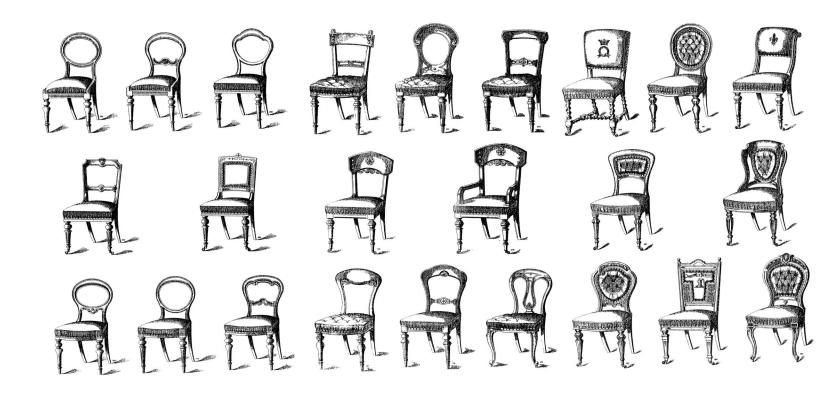

Choice: dining room chairs – 32 out of 48 designs – illustrated in the catalogue of the London firm C. & R. Light, *c.* 1880. It featured a total of 1,911 items of furniture.

colourlessness'. Altogether, 'a splendid house always presents to us a happy man'. Notions of décor appeared intimately tied to the other major qualities of luxury and comfort, as shown in many glib formulations, such as 'elegant comfort', or the upholsterer's efforts 'pour le confort et la décoration'.[18] But there was also something fundamental and self-evident about décor: together with size and overall quality of workmanship, the amount of décor indicated the social and economic status of the dweller. The combination of these two factors traditionally represented a so-called 'hierarchy of decorum'. Dwellings, along with dress, were the most ubiquitous manifestation of this hierarchy. All this, then, helps to explain the enormous increase in décor during the century: quite simply, so many more people were now rich.[19]

In searching for the most basic explanation of how the modern dwelling came about, plain statements about wealth would lead one straight to an understanding grounded in economics. In terms of classical economics – that is, capitalism – house-building and furnishing were among the most important sectors, both as regards employment and capital formation. The result was that 'the quality of dwellings is steadily improving … which does not mean that they are dearer'.[20] Harder to tackle is the issue of how much was spent on the dwelling, on convenience as well as décor in proportion to other expenses, but there was some agreement that it also increased.[21] One visible sign of this growing housing economy – or, more precisely, of the economization of processes – was a certain standardizing of dwelling types as well as of décor, although it was more than matched by a greater variety in the choice of detail.

To sum up: a good modern dwelling is large; there is plenty of light and healthy air; there are a good number of rooms, carefully differentiated in use; there is a good amount of well-functioning technology; the whole is suitably decorated, even beautiful; and, of course, all this is – has to be – affordable.

Anti-modernity

The very way in which this definition of a good home has been formulated will challenge many basic 19th- and 20th-century values. Surely it cannot all be so simple. Plain statements of rationalism and utilitarianism cannot suffice. Of the factors already discussed, only the first, convenience – and that only in a purely technological sense – obeyed a linear trajectory from the later 18th through most of the 20th century; it is only since the 1990s that doubts have

been voiced about certain elements of this technical advance. In the case of the other two factors – comfort (taken in the widest sense of the term) and décor – a notion of straightforward linear progress has never applied.

To begin with non-rational and non-technological judgments, we may state that a large room does not always feel comfortable. The principle of having many separate rooms is fine if one seeks only personal privacy, but usually the dwellers constitute a small group. Thus we find in some later 19th-century English plans a renewed stress on the living room as the proper place for normal family gatherings, and in the United States the 'parlour' seems to have had a multifunctional purpose throughout. The trend of providing a room for family togetherness was strongest in Germany and led to the (re-)introduction of the *Wohnzimmer*. In larger French dwellings, the *petit salon* became the venue for less formal gatherings. Finally, from about mid-century onwards, we note the new English and especially American desire to create one large central space, the hall, which then led to a general new openness of the plan.[22] This, however, applied mostly to the freestanding house, while urban apartments changed much less in plan over the course of two centuries.

Besides 'comfortable', there are many terms of similar meaning, of which the German *gemütlich* is the best known and, arguably, the least bound up with modern ideas of convenience. By the later 19th century, entirely new notions of comfort gained acceptance: to feelings of

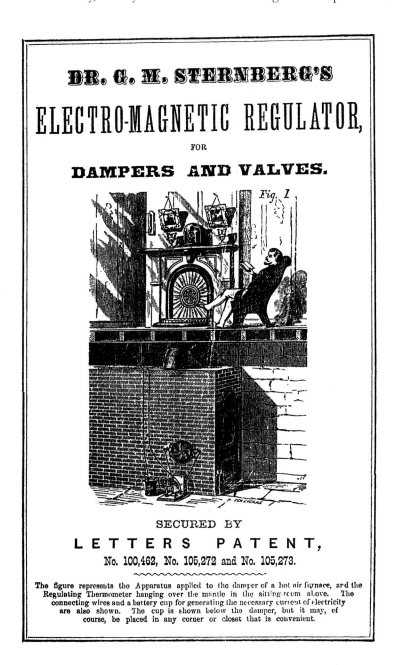

An American advertisement for thermostat-regulated heating, 1870.

comfort within an ornate and ordered environment was added a new preference for less ordered surroundings; and darkness could be more conducive to comfort than light.[23] The compulsory association of comfort with luxury, with material provision, began to be doubted. A strong image of comfort could also emanate from the 'simple', even the 'primitive'.

This leads directly to the further proposition that progress can be effected through greater visual attractiveness, through more décor. As soon as one leaves behind the plain quantitative equation of décor with income levels and tries to associate it with class labels instead, one encounters problems. The acknowledged dominant class of the 19th century was the bourgeoisie, or *Bürgertum*, and most historians would label the trends discussed here as bourgeois – mindful, though, that in Britain 'middle class' sounded more vague and less rhetorical, and that in the United States class terminology tended to be played down altogether. In fact, the situation was much more complex, even contradictory. Until the 1830s or even the 1860s, depending on the region of Europe in question, the Bürger's house was not supposed to show any décor. Then, by 1880 or 1890, a quite richly or even very richly decorated new house could well be, and mostly was, dubbed 'bourgeois'. Wholly unornamented dwellings would now be built only for the poorer working classes.[24] Confusingly, however, until the early 20th century only the smaller Berlin flat was classified as *bürgerlich*, and anything that showed a slightly more lavish size and décor was still labelled *herrschaftlich*, that is, belonging to the 'ruling' classes.[25] Strictly speaking,

Status and décor: features such as bay windows were available for large purses, like an example from the 1879 Berlin Trade Exhibition (*opposite*), as well as for medium-size budgets, like the built-in 'oriel' designed by Robert Schumann of Leipzig in 1885–87 (*above*). By the 1880s new kitchens were also likely to show décor, but the rooms' more lowly status meant that only a meagre amount was permitted, as in another design by Schumann (*above right*).

this classification was not as misplaced as it may sound, since the original class significance of most décor – certainly of any classical form, say a column – would have been not bourgeois but aristocratic. And yet this term hardly seemed to fit the 19th century as a whole.

Henceforth the association of décor, or amount of décor, with class became ever more complex and contradictory. From 1900 onwards German and Austrian art historians and collectors called the phase around 1810 to 1840 'Biedermeier', a word that was not known and would not have been understood during the period itself. Their British colleagues soon applied the term 'Regency' for the same period in their own country. The early 19th century was believed to have practised a conscious restraint and simplicity, and it was now characterized (in Central and many other parts of Europe) as virtuously *bürgerlich*, conforming to the perceived central bourgeois ethos of moderation, while the rich décor of the later 19th century was now sneered at as either parvenu or petit-bourgeois.[26]

In actual fact, the denigration of lavish décor as exuberance and trumpery was not a new trope at all. It had occurred at intervals for a very long time, precisely at those moments when the hierarchy of decorum appeared upset by sudden bursts of splendour lower down the social scale – hence statements such as 'real gentility rests exclusively in practising moderation and in remaining truthful',[27] so long as this moderation relied on solidity and 'genuine' materials. In the late 19th and the 20th centuries, many of the art-loving elite sneered at the new 'suffrage universel du goût'.[28] A somewhat different story follows a purposeful and sophisticated simplicity dating back at least as far as the retreats that featured in 18th-century landscape gardens; it then fed into the rusticity of the English Arts and Crafts movement and other European and American revivals of peasant art, and finally into some radical modernisms. However, such radical kinds of simplicity were hardly associated with the 'average' bourgeois.[29]

Class labels, therefore, will be employed here only very cautiously. What one has to remember above all is the increasingly dynamic nature of these distinctions; stable meanings could no longer be expected. There are of course other kinds of labels, such as 'smart' and 'popular', which will occasionally be used here – terms that rarely entered the sociologists' or social historians' discourse – but to analyse them would again raise the same problems. In the end, one is tempted to reject all this terminology and simply return to the trade, to the theme of 'supply': here, we again meet a more straightforward, quantitative point of view, where what mattered was not so much the client's standing, but simply the size of his or her purse. The lavish décor in so many interiors shown here could be then taken as literally the celebration of newly acquired economic and social powers. On the other hand, the new elevated discourse surrounding art in the home aimed to disregard any quantitative understanding of décor and was indifferent to considerations of social status, too.

All in all, the 19th century's lavish décor, produced by new technologies and newly effective organization, could raise the same doubts as the physical comforts achieved by similar means. 'Art' and 'poetic' appeared quite rigorously to exclude anything rational or utilitarian. Crucially, by the later 19th century the very word 'home' had acquired so many psychological or even emotional overtones that it appeared totally opposed to the modern rational, professional world. Indeed, 'home' was principally defined as opposed to that world. Nothing could have been aimed more explicitly against the modern than the ever increasing attractiveness of the old (the way in which the evaluation of the 'simple old' developed into something very sophisticated is the subject of a later chapter). From at least the middle of the 19th century onwards, there was an increasing belief that adherence to the everyday 'old' gives us more comfort than the everyday 'new'.

A sharp rationalist reaction set in from the later 1880s, when a rapidly increasing number of critics declared all mid- to later 19th-century interiors as mistaken or worse. For most of the 20th century, until around the 1990s, this amounted to the accepted wisdom and pervaded all art history books, as demonstrated, for instance, in the Dutch exhibition catalogue *De Lelijke Tijd* ('The Ugly Period').[30] International-Style modernism radicalized this position: why do we sentimentalize the dwelling at all? Modern functionalist design does not need to designate art as a special issue, either. The modern user, it was argued, does not shut himself or herself away, but looks out to the wider community and the great outdoors. The result of these avant-garde manifestos was that millions were declared to be living in a condemned environment, which was totally unsuitable and damaging to body, soul and taste. According to Freudian and Marxist approaches, it all appeared even worse: the interiority typical of the later 19th century amounted to a phantasmagoria.[31]

Can these dilemmas ever be resolved? How can such polarized positions be reconciled? Are we stuck with opting either for the 19th century against the modern, or for modernism against the 19th century? Two ways of dealing with the dispute can be proposed: either one takes the polarity between modern and anti-modern as necessary, as a given, even as natural, or one simply dispenses with the term 'modern' altogether.

Surely, the opposition between modern and non-modern relates to some of the most common ways of perceiving and evaluating the world: the objective versus the subjective, the physical versus the mental, technology versus art, to cite only a few of the most familiar binaries. The same might apply to the polarity 'new/old'. It ought to be noted that the modern concept of subjectivity itself developed around 1800, at exactly the time when the rational understanding of 'modern' consolidated itself. And yet some of these polarities were less solidly fixed than they at first appeared, at least as far as the fashions of design were concerned. Evaluations of art could change radically, often arriving at the diametrically opposite. High modernism's judgment about the 'terrible' 19th century was gradually suspended during the later 20th century. Prompted by milder versions of 1930s Surrealism – for instance the work of the painter John Piper – Britain came to rediscover much of its Victoriana during the 1950s to 1970s. Such shifts were nothing new: after all, much the same had happened earlier in the 19th century, when pure classical taste judged Elizabethan or Mannerist décor and their vernacular versions to be horrific and mad. With time, however, they were viewed as grotesque, then as picturesque or quaint, and soon most fell completely in love with them. The polarities stay with us, but we can never be sure that they remain exactly the same.

Another way out of the dilemma is to give up the idea of a specifically 20th-century modernity altogether. Divesting the 20th century of both the proud rhetorical labels 'modern'

The modernists' condemnation: 'How to Live? The Dwelling', a poster by Willi Baumeister for an exhibition of the Deutsche Werkbund, Stuttgart, 1927.

and 'anti-modern' will take us back to the 19th century in many respects. The love of the old has, if anything, increased since then, as witnessed by our recent desire for second homes in rural areas of one's own country or in far-flung places overseas. On a wider front, designing interiors in the 21st century in any style, regardless of whether they are meant to look old or modern, means using a language of form, space and textural effects that largely developed during the later 19th century. As far as the term 'poetic' is concerned, it may even be argued that certain images of heroic modernist life appear far from prosaic – as with Futurism and Purism, for instance. Lastly, there is the modern infrastructure of interior decoration – exhibitions, shops and journals, to name but a few of its manifestations – all of which was fully developed by the end of the 19th century, regardless of whether the products looked modern or not.

All in all, the 'common' user today may be excused for no longer bothering much about those burning debates, about the new versus the old, about modern or anti-modern. But the designers and the critics certainly do, or did, and that is what this book chiefly concerns.

I

A Poetic Everyday Home?

A meticulously constructed image of an 'ordinary' home by an unknown artist, on the cover of the 1892 edition of *Spemanns Schatzkästlein des Guten Rats* ('Spemann's Little Treasure Trove of Good Advice'). It presents a young, nuclear family cosily nestled in their home; their furnishings, and even their clothes, are carefully designed in the new Altdeutsch style.

Human habitations make a sterile subject, wrote the renowned architectural theorist Étienne-Louis Boullée. Churches and public buildings will always have a special meaning, but dwellings are considered only in a rather quantitative way: one merely takes note of the amount of decoration. This leads Boullée to conclude: 'With houses … it is difficult to introduce the poetry of architecture.'[1]

Boullée clearly valued the poetic above mere routine decoration. In a similar way, 'home' may be said to rank above 'house'. But the former was a term that Boullée, writing in the late 18th century, did not use and perhaps had never even heard of, since it derived from the Germanic languages and was adopted by the French only a few decades later. The present book in fact agrees with Boullée: there seemed no possibility of a poeticized ordinary house in 1800, but seventy or eighty years later a poetic element had moved into the dwelling, which by now had been reconceptualized as the home.

How had it been possible to link the loftiest branches of high art with a traditionally low sphere, the dwelling? Naturally, there had always been palaces with artistic and evocative interiors, but this had never applied to the living rooms of the majority. The answer lies in the way the home was elevated by moralists, sociologists and poets, as well as by designers, to a position where the notion of lowness no longer applied. Now the ordinary house could be, even ought to be, interpreted as something special, precisely because it was the home. There was of course nothing new in propounding all kinds of practical as well as moral advice for the good running of a household. But the 19th century placed a special stress on the good home, the happy home, by using sociology's new definition of the 'normal' family. Domesticity was then declared a major sphere of the poetic, and the main task of art and poetry was to affirm and to praise the moralists' and sociologists' stance. One hundred years after Boullée, a French book on the home could assert, even with quite unpoetic brevity, that 'an apartment [meaning also a room] resembles a poem'.[2]

At times, the new rhetoric was so successful that these characterizations were extended to all 19th-century homes: the 19th century, we are told, was simply *the* period of the homely home. Statements of this kind cannot be subscribed to here. This book's starting point is a much more modest question: how could the 19th-century domestic interior be characterized as poetic? Doubtless the process was helped by the innumerable images and texts that depicted fictional home scenes. The chief topic here, however, is the look of the interiors themselves, or, more precisely, the texts and illustrations that communicate these interiors. 'Poetic effect' will refer to the rooms' designs – their overall shapes, textures, colours and lighting – as well as the way in which certain styles of décor are used to conjure up other cultural worlds. Part and parcel of this effect is the question of how a room's appearance may influence the mood of its occupants. The 20th century's term for this convergence of shape and mood would be 'interiority'.

Poetics

'Poetry', 'home', 'design', 'art' – all these words have mighty backgrounds. Chapter IV will discuss the diverse issues bound up in the term 'home' in more detail. Most urgent here is an explanation of 'poetry'. Do we use the description 'poetic home' in the same sense as 'poetic landscape', or 'I am in a poetic mood'? In those cases we might be rather reluctant to provide a detailed definition. 'Poetic' here serves as a loose metaphor, or simply as an ornament of speech. We might then face the reproach that 'poetic home' amounts to no more than a harmless phrase, and that it cannot serve serious kinds of investigation.

The reader might also understand the phrase 'poetic home' in a material sense: there might be a shelf containing books of poetry, or the occupant might have decorated the house with tablets bearing little sayings like 'home sweet home'.[3] More serious collectors might have acquired sculptures or pictures depicting scenes from poetry:[4] it can be assumed that a fairly large number of smart European houses exhibited wall paintings of poetic or epic subjects. But to analyse poetic messages of this type would make for a quite different story. The emphasis of this book is on the design of the interior as a whole.

The best way of understanding the term 'poetic' is surely to consider the literary sphere, to which it primarily belongs. As has already been implied, nothing in our environment is barred from poetic representation, certainly not from the mid-19th century onwards. In any case, literary analysis is the traditional master discourse from which most discourses on the other arts are derived. What can be said of the home in literature applies also to the home as represented in painting and the graphic arts.

Definitions of 'poetry' in modern English, French and German dictionaries are by no means consistent, but 'a quality of beauty and intensity of emotion'[5] is about as straightforward a wording as one might hope for. Of primary interest here is the way two factors, art and the mental sphere, are linked. Indeed, 'poetic' appears related precisely to the making of connections. To understand the 19th century's application of the word to an increasing number of spheres of life, one should first note how, around 1800, it was linked to subjectivity by the Romantic critics. The meaning of 'poetic' now overlapped with that of 'romantic'; it no longer signified merely complex artifice created according to generally accepted rules, but increasingly referred to a freer, stronger and more individualized expression. The German term *Innerlichkeit* indicated this very step, from the physical and/or spatial to the mental, from *innen*, meaning 'inside', to a psychological interiority.[6]

Second, in the wake of revolutionary egalitarianism, notions of the audience of the poetic also changed considerably. So far, only those of a higher social status had been deemed capable of understanding poetry, whereas now all people were addressed. The German word *gemütlich* ('comfortable', 'cosy') as applied to the domestic interior was largely a 19th-century literary invention and can be traced directly back to the Romantic poets' stress on *Gemüt*. The latter was, and still is, a term that combines elements of soul and mind, of a subconsciously acting psyche as well as conscious reflection. But from the middle of the century the word *Gemütlichkeit* signified almost exclusively the enjoyment of the domestic interior – something that could be experienced in all homes.

Out of all this, a constant dialectic arose: traditionally, poetry had depicted high drama as experienced by remote heroes. But readers now strove to find romantic or poetic elements also within their own, very mundane, world. Increasingly, man-made objects in their own environment could also be experienced poetically. Among the first such manifestations were the exceptional and often outlandish buildings created in the new landscaped gardens of the 18th century.[7] Marking a decisive step away from the definition of poetry as high drama, acted out in remote spheres, was William Wordsworth's celebrated choice of 'incidents and

Detail of an illustration by Otto Speckter for 'The Frog Prince', a fairytale by the Brothers Grimm (1857).

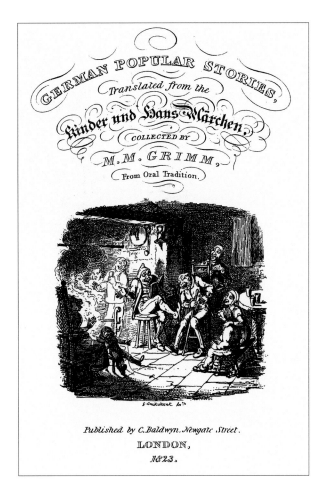

The title page of the first English translation of the Grimms' fairytales, published in 1823.

situations from common life'.[8] A little later, Hegel maintained that, in order to penetrate man's innermost spirit and feelings convincingly, the Romantic artist had to render the 'exterior in the shape of the common world, using empirical human factors', claiming: 'it is that homeliness in the common world by which romantic art enticingly attracts attention'.[9]

For a long time the 'poetic' had been extended to a special sphere of simplicity: the pastoral. During the 18th century a new emphasis on sensitivity, on the definition of moods, gave this old literary genre a new intensified meaning. Originally, the pastoral, or idyll, referred to a state of being that was exceptional; during the 18th century this, too, began to be turned into something that was close to the everyday world – for instance the countryside, or the landscaped garden. The 19th century proceeded to apply the idea of the idyll to the common home environment and to the family gathering, as seen in several popular poems by Schiller and Goethe. From the 1840s, illustrators of children's rhymes such as Ludwig Richter created a verbal and pictorial world of comprehensive tranquillity; it displayed a sophisticated ordinariness and naivety, and centred on the home as its seemingly obvious setting. The meanings of 'poetic' and 'romantic' remained linked, but the relationship of the former with the ordinary became stronger, while the word 'romantic' continued to carry notions of the exceptional.

The new Realist school – represented by the novels by Balzac and Dickens, as well as by paintings and illustrations between the 1840s and the 1880s – concentrated on a middle ground between drama and peace, between action and contemplation. In its most general sense, 'realistic' implied an increase in the number of artefacts represented in works of art or literature, and, in its more specific mid-19th century sense, the deliberate choice of themes and environments from the contemporary world. 'Poetic' and 'romantic' could now be applied to the whole range of human actions and feelings that unfolded in an everyday world, and to the multitude of objects it contained. When early in the century William Cowper was labelled as the 'poet of domesticity',[10] this referred largely to a generalized religious and moral message.

Realism, one might argue, ultimately rendered any object suitable for poetic treatment, thus ennobling the whole of the domestic environment.

After 1870 there appeared a new genre of books dealing in the greatest detail with the design of the domestic interior, including those well below the top class. Here, a notion of the poetically designed home, potentially of every home, emerged fully. Jakob von Falke, a German–Austrian writer on the history of the applied arts and material culture whose texts will be referred to throughout this book, linked the poetry of the domestic interior primarily to the woman of the house, who brings 'poetry into life … reflecting her position … according to which she takes on one half of human life, *Gemüth* [sentiment] and domesticity, which she nurtures and represents'.[11] In a somewhat complicated way, Falke here refers back to the favourite Romantic topics of the medieval knight and the medieval woman. By the early 1870s, much of this Romantic medievalism was cast aside in favour of simple formulations like 'die Poesie des Hauses'. The English architectural magazine *The Builder*, in an article on domestic wall décor, likewise wrote very plainly of 'homely poetical feeling'. Georg Hirth, a Munich author who contributed substantially to the definition of domestic interior design, wrote about 'the continuous pleasurable feelings of assured comfort, the deeper, artistic poetry of homeliness'. In a discursive little essay in the *Art Journal* of 1877, we read that 'the Perfect House' may look old and 'awkward', but will come across as 'a romance, a poem'. The most eminent of all the writers on the domestic interior – Charles Blanc, the French art theorist and secretary of the Académie des Beaux-Arts in Paris – concluded his lengthy book on the decorative arts in the house (*Grammaire des arts décoratifs: Décoration intérieure de la maison*, 1882) by stating that the 'foyer domestique' can never be too graceful, and that abandoning all this, 'pretending that these [values] are pure illusion … would also mean renouncing poetry'. Much later on, the French sense of cherishing the intimacy of the house found another celebrated text in Gaston Bachelard's *La Poétique de l'espace* (1957).[12]

However, the notion of the 'poetry of the ordinary' cannot be taken on board quite so straightforwardly. For scholars of 19th-century literature, the issue is tied in with some complex socio-literary problems. Most basically, the question was still how 'the ordinary' could be married with high art – or, put another way, how one could have a popular consumption of high art. There had of course always been the genre of the burlesque. But it no longer sufficed to treat the lower classes as grotesque or comical. The literary world had just begun to revive, or construct, a body of 'people's poetry' by retelling popular legends and fairy tales. The *Kinder- und Hausmärchen* ('Children's and Household Tales', 1812) by the Brothers Grimm stressed the homely sphere in the title itself. But such stories hardly described the everyday world of their readers. From about 1840 onwards, some German authors such as Berthold Auerbach made a new realistic and moralistic view of the 'small people' in towns and villages their main subject. At the same time, it was noticed that the appreciation of high literature was spreading rapidly down the social ladder. Much writing emerged that was considered cheap, of poor quality and amateurish, including, for example, the type of quasi-homemade verses for adolescents that featured in the so-called *Poesiealbum*.[13]

All this affected the value of the term 'poetic'. Around 1800, the word had enjoyed perhaps its strongest reputation. But after the middle of the 19th century, when it proliferated into many spheres, a negative perception began to emerge, which applied even more strongly to its sister terms 'romantic' and 'idyllic'.[14] From the 1870s onwards, Realism – which initially had helped to sanctify the ordinary – began to question the rhetoric of sanctity itself. Solid praise and plain moral judgments, 'simple' devotion to the 'happy home', or any straightforward, 'normal' morality could now appear hackneyed. Instead, 'high' and stylistically advanced literature – Naturalist works exemplified by Ibsen's plays and Zola's novels – would now just as likely stress the problematic, even the ugly, aspects of the home. Furthermore, much of this new

A scene in an upmarket home, from the richly illustrated *Contes à ma fille*, by J. N. Bouilly (1814).

Ludwig Richter, 'Mother and Children Laying the Table', 1851. Even the most mundane domestic activities at lower levels of society could now form the subject of poetry and attract the attention of eminent artists.

literature and painting now focused on reality at the very lowest social levels, worlds where the notion of a 'home life' hardly seemed to apply. Those who read this new literature, however – and herein lies the rub – were more likely to see themselves as members of an advanced elite of connoisseurs, placing themselves above the 'normal' citizen. Clearly, books on artistic home design of the 1870s and 1880s could not associate themselves directly with this new literary trend, and could never engage in any talking down of the happy home. But they would nevertheless refrain from using the term 'poetic house' or 'poetic home' in the title, or even chapter heading, of a book. Henceforth, 'poetic' remained a term of high praise and special emphasis in an older sense, but it was now no longer a term that appeared to require special analysis.

Such problems eventually resulted in 20th-century modernist literary historians – especially in Germany – defining a category of 'lesser' 19th-century novels and poetry as *Trivialliteratur*. Sociologically orientated literary and cultural studies subsequently reinforced earlier negative judgments, seeing the popularization of the poetic not only as 'inferior' literature, but also as fetishism, as a manifestation of a flight from reality and from the perceived complexities of modern society.[15] This view appeared to tie in neatly with most 20th-century art historians' notions of 19th-century painting and design as sentimental or simply bad.

Is it thus futile to construct a poetics of domestic interior design? Of course, there is a mismatch when one imports a term from the largest sphere of art discourse – literature – into a sphere where writing plays only a minuscule role by comparison. Or, to put it even more starkly, there was one world of writing and depicting, and another of making things. In the old hierarchy of the arts, the crafts still occupied a lowly position. But such a line ought not to be followed here, since it was the cherished aim of the later 19th century, and then of modernism, to consider all branches of the visual arts on an equal footing. In any case, this book cannot deal comprehensively with the problems surrounding representations of the home in literature and the visual arts, nor with the complex issue of the hierarchy of the arts. Instead, its focus is the poeticization of the interior through design, using methods that were verbalized only very gradually during the course of the century, with or without the actual label 'poetic'.

However, the question still remains: should most of what is reported here be classified as 'trivial art'? A simple view based on economics would stress that while every self-styled intellectual can buy a book of high-art poetry cheaply, he or she is much more rarely in a position to afford a genuine high art object, let alone a complete new set of stylish furnishings. Thus the modernist critic should be warned of arrogance and not simply sneer at 'popular' or 'mass' décor. During the 19th century the situation was more complex: the new proliferation of seemingly competent, professional décor was greeted by many – by almost all the authors cited in this book – as 'la démocratisation du luxe', while a few others, including John Ruskin, bitterly regretted it as inauthentic and therefore vulgar. Today, we can hardly consider the problems surrounding the popularization of art to have been solved. All that can be proposed is a compromise: while respecting the elevated nature of the discourses of high art and literature, one is entitled to use some of their terms for 'lowly' purposes as and when it seems apt.

Poetry, decoration, design and art

'Poetic' is here applied to works of decoration and design as a word of praise. 'Decoration' is a relatively unproblematic term, and can be connected with poetry in the most direct way – in actual volumes of poetry, for example. Earlier in the century, poems tended to be read from small, mostly paperback, books that contained a few engravings at best. After 1850, poetry was increasingly published in larger volumes lavishly illustrated with chromolithographs and bound in gilt-edged embossed leather, 'lying on the toilet table for a year'[16] – material culture linking up with literary content in a way that the high-minded literary critic would not normally wish to notice. On a most basic level, the new phrase 'poetic home' may be identified with the rapid increase of any kind of décor in the house.

The Vitruvian definition of architecture, which held that a building should be durable and useful as well as beautiful, had sufficed also for applied art and product design long into the 19th century. In practice, beauty equated simply with the addition of décor. That said, by the time Boullée was writing, this straightforward discourse was already being supplemented by much more complex theories surrounding the relationship of art or beauty with construction and convenience. As we have already seen, for Boullée poetry in architecture meant more than décor, more than sets of smallish forms attached to a building. However, for most theorists, including Boullée, 'poetic' had to refer to the grand or the exceptional. Principally it concerned the grandiose effects of the whole mass of a building, preferably of the largest kind, together with contrasts of light and shade.[17] Boullée wanted us to see buildings as they might appear in dramatically conceived paintings. In Chapters III and IV we will turn to these elements that English discussions of art called 'picturesque' and 'sublime'.

Clearly, the simple term 'decoration' was no longer suitable, and 'design' – one of the most difficult of artistic terms – was increasingly preferred. In the 19th century the word 'design' was used much less frequently and less emphatically than during the 20th century, and there was very little theorizing involved. Most commonly, 'design' in English either simply equalled 'decoration', or was used in the everyday sense of a preliminary drawing for an object – the principal use also of the French *dessin* and the German *Entwurf*. But the Renaissance source word, *disegno*, always carried an extended meaning that stressed the intrinsic value of overall preconception and control. However, before the early 20th century this meaning attached chiefly to high, figurative art and much less to décor, and it was only with the arrival of modernism that it was applied to all spheres of product design. Naturally, the increasing trend during the 19th century to show proposed rooms as ensembles contributed to notions that ultimately found expression in the term 'interior design' – even if this crucial phrase was as yet hardly used. As will be explained in Chapter III, discussions were still dominated by the technical language of the individual trades on the one hand, and by the old architectural nomenclature for larger decorative schemes on the other. By the 1870s the abstract notions of form, of light and dark, of mass and, a little later, space, were expressed explicitly and began to be adopted for the domestic interior. Thus Chapter III also covers the principal attempts to distinguish between decoration and design, and the 19th-century trajectory that led from 'interior decoration' to 'interior design'.[18] It was the increased use of abstract formal terms that prepared the way for 20th-century modernism.

The carefully coordinated interior was thus fit to receive the epithet 'poetic', which referred to something more than just applied décor, to something comprehensive. It was then taken up in expressions such as 'poetische Stimmung', 'poetic atmosphere',[19] which may finally be understood as characterizing a 'poetically designed interior'. Here, at last, we encounter something that may serve as a very modest equivalent of the literary poetics of the home. During the 19th century the concept branched out into diverse historical styles and themes. Interior décor and interior design here allied themselves ever more closely with art, literature and history – and in particular with historical novels and history painting.

Similarly, 'designer' was a term used, but hardly ever defined, by the 19th century. The label 'interior decorator' slowly gained currency during the late 19th century (just 'decorator', as we shall see, did not carry quite the same meaning), while 'interior designer' hardly emerged at all: the full professionalization of interior design took place only during the mid-20th century, and hence this book uses the term 'designer' only in a very general sense. In many cases, the role of coordinator was assumed by the architect of a house – a profession with which the term 'design' had become associated a long time before. Regardless of all these complexities,

Das deutsche House im Schmucke der Poesie und Kunst ('The German House Embellished in Poetry and Art') by K. Dorenwell (1893), an author of religious and moral tracts. The cover features a muse with composite attributes presiding over house and garden.

Advertisement for an interior design firm, London, 1887.

A French view of how 'Yankees' make themselves comfortable – 'in positions as ingenious as they are picturesque' (Henry Havard, *L'Art dans la maison*, 1884). By the end of the century, the discourse of the home had split into several threads: high-flown moral and cultural exhortations; advertising and posturing by designers and tradesmen; and the world of the actual user, who sought comfort but may not have cared much about anything else.

one general notion gained ground continuously: that of the individuality of artistic agency, of artistic creation. As the trade journal *Furniture Gazette* remarked in 1887: 'every work of art – including furniture – should be stamped with an individuality'.[20]

This brings us to seemingly the simplest and most traditional classification of the 'poetically designed home', to a definition that could comprise everything that was valorized: that briefest of words, 'art'. While academic attempts at its definition filled hundreds of volumes, its basic ethos hardly ever seemed to demand an explanation. This is the reason why most books on any field of art history do not bother to define it. Furthermore, throughout the 19th and most of the 20th centuries, the term 'art' never appeared overused or hackneyed. Like the description 'poetic', 'artistic' always implied a value judgment, but one that could usually be clearly defined and easily measured. At its simplest, one might say that the domestic interior as described in this book acquired 'art', or developed into a work of art. Hegel, writing around 1830, was still trying to deny this, although the actual words he used do make one wonder: 'the house … a human … not yet an artistic invention'.[21] But once it had become established, the 'art in the home' slogan never lost its validity. Most books on the décor of the domestic interior from the late 19th century included the word 'art' in their title.

There were, however, some problems with the term 'art', too. In this book, 'art' is limited to the visual and material sphere, and thus is tied in with the artefact, with materiality, and thus with a hierarchy of costs and status. It was almost always better to spend more rather than less, and it should be noted that simplicity – in the sense of noble or elegant simplicity – usually cost more than heavy décor, which could be procured cheaply. While in theory the heightened discourse of 'art' denied these material ties, in practice the designs and objects were created by the trades, by professionals, or by bona fide artistic designers. Although the client was deemed to appreciate and understand at least some of art's techniques and meanings, he or she remained largely a passive recipient, or even just the paymaster. In any case, through much of the 19th century the old, pre-Renaissance hierarchy of the arts persisted, with poetry at the top, the *artes mechanicae* at the bottom, and 'design' somewhere in between. Yet in the end it was poetry that also had more direct access to the 'ordinary' world. In spite of all the rhetoric of 'art and the ordinary', the connection between the two remained tenuous because of the material costs involved. Not so with poetry or fiction, at least from mid-century onwards: to partake in poetry never costs much. While, as we saw, this could lead to doubts surrounding the worth of 'lesser' literature, it was taken for granted that poetry always involves the recipient's subjectivity. The concept of the 'poetic home' had a clear destination – its clients, or 'users' – and was closely bound up with certain recurring domestic situations, such as the quiet evening atmosphere. In what follows, questions relating to the design and construction of the interior come under the heading 'art', while discussions of its wider meaning and intended reception come under 'poetic'.

1re ÉDITION

Ameublement Parisien

ALBUM

GÉNÉRAL

II

Art in the Home: A New Discourse

The cover of the *Album Général de l'Ameublement Parisien*, a folio volume of *c.* 1890. Several of the illustrations included here are drawn from its pages.

When we visit beautiful homes in person or look at glossy illustrations in a journal, we are not usually aware of how many diverse elements of design, production and propagation were involved, nor do we realize what powers of control were needed to bring them together. For the very richest interiors there had always been somebody who was in charge of assembling them. But it was only in the 19th century that the coordination of any type of domestic interior emerged as a recognized skill. This chapter surveys the many different agents – traders, designers, critics, shops, and so on – that were involved, with a special emphasis on the emerging discourse of the artistic and unified domestic interior.

The trades

How could one achieve a complete and harmonious interior through the use of 56 crafts or businesses, which could be further subdivided into 146 specialized activities? These are the numbers listed in the 1877 edition of the *Post Office Directory of the Cabinet, Furniture and Upholstery Trades*, published by Kelly's. In 1845, construction of the Kaiser Salon at the Austrian Trade Exhibition had involved 31 separate trades, and even making a copy of a complex piece of Rococo furniture required the participation of ten different crafts.[1] It hardly needs stressing that the furnishing trades – from the jobbing craftsman or craftswoman to the powerful manufacturing conglomerates and international suppliers of materials – constitute a major sector of the economy. During the 19th century many of these industries were going through a rapid process of modernization. The earlier goal of trying to attract the outstanding patron was if not replaced, then decisively supplemented by the efficient fulfilment of large institutional orders and by production of stock. Optimism sometimes knew no bounds: 'We may justly state that the cheap machine work of the German art industries supplies everything that belongs to the artistic furnishing of the dwelling.'[2]

Strictly speaking, however, 'trade' could not mean 'art'. In commissions for the richest households, it was the patron, the architect or an artist who did the talking, but there was otherwise no need for many words beyond the strictly technical. Between the 1820s and 1870s, the number of words describing the domestic interior grew considerably. A primary requirement was for generally recognized terms of praise, and their meaning has remained surprisingly stable in all the main Western languages. Chief among them is 'elegance', which in the hierarchy of art terms has always occupied a rather low position and has appeared eminently suited to the mundane sphere of fashion and décor.[3] A number of other popular terms meant much the same: 'graceful', 'charming', 'delightful', 'exquisite', 'pure', 'chaste yet striking', etc. A word with much wider connotations was of course 'taste', which until at least the middle of the 19th century was tied firmly to the class hierarchy. Later on, the word's power was much weakened, although its negative – 'bad taste' – remained in widespread use. Apart from its dominant meaning as 'artistic value', the term could also be used neutrally as a synonym for style: 'in the Chinese taste' means the same as 'in the Chinese style', for example. Finally, traders could appeal to a desire for novelty. Whereas taste is something that is, or ought to be, shared by both trader and client, to know what is novel is the trader's foremost expertise. In this context, furnishings were often seen as the equivalent of fashionable dress: according to Mrs Parkes, a writer of home advice books, the décor of the drawing room was 'almost as changeable as fashions, as female dress'.[4] The traders and their spokespersons effortlessly combined such praises into tempting labels: 'in französisch-modernem Geschmacke' ('in French modern taste'), for example.[5]

Increasingly, the traders felt that they had to draw attention to their work through publications.[6] But lavish books on art and antiquities were unaffordable for many, and the trade's early technical manuals, produced for their own use, were rather unattractive little tomes.[7] In the early decades of the century, a number of general journals carried pictures of the newest fashions and items of furnishing – the Parisian *Journal des Dames et des Modes*, for example – which were, in an innovative way, addressed mainly to consumers.[8] The principal source of illustrated novelties were the pattern books, known in Germany as the *Musterbücher* or *Ornamentvorlagen*. They could be specific to a particular craft, or they could show a model for decoration that might be used by several crafts. Most numerous were pattern books for cabinetmakers and window drapers. But the publishing of all trade literature was haphazard (a nightmare for bibliographers).[9] Its cheapness was often given away by poor-quality illustrations, partly the fault of high production costs. A calculation from the early 1880s reveals what could be afforded: the earnings of a small trader came to £1 or £2 per week, while each printed copy of a single picture retailed at between 1 and 3 pence. In other words, the cost of the image amounted to 1–2% of the trader's wage. This may not sound much, but if one projects this ratio forward in time, a trader today on, say, £500 per week would have to spend £5–10 for his picture.[10] However, during the 1880s the number of journals for individual trades did expand very rapidly, in Central Europe, Britain and the United States (less so in France). They contained all kinds of information: technical matters, news relating to the trade's organization, articles on the theory of décor and on the history of the craft, and so on.[11] At the same time, more and more firms brought out their own catalogues, which were often lavishly illustrated.[12]

All these developments can certainly be characterized as steps towards the professionalization of the crafts and trades. Did they also accord with a stricter definition of 'art'? The previous chapter briefly addressed some of the difficulties of the term 'design'. Now the question is: who devised the artistic element of an object, its decoration? Clearly, richness of décor was a constant challenge to the inventiveness of those who operated in the trades' higher echelons, while at the lower end of the market the maker would most likely supply a repeat pattern or copy an illustration. Increasingly – especially in the large textile manufactures – there was an 'ornamentist' or 'dessinateur' whose responsibility was to invent the décor. But their names hardly ever became known, since the product was always sold under the firm's mark.[13] The French luxury manufactures provided the *pièce de résistance* of this system: the vastly expensive creations of Fourdinois, Christofle, and so on marked the acme of craft perfection, and they often bristled with new kinds of decorative motifs. At the same time these 'fabricant artistes'[14] were enlarging their production on an industrial scale, and yet we have no notion of who the pieces' actual designers were.

By the 1880s a small number of men and women had emerged in London whom one might call specialist furniture designers (essentially they were freelance consultants), but who also supplied designs for whole interiors. Almost all of them, however, remained in relative obscurity because their designs were published only in the trade press.[15] One of the main reasons for the huge and lasting success of Morris, Tiffany and a very few others was the way they went one step further. A product, say a textile, became well known because of a particular designer's name that counted for more than the firm that made the product or the shop that sold it (in the case of Morris, one name covered all three). These designers were therefore decisively elevated to the rank of artist, leaving the ordinary trade behind. A somewhat similar situation had arisen in Munich, where some fine art artists, such as Lorenz Gedon or the father-and-son team of Franz and Rudolf von Seitz, turned their hands to the design of all kinds of objects and environments.

The decorator

The trades clearly tried their hardest to aspire to 'art'. At the same time, the process of professionalization led to each trade being defined much more strictly. How did that affect the task of coordinating a complex interior? A fine art artist, an artist-designer (that is, an artist who designed ornaments, such as Owen Jones) or an architect (the contribution of architecture will be discussed below) could be in charge of a project. However, from the 18th century onwards a number of agencies whose specific task was the coordination of the trades had also emerged. Where decisions were made mostly by the client, shops could help with coordinating whatever objects he or she had chosen. One of the trades almost always stepped beyond its sphere of production, such as happened with the *marchand menuisier* (woodworker-cum-dealer) or the

A treatise on upholstery, incorporating a teaching manual, patterns and advertisements for traders (1886).

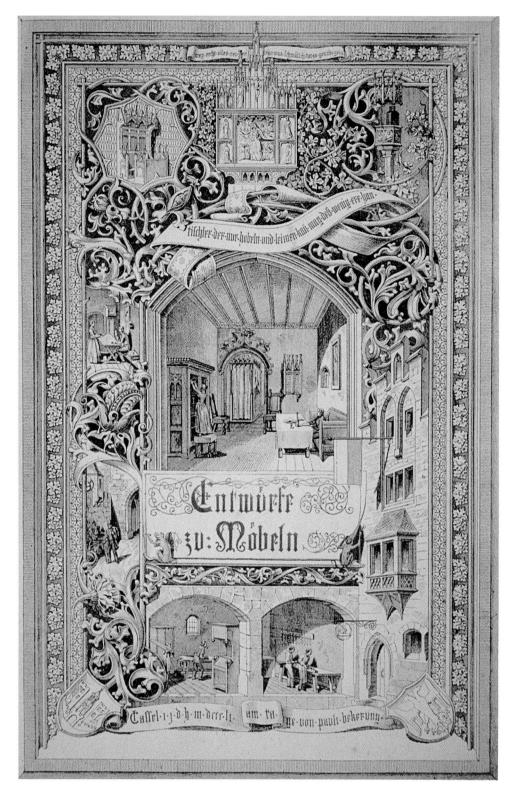

Frontispiece for *Entwürfe zu Möbeln* ('Designs for Furniture') by Georg Gottlob Ungewitter (1851). A strict Gothic Revivalist, this architect and designer here devised a cosmos spanning everything from basic workmanship to high religiosity. Ungewitter was a keen adherent of the rationalist views of Viollet-le-Duc and the religious fervour of Pugin, while this multi-scene composition displays the influence of German Romantic painters and illustrators (see pp. 159ff.)

marchand tapissier (upholster-cum-dealer), although they could also adopt other, more neutral names like *marchand mercier* (dealer in all luxury goods), *ensemblier* or *assemblier*.[16] By the end of the 18th century, London firms who were primarily furniture-makers, such as Seddon's, were already giving the impression that their workshops made everything else too, as did the Viennese workshops of Danhauser between the 1820s and the 1840s. In France, the furniture-maker Fourdinois also advised on decoration. Later on, firms such as Jackson & Graham in London and, from the 1870s, a handful of New York furniture-makers like Herters rose to great prominence on account of the completeness and lavishness of some of their jobs. Several London shops eventually set up furnishing and decorating studios, such as Liberty's in 1883.[17]

There was one profession that increasingly undertook to fit out an interior on the spot: the upholsterer (*tapissier* or *Tapezierer*). From a narrow viewpoint, it could be said that 'the upholsterer is at the same time the tailor and the milliner of the room'.[18] In the period of Louis-Philippe (1830–48), it was the *tapissier* who was held to have assumed charge of the whole. By 1845, according to the art historian Eva Ottillinger, 'the *Tapezierer* ruled Vienna'. Mrs Haweis insisted in 1881 that 'the furniture and scheme of decoration [are] now provided by every upholsterer'.[19] But there was a second trade in a position to take up the task: that of the painter (in France, the *peintre-décorateur* or *dessinateur-décorateur*), the 'house painter who dignified himself by the name of the decorator'[20] – who obviously undertook more than today's 'painter and decorator'. A well-known example was the London firm of Crace, which through high patronage and careful historical research rose to an unusually high position in the art world.[21]

Lastly, by about mid-century, a separate term became established: that of 'decorator'. Outsiders were not normally told his or her actual trade background. Decorating was slowly recognized as being a task in its own right.[22] Julius Lessing, the Berlin applied art supremo, stresses repeatedly the new London and Paris profession of the *décorateur*; first, their 'magasins' contain absolutely everything that is needed, and second, the decorator 'manages to link the individual trades together in a unified achievement'.[23] 'Have one fixed mind preside over the rooms', someone who possesses both 'a deep knowledge of style' as well as 'a personalized taste'. The 'skilful decorator' also deals with 'the play of the curtains and with the lighting'; what is needed is 'dexterity, taste and a good eye'.[24] However, searching for the names and handiwork of these decorators is not an easy task. Eugène Prignot, who we know worked for French and English furnishing firms, was called a 'a celebrated French artist', but all that can be cited here are his books with their lavish plates.[25] In London, the Garrett cousins, Rhoda and Agnes, were known as 'house decorators', but only traces of their seemingly modest work have come to light, and the illustrations in their book are not very revealing.[26]

It could be argued that a real profession of domestic decorator never emerged. Much of the work had to be done on the spot, improvised, and often needed to be completed quickly (in 'some weeks', according to Havard),[27] requiring a kind of dexterity different from that of the long-established crafts. In *Laxton's Builder's Price Book* of 1894 we read that it could be difficult to establish adequate estimates in this field, and in the massive *Post Office Directory* of 1877, cited above, the category hardly occurs[28] (discussions at the end of this chapter will return to the issues of coordinating and marketing interior decoration). The great names in the English reform movement – Owen Jones, Robert Edis, Lewis F. Day and others – certainly did not want to be associated with commercial decorators, instead calling themselves 'decorative designer'.

The architect

Compared with the discourse of the lowly tradesmen, the world of architecture appeared almost on a par with that of the fine arts. The most lavish and architecturally integrated interiors – certainly those that were palatial in scope – lie beyond the current frame of reference. And yet architects contributed immeasurably to the development of the domestic interior at all levels. Mostly this is attributable to the fact that architecture had for a long time recognized a clear definition of design, and in any case many of the rules and patterns of architectural design applied also to interior décor, especially during the Neoclassical period. One key figure, Robert Adam, rose to prominence through the way he exercised strict control over the stucco work and furniture in all his interiors.[29] Closely allied to the issue of design was style. 'Historical' styles in the 19th century were largely architectural, and where an identifiable style was applied to an interior, it was most likely an architect, or a trader or decorator aspiring to the ways of an architect, who supplied the design. In 1850 the American landscape designer and critic Andrew Jackson Downing clearly summed up this close relationship between architecture and interior design: 'It is almost needless to remark here, that a certain manner of treating a subject architecturally, which we call style, and which is nothing more than making the general spirit of the composition pervade all the lines and forms, may be exhibited in the smallest details, as well as the boldest outlines of a building; that it governs the form and proportion of the least molding upon a table as well as the strongest lines of tower and roof.'[30] Seventy years before Downing, the French architect and critic Le Camus de Mézières had written that the precise rules and characters of the orders should determine the décor of the living rooms: Doric for the library, Ionic for the dining room and Corinthian for the boudoir.[31] At the peak of the Italian Renaissance revival between the 1840s and the 1870s, Gottfried Semper's palaces and villas in Dresden[32] and those by top Viennese architects along Vienna's Ringstrasse adhered to the same rich Renaissance motifs inside and out – an approach that also directly influenced architects' control of furniture designs under the stern eyes of the Austrian applied arts reform movement.[33]

One key factor architects had in their favour was the lavish publications they were able to produce, often showing their own work. Long before the trade could afford impressive books, Robert Adam published his own designs, which included many kinds of interior fittings. The next major book, and the first devoted entirely to the domestic interior – naturally, in this period, of the very smartest kind – was the *Recueil de décorations intérieures comprenant tout ce qui a rapport à l'ameublement*, published in Paris between 1801 and 1812 by the top French architectural team of Charles Percier and Pierre-François-Léonard Fontaine. In their perceptive introduction, they made it quite clear that only the architect should be in charge, only he can 'improve' matters, and already they use a term that was to dominate discussions of applied arts design during the 19th century: 'reform'.[34] Six years later, in 1807, the London collector and amateur architect Thomas Hope published the interiors of his own house as *Household Furniture and Interior Decoration Executed from Designs by Thomas Hope*, a title held to contain the first proper use of the term 'interior decoration' in the English language. The star architects of London and Berlin, John Soane and Karl Friedrich Schinkel, kept publicizing their striking interiors. This tradition was kept up by Schinkel's followers in Berlin into the 1880s.[35]

There was a consistent element of posturing on the part of the architects. Often they felt they had to put a special stress on their superiority over, and contempt for, the trades, as in the case of Le Camus early on,[36] or, most explicitly, in Leo von Klenze's comment on his new interiors for Munich's Königsbau, the new royal residence (see p. 67).[37] It should be remembered that, during the 1830s, London architects were also trying extremely hard to emancipate themselves from the speculative house building process: Pugin, for example, attacked both the building trades and some of the applied arts manufacturers. In Paris, architecture's main critic, César Daly, was usually more cautious, but in an 1862 edition of his journal, the *Revue générale de l'architecture*, he pronounced squarely: 'First among the *décorateurs* is the architect.'[38]

From the 1870s, architects took the lead by publishing whole interiors and furnishings in their journals, of which there was a considerable number in each country; these interiors were almost always designed by architects and, at least in England and the United States, by younger, avant-garde practitioners. 'Now the internal fittings in our houses are carefully designed and admirably worked out': so wrote the architect J. M. Brydon, a pupil of Richard Norman Shaw, in 1877. In 1870 Charles Eastlake, the early spokesperson of the English furniture reform movement, compared the current situation with past practice: '50 years ago no architect would have considered designing the interior in this way', but now 'younger members of the profession readily accept commissions for such supervision if they were adequately remunerative'.[39] In New England, the 1870s brought a sudden concern on the part of some architects to distinguish themselves in interior design. Upon his death in 1886, the United States' most celebrated architect, Henry Hobson Richardson, was given the designation 'interior designer', no doubt one of the earliest uses of the term.[40]

A decorative page from the large *Der decorative Ausbau* ('The Fitting of the Interior') by the designer and furnisher Martin Kimbel. Containing many views of whole rooms, the book appeared during the 1870s (this edition *c.* 1880). Kimbel had an unusually cosmopolitan career, working in New York between 1856 and 1864 before settling in Prussian Breslau (today Wrocław). Some of his plates stray into the grotesque.

Occasionally the trade tried to fight back. In 1840 Arrowsmith, a London decorator, warned clients not to 'apply too much exterior classical architecture to the interior'.[41] Critics in Berlin and Munich suggested that architects should perhaps not become too involved in the applied arts, since the results might lack liveliness.[42] Sometimes the architects themselves were not too sure of their role. For the immensely lavish new interiors of Windsor Castle (1824–40), the architect, Sir Jeffry Wyatville, wished to distance himself from many of the details: textile work in particular he considered too impermanent for an architect's concern.[43] In the 1880s several London practitioners maintained pragmatically that it was not always clear how much time an architect would have for subsidiary elements in the design and building process.[44] It was only at the very end of the century, when the culture of the medium-sized detached house had developed fully, that some architects like Baillie Scott tried their utmost to prove themselves as interior designers as well.

The architects' reinforcement of their superiority – in which they often tried to elevate their sphere even further by calling it 'art' – effectively confirmed the trade's subordinate position. However, for 'art in the home' to emerge fully, other agents had to be involved – agents that came from outside the professional design and making processes altogether.

Books and periodicals

An impetus from below: home and architectural advice books

Art and architecture invariably direct from above. But the ideology of the home was meant to include all social classes in like manner. Indeed, a new emphasis was placed on how the happiest homes can be found in the most modest circumstances, whereas the upper classes, because of their more scattered interests, are less likely to conduct such a close-knit home life. To somehow marry the higher with the lower was also one of the chief aims of the new 'art in the home' movement. Inevitably, it was obliged to look well beyond the high sphere of 'art'.[45]

Home advice books were based on an old type of husbandry manual, which dealt comprehensively with the running of a self-sufficient house and farm. As with the new technical manuals for the trades, there was a general sense that running something, running anything, was becoming more complicated and scientific by the day, and advice could sometimes fill over a thousand pages. Many of these books were written by women and claimed to be based on their authors' comprehensive practical experience. Usually a wide range of incomes was addressed: for instance J. H. Walsh, in 1856, presents a scale of annual incomes from £100 to £1,000.[46] Unmistakable in all such manuals is a tone of a moral and economic rationality, which urges every income bracket to make the best of what it has.

Many mid-century home advice books offered at least a few pieces of advice on how to decorate rooms, sandwiched somewhere between health matters and cookery. As in the writings of the educator Catharine Beecher, the stress is usually on the initiative of the householder – largely the housewife, that is – who is encouraged to use decorating materials of the cheapest kind that could be made in the home, such as flower arrangements or items of textile décor.[47] In the wake of these manuals, more and more journals, like *Godey's Lady's Book* in the United States (published from 1840), also included copious advice on home decorating. The integration of wood engravings – a new, cheap technique – into the text helped greatly, though in their sketchiness – even crudeness – these illustrations differed substantially from those in the trades' and architects' pattern books.[48]

To extend such advice on the home into building and architecture was the aim of the indefatigable John Claudius Loudon. His *Encyclopaedia of Cottage, Farm, and Villa Architecture and Furniture* of 1833 deals with all, literally all, thinkable aspects of the house, in everything from the smallest cottage upwards, although it rigorously excludes all denser, urban kinds of dwelling.

Since his original and principal interest was gardening, Loudon propagated the ideal of the self-contained country home. About one fifth of the book is taken up by a detailed consideration of interior decoration and furniture, including the minimal décor of the smallest cottage. But on the whole Loudon has most to say on smart villas, small country houses and their architectural styles. Ultimately he does not forget to remind his readers of the advantages of 'the building and furnishing of the house being under the control of the same mind' (meaning of course the architect), at the same time recognizing that, in practice, individual trades might be in charge.[49]

A very concise version of Loudon's viewpoints appeared in Andrew Jackson Downing's somewhat misleadingly entitled *The Architecture of Country Houses* of 1850. Above all, it concentrates on the individual house, of small to medium size, belonging to the nuclear family, thus somewhat breaking away from the customary upmarket focus. For Downing, the ideal interiors are 'cosy rooms, where all kinds of fireside joys are invited to dwell'. Nonetheless, his section on the interior limits itself to the discussion of styles that can be found in more elegant houses.[50] In England, and even more so in the United States, volumes on the larger detached house soon became a major category of architectural publishing, but extended discussions on the interior were still very rare.[51]

Applied arts and reform

What Loudon and Downing had preached was a belief that virtually all citizens could aspire to a tasteful environment if both producers and users were properly educated. After the middle of the century, this new ethos of 'art for all' was officially adopted by many governments, who in one of the most impressive public efforts of the 19th century undertook to 'reform' the applied and decorative arts, known in Germany as the *Kunstgewerbe* (these very terms were new). To the traditional craftsman or manufacturer, such generalized labels might not have seemed necessary at first; but nobody appeared to object to the idea of defining and thus ennobling the trades as 'art'. In this way, the Renaissance goal of elevating more of the 'mechanical arts' (which originally had included painting and architecture) to the level of the 'fine' or the 'free' arts, such as poetry or music, was fulfilled.[52]

Alongside the many journals and innumerable cheap instruction books in circulation, all the new museums and specialized schools – those in South Kensington in London (later to become the Victoria and Albert Museum and the Royal College of Art) in the 1850s, Vienna's Museum für Kunst und Industrie, and Prussia's applied art museums in the 1860s – professed the aim of teaching the 'right' kind of ornament.[53] This could be achieved either through the study of historical examples shown in the museums, or with the help of the so-called South Kensington system of formal and geometric training. The latter favoured abstracted plant motifs,[54] which were contrasted with the 'tasteless' desire for three-dimensional illusion – particularly among the trades, of course. There was therefore now a 'reformed' taste and a bad, 'commercial' taste. The arbiters were the officials of the applied arts museums – the 'taste professionals' like Jakob von Falke[55] – and those who wrote and illustrated books on the theory of ornament, such as Owen Jones. Crucially, taste was now viewed as independent of cost: as a popular German encyclopaedia explained in 1877, 'significantly increased value is created … requiring no special expense in work and materials … but only more taste'.[56]

A flood of new texts

The sudden appearance, in the 1870s and 1880s, of a mass of writings devoted exclusively to the reform of the design and décor of the domestic interior has no parallel. They may certainly be viewed as one of the major outcomes of the applied arts reform movement. Before 1868, there was literally no book that dealt with the subject comprehensively, either in text or in pictures. 'Art in the home' or 'art in the house' would not have appeared a specially revealing

A volume from the 'Art at Home' series (1880), which was devoted to various aspects of home decoration and the applied arts. It was initiated by the London publishers Macmillan in 1876.

topic, since it was expected that rich homes would already contain valuable works of art and décor, while in lower-class houses such products would be totally absent. 'One had no conception', one critic commented retrospectively, 'that domestic implements could demonstrate a sense of art.'[57] In the 20th century, few major architectural or design critics addressed it as a theme: 'house and home' belonged once more with the furnishing trades and their popular illustrated journals, or it was taken up by social reformers and sociologists.

Some important books on interior décor with an architectural background have already been cited: Percier and Fontaine's studies of decorative motifs and a few ensembles of décor, although books by their followers should be classified as pattern books and thus as trade; and Thomas Hope's pioneering work on 'interior decoration', which showed the house of one collector. Andreas Romberg produced a complete set of illustrated palatial interior pictures, and David Ramsay Hay, who had started out as a house painter, wrote a work devoted entirely to the domestic interior; even though his advice is limited to house painting and colour, it occupies an important position as a serious early text. Loudon's and Downing's contributions to interior décor were substantial but did not represent the main focus of their books. Perhaps

Ella Rodman Church's *How to Furnish a Home* (1881), one of the 'Appletons' Home Books' series published in New York.

a little anonymous text of 1853, *How to Furnish a House and Make it Home*, from the home advice genre and aimed at a low- to middle-level readership, comes closest to a complete book on interior design, but it seems to have made no impact. One exceptional text is the short essay 'The Philosophy of Furniture' by Edgar Allan Poe, published in 1840.[58] An 1866 lecture called 'De l'ameublement et de la décoration de nos appartements', given by Édouard Guichard, one of the early French designer-reformers, presented probably the first systematic overview of the subject, but it too was very modestly presented.[59] France had to wait until the 1880s for significant texts. In Germany, the otherwise obscure teacher A. Scheffers[60] and the noted Berlin architect Richard Lucae both made important early theoretical contributions.

Of vital importance in establishing a discourse of art in the home were historians – the 'antiquarians' in Britain; the architect Gottfried Semper in Germany, with his studies of ancient building and craft methods; and above all Eugène Viollet-le-Duc. From the mid-1850s Viollet-le-Duc published countless secular objects from the Middle Ages and numerous imaginary medieval domestic interiors, taking pains to explain their practical applications. In a similar way, Nuremberg's new Germanisches Nationalmuseum partly devoted itself to what today would be called material culture studies (see Chapter V). However, because of their aim of explaining objects 'historically', such studies implied that present times were different. Fascinating as the Middle Ages appeared, by the 1850s it was increasingly stressed that medieval homes lacked the comforts necessary for the modern age.[61] Nonetheless, underpinning the topic of the domestic interior with an extensive history did lend it a massive dose of legitimacy.

The uniting of the 'home spirit' with the applied arts reform movement also gave a new impetus to the desire to 'improve' the domestic interior: 'The furnishing of our habitations is the real provider and educator of our modern applied arts.' Another writer claimed that 'art will become a common property of the whole people only when it finds a place also in the home'. An English voice placed the onus slightly more on the receiving end: do not lay down 'fast laws', but 'lead people to think for themselves'.[62] What was required was a combination of the ethos of the advice books with discussions of design.

Journalism, not mentioned thus far, also had a part to play. The arts sections of newspapers and some of the countless highbrow magazines (later also the more popular journals) carried pieces that were critical, even satirical, in tone; but this criticism was held to be legitimate and for the common good. It seemed the writers had no axe to grind for themselves, especially since many of the articles appeared anonymously.[63] Both Eastlake and Falke, the most influential authors in Anglo-American and German-speaking territories respectively, first wrote in general interest journals during the 1860s. Their texts are ostensibly aimed at the layman, at the consumer. Falke and, a little later, historians-cum-critics such as Charles Blanc, Henry Havard and Ferdinand Luthmer all took great pains to familiarize themselves with the various trades so that they could explain technical matters in a language accessible to the non-specialist (an accessibility from which the present book also profits greatly). However, all these articles maintained a professional tone, avoiding anything that sounded amateurish, such as the 'ladies' work' advocated especially in American books on household décor up to that date. Many a trader in, say, the 1880s, when faced with numerous new, weighty tomes on décor, must have wondered whether all those words were really needed. Was it not enough to just make things, or at most produce a good picture? However, the trader might not have realized was his trade language could never have aroused a client's interest in the same way.

No other writer became more involved in the topic than Jakob von Falke. From the early 1860s, Falke was the authority on applied arts in the Austrian Empire, working closely with all the institutions that were aiming for reform of the *Kunstgewerbe*. He first studied history, which brought him to the new Germanisches Nationalmuseum in Nuremberg, although he was not an enthusiastic convert to German medievalism. Falke's preference was for South Kensington rationalism combined with the international Italian Renaissance style. He also came gradually to know and to love many European folk idioms, to which we shall come later. The only culture he strongly disliked was that of the 'tasteless' French Louis styles. Falke lacked Viollet-le-Duc's assiduousness and Semper's depth and breadth, but his writings exceed theirs in clarity and user-friendliness.[64]

Based on articles he had written from 1860 on, in 1871 Falke published *Die Kunst im Hause. Geschichtliche und kritisch-ästhetische Studien über die Decoration und Ausstattung der Wohnung* ('Art in the House: A historical and critical-aesthetic study of the decoration and fitting out of the dwelling' – note the last word, which signified mainly, though not exclusively, an apartment). It went through six German editions, plus American, Swedish and Hungarian versions.[65] Falke devotes just under half of the book to the history of the dwelling from Greek antiquity to the 18th century. He then progresses to a systematic consideration of various kinds of rooms, which are subdivided into the basic units of walls, floor and ceiling. Unity of design is stressed throughout: 'vessels and utensils are single items … they constitute a full work of art only when combined in the human dwelling'.[66] Falke does, however, betray a literal approach to the term 'art': having discussed fabrics, furniture, wallpaper and much else, at the end of the book he pulls out all the stops of Classical idealist language: 'the language of beauty, the most beautiful happiness … that nectar which Minerva brought down from heaven for her lover Prometheus … and who has thus a share in the most beautiful happiness, art'.[67] Much of the book is dedicated to decorating the house with paintings and sculpture, and at one point Falke seems to step back from the whole new concept of art in the home: 'house and apartment should be artistically decorated, but hardly [constitute] a work of art in the highest, monumental sense'.[68] Thus, for Falke, until the late 1870s at least, 'art in the home' means literally works of fine art in the house.

Other major books in German appeared only at the end of the 1870s. The Leipzig architect Oskar Mothes brought out *Unser Heim im Schmucke der Kunst* ('Our Home as Beautified by Art') in 1879, a lively illustrated volume stressing the diversity of rooms and also advertising numerous traders; and in 1879–80 Georg Hirth published *Das deutsche Zimmer der Renaissance*, the most successful work after Falke's, which opted strongly for a particular style, Alpine Bavarian Altdeutsch. The 1880s brought many more books, especially by the circumspect Ferdinand Luthmer, who even more than Falke excelled with the clarity of his technical explanations.[69]

England prided itself on leading with the first proper book on the interior: Charles Locke Eastlake's *Hints on Household Taste in Furniture, Upholstery and Other Details*, published in 1868. Written from 1864 as a series of articles, it became the key text for a number of years.[70] Above all, Eastlake felt free to chide the trade as pretentious and dishonest and most customers, women in particular, as too gullible – a viewpoint he borrowed, as a member of the neo-Gothic school of architecture, from Pugin and Ruskin. (The perplexed *Athenaeum* wrote, 'If any "upholsterer" murders Mr. Eastlake, he will be a martyr for art.'[71]) However, Eastlake's book was far from being systematic or from offering comprehensive advice: one searches in vain for extended discussions, or major illustrations, of complete rooms. Furthermore, Eastlake does not seem to care much for history. He does not highlight a particular old style, but recommends a very heavy wooden, vaguely Gothic type of furniture to combat what he saw as modern flimsiness. Easily recognizable, the 'Eastlake style' (as it was dubbed) contributed greatly to his fame, especially in the United States. Forming almost a supplement to Eastlake, an equally influential London book was Bruce Talbert's *Gothic Forms Applied to Furniture, Metal Work and Decoration for Domestic Purposes* (1867), which gave some complete interior views in an ornate and at the same time severe style.[72]

In England, architectural journals from the late 1860s supplied many designs of whole interiors, as well as incisive texts, some written by the architect E. W. Godwin.[73] Two books by

Georg Hirth's *Das deutsche Zimmer der Renaissance: Anregungen zur häuslichen Kunstpflege* ('The German Room of the Renaissance: Hints for the Domestic Cultivation of Art'), first published in 1879–80, was Germany's most successful art in the home book of the time, and also the most scientific. The title page was probably designed by Lothar Meggendorfer (see pp. 224, 309).

a disciple of the South Kensington theories of ornament, Christopher Dresser, provided prescriptions on matters of colour and flat décor.[74] One really new kind of publishing venture was the 'Art at Home' series, begun in 1876 partly in cooperation with American publishers and illustrators. These little volumes are characterized by their corporate look: they are artily designed, informally illustrated and 'reasonably' (but not very cheaply) priced at 2*s.* 6*d.* They steered clear both of high theory and of practical householder's advice. In a rather Eastlakean sense, 'art' here implied a suspicion of 'bad taste' and of all 'showiness' and 'commerce' generally. Much more explicitly than before, these slim texts were intended for the homes' users, and most especially for women: as the cultural historian Emma Ferry has underlined, they were not without some sideswipes at the misogynous Eastlake and Dresser. The architectural press in turn criticized the little volumes as ephemeral. The first, *A Plea for Art in the House*, was written by Revd W. J. Loftie, an eminent preacher as well as an ardent collector; it turned the tables on furniture manufacture completely by giving advice principally on the 'the prudence of making collections'. A more systematic account of decoration was found in the second volume in the series, *Suggestions for House Decoration* (1876), by the already mentioned decorator-team of Rhoda and Agnes Garrett. Although women writers had already contributed to the sphere of home advice books, here the Garretts branched out in providing their own designs. The next three volumes, written in an ever lighter tone – *The Drawing Room*, *The Dining Room* and *The Bedroom and Boudoir* – were also supplied by women.[75]

During the 1880s, numerous books and articles spread a sense of the topic's importance. The longest was Mrs H. R. (Eliza) Haweis's *The Art of Decoration* (1881); other books, such as those by the architect Col. Robert W. Edis and by the decorative designer Lewis F. Day, relied on both text and illustrations. The general tone became ever chattier, for instance in Mrs Panton's many works, so that by 1890 the whole topic appeared both saturated and once more restricted to the woman's sphere.[76]

By 1880 a new movement had appeared in London, called the 'Aesthetic' or simply the 'Art' movement, which distanced itself from the strict institutions at South Kensington and from all kinds of prescriptive, rigid reformist pronouncements. It consisted of a rather free grouping of artists and critics, including James McNeill Whistler, Oscar Wilde and William Morris.[77] Many of these names achieved worldwide acclaim with their designs as well as through their self-publicity. ('Old France', on the other hand – despite its global reputation in the applied arts before the late 1880s – produced no names even remotely comparable with those in London.) To these London artists, commerce at all levels appeared beyond redemption. Objects of low intrinsic value, such as a 'Japanese' peacock feathers, may be worth just as much as richer artefacts. As Lewis F. Day commented about 'everyday art': 'humble … as it may be … it was indeed art'. At the same time Wilde was pleading for a new 'refinement'. The old hierarchy of decorum had been thoroughly upset, so that its upper and lower levels could seemingly touch each other. Soon, however, the term 'art' itself appeared hackneyed. When William Morris spoke and wrote (briefly) on the subject of interior décor, in his lecture 'Making the Best of It' (*c.* 1879), he foregrounded neither 'home' nor 'art'; and somewhat later Day warned against 'too much art': 'distrust the word'.[78]

For the most diverse and thorough investigations into the art of the domestic interior in the 1870s we must turn to the United States.[79] Eastlake's moralist language, together with his 'honest' wooden designs, had a huge impact there,[80] pushing aside the copious models for 'pretty' domestic ornament provided by *Godey's* publications and others. Interior design was now a topic to be discussed in a critical language. In 1874 Moncure Daniel Conway, a firm Anglophile, presented a glowing report on the new English art movement – on Owen Jones, William Morris and others.[81] The following year saw the commencement of a seemingly never-ending series of articles in major magazines (those by H. Hudson Holly in *Harper's Monthly* are typical), and from 1876 there was a veritable flood of books. The English 'Art at Home' series was coproduced in the United States, to be followed a little later by an all-American sequence of handsome little volumes called 'Appletons' Home Books'; and the Philadelphia World's Fair of 1876 was widely celebrated for its English and American interiors. The United States' first fully professional architectural journal, the *American Architect*, appeared the same year and included both thoroughgoing texts – especially those by Henry Van Brunt – and superior illustrations of whole interiors.[82]

Two years later, several series that had begun in journals matured into books, of which Harriet Prescott Spofford's *Art Decoration Applied to Furniture* stands out: well illustrated, historically researched (Spofford relied on the English antiquarians and on Viollet-le-Duc), and with formal descriptions that successfully convey the character of materials and ensembles, it is quite probably the best text on the subject so far. The same year, 1878, also saw books by the idiosyncratic Eugene Clarence Gardner, which combined profound statements with the kind of practical advice found in earlier manuals. For good measure, Falke's *Die Kunst im Hause* was issued in a lavish American edition. In *The House Beautiful: Essays on Beds and Tables, Stools and Candlesticks*, Clarence Cook, the most prominent art critic in the United States, adopted a specially light tone: history and morality were replaced by nostalgia (an issue to which we shall return). Somewhat to their surprise, the Americans now felt a degree of independence from the Old World, although Oscar Wilde reunited the countries once again during his famed lecture tour of 1882.[83]

France joined the chorus only during the 1880s. It had also come round to the applied arts reform movement rather late, its powerful manufactures, with their reputation for high-quality work, seemingly not in need of reform. Viollet-le-Duc had investigated Gothic like no one before him, but he did not preach it as assiduously as his English confrères. In 1882 the country's most respected author on art, Charles Blanc, brought out his somewhat unclearly entitled *Grammaire des arts décoratifs*, subtitled *Décoration intérieure de la maison*. Was the publisher afraid of putting 'house' in the main title? Essentially, Blanc offers an account of the various 'industries' involved in producing décor, having patiently acquired technical knowledge in each field.[84] The art historian and later art administrator Henry Havard ('an uncontested moral authority among art writers') provides more detail in *L'Art dans la maison: Grammaire de l'ameublement* (1884). He attempts to address all aspects of art in the home systematically, dividing the work into four sections. These comprise a short history; details on all crafts and trades; the actual *grammaire* on the subject of furnishing, which gives advice in the form of fifty rules for a 'harmonie intelligente' and a 'logique aimable', and which could be called the first extended theory of the domestic interior; and, lastly, the by-now familiar consideration of the interior room by room. Havard's subsequent *Dictionnaire de l'ameublement et de la décoration* (1887–89) – a massive 4,000-page work with some 2,800 illustrations – provided a remarkable wealth of historical information about the domestic interior and all its objects, chiefly French in scope.[85]

Havard's *Dictionnaire* already marks an endpoint to this phase of home art books, in that the historical account now begins to edge out the decorator's recipes, the do-it-yourself aspect. The initial impetus for this first phase of texts had come from a conviction on the part of the art writers-cum-taste officials that the general public needed to be informed in order to deal critically with the trade. In addition, many books carried a special chapter on the involvement of the woman of the house, particularly Falke's. But once the notion of 'art in the home' appeared fully established, the subject divided into quite distinct branches. Detailed technical works, such as Ferdinand Luthmer's, were again aimed more at the professions, while books that benefited from exhaustive historical research were destined for the insatiable antique collector and the museum curator. At this point, however, the decorative unity of the interior was once more lost sight of. For the new kind of art guru – William Morris or, later, Alfred Lichtwark[86] – 'home décor' was too narrow a concern, even if they continued the onslaught on bad taste. Indeed, 'art in the home' as the embodiment of values subscribed to in all dwellings never regained the intellectual and artistic vigour it enjoyed around 1880. The new 'designer power' that appeared from the 1890s onwards had no need of advice texts either.

Folio volumes and journals

Picture-based publications by their very nature hardly ever served a single type of user. From the 1860s and 1870s in France, and especially in Germany, a large number of folio volumes offered elaborately created views of whole interiors: one thinks of publications by Eugène Prignot or Martin Kimbel, which could in fact be considered works by designers rather than by the trade. Other volumes were brought out by manufacturing firms or even initiated by publishers themselves, such as C. Claesen of Liège, who – remarkably – also had offices in both Paris and Berlin.[87]

Considered together, journals demonstrate the sheer diversity of agents more than any other source. We have already mentioned publications with views of domestic interiors that

Henry Havard's *L'Art dans la maison* ('Art in the House'), published in 1884 – the most comprehensive work on the domestic interior then available.

were produced by the individual trades, by architects, by applied arts organizations or by fine art journals. The United States excelled in this area, while France, with its entrenched traditions of craft and manufacturing, lagged behind. Initially, however, few journals catered to the mix of trades needed for the complete interior. In London, *The House Furnisher and Decorators' Upholsterers' and Cabinet-makers' Monthly Journal*, begun in 1871, was cheap and short-lived. Subsequent English periodicals reverted to a focus on individual trades, although they often showed whole interiors, such as the comprehensive *Cabinet Maker and Art Furnisher*, first published in 1880. From 1883, the mainly trade-oriented *Decorator and Furnisher* appeared in New York: although it shared quite similar content with other journals, which were aimed either at the 'amateur' (that is, mainly the collector) or at individual trades, the *Furnisher and Decorator* has a claim to be the first organ devoted to the domestic interior in its entirety, addressing both users and professionals – a forerunner of hundreds of its kind.[88]

A telling illustration of the way interior décor gradually became considered as a whole was the *Innendekoration*, Germany's most successful periodical on the interior. In its first year, 1890, it was entitled (in German) *Professional Journal for Interior Decoration, especially for the Furniture, Carpet, Wallpaper, Curtain and Upholstery Fabric Industries*, mentioning just about every conceivable element. But from the journal's second year, the publisher, Alexander Koch of Darmstadt, realized that its readers also included many clients and dropped the trades from the title, which now read: *Illustrierte Kunstgewerbliche Zeitschrift für Innendekoration*. The contents are a clever mix of veiled advertisements, technical information, art journalism – much of it inspired by the applied arts reform movement – and copious illustrations of an equally varied kind. The journal was still a mouthpiece for the trade, but that did not need to be made explicit: instead, *Innendekoration* was now presented as something of interest to everyone.[89] By 1897 Koch, one of the most astute art publishers of the day, raised the stakes yet again, featuring top-class designer interiors in a new kind of glossy art journal entitled *Deutsche Kunst und Dekoration*. By this point, a large body of easily accessible information was available, ranging from the artiest to the homeliest publications – even though the golden age of unity between 'art' and 'home' had arguably already been left behind.

A calendar advertisement for *The Cabinet Maker and Art Furnisher* (1885). The journal's editor was John Williams Benn, founder of the Benn political dynasty.

Shops and exhibitions

Whether it was defined as art or not, the quantity of home décor had grown immeasurably by the 1870s and 1880s. In large cities, each year tens of thousands aspired to a higher status in their newly built dwellings, and their needs and wishes had to be served ever more efficiently. In addition, we can assume that there were now far more customers who wanted to purchase a complete interior in one transaction. The trades – initially characterized as unorganized, each one closeted in its own area of expertise – needed to find more effective ways of reaching clients in a united fashion.

As with other products during the 19th century, the marketing of the interior was marked by the rise of the middleman, who operated between the craftsman-manufacturer and the purchaser who might not have the time or inclination to go directly to the producer. The 18th-century *marchand mercier*, who was able to supply most of the required items, has already been mentioned, as has the *décorateur*, whose role was not only to coordinate décor in the room, but also to advise the client in the act of purchasing objects and materials. By the middle of the 19th century, the making and the selling of furniture in London had become separate businesses. In Central Europe it took somewhat longer, since the last of the old guild restrictions controlling and restricting the roles of individual trades were removed only in the 1860s. Ostensibly, the main sphere of commerce was the 'point of sale', or the contact with the purchaser; but there was also a growing sphere of decision-making between commerce and production. It was the buyers of the large shops who communicated to the manufacturer what would sell.[90]

The display of whole rooms in exhibitions and shops became more sophisticated as the century progressed, great advances being made at the World's Fairs. The main aim of commercial displays was to demonstrate completeness and variety. Whereas most early examples consisted simply of a loose arrangement of furnishings, concepts of visual coordination and of the grouping of items so that they resembled a complete environment slowly gained ground. Whole rooms were shown, with all décor and even ceilings in place, so that eventually they felt like actual living rooms (*see overleaf*).

right Showroom of the London Marble Working Company, Westminster, 1841. In the earlier kind of commercial display, all items were simply placed one next to another.

below Advertisement for cast-iron fireplaces, Manchester, 1887. Here, attempts have been made to unify the exhibition stand.

below right This room at the Philadelphia World's Fair of 1876, by James Shoolbred & Co., London, still shows the furnishings arranged rather casually.

By definition, commerce – like trade – could not come under the heading 'art'. The applied arts movement from the 1850s and 1860s onwards rubbed this in: 'O holy Falke, grand inquisitor of all industrialists', quipped a colleague in Munich.[91] A number of English traders tried to get round the problem by simply attaching the word 'art': in the 1870s 'art-cabinetmakers' and 'art-manufactures' of all kinds mushroomed in London without it being very clear how they distinguished themselves from their non-'art' brethren, except perhaps in their prices. Predictably, this attraction did not last for very long, and in fact the English decorative art gurus saw it as counterproductive.[92]

And yet the official world of the applied arts was in the end not so far removed from the world of business, at least in Central Europe. The promoters of applied arts, the museums and the industries all strove to increase national production. Occasionally Falke could sound like their spokesperson: '… the most modern dwelling, as it grows out of the efforts of the art

A much-publicized 'complete' interior at the Philadelphia World's Fair, 1876, by the New York firm Kimbel and Cabus.

industries …'[93] While many traders had initially been sceptical of the new state interference, they soon realized that these public bodies provided added publicity. One might even find traders who chimed in with the reformers' demand for restraint.[94] Traders and officials worked particularly closely on the innumerable exhibitions that were popular during the period, and the plethora of prizes and medals given to firms were entirely welcome.

We are interested here less in the quantity of merchandise available in the shops or in their pricing methods (William Burton of Oxford Street,[95] for example, sold fireplaces ranging from £1 12s. to £109) than in the way some shops tried to predetermine the arrangement of a complete interior. Traders enabled the public to select paperhangings and curtains that were in harmony with each other.[96] In the early 1860s Falke was immensely impressed with the 'colossal' shops in London, and with the way they sold 'ready-made all the furnishings for different kinds of rooms, each put together separately, and in different sizes and in different prices; and thus English dwellings show far more stylistic unity than is usually found in German interiors'.[97] After 1900, the sale of unified interiors was widely taken for granted in Central Europe as well, so that even 'middling consumers' demanded to see 'model rooms'. Some shops styled themselves as 'exhibitions', trying to avoid the look of a 'bazaar' – and in 1882 one Parisian shop even called itself 'un musée'.[98] Some store catalogues developed from a mass of small pictures of individual items into proper books, presenting a number of complete interiors and chatty comments in the manner of the 'art at home' books.[99]

Were the shops' room ensembles influenced by those on display at the large trade fairs or even the exhibitions? Illustrations of such rooms have survived from the French Industrial Exposition of 1844,[100] whereas the giant Great Exhibition, held in London in 1851, showed much furniture but hardly any domestic ensembles. It was the 1867 Exposition Universelle in Paris that promised to exhibit 'all manifestations of life', especially in the 'Gallery of furniture and other objects destined for the dwelling'.[101] Unity of design was, however, most evident in the richer, more official displays, especially the 'Pavillon de l'Impératrice', which had been designed inside and out by Henri Penon. 'La conception était parfaite' was one judgment – and the whole was a snip at just 500,000 francs.[102] At the Vienna World's Fair of 1873, it was again the pavilions of the emperor and the empress that were 'designed by one hand, their execution directed by one head'. Already in 1871 Falke had boasted of something 'wholly new', which 'we' had installed in the newly opened Museum für Kunst und Industrie in Vienna: namely five 'complete artistically conceived apartments', each supplied by a different firm.[103] Several years later, the Philadelphia Fair of 1876 featured a large number of rooms mainly by North

The interior of a Paris antique shop, 1886. Here, all signs of a commercial environment have been completely expunged.

The Schäffer & Walcker furnishing store in Berlin, 1890.

American and English firms. Two ways of exhibiting an interior emerged (something that can be observed also in trade catalogues, such as those produced by Shoolbred & Co. in London): first, the simple grouping of items of furniture, and second, an attempt to create the sort of complete interior that might be found within a dwelling, with a ceiling and even a window included. In the great German art and applied arts exhibition at Munich in 1876, an architect's interior, the 'Seidlzimmer', stole the show with its meticulously unified design. Thereafter, regional German and Austrian trade fairs abounded in complete rooms, each set up under the name of a firm; sometimes the name of the architect was given as well.[104]

The purchaser

The following chapter will be concerned exclusively with what the shops, the craftspeople and the designers provided; the users play only a subsidiary role, in that they were urged to keep interiors in the state in which the makers left them. In Chapters IV and V the user appears once more, but chiefly with regard to the way designers and their spokespersons imagined him or her responding to the meanings they supplied. Here, however, we need to consider exactly how we should view the agency of the client at the point of sale. Does a domestic interior represent what the user had in mind, or is its appearance simply the result of what the producers wanted to and were able to provide or sell? There is also a secondary question: does the interior spring from the artist-designer's or architect's convictions, or does it result merely from what industry and commerce offered? The plethora of ideas that follow constitutes the main and certainly the most novel characteristic of the debates that took place in the later 19th century.

Classical capitalist economics posits an unproblematic automatism in the relationship between production and consumption: what is produced is needed, and what is needed is produced. Where art and design are concerned, the classical art tradition, as well as the modernist view, come out rather differently: here, the balance is tilted away from the client and the user: what has been designed ought to be respected as bona fide art.

Producers, on the other hand, entertained the most complex views about this relationship. As we have seen, commerce had grown into a major power in its own right. At the same time it felt that it had to stress the agency of the purchaser. Originally, the relationship between producer and client had been determined entirely by the class structure. In the case of the richest patrons, like the British 'gentleman architects', his or her input could be very considerable, even decisive, and the producers and even the designers could be downgraded

almost to the level of the patron's executants. In the later 19th century, traders considered all purchasers to be knowledgeable and choosy 'customers'. Naturally, purchasers were still categorized according to their status, and trades still elevated some clients above others with statements such as: 'la clientèle des mondains les plus délicats …'.[105] The new mass displays in the shops were aimed at what were assumed to be the clients' diverse requirements, by stressing the many different types and combinations of object available for their interiors. 'The vast majority of our furniture is produced for stock'; 'the purchaser wants to see finished pieces of furniture and, within a short period, receive the ordered goods' – such were the shops' refrains. Statements like that of Mrs Haweis – 'what [customers] want … they will assuredly get' – were, strictly speaking, redundant in a capitalist world, but they indicated a growing sense of the agency, or some kind of empowerment, of the mass of purchasers. One factor, of course, were the very books that Mrs Haweis and her colleagues were writing, which provided an independent source of advice for the clients. 'Customers became astute purchasers', claimed the historian David Handlin, and Henry James spoke of the 'power of purchase'. According to some, it was neither the design elite nor the producers who determined the course of fashion, but the multitude's 'Kauflust' – its desire to buy things and its pleasure in doing so.[106]

Did commerce succeed in convincing others of its art credentials? At times it appeared so, but not according to many members of the new reform movements. Critics of commercialism, from Pugin, Ruskin and Eastlake onwards, had seen most of commerce's pursuits as anti-art and as conducive to bad taste. The ordinary client was also held to be an ignoramus, and the way he or she simply swallowed what commerce rammed down their throats appeared little short of a cultural disaster. Underlying this kind of condemnation was also the old fear that the hierarchy of decorum was being upset, that the lower classes were using 'too much' décor. This argument provided one of the bases of the Continental applied arts reform movement, although its protagonists also believed that the masses could eventually be led to good art. Meanwhile, a new type of designer–guru, exemplified by William Morris, preached anti-commercialism under the somewhat vaguely worded banner of 'common sense'. The history of the applied arts of the 19th and 20th centuries was subsequently written almost entirely on the basis of these gurus' agendas.

What has been little noticed thus far is the way in which, in the late 19th century, discussions surrounding art in the home also generated a new concept of the user as semi-independent. The client in his or her own home should, and did, try to exercise judgment independently of commerce, and even, astonishingly, independently of 'art', at least in England in the 1870s and Germany in the 1880s – an issue that we will touch on briefly in Chapter VI.

The notion of user independence resurfaced in the 1960s in the form of 'user studies' – a late modernist trend in the field of design theory. Economists, sociologists and anthropologists subsequently developed much more complex views on the role of the recipients, within what

'A Furnishing Showroom in the Nineteenth Century', from an 1886 issue of the *Cabinet Maker*. The image captures customers hesitating and deliberating.

are comprehensively called 'consumption studies', using psychological approaches to analyse the symbolic uses of the interior. In a recent major study on the retailing and consumption of furnishings, the design historian Clive Edwards has attempted to shift the emphasis back somewhat, claiming that in order to arrive at their own decisions, customers often actually needed the seller's specialist advice. Wishing to counter the art world's (and modernism's) distrust of commerce, he ends by stressing various unifying factors within a 'retail–consumption interface'.[107]

Women and interior décor

Critics of the 19th century did newly define one of the user–agents with great precision: the woman of the house. Her role now assumed a considerable degree of specificity and thus autonomy. In the richest houses, either the man or the woman of the house could traditionally pursue its decoration, since their time was their own. But for classes further down the social scale, the man was 'excused' as someone who did not normally have time to spare for such home matters. It was the woman, now conceived as confined to the house, who had to be in charge. Playing with an oft-repeated saying, one female French writer opined that 'le style, c'est l'homme – l'installation intérieure, c'est la femme'.[108] Discussions of 'beauty' only emphasized this distinction, since it was considered that this was women's chief innate quality.

A problem arose, however, with the issue of how independent, or otherwise, women were of commerce. In a new kind of toing and froing, women were courted by the shops on the one hand, and on the other urged by reformers to resist the sales talk. Commerce increasingly

below The catalogue of Carl Müller & Comp., Berlin (1894).

below right Frontispiece of the New York-based *Decorator and Furnisher* (1883).

assumed that much buying for the home was done by women and hence tried to give women the impression that they themselves were 'in the know'. At the same time, it was felt that shopkeepers were 'versed in the ways of leading her'. When they chided the trade, the reformers thus implied that women customers were particularly gullible: 'Ladies are principally responsible for the evil, it is they who mainly determine the various household arrangements.'[109] Several of the institutions that were occupied with reform of the applied arts, such as art schools and exhibitions, devoted themselves exclusively to the art education of women.

But the apparent strength of the woman's position, with her widely agreed-upon gender characteristics, transcended these limitations. The sociologist and philosopher Georg Simmel declared steadiness and unity as important female qualities that paralleled supra-personal forms such as works of art.[110] A more direct and detailed analogy evolved between décor and what were defined as a woman's inherent physical characteristics. Very simply, the female body appeared to guide the forms of decoration in the home: 'gentle undulations, insensible transitions, smooth and soft surfaces, circular and conical forms, are all considered beautiful'.[111] It also seemed natural to discern a close correspondence between women's flowing garments and the fall of decorative textiles; and colour and lighting could, and should, be devised in such a way that they suited a woman's complexion.[112]

Definitions of the woman's influence on the interior could not stop at such passivity, however. Within the comprehensive approach of the applied arts reform movement, a policy had to be formulated that recognized the active involvement of women. In many ways it reflected Schiller's view of beauty as tied in with, and conducive to, happiness and even to the moral good. A woman's beauty did not just exist by itself, but was linked to an eagerness to nurture beauty in general, and thus – especially in Germanic discourses – it became associated with the whole home ethic, with the 'woman's sense for comfort and the enjoyment of beauty' within the home.[113] The *altdeutsche Frau* could be depicted as elegant even when performing such mundane tasks as ironing (see p. 227). In turn, this concept informed a general trend towards viewing household cares and housework not as drudgery, but as a sphere suitable for poetic interpretation.

At this point Falke introduces his conviction that it is the woman who is properly responsible for the unity of domestic interior décor, or at least for its vital final touches. To the lengthy final chapter of his book *Die Kunst im Hause* he gives the title 'The profession of women in the furthering of beauty', and embarks on a wide-ranging and part positive, part restrictive analysis of the female contribution to the fine arts. Underlying this viewpoint is, again, the rationale that women possess a generic capability to form 'a comprehensive view, a feeling for harmony, a receptivity to artistic effect'.[114] The woman's particular task, when the trades and the decorator have completed their work, is to devise and arrange the countless smaller elements of décor within a room – the hanging of pictures and suchlike. Some French writers agreed, stressing these 'womanly activities' and 'the decorative sentiment innate in the other sex'. She might even relieve the decorator of some of this duties, draping the curtains, for example. The author, Ris-Paquot, does not want to do the professional decorator an injustice: the latter's work displays an 'irreproachable Classical regularity', yet is liable to produce a 'monotony engendered by banality'.[115]

Aside from these still rather vague definitions of 'womanly activities' in the home, it was also recognized that women actively created beautiful objects. Although mostly small, such artefacts could be crucial to a room's appearance. In the early decades of the century, it was understood that gentlewomen produced handiwork largely to pass the time, availing themselves of a plethora of materials and techniques. Women were making 'innumerable implements of domestic life'.[116] But as far as the applied arts reformers were concerned, these activities were not serious enough, merely simplistically diligent and mindless (Berlin woolwork, or *Kreuzstich*, was one example given). Following these denunciations, the characterization of women was subtly changed, or rather it was purged of lightness or superficiality. Instead, the applied arts reformers began to identify serious-sounding female capabilities, which centred almost entirely on textile work and on its technical, as well as historical, expertise, especially in more complex kinds of embroidery. Finally, women's textile work was viewed as almost fully professional, allowing it to leave the confines of the home.[117]

A more comprehensive view of the role of the woman in the home, encompassing not only art but also the practical and psychological spheres, will be set out in Chapter IV. The specific concept of the woman as home textile craftswoman or creative artist did not, however, outlast the 19th century. In the 1890s it was hit both by the more leisurely smartness of the Belle Époque[118] and by new emancipatory movements that stressed the woman's influence in the wider world. As for forms and textures, the fashion for lavish fabrics and their 'feminine' curvaceousness was also disappearing around the same time. Ultimately, the role of the agent could be extended from the woman of the house to other members of the family, to the father and the children, and perhaps even to the servants who were all supposed to imbibe the cultural and moral values of the artful house. The new home was a completely mutualist, holistic concept.

The dynamics of the illustration

The domestic interior had become a wordy topic. Was it not much more instructive, as well as more pleasurable, to look at an image? According to collector and historian Charlotte Gere, 'The art of depicting the interior reached its highest point of refinement in the nineteenth century.'[119] Initially, however, high-quality pictures of domestic interiors were quite rare. In the European tradition of painting, the domestic interior had played only a minor role (except in the Netherlands) on account of its relatively lowly status. In the 19th century itself, only a handful of famous painters – Adolph Menzel, James Tissot or Édouard Vuillard, for instance – excelled in works where the domestic interior formed the main subject.[120]

Issues surrounding the representation of interiors are discussed throughout this book. As mentioned earlier, commerce had a significant role to play in the dissemination of images, although one should remember that tradesmen in the applied arts were not nearly as wealthy as their architectural brethren, from whom a far larger number of high-quality pictures, mostly of lavish interiors, have come down to us.[121] To draw an interior – rendering the whole room, with all its contents, in a spatially convincing way, and catching all the nuances of colour and tone – is a particularly difficult task, for which a fully trained artist would normally be required. The type of image Gere is mainly referring to above forms a rather special category, which

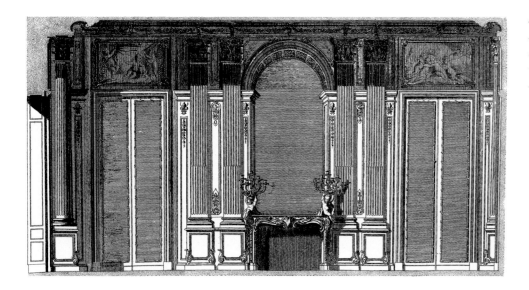

The elevation of one side of a room – usually the wall containing the fireplace – was a type of image employed by all trades and designers since at least the 18th century. This example is from the *Grande Encyclopédie* of 1762.

one might call the chronicle picture. Throughout the first half of the century, the Central European nobility commissioned artists to make renderings of their lavish rooms; more modest interior views by amateurs have also been preserved, which later charmed so many art historians, Mario Praz in particular.[122]

The topic here is the diversity of images procured by or for the trades and the designers. By the 19th century several standard methods of conveying designs had been formulated. We may begin with what architects, especially in France, had provided for a long time: sections through buildings, which allowed one to see the full wall decoration, including the fireplaces, of the principal rooms, but not usually their movable furnishings. A method more common in the 18th century but still practised in the 19th was to accompany the plan with elevations of all four walls.[123] The most convenient and most frequently used technique, which combined both the architect's and the decorating trade's conceptions, was the elevational rendering of just one wall. A derivative is the upholsterer's elevational rendering of a window or a door in order to show the folds of the curtains and or the portières – probably the 19th century's most ubiquitous kind of illustration of the interior. Furniture producers, however, required images of a different kind: their preferred mode was a perspectival or axonometric rendering, although it looked rather stiff to eyes outside the trade. Naturally, the trades also aimed to show the effect of their products in the room as a whole, at least in the more expensive types of publication. This was normally achieved through perspectival renderings, which assumed a viewing point outside the actual space – peepshow-like – and usually from a slightly elevated position. The technique resulted in a wide, panoramic image that made the room look large, but once more the effect was quite stilted. Slightly off-centre and lower viewpoints helped to liven up the views.

On the whole, few original drawings produced by the applied arts have come down to us. Visual evidence for their designs consists almost entirely of books – the trade's pattern books –

Section through a building showing wall décor but no furniture – a type of drawing invariably provided by architects. For a villa near Paris, 1867.

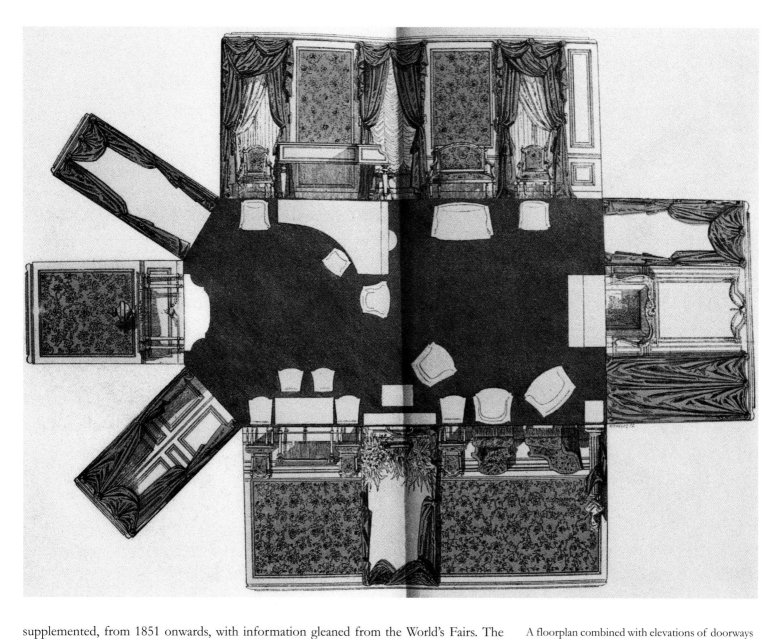

A floorplan combined with elevations of doorways and all four walls; few of these survive from the 19th century. From Henry Havard's *L'Art dans la maison* (1884).

supplemented, from 1851 onwards, with information gleaned from the World's Fairs. The nature of these illustrations was to a very large extent determined by the choice of printing methods. Early representations displayed an outline style that conformed to the appearance of traditional copper engraving, and soon to the more finely detailed steel-engraving methods. Artists turned to fine engraving to render textural effects, which culminated after mid-century in the delicate plates produced by the Parisian Rodolphe Pfnor. By contrast, the much cheaper processes of woodcut and wood engraving, which appeared in the 1830s, gave less definition but a more lively character to the illustration as a whole. Lithographs looked very different again, smoothing contours and providing infinite gradations of tone. Colour was crucial to some trades, notably textiles, but it was very expensive, since it had to be added by hand to each copy of an engraving, resulting in strong, often garish effects. From the 1840s colour lithography ('chromos') solved the problem.[124]

By the late 1870s a multitude of reproduction techniques were appearing side by side, as in the important publications of Havard and Falke.[125] What was required of an illustration of an interior, an object or a building began to change fundamentally. There was now a new demand for immediacy, for what one could loosely call an impression, rather than a faithful drawing of outlines. A view of the whole was not always needed – ironically, just at the time when there was a heightened concern for the design of complete interiors. A partial view could be quite effective, particularly in spatial terms, since it could suggest a sharp contrast between nearness and distance. Conversely, an object in a room was usually shown off to greater advantage as

opposite This more sophisticated use of perspective (possibly based on a photograph) combines meticulous detail with a look of immediacy (compare the earlier, stiffer view overleaf), all reproduced in full-colour lithography. Such folio plates were still largely produced by the trade for the trade, and of their creators hardly anything is known. By H. Kolb and T. Seubert, Stuttgart, 1885–88.

A strict use of perspective, of the kind used earlier by the trade. Design for an *antichambre*, from the *Magazin des Meubles* (1865).

part of a wider group than in isolation. Textures, too, could appear more convincing if rendered casually rather than diligently. Light and darkness were also crucial factors: whereas earlier interiors had appeared evenly lit, carefully controlled lighting and shading now made frequent appearances (to be discussed in detail in Chapter IV).[126]

These new methods of representing interiors were clearly derived from centuries-old techniques in painting, drawing and etching – impasto and strong colour contrasting with a diligent outline, for instance, or the trend of the picturesque towards conveying immediacy and surprise. Illustrators were keen to leave behind their role as servants to the trade and to ally themselves with painters, or at least with graphic artists. Illustrations also reveal an influence from below, in the sketchiness and immediacy that were borrowed from cheaper wood engravings, by now very widely available. All the 'art at home' books, as well as Clarence Cook's *The House Beautiful* in the United States, adopted wood engravings so that they could include lively pictures close to the text. The most prominent author of the new, casual type of picture was T. Raffles Davison, a regular contributor to *The British Architect*. In addition, most designers, and sometimes even the trade, further livened up their pictures by including figures.[127]

In the late 1870s photography began to make its impact felt. Thus far, it had not seemed practical for the trade to employ this still very cumbersome and expensive medium, although some home owners had already started to use it privately. The most obvious advantage of the photograph was that it was 'real': one writer praised its 'truth to life and lively rendering, the full truth'. Undoubtedly, photographs removed the difficult task of judging the correct spatial positioning in order to achieve a natural perspective and tonal precision, and viewpoints could be chosen with much more care. By showing actual interiors, photographs also boosted the trade's credibility: many early examples were taken at the new kinds of exhibition mentioned above.[128] The adoption of photography was not advantageous in all respects, however. Photography could not yet provide colour, although this was perhaps a relief to those who had become tired of the unsubtly bright hues of the ever cheaper chromolithographs. Another great problem was lighting, and the contrast between light and dark tones in an interior was usually vastly exaggerated. Patterns and details were hard to reproduce, as were large surfaces, which needed even lighting; this is probably why the English hardly used photographs for showing designs, or at least hardly published them. The Americans and the Germans, on the other hand, frequently published photographs in large volumes.[129] In Germany, the new medium seemed particularly well suited to the plasticity and bulk of the neo-Renaissance, as well as a desire to reveal textures patchily but intensively. With the new delight in the overall manipulation of light and dark, it

Immediacy and individuality through sketchiness: 'A quiet corner in L. H. Caliga's Studio, sketched by Mr. Caliga', from *The Decorator and Furnisher* (1885).

seemed that only the photograph (and possibly the etching) could produce real blackness, real darkness.[130] Finally, the sudden inclusion of photography in books can be explained by the greater availability of new automated reproduction techniques like photolithography, whose successful rendering of subtle tones played a specially important role.[131]

In about the mid-1890s, the creation of competent and striking images of whole interiors became even easier. Photographs were now much lighter, more evenly lit, and more faithfully reproduced in glossy periodicals. But there were rough sketches and individualized coloured fantasies, too. In the case of some architect-designers, such as Baillie Scott and Hermann Werle, both their interiors and the way they drew them were recognizably theirs.[132]

III

The Unified Interior: From Decoration to Design

Competing materials

César Daly, France's most influential architectural journalist, somewhat unexpectedly devoted a large publication to the work of the common housepainter. He had a very specific agenda, however: to praise the excellence of classical décor, for which – he claimed – the architects were responsible. From Daly's *Décorations intérieures peintes* (1877).

'It's all very well to talk about art when one is not actually doing it …' One can be sure that the old adage rang true for many a decorator or tradesman. For them, the 'who' and the 'why' were secondary to the 'how'. This chapter focuses on how décor was made and what it looked like. It does not deal with the detailed meanings of the motifs used in décor, and hardly touches on the question of styles. In most cases, preferences relating to form or colour can come under the heading 'fashion'. Instead, the principal aim of this chapter is to understand how each method of décor contributed to the look of the room as a whole.

Even today, most householders who are fitting out their homes consult a number of trades separately. To a greater or lesser extent, one expects these trades to work with each other, and the richer or more architect-dominated the interior, the more likely they are to do so. But we should begin by recalling the near absolute separation of the trades. Isaac Ware, in his influential treatise *A Complete Body of Architecture* (1756), wrote of three basic, and to him very different, kinds of interior fittings: stucco, the noblest, the most architectural kind; wainscoting, that is, covering the walls with wood; and lastly, 'hung' – covering the walls with paper or fabric.[1]

One factor may be taken as both symptomatic of the rivalries between trades and as confirmation of each trade's specificity, namely the way in which one craft encroached on the territory of another by imitating its materials. The most commonly substituted material was gilding on furniture or on plaster, which was not applied by a metalworker but painted on by the painter or gilder. In the 17th and 18th centuries, gilding had constituted decidedly the most important element of décor, far more so than colour; it continued in Empire and in many neo-Rococo interiors. For Jakob von Falke, gold still signified a 'glänzende Gesellschaft' – a 'brilliant society'. But already by the 1830s some critics, including John Claudius Loudon, advised that is should be used sparingly, so as to avoid the 'gaudy and vulgar'.[2] From the later 18th century many more kinds of substitutes became common, notably painting on walls to imitate textiles, and 'graining'– painting patterns on cheap wood to make it resemble a smarter variety. Wallpaper and papier-mâché became the best known of the imitation materials. Until mid-century and even beyond, all these methods were employed even for the very richest interiors, such as Buckingham Palace in London. The Bavarian royal architect Leo von Klenze proudly cites the 'imitated lapis lazuli … [used] to the greatest degree of deception' in the living rooms of the Königsbau in Munich.[3] Indeed, the very dexterity needed to carry off these imitations was held in great esteem. Later on in the century, with the enormous widening of the market and the increase in the range of materials and techniques, many new substitutes came to the fore, such as the extremely economical moulded zinc (*Zinkguss*), ideal for sculptured work and relief patterns,[4] or the coloured and patterned paper used to imitate stained glass.[5]

But during the 1850s to 1870s decorators and clients began to shun this kind of substitution. It now came to mean cheapness, recognizable to anybody 'in the know'. Initially, this dislike was due to the fervent preaching of theorists of 'architectural truth' such as Pugin and, later, Gottfried Semper, but it could also be linked to a new process of professionalization among the trades. Genuineness – of any material, not just the most precious – was claimed as an asset ('noble fabrics – smart people, no surrogates'). German *Handwerk* masters (skilled tradesmen) in particular laid great stress on their 'traditional', 'honest' working methods and

H. TOUSSAINT

Imitation, imitation, imitation: papier-mâché furniture by Jennens & Betteridge (*opposite*) for the Great Exhibition, London, 1851; and a dressing room by Leo von Klenze for the Königsbau, Munich, 1826–35 (*above*). Klenze's overriding principle in this addition to the Residenz was to avoid any kind of trade look, '*absolutely* eliminating any covering of the walls with silks or other fabrics, open fireplaces, mirrors, window draperies and floor carpets'. The architect's chief aim was to devise 'decoration in the manner of high art, in which, however, the character of a cheerful dwelling was not to be lost sight of'.

contrasted them with the alleged bad quality of factory mass production. A new emphasis was put on precisely the specific, the different look of each material and its related technique: 'every material carries with it its style and treatment'. Each major trade would now proclaim its ability to create a successful whole by praising the effects of the textures and colours of its own material.[6]

By the later 19th century a new pride and assertiveness among the major trades can be felt – even a kind of rivalry and jealousy, as each trade tried to claim as large a share as possible of the lucrative home decoration market. It is, however, necessary to remind ourselves once more of the relatively low perception of all trades. Wood was an altogether inferior material, except for its very expensive exotic varieties; textiles, unless they were of the most expensive kind, could be seen as temporary, even flimsy décor; stucco was in any case considered to be merely architecture's handmaiden; and painting was fine if associated with the fine art of painting, but ordinary housepainting was something very ordinary indeed.

Plaster

Some trades appear to have very little to offer in terms of a history. Rough plastering does not really belong to interior decoration but to the building process, and thus cannot come under the traditional definition of art at all. Plaster, or stucco décor (these terms are usually interchangeable), was the most ubiquitous mode of decoration, yet no material figures less in 19th-century discourses about the domestic interior. Only Loudon, who concentrated some of his analyses on that lower sphere, had praise for it: 'Without a cornice no room can have a finished appearance'; in addition, at the price of 7s. a ceiling rosette for the cottage would be 'no extravagance'. Earlier in the century we read that in Germany, then a much poorer country than Britain, 'the small rosette on the ceiling of the parlour was greatly admired'. Nobody could deny, although this was hardly ever expressed, that 'every décor … meets in a natural way in the centre of the ceiling' – especially when many rooms later used central gaslight fittings.[7]

The study of any of the crafts ought to begin precisely with what is most taken for granted: the dexterity required to produce a basic neatness of execution. An even wall surface is a precondition for the successful application of all décor and fittings, although a considerable range of finishes was available, from the rougher covering of internal walls with cement – practised in all buildings, even in the lowest kind of cottage – to the additional application of much

Floorplan of a villa in Leipzig, drawn in 1882, showing the scheme for the plaster ceilings.

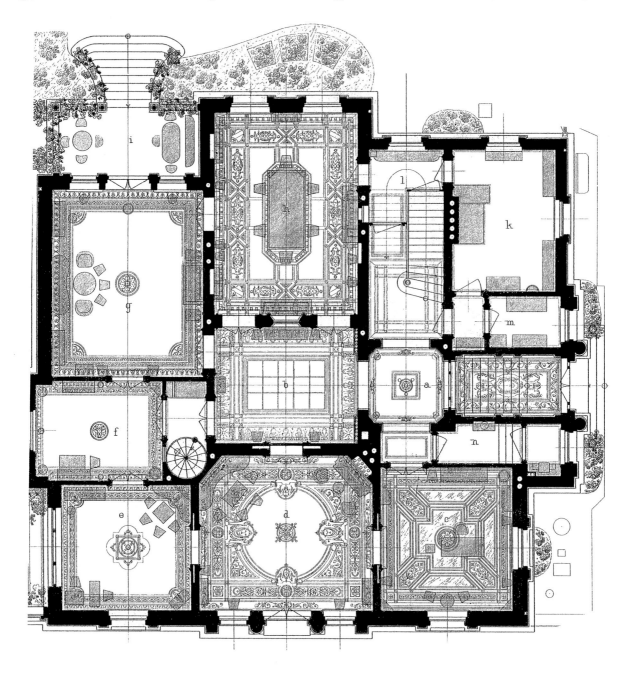

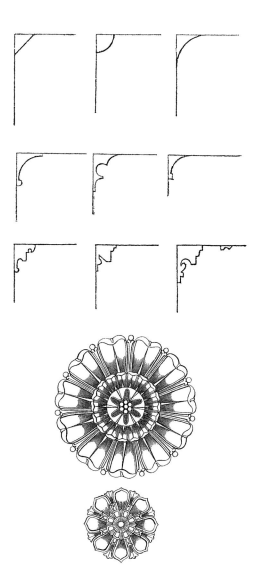

smoother layers of stucco. The wall or ceiling was then ready to receive ornaments, which could be either pre-cast and fastened onto the wall or the ceiling, or moulded *in situ*.

Plastering never did exude an aura of a novel technology and manufacture. Very few technical descriptions of it were published, except for those relating to substitutes;[8] the issue of colour hardly arose; and its motifs appeared more standardized than in any of the other crafts, presumably because plaster décor was restricted mainly to the ceiling. Plaster had to compete increasingly with all the other materials – with painting, with wood, and even with wallpaper and textiles – all of which were usually considered smarter. Even worse, perhaps, some select interiors of the early to mid-19th century were designed with completely flat ceilings that showed no relief at all.

This trade's neglect came after almost two centuries of the most remarkable craftsmanship: intricate and vigorous floral and figurative plasterwork that had superseded the wooden interior décor of earlier centuries.[9] But in the late 18th century, plastering in the better neo-Palladian, Greek Revival and Neoclassical interiors came to be governed strictly by the architectural scheme, and instead of demonstrating absolute whiteness was painted to look like stone or marble. Robert Adam in particular insisted on the plasterer following his, the architect's, designs, thus severely reducing the trade's sense of independence and pride: 'Adam brought death into the world', wrote one craftsman. Neither was the preference of the Classicists and the mid-Victorian reformists for pure geometry and flat surfaces propitious for stucco's three-dimensionality. Any kind of figurative sculpture provided by the plasterer had to make way for 'real' Antique sculpture (or copies thereof). What did continue was routine classical décor in cornices and in frames on the ceiling. By the 1850s to 1870s the conception was that 'the plasterers' methods were not artistically schooled' (Luthmer). Plaster's customary whiteness, or off-whiteness, was 'hated' by many by this point, and features such as 'centre flowers' appeared an 'intolerable ugliness' to the Aesthetic Movement designer E. W. Godwin.[10]

The plasterers' craft was also severely threatened by the fact that much of what was attached to the walls could be made of materials other than plaster. A central feature in ordinary British

interiors that delineated the lower edge of the frieze – the picture rail – was invariably made of wood. More prominent three-dimensional décor might also be made of substitutes like papier-mâché (not necessarily cheaper but easier to handle) or relievo papers that could simply be stuck to walls and ceilings.[11] Conversely, in the never ending story of imitation, plaster was used extensively later in the century to imitate wood, especially on ceilings.

And yet, after it reached its lowest ebb around 1860–70, the trade of the plasterer did pick up again moderately with the arrival of the neo-Renaissance style, which was generally welcomed as a richer alternative to Neoclassical 'monotony'. Northern versions of the Renaissance, and also neo-Rococo, demanded fine and varied work, and the Arts and Crafts movement in Britain finally revived coarser kinds of décor.[12] At the very end of the century, William Millar, a 'plasterer and modeller' (that is, somebody concerned not just with copying ornament, but with creating the models for it) spoke with some pride – albeit somewhat belatedly – on the subject: 'plaster work is the natural covering of walls and ceilings. It is not governed by coursing or jointing as in stone or brick, and there is no piecing or framing as in wood. The full face of plaster presents a breadth of field such as no other building material possesses.'[13]

Paint

Alongside plastering, painting constitutes the plainest, most necessary element of décor in any room. The profession of housepainter was therefore the lowest of all the trades discussed

Pompeian-style room with gloss paintwork, from Lübeck, completed in 1835; now in the Museum für Kunst und Gewerbe, Hamburg.

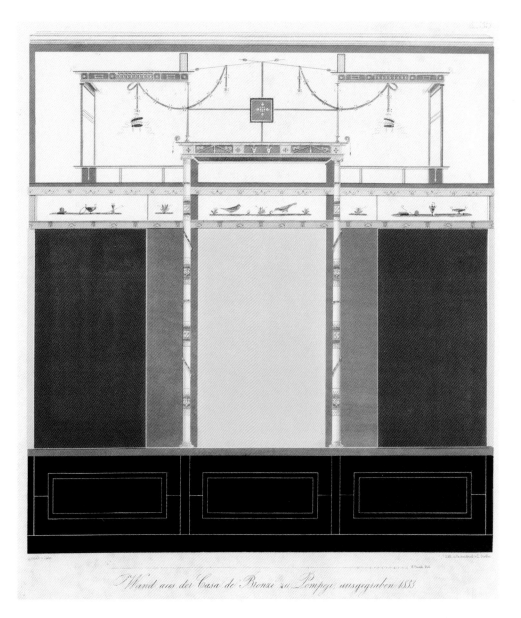

Wand aus der Casa de Bronzi zu Pompeji, ausgegraben 1855

Wall decoration from the Casa dei Bronzi in Pompeii, drawn by Wilhelm Zahn, 1842. Zahn's *Die schönsten Ornamente und merkwürdigsten Gemälde aus Pompeji* was a work of enormous folio plates that appeared in three volumes between 1828 and 1859. In his review of 1830, Goethe highlighted the quality of unity that was apparent in all the décor: 'The decorations originate in one mind and are painted out of one and the same paint pot.'

here – or, to be more precise, it comprised both very low-ranking and very high-ranking craftsmen and artists.[14] But it was not viewed negatively or neglected, as was plastering – certainly not during the earlier decades of the century, when painting served a new preference for flattish but brightly coloured surfaces. Colour science evolved as a new influence on the interior (to be discussed in a separate section), although choice of colour was always limited by the vastly differing costs of pigments. Because of their special interest in colour, painters generated considerably more literature than plasterers.

Paint chemistry affected cost and perceived overall quality as well as the medium's practical usefulness. For walls and ceilings, the very cheapest types of cover were whitewash and milk colour; water-soluble distemper was also common. Oil paint, on the other hand, was 'far more durable, more beautiful and cleaner' than distemper, but about twice as dear; it also required an extra-smooth undercoat of plaster. What housepainting seemed to lack, in contrast with all other home décor materials, was a sense of materiality and associated demands for a pronounced dexterity of craftsmanship. Technique also appeared of little significance, although there was one relatively cheap and easy method of decorating an already painted surface (or for that matter, paper) that had been practised for a long time: stencilling, or the application of colour using cut-out templates held against a wall.[15]

Paint was very much needed in the business of substituting materials. It was widely used to imitate textiles hung on the walls, or marble slabs. As already mentioned, the skilful application of oil paint on cheap woods produced the colour and figure of more precious woods. In

Illustration by Marie Rehsener for *Euphorion*,
a poem about Pompeii by Ferdinand Gregorovius
(1882). This is a late example of the Pompeian style;
strong colours were by now going out of fashion.

Britain, 'graining' was common on doors that were not made of mahogany; it was even argued that a surface thus painted would perform its task better. A rather different way of deceiving the viewer was to suggest that a room was open at the top by painting sky and clouds – a task requiring the utmost delicacy.[16]

There were three types of 'art' with which the high-class interior could be fitted out: architecture, sculpture and painting. In the early 19th century, it was realized that while all three could be integrated neatly, they could also be treated as completely discrete elements. One could have a room consisting solely of almost colourless classical architectural features, such as columns and arches; a room with a few works of (likewise colourless) sculpture in otherwise bare surroundings; or a room that was devoid of sculpture and prominent architectural features but colourfully painted with imitation architecture and sculpture. Much of this derived from research into the architecture and arts of Roman and Greek antiquity, as well as the frescos of the Italian High Renaissance. Studies increasingly focused on the actual techniques of painting, and the archaeologist-architects themselves began to experiment, with the chief aim of creating a 'force and brilliance of colouring' (Klenze).[17] The ruins of Pompeii, with their plethora of figurative décor and colour schemes in what appeared fairly common kinds of houses, made the strongest impression on decorators well beyond the middle of the 19th century, especially in Central Europe.[18] It was relatively easy to paint horizontal and vertical lines, which greatly helped with the overall coordination of a room; small elements of figurative or other kinds of décor – often exceedingly delicate – could be placed judiciously within this framework, but a brightly coloured surface without décor could be just as impressive. In mid-century France, the Pompeian style was followed by a more vigorous 'Néo-Grec'.[19]

Under very different auspices, housepainting could merge into fine art wall or ceiling painting, which was probably more common than one would assume; only some outstanding examples (such as the work of fine art circles in Britain between the 1860s and 1880s) have become well known.[20] A very few artists – Whistler was one – 'condescended' to paint on walls, while, conversely, some housepainters aspired to fine art work. More than with any other material except wood, painted decoration on walls was subject to the century's historical style choices and, even more importantly, to new theories of ornamentation. Two major modes had arisen by mid-century. First, lively human, plant and animal forms, largely based on Raphael's grotesques of the early 16th century and on antique acanthus motifs. Second, there was a trend towards flatness – a formal doctrine of abstracted ornament, to which we shall return later. A number of architects also had a hand in directing the painted decoration, as can be seen in numerous examples from Berlin and in the lavish pictorial work on housepainting produced by César Daly, France's premier architectural journalist. The new printing method of colour lithography reproduced all styles of décor splendidly.

The trades' situation with regard to wall covering was becoming ever more complex. Although the papering of walls could be seen as a serious threat to painting, the trades of painter and paperhanger in fact greatly overlapped. Increasingly, some kind of three-dimensional relief was preferred to entirely flat walls, and – as we shall see – paperhangers could supply this as well. Some painters now began to make explicit claims about their role as coordinators on account of their understanding of colour science. For example, in 1836 David Ramsay Hay, whose book on the *Laws of Harmonious Colouring* was exceptionally well known, protested against 'gaudy' paper hangings and maintained that the painter's task was to introduce tints on ceilings and walls in order 'to unite whole in perfect harmony'. A later text stressed the way paint can manipulate the effect of a room as a whole: 'lighter or darker, more friendly or more serious, moving the objects closer or distancing them'.[21] In 1888 the professional journal *Der Dekorationsmaler* made a desperate attempt to attack rival wall coverings, namely textiles and unpainted wood: 'One is almost tempted to advise that the opulent creativity of the textile trade should restrain itself … Ceiling, wall and floor [should be] kept in a simple and quiet tone, while furniture should receive coloured décor.' But in London there were already signs that plain paint was being revived, for both its colour and its surface effect, and in the 1870s E. W. Godwin had exhibited a penchant for plain distemper in single pastel colours.[22]

A new sense of surface qualities began to emerge; after all, paint did appear to possess a materiality of its own. But it was a trend that originated with the architectural and design elite rather than with the trade itself. By 1890, some architect-designers in England and Germany were once more opting for plain whitewashed walls.

Wallpaper

'The wallpaper industry had triumphed in making its product the universally preferred wall finish', Catherine Lynn proudly concludes in the most incisive of many recent analyses of this topic. The history of wallpaper in the 19th century is a breathless one: it was a product that could be incredibly cheap or vastly expensive, and it could look either like itself or like something else entirely. Among all the major trades, only wallpaper primarily served the dwelling.[23] Two factors have made this material the subject of copious histories: the striking artistic décor seen on some papers, and the story of its industrializing production, which was viewed as something 'tout moderne' (Henry Havard, 1884).[24]

The terminology relating to wallpaper in the major European languages was wholly confused. The word 'wallpaper' is the only one that supplies a clear definition of the product.[25] From a technical perspective, the main advance occurred between the 1820s and the 1850s, when roller print superseded block print – a fact which, combined with the lower cost of raw materials, greatly reduced the price of the product, the cheapest versions in England reputedly costing 1¼d. per yard, or even ¼d.[26] By 1860, even a 'a simple burgher's dwelling' in Germany was said to show at least one room with wallpaper; the décor could mark the very threshold between ornament and no ornament, as well as between 'cold and uncomfortable' and 'clothed, warm and comfortable'. Moreover, the relative ease with which a new layer could be applied was, as Clarence Cook pointed out, a quick way for those with 'migratory habits' to 'change their coat'.[27]

Wallpaper has two basic histories. The first concerns its chameleon-like behaviour, while the second is that of the décor itself. Undoubtedly, its initial role was to imitate. A special substitute for expensive wall textiles was flock paper, in which the main pattern was created by gluing on a layer of powdered wool in order to give the appearance and feel of velvet. Another sign of smartness early on was shine, especially the 'satin papers'. Soon any number of textile fabrics could be evoked: brocade, moiré, even chintz and Gobelin tapestry.[28] Wallpaper could imitate practically any other material that was costly, be it marble, plaster or wood. It was ironic that later in the century wallpaper imitated wooden panelling and wooden ceilings, the very materials it had helped to oust in the 18th century. Finally, there were the so-called 'scenic' wallpapers, reigning from the early 1800s to the 1860s, almost all of French production, which transformed a room into a landscape view or a garden and whose exceptional skill lies outside the remits of this book. Here, especially, *papier peint* was both itself and something else.[29]

'Paper' eventually expanded beyond its traditional definition when it began, from the 1860s, to include pulp and textiles; a *Naturholztapete*, for example, could consist of thin layers of wood. By that time some manufacturers such as Paul Balin were creating ever closer equivalents to textile fabrics, although, ironically, some of these imitative wallpapers could cost just

Sprigged wallpaper in Central Europe, *c.* 1850. The principal aim of this amateur watercolourist was to convey the room's likeness. He was clearly not able to give his image a unified character: the motifs applied to the walls and to the ceiling appear far too prominent.

Whole-wall decoration: pilaster and panel sets in wallpaper, by M. Bezault, Paris, 1867.

below Wallpaper imitating wall hangings in a lady's bedroom. Note the real curtains on the right. From the Schillerhaus, Weimar, *c.* 1802.

below right Checked German wallpaper from the early 1830s.

as much as the real thing.[30] When old leather wall coverings became newly fashionable (*cuirs repoussés*, or embossed leather) in the context of the Henri II style, these too were imitated.[31] All this culminated in the English Lincrusta, launched in 1876, and in Anaglypta, from a decade later, both of which pressed pulp into moulds – taking up the by then dying practice of papier-mâché décor – chiefly in order to imitate stucco. The popularity of Lincrusta and Anaglypta was also tied to the increasingly fashionable Northern Renaissance, especially the Jacobean style.[32] Here, however, three-dimensional wallpaper had competition: cheap stamped zinc.[33] A more expensive American process applied mother-of-pearl to the paper, as well as to the paint on friezes and ceilings, and combined it with mirrors and stained glass, lending the whole an iridescent quality and creating environments in which real materials and imitations could hardly be told apart (Tiffany specialized in such effects; see p. 153).[34] It is remarkable that, in spite of all these developments, wallpaper's imitative function was hardly ever denounced, even during

By Owen Jones.

By W. Burges.

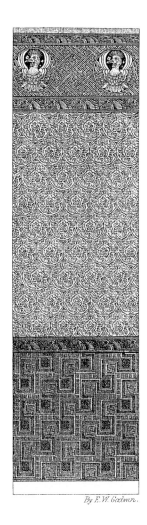

By E. W. Godwin.

Wallpapers by (*top row, from left to right*) Owen Jones, William Burges and E. W. Godwin; (*bottom row*) Christopher Dresser, E. W. Godwin and C. L. Eastlake. All were designed by architects (with the exception of Dresser's), and were published in the avant-garde journal *Building News* in 1872 and 1874.

By Dr. C. Dresser.

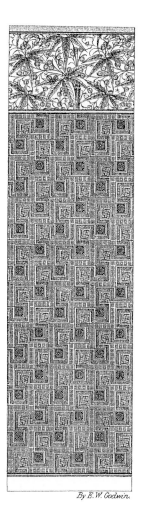

By E. W. Godwin.

By C. L. Eastlake.

the 1880s when critics argued most loudly against surrogates. It was simply that wallpaper's material – paper – could not possibly assume a specific materiality of its own, so there was no cause for accusations of falsity.

The continual story of one material usurping another may lead one to forget wallpaper's other function, that of furnishing a surface with ornamentation. Flowers were considered most attractive: 'the constituent element of the wallpaper industry is the flower'; it serves 'to transport into the interior of our habitations a little of the charms of nature'.[35] But in fact there was a boundless variety of patterns; as with textiles, 'fashion [changed] so frequently'.[36] Papers were available in an infinite range of sophistication – from plain vertical stripes to the most complex vignettes of illusionistically rendered flowers – and in any historical style. In addition, wallpaper was probably best for providing vivid colours, popular especially around mid-century.

However, as with domestic painting, a reaction was setting in, which led to abstract and less varied décor. Initially, the influence came from richly patterned, highly abstracted textile décor, such as the work of the ornamentist C.E. Clerget. From the 1840s on, the history of paper – in

Lewis F. Day, design for a room, 1881. Some wallpapers displayed large motifs, such as William Morris's celebrated plant forms, while others featured patterns so small that one could hardly make them out individually (see the examples opposite). Day's décor steers a middle path.

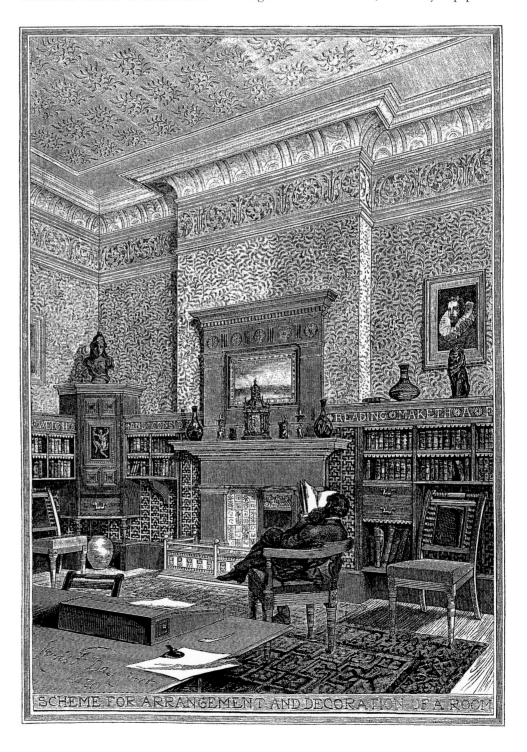

SCHEME FOR ARRANGEMENT AND DECORATION OF A ROOM

opposite Wallpaper and stencilling at Wardlow House, Parkville, Victoria, 1888. There are a number of surprisingly well-preserved later Victorian interiors in Australia. Their wallpapers were mostly imported from Britain.

England at least – is virtually identical to that of decorative wall painting outlined above: an increasingly precise use of historical sources, and an adherence to new theories of flat ornament, echoed on the Continent from the 1860s.[37] Morris then mixed this grammar of flatness with recognizable flowers – a winning combination. He and his colleagues also allied themselves closely with the powerful printing firm of Jeffrey & Co. (who reputedly paid the young artist Walter Crane £200 for one design); as a combination of artistic originality and industrial prowess, it marked a peak of 19th-century decorative art production in any material. England was now playing the leading role, having overtaken the French and their illusionistic artifice.[38]

In the final analysis, there was surprisingly little discussion of wallpaper's effect on the room as a whole. With the stencilling and the immensely strong wall designs of a Pugin or a Morris, and possibly with some strongly patterned paper on the ceiling, too, the character of a room was pretty much determined. As Robert Edis indicated: 'Amongst the patterns now made, there are many which may fairly be accepted as decoration complete, while others are more adapted to form the background for pictures and engravings.'[39] Wallpaper can of course make a room lighter or darker, and can also influence its perceived size. In contrast with Morris's large figurations, Lewis F. Day and Edis himself mostly devised tiny repetitive features, achieving a quiet evenness in their papers.[40] In England and the United States, wallpaper designers addressed the issue of the horizontal division of a room, varying the heights of dado, wall and frieze – the 'structural' divisions normally installed by the plasterer or the joiner (to be discussed later in this chapter).[41] At the same time, by the 1870s one begins to sense an eclipse of the fashion, the habit, of wallpapering. Nonetheless, one shopkeeper in 1890 was full of praise: 'no housepainter can approach [the wallpapers]', and even cheaper papers could present qualities that 'no paint can match'. A hygiene scare had flared up during the 1880s, fearful of dangers lurking behind the patterns, but others claimed that wallpaper was still

Textile-effect wallpaper functioning as an almost neutral background in a bedroom design by Jean Pape, Dresden, 1887.

more 'healthy than textiles'.[42] Finally, a distaste for mass-produced roller-printing resulted in attempts to re-establish woodblock-printed papers for the smartest jobs.[43]

More fundamental was a general tiredness with the whole concept of patterned décor. Wallpaper should not foreground its own décor, but play an 'essentially secondary [role] in the ensemble', wrote Richard Redgrave when he attacked the many abundantly floral papers of the Great Exhibition of 1851.[44] In Austria, Falke went further: 'the pattern is of no importance, what matters is the impression of the whole'; and a little later Robert Dohme emphasized an 'atmosphere of colour', whereby the design can be neglected. German and French wallpapers essentially continued in their imitation of textile patterns, although these were now darker and more uniformly coloured. In England, by contrast, Godwin went for an effect of lightness; he now complained that many rooms were 'very much overpapered and overpatterned'.[45] For him, as for many on the Continent (although in different ways), it was the three-dimensionality of the furniture, textiles and other objects that should dominate the room. The walls had to look entirely flat and even.

Textiles

While an accepted aspect of domestic design today, textiles in the home have not always seemed so commonplace. Indeed, as recently as the late 18th century, when most home textiles as we know them were first conceived, they appeared nothing short of revelatory. Fabrics in general (except, that is, for the coarsest cloths) traditionally had a high material value in themselves – far more than basic wood, let alone paper. Thus, amid the 19th-century confusion of one substance imitating another, textiles occupied a special position, for no fabric ever

A room before the upholsterer's work has begun. From Jules Verdellet's *Manuel géométrique du tapissier* (1851).

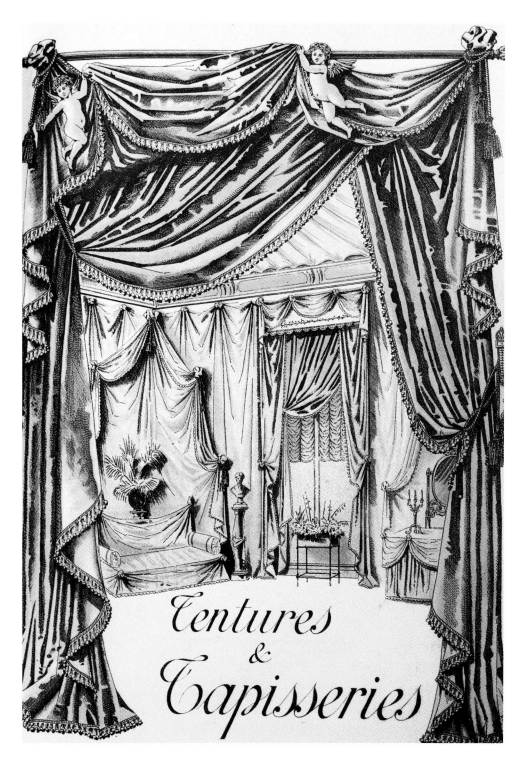

Centures & Tapisseries

A frontispiece from the series *Ameublement Parisien*, published in Paris (*c.* 1890).

attempted to look like another material. Quite the contrary: textiles were among the most often imitated materials, as shown by the painted draperies of Neoclassical interiors or wallpapers printed to resemble silk.

The alluring visual features, strong colours and soft touch of textiles embodied an image of luxury. The way in which such luxuries became available to a wider public forms a crucial part of the story of early capitalism, and the upholsterer was just one link in an extensive chain of production and consumption. Unlike many other trades that furnished the home, domestic textiles, like dress fabrics and fashions, were a thoroughly international undertaking, albeit one dominated by France and Britain. To be more precise: heading the industry in Europe was the centuries-old manufacture of silks in Lyons, while cotton became the principal British product and largely occupied the lower price range. When it came to employing textiles decoratively, French fashions ruled supreme well into the later 19th century. After mid-century, however, many newly fashionable fabrics came directly from Asia.[46]

The ready supply of ornamented textiles put upholsterers and decorators into a different position from that of woodworkers or painters who created their own décor, even though the upholsterer's task of selecting from a vast range of fabrics was in itself demanding. Altogether, theirs was a 'complex enterprise', almost like that of building contractors.[47] Once the fabrics had been chosen, the work of the upholsterer – who could also call himself by the grander title of 'decorator' – was chiefly one of 'nimble fingers, taste and a good eye'.[48]

As with most other materials there was a hierarchy of perceived quality, which initially depended on the natural source of the material. In time, this situation was partly superseded by the increasing diversity of automated manufacturing techniques, such as the Jacquard loom, roller printing, and so on. Dyers teamed up with industrial chemists, and artificial, aniline-based colouring began to make headway. Further chemical processes were introduced to render the fabric strong as well as shiny (mercerization). By the end of the century it was reckoned that nine-tenths of decorated textiles were machine-produced.[49]

Materiality

During the 19th century a tremendous dynamic of pricing arose, with an associated plethora of confusing names. At the top were the venerable variations of silk-weaving: shiny satins, heavy brocades and flowing velvet (the dearest of all fabrics), with its derivative, plush, which forms a carpet of thin hairs: all 'solid splendour' (Falke).[50] However, the same – or almost the same – look could be had for a fraction of the price: the Vienna World's Fair of 1873, for example, reported staggering scale of prices: hugely expensive 'luxuriöse Seidenbrokate' (silk brocades); similar curtains in cotton for a quarter of the price (or less); and paper imitations by Paveys at just one tenth of the cost of the silks. Early in the century coloured chintzes had been relatively smart, having replaced unpatterned wool; by the end of the century, however, chintzes had been relegated to the lesser rooms. Damasks or brocades could be imitated in cheap heavy jute. Wool could now be given hardness and shine, and mass could be lent to both silk and wool by the addition of 'mungo', that is, recycled rags. It thus became ever harder to distinguish between original materials, and fabrics were increasingly chosen on the basis of looks rather than for the materials themselves.[51]

Unlike most other decorative finishes, the materiality of textiles had been accepted for a long time. For several centuries painters had used immense artifice to render fabric as fabric, its weight, its dynamic shaping, its softness and precious shine and its strong colouring. There is no discussion here about an emerging 'sense of the material', as with wood, because a strong sense of tactile effects had always existed. The continuity between home textiles and dress fabric was of great significance for the appearance and use of textiles generally. 'Drapery is to a room what dress is to the human figure', wrote an English manual of 1853. Decorators 'make … warmth beautiful', not only visually, but also through 'the feeling caused by touching the skin'.[52]

Because of the established materiality of textiles, and perhaps also because of the vast number of patterns available, we note a certain indifference towards the meaning of the ornament itself. Historical styles mattered far less than in furniture or paint. In 1873 a German critic could maintain that the patterns on fabrics were 'meaningless'. French silks tended to continue with designs from the 16th and 17th centuries; more novel were naturalistic plant forms, especially on printed chintzes.[53] 'Severe' medieval patterns were also revived. The South Kensington Reform Movement was adamant that illusionistic nature should be phased out, endlessly asserting that 'you can't walk on flowers'. Oriental textile patterns, normally abstract, were increasingly popular – especially their 'gorgeous yet harmonious colouring', which helped to take one 'away from European studiousness' (Julius Lessing).[54]

Textiles in the home had a number of distinct applications, related to their 'behaviour': they might be thick and laid flat on the floor or any larger surface; they might be delicate and

Bedroom from the Munich Residenz, before 1820.
The décor centres on the carpet design.

stretched tightly over flat or rounded surfaces; or they might fall or hang. From about mid-century onwards, the differences between these three treatments became highly pronounced.

Flat coverings

One could argue that carpets changed little between the late 17th century and today: heavy tapestry fabric gradually went out of fashion as a wall covering and was restricted to floors (still evident in the French word *tapis* for carpet). A complex system of brand and genre names arose during the 18th century; derived from the carpets' original places of manufacture, they were used to denote price range and technique.[55]

Unlike other elements of the domestic interior discussed here, carpets were never de rigueur. Parquet remained the most prestigious kind of floor covering in much of Continental Europe, certainly for the more festive and elegant kinds of room. At the lower end of the market was patterned oilcloth, or floorcloth.[56] In 1856 wall-to-wall carpeting was said to be 'almost universal' in England. By this time carpets were on the increase in Central Europe, while in England some reformists advocated a limited return to wooden floors.[57]

The early 19th century was the period when the relationship between a patterned carpet and the rest of a room's décor was observed most carefully, both in terms of colour and design (sometimes a central feature would be echoed by the ceiling rosette, for example). Towards the middle of the century motifs – as with most other textiles – became more lively; all-over flower patterns were much preferred, 'with rich brown colours, and flowers etc., of glowing tints as though we were treading on something warm and comfortable, and like home'.[58] This approach was sharply condemned by the reform movement, which – especially in Britain – demanded geometrization. In any case, with the onset of the fashion for darker rooms, all floors became darker, too, which rendered colour and ornament less visible. The demise of the European naturalistic flower motif was accompanied by an ever greater admiration for Oriental décor: expensive Persian carpets, the long-familiar and much cheaper Turkey carpets, and all their European imitations. 'Oriental rugs will never fail to look right', was one critic's judgment.[59] Alongside the greater presence of thick textiles, the materiality of the carpets – or rather of individual rugs, large and small – became more important: some preferred the thick, soft, even shiny velours for their velvety surface, while others liked the toughness of knotted weaves. The rugs' random placement corresponded with the new casual arrangement of the rooms in general. In Central Europe these thick fabrics were sometimes also draped over part of the table. Viewed in this light, carpet design, or rather the way carpets were used, had come a fair way since the early 19th century.

Stretched coverings

When fabric is stretched over a surface, it has a very different 'feeling' from other types of application. Wall 'hangings' – like carpets – are ultimately the descendants of tapestries; but during the course of the later 18th century they assumed rather different forms. As part of a move towards light, unified interiors governed by clear, rectilinear divisions, walls were now covered with thinner fabrics that were either attached directly to the wall or fastened onto removable frames. The panels were invariably of silk and mostly exhibited strong colours, which silk carried particularly well. Most importantly, stretching helped to bring out the material's natural shine.[60] All this continued to be an important option for very rich-looking interiors.

Using textiles on the walls provided obvious opportunities for coordination, since the same fabric could be applied also to the upholstery. In conjunction with classically, symmetrically arranged furniture and with curtains and carpets containing similar colours, upholstery textiles contributed to a very high degree of unity.[61] Of course, the same kind of coordination could be attempted with cheaper materials such as chintz.

By the 1830s and 1840s, when textiles on walls went somewhat into decline, curtains and upholstery assumed greater prominence. More and more the latter took on a life of its own, particularly in France, which was dominant in this field (hence the term 'French stuffed'). The padded seat exuded an aura of luxury: there was an enormous variety of types of armchair and and sofa, all with fanciful names, which benefited in terms of comfort from the recent introduction of steel springs. Whereas proper Neoclassical shapes had to be straight and moderately flat, by the 1840s bulbous forms knew no limits. The upholsterer's pièce de résistance was the chair in which the textile completely covered the wooden frame. New methods had to be developed to fasten the padding and the covers, which became known variously as *capitoné*, tufting, buttoning, *pikieren* and *abgeheftete Polster* – all of which heightened the stretching effect and optimized the fabrics' surface qualities.[62]

By the 1870s, however, bulbous forms had gone out of fashion. Furniture had begun to straighten again and to become heavier, and wood was shown once more, but the seats and bolster could still be quite rounded. At the same time, the Near Eastern ('harem') fashion for the casual draping of seat furniture came into vogue (see p. 205), alongside a new preference for loose cushions, resulting in even greater opportunities for textiles in the home. For the West, it also meant a return to an earlier age when individual items of fabric were as yet far less differentiated from each other. These fashions can be summarized as a new adherence to the Renaissance, or even a new medievalism, pushing out the Rococo, but the driving factor was

Advertisement for armchairs, from the *Cabinet Maker*, 1889.

a preference for heavy over delicate materials. This went hand in hand with a predilection for voluminous folds.

Hanging fabrics and the all-textile room

Undoubtedly the most characteristically 'textile' forms of the later 19th-century home were not flat, tightened or fixed, but hanging and free-flowing ('curtain' is far too limited a word). Draping and festooning of course have a long history – drapes surrounding state beds (*lits de parade*) were among the richest items in a palace – but they hardly featured within smaller domestic surroundings. While the customs associated with these formal beds were dying out, their grandiose forms lingered on.

Curtains became an ever bigger issue simply because windows had increased in size, while light needed to be kept out. Among the many simple arguments that were introduced to explain the practicality of heavy curtains was the somewhat paradoxical notion that they prevented the sun's rays from damaging other textiles and their colours. One French popular journal wrote of double draperies that 'hermetically seal the window',[63] while from early in the century various kinds of light curtain made of cotton muslin or lace had also become common, allowing for more control over how a room could be lit from outside.

For purely formal reasons, from the late 18th century onwards curtains appeared absolutely necessary to soften the transition between the walls and the glare of the opening (see p. 193). Moreover, long curtains could make a room appear taller. More and more drapes were added, either slung around the rail or allowed to hang at full length. By the 1820s and 1830s some windows displayed a vast, multicoloured combination of textiles, 'an infinite variety in the ways of adjusting the drapes',[64] which could even be composed asymmetrically. The custom of the double set of curtains, the inner set lightly coloured and the outer darker in tone, appears to have come in by about 1840.

The rail from which the curtains were hung was greatly elaborated, which no doubt harked back to the way the drapes of state beds could be fastened together at the top and ultimately to

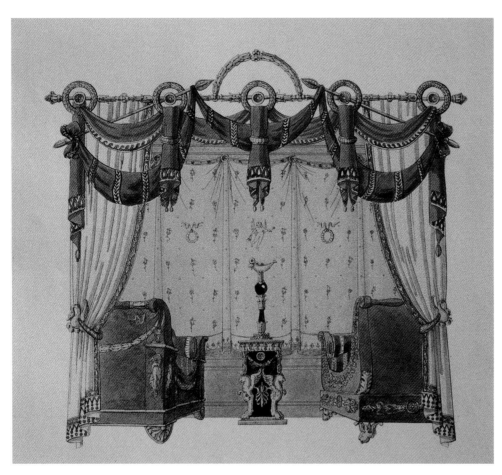

left Alcove with two beds, by M. Santi, Paris, 1828. In the 1820s, the configuration of the drapes around the rail often appeared more important than the curtains themselves.

below His Majesty's Writing Room at Windsor Castle, designed by Morel's office for Seddon, *c.* 1826. The silk was budgeted at 40*s.* per yard. Did grandeur have to mean regularity?

forms of dress. Alternatively these fastenings could be covered by a length of ornate fabric known as a valance or pelmet, which was sometimes continued across the wall between windows. Indeed, the *goût tapissier* expanded textile décor over almost the whole wall, so that draperies could be hung over the edges of a mirror or even from the mantelpiece or over a clock. Even the tablecloth could be treated as draped, especially when it was made of the same heavy fabric as the curtains or the portières. The latter, which were hung over internal doorways, became ubiquitous in the 19th century and could even take the place of doors

Curtains by A. & L. Streitenfeld, Berlin, 1888. The drapes are relatively cheap, but arranged with late 19th-century improvisatory flair.

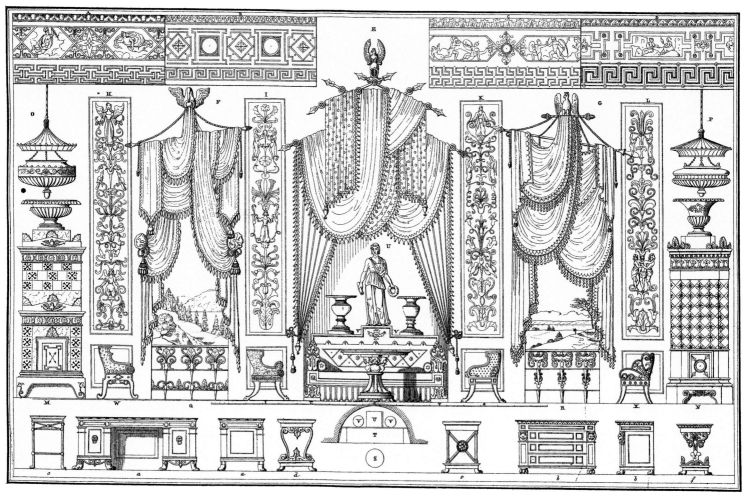

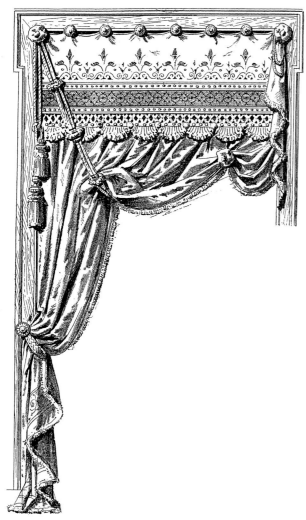

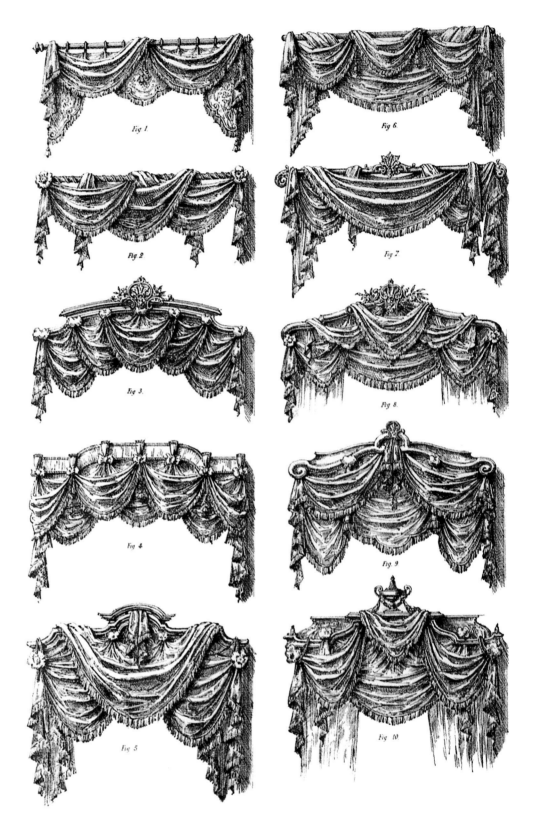

themselves, for instance between a stately dining room and an inner corridor.[65] Along with single, tall displays of window drapery, they constituted the 19th century's most frequently repeated and varied image of the interior, especially in France.

A singular fashion arose around 1800 that has not thus far been sufficiently explained: the tent-like interior. Napoleon I used the conceit to fit out a lowish room as his Salle de Conseil in the small suburban palace of Malmaison, thereby evoking associations with the important temporary meeting places of his military campaigns. Schinkel later reprised the idea for a bedroom.[66] To cover walls with freely hanging draperies, often arranged in a severely symmetrical fashion, was also held to be a feature 'after the Antique' (George Smith)[67] – something which, as we have seen, lent itself to painted imitations. A more structured use of textile covering can be found in later 19th-century boudoirs; as mentioned in the previous chapter, a notion that textiles and women – and more especially loose drapes and women – belong together was prevalent throughout most of the 19th century. The 1860s to the 1880s, on the other hand, witnessed rooms in which almost all of the walls and the ceiling was covered in fabric, usually pleated, while the rounded parts of the architecture, such as the coving, were lined with buttoned cloth. Here, the victory of textiles seemed complete.[68]

While the basic appreciation of fabrics remained the same throughout the century, a slow but significant shift in people's sense of materiality did occur towards its end. The elaboration of curtains, valences, and so on around 1840 made a great impact, with their vivid colour contrasts and often immensely complicated configurations of overlapping folds and gathers. These were joined by ornamentation on the borders, seams and tassels, which kept increasing in boldness: 'tassels large like pumpkins',[69] Lessing quipped. Indeed, a Danish term for that period of décor is *klunketid*, or 'tassel-period'. Early in the century these arrangements were strictly symmetrical, as was everything else in the room, but by the 1840s asymmetrical draperies were common, and by the 1870s wildly asymmetrical arrangements prevailed.

below and opposite Curtains by T. Pasquier, Paris, *c.* 1840, showing the upholsterer's intention to extend his work across the whole wall. The pelmets have become less elaborate, however. Note the toilet table: for the next three or four decades, an increasing number of items of furniture were covered with drapes.

'Drapery is art; the textile is just cloth', Gene Doy has written.[70] Later in the century such a view would appear somewhat simplistic, as the ever greater diversity of cloth itself became more appreciated. The art of arranging folds and of thereby creating an impression of verve certainly continued to flourish: 'the judicious disposition of folds … beauty of the stuff … play of light and shade, and reflection'.[71] The creation of folds was subjected to the most penetrating geometric analyses, and Jules Verdellet (France's most eminent theorist of textile décor), Luthmer and others began to set out the art of *Aufmachung*, the draper's skill in arranging curtains on the spot.[72] With the fold itself the focus of interest, the pattern on the cloth, and even its colour, became secondary; vivid colours were now mostly rejected. It was the 'materiality of the cloth' that was at issue. Somewhat influenced by Semper's mighty investigation into the history and theory of textiles, Falke placed a new stress on the 'the optical effect of various cloths'.[73] Folds should not be affected by pattern: in fact, in order to prioritize the folds one could dispense with decorative patterns altogether. Another German critic had a slightly different emphasis: 'one usually takes too much note of the contours of the curtains … the impression they make is due to the folds and the colours of the fabric.'[74]

Draperies by Bernhard Grünstaudl for the Munich Exhibition, 1888. Earlier in the century elaborate curtains were strongly coloured, whereas later displays would highlight textural contrasts.

Designers now paid great attention to the way different fabrics fell and folded. Folds in silk could be impressive, but they were also 'crumpled'; wool, on the other hand, showed a 'suppleness and softness' in its fall, combined with its own kind of shine, making it ideal for the 'massive, the great round throw … in the style of the Renaissance'.[75] Extra filling often helped in providing the right weight and thus helping materials to fall correctly.

But yet another change in fashion was on its way as informality gained in popularity. Elaborate shapes were replaced by a new ideal: the gently hung curtain that displayed soft but essentially only vertical folds. This look was greatly influenced by medieval hangings, as well as pictures of the heavily clothed rooms of the Near East; early signs appear in Eugène Prignot's designs of the 1870s.[76] The fabrics themselves were now turning lighter again, and the general informality concurred with the rejection of puffy upholstery shapes and stretched coverings.

right Wall of a study hung in 'silk or wool and silk', by E. Maincent, Paris, *c.* 1886. By the 1880s, the hanging of fabric flat, or relatively flat, on walls had gone somewhat out of fashion. Maincent, one of the most original designers of the decade, has here reintroduced it, but in a completely different way.

below Boudoir (also called a 'Grand Salon') by the decorator and gold medallist Henri Penon, designed for the Paris Exposition Universelle, 1878.

below Drapery by Eugène Prignot, one of the better-known Parisian designers and decorators, 1870s. Here, one can see the beginnings of a new fashion: a move away from the more riotous diagonal drapes.

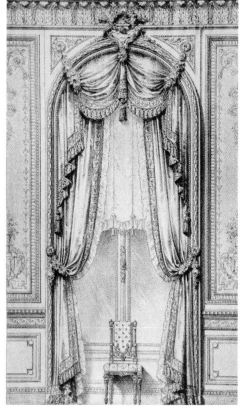

To a small degree, leather gave the textile producers some competition. Relatively smooth in texture, it was usually applied to flat surfaces, as well as forming a part of the 'archaic roughness' of the Northern Renaissance revivals.[77] In addition, leather was considered suitable for male rooms, which in turn reinforced the conception of fabrics as 'female'.

Textiles appeared indispensable at every level: 'What an air of snugness and comfort they import to a room.' In 1830 the trade's pride was fully evident: 'the upholsterer surpasses the cabinetmaker'. 'The textile ornament will prevail', wrote the *Monatsschrift für Textilindustrie*, perhaps not surprisingly, while Luthmer, discussing smaller pieces of textile draped over easels or statue bases, remarked that 'the art of the upholsterer has here … tried to conquer another sphere'.[78]

And yet an eclipse of the *goût tapissier*,[79] of the whole of the *tapissier*'s work, was on its way. Many architects had been unsympathetic from the start, including Le Camus de Mézières and Schinkel. The latter complained of a 'barbaric opulence' and a fashion that only considered

Portières by E. Foussier of Paris, *c.* 1896. The modernist demotion of textiles in the interior has begun.

'the value of the fabrics', while others wrote of 'the death of art and taste'.[80] Health considerations rapidly gained ground in the 1880s, some counselling that carpets must be removable to allow for beating. Finally, a new kind of competitor, or part competitor, to the upholsterer could be conceived: whereas the upholsterer did the draping perfectly, the woman of the house did it *naturally* (Ris-Paquot).[81] By 1900 most of the heavy draping, puffy upholstery and soft carpeting had gone out of fashion. The work of the upholsterer, like that of the wallpaper-hanger, smacked too much of temporary profusion for a time that craved a new solidity and a more linear kind of refinement (to which we shall come towards the end of this chapter). The 19th century's mightiest fashion in interior décor had now become much reduced. The Arts and Crafts movement and most brands of modernism cut furnishing textiles back to a minimum.

Wood

Of all the materials, wood is the most basic, as well as being the most versatile around the home; in fact, the whole house and virtually everything inside catering to domestic necessity could be, and at some stage was, made of wood. *Zimmer*, the principal German term for a room in a dwelling, is related to the word for 'timber', while the Dutch for wainscoting is *betimmering*. Thus, in contrast to the conception of textiles as always 'modern' and elegant, the world of wood was held to be an ancient one. And yet the history of wood inside the smarter dwelling

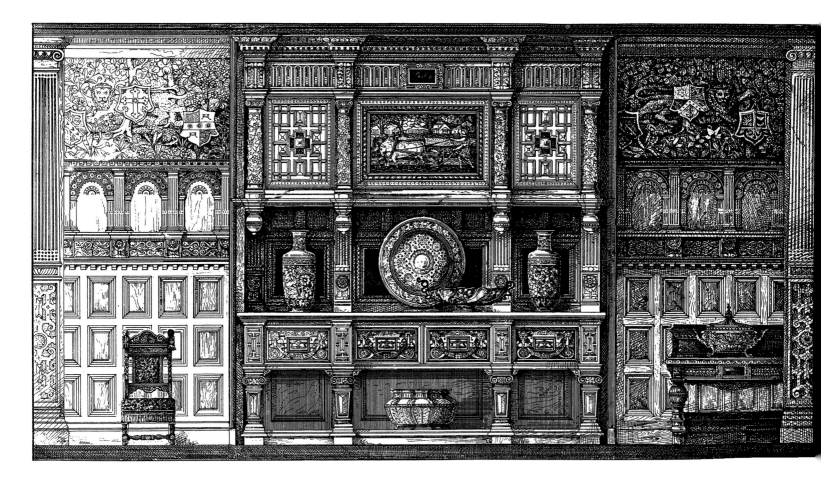

was full of ups and downs. The period around 1800 must have marked its absolute nadir: all joinery in a room could be covered thickly with paint, the floor was concealed with carpets, and most of the furniture, if not painted or gilded, was veneered with costly exotic woods that completely covered the baser wood of its construction. Eighty years later we might have been able to enter a new room where not only the floor and the furniture, but also the ceiling and the walls, were of exposed wood, of relatively cheap, untreated timber at that. By 1900 some avant-garde Scottish and Viennese designers were once more hiding wooden surfaces completely.

However their products might appear, the joinery and furniture trades were among the noblest. By the later 18th century the precision crafts of the great Paris *ébénistes* and of sophisticated English designer-manufacturers had gained a degree of fame approaching that of any of the fine arts to be found in the home. The ultimate way of enriching wood in the mid- and later 19th century was the direct application of sculpture or carving, as in many of the spectacularly elaborate exhibition pieces shown at the World's Fairs by Leistler of Vienna or Fourdinois of Paris.[82]

It seemed natural that, of all the artefacts in the house, furniture should be the one most strongly tied in with architecture. The largest sub-group of pattern books dealt with furniture, and the professional literature on woodworking often contained highly theoretical accounts of geometry, akin to those used for construction in stone. Furniture styles mostly went in tandem with architectural styles. Architects not only designed individual items of furnishing, but also embarked on theoretical and historical research (Viollet-le-Duc and Semper in particular), although, surprisingly, comprehensive histories of furniture really only began in the 1880s, when they were written largely by collectors and their aides, the dealers.[83]

Timber and its industry

The many kinds of wood varied enormously as far as cost and fashionableness were concerned. By the later 19th century, upwards of fifty kinds of wood were available.[84] Probably the

above Wall décor and sideboard in oak by Marsh, Jones & Cribb of Leeds, shown at the Paris Exposition Universelle in 1878.

below Frontispiece of Ernst Plassmann's *Designs for Furniture*, published in New York, 1877.

most enthusiastic preference for foreign, exotic woods occurred during the later 18th century: rosewood, for example, or Sheraton's favourite, satinwood, which he called 'cool, light and pleasing'.[85] Another exotic variety, mahogany – red-brown, darkish, evenly grained and smoothly finished – became the staple smart wood in England and France during the 18th century and soon thereafter in the United States; initially, it was about two to three times dearer than oak and fifteen times dearer than pine. Yet by the 1880s its dominance was on the wane, though it remained popular with the lower middle class.[86] By that time oak had made a comeback. Hard, heavy-duty, long-lasting, 'not polished' and demonstrating 'simple propriety of treatment, admirable construction and cleanliness', oak appeared in most respects the opposite of glossy mahogany. Loudon already recommended it for the dining room, but for others it still had a 'rather cold look'. It soon became closely associated with national architectural history, especially the Elizabethan and Jacobean periods in Britain. Germany followed the trend but more slowly, while in France oak – often the so-called 'old oak' – held sway in Northern neo-Renaissance work.[87] Much in vogue in the last decades of the century was Hungarian ash (*ungarische Esche* or *point d'hongrie*), with its 'glowing golden colours'.[88] Perhaps most astonishing was the sudden rise of pine from the 1870s. This soft wood was a close relation to the very commonest all-purpose building timber – deal, i.e. fir or pine wood – and never appears in any earlier accounts of stylish furniture. Now much of the pine came from America and was often called pitch pine, in the American fashion.[89] Its grain shows a great deal of patterning, the wood appears full of sap, and in fashionable work it was often left unpainted, its golden yellow colour now appearing highly attractive. Some Alpine provinces viewed pine and fir as essentially local woods; we shall return to their revival in Chapter V.

above 'Art Furniture', a publication by the London architects Watford and Donkin (1868).

right Sideboard by H. W. Batley, exhibited at the Exposition Universelle, Paris, 1878. Between the late 1860s and the 1880s, avant-garde English furniture makers oscillated between heaviness and delicacy; in the end, the latter won out.

Dining room by Phillip Niederhöfer, Frankfurt am Main, 1884 (see also p. 140).

The timber industry formed a considerable section of the economy on a thoroughly international scale. During the later 19th century, the wood trade – or, as the Germans increasingly termed it, its *Handwerk*, its 'craft' – was seen as in the ascendant: 'carpentry presents itself as … Germany's favourite national trade'.[90] In Paris, the furniture industry alone employed around 100,000; much of its production was destined for export. Grand Rapids, Michigan and Berlin

Settee by Bembé & Co., Mainz, *c.* 1880. Here, furniture has become architecture.

Intérieur exécuté en bois de chêne, les panneaux en racine, les encadremens en citronnier et les filets en bois d'amaranthe.

This design, from 1837, is a very early example of a room completely finished in wood. Described as an 'interior executed in oak, with panels in root-wood, frames in citron-wood and lines in amaranth', it clearly takes its cue from furniture inlay. The Parisian designers, Thiollet et Roux – also, one assumes, the makers – are most explicit about the general virtues of the design: it gives 'the eye a rest from the profusion of gilding and sculpture, the abuse of which from day to day becomes more reprehensible'.

were major centres for the middle market, producing 'good average' work 'cheaply'.[91] Yet wood was not subject to the dramatic economic fluctuations that affected wallpaper or some textiles. Rather, progress lay in the way the material was worked. The steam sawing of rough timber had begun in England early in the century, followed by machines that cut profiles, mouldings and chamfers for furniture and for all kinds of joinery; knobbly legs became far more frequent. There were also firms that specialized in producing just small elements of decoration, sometimes in imitation materials. In general, however, mechanized carving was considered much less successful than hand-carving. Initially, the greater precision of machine work had been much praised, but critics subsequently maintained that 'the machine' led to everything that was cheap and nasty. Very recent historiography, however, has been of the view that machinery did not really affect design or overall quality.[92] The simple conclusion here is that new mechanized processes did help to bring more wood into every part of the home.

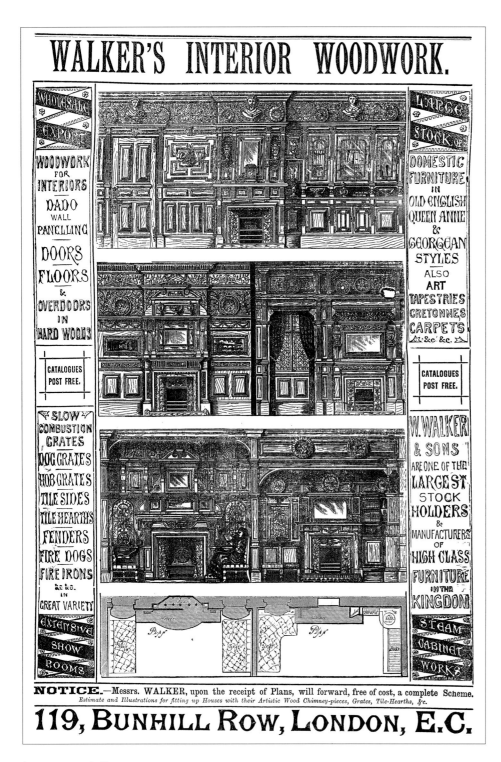

Advertisement for woodwork from *The Builder*, 1885.

A new materiality

A piece of wood in its raw state was not normally considered a particularly beautiful object. There were many ways of enhancing its appearance: from the 17th to the early 19th centuries, the attachment of gilded metal had guaranteed the ultimate distinction; veneering and marquetry (the gluing of a thin layer of a wood onto a cheaper carcass) were other means of improving on the raw material. Occasionally the wood was soaked with chemicals to change its colour; cheaper woods were frequently stained black in imitation of ebony, for instance. Most woods seemed to require a strong polish. 'French polish', available from the 1820s, achieved a virtually transparent cover that consisted mainly of shellac. 'For our furniture makers polished wood surfaces were the acme of perfection', wrote one critic; an analogy with the preference for shiny textiles can be drawn here.[93]

The development of wooden furnishings may be understood as a recovery from the nadir of 1800, when natural wooden surfaces were so often in hiding, with the exception of only the

Library in black walnut, designed *c.* 1875 by the architects Sturgis & Brigham, Boston, Mass.

most precious varieties. At this point, one should be aware of a distinction between the trade and a 'higher' sphere of design. As far as the former was concerned, wood could never be dispensed with, and the fact that it was not properly visible did not trouble the suppliers unduly. The re-evaluation of wood's structural and surface qualities originated less with the trade than with designers and architects.

The first significant step towards a rehabilitation of wood in the interior took the form of certain 'heavy' look. Architect-orientated publications and illustrations produced by the trade were clearly distinguishable: until late in the century, trade images of chairs and settees displayed a delicate structure, continuing the mid- to late 18th-century emphasis on refined workmanship. The change that occurred in the 1840s was due mainly to Pugin, who insisted categorically on what was later called 'the nature of the material', rejecting lightness, veneers or any other coverings in his designs in order to show the material's basic solidity;[94] Loudon, on the other hand, was able to appreciate a wooden object's psycho-physical qualities even when it was 'painted in a warm tone of colour'.[95] The play of light and shade was now more appreciated on rough than smooth surfaces, with one source maintaining that 'polishing, finishing etc. destroys surface'; and by 1894 a trade guide claimed that wood inside a building lasted longer if it was left unpainted.[96] These developments mirror the trend towards an appreciation of 'natural' qualities rather than those that depended on elaborate treatment. The emerging love of the old further advanced and complicated textural preferences.

For such designers, the French Rococo habit of applying curves to all outlines was disastrous: 'it makes a mockery of the structure of timber'. Eastlake, with his heavy moralistic tone, weighed in against all curved furniture, veneering and polish, demanding square outlines, flat surfaces and the show of the 'natural "vein" of the wood'. Even more influential was Bruce Talbert's *Gothic Forms Applied to Furniture ...* (1867). A woodcarver by training, Talbert was also an architect who came directly out of the school of High Victorian massiveness; he, too, fulminated against 'wanton curves' and the 'glitter' of French polish, asserting that 'the natural flow of fibre in all woods is very beautiful'. A little later, the German architect Edwin Oppler wrote of the 'expression of "woodenness"'; avoid any kind of 'sugary, minute execution' and adopt a 'certain toughness and roughness'.[97]

However, wood also provided a good example of how the philosophy of 'the nature of the material' could be turned and twisted. Eastlake and his 'packing case' school of design soon

Buffet and wooden wall-covering by A. Schill, Stuttgart, c. 1879. It is now impossible to distinguish between the furniture and the 'architecture' of the wall décor.

encountered opposition. There was no reason (it was argued) why furniture in honest wood could not also be light, as long as it adhered to rectangular outlines. The staunch defender of the 'slim sticks' school of furniture – which was mostly ebonized, and thus hardly showed any grain or characteristic texture – was E. W. Godwin, Talbert's and Eastlake's exact contemporary. He advocated 'a light and wooden appearance, and one we cannot mistake for any other material'.[98]

This re-evaluation of wood extended beyond issues of colour, shape and moralist demands for truth to material into the tactile and even the psychological realm. Crucial was the realization that timber always feels warm because it is a bad conductor of heat: 'Do we not favour wood for our furnishings for reasons of our frequent contact with it, which demands a relative elasticity and a temperature close to that of the human body?' (Édouard Didron).[99] In fact, these sensibilities were subject to variation, for instance when questions of gender were involved: in contrast to 'feminine' soft textiles, hard wood was held to be especially suitable for the man's rooms.

Furniture and the room

Whether of light or heavy construction, a piece of wooden furniture always appears obviously three-dimensional. A perfectly obvious fact, one might say, but one that received critical attention later in the century, when three-dimensionality was contrasted with flat patterning. We have already quoted Godwin's complaints relating to over-patterning, and indeed he sometimes voiced a vaguely worked-out theory of three-dimensionality, expressed as the alternation of 'solids and voids'.[100] Mrs Spofford employed another important word when she advised readers to 'arrange the furniture with a view to masses'.[101] The cumulative effect of solids and voids in an interior was subject to many complex considerations and will be dealt with later in this chapter. The most basic choice was between ordered and casual display, the first gradually giving way to the latter. In the richest and most stiffly arranged Neoclassical interiors, all wood – whether doors, door frames or furniture – could be coated in white (or white and gold), with the ceiling and walls treated similarly. The mostly smallish-looking furniture would be equally straight lined, and it would be placed symmetrically against the walls.[102]

Furnishing 'en suite' was an important trend throughout the century. Germans use the term *Garnitur* for a set of matching armchairs, sofa and table, all to be placed in the most ordered fashion.[103] By about the 1850s a counter-tendency developed, according to which furniture was arranged casually (for a time, there was even a vogue for buying items of furniture piece-meal).[104] In any case, furniture types continued to diversify. Whereas early in the century two types of chair might have sufficed for a moderately formal room, by the middle of the century a good salon was distinguished by a plethora of types of seating: larger, smaller, higher, lower, etc. There was a practical reason: modes of sitting vary greatly, and so should the shape of seats, accommodating different heights, angles of recline, number of people, and so on. Here, of course, the chairmakers acted in cahoots with the upholsterers.

The timber industries also attempted to promote increasingly bulky items, such as the grand, showy *meubles de parade*.[105] They revived the sideboard, partly to provide practical storage in the dining room and partly to allow for the display of silver or ceramics. In Germany, a massive kind of *Büfett* soon became standard. Sideboards also formed the most spectacular English exhibition pieces: sometimes they were incredibly massive (like those designed by Talbert), sometimes lighter (like those by Godwin), but in each case they bristled with invention.[106] The settee (to use the most common English term) was also of major impor-tance. The Germans in particular continued to design big sofas, which had been de rigueur from earlier in the century; by 1880 they could incorporate shelving and appear almost fixed to the wall.[107]

Dining room by Bembé & Co., Mainz, for Peleş Castle, Sinaia, Romania, 1875–83. The Romanian king's summer palace contains probably the richest, and certainly the best-preserved, interiors by German and Austrian designers and makers of the period.

The all-wooden room

Wood began to take over ever greater parts of the room. After the giant sideboard, it was not long before combined items of furniture – so-called 'fitted furniture', or 'fitments' – covered the best part of a wall.[108] This trend culminated in the walls being completely lined with wood. Wainscoting or panelling had been used to fit out medium-sized rooms for centuries, to provide warmth, but also because the wood could easily be lined up with the joinery around door frames and window surrounds.[109] Such 'door-furniture' was in fact crucial in shaping the character of an interior, although the placement of doors and windows is outside the realm of interior design. The art of the late 19th-century decorator often resided in overcoming, or in compensating for, the awkward positioning of doors and windows. Earlier in the century there were attempts either to hide an unwanted door or install a blind door for the sake of the overall symmetry of a wall. But these doors did not reveal much wood, blended in as they were with the surrounding stucco ornament.[110] In the later 19th century, by contrast, all doors would be lent emphasis through the addition of elaborate frames and overdoors, all proudly displaying the material from which they were constructed.

Somehow during the 19th century the general perception of most materials was overturned. Wallpaper became cheaper and cheaper, stucco went out of fashion, and ornamented panelling showing real wood was now considered smart again – although for its makers new machinery had brought down production costs. Wood was now also considered as something

Ceiling of the Great Hall at Schloss Hummelshain, Thuringia, by the architects Ihne & Stegmüller, Berlin. It was begun in 1878.

ancient, harking back to Jacobean, Elizabethan, Henri II or German Renaissance styles, and even back to Gothic. Extensively timbered interiors made an early appearance in spectacular mansions such as Fonthill; Pugin then introduced them to the Houses of Parliament; and from 1870 examples in most styles abounded. In France, we can perhaps discern a certain continuity in old-style smoothly painted wainscoting. Havard distinguishes between *lambris de hauteur*, which covered the whole wall, and *lambris d'appui*, which reached about halfway up.[111] The medievalists were keenest of all, especially Viollet-le-Duc, and were enamoured of one of the most frequent motifs of Gothic décor, the linenfold pattern. In a remarkable early statement, dating to 1837, Thiollet & Roux – presumably woodworkers themselves – assert that completely lining a wall so as to show 'the natural nuances of the wood' (albeit in this case quite precious woods) can 'give the eye a rest from the profusion of gilding and sculpture, the abuse of which from day to day becomes more reprehensible'. This is of course an example of one trade preaching taste reform at the expense of other trades.[112]

Naturally, the later, wooden-built suburban houses in the United States would show timber most strongly, but it was probably within richer German houses that wooden fittings were applied most fervently. Here, as elsewhere, wood seemed especially appropriate for dining rooms. Around 1860, Falke forcefully championed the complete wooden interior, particularly for smaller rooms, which at the same time satisfied the formal need for unity: 'the whole room all of a piece …'.[113] At one point Luthmer even stipulated that an all-wooden room should have no curtains.[114]

Crowning the wooden room was the wooden ceiling: here, too, a mass of good, solid wood had become a sign of expense, since a ceiling with 'densely laid beams' could cost ten times more than a stucco imitation. Earlier in the century ceilings could not look light and airy enough; now they might appear as heavy as possible: 'wainscoted walls' and a 'heavy ceiling' made of dark wood gave 'the impression of being comfortable, of seriousness and solidity',[115] although such effects were still mostly restricted to the dining room and the gentleman's room. In addition, there was a contest between flooring materials, this time between wood and textiles, although Anglo-Saxon and Continental practice differed, the latter mostly preferring parquet, that great product of precision craftsmanship.[116]

In 1840 a member of the woodworking profession claimed that carpenters, joiners and cabinetmakers were 'feeling a desire to hold on to their pre-eminence'. By 1875, the *Furniture Gazette* expressed the sentiment more explicitly, demanding a oneness between furniture and fixtures: 'we have not much sympathy with lath and plaster and whitewash; we would rather see beams and joints and boards'. Ten years later the *Cabinet Maker* enthused about the wooden fire surround, which had 'been rescued thanks to the enterprise of the cabinetmaker from the hands of the builder's marble mason'.[117] But envy was mutual, and a housepainter's journal maintained that 'décor and harmony today is produced … far less by furniture than by the other crafts', recommending variously painted ceilings.[118]

Objects and their display

Products

An abundance of objects, large and small, greets the eye in many later 19th-century interiors. This section deals chiefly with the ways in which they were visually coordinated. Its main argument is that assemblages of great numbers of objects may help to unify the visual character of a room, or to create areas of coherence, just as much as any of the other furnishings presented so far. Writers of the 'art at home' books made a point of dealing comprehensively with a wide range of manufactures, underlining what they saw as the necessity of diverse artifice, and none more so than the French art philosopher Charles Blanc in his *Grammaire des arts décoratifs* (1882),

An 'architectural fantasy in Pompeian style' by Félix Duban, *c.* 1830. The young architect has here indulged in an improbable abundance of Classical artefacts, thereby creating a new vision of 'Pompeii' in which flat décor no longer prevails.

which bore the subtitle *Décoration intérieure de la maison*. For Blanc, the home is virtually the sum of the different objects in it. The trades discussed so far fill only half of his book, the remainder being taken up with metalwork, ceramics, glass and book cover design.

Dealing strictly with the decorating trades means leaving out two fundamental ways of beautifying any home. First, pictures on the wall. For the purposes of this discussion, we may disregard the fact that their overall numbers increased vastly in the 19th century, and that questions relating to the shape and colour of frames fell into the decorators' sphere. However, the choice of the pictures themselves was not normally the concern of professional decorators or designers, and leading writers on art in the home sometimes voiced their dislike of too many pictures on the wall.[119] The second way in which the home could be made more attractive was through flowers, whether fresh or artificial. They were not part of the professional decorator's remit either, except for the later 19th-century custom of displaying dried plants, among them the notorious *Makartbouquet*.[120]

Without a doubt, the highest category of domestic ornament was metalwork. In France, the term *orfèvrerie*, meaning goldsmith's work, was in fact rather broader, including also *orfèvrerie courante*, the manufacture of larger objects in bronze and even much cheaper metals. Some of the objects served a practical purpose, while many others aspired to the highest realms of figurative sculpture (*bronzes d'art*), copying the works of notable artists or the time-honoured

Display of ceramics from *At Home Again* (1886),
a children's book by Eliza Keary.

statues of Classical antiquity.[121] The new chemical process of the electrotype (*galvanotype*), from around 1840, enabled the automated reproduction of eminent artworks, while the closely related electroplating (*galvanoplastie*) allowed for economic gilding and bronzing. The original hierarchy, comprising in descending order gold, silver, gilding, copper alloys (bronze and brass) and pewter, was now joined by further metals at its lower end. Early in the century, the Berlin cast-iron technique known as *Eisenkunstguss* had been employed for artworks, as was the extremely cheap *Zinkguss* later on, which was plated with bronze and which worked out at about one sixth of the price of real bronze.[122] All these domestic art objects were trumped in terms of sheer availability by the claim that, in 1900, reproduction paintings cost just one hundredth of their price in 1850.[123]

None of this seems to have affected the established hierarchy of decorum – at least not until the 1890s. The more décor, the better. As Charles Blanc wrote, 'the dignity of life extends to the greatest number'.[124] Alongside goods of the most expensive kind, Emperor Napoleon III commissioned a service in cheap *metal d'argent* (i.e. electroplating) from Christofle – a prestigious firm, but one that was also in the process of expanding to factory size.[125] And yet, as in the case of textiles and other manufactures, the 'art' aspect of metalwork did shift somewhat, from prioritizing figurative elements to displaying a greater interest in the material itself. Blanc and others pleaded for the restriction of figurative décor in favour of a variety of surface effects, the 'glint of light reflected from its embossed surface', which could be matched by the matt shine of other types of surface. Critics were tired of the 'glaring cold shine' of earlier gold and silver.[126] Interest also turned towards methods of fixing colour on metal, as in medieval and Oriental enamel work.

A 'Room Containing Greek Fictile Vases' in Thomas Hope's house, London, 1807.

Three bad ways and one good (*bottom*) of arranging objects on a mantelpiece. The top two examples are taken from Henry Havard's *L'Art dans la maison* (1884), while the bottom two were published in *The Decorator and Furnisher* (1892), which comments: 'lines whose apices point downward … cannot fail to be pleasant and cheerful'.

Japanese fretwork cabinet and overdoors by Paul
Hasluck, London, 1882 and 1883.

Second to metal in its apparent preciousness was glass, especially sparkling, deeply cut
crystal; prevalent during much of the century, it was imitated from the 1820s by the American
invention of cheap pressed glass. On the whole, however, glass was more limited in its aspirations to fine art and rarely carried figurative meaning.[127] Its great competitor was ceramics,
which arguably demonstrated the widest spectrum, ranging from works of high art through
the trade to purely utilitarian wares. Around the middle of the century English and French
ceramic manufacturers broke the monopoly on smartness enjoyed by hard-paste Meissen or
Sèvres porcelain, reintroducing coarser, more colourful and – most importantly – more
diversely textured wares such as majolica and stoneware, thus widening their historical and
geographical remits enormously. 'Next to our pictures our china is our most valued movable
decoration', claimed a British writer late in the century, referring to the mania for 'blue and
white', which was indeed one of the most effective types of unified décor ever devised.[128]

Meaning

Aside from issues of production and form, one can assume that a movable object normally
carries more complex meanings than fixed kinds of décor – than, say, the profile of ceiling
plaster or the ribbon on the back of a chair. These latter examples may be regarded as mere
decoration – attachments to an object whose chief meaning resides in its practical purpose.
With objets d'art, however, figurative meanings were becoming ever more diverse. The high
value of the material itself was also a consideration (disregarding for a moment the growing
number of imitations).[129] But their principal meaning, in the context of this chapter, was that

they served as generic fine art objects. These artefacts elicited 'feelings of the possession of beauty' (Charles Blanc). Falke would have agreed heartily: as has already been stressed, 'art in the house' for him largely meant the assembling of works of fine art.[130]

In time, discussions surrounding the relationship between objects and humans – the 'rapport entre les hommes et les choses' – assumed wider implications. One could differentiate between an individual's appreciation, 'which favours the liberty of one's spirits', and social use: 'The salon requires a certain diversity of objects … not only to show the wealth and cultural aspirations of the owner, but also to animate conversation and create entertainment.'[131] In addition to the significance of each individual object, there are further levels of comprehensive meaning. The hierarchy of decorum forbade any area in the richest palaces from being left bare. In all lesser houses, displays were first and foremost related to the rooms' functions, for instance the arrangement of valuable plates and related objects on the dining room dresser or at the centre of the dining table itself. Charles Blanc still uses the old phrase *de parade* to refer to these displays.[132] Many had become influenced by issues of gender, such as the array of small bottles on a dressing table in the bedroom, or the assembly of armour in a male collector's room. One may understand these displays in a ritual sense, even if the objects might be

Boudoir by A. & L. Streitenfeld, Berlin, 1888: a late example of objects being displayed in rows.

Study at Schloss Hummelshain, Thuringia, by Ihne & Stegmüller, Berlin, begun 1878.

Overleaf
Four schemes that sum up the possibilities of various materials for decoration and coordination. All were entries in a *Building News* Designing Club competition for 'A Dining Room showing Door and Buffet', 1877.

left Walls in wood panelling (above: a debut by the young W. R. Lethaby) and in painted plaster (below).

right Walls in leather panels (above) and wallpaper and stencil (below).

used only rarely, if at all. Lastly, these items could all hark back to the old iconography of the *memento mori* and the still life, even though their principal, ancient allusion – to death – was hardly remembered. What remained was simply the image of a casual assembly.

In the users' justifications for surrounding themselves with a plethora of objects, more relativistic views were gaining ground. What hardly seemed to matter was size. Smallness need not be a hindrance, and may actually help create an impression of higher material value, although not necessarily so. 'Trifles make the sum of life … so that it is trifles that make much of the effect of furnishing,' wrote Mrs Spofford: 'lovely outline, pure colour … they go very far towards securing beauty as a whole'. One French writer spoke of 'the little nothings which are the eye's pleasure and mark the quality of the home'.[133] This brings one to other spheres of meaning; 'collecting', for example, leads us to the amassing of objects of the same kind, as the term implies. If this analysis is extended, the notion of the home may become usurped and the whole turned simply into a collector's abode. But one could also collect less serious kinds of articles, which were now given special terms: *bibelots*, bric-a-brac, knick-knacks, *Nippes* or *Nippsachen*.[134] In any case, none of them could clearly be defined as art. In 1868 a British observer remarked: 'bric à brac includes all that is precious and beautiful as well

"BUILDING NEWS" DESIGNING CLUB : DECORATION OF DINING ROOM :

"Building News Design Club" ‖ SKETCH for the Decoration of a DINING ROOM ‖

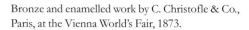

The 'Musée Rétrospectif' – a huge display of
objects from the past – formed part of the Galerie
de l'Histoire du Travail at the Paris Exposition
Universelle, 1867.

as mediocre in art'.[135] These minor objects could even be considered in the same category as the
more ephemeral *articles de Paris* or *Galanteriewaren* (fancy goods), which also included cheaper
fashion accessories.[136]

Modernist critics and some of their predecessors doubted the artistic value of much of this
décor, condemning as meaningless the assembly of such objects in the home and insisting on
a rigid philosophy of art that strictly divided the 'artistic' from the 'useful'. Following Marx,
some modernists feared the alienation that would result from being surrounded by quantities
of objects bought from a trade that supposedly did not care for meaning. By contrast, more
recent researchers, working chiefly in the fields of anthropology and social psychology, but
also in literature and studies of material consumption, have tried to (re-)claim a profound relationship between objects and users, and to assert the meanings represented by these objects in
everyday life.[137]

French 16th-century tin-glazed pottery ('faïence dite d'Orion') from *L'Art Pour Tous* (1868). This periodical, which appeared over several decades, presented an unusually diverse array of old objects, often drawn in a striking manner.

Mass display

Within this account of the various ways in which coherence and unity could be created in the domestic interior, the producers should still be viewed as the chief agents responsible for décor. Later in the century, the person with this remit was given the label 'decorator', as explained in Chapter II; in practice, it was mostly the upholsterer, whose work could now include the distribution of the *orfèvrerie*.[138] Sometimes these decorators feared for their artistic independence, resenting any contributions by the client.[139] The client did have the opportunity to judge the decorator's work in advance, however, at the decorator's own shop and at exhibitions. From the 1850s, images of grouped objects from the World's Fairs increasingly served as models. Late 19th-century shops and department stores presented several kinds of display, including objects of the same kind amassed together ('hundreds to be chosen from …'),[140] and the room settings discussed above, with all objects preselected and positioned with care.

Throughout the 19th century the display of objects in metal, glass or ceramic followed much the same trajectory as the other decorating techniques. In the Neoclassical interior, it was the architecture, or the main lines of the wall divisions, that dictated where objects should be placed. In the very smartest interiors, works of fine art – the paintings or sculptures – provided the principal décor; a very small number of other objects, such as a few candlesticks, were treated as relatively precious, but they appeared small and corresponded rigidly to the lines of the overall scheme. In an interior with more objects than usual on display – a collector's house such as Thomas Hope's in London, for instance – everything nevertheless appeared neat and extremely carefully organized. The same essentially applied much later to the blue-and-white collections of the Aesthetic Movement in England in the 1870s: superior Nanking ware 'for the purpose of decorations reigns supreme'.[141]

From the long-established kind of ordered display we move to what has been termed the 'romantic interior'. This was a newer world belonging to the collector of mainly Northern (that is, non-Classical) antiquities, which often appeared as a den of darkness and disorder, almost of neglect – at least in some carefully staged paintings. It is very hard to make out any individual objects, though one may suppose that this was the ostensible aim of any collection. Nevertheless, these interiors could hardly be called 'homes' in any usual sense of the word.[142]

Later in the century the disordered interior was adapted for another special user: the fine art artist. Until well into the 19th century studio spaces were seen as rather sparse rooms, but by the 1870s the more opulent artists of London or Munich surrounded themselves with the paraphernalia they depicted in their realist genre paintings, including peasant gear, all kinds of antiques, and more ephemeral artefacts like dried palm trees and so on. Bohemianism led to a preference for very casual arrangements that nonetheless exuded artistic imagination and verve. An artist, writes Blanc, 'needs to be surrounded with varied and numerous objects which support the freedom of his thoughts and which provoke them through their unexpected proximity and through the strangeness of their contrasts'. The most outstanding example of this sort of bohemian interior was the giant Vienna atelier of the Munich-trained Hans Makart.[143]

Again, in spite of the contention that they constituted actual homes, these romantic artistic interiors, with their look of extreme casualness, cannot be taken as normal dwellings. But some elements from the studio found their way into many homes, such as the device of the painting displayed on an easel and the bunches of dried plants and flowers (henceforth called the *Makartbouquet* in Central Europe and beyond). Most significantly for the development of the interior, these features demonstrated 'the right instinct for the visual coherence of all objects' (Alfred Lichtwark).[144] The spread of bohemianism did correspond with general changes in the notion of comfort and with a new informality. A German women's magazine of the 1850s opined that French salons were not 'tidy', but that they were 'comfortable'. The critic R. Bergau argued very simply that the arrangement of objects in the salon should be varied and informal, just like the room's different uses.[145]

The homes of eminent artists in many capital cities were much admired by the later 19th century, the best documented being the studios of Munich. The chief principle governing their interior design was a highly contrived disorder, as in this atelier belonging to the Polish painter Józef Brandt, 1876.

As the century progressed, the mass of smaller objects in a room could begin to dominate, almost directly paralleling the efforts of the wallpaper or textile trades to promote their wares. One problem was finding enough surfaces on which to place the objects. Fireplaces in England and the United States, and to a lesser extent in France, were for a long time surmounted by a mantelpiece, a shelf mostly for holding a clock and candlesticks. By mid-century, however, this fashion was viewed as somewhat amateurish.[146] From the late 1860s some English architects constructed complex overmantels for the display of copious objects, mostly ceramics. One way of emphasizing the objects' value was to put them in a cupboard behind glass. By 1859, though, we read that in Germany 'the vitrine [glass cabinet] is going more and more out of fashion';[147] the freer and more expansive displays on the *Nippestischchen*, the 'knick-knack table', became popular instead. There was now a mushrooming of étagères, small sideboards, shelves on the wall above tables and so on, all supplied by the woodworkers. High shelves above the wainscoting and over the doors (the 'overdoors') were also increasingly popular. Lastly, the corners of rooms were considered suitable places for display ('corner potpourri').[148] Manufacturers and shops would stress that items of furniture belonged with particular objects; Jackson & Graham even advised customers that an ebony cabinet was destined 'for the purpose of showing objects of art and virtu'. Perhaps a little stranger was a statement implying the reverse, advertising the sale of 'a large amount of china articles specially adapted for decorating cabinets'.[149]

Every time a new place for showing off objects was discovered, questions of overall coordination became more pressing. These new modes of display may be summed up by the

The Munich atelier of Hermione von Preuschen, 1889.

Decorative motifs for a music room and a hunting room, by Martin Wiegand, 1893.

ubiquitous word 'picturesque' (a term to be explored below), and items were praised for 'their congregated beauty ... for the sake of their picturesque charm when united'.[150] This signified an abandonment of symmetry and a central viewpoint, as well as a new stress on body and surface rather than on the outline of an object – a phenomenon that has already been noted in the case of timber and textiles. The aims of this kind of display basically remained the same: the individual object should not force itself onto the onlooker, but should appear integrated with its surroundings.

'Chairs, sofas, tables, stools, chiffoniers, articles of vertu, a few elegantly bound books, vases for flowers, musical instruments, with other elegant articles of refinement, taste, and ornament, should be strewed about the room in most picturesque disorder', wrote the young radical architect Edward Buckton Lamb in 1834.[151] In France, the young architect Félix Duban indulged in highly coloured fantasies of diverse objects.[152] By the 1880s writers and critics were fully considering the new, casual kind of display, and none more so than Henry Havard: 'thousands of art objects' belong to 'mobile finery' rather than 'fixed finery', although all this by no means prevented him from offering some very precise advice on how to arrange them.[153] But time and again we are told that the placement should appear accidental: 'the accidental nature of their presence … '. To one woman who said: 'You have just come in time, Mr Wilde … to arrange my screens for me', it is claimed that Oscar Wilde replied: 'Oh, don't arrange them; let them occur.' The more one discusses this kind of picturesqueness, the more acute the conundrum of the picturesque aesthetic becomes: should the 'picturesque disorder' (Luthmer) be intentional or not? Do we see it all as 'willed disorder' (Havard), or do the best effects come about unconsciously, 'by instinct' (Mrs Haweis)?[154] Occasionally authors asserted the opposite, as did Lewis F. Day: objects, especially knick-knacks, 'should not look as if they had come together by accident'. Neither did it mean that a 'free' arrangement could not very easily be disrupted: 'not infrequently, even a single piece disturbs the harmonious overall effect of a room'.[155]

The way in which such smaller objects could be arranged was thus more important than their meaning or value ('a good arrangement is more important than the choice of the individual objects'). As important as shape and colour were the effects of light, and various writers between the 1870s and the 1890s gave the following advice: 'these little precious objects are

Perhaps the *ne plus ultra* of varied, picturesque décor: an 'arrangement for a boudoir' designed by Karl Hammer and executed by J. A. Eysser for the Munich Exhibition, 1888.

the shining points and the highlights of the room'; there was no 'merciless silhouetting; now and again the outline is intermingled in a pleasant dusk'; and 'china glass' should be kept 'where it will make a cheerful show of blinking light and colour'.[156] The casual look – in reality devised most carefully by the professions – had become one of the principal visual formulas for the domestic interior, applicable to all rooms regardless of use. Only the dining room had to maintain a more formal character.

Inevitably, criticisms of the new way of displaying many diverse objects together were not slow to appear, and usually began with the old warnings against upsetting the hierarchy of decorum. It could not be expected that meaninglessness would be welcomed as something positive for long.[157] By the 1890s, there was a new attitude: avoid décor for its own sake, and stick to fine art or to useful objects only. From this point on, the serious 'antique' was understood as a single piece or a matching pair of items, preferably placed in front of a neutral background. But there were also designers who created very specific and effective kinds of meaning for the whole room by coordinating carefully selected objects within the broader framework of walls and ceilings, with everything adhering to a single style (see Chapter V).

Upkeep

After completing their work, the designer and the decorator leave, and the client takes over. But in the 19th century, the way the more elaborately fitted homes were inhabited remained deeply connected to the producers' work. Values in society as a whole informed the way in which one's interior décor was perceived, and one's home had to meet those standards. Hence the processes of protecting, cleaning, renovating and supplementing the décor of a room can be seen as a direct continuation of the designing and making processes. Indeed, when difficult furnishings or objects required cleaning, mending or altering, they could be returned temporarily to their makers.

Running a home in the 19th century was circumscribed by very detailed guidelines. With the exception of the richest households, it was the woman of the house who was in charge. The line invariably taken by the new moralistic home advice books was that the 'mistress' should make it her duty to direct all activities: in contrast to the perceived leisurely existence of earlier days, there was no longer spare time to waste. Furthermore, as we saw in Chapter II, women were seen as agents in the art of the interior – almost professional creators of home textiles, but also coordinators overseeing those final details that Falke claimed were so important for the look of the whole.[158]

According to the advice books, thorough cleaning had to be done in a certain order that involved a considerable shifting of all objects. Nothing could make one more conscious of the whole than having to put it all back together again.[159] The mistress could of course rely on countless servants. Can it be calculated that the increase in the domestic servants per household paralleled the boom in home décor? In 1891 their total number in England had peaked at over one and a half million (the figures in Germany and France were somewhat lower). The minimum annual income that enabled a family to keep one female servant was put at £150–200, and a 'maid of all work' typically received just 7 guineas annually, apart from shelter (of a kind) and food. Rates of pay did rise during the century, but in terms of income and drudgery domestic service always represented one of the lowest strata of the social economy. This growth in service was matched by an increased specialization in different kinds of cleaning, as well as by the appearance of a more precise hierarchy among the servants of larger houses. Servants' expected performance was set out in immense detail; for example, their hours of work – or of being 'on call' – were 5 or 6 am to 12 midnight. Equally complex and precise (according to the books) was the order in which the various types of cleaning should be carried out, as was their division into daily, weekly, monthly or half-yearly tasks. The more

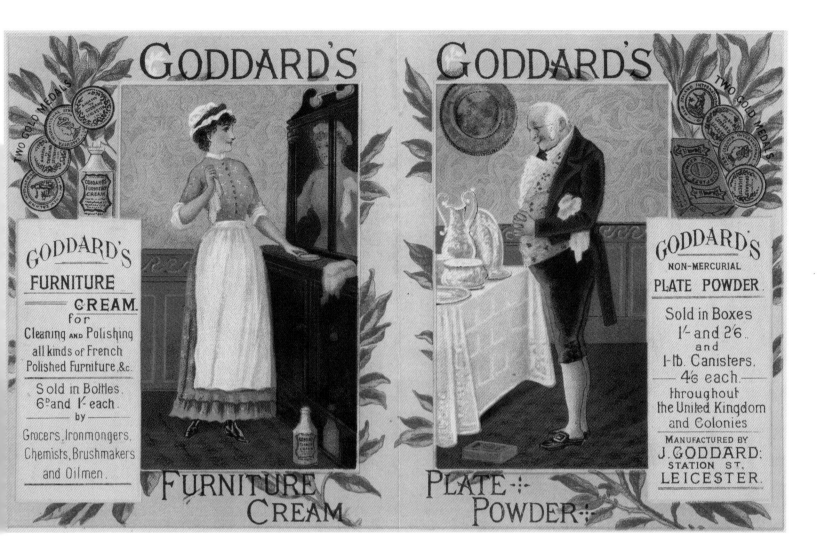

Late 19th-century advertisement for cleaning products. Regard for workmanship did not stop with the completion of an interior but continued long afterwards. The cleaning of each material required a special expertise, with the hierarchy of the trades reflected in the way jobs were allocated to different ranks of servant. The polishing of precious metals, for example, could come only under the butler's jurisdiction.

delicate the object, the less its cleaning could be entrusted to lower-class servants, and real collectors would insist on caring for their objects personally.[160] The cleaning of some materials had to be left to specialized professionals, and even the word 'art' could creep in here ('the delicate blue of the muslin curtain' resulted from 'the art of the washerwoman').[161]

The home could be comprehensively cared for in a number of ways. One was simply through non-use. The apparent increase in rooms reserved 'for best' served those who could afford to buy the décor but not to renew it frequently. Copious use of antimacassars also helped in this respect.[162] The long-established signs that reliable cleaning had taken place were polished silverware for the table, the gleaming metal parts of a fireplace, or the whitened stone steps at the entrance to modest and even poor houses. Whiteness was a universal indicator of 'cleanness' (Goethe), and a demand for cleanliness throughout the house was common, it appears, by the early 19th century ('cleanliness, freshness and elegance').[163] Clearly, more and larger objects and a new preference for darker areas in the rooms incurred more work, indicated by endless admonitions to sweep underneath the furniture and so on.

Many cleaning practices had to be tailored to the nature of the materials. The cleaning and pressing of textiles was the most complex task, and a proportion of the cleaning and certainly of the renovating was performed by the upholsterers. Dry cleaning appears to have come in around 1870. Movable carpets had to be beaten, while fixed carpets were spread with old tea leaves, to bind the dirt. Upholstery also needed to be gently beaten, and coloured fabrics required careful protection.[164] Most onerous was the cleaning and especially the rehanging of voluminous heavy curtains. As already noted, Ris-Paquot extolled the genius of the arty house-wife in curtain-hanging: 'it is the manner of composing a drapery that reveals the genius of the woman in this truly artistic kind of work'.[165]

Another area of maintenance requiring complex expertise was wood, especially its polish. Different woods required different chemicals and different ways of rubbing them in. French polish in particular was the cabinetmaker's pride, but its reapplication was also an important task for whoever was in charge of maintenance. Ris-Paquot was again most emphatic: 'to conserve all the furniture in its freshness and original beauty … a large number of indispensable precautions … methodical cleaning …'. Baroness Staffe claimed that 'a single layer of dust on a piece of furniture takes away half its beauty'. Polished wooden floors needed 'constant and intelligent care', too. In his extensive 1856 *Manual of Domestic Economy* John Henry Walsh went into French polishing in great detail. Pointing out its artifice and complexity, he then also recommended a simpler technique, based on the application of butter of antimony, vinegar, 'spirit of wine' and linseed oil; its effect was 'very fair' but 'not quite equal to the brilliancy of French polish'. Clearly, the amateurs' efforts might come close to the trades' but could never equal them.[166]

Basically the cleaning processes were not questioned. Where there was décor, there were servants whose almost natural task, so it seemed, was to keep it clean. It made no difference in principle whether the objects were dark, complex or heavy. The act of cleaning was something that polite society took for granted. The advice books' copious admonitions were thus probably largely rhetorical, and some of their obsessive complexity very likely exaggerated. It seems, though, that their assessment of the total amount of work required was not. We may thus cautiously conclude that the 19th century's increase in décor did not result in diminished standards of cleanliness.

Eventually, by 1890, a new perception began to emerge. The cleaning tasks and the frequency with which they were carried out appeared cumbersome and inconvenient – certainly for the master of the house, if he happened to be present.[167] Some writers now asserted that elaborate décor by its very nature harboured dirt. All this coincided with never-ending discussions of the new shortage of servants. 'Who is doing the dusting here?' a lady from sober Hamburg asked when on a visit to showy Berlin. Equally important was an increased desire for family privacy, which tended to find the presence of servants embarrassing. In any case, nothing could really be done about the dirt, which the city as a whole created. New fashions arose for thinly built, less bulky furniture, for curtains that hung straight, and once more for light-coloured interiors overall. By the early 1890s a conviction voiced by E. W. Godwin as early as 1876 had become widespread: cleanliness was 'the first consideration in all domestic design'.[168] This is almost the opposite of what had been argued thus far – in order for décor to be clean, it had to be cleaned. More broadly speaking, Godwin's statement about applied décor chimes with a comprehensive, more abstract notion of 'design', to which this chapter now turns. At the same time, the differentiated cleaning practices outlined above illustrate once again the significance of the materials themselves, their associated production techniques, and the effects of their textures and colours.

Colour

Materials

'Colour, lovely colour of itself would make our rooms charming', wrote Christopher Dresser in 1873.[169] Vivid colours were a distinguishing feature of domestic interiors for much of the 19th century. Before that, a special notion of applying or coordinating colours in the home did not seem to exist, whereas after 1910 the use of colour was severely curtailed by many orthodox modernisms. However, when viewed in the context of the colour industry and colour science as a whole, the domestic décor was but one of many applications – probably one reason why it has hardly been investigated, excepting Ian Bristow's extensive study of the British situation until 1840.[170]

Colour science was very much a field in itself. At the same time – especially in the 19th century – it stimulated the interest of a great number of professions, scientific as well as artistic. As with the other media used to decorate the home, the material itself came first – in this case the colouring agents, pigments and dyestuffs. From the viewpoint of later advances in the 19th century, obtaining reliable pigments was a hit-and-miss affair and their nomenclature was confusing. As with other materials, only infinitely more so, there was a gap between the cheap and the expensive. As late as 1894, at a time when others were claiming that all colours were now readily available, *Laxton's Price Book* still made the basic distinction between 'common colours' and 'ornamental colours'. The former included lamp black, white lead and 'any of the common brown ochres', while the latter category consisted of all those colours one might call attractive or striking, such as green, blue and pink. Vast differences in price could apply also to individual colours. The most expensive red, vermilion, was twenty times dearer than red lead.[171] Further uncertainty arose through the mixing of cheaper with more extensive pigments, across an 'ill-defined boundary between legitimate material and adulteration' (Bristow).[172]

The chief purpose of these colours was to relieve the common world of drabness, as with the new cheerful wallpapers and chintzes already discussed. The speed at which colours could be 'improved' and made cheaper through the use of new substances and mixtures accelerated during the early 19th century, as witnessed by the introduction of chrome yellow and the intensive work undertaken on practicable greens. Apart from the development of pigments and dyestuffs, the colour industry also constantly refined the ways in which they could be adapted for house paints and textiles.[173] The spread, from the 1840s onwards, of brightly coloured

Probably no other period was as keen on the multicoloured interior as the 19th century – or so it would seem from the popularity of chromolithography, one of the century's new printing methods. This design is from Jean Pape's *Mustersammlung* ('pattern book') of 1888 – perhaps the most striking set of interiors to come out of Germany in the 1880s. Pape, now almost completely forgotten, came from Cologne, trained as an architect at the Berlin Bauakademie and then taught for the rest of his life at the Dresden Kunstgewerbeschule.

pattern books reproduced through chromolithography also influenced the colour climate. All these factors soon underwent a fundamental shift when old empiricism turned into modern science. A new *Farbenindustrie* – the word covered all types of chemical colour production, on which Germany enjoyed a monopoly for some decades – largely abandoned mineral, vegetable and animal substances and produced colours synthetically, mostly from a tar base ('aniline' dyes). From their beginnings in 1826, synthetic colours developed rapidly after 1850. By the 1870s 'tar colours … now reign completely in wool and silk colouring',[174] and according to some critics they were 'extremely beautiful'. By now there was a reliability of nomenclature, applicability and cheapness, a wide choice of colours ('a complete choice') and, for the home, paints that could be 'purchased ready for use' rather than mixed on site.[175]

An extreme example of the pale interior, in which everything – apart from the small amount of wood on view – is painted white or light grey. This Viennese room dates to 1836 (compare the illustration on p. 183).

Early use

For the rich, all colours were notionally available ('in the higher class of houses … different colours [were] employed for … decorating different rooms').[176] In fact, even here colour was something relatively new. Earlier on, the decorative schemes of the most palatial kinds of room had been determined completely by architectural elements, usually executed in a 'colourless' neo-Palladian manner. In slightly lesser rooms, colour could be found in paintings in any medium, and perhaps in non-conspicuous tones applied to wainscoting and in the room's textiles. Stuccoed ceilings were invariably kept a neutral brilliant white. Only in ladies' rooms was one likely to find any 'gaudy' hangings.[177] In other words, colour, or the lack of it, was what the individual trades produced, since it all depended on their materials and techniques. According to Bristow, there is no sense in even asking the question 'how were colours harmonized in the eighteenth century?'[178]

Nevertheless, it appears that the trades in France did gradually bring in a greater variety of colours during the 18th century, chiefly through the use of textiles. Colours were increasingly varied within a single textile cover or hanging (silk was particularly good at showing brilliant colours).[179] At the same time, the smartest furniture also featured woods of different colours. More radical steps were taken in the design of British interiors from the 1760s, especially in the work of Robert Adam. He restricted textile décor on walls, eliminated old-style wainscoting, broke the rule of the proud, independent plasterers and condemned the 'glare' of their white ceilings. But principally it meant that there was now someone else to choose and coordinate the colours.[180]

The commonest method of bringing more colour into rooms was the application of distemper to the walls: in the 1830s, 'distempered blue, red, [and] yellow' could present 'new delights'. Painted décor soon became 'the chief vehicle for embellishing the interior'. The Neoclassical insistence on the complete flatness of walls now contributed in its own way to a new rule of colour, for the simple reason that colour was the only decorative element the flat surface could display. From this point on, the praises of colour could be heard throughout the rest of the century: 'colour is the main factor for the whole of furnishing', claimed one writer in 1889. In 1858 the architect and decorative designer George Aitchison maintained that 'thirty years ago' architects were simply 'against colours'. Contemporary comments also stressed easy availability: 'carpets … now [come] with almost an infinite number of shades and colours' (1856).[181]

On the whole, rooms at the turn of the 19th century tended to display one colour and a narrow range of tones.[182] A long-standing preference was 'royal red', or scarlet, and also crimson; green had been a popular and elegant choice in the later 18th century. Under the influence of Napoleon, the fashion for light blue became widespread: the Germans favoured *Königsblau*, a light royal blue.[183] The extraordinarily lavish refitting of the Prince Regent's Carlton House in London and of Windsor Castle in the 1820s was ruled by the contrast between rooms: the 'Large or Crimson Drawing Room', the 'Green Drawing Room', etc.[184] Increasingly, however, delight in colours meant mixing them in the same room. Probably the

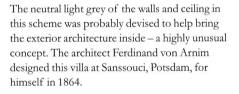

The neutral light grey of the walls and ceiling in this scheme was probably devised to help bring the exterior architecture inside – a highly unusual concept. The architect Ferdinand von Arnim designed this villa at Sanssouci, Potsdam, for himself in 1864.

A refined grey used to set off colourful accents in a scheme by Wilhelm Kimbel, Mainz, *c.* 1843.

wildest display of juxtaposed colours occurred in French books of around 1830–40, which showed all manner of strongly coloured curtains (see pp. 86, 90–91).[185] Publications focusing on furniture, such as the serial *Le Garde Meuble*, coloured their plates seemingly arbitrarily. On a much more modest level, a small strip of paper could mark the frieze on a distempered wall in a strongly contrasting colour, or, with the same intent, a gaily coloured ribbon could be added to seat upholstery.[186]

But there still seemed to be no principles guiding coordination: texts recommend 'colours as fancy or taste may direct' without devoting too much attention to how they would look side by side. In 1807 Thomas Hope presented the simplest alternative: 'harmonious blending or gay opposition of the various colours'. Recent findings in 19th-century upper-range Swiss interiors have concluded that their palettes oscillated between harmony and disharmony.[187]

Alternatively, there always remained the option of whiteness. But this, too, became a complex matter. First, white walls and ceilings formed a good basis for all those who wanted bright colours in their furnishings, as is conveyed by many illustrations from cabinetmakers and upholsterers. Furthermore, the continued preference of some for all-white rooms did not necessarily mean that colour was not understood. There was still a hangover from the neo-Palladian sense of the smartness of colourless high architecture, as well as of white stucco splendour: the grandest room in a rich house (the *Prachtsaal*, or 'room of magnificence', often the ballroom) could still be all white. There was also a more recent argument linking lightness with health, and the visual rule that a light room looks larger than a darker one.[188] In smarter houses, the light colour might not necessarily be bright white (after all, everybody knew that lead white was one of the cheapest colours available) but carefully prepared tinted or 'broken' whites; a frequent label in early 19th-century Britain was 'French white' or 'French grey'.[189] However, the most noticeable trend from mid-century was for darker main reception rooms, to which we shall come. The white ceiling in particular was now ridiculed by many as 'a plain white shroud' suggesting 'cold utility'.[190]

History and science

Much more precise discourses on the subject of colour had taken place in areas of art and science for centuries. From the early 19th century onwards, the traditional debate between form (*disegno*) and colour (*colore*) with which much art theory concerned itself tilted towards the latter, in that two of the most important artistic movements, Romanticism and then Realism, assigned themselves to the colour group. Historical studies of the use of colour in architecture,

Stronger – and cheaper – colours: a German living room in Rügen, designed in 1828.

under the heading of 'architectural polychromy', also gained in importance. Between the 1820s and the 1840s in Germany, France and England, the most celebrated names in Classical revival architecture and in archaeology engaged in friendly battles over the coloration of ancient Greek temples. The outcome here, too, was the eventual silencing of those who maintained the whiteness of these hallowed buildings.[191]

One historical use of colour became increasingly popular, especially in Central Europe: that suggested by Pompeian wall paintings. When they were rediscovered in the 18th century, the remains of the Roman city of Pompeii were cherished for the wall paintings themselves, but after 1800 interest turned more and more towards entire interior decoration schemes. Here was a Classical model that had been employed in relatively small houses. Figurative elements could be reduced to very small vignettes, and the gently illusionistic architectural motifs to a few lines. This meant that colours were particularly prominent. As Goethe remarked, 'there was no lack of unity in these rooms … a large area of the wall painted in one colour, pure'.[192] By contrast, a more vivid mixture of colours was revived in neo-Byzantine and neo-Gothic churches, including the intense colours conveyed in the medium of stained glass.[193] Colourmania likewise influenced a new Orientalism (see p. 204), beginning with the Moorish and Chinese extravagancies of Nash's Royal Pavilion in Brighton. Soon a love of carpets from the Near East enriched the stock of strongly coloured artefacts, and colour intensity appears to have reached a peak between the 1850s and 1870s.[194]

Art history was one way of legitimizing the study of and enthusiasm for colour; more significant, however, were attempts to pin down absolute, scientific certainties. Artists allied themselves to physicists, chemists and physiologists; they tried to profit from their experiments and theories, participating in their controversies and hoping that this might provide them with

A strict one-colour scheme for an official's residence in Transylvania, c. 1840.

The Princess of Prussia's sitting room, Schloss Babelsberg, Potsdam, designed mainly by Karl Friedrich Schinkel (1830s); lithograph after Carl Graeb, 1853. Although based around one principal colour, this scheme is less rigorous, with adjacent rooms painted in a contrasting hue.

a new kind of rightness in their artistic pursuits. There were two major issues at stake. First was an attempt at classification, which examined the constitution of individual colours, their names, their division into primary, secondary and tertiary colours, their mixing with white or black, and how they could be coordinated with the help of the colour circle. The name of Isaac Newton loomed large over all such concerns well into the 20th century. Second was an attempt to solve the problems that arose from the juxtaposition of different colours. Here, especially, psycho-physical arguments came to the fore: how colours were received by the eye, and which colours made the most pleasing combinations – in other words, how one could achieve absolute colour harmony. The universally agreed solution, which emerged fully only from the 1820s, was that harmony could be achieved by the juxtaposition of 'complementary' colours – a relatively new term that described colours appearing on opposite sides of the circle.[195]

Discussions relating to colour theory in the home got off to a very slow start. Goethe, who apart from being Germany's major poet was also a writer on art and on many areas of the natural sciences, devoted much attention to the colour schemes in his own house, recommending a restful green for the most frequently used rooms. In his lengthy *Farbenlehre* of 1810, however, he touched only briefly on colour in decoration.[196] The same is true of the Scotsman George Field in his treatise on *Chromatography* (1817), but Field's insistence on precision in the calculation of comparative colour intensities ('blue 8, red 5, yellow 3', etc.) would become a discussion point in the applied arts.[197] The utmost accuracy and assurance of verifiability were the

Contrast according to the rules: the Empress Eugénie's study at Saint-Cloud, c. 1860.

principal aims of the French chemist Michel-Eugène Chevreul, who in the late 1820s pro-moted a widely accepted 'Law of Contrasts', which purported to be based on scientific experimentation as well as everyday experience. A story cited innumerable times for the next half-century was Chevreul's observation of a seller of textiles, who complained that prospec-tive customers tired quickly when shown just one colour, such as red. When they were shown material in the contrasting colour – in this case green – the customers' enthusiasm for the orig-inal colour was soon revived. 'The apparent brightness of a given colour', Chevreul maintained, 'depends more importantly on the colour surrounding it than on the intensity of the dye itself.' In his *De la Loi du contraste simultané des couleurs* of 1839, Chevreul presented innu-merable applications for his rules: textiles, wallpapers, picture frames, anywhere where colour would be present. With its colour charts featuring 14,400 different shades, Chevreul's book became the most widely used manual in the field, although there were still only relatively few references to the domestic interior as a whole.[198]

It was in Britain that applied colour theory enjoyed an early prominence. This may have been due to the fact that the discourse of interior décor was kept above the level of mere trade. At the same time, a few tradesmen did contribute to the scientific discussions surrounding the issue of colour. David Ramsay Hay was a housepainter in Edinburgh who had risen to a social rank and independence unusual for his profession. His *Laws of Harmonious Colouring Adapted to House Painting*, a very short book when first published in 1828, had grown into a much amended work by the time of its last edition of 1847, involving subtle changes of title along the way. Hay devotes nearly half the book to colour matters in general, followed by a chapter

CARPET.	WOODWORK.	WALLS.	FRIEZE.	CORNICE.	CEILING.	UPHOLSTERY.	DRAPERY.
Black bear rug.	White mahogany and bronze.	Yellow striped paper or silk.	Painted.	Different tones of yellow.	Light yellow.	Yellow self-tones, rose.	Red and ivory
Chocolate.	Ivory enamel	Ecru, warm.	Old rose.	Chocolate, ecru, old rose.	Light warm ecru.	Old ivory, ecru and chocolate.	Capote blue.
Citron.	Bronze.	Old gold.	Citron.	Light gold, citron, old gold.	Light gold.	Old gold, red and citron.	Empire blue.
Claret.	Antique oak.	Olive green.	Gold.	Antique oak.	Vellum.	Red.	Bronze.
Deep sienna.	Antique oak.	Bottle green.	Indian red.	Deep sienna.	Deep ecru	Brown and Indian red.	Indian red.
Ecru or fawn.	Old ivory.	Light old ivory.	Ecru.	Deeper ecru and Indian yellow.	Very light ivory.	Ivory, with Indian yellow.	Blue and ivory.
Gobelin blue.	Fawn color or antique oak.	Dull drab (dark).	Gobelin blue or red.	Dull drab, Gobelin blue, or red.	Light drab	Drab, Gobelin blue, & little Gobelin red.	Rose and Nile.
Golden brown.	Black walnut.	Sage green.	Golden brown.	Ochre.	Light ochre.	Sage green & brown	Red and bronze.
Indian red.	Yellow brown.	Deep dull olive.	Indian yellow.	Olive.	Yellow olive.	Indian yellow & red.	Indian yellow.
Indigo.	Mahogany.	Deep Pompeian red.	Bright deep olive.	Olive, red, blue.	Light olive.	Deep Pompeian red.	Yellow.
Indian yellow.	Oak or cherry.	Indian yellow.	Deep Indian yellow.	Indian yellow.	Light Indian yellow.	Ind. yellow, cardinal red, olive or blue	Heliotrope.
Leather.	Antique oak or cocobola.	Bottle green.	Maroon.	Leather.	Deep ecru.	Deep bottle green and maroon.	Orange.
Old green.	Antique oak.	Dull sage.	Pompeian red (dull).	Dull sage, ochre.	Light greenish ochre.	Brown, with Pompeian red.	Capucine red
Old rose.	Rosewood.	Sea green.	Old rose.	Old rose and sea green.	Light sea green.	Sea green, grey, old rose.	Old rose, with sea green.
Olive.	Black walnut, cherry or mahogany.	Indian red or Indian yellow.	Dark blue, dk. Indian red, dark Indian yellow.	Olives	Light olive or ochre.	Deep Pompeian red or Indian yellow.	Copper bronze or Empire red.
Oriental rug.	Mahogany.	Pompeian red.	Same as wall.	Mahogany.	Buff.	Deep yellow.	Oriental stuffs.
Pompian red.	Olive.	Dull blue.	Dark Pompeian red.	Olive.	Cream.	Olive and red.	Tones of Pompeian red.
Red orange.	Ash.	Ochre.	Bright olive.	Ochre and light dull orange.	Pale ochre.	live, yellow and orange.	Two tones of olive.
Sage green.	Cherry.	Ochre.	Pompeian red.	Sage green, ochre.	Light sage green.	Pompeian red, dull blue, olive, sage.	Pompeian red, Nile or sage.
Violet.	Butternut.	Violet and yellow.	Violet and gold.	Violet and gold.	Yellow.	Warm green.	Old gold.

Two tables of suggested colour schemes, the first from *The Decorator and Furnisher*, 1895 (*above*), and the second from J. W. Facey's *Practical House Decoration*, 1892 (*right*).

SKIRTING	DADO	BAND	FILLING	CORNICE
Black.	Marone.	Straw colour.	French Grey.	A.
Brown.	Olive Green.	Orange.	Pompeiian Red.	B.
Olive Green.	Red.	Cinnamon.	Lilac.	C.
Black.	Brown.	Light Salmon.	Pale Green Tint.	D.
Dark Brown.	Light Brown.	Blue.	Salmon Tint.	E.
Black.	Marone.	Light Salmon.	Cream Tint.	F.
Dark Green.	Chocolate.	Blue.	French Grey.	G.
Dark Green.	Olive Green.	Deep Cinnamon.	Pink.	H.
Black.	Purple.	Green.	Red.	I.

on the more common topic of the technicalities of applying paint. There is thus relatively little discussion on the actual choice of colours in the home.[199] Others, including John Claudius Loudon and Andrew Jackson Downing, soon copied long passages from Hay's book.[200]

'I always design in colour', Owen Jones is reputed to have said. In his celebrated colour volume the *Grammar of Ornament*, Jones largely followed the axioms of Chevreul and Field. The South Kensington design reformers combined strong colours with 'flat' décor, a style that Owen Jones practised in a number of spectacularly rich London apartments. From the 1860s into the 1870s, published texts on colour in the applied arts proliferated.[201] A firm belief in laws prevailed: harmony, 'une science certaine', meant that 'the linking of complementary colours

opposite Colour contrasts that follow the standard formulae: a library by Berlin architect C. Schnitzler, 1881, and a living room by C. Grosser, 1877.

right and below The natural hues of the materials begin to dominate and the colour rules are relaxed: a living room and a dining room, both by Jean Pape, Dresden, 1887.

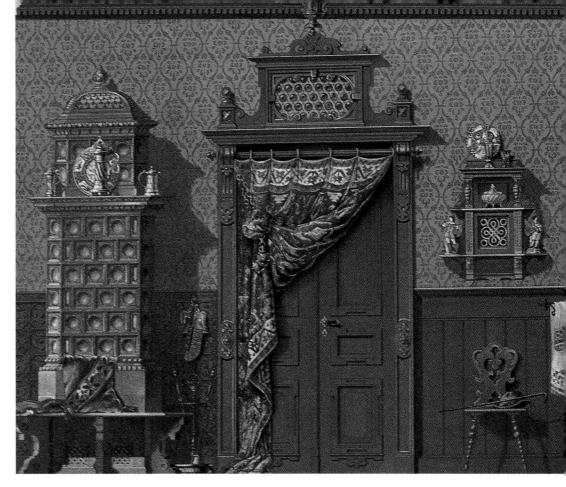

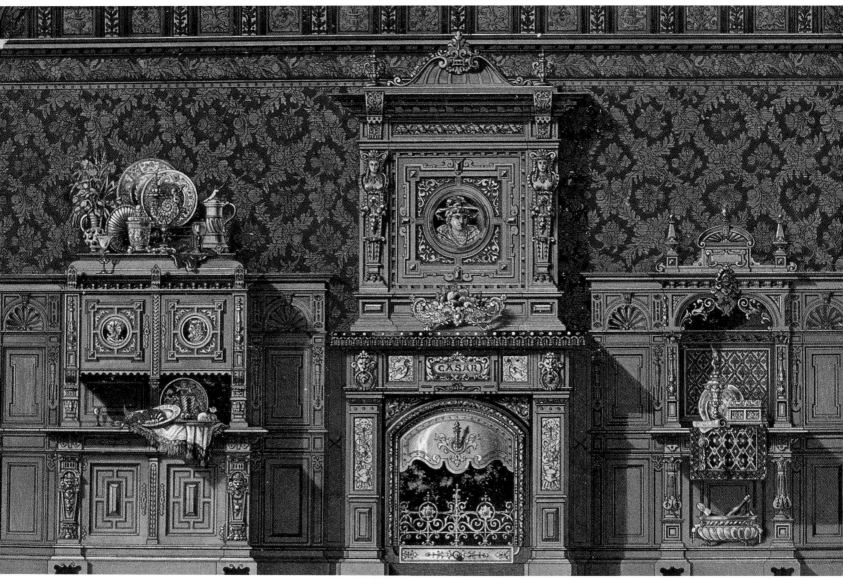

A new kind of luminosity prevails over colour rules in these two boudoirs designed in Karlsruhe in the early to mid-1880s (see also Chapter IV).

is, as the harmony of contrasts, superior to any other'.[202] It was Georg Hirth, the prominent Munich publisher and writer, who in *Das deutsche Zimmer* (1879–80) set out the most elaborate colour theory in any book on the interior. He fervently wanted to avoid 'appearing an insecurely groping hack', and thus based himself on many of the latest theories, including those of one of Germany's most noted scientists, Hermann von Helmholtz. For Hirth, 'everything we see is colour', including black and white, and there is no 'form'. In the end, however, he displays a preference for one colour, brown, for sentimental and nationalist reasons (issues to be taken up in Chapter V). Moreover, this colour was not a product of human intervention but inherent in wood itself.[203]

How was theory converted into practice, and science into art? It should be remembered that, for most, a strong colour was something positive in itself, something that indicated wealth. Does one need to understand it all in terms of rapidly changing trends for particular colours, Goethe's 'so-called fashionable colours'?[204] Bristow maintains that by the 1830s, in Britain at least, colour theory was being widely applied in the design of interiors, with fully coloured rooms, coordinated according to the proper rules, replacing neutral architectural frameworks.[205] The ever-cautious Loudon introduced his remarks on colour in interiors by saying, for the benefit of those 'who did not know the word "harmony"', that it consisted of 'colours that harmonize, or, in other words, that look well together'.[206] A key question that now had to be asked was: where does one begin planning one's choice of colour? Frequently, the answer was to start with the furniture covers or the fabrics in general, and then to decide on the décor of the walls accordingly.[207]

Earlier in the century, designers and users preferred one strong colour for all textiles, whether for furniture, carpets or wall-coverings and whatever the material. Edgar Allan Poe still recommended such unity in the 1840s, suggesting for instance a scheme of crimson and gold that even took the rosewood of the furniture into consideration.[208] But 'uni' – to use the French and German term for single-colour schemes – was soon considered monotonous. The possibilities opened up by the increased range of available colours presented a challenge few could ignore. English authors and designers adopted the rules of complementarity as early as

1810 or thereabouts, at the time when Goethe had just formulated his own version, the essence of which ran: 'yellow demands a reddish blue, blue demands a reddish yellow, purple demands green'.[209] Hay's main stipulations were as follows: avoid situations where no particular tone appears to have been chosen; beware of a 'predominance of some bright and intense colour'; refrain from 'introducing deep and pale colours'; and avoid a 'confusion of parts of equal strength'.[210] Some writers made recommendations that were often highly complex, taking into account all possible scenarios: 'With walnut red green, dark blue or violet go best; with rosewood light crimson, amber, or blue of medium tone; with maple wood light blue or violet, or plum colour', and so on.[211] However, in spite of so much scientific stringency, or perhaps because of it, 'contrasting views of contrasts' (John Gage) still seemed unavoidable.[212]

Eclipse

From the 1850s and 1860s, colour science itself became ever more complicated. While it continued to play a role in fine art, its influence on applied art theories had by now diminished.

An attempt to integrate the décor with the colour of the wood: John D. Rockefeller's dressing room, New York, c. 1880.

Moreover, the growing richness and the multiplicity of objects in the home made strict rules of colour impracticable. Neither did the new trend towards natural materials, especially woods (although of course they also constituted colour preferences) leave room for much precision. Semper attacked the 'colour scales' of 'modern European colour harmony' – itself a very unscientific statement – and, as Morris did somewhat later, demanded a revival of the 'undefinable' and 'deeply harmonic natural colours'.[213] In effect, all this signalled a return to the situation that had existed before the 19th century, when the colours of a room arose simply from the different materials supplied by the different trades.

'Ladies' room in the English manner', designed by Jean Pape in 1887. It demonstrates a unifying pastel tone and a lighter palette overall.

Other eminent authors also voiced their scepticism. Ruskin liked the 'indescribable tints', and in 1867 the decorator John Gregory Crace warned of the 'popular delusion that contrast is harmony'.[214] Many writers on home décor now avoided detailed scientific discussion altogether. Falke had shown some interest early on, but by the early 1880s concluded that, although it is useful to know something about the physical and chemical sciences, within the 'infinite realm of tints and tones' a happy choice of colour amounts to a matter of 'feeling'. Havard likewise expressed his scepticism of colour science.[215] Nevertheless, these authors were not advocating colourlessness.[216] The more subtle or sombre colours needed just as much care in their selection, if not more. Already in 1836, Hay had written that 'the colours of the house painter and the manufacturer are all liable to be placed in full light', which for him gave them an 'unnatural crudeness so annoying to the eye'. This led Hay to consider at length the different dispositions of tone – the 'degree of warmth or coldness', for example – that 'are regulated by the use, situation, and light of the apartment'.[217] By 1881 Ella Rodman Church was focusing on 'tone' as the most important consideration in any colouring scheme, to which all other elements in a room should be subjected. In the 1870s and 1880s many writers laid great stress on 'restrained tones'; in Germany perhaps more than elsewhere decorators used browns, even though it was known that Goethe had disliked them, calling them 'excremental'.[218] In France, Havard opted for 'warm deep-red ruby' and suggested contrasting it with any 'fine, cold shade, light green [or] blue'. In England, decorators demonstrated a further rejection of everything sharp and shiny, of 'luminous colour, coruscating lustre and brilliancy'.[219] The increased concern with overall tone and with relative darkness, as well as the assumed psychological effects of colour, will be covered in a later section.

The Aesthetic Movement in London maintained a special interest in colour, but this could hardly be called theory-based: it simply meant voicing a number of preferences, namely for tertiaries and their minute differences – no good for somebody with an 'an untried eye'. In some paintings by the 'arch-aesthete' James McNeill Whistler, (off-)whites, light blues and yellows are declared as the actual 'contents' of the paintings. One dislike that united Continental lovers of the dark and English lovers of muted light was the vociferous rejection of bright 'shrill' white, even on ceilings. It was held that 'the paler tints blend more harmoniously'.[220]

In the 1880s it becomes impossible to make out a unified trend. Strong condemnations abounded, which frequently ended in contradictions: 'against white a violent war has been fought by the leaders of taste because it does not tolerate any strong and decisive hues next to it, without their appearing common and trivial'; and yet: 'for certain purposes, such as net curtains, table cloths and underwear, white is now the sole ruler because it allows for the easiest control of cleanliness.'[221] Notwithstanding the Aesthetes' claims to avoid absolute whiteness, the interiors of Whistler, Godwin and Oscar Wilde did appear extremely light overall. By the mid-1880s pure white was gaining recognition once again in Queen Anne Revival circles, as seen in Philip Webb's Clouds House in Wiltshire. In Munich, Gabriel von Seidl had introduced a white frieze above his wainscoting by 1876, to the chagrin of some critics.[222] By 1890 many Germans had begun to reject their 'deutsche Chocoladensauce'. At the same time, many condemned the new aniline dyes as too harsh. Used to the 'brown sauce' of Germany, Robert Dohme praised England's 'fresh, clear colours' in his book *Das englische Haus* of 1888. In Germany, the 1890s also saw a renewed taste for sharper colours ('… today one aims for the enjoyment of colours'), which led to the lively spectrum of Jugendstil and Vienna Secession interiors.[223] The English Arts and Crafts movement aimed at precisely the opposite: natural, earth-coloured materials. The stained glass of Tiffany and La Farge in the United States introduced new colour accents of a hitherto unknown luminosity. Finally, in 1896 a French home advice book discussed the issue of the 'Grand Salon': 'When it comes to the colour of the drapes and the seat furniture, it depends on you, Madame' – that is, on the user herself.[224]

Opposite
left An extremely pale interior influenced by developments in Munich (see p. 266). The design is by Phillip Niederhöfer, Frankfurt am Main, 1883.

right Pale Aesthetic Movement décor by Christopher Dresser, 1873.

And as for scientific colour theory? Oriental rugs and carpets and Indian cotton fabrics, which were made with 'natural colours' and an 'undefinable natural tone', were further nails into its coffin. Although some writers attempted to guess at the principles underlying their composition ('arrangements in diagonals …'), Eastern carpet-makers were held to be completely unaware of colour science. This conception was soon applied to the folk textiles of the remoter parts of Europe, too, whose colours could now be dubbed, again most unscientifically, as 'simple colours'.[225] This was the judgment of none other than the astute Berlin design critic and museum director Julius Lessing, at a time when one of the most influential physicists of the day, Hermann von Helmholtz, was teaching advanced colour science only a few steps away.

Form

Thus far, a room's overall appearance has been considered in terms of the contributions made by individual trades or crafts. In a spirit of fierce competition, the upholsterer might cover all surfaces with fabric, allowing no wood to show anywhere, while those who produced interiors furnished completely in wood might banish curtains altogther. Increasingly this fed into an emphasis on pure materiality: it was the colour and the intrinsic textural effects of the materials that were seen as the unifying factors.

But the unity of interiors was also now understood in a totally different way. In a process of radical abstraction, all aspects of production were sidelined: individual forms, the shape of the room and how to coordinate them became the sole focus of interest. It was not a new discourse at all, of course: general statements about the desirability of harmonious interiors are not hard to come by, especially in French writings.[226] Jacques-François Blondel, the revered 18th-century author on architectural planning and interior décor, quoted Horace's view that the fundamental principle in all the arts is formal unity. A German writer on the applied arts, C. H. Terne, suggested in 1839 that the interior was a self-contained work of art.[227] French writers of the mid- and later 19th century maintained that overall unity was more important than the value of any individual element: 'The great luxury of an apartment is its ensemble.

Linearity in the early 19th century: a Parisian drawing room from Percier and Fontaine's *Recueil de décorations intérieures* (1801–12; *left*), and a drawing room in London by Thomas Hope (1807; *right*). Many Neoclassical interiors have become familiar through black-and-white engravings, but the rooms themselves were usually highly coloured.

An expensive piece of furniture has no value if it is not in harmony with those that surround it', thought one such critic. Unity is composed of everything down to the very smallest detail, wrote another: 'in order to apply justly the term decoration, it is necessary to consider all parts of the ensemble, from the most infinitely small detail to the object that forms the key of the work.' Ferdinand Luthmer gives a long list of what should be considered necessary for the salon, including even small items like bric-a-brac.[228]

Statements of the period sometimes betray a notion that the unified interior was something that had not occurred before. There is a broad agreement among modern historians that Robert Adam was one of its initiators.[229] In 1827 John Britton was still writing that 'interior … architecture [is] not much attended to in this country', whereas in 1914 a commercial investigation into furniture selling found that the furnishing of whole interiors was 'today taken for granted'.[230] A closer examination makes one sceptical of such statements of novelty. Peter Thornton has maintained that the Western demand for unity in the interior essentially dates back to Renaissance times. His books, however, do not follow up the issue in any systematic way, and the same may also be said of many other writers on the interior. Among the most forceful was Havard, who considered 'unity of conception', 'completeness of conception' and 'logical progression', and yet assembled the fifty main points of his section 'Grammaire de l'ameublement' in a very random order.[231]

Attempts to define unity became more precise as the century progressed. Although Neoclassical or Empire interiors appeared unified to a large degree, in fact this was due mainly to their overt use of grand architectural motifs. But this was not an option for many of the trades, who, unless they created elaborate imitations of architecture, were narrowly restricted by their materials. As the textural individuality of materials became more appreciated, this type of disguise was no longer desirable. On the other hand, the complete dominance of one trade, of one material, would be the exception rather than the rule.

It thus became apparent that someone outside the trades was needed to direct the whole enterprise. Chapter II considered the label by which that person was known – be it *décorateur*, architect or even 'designer' – but by 1890 a clear role of the 'interior designer' had still not

emerged. What had developed, so to speak, were new vehicles of expression, in both pictures and words. This section is thus principally concerned with the gradual emergence of a more purely formal language for describing any interior. This new language abstracted its terms from descriptors of each material and from architectural tectonics. While some terms may seem identical to the nomenclature of particular historical styles, their chief sense was one of entirely neutral, abstract, 'formal' preferences. To consider an interior, or in fact any artefact, in terms of form entailed a different way of looking, both more basic and more complex. For Loudon, setting out his analysis quite clearly in 1834, a description 'guides in the general composition of lines and forms'; he himself aimed at an 'art of combining artificial forms, lines, shades and colours; without reference to the uses of buildings, or to particular styles of architecture'. As it happened, Loudon hardly ever followed his own principles in his books, but proceeded often by way of a series of historical styles.[232] From the 1840s and 1850s, abstraction was pursued ever more forcefully by the South Kensington theorists in their ornamental patterns. In 1871, Falke stated quite sharply that form, 'as noticed by our knowledgeable eye', does not mean style: 'to repeat, [it is] not a historical style'.[233] 'The play of forms and colours'; 'artistic harmony is based on two elements, form and colour'; 'unity in form and colour' – writers were talking in such terms more and more frequently, although they were still likely to have baffled anyone outside the circle of historians and critics.[234]

At the time when verbal discourses surrounding matters of line, surface, texture and space were growing more sophisticated, we also note a massive increase in the number of pictures of whole rooms being published. Thus far illustrations of interiors had been an essential tool for showing objects as solid and three-dimensional; now they were perceived as conveying the composition of whole rooms. All this meant that the visual impact of an interior became more and more detached from its materiality – the theme with which this chapter began. A room was increasingly understood 'like a picture'. Unity is most conveniently rendered through a comprehensive image, as in the German phrase *ein harmonisches Gesamtbild*, which implies both an actual ensemble, harmonious and complete, and a picture of such harmonious totality.[235] By no means did this run counter to the new materiality referred to previously, and in fact the comprehensive image embraced this liking for surface effects – including, say, the shine of metal or of a fabric. These representations of furnishings clearly mirrored the latest trends in fine art painting, which were culminating in Impressionism.

Traditionally, there were two ways in which a room could be unified. The first was through splendour. Many of the interiors commissioned by Ludwig II of Bavaria – among the most

above left Parisian dining room, from an architectural journal, 1859. With most of the furniture removed, the architectural lines are even more apparent.

above Dining room displaying a 'oneness between furniture and fixture', in which all the lines have been coordinated; from the *Furniture Gazette*, 1875.

Dining room by Bruce Talbert, 1867. The lines marking out the interior have here acquired a three-dimensionality.

exuberant of the period – are full of furnishings in diverse materials, which must have required an immense effort of coordination. The second way of achieving great unity was to choose a particular style, and then to stress its specificity, its singularity, as with William Burges's '13th-century medieval' interiors. This book essentially deals with the issue of unity not as a special consideration but rather as a set of recipes or formal conceptualizations that could be applied even in quite modest circumstances; for 'recipes', one may of course substitute the term 'design', or 'modes of design'. A further chapter will deal with the way historical styles were linked to users' moods, resulting in a notion of a specifically 'domestic' wholeness.

Design from Henry Van Brunt's 'Studies in Interior Decoration' (Boston, Mass., 1877). Both Talbert and Van Brunt trained as neo-Gothic architects, seeing little difference between interior and exterior architectural décor. Their forms derived largely from High Victorian church design.

A seemingly straightforward principle of coordination was offered by all the classical styles: symmetry.[236] But often symmetry could not be obtained in the rooms of less palatial houses or flats. Also aiding the quest for unity, as discussed in the previous section, were the principles of colour science; but, as has been pointed out, one of the many problems here was where to begin with the choice of colour – with the furniture or with the décor?

A more systematic approach – and one more in tune with the 'shell' of a normal room – was to proceed by analysing its basic components in turn: floor, ceiling and walls. This was Falke's way of approaching matters of coherence and interdependence: 'the delimited, enclosed room with its four walls, floor and ceiling'.[237] These components have so far been mentioned in the context of materials, but now they have to be judged independently. Many early 19th-century floors displayed elaborate ornamental patterns – in wood, stone, oilcloth or its derivatives, or woven into the carpet – that corresponded with the general symmetry of the room. After mid-century they were treated as something more neutral: they were darkish and evenly coloured; one should avoid 'anything that can hinder our steps, or affect them in any way'; and the floor should be 'quiet, not too light, not especially attractive to the eye'.[238] For the more elaborately conceived interiors, there was a considerable variety of ceilings to choose from. They ranged from very light and unornamented to very heavily decorated schemes in the darkest colours. In the early decades of the century there was a fashion for completely blank

above left Boudoir illustrated by H. Hudson Holly in his series of articles for *Harper's New Monthly Magazine* (1876).

above E. W. Godwin's almost transparent but strongly three-dimensional rendering of furniture in a room, from William Watt's catalogue of Godwin's furnishings, 1877. Godwin's linear designs were often described as 'Anglo-Japanese' (see Chapter V). This set was also labelled 'economic furniture'.

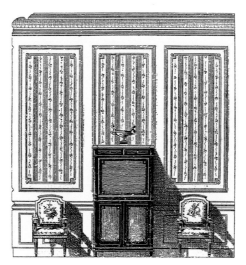

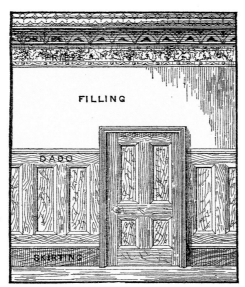

Dado walls, from J. W. Facey's *Practical House Decoration* (1892).

Opposite
far left and centre These two illustrations from Henry Havard are designed to show contrasting effects of horizontality and verticality. Havard claims that 'lines can alter the apparent dimensions of a given surface', making walls seem either taller or lower. He also speaks of 'expression': 'lines express a language', so that verticals appear 'slim' and horizontals 'heavy'. From Havard's 'Grammaire de l'ameublement', the central section of his *L'Art dans la maison* (1884).

right above and right below 'An ordinary room just as the builder left it' (above), and 'some improvement in its proportions by a few simple lines' (below); from *Harper's New Monthly Magazine* (1884).

ceilings, even in rooms that were otherwise richly decorated. In order to provide the greatest illusion of light, a blue sky with or without clouds could then be painted.[239] In the 1850s George Gilbert Scott noted the three major solutions for ceilings – paint, plaster and joists – and in his usual deadpan way found them all acceptable. Falke found completely flat ceilings regrettable, and Dresser, that producer of striking decorative motifs, predictably found the 'invisible' ceiling a bad idea. For others, ceilings should be darkish, because we desire 'shelter'. For timber suppliers, there was no reason why rooms should not be covered in woodwork of the utmost heaviness.[240] By the early 1880s, collections of photographs of American 'artistic homes' show a dazzling array of ceilings.

Line and surface

The most complex formal language emerged in relation to the design of the walls. Once again, discussions of the elevation of a room took architecture as their starting point: 'The general characteristics of a room depend on the architectural forms and lines which compose its walls, ceilings, doors and windows.'[241] A classical elevation begins with a base on which the main elements rest, which in the best buildings consist of columns or pilasters. All this is crowned by the entablature, with or without a frieze. In basic domestic interiors this architectural order was downgraded to the language of the joiner and the practical user, at least in English and German. The base and the plinth became the skirting-board, or *Scheuerleiste*; the entablature was effectively reduced to its lowest demarcation line, the architrave, which was the picture rail; and the empty space above it represented the frieze and even the cornice in simpler interiors. The main part of the wall in smarter houses could also be divided vertically through panels or shallow strips of various materials, again faintly reminiscent of columns or piers and their intervals.[242]

A further horizontal division – the dado – became popular, especially in Britain; it, too, derived ultimately from a classical habit, that of placing the columns on a very high pedestal (in Italian, *dado* means cube). Early on, Loudon stressed the double role of the dado – 'to prevent injury, to give importance' – recommending a height of 2 feet 3 inches and 2 feet 9 inches (69 and 84 cm) above the floor . In the 1870s a great 'dado movement' arose, which saw the dado area in richer houses covered with wood, leather or fabric and surmounted by a narrow batten. It was now also matched by an elaborate frieze on the upper part of the wall. English wallpaper designers took a special interest in these horizontal divisions, marking them out with changes of pattern and thus demonstrating their own facility in all aspects of wall décor (see p. 76).[243]

The architectural, three-dimensional viewpoint – that an elevation was something that grew from the ground up – thus gave way to a more abstract, formal conception in which an elevation comprised merely a series of horizontal lines. Although Morris was not much in favour of the dado, it was said that 'horizontal lines [were] so dear to his heart'; Clarence Cook, in his small book *What Shall We Do With Our Walls?*, wrote of horizontal shelves that help with 'the horizontal divisions of the wall itself'. From about the mid-1880s, however, when wainscoting – which often included an emphatically horizontal top shelf – gained a new popularity, the dado went out of fashion.[244]

To speak of and to stress mere 'lines' was clearly a step towards abstraction, but in fact it had a history in 18th-century writings on the theory and practice of drawing. Sharp outlines, strictly rectangular edges and plane surfaces characterized much design around 1800: 'simple lines, pure contours [and] correct forms replace mixed lines, irregular contours', wrote Percier and Fontaine early in the century. Thomas Hope adopted a radical 'mere outlines' mode for the illustrations in his *Household Furniture and Interior Decoration* of 1807.[245] Other publications followed suit, whether the room was in the classical or the Gothic style. Much later, Bruce Talbert developed his lines into vigorous mouldings that ran horizontally and vertically – not only in their traditional positions (the frieze or the skirting-board, for example), but virtually everywhere in the room: 'It was by studying lines … that … Talbert was able to revolutionise our furniture as he did.'[246]

Once such parlance becomes established, everything can be defined as lines. For Edis, 'A decoration is always a combination of lines, colours', which serve in 'marking … the proportions of the surfaces' – a reason why there should always be 'strong containing lines' or, as Victor Ruprich-Robert phrased it, 'lignes envelopantes'. These lines were to be 'conducted' ('Linienführung'). We also read of the 'lineal harmony of a room'.[247] The Anglo-American stress on the straight line later in the century was to a large extent a rejection of the curved styles that were seen as originating in the dreaded French Rococo, hated by all Gothic Revivalist and South Kensington-influenced designers. 'The best of a straight line is that you cannot vulgarize it', wrote Mrs Haweis.[248] Whistler praised the delicate, plastic, 'lovely lines' of Thomas Jeckyll's original wall décor for the Peacock Room. In the United States, Hudson Holly's renderings of more modest interiors – which simplified Talbert's style – further popularized strong linear divisions. During the 1870s styles of illustration diversified considerably. Quite sophisticated tonal renderings could be reproduced, but there also seemed to be a special attraction in reducing the principal framework of a room to thin, straight lines. The Boston architect Henry Van Brunt followed Talbert and Holly in designing vigorous, continuous mouldings on walls and ceilings; later he remarked: 'abstract lines are the most concentrated expression of human ideas.'[249]

Surface, the correlate of line, likewise became a major point of discussion during the 19th century. Traditionally in classical design, relief would be given prominence where it could be afforded, and strong plasticity – or even fuzzy outlines – were preferred over flatness. But Neoclassicism's desire for sharp outlines also included a liking for clear geometrical solids and smooth surfaces. Greek art, especially in vase painting, was valued for its reductivity, since it relied mainly on outline. In Klenze's words, 'the entirely flat representation of surface is the chief requirement'.[250] Increasingly, colour also seemed to demand flatness. One should remember that certain materials – including stretched silk, marble and all their cheap imitations – were also dependent on flat surfaces for their effect.

This new appreciation of flatness then grew into a major concern – one may even call it a worldview. It manifested itself, as we have seen, in painted wall décor, in wallpaper design and, to a lesser extent, in fabric décor, all of which aimed at the appearance of 'truth' and the expurgation of illusionistic motifs. It eventually affected the décor on all conceivable

'Diagram of a staircase as the builder left it' (*above*), and a 'design showing a simple solution to the difficulty of decorating a builder's staircase' (*opposite*); from Lewis F. Day's *Everyday Art* (1882).

kinds of objects and on all parts of the domestic interior – prohibiting rich floral designs on the carpet or the illusion of sky on the ceiling – but above all it influenced the treatment of the wall. The new doctrine of flatness, already alluded to in the sections on paint, wallpaper and colour, originated after 1800, when the search for the archaic, the 'primitive', turned to the Middle Ages ('Primitive' was also a general label for the painting style that predated the early Renaissance). Some architects and painters, overwhelmed by the colourful interiors of Byzantine and Early Christian churches, applied this mode to new churches in Munich from the 1820s. John Gregory Crace then took the style to England, encouraging Pugin's flat yet intricate Gothic décor for fabrics and tiles. The South Kensington theorists, especially Owen Jones, codified flatness further and considered it in conjunction with all issues of colour and historical styles, including, most significantly, those from the Orient. All floral décor, so popular mid-century, was now also subject to the 'rule of flatness'. Central Europe (Austria more than Germany) followed on in the 1870s, while France took somewhat longer.[251]

Flattish décor could nonetheless assume an almost endless variety of forms. Motifs could be large, even coarse, or they could consist of the repetition of extremely small elements ('all decorative work must consist of small parts if refinement of effect is to be attained').[252] In New York, Tiffany's patterns of 1880 present a lively two-dimensionality (at least, that is how they come across in black and white) and an exceptional consistency, extending over all objects in all materials and thereby also denying the old Classical tectonic order (see p. 153). Clearly, the extent to which an overall 'flat' character could be achieved was dependent to some extent on which materials had been chosen, although the later wallpapers and certainly stencilling lent themselves particularly well.

Domestic wall décor then underwent another astonishing change: it moved from being highly visible, with strong, intrusive patterns, to being very discreet or almost invisible. In Continental Europe, the designs of better kinds of wallpaper continued to be derived from textiles, which included patterns of a weak directionality. From here we move to a view of wallpaper not as providing striking forms, but the opposite: the wallpaper as a neutral, even an unobtrusive background. Falke put it quite radically: 'walls form ... only the background for the inhabitants and do not present an individual element'. As for the décor itself, 'simple patterns' were needed.[253] The wall should not appear prominent and, like the floor, it was to be kept fairly dark.

By 'background', Falke meant that the wall was seen as a foil for the increasing mass of objects in a room. Considerations of surface, flatness and three-dimensionality had by now become very complex. While flatness and pronouncedly flat décor were a cherished formal principle, a room that showed principally smooth walls, however elaborately and strikingly decorated, did not satisfy anymore. German designers in particular began to lament the increasingly tedious 'tapezierte Kiste' – the type of boxy interior that reminded them of the paper-lined insides of a crate.[254]

Picturesqueness

Just as important as the solids in a room is what lies in between. One experiences a room not only from a static viewpoint, but also from moving around. The term 'picturesque' is closely related to the landscaping and buildings of 18th-century English parks, in particular the notion that a building can vary in appearance, and that in fact we like it to vary. In the context of the interior, this concept translates as asymmetrical shapes that form unexpected groupings, in contrast to the highly regularized, symmetrical room viewed from a fixed point. By the later 19th century the term 'picturesque' was being used more rarely in elevated British architectural and applied arts discourse, but its main tenets still held sway. In France, the *pittoresque* enjoyed a certain popularity: 'unforeseen contrasts ... the picturesque character of the decoration increases accordingly' (Havard). For the Germans, the so-called *malerische* ('picturesque')

left 'A few suggestive hints for economical decoration', from the New York *Decorator and Furnisher* (1883).

below The emphatic lines and pale colours of the Aesthetic Movement make an appearance in Eliza Keary's *At Home Again*, a children's book published in 1886.

arrangement gained acceptance as the century progressed, as did the *schilderachtig* ('picture-like') in the Netherlands.[255]

Mass

The most important term in all discussions of the picturesque was 'mass'. This apparently simple word had two separate meanings that need to be distinguished from each other. First, it signified solidity and materiality (emphasized from mid-century onwards), whether in stone walling, solid woodwork or heavy curtains. (The next chapter will go on to consider the psychological and physical effects of these elements in a room.) Second, in more general and abstract terms, 'mass' refers to any shapes around the room: 'The harmony of the ensemble … from which spring the large masses that give character' (Le Camus de Mézières). Such language goes right back to the way in which painting was discussed, most famously in Joshua Reynolds's *Discourses*.[256] 'Mass' could thus also be understood in an evaluative sense. Later in the 19th century the word proliferates in writings on the interior: Falke refers to the 'forceful effect of the masses' ('kräftige Massenwirkung'), and Spofford advises that 'the patchy look is prevented by arranging the furniture with a view to masses and then combining the masses themselves with a view to harmony'.[257] Occasionally, German writers also used the term *plastisch* in this very abstract sense.[258] 'Mass' thus became an important term for characterizing the main shapes inside a room. Many were there to be manipulated, to be shifted around – as a painter might do with forms on a canvas.

A latecomer in architectural and interior design terminology was 'space'. Anyone analysing the history of interiors should bear in mind that the immense value attached to the word in modernist discourse would simply not have been understood earlier on. In its very abstract sense – as the correlate of mass – the term was introduced only in about 1870. It became widespread in writings about building interiors only from about 1890, and at first only in German – which is why this text does not place too much stress on it either. A closer analysis would reveal that much of what was labelled as 'space' or 'spatial composition' before the end of the century was simply a continuation of the issues examined under the heading of 'picturesque'.[259]

above Room from the 'Pavilion of the Empress', designed by the *tapissiers* Penon Frères for the Paris Exposition Universelle, 1867. In high-ranking interiors of the late 1860s, it was architectural décor that still provided the main type of embellishment.

above right Large, straightforward spaces, high ceilings and all furnishings arranged in an orderly fashion had been the hallmarks of smart rooms for a long time. From a sales catalogue produced by C. & R. Light, London, *c.* 1880.

As far as the overall shape of a room was concerned, architects from Palladio onwards had subjected houses to squarish forms, creating sets of rigidly ordered boxes inside, and 19th-century theorists, too, had rules that ensured satisfying proportions within the domestic room: 'the height must be somewhat less than the width of the smaller side of the room', and so on. Traditionally, the most obvious elements of beauty in a room, and what gave it distinction, were size and a comparatively great height. Loudon demanded that the drawing room of a large villa should be 13–18 feet (4–5.5 metres) high. In smart houses, the smaller rooms also enjoyed a certain height, which made their proportions very narrow. Interiors in smart German flats of the late 19th-century were also of a great height – at about 4 metres, they were higher than their Parisian equivalents (usually 3 metres).[260] A German critic found Parisian rooms 'zierlich' ('delicate').[261] In addition, decorators had devised means of making rooms

This drawing room 'in the Norman Style', by the young architect Edward Buckton Lamb (1834), is an early example of the picturesque interior, in which all the forms are diverse and highly unusual.

appear larger or higher, for example through the use of linear patterns or the proportions of curtains.[262] In 1870s England, however, E. W. Godwin maintained that a height of 9 feet (2.74 metres) was enough.[263] The trend towards low domestic interiors, to be discussed in the next chapter, had already begun.

Impressive height and size (or at least the appearance of height and size) were thus important signals of quality – and they were precisely what the picturesque was beginning to leave behind. These factors matter so much less when the static view is abandoned: 'one does not stay in a room in order to continuously enjoy a good view, which one soon gets used to; but one is surprised when faced with a vista that comes to us for a only moment.' According to H. J. Cooper, 'we much prefer not being able to see all over the drawing room at a glance'; and one German critic urged decorators 'to create as animated a picture as possible'.[264] In the renderings produced by some Munich-based designers like Franz Brochier or Hermann Kirchmayr, movement seems to affect the objects as well – indeed, a constant gale-force wind appears to be blowing through the house.[265] One good way of ensuring a diversity of viewpoints was to look in from another room – an approach that perhaps reached its apogee in plates by Hermann Werle from the mid-1890s ('vistas … not a row of cells for hermits').[266] From the mid-1870s Americans favoured a larger central hall and adopted complex ways of linking it with adjacent rooms, thus rendering the interior spaces of the detached house more varied and picturesque than ever before.[267]

'Sameness can be avoided only by breaking up the room into parts', claimed Mrs Spofford. 'Symmetry [is] the arch-enemy of all that is picturesque and characteristic', raged the *Deutsche Tapezierer Zeitung* in 1887, and of course any kind of 'axiality' or enfilade had to be avoided. Corners were popular (they lent 'poetry and grace'),[268] and there was an 'attractiveness' in 'different floor levels'.[269] If the room was boxy, as most rooms invariably were, then it could be improved through the addition of a bay window or, in Central Europe, an oriel window (i.e. a bay window that does not extend to the ground). Failing that, the room itself could be divided up by the installation of wooden quasi-oriels – the so-called *Zimmerlauben* or 'cosy corners', widely introduced in Britain (according to Helen Long) in the early 1890s.[270] In their simplest form, they could consist of just a couple of screens, either fixed or moveable and usually partially see-through.[271] Even without these additions, the squarish box of a room could be livened up through the arrangement of the furnishings. Critics condemned any kind of 'standardized furnishing'.[272]

Picturesqueness in the later 19th-century was closely linked to a *horror vacui*;[273] one French writer went as far as to state that rooms 'must be furnished in order to give them the beautiful

An early attempt at informal display: the furniture here was designed in 1834 by Joseph Danhauser, a Viennese painter of domestic genre scenes who also acted as a designer for the family firm of furnishers.

The 1880s marked the height of picturesque interiors, with their free grouping of diverse objects (see also the boudoir on p. 119). Design by Hermann Kirchmayr, Munich, 1888.

right By 1890, one of the designers' principal aims was to avoid any feeling of 'boxiness' in a room. This interior, with 'latticework décor in the American fashion, adapted for German use', was devised by the German Hermann Werle in 1894.

Three examples of advanced informality: a scheme by the celebrated Munich designer Lorenz Gedon (late 1870s; *right*); a London living room by an anonymous designer (1887; *below*); and an 'example of movable décor' in Paris (early 1880s; *below right*). The interiors in Munich and Paris feature in the two most important books of the 1880s, by Georg Hirth and Henry Havard respectively. Yet one is hard pressed to detect any principles that might have governed the arrangement of the furnishings, or any obvious historical styles. On the contrary, the designs appear entirely casual and the viewpoints have seemingly been chosen at random. Compare this informality with the simple order of the room by C. & R. Light on p. 147, and with the highly contrived display of objects by Christofle on p. 114. The unidentified London interior comes from an article by Mrs J. E. Panton entitled 'Artistic Homes, and How to Make Them', which emphasizes the input of the users over that of the trade (see Chapter VI).

A 'music room in Louis XVI style' by Adrien
Simoneton, Paris, 1893–95. By the mid-1880s,
views of whole interiors had reached a considerable
level of sophistication, with many illustrations
reflecting a renewed stress on 'elegance' in the sense
of 'lightness'. Most were still produced within the
trade, however, which means that their designers'
names have been almost totally forgotten.

disorder that is one of the effects of art'.[274] And yet the picturesque interior should not – or so
its chief theorists maintained – be understood simply as a disordered accumulation of objects:
on the contrary, it was a more sophisticated method of coordinating a room. Mrs Spofford
constantly oscillates between praise for unity and asking for it to be divided up, while her
German near-contemporary A. Scheffers talks in rather more abstract terms of 'the principles
of organic design' – 'organic', along with 'space', being a concept that would assume the greatest importance in 20th-century design. Havard, as so often, said it most effectively: 'variety
within unity'.[275]

So far, linearity, flatness, mass and the picturesque have been dealt with as purely formal
options for the room and its contents; they constitute a running commentary on the work
of all the trades and crafts – at least in the writings of the more eloquent critics and historians.
In the next chapter some of these issues will be taken up once more in a psychological context:
how the user not only sees the interior, but also feels it.

'Peacock Room' by E. Maincent, Paris,
mid-1880s. The designer described this 'Moorish'
interior as 'not an archaeological study', but an
application of 'new ideas and forms appropriate to
the civilization of today'.

Design from the early 1890s by the young Georges Rémon, who went on to practise in the Art Nouveau style.

The new 'refinement'

Agency and innovation in domestic interior design had been increasingly linked with a coterie of writers and illustrators who had created a wholly new discourse of the interior. But by the mid-1880s in England, this wave of advice, urging people to choose one form and not another, was abating. Robustly worded admonitions on the subject of taste *à la* Eastlake no longer appeared apposite. It therefore becomes more difficult to make out which new trends succeeded those of picturesqueness and muted colour. Most historians would resort to the statement that the 1880s and 1890s were 'all things to all men'. Yet this does not preclude the existence of certain lines of argument and the continuing expression of strong convictions, at least in some quarters. In England, one question that gained in urgency was that of a national idiom, and Chapter V will debate the way in which a wide spectrum of styles, from heavy, rough and cottagey to ultra-delicate 'Sheraton', could all come under the label 'Old English'.

Drawing room by the otherwise obscure London architect G. Freesh-Roper (1880). The pale colours and delicate lines of the Aesthetic Movement are here combined with neo-Neoclassical decorative motifs. Note the inglenook, although there is little sign of cosiness.

But to explain further what happened in 1880s England, one also has to shift the focus somewhat away from the writers and the named designers, and back to the group they considered their adversaries: the trade or, rather, the high-class trade. But what we cannot expect from this sphere as yet are longish pronouncements on particular fashions – one can merely follow their work in illustrations. Here one notes, above all, lightness, especially in furniture. This was partly due to the cabinetmakers' long-standing dexterity in rendering all items of furniture with the utmost delicacy. The trade itself would thus have vigorously opposed the kind of heaviness espoused by Eastlake and Talbert. In that sense, it could be seen as agreeing with most post-Eastlake reformers and with the much-caricatured Aesthetic Movement and its 'Anglo-Oriental' work. However much Oscar Wilde's ideas of 'refinement' might have belonged to a rarefied Aesthetic world, few high-class manufacturers would have wanted to quarrel with a statement he made in 1883, that although the Gothicists had made important contributions, their furniture was too heavy for ordinary use. All this led him to demand 'furniture made by refined people for refined people'.[276] Likewise, both the Aesthetes and the 'refinement' party would have eschewed the more extreme kinds of picturesqueness. These two groups differed in one crucial respect, however. Designers like Shaw, Day or Morris no longer emphasized style in the sense of attaching precise historical labels to their work, whereas the trade, as seen in Chapter II, increasingly thought it necessary to demonstrate their academic seriousness by attaching style labels to all their products. In any case, for both sides the trend towards refinement led to an ever deeper appreciation of 18th-century work. There was a strong and widespread conviction that the quality of late 18th-century design and workmanship – the 'constructiveness' of Sheraton's furniture, for instance – was unsurpassed. Put simply, the later 18th century was deemed to have been a period 'devoid of any suspicion of vulgarity'.[277]

In the United States, the lines between trade and art or design, between anonymous manufacturers and named designers, had never been as sharply drawn as in London. From about 1880 New England joined the general chorus with its own (relatively) smart 18th-century furniture, in the 'Old Colonial' style; and at the same time Orientalism appeared more influential than in England. A deft amalgam of many elements can be discerned in Tiffany's interiors

Morning room at No. 2 Albert Gate, Kensington, London, completed in 1885. It was designed by the decorator G. Jackson & Sons for the banker Arthur David Sassoon. Interiors for wealthy clients had begun to show a new restraint, combined with an emphasis on expensive materials and on delicate workmanship. Yet the continuation of straightforward classical décor made such interiors also appear old-fashioned.

of around 1880.[278] In the 1890s, the influential decorating team of Edith Wharton and Ogden Codman moved decisively towards whiteness in their interiors; this also entailed a need for order and a return to architectural kinds of symmetry that to many must have seemed an explicit abandonment of the picturesque. In France, the starting point for a new gentleness was a return to the styles of Louis XV and more especially Louis XVI (to be debated further in Chapter V). In any case, neo-Gothic or neo-Renaissance massiveness was never as popular in France as in Central Europe or London. Most illustrations of 18th-century interiors in Havard's work of 1884 show a striking evenness and lightness. From the later 1870s a number of French designers rose to prominence, though not nearly as much as their London counterparts; they made their names mainly by publishing illustrations of whole interiors. Eugène Prignot, who worked in both and London, seems to have practised restraint already in the late 1860s. E. Maincent demonstrated the most vigorous and yet controlled eclecticism during the 1880s. From around 1890 Ernest Foussier, Paul Planat and especially Georges Rémon began to show a lightness and delicacy hardly seen before.[279] In Germany, the whole trend started somewhat later, just before 1890, and was strongly linked to imitations of light and straight-lined Anglo-Japanese furniture as well as to a newly revived Rococo, although the latter appeared more fulsome than the best new interpretations from Paris.[280]

The discourses of domesticity showed an ever greater breadth and complexity. Lightness was of course associated with informality, but it also, conversely, represented a new formality – a gentle one, though, and not a return to early 19th-century stiffness. Terms such as 'elegance' and 'Belle Époque' immediately come to mind. One has to consider that by the end of the century the number of rich households had grown enormously, and most of their inhabitants simply wanted to appear smart. This trend contrasted sharply with the 'folksy' or 'primitive' movement, which will be discussed later, yet one may see them both as sharing, in a very generalized way, a new appearance of quality through concentrated craftsmanship and restraint. As William Morris remarked in his lecture 'The Prospects of Architecture in Civilization': 'simplicity of life, even the barest, is not misery but the very foundation of refinement'.[281]

Decoration for a parlour in New York by Louis C. Tiffany & Co., *c.* 1880. Tiffany had a highly distinctive way of using tone to unify many different textures.

IV

Atmosphere

Detail from Franz Pforr's *Shulamit and Maria* (1811; see p. 159) – a highly idealized view of a female figure within an intimate domestic setting.

Enter the imagined user

'Not every house is necessarily a home', or so runs one of the most enduring maxims of the 19th century.[1] We shall now move from considering the domestic interior as an artistic 'artefact' to an investigation of what its inhabitants feel and do within it. When the trades finish their work, they await payment, crave a word of praise from their client, and start preparing for their next job. At this point, claims Charles Blanc, 'the reader may declare: ... let the joiners plane and assemble their timbers ... human happiness does not depend on something so small.' However, he goes on to say that it does 'contribute to the comfort of the soul, to be surrounded by well-designed objects'.[2] The experience of 'home living' formed a vast discourse in the 19th century, which one may see as lying completely outside the world of traders and designers. The aim of this chapter is to begin with this broad background, but gradually to return to the issues of design.

Imagining the home was one the 19th century's main preoccupations. The basics of this 'home' – which pertained also for most of the 20th century – hardly need repeating. It was a place clearly separated from the outside world and from one's daily work; it was a prime place of moral conduct, even a bulwark against revolutionary movements. The old practical discourse surrounding husbandry and household matters was increasingly seen in complex legal, political and economic terms. What had always seemed biologically and socially obvious now appeared to be 'one of the most burning questions of the social sciences', according to a Viennese economist of 1873, who also stressed not only that the dwelling was an 'expression' of society, but that, conversely, the dwelling greatly influenced human beings.[3] Another oft-repeated phrase linking the social with the material was 'das ganze Haus' ('the whole house'), coined in the 1850s by the sociologist Wilhelm Heinrich Riehl. Home privacy and salubrity became the subjects of a huge public debate, which was later dubbed 'the housing problem'.

Historians of the 20th century frequently pointed out that the 19th century constituted the high point of home-making. Walter Benjamin's oft-cited remark that 'the nineteenth century was home-addicted like no other' was confirmed by the foremost historian of interior decoration, Peter Thornton; for him, the period between the 1820s and the 1870s was the 'age of great domesticity'.[4] However, we ought to be cautious with such statements, for the simple reason that we know very much less about what previous centuries had thought and felt about home life. What is certain is that the 19th century witnessed an abundance of writings about, and illustrations of, 'the home' – far more than any earlier period. Growing realist tendencies within art and literature declared 'ordinary' contemporary domestic life the principal arena for many kinds of narratives. By the middle of the century 'domestic genre' was becoming one of the most popular subjects for paintings and novels. Most significantly, the rise of the home discourse coincided with the rise of the illustrator. Their products clearly ranked below the bona fide art of painting, but they reached an infinitely wider audience, especially once cheap journals adopted the revived techniques of the woodcut and wood engraving from the 1830s on.[5] Some of the popular journals actually described themselves as suitable for reading in the home: one of the best known was the German *Die Gartenlaube*, which referred to the domestic garden shelter or summer house in its very title. This rapidly developing discourse of the home reveals to us exactly how its users should behave, how they should feel about the home, and in what ways the general character of its rooms should correspond to their activities.

Privacy

The way the family appeared central to the social concept of the home may make one forget that it was also meant to serve as a refuge for the individual. An article that appeared in *Die Gartenlaube* in 1864 entitled 'The Poetry of Our Four Walls' – a pivotal analysis of home life and home décor – addresses only one of four categories of comfort to the family, while two deal with rooms for the individual, male and female respectively (the fourth is concerned with décor and elegance).[6] A Frenchman who commented on the usefulness of the English term 'home' took it to mean 'a way of perfecting the equipment of private life'.[7] Indeed, the term 'private' – used in all major Western languages – underpins all these new socio-psychological discussions. Many historians have investigated what they see as the relatively recent emergence of the individual's desire and stated need for privacy; Philippe Ariès went as far as to claim that 'until the end of the seventeenth century nobody was alone'. By the late 19th century it appeared that 'rooms for individual family members now [occupied] more space'.[8] Significantly, the new emphasis on family togetherness meant that there was now (in the better-class house, at least) an added reason to desire privacy, as a refuge from the family: 'A room of retreat where the master at least may shield himself from the exuberant spirits of the boys, or the insistence of domestic routine'.[9]

Gendered rooms: the boudoir and the study

In Chapter I, the plan of the average well-situated dwelling was briefly discussed in terms of its differentiation according to purpose and gender. This was a new development, first

Boudoir (*left*) and study (*opposite*), both from Oskar Mothes's *Unser Heim im Schmucke der Kunst* ('Our Home as Beautified by Art'; 1879). One new task for the 19th-century designer was to distinguish clearly between rooms reserved for each gender. This was achieved principally through the use of harder textures and more angular forms in 'male' interiors, and soft, rounded furnishings in their 'female' equivalents. Mothes also took into account the householders' different occupations: the master of the house might worry over work-related matters while the woman was more likely to be concerned with her finery.

expounded in French architectural treatises of the later 18th century; already 'by the end of the eighteenth century the gendered role of rooms was apparently understood'.[10] A new type of room that emerged from these considerations was the boudoir. Its name derived from the verb *bouder*, 'to stay away, to sulk, be moody'; more often than not, this had erotic connotations.[11] The boudoir became the epitome of the secluded room. Its close association with the female gender was held to be evident in its design, which conveyed notions of delicacy, softness and roundedness, but also of the mysterious – all of which resulted in the richest kind of décor,[12] explicitly combining smallness with *luxe* and, of course, executed in the utmost 'taste'. The room somehow remained linked with a nostalgia for the later 18th century, which in turn strengthened the view of the Rococo style as 'female' – issues we shall return to later.

By the mid- to later 19th century the room's erotic connotations received less attention. Yet most books on home art still dealt with the boudoir, repeating the same formulae. In his programme for the complete home, Oskar Mothes refers to the 'Poesie des Boudoirs', calling the room 'a cosy nook', a 'little nest' that serves 'the purely psychological needs' of a woman's life; furthermore, Mothes maintains that the room should be entirely private and not semi-social, as it was in Vienna and Paris.[13] In other respects, though, the nimbus surrounding the boudoir did appear somewhat in decline, while in the Protestant Anglo-American world the importance of the room itself seemed altogether reduced, since the smartest drawing rooms – in England, at least – appeared sufficiently 'female' in themselves.[14] Elsewhere the *petit salon* or *Damenzimmer* often took the place of the boudoir, and the growing preference for running a household in a more relaxed fashion affected most rooms of the house, together with the widespread adoption of rich, free-flowing textiles that were increasingly seen as possessing 'female' qualities. The ideal of the woman dressed in ample fabric and in repose became almost fused with images of draped domestic textiles, cushions or hangings, all of which could be fetishized in the same way. The painter Albert Moore celebrated states of extreme langour with a veritable feast of drapes. However, his foregrounding of materials to this extent, combined with his preference for a light palette, meant that much of the sense of an enveloping interior was lost.

According to the ideal of the home based around the nuclear family, men were expected to work in the outside world; even so, as an antidote their place in the home was assured. Men were often obliged to do paperwork or to worry about their jobs when at home, and it was

Two gendered interiors with sharply contrasting atmospheres: *A Forestkeeper's Home* by Ludwig Knaus (1886; *above left*), and *Jasmine* by Albert Moore (1881; *above*). Despite their obvious differences, a mood of solitary contemplation characterized both the male and the female types of secluded interior.

natural that they should require a quiet place in which to do so ('One gets away from all domestic matters … nobody is allowed to enter', etc.). In terms of importance, the man's room came directly after the *salon* or living room and the dining room and even before the boudoir. In spite of what was written about the singularity of the boudoir, it was the man's room that bore the strongest mono-functional characteristics in the home – that is, it was the room that could be used least flexibly. The study had, moreover, a much longer pedigree than the woman's equivalent, stretching back to the monk's cell and the Renaissance *studiolo*. The greatest proof of the room's private nature was that, in contrast to the rest of the home, it did not have to be tidy. Not surprisingly, the marked distinction between male and female roles in the 19th century strengthened the room's special character: visually, its overall effect – again, in opposition to the female room – was sedate, serious and dark, a 'library solemn and grave'. One should avoid ostentation, but of course solidity and heaviness would themselves convey the impression of expense. Tough leather upholstery provided comfort here, rather than the soft padding of the boudoir or drawing room. The prescribed style was usually Renaissance, but the link between style and gender was less fixed than with the boudoir. In any case, the individual choices of the occupant carried much more weight than in the case of the woman's room.[15]

Within the dwelling the male sphere could extend much further than the female: it could comprise the study, the gentleman's room or the library, to which could be added the mainly male *Jagdhalle* (hunting room), the billiard room and the *Trinkstube* (drinking den; see pp. 228–29).[16] 'Masculine' characteristics could spill over into other parts of the house, such as the dining room, with its 'serious' character. In small homes male and female spheres could of course be expressed just in the style of a piece of furniture – a heavy Renaissance writing desk with leather chair, for instance, or a delicate Rococo sewing table. Gender-specificity could be attached to a whole room as much as to the objects within it.

Idylls unlimited

Clearly, the wealthier the inhabitants, the more likely it was that their home would have several rooms for individual use and the more décor these rooms were likely to display. In addition to

serving a specific psychological need, a proper boudoir also represented a celebration of its occupant through luxury.[17] However gender-specific it may have been, a room of this type was ultimately also linked to the general splendour of the home. The décor in many Neoclassical palaces was not required to show any specific 'domestic' characteristics and may be called wholly conventional, in the sense that rich houses had always been richly appointed. The design of the new 19th-century 'home', however, was meant to move beyond this conventionality. We now encounter a concept of the interior that stressed intimacy and sought to influence the occupants' mood by enabling contemplation – to be effected through the manipulation of overall atmosphere rather than tangible décor. This brings us to a crucial point: the professed aim of the new holistic movement of the home was to foreground the users as individuals, or as precisely defined small groups, acting more independently of society, etiquette and other constraints. This is what is meant by 'interiority': tailoring the environment to mood and atmosphere and not merely to the user's position in society.

While 'privacy' is a concept formulated by modern sociology and psychology, the desire to be alone, to rest alone, to contemplate has been around for a long time: we have known about it at least since Roman antiquity, when, combined with a sense of landscape, it was termed an 'idyll'. However, in its early forms it appeared not so much a sociological or psychological reality as a poetic genre. What is of fundamental importance here is the idyll's liminality – the sense, common to poetry and to all kinds of representation, that at one moment we are faced with fiction and at the next with real life.

Traditionally, the preferred place for seeking refuge was in nature, even wild nature, where one felt both exposed and sheltered. One's psychological state should be a mix of solitariness and loneliness (indeed, the German term *Einsamkeit* covers both).[18] The stereotypical idyll-seeker was at first not associated with any gender in particular. The hermit formed a Christian subspecies, also living in wild nature, as did the monk, sitting and contemplating while secluded within his cell. Renaissance humanism turned the monk into a secular learned man and his cell into a *studiolo*, mentioned above; Dürer's woodcut of *St Jerome in his Study* (in German, 'Hieronymus im Gehäuse', the latter word deriving from *Haus* and meaning 'housed' or 'boxed in') has, perhaps somewhat rashly, been declared the archetypal image of domesticity.[19] During the 18th century the poets' analyses of sentiment became more searching, and the experience of intimacy and its associated erotic innuendo appeared more intense. A stronger genderization seemed inevitable: it was primarily the young female who sought seclusion while really waiting to be 'discovered' by the male.

Illustration by Gustav Heinrich Naeke for a novel by Friedrich de la Motte Fouqué, *c.* 1820.

And yet a communal element did not necessarily have to be excluded. Nature could be enjoyed just as much in the company of friends, and, in the context of the new definition of the family, to which we shall come below, even the nuclear group of mother, father and children could all indulge in a *fête champêtre*. Further ancient literary terms related to the idyll were 'arcadian' or 'bucolic', signifying the remote countryside; here, one might meet those who were considered Arcadia's original inhabitants – peasants or shepherds, with whom the person seeking refuge could associate, albeit on a strictly temporary basis. (The implications of this particular trope for design – the 'peasant' look – will be discussed later in this book.) After all, the idyll was something to be experienced only by the well-to-do. The 19th century's great contribution was to spread this ideal, under the banner of the universal model institution: the home. One may call it the idyll's utopian dimension.[20]

But how precisely does the notion of escaping the everyday world into a distant natural environment become linked to the desire not to escape or break out, but to withdraw into the 'ordinary' world of house and home? The idea, and eventually the design, of the home as a refuge is obviously complex. Its beginning is marked by the 18th-century fashion for erecting small structures in parks and gardens in diverse styles, in order to conjure up different moods, pleasurable as well as contemplative. It was a great help if these buildings exuded a feeling of 'ancientness', since this seemed to aid contemplation. The 'hermitage' – a common building of this kind – took many of its cues from the idea of the monk's or nun's cell in a medieval abbey, and a further influence was the even more potent image of castle dungeons or ruins. It all formed a powerful brew that contributed to a psychology of seclusion, of forgoing the amenities of the modern, well-lit house. A new literary genre had also emerged, influential until the present day: the 'Gothic novel', whose stories told mainly of females incarcerated in haunted old castles. The related theme of darkness in the interior will be dealt with below; what matters here, as with the idyll, is the basic concept of an environment matching the user's mood, even if the 'Gothic' mood itself was the very opposite of the old, pleasant idyll.[21] All this happened at much the same time as the development of the boudoir; indeed, the boudoir's occupant could appear as a 'mixture of the Magdalene and Mme Pompadour'.[22]

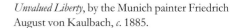

Unvalued Liberty, by the Munich painter Friedrich August von Kaulbach, *c.* 1885.

Looking ahead, neither the secluded spot in the wilderness nor the image of the monk or nun in a cloistered cell, let alone the dungeon, could be transferred directly to the home. Just after 1800, the painters of Romanticism added new variety to the image of seclusion, depicting the Virgin Mary in her 'Kämmerlein', her 'little chamber'. Here, two religious trends were merged: Pietism, a moralist–contemplative branch of Protestantism, and a new fascination with 'medieval' Catholic sanctity and ritual. The image of Mary in her small abode, alone or with the Angel of the Annunciation, can thus be linked to that of the monk's cell and the study, as well as to the home and the family. While the hermit, the nun or the imprisoned maiden had

Bedchamber in a 14th-century castle, from Eugène-Emmanuel Viollet-le-Duc's *Dictionnaire raisonné du mobilier français* (1858–). In his reconstructions of medieval life, Viollet-le-Duc emphasizes the fact that the rooms of old houses were not marked out by different functions or groups of inhabitants, unlike modern compartmentalized ways of living. Neither did there seem to be space for the Romantics' notion of contemplative seclusion.

The Delights of Motherhood by Jean-Michel Moreau le Jeune (1777). This gathering of a virtuous family is treated as an 18th-century *fête champêtre*.

to forgo most amenities, Mary's room was now marked by at least some elements of domestic comfort. Excitement and restfulness could somehow coexist, and the senses of being threatened and of security probably reinforced each other.[23]

During the first decades of the 19th century images of young women sitting in a small chamber, with or without religious overtones, became popular, although few were as precisely programmed as Nazarene painter Franz Pforr's picture of his intended bride, Maria.[24] We can now begin to speak truly of the domestic idyll: 'Happiness dwells in quietness', the advice book writer Henriette Davidis tells the 'Jungfrau', the young maiden – exactly what is needed 'for the preparation of her profession', the running of the family home.[25] A state of contemplation and thus happiness may be achieved by anybody, within any home. Politicians and sociologists, too, were defining the home as 'other' to the threatening outside world. Two age-old conceptions of life, the *vita contemplativa* and the *vita activa*, were now allowed to combine: the young mother would work and watch over her family while still indulging in a contemplative mood. Historians of chivalrous life in the Middle Ages extended this poetic sphere, conjuring up the image of a woman who fulfilled a multitude of tasks, as wife, lover, muse and organiser of the household; her room or rooms were presented as benefiting from advanced comforts such as heating, while the menfolk occupied the rougher quarters.[26] Sociologists of the 19th century, as well as its novelists and painters, formulated an extraordinarily complex idyll of the woman in the house, with the rest of the family grouped around her – a seemingly inexhaustible formula.[27]

Domesticity

Literature and illustration

Privacy and secludedness were values that found expression in the gendered rooms for both sexes. The idyll – initially a purely 'poetic' conception of an environment – seemed to find its way into the actual rooms of the home. Again, one asks how it was possible to consider domestic spaces and the predominantly mundane activities of ordinary family life as idyllic. Certainly, a new, persuasive trend for family privacy had emerged. The combination of the poeticized ideal of the idyll with the more social, moral and practical notions of privacy was the single most decisive factor in the development of the 19th-century concept of 'home'.[28] And yet,

'Homeliness' and domestic furnishings in popular graphic works. Here, a carefully constructed vision of the family, from *The Family Economist* (1849). It is addressed to the 'Cottage Homes of England! by thousands on her plains'. The interior fittings, however, are of significantly better quality than those usually affordable by cottage-dwellers.

while suitable fittings for the boudoir or the study could be readily supplied by the furnishing trades, formulating the visual or design aspects of the idyllic family room appears to have taken somewhat longer.

From the later 18th century on, the presence of the 'family home' in literature and painting is overwhelming. Earlier, the family had appeared primarily in portraits (with the natural exception of the Holy Family). Now the nuclear family was depicted as universal and statusless. The activities chosen for it tended towards the contemplative – quietly eating together, sharing prayers, reading in relaxation. Typically, the family takes the form of a young couple with a small number of young children, preferably of a still angelic age and including a baby. The

Plates 1 and 5 of George Cruikshank's series *The Bottle*, first published in 1847. A respectable and morally upright existence was seen as synonymous with the possession of a minimum of décor and a certain standard of completeness. The disappearance of these attributes marks the family's complete degradation.

A vision of 'Happy People in the Palace' (*above*) and 'in the Cottage' (*above right*), from *Die Gartenlaube*, 1867. They typify the rhetoric of dignified poverty.

image of the naive but lively child became a crucial ingredient in the image of the home as a whole.[29] Grandparents, too, appear frequently, clearly related to the young family but also somewhat detached from that nucleus. They usually sit around passively, signifying stability at the centre of the home.[30] The home-dweller could be sure to relax in the company of the family; as Hegel wrote: 'the individual, seeking the enjoyment of his individuality, finds it in the family'.[31]

Literary and pictorial images of family life varied constantly, but it took some time for the material aspect of the domestic interior to become a legitimate topic. Of course, in fiction much of the action had always taken place in the characters' homes, but that did not mean that the domestic environment itself would be characterized in detail – except, of course, for representations of the highest class. At first, writers hesitated to pay much attention to these surroundings: Goethe, for instance, considered domestic scenes unsuitable for high art.[32] Likewise, in Jane Austen's novels – intensely domestic, one might claim, in their content and message – actual details about the rooms are mostly absent.[33] Indeed, this situation reflects one of the main tenets of this book: that the older kind of house simply did not contain much to discuss. In an investigation entitled *Das deutsche Haus in der Poesie* of 1892, we read all about its inhabitants and the diverse moral issues affecting a family – especially the housewife – but still very little about the actual *Haus*.[34]

The work of the early illustrators points in the same direction. The happy families of the 18th-century French painters and the moralising book illustrations of Prussian-Polish artist Daniel Chodowiecki usually show a well-appointed but somehow standardized décor.[35] Representations of actual interiors from the early to mid-19th century, already characterized as 'chronicle pictures', demonstrate more knowledge of the variety of décor, while many amateur pictures of the 1820s to 1840s from Central Europe and Scandinavia also include the occupants. After 1900 such interiors were dubbed 'simple Biedermeier homes', but the images, often clumsily drawn, served mainly as portraits and should not necessarily be interpreted as comprehensive manifestations of a 'simple' home.[36] It was the writers of high literature, painters and some professional illustrators who assumed the responsibility of conveying the ideal.

Attempts to define the 'ordinary' became ever more complex. The relationship between the inhabitants' moral state and their relative wealth had entered a new dialectic. Strictly

Die Hausfrau.   Friede.

Heilge Ordnung segenreiche Himelstochter!

moral behaviour was no longer related to, or dependent on, a rich or interesting environment. In the works of Greuze, painted in the 18th century, happy and virtuous families are invariably located in poor, dark and even dirty surroundings in the manner of old Netherlandish low-life scenes. For Diderot, Greuze's subjects were virtuous in spite of being poor.[37] The next step, during the 1830s and 1840s, was to argue that a moral life could actually be brought about through a specific kind of interior or a specific kind of appearance. This new look was characterized by the removal of all signs of disorder, dirt or neglect. What was left was bareness, and it was this new bareness that was now taken as a sign of cleanliness, and therefore of order, virtuousness and solidity. Thus a new subspecies of the idyll was emerging, in which the simplicity of the bucolic or arcadian could be transferred to modest interiors. Wordsworth's turn towards the 'ordinary' was noted in Chapter I; in Germany, a well-known definition of the idyll followed similar lines: 'complete happiness through restraint'.[38] It should be noted that George Cruikshank's and Charles Dickens's depictions of the small home represent an intermediate stage: in Dickens's stories, and in many of Cruikshank's illustrations, the happy family demonstrates order and care plus a certain amount of modest wealth; when the family goes down, say, through drink, the home shows neglect as well as depletion.[39]

The master of transforming the Wordsworthian claim of the significance of the ordinary, of bucolic 'simplicity', into a highly specific and recognizable image of the home was Ludwig Richter. Richter was ostensibly a producer of illustrated children's books, but the main themes

Ludwig Richter, 'The Housewife' (*above left*) and 'Peace' (*above*), from his *Schillers Lied von der Glocke* (1857). The inscription in the second image reads: 'Holy love of orderliness, blessed daughter of Heaven'. Friedrich Schiller's 'Song of the Bell' (1799) was Germany's most popular didactic poem. Here, Richter ennobles a humble populace through his use of a Raphaelesque classical style, at the same time identifying the small town environment as typically German (see also p. 31).

Eigen Haard ('Our Hearth'), published in Haarlem from 1875. The numerous illustrated journals aimed specifically at the family sought to introduce issues from the world at large at the same time as focusing on the secluded home life of their readers.

below Illustration by Oskar Pletsch for *Die Kinderstube in 36 Bildern* ('The Nursery in 36 Pictures'; 1860).

below right T. Raffles Davison, *Children in a Dining Room* (1885). By 1880, many artists were less preoccupied with projecting idealized images of absolute seriousness.

of his vast corpus of illustrations, appearing from the 1840s to the 1870s, were the family and the house.[40] 'Simplicity' was indeed the most frequently commented on, and praised, characteristic of his work, 'Germanness' the second most frequent; equally important was the ingredient of the old, aspects of which will be debated further in the following chapter. Many further epithets could be applied by the critics to his images: 'depths of mood, tenderness and truthfulness of feeling', 'poetic beauties', etc. However, rather surprisingly, on closer inspection the 'simple German' scenes and people, their angelic little faces and their bodily movements turn out to be derived directly from Raphael and the classical style of the Italian Renaissance. Richter had been associated with the German Nazarene painters in Rome; once back in Dresden he largely gave up painting in favour of illustration but essentially kept to the Italianate style in his figure drawing. Not only are his children angelic, but also the mothers and fathers, who are invariably very young and starkly contrasted with the elderly. Even his small dogs have a certain air ('Richter's spitzes also have a family sense'). People of a 'normal' professional age occur much more rarely. For a reproduction process, Richter turned to the newly revived (likewise 'simple') English technique of wood engraving.[41]

What Richter does most determinedly is to devise a frame for the idyllic existence. His method is derived from the vignette: the small illustrative scene framed by modest ornamentation. The Romantics, such as Clemens Brentano, Moritz von Schwind and Eugen Napoleon Neureuther, had begun to combine several of these vignettes into one large multiple composition (a technique that we have already noted in later publications by the trade: see pp. 38, 80),

providing an anti-classical, bitty kind of narrative, held to be particularly suitable for fairy tales. Thus the genre of the vignette itself contributed directly to a new love for the small interior.[42] Richter then fits his tiny houses so snugly around their inhabitants that one thinks of Walter Benjamin's description of the dwelling as being 'like a case' [e.g. for one's glasses].[43] It appears that Richter's subjects live in only one, or at most two, rooms. Often he shows a room together with the whole exterior of the house, thus transferring the in-built restrictiveness of the traditional idyll to the dwelling as a whole, to the 'kleinste Hütte', the smallest cottage.[44] Inside, he devises furnishings that look basic but are solid and complete, and thus prefigures the Arts and Crafts preference for far greater solidity than was practically necessary. Above all, Richter avoids Cruikshank and Dickens's association of bareness with poverty in the sense of deprivation; the old association of simplicity with poverty is decidedly broken. A few decades later, Kate Greenaway eagerly took up and developed Richter's poetry of mundane life and transferred it to a subtly gentrified, English view of 'cottage life' (see p. 247).

But of course there was no way of ignoring the fact that this perfect version of simplicity arrived at a time when just about every aspect of the real modern Continental dwelling was developing in the opposite direction – most characteristically in the new, dense urban apartment blocks. A sharper contrast could not be imagined: smart parents sporting modern urban dress, sitting in a puffy armchair in the well-appointed rooms of their *bel étage* flat, enjoying with their elaborately dressed children Richter's pictures of ragged infants in their village cottage. However, the already familiar concept of *Volkstümlichkeit* (folk character) would help bridge the status gap and serve as a reminder that 'home' was a concept meant for all classes.

Pierre Revoil, *The Convalescence of Bayard* (1817), Musée du Louvre, Paris. The events depicted in early 19th-century history painting were either violently dramatic or ramblingly contemplative, and usually accompanied by miscellaneous details vaguely related to the period in which the story occurred – here, the Renaissance.

Another way of looking at Richter would be to consider him as ahead of his time; indeed, from the 1880s Central Europeans built more and more small villas in green surroundings while using new kinds of folksy décor.

As everybody noted, Romanticism and other-worldly idylls were followed by a new trend: realism. Effectively this meant more detail, and new sets of more diverse meanings. In the earlier home idyll, the environment was of critical importance, but it was also standardized, typified. Now the 'pure' idyll began to lose its appeal. As was hinted at in Chapter I, the notions of the 'romantic' and the 'poetic' (but chiefly the former) were in danger of becoming hackneyed. The bucolic country atmosphere was likely to have been devised by a 'city poet who knew nothing about the life of nature'.[45] The same could be said of the low-life pictures that David Wilkie continued to paint into the 1820s, which still essentially adhered to the Old Dutch manner, their surroundings indicating a highly stereotyped poverty or meanness. But now these generic scenes (as well as those concerned with subjects of a higher social status, especially 'bourgeois' ones) were transformed into 'genre'. A confusing term, 'genre' in this case essentially means that each image of ordinary life, each event, was constructed as an individualized situation, made specific through the careful study and inclusion of circumstantial details, which of course became ever more diverse.[46] Moreover, a genre picture required a 'unity of *Stimmung* [atmosphere/mood] and a certain historical thread'.[47] The scene could be situated in the past or in the present; altogether, the sense of history was greatly sharpened. Among the plethora of topics, the 'domestic genre' became one of the most sought-after.

Jean-Louis-Ernest Meissonier, *Young Man Writing* (*c.* 1852), Musée du Louvre, Paris. By mid-century, realist historical genre paintings tended to show anonymous protagonists in 'ordinary', undramatic scenes. The emphasis is now clearly on the surroundings, which were painstakingly researched. The work of Meissonier, France's most prominent painter in this style, exhibits a keen sense of the materiality of all furnishings and an eye for the signs of age.

Yet even here the 'advance of empiricist description' was slow.[48] The environment continued to be instrumentalized in different ways. In Dickens's novels the home plays a crucial role, but since he writes so much about events in modest homes, there is still a paucity of detail regarding the furnishings. Balzac's realist novels on life in Paris abound in descriptions of decorative domestic objects, but he does not appear to share Anglo-German notions of the value of domesticity as such. His richer interiors appear mainly as reflections of the decorators' and manufacturers' work, and his judgments mostly concern 'taste' or 'elegance'. Very clearly, the décor is seen as serving the characters: 'those people without an ambience of décor … seem like colourless walk-on parts'.[49] Much the same applied to new developments on stage. Whereas previously it had been actors' words and actions that carried the performance, now the elaborate *mise en scène*, with its historical and geographic specificity, played an increasingly important role.[50] Conversely, some editors of books on interior decoration, such as Mothes's *Unser Heim* of 1879, explicitly styled their illustrations as 'livened-up pictures'.[51]

By about 1880 this sense of detail was already changing once again. Domestic scenes could include again actors who possessed very little, the urban poor, or the lowest class of peasants. Fiction began to interest itself in existential, often tragic themes.[52] This new trend focused less on factual and narrative detail in favour of the characters' broader psychological states. But here the unity of the whole, 'unity of atmosphere', mattered ever more. In the end, whatever the message, be it celebratory or critical, anyone seeking to represent the home needed to understand how to 'lighten the ordinary sphere with the magic light of poetry'.[53]

Family rooms

How could these themes be expressed in actual plans and fittings? How exactly should one interpret César Daly's description of 'the house' as 'the family's dress'?[54] In the Introduction we dealt with the basic plan and the designated use of some of the rooms. This section, on the other hand, is concerned with psychological and sociological issues rather than material, practical ones. As Wolfgang Brönner has pointed out, there was a new preference for enclosure and privacy in the rooms that served family life, as pronounced as it had been in the rooms that offered personal seclusion.[55]

Living room ('bürgerliches Wohnzimmer') from Mothes's 1879 book on art in the home (see pp. 18–19). This image reveals a very carefully constructed sociological agenda. All the family members are present and are placed close to each other, but each has his or her own occupation. The servant indicates a social level above the average, but the fairly meagre décor suggests the opposite.

Living room by Phillip Niederhöfer, Frankfurt am Main, 1884. Niederhöfer's was one of the first catalogues explicitly to include a cheaper range of furnishings for the whole room. The table in the corner next to the sofa became a major symbol of family togetherness in Central Europe, representing a modest amount of comfort and coordinated décor for those who could afford only one living room.

However, on the plans of many 19th-century dwellings it is far from clear which of the common reception rooms constituted the actual family living room. The wealthier the family, the more likely its members were to use different rooms at any given time; the shared meal provided the most important occasion for togetherness, taken in the most formal room of the house, the dining room. In larger English houses the family could also meet in the morning room, while in somewhat smaller dwellings, particularly in the United States, the parlour could serve as a kind of formal family room. In France, the need for the family to be together was served by the *petit salon* as well as the dining room. In 1870s England, the term 'living room' – or, more rarely, 'sitting room' – was revived as a replacement for 'drawing room', which sounded too formal.

The family could also come together in specific parts of a room, such as next to the (largely Anglo-American) fireplace or, in Continental Europe, at the table in the corner, around which it would sit in the evening. Furthermore, there was the concept of the central hall, which had been revived for some large country seats by 1840, principally by the medievalists. This room contained the central fireplace and was meant, in a somewhat neo-feudal spirit, as a meeting place for the extended household. Later, the Americans in particular cultivated the central hall, which in smaller detached houses also contained the staircase and a fireplace.[56]

The Germans took the issue of the family living room more seriously than others. As Ferdinand Luthmer wrote: 'for the daily togetherness of the members of the home', one should 'assign the best location in the whole house. Without doubt we can preserve the old intimacy of family life if we can provide a pleasant and comfortable room where it can develop.' This later 19th-century emphasis on the *Wohnzimmer* was largely a question of redefinition. The term itself had always existed as a synonym for *Wohnstube*, which referred to what in the smallest dwellings was the one and only living room, but it also appeared frequently on the plans for larger dwellings where the room designation was left vague.[57]

From the 1850s onwards, the views of sociologist-cum-cultural historian Wilhelm Heinrich Riehl on the nature of the family gained widespread recognition.[58] Riehl's 'das ganze Haus' ('the whole house') fused the notions of family and home: 'The family house and the real customs of the house are mutually dependent.' Over the course of the century, the Germans gradually adopted the term *Salon* for the 'best' room, but Riehl regretted this modern

European separation of room uses and suggested the adoption of a general family meeting place: the 'altdeutsche Diele' (an extended corridor; not the same as the English 'hall', he adds) or the 'Herd', the hearth. Riehl frequently engaged in nationalist polemics, taking on the 'French' fashion of the *bel étage* (the first floor) in new urban dwellings, which for him disturbed 'the image of German unity' found in the old 'idyll of the German house'. Notwithstanding all this nationalism, nobody in France (nor in Britain, for that matter) would have taken issue with Riehl's remark regarding German sociability: 'The real *bonne société* is the house that is extended towards a circle of friends'.[59] Moreover, his ideas were publicized from quite early on in the principal architectural journals in England and France, and the extent of their influence ought to be investigated further.[60]

It should be a simple matter to determine the basic functions of the rooms in a home. But this certainly was not the case in the 19th century. Adapting, or rather side-stepping, Riehl's formulation of *bonne société*, in the final decades of the century the Germans became increasingly convinced that it was the English who did not differentiate to a great degree between spaces for the family and spaces for guests.[61] The discussion on room labels in the Introduction emphasized precisely that differentiation, as an element of progress and as a sign that greater comfort and convenience in the home had been achieved; all human activities within the house ought to be separated carefully. In this context Riehl's 'Diele' or the English neo-Gothic 'great hall' in large, newly built houses could be seen as newly defined communal rooms to be used alongside the modern rooms whose individual functions were so carefully circumscribed – making it all even more complicated. Finally, the end of the century saw a general indifference towards room distinctions. It was now claimed that the 'pattern of use' of the German *Wohnzimmer* was 'not very much fixed'.[62]

Ultimately, one can conclude that 19th-century demands for togetherness, for special enclosure, do seem to have had an impact, and that *Wohnzimmer* became the common term in the 20th century for this reason. German gradually dropped other words such as *Salon*. In Britain, 'living room' had regained its use, though mainly in smaller and medium-sized dwellings. One major issue remained: the distinction between rooms used on a daily basis and those reserved 'for best'. For some 19th-century and later ideologists, 'home', the ordinary home, should mean the abandonment of this separation, although it took much of the 20th century for this idea to take hold. Only the French never seem to have problematized the issue, conceiving of a dwelling as a seamless gradation between public openness and secluded privacy.

Small children were the mainstay of the nuclear family and of domestic togetherness, yet they, too, were 'divided off' as the nursery became popular in larger English houses during the course of the 19th century. Even by 1900 the room's main design characteristics were based on practicality ('simple and rough and ready, serviceable and clean').[63] By then, however, a notion of child-specificity and child-centredness had emerged, which held that all children were entitled to naivety, even to mischievousness, as well as to relaxation, contemplation and art. In the 1870s a few English artist-designers like Walter Crane had begun to design child-orientated wallpapers, in effect borrowing elements from their illustrations for children's books, but only in the 1890s, with the designs of C. F. A. Voysey and Baillie Scott, did the décor of the children's room attain a specific character (see p. 271).[64] Rooms for grandparents did not appear to be much different from others in the house, even if the grandparents themselves lent a special sense of rest to pictures of the period (particularly when sitting next to the newly revived large ceramic stove).

Thus far, the secluded happy family home had provided some potent images, backed by moral and social exhortations; and yet somehow the generalized home idyll did not provide the spaces assigned for family life with a distinct atmosphere or character – especially when compared with the boudoir or study. The following sections consider the efforts of designers and critics to create features and styles for a more intense, but also a more adaptable, domestic interiority.

Poeticization through design

Comfort

Enter the designers again, but also the users in a different role. In the domestic interior we are concerned both with an 'objective architectural impression and with our subjective experience', as the Berlin architect Richard Lucae wrote in 1869.[65] Thus far the definitions of home have been connected to external factors: social stratification, the division of gender, and the institution of the nuclear family in society. Yet each user may have a number of quite different preferences: 'for splendid company … radiant rooms … or a cosy nest, warm, quiet and comfortable, which fits around him like a well-cut costume'.[66] With careful

Dining room with a bay window, by H. Kolb and T. Seubert, Stuttgart, 1885–88. By the 1870s, the bay window had become favourite motif of Central European decorators. Illustrations invariably show a diagonal view, and the skills of the upholsterer in managing light are conveyed through the complex arrangements of curtains.

planning and the right technical equipment, all these demands could be met within a well-appointed dwelling.

Of critical importance for the 19th-century experience of the interior was the sense that one needed a place in which to rest. The main German term for 'rest', *Ruhe*, includes physical quietness, mental repose, serenity and privacy. Many factors could contribute to a restful experience: having one's own room, using carpets that 'avoid the noise of footsteps', or fixing 'silent door springs', for instance; and luxury in general could help encourage 'happy, refined rest'.[67] But these diverse elements still do not go directly to the heart of the matter of domestic interiority: they do not explain a user's intense physical and psychological experience of a room independent of its assigned function. Even 'art', in the traditional, Renaissance understanding of splendid décor, may not be necessary for the achievement of interiority – one's subjective, psychological contentment in an interior.[68] Although 'The Poetry of Our Four Walls', the *Gartenlaube* article of 1864 mentioned above, considers the general issue of comfort in the home, using four types of room as examples, the characteristic of *gemütlichkeit* is mentioned in connection with only one: the personalized interior of the whimsical old lady. It is seemingly not found in the richer, more carefully decorated kind of room.[69]

The increasing desire for privacy and the stronger polarization between the private home and the outside world clearly did contribute to an appreciation of interiority, narrowing definitions of leisure to self-indulgent, quiet activities that could lead to a contemplative mood. The concept of the idyll was of course one of the main influences in the construction of interiority, although the psychological element could be obscured by literary ballast. Crucially, it was now believed that every human being was entitled to such relaxation at home.[70] Furthermore, this view was linked to an older concept of security: 'My home is my castle.' Originally a legal phrase, it now became an assertion of the complete individuality of the home.

This notion of subjective experience had a long philosophical history. The Romantics' concept of 'sich innewerden' – 'to become aware of oneself' or, according to Hegel, 'the desire to enjoy one's individuality'[71] – had by the 1880s turned into a more intense kind of psychologizing that manifested itself in a new 'cult of the ego'.[72] For the city dweller, it was thought to help the escape from the menace of modern anonymity. But were these experiences not just exceptional and fleeting, valid and available only to artists and intellectuals? A Parisian critic invoked Hamlet by posing the dilemma: 'être artiste chez soi ou ne pas l'être' ('to be or not to be an artist at home'); for him, this was a decision to be made 'daily'.[73] Charles Blanc also addressed this very issue: impressions gained in the home are 'fleeting moments, no doubt, but out of these minutes the agenda of life is composed; these moments constitute three-quarters of our existence'.[74] Many home art books now defined the effects of the interior in vague psychological terms, some even claiming that domestic happiness imbued one unconsciously.[75]

'Gemütlichkeit' and 'Stimmung'

The language of the critics and philosophers may not have been accessible to many, but during the 19th century adjectives that underlined the personalized, psychological qualities of the home greatly increased in circulation. Among all the rhetoric, pride of place (at least in the Western languages) was occupied by the word 'home' itself.[76] Germans, who so often boasted their pre-eminence in all matters of domesticity, do have their version of the 'old Saxon word' (as an American put it) – namely *das Heim* – but that term had largely been abandoned by the later 18th century (as was the Dutch *heem*), enjoying only a limited revival in the later 19th century under the influence of its English counterpart.[77] Another relevant word is 'homely' ('homey' in the United States), although its original meaning was much wider than it is today.[78] 'Cosy' and 'snug', from the 18th century onwards, refer more to states of mind and (importantly) to intimacy. By contrast, the detached-sounding 'interior', in the sense of domestic interiority, does not seem to go back beyond the early 19th century.[79]

The best known of all nationally specific terms is *Gemütlich*; the Frenchman 'has not even a word for it', the Germans claimed.[80] Were they right? *Chez soi* does rather appear to be an equivalent to 'at home', *zu Hause* or *daheim*. The French had also imported 'home' by the early to mid-19th century, but it remained a foreign word.[81] Like most other languages, French also borrowed *confortable* from English, which became the most widely used term, even though it continued to refer to purely physical as well as mental qualities.[82] The Germans had numerous terms that covered a wide span between physical comfort and psychological states. Modern *komfortabel* and the old word *bequem* (in French *commode*) both signify the former, while *häuslich* and *wohnlich* (from *wohnen*, 'to dwell') come in between. There is also *behaglich*, which conveys a strong sense of containment (from *Hag*, 'enclosure'), and *traut* (related to *trauen*, 'to trust'). *Gemütlich* has a more complex history, beginning to acquire its dominant meaning only in the late 18th century. It is directly related to *Gemüt*, the hard-to-translate term for 'state of mind', 'feeling', 'sentiment', the contemplative sense. *Gemütlich* then had a brief negative phase before mid-century, used to satirize the self-satisfied German who shuts himself away from public life. Only thereafter did its meaning become restricted to the domestic sphere. It could refer to the individual, to the nuclear family or to the company of friends (compare the Dutch *gezellig*, which has similar connotations of friendly cosiness). Thus, like all notions of 'home', *gemütlich* was inseparable from a wider socio-political discourse. After 1900 both intellectual and modernist design discourses turned away from the word, although this in no way diminished its importance in everyday speech.[83]

Subjectivity of course plays a large part in how one experiences an interior, as can be seen from frequent phrases such as 'wir machen es uns gemüthlich' ('we are making ourselves comfortable'). The issue here, however, is not primarily how any actual user feels, but how he or she is intended to feel. This chapter is concerned with what the designers were aiming for, and with qualities that should be demonstrated within the design of the room itself. What will help at this point are more exact terms, like the German *Stimmung*. French, English and most other European languages translate *Stimmung* as 'atmosphere', but its meaning in German is wider: like 'atmosphere', it signifies the overall impression received from a landscape or a room, but the Romantic critics also related it to moods ('I am in a good *Stimmung*') and thus added a purely subjective element. To say that a space creates *Stimmung* or 'atmosphere' means that a space or room can create both an atmosphere *and* a mood.[84] As Luthmer states: 'There are moods of the soul that are analogous with a room … our mood and our emotions are dependent on the objects that surround us.'[85] According to Julius Lessing, the 'Pavillon de l'Impératrice' at the 1867 Paris Exposition Universelle (see p. 147) – a work renowned for its integration of all décor – 'produced through its furnishing a specific character and the expression [*Stimmung*] … of a sweetly dreaming restfulness and relaxation'.[86] Mrs Haweis used copious words to convey this quality in her book's concluding sentences: 'Let, then, our homes reflect our warmest and most sympathising moods, as far as art has the making of them, and let the art be the very best of its kind, however little. Let them fit our daily wants as the shell its fish and the plume its bird.'[87]

The value-laden rhetoric was heating up. From *Stimmung*, we move finally to the soul, and to the poetic. In Lucae's 1869 article 'The Power of Space', we read: 'Light is the soul of the room; colour, on the other hand, will give it a specific atmosphere; it will touch us lyrically and will affect our soul [*Gemüth*] in particular.'[88] Falke phrased it, as usual, more directly: 'give the room that poetical attractiveness, that unconscious gripping magic, which in a picture we call atmosphere'.[89] Should one attempt to analyse these general romanticized terms further?

In Chapter I we saw a reluctance to do so on the part of later 19th-century writers on the home. We also note, from the 1880s on, new scientific methods in psychology and physiology that looked beyond these older terms (see below). For the designer, there was always the core consideration of the room as a whole, and the goal of achieving a 'total harmonic effect' that would 'unconsciously touch whose who are occupying the … rooms in comforting, cosy ways'.[90]

Inside/outside

In this section, the discussion narrows down to consider a strong sense of interiority – one may say, a 'pure' interiority. It naturally presupposes a particular conception of the relationship between interior and exterior. Of course, much depended on the home's immediate surroundings and on whether it was in the country or in town. More significant here, however, are the considerable changes that took place over time in what those who dwelt inside any type of dwelling expected to see of the outside.

Very early on, what was outside did not seem much of an issue. One may assume that in a very basic sense dwellers wanted to keep out anything unwanted. But by the later 18th century there was a definitive trend towards letting in as much light as possible and catching the best view of the surroundings. It gradually became smarter to live in an outer suburb where the house could have direct access to a garden or to the in-between space of a winter garden or a conservatory, constructed in a new way in metal and glass. The living room needs 'domestic bliss, a view into nature'.[91] In the best new urban districts, large windows also gave out onto the street – a street that was clean, ordered, and populated by people as smart as those looking out of the windows, who wanted to enjoy a 'pleasant and entertaining view'.[92] Conversely, window curtains served to 'show order to the outside' even in more modest streets. French writers in particular emphasized the householder's obligation to maintain a good façade for the public to look at.[93]

But ideas of what formed a desirable view from the urban house or flat soon changed fundamentally. At first, the polarization between the home and the exterior world was understood economically and sociologically, but it soon turned into a psychological and perceptual issue too. More and more, the perceived nervousness and discomfort of the times centred on the town, in spite of the modernization that was taking place in all its public institutions, theatres, restaurants, offices, and even in its factories. It was the communication networks, the thoroughfares, that seem to have caused the problem. In fact, the great increase in mobility meant that a good street could turn into one that should be avoided. After mid-century, better-class houses turned away from main thoroughfares to quiet side streets. Furthermore, the average 'modern' urban house, which so far had carried little exterior decoration, now appeared monotonous, although this view did not change when more décor became fashionable. The outside of one's abode in London was 'as a rule irretrievably ugly'. Apartments in Paris, too, now became decisively introspective, their exteriors appearing impenetrable.[94]

Writers on home art, such as Falke, took up the topic: 'There is no need for a good view of the outside from the dwelling, for all its attraction must be directed inside.' Falke realizes that earlier on 'ladies sat there, seeing but unseen', watching what was going on outside; but 'today that is different; we have neither the time nor the inclination, and it is not even respectable to be concerned with small events on the street'.[95] For Oscar Wilde, to look into and out of the house were both 'extremely bad habits'.[96] However, the matter was complicated by the infinite possibilities for interchange between inside and outside. So many houses and flats now sported verandahs or balconies. Dwellers now had it both ways, enjoying a sense of interiority and contact with the outside world when desired.[97]

Soon, however, the dominant trend was to live away from dense urban centres, choosing the spacious, low-density suburb instead. Here, the need to enclose oneself was considerably less pressing (a point to come back to at the very end of the book). The general 19th-century notion of interiority, whether in town, country or suburb, is perhaps best summed up in one of William Morris's inimitably plain comments. In pleading for more glazing bars in windows, he wrote: 'we shall then at all events feel as if we are indoors'. Of course, the word 'interiority' was not known to Morris, but he does foreground the smallest spatial unit in the dwelling – the room – claiming that the modern house as whole has 'neither centre nor individuality'. He underlines this point by writing: 'the unit I have to speak of is a room rather than a house'.[98]

Tight enclosures

When we appreciate a satisfying interior, wrote Lucae, we do not usually ask how it all comes about. Only those who possess a 'finely organized sensitivity' understand the processes of creation. Part of Lucae's expertise is the formulation of highly abstract concepts of design: for him, the artist's task is to manipulate the principal elements of 'form and light'. Their combination results in the even more abstract, and at times baffling, term 'space', hence the title of his article, 'The Power of Space'.[99] The previous chapter showed that this term did not really gain wide currency before about 1890, and at first only in Central Europe; in Lucae's case, too, it was the individual components – proportion, line, surface and tone – that were discussed.[100] Most of these formal elements have been dealt with already in Chapter III, but here they are taken up again in relation to the influence they had on the user's moods.

How does one design for the size and proportions of a room as a whole? As with the desirability of copious ornament, here the starting point was the sense of contentment that could be derived from a large room: the richer the house, the bigger the spaces. However, the concept of the psychologically satisfying idyll could also demand the opposite: a closely contained space, the desire 'to make my small room into a little treasure chest', as Goethe wrote.[101] In small but still relatively smart Paris flats a salon could measure 2.5 by 4 metres (8 feet 2 inches by 13 feet): 'What is being realized in Paris … so comfortable, so pretty and so

Two small, low-ceilinged rooms: a library by Charles F. McKim, New York, *c.* 1876 (*below left*), and a recess in a study by Gabriel von Seidl, *c.* 1883 (*below*).

Small enclosures similar to the bay window could be constructed within the room itself, as in this example by Gabriel von Seidl, Munich, from the late 1870s.

lovely in the small spaces, by way of ingenious interior arrangements and intelligent distribution, is unimaginable.'[102] Thus the boudoir could now be called 'le nid' ('the nest').[103] It must be noted, though, that these Parisian rooms were mostly quite high, usually measuring a standard 3 metres.

While small enclosed areas within a room became common, a whole room was rarely praised for being small: size was still valued greatly in a period when the average home was growing, as indicated at the beginning of the book. One widespread new fashion from the 1870s was for low ceilings – surprising when one considers that height, too, was one of the main signifiers of affluence, not to mention the fact that an ever greater amount of breathing

Canopied settee and corner seating arrangement by an unknown designer in suburban London; from *The Lady's World*, 1887.

space was demanded for health reasons. Ceilings, as we have seen, were originally discreet and underemphasized, but later in the century they became heavier and darker. White ceilings could give 'an exaggerated idea of height'.[104] John D. Crace cleverly remarked in 1882 that 'People seem to think that every room should be made to look as high as possible. Now I am all for having plenty of actual height for health's sake; but it cannot make much difference to one's health whether the room merely looks high or low.' Reception rooms should be high, but libraries and studies 'decidedly look all the more comfortable for seeming low rather than high. A really cosy room must SEEM to be a low room … It would be difficult to trace the chain of association by which this postulate is arrived at; but it may almost be called essential to the "sentiment" of the place if it be a room of quiet retirement.'[105] Hermann Muthesius later recommended a relatively low ceilings, of 2.5 metres (8 feet 2 inches), 3 metres (9 feet 10 inches) or 3.5 metres (11½ feet) at the most. E. W. Godwin pleaded for '9 feet fine' (2.7 metres).[106] The 'English cottage' type of interior and the American Colonial style introduced further variations on the low interior. Karl Henrici was fully converted by 1889: 'only the horizontal is comfortable; the room must be of a lying character … [giving] the impression of spatial restfulness. The walls should not be higher than their length; the ceiling should not be so high in the air that one no longer feels protected by it.'[107]

As we saw in Chapter III, a major aim of the picturesque and of accumulating objects large and small was the break-up of rectangularity. Picturesqueness could now also be equated directly with comfort, even with warmth: 'The art [of the interior] resides in the way an animated picture is created, which receives the person stepping in with a warmth that does him good.'[108] The most obvious way to break up the straight contours of a room was to add an extension: a bay window or oriel (*Erker* in German). In the early years of the century this small addition served chiefly to allow users to look out, to step out partly of the room; now it became the opposite, so to speak: an element of interiority. One may withdraw from the room into the bay window while still being able to observe what is happening in the rest of the room (see pp. 164, 304). Within the normal boxy room itself there were also ways of creating small subsidiary spaces – 'cosy corners', a term that gained wide currency in the 1890s.[109] In Germany, a 'Zimmerlaube' (an expression adapted from *Gartenlaube*, a small summer house) could be 'built into ordinary rooms … starting from 150 Marks',[110] and there were many other even more modest ways of screening off parts of a room. A similar space for withdrawing into was the Anglo-American inglenook, which will be discussed below in the context of the fireplace. A much smaller but still potent form that provided a feeling of protection was the cove or concave horizontal moulding. Known from earlier medievalist illustrations, it emerged prominently in Bruce Talbert's interiors and then in American designs in particular. Coving could be applied where the wall meets the ceiling, at the top of a mantelpiece, or above a large settee. For Hudson Holly, this 'canopy effect' lends 'an air of snugness to the apartment' (see p. 142).[111] Lastly, a room's floor levels could be varied: the Continental oriel was usually one step up. Failing all that, the designer could 'break up the hard angular lines of the four square walls that form the boundary line of most dwellings' with the help of temporary partitions. These could be portable screens in the form of light *paravents*, but fixed partitions were also increasingly used, partly influenced by Oriental models. All of these elements 'add an air of coziness'.[112]

Naturally, the quantity and diversity of applied décor continued to play a major role ('The eye demands an interruption of the smooth surface', says Luthmer), although we find that the opposite – a restraint in ornament – was also argued.[113] Meanwhile, a more detailed psychology of form had emerged, chiefly within French art teaching, which characterized arrangements of lines and surfaces according to the way in which they were held to affect the psyche. Such recipes appeared straightforward enough: groups of horizontal lines suggest

Internal bay of a dining room, from the Berlin Trade Exhibition, 1879. Its design involved both an architect, A. Schütz, and an 'artist–painter', M. Meurer.

right and far right Design for a house with an oriel window, by Georg Gottlob Ungewitter, 1856.

below Bay window by H. Kolb and T. Seubert, Stuttgart, 1885–88.

rest; vertical lines excitement; the curved line softness, pliability and devotion; the broken line, by contrast, implies liveliness; and parallel lines represent the character of friendship. Havard in particular and, following him, Luthmer experimented in juxtaposing schematic elevations and strong horizontal or vertical lines (see p. 143).[114]

All this psychological theorizing brought with it an ever greater degree of abstraction. This was of course perfectly in line with the trend for psychologizing symbolism in painting and sculpture. In their exteriors, architects in New England (such as Henry Hobson Richardson) and soon in Germany, too, increasingly employed plain, massive formations. In Germany, philosophers and art historians such as Heinrich Wölfflin subscribed to the concept of the empathetic appreciation of architecture – namely the view that one's experiences of a building concur with basic physical sensations (weightiness, lightness, etc.). We have already noted similar discussions surrounding the need for quiet, low-impact patterning on walls and floors.

By the later 1880s, the term *Raum* ('space') had gained considerably in importance: 'space … the explicit symbol of secludedness', writes A. Scheffers.[115] Space is created principally by enclosure, by the arrangement of (preferably) 'uninterrupted wall surfaces'. This results in *Raumruhe*, or 'restfulness of space'.[116] A room must contain a fair stretch of uninterrupted wall; if it has too many windows or is intersected by paths leading from one door to another, or if any of its walls is divided up into too many small sections, this will lead to grave problems: 'we do not feel comfortable … Nowhere do we feel that our backs are covered, and we feel that any moment we might expect an attack.'[117] Furthermore, the windows should not be situated

Lawrence Alma-Tadema's *My Children*, reproduced in the *Art Journal* (1877) – an image of enveloping comfort.

Four enclosed spaces by the architect Carl Panke, from *Innendekoration* (1893).

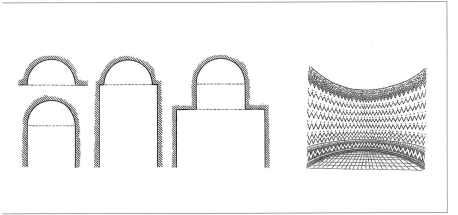

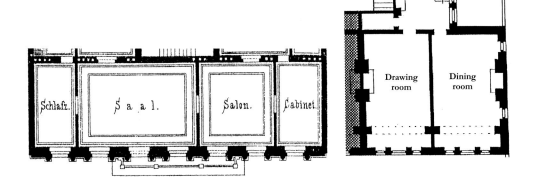

above Drawings by A. Scheffers for types of 'circular enclosed space ... it is the place for contemplation and the most emphatic symbol of seclusion'; from the *Architektonische Formenschule* (1880).

above right Eugene Clarence Gardner, 'Where shall the Pictures be?', from *Home Interiors* (1878). In addition to showing the difficulty of hanging pictures on interrupted walls, it seems likely that Gardner also wanted to illustrate how too many doorways militate against a satisfactory sense of enclosure.

A flat in Vienna from the 1870s (*right*), and Albert Hall Mansions, London (*far right*), by Richard Norman Shaw, 1879. Plans of late-19th century apartments can be very diverse. In older types of building like the Viennese flat, the principal rooms at the front of the block are arranged as an enfilade, thus allowing a view through the centre of the apartment from one end to the other. The middle two rooms can each be entered through any of three doors, meaning that the walls are frequently interrupted. In the newer type of room plan – the London block of flats, for instance – there may be only one access to each room, resulting in long stretches of continuous wall.

too close to the side walls, so as to avoid the impression that the wall is about to end. All these considerations were summarized under a new term: *Geborgenheit* ('feeling of security') and the related *Geborgensein* ('being saved, contained, sheltered'). *Gemütlichkeit* had been turned into architectural and psychological factors. Critics might even describe the effects of elements of design as an 'activity'.[118]

The new darkened interior

Light

For most inhabitants, light in the domestic interior could hardly be a contentious issue. Does one not hope for as much of it as possible in a modern dwelling? Good rooms needed a 'blaze of light and colour'; 'without light' there was 'no cheerfulness'.[119] As the 19th century wore on, many factors contributed to a general change from dark to lighter dwellings. Throughout the 18th and 19th centuries windows were becoming larger, and already by the later 18th century the desire to step directly from the main rooms of the house into the garden through glazed doors had become widespread. The façades of many terraced houses on major London streets built from the 1820s to the 1850s (not to mention many houses in the Netherlands) have such large window openings that one wonders how the buildings can stand up; and from about the 1850s the much lower price of glass led to brighter dwellings for everyone, even the poor. In addition to windows of whatever size, large mirrors were widely used in the 18th and early 19th centuries to increase the amount of light in an interior, to provide another apparent light source and to make the room appear larger. Moreover, mirrors spoke of great expense. After mid-century this usage began to die out, partly on account of the new liking for solidity, and partly because glass was now cheaper.[120] One characteristic of many illustrations of interiors from the first half of the 19th century was that they tried their hardest to eliminate darkness; the result was that the room inside appeared as light as the world outside. 'A large amount of

Differing approaches to interiority, drawing in or excluding the outside world: title page from F. Robinson's *Sketches for Ornamental Villas* (1830; *left*); and large-windowed terraced houses on the City Road, London (*c.* 1840–50; *above*).

even light' was de rigueur.[121] During this period the relationship between light, air and health was being studied scientifically for the first time. Furthermore, the development of artificial lighting followed as a simple linear progression, so that more was now available at less cost. Any kind of small, dark room now signified age, poverty and backwardness. Humphry Repton, the architect and garden designer and one of the most influential manipulators of any kind of environment, captured this feeling succinctly in 1816, when he contrasted the 'cedar

below left A suburban house, London, 1885. Many new vernacular-inspired houses show an astonishing decrease in the size of the windows.

below Design by E. W. Godwin for a sash window with a small-paned upper section (1874) – a style that became widespread in Britain and the United States. The lower half is for looking out, while the upper half provides a sense of containment. This published design by a noted figure also demonstrates the way in which architects were now concerned with seemingly the most mundane details relating to exterior and interior fittings.

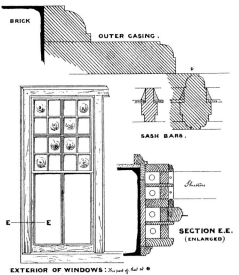

right Perhaps the brightest of 19th-century interiors: an etching of a German children's playroom by Johann Michael Voltz, 1823.

below 'French Window Curtains', from Ackermann's *Repository of Arts* (1811). The room's décor makes reference to the view outside.

parlour' – dark, old-fashioned and even empty – with the 'modern living room', which was bright and full of happy people.[122]

From colour to tone

'Colour is the most powerful mental influence in the home', wrote Candace Wheeler in 1893.[123] But by the later 19th century it had become subsidiary to questions of tone. In Chapter III the discussion of colour concentrated on its historical, natural and scientific aspects, as well as on the artistic rules that governed its application, while the psychological effects of colour had been taken for granted for a long time. The old dichotomy of form versus colour – or, to use the Renaissance terms, *disegno* and *colore* – could now be employed to underline the special value of the latter: 'it is design that gives beings their form; it is colour that gives them life', claimed Diderot.[124] Romantic critics agreed, writing endlessly on 'the pleasures of colour' and the 'effect of colour on practical life'.[125]

For centuries certain characteristics had been assigned to particular colours, such as blue being 'cold' and red being 'warm', to give the most obvious examples. Goethe tried to be more precise: 'yellow, red-yellow and yellow are alerting', and put one in an active mood; yellow was 'warm and comfortable'; and blue was seen as 'empty and cold'. Green was already understood as restful in the later 18th century.[126] David Ramsay Hay proposed a detailed list of the effects of certain colours, such as 'gay', 'lively', 'sombre', 'solemn', etc. However, discussion of a room's colour symbolism was made difficult when the décor contained more than one colour. It is notable that Hay and, following him, Loudon rarely named actual colours when advising on the character of a room, but instead stressed the general tones or effects mentioned above.[127] Increasingly, 'warm' seemed to suffice as a recommendation. During the 1870s and 1880s the 'warmest' colour in domestic interior design – certainly as far as Central Europe was concerned – was brown, often with 'a tendency towards red'. Was this choice of colour influenced by the fashion for wooden interiors or vice versa?, asked Luthmer, but he could not give an answer.[128] Certainly the dominance of colour as an issue in the middle of the century was pushed aside by the new emphasis on materiality, on textures; in practice, this meant a lack of interest in, even a dislike of, bright primary colours, and a predilection for the many new broken and subtle shades.

Attention now also turned to a further vehicle for colour: glass. Stained glass was an artistic medium of considerable importance in the 19th century.[129] During the 17th and 18th centuries the practice of colouring glass had practically died out, but it was revived in the context of antiquarianism and religious medievalism. It offered a darkish atmosphere, and in the home its strong colours gave a 'softened light' that was much sought after. From a practical point of view, filling windows with coloured glass also provided a degree of opaqueness that was useful in situations where 'the view is actually ugly'.[130] For Falke in 1883, clear glass implied 'nothing, sobriety, banality', but now stained glass 'lends poetry to the room, adds solemnity, life and warmth, a touch of serenity'.[131] The most popular kind was probably 'cathedral glass', which was opaque, mostly light green in colour and slightly textured. The most heavily worked glass was produced in Germany – 'bottle glass' (*Butzenscheiben*), supposedly made from the bottom of bottles and taken to be Altdeutsch – and in the United States, where Tiffany and La Farge created new kinds of brilliantly luminous glass décor.[132]

The changing meaning of darkness

One of the most astonishing developments in the later 19th century was the abandonment of light interiors in favour of a completely new preference for relative darkness. This change was clearly related to a number of factors already mentioned, particularly the fashion for small spaces, low ceilings and a look of massiveness. First, however, one should consider the liking

A Romantic conception of a dark religious interior: the Oratory at Fonthill, designed by James Wyatt for William Beckford, *c.* 1810–12.

Ut disciplinam Christi capiat Nicodemus,
Ipsi nocte adiens dogmata cuncta capit.

Night, an 18th-century illustration from Cesare Ripa's *Iconologia*, first published 1593 and 1603. The inscription reads: 'In order to comprehend the teachings of Christ, Nicodemus visited him by night and learned them all.'

for darkness in connection with the picturesque. Chapter III discussed how picturesque elements could be used to add variety to the interior and to introduce unusual configurations that could be enjoyed from shifting viewpoints. The appreciation of a room was thereby identified ever more closely with pictorial representations. Ultimately, a room, any room, was to be seen like a painting – 'almost identical', wrote Havard[133] – so that the manipulation of light inside the domestic room was intimately tied up with the history of painting. In addition, by the later 1870s a new medium began to be used more extensively for the representation of interiors: photography, whose tendency to produce a sharp contrast between light and dark was one of its preferred effects.[134]

According to the older traditions of art, light signified holiness and dark its opposite. Clearly the main problem is to explain how something that symbolized evil should have become a visual and mental asset in an everyday context. It began with the way many painters made a speciality of producing dark scenes. By the 17th century the genre of the nocturne had turned the night into something that seemed both threatening and exciting. At the same time those who sought religious meditation might opt for the night as a period of calmness and repose.[135] But this did not mean that artists wanted to divest darkness of its threatening character. Quite the contrary: during the 18th century the nocturnal subject attracted more and more attention, and it now became firmly connected to the new, completely secularized theory of the Sublime. Edmund Burke made a special point of ascribing aspects of the Sublime to large buildings with dark interiors. Thus one might have an actual experience of the Sublime rather than a fictional (literary or pictorial) one. It need not induce real terror, however, and this is Burke's famous trick: one is excited, even frightened, at the same time as knowing for sure that one will not be physically affected. In this way Burke established the possibility of a 'well-managed darkness', for instance in an old Gothic cathedral.[136] One such kind has already been mentioned: the interiors of the Gothic novel, which match a room with a person's mood. In the case of 'Gothic' darkness, the correspondence between design and mood is very close, precisely because both are so extreme. Some literary commentators even see the architecture as the main agent of the narrative ('the protagonists are so very much tied to the architecture'[137]). Essentially, the reader was titillated by the frightening stories while sitting comfortably in his or her well-lit, modern drawing room.

The rougher, older type of environment could be desirable particularly for the collector who amassed diverse non-Classical objects, as has been shown in Clive Wainwright's book *The*

The Antiquary's Cell by E. W. Cooke (1835). The interiors of collectors – at least of those devoted to non-Classical antiquities – evoked the darkness of old houses and the distant past from which the objects came.

above Alcove for the dining room of a villa in 'thirteenth-century' style, by Edward Buckton Lamb, 1835. Severity, even sombreness, became the rule for dining rooms, although they do not usually remind one of churches.

above right *Sir Walter Scott in his Armoury*, by Henry Stisted (1826).

Romantic Interior. From a merely technical point of view, creating darkness is not a difficult job for an architect or decorator. William Beckford's Oratory (his small domestic chapel) at Fonthill was almost pitch black. At Walter Scott's Abbotsford it was the Armoury, also relatively small, that was kept dark. The French Troubadour style of painting also employed dark interiors for a variety of historical scenes. Sometimes antiquarian grime was combined with old cottage grime – to be distinguished from the merely old and dingy that reign in many of Dickens's interiors, indicating that for him age and gloom were still largely negative qualities.[138]

A Scottish antiquarian interior: Joseph Noel Paton's 'cottage ornée' at Wooers-Alley, Dunfermline (1848).

The Melancholy Nun, an illustration from a German almanac (1815; *left*); and *The Ghost Story*, an engraving by R. W. Buss (1840s; *right*). Although both these interiors are gloomy and threatening, the role, or function, of the dark is rather different in each. The first, highly unusual, interior corresponds exactly with the character's exceptional mental state; in the case of the young female reader, there is only a momentary association of the extraordinary fictional content of the book with ordinary late-evening darkness in an everyday domestic interior.

Lullaby, an illustration by Johann Christiaan Bendorp for a Dutch edition of songs by Matthias Claudius (1833; *left*); and *Homely Happiness* by Daniel Chodowiecki, from a moralist tract on marriage (1774; *right*). In contrast to the previous two scenes, these images – and the painting overleaf – reflect an entirely straightforward use of the theme of darkness, allied to the time of day.

Remarks by early 19th-century French writers like Alfred de Musset or Chateaubriand indicate a transition from mysteriousness to solitariness and meditation, to at least a limited recognition of the usefulness of the dark in one's house. In the 1820s and 1830s, the *style cathédrale* and the darkly antiquarian interiors spread further. The mysterious aspect of darkness pertained in some French interiors into the latter part of the century, when it became linked with a more advanced kind of psychology – notably in the home of one of its most eminent practitioners, Jean-Martin Charcot.[139] On the other hand, continued interest in less extreme forms of darkness and their adaptation for the ordinary everyday interior can perhaps be compared to the way elements of violent 'Gothic' were taken up by writers of popular fiction to give their novels a frisson of manageable fear and excitement.

The cautious Andrew Jackson Downing addresses these issues under what he now calls the 'domesticity' and 'home-like expression' of Gothic. These qualities arise 'mainly from the chaste and quiet colours of the dark wood-work, the grave though rich hue of the carpets [and] walls': 'Those who love shadow, and the sentiment of antiquity and repose, will find most pleasure in the quiet tone which prevails in the Gothic style; as those who love sunshine, and the enjoyment of the present moment, will prefer the classical and modern styles.'[140] Here 'shadow', 'sentiment' and 'antiquity' have been almost completely purged of anything threatening. 'Antiquity' in this instance also referred to the old buildings of one's own country (to be explored in the next chapter), and the materials themselves now seem important ('the dark wood-work'). One is reminded of the medievalist Franz Pforr's description of his bride's bedstead: 'according to the old ways, the bed frame is made wholly of dark brown wood'.[141] However, Gothic soon fell out of favour for domestic architecture. To some extent its place was taken by the 'Oriental', meaning largely Arabic or Moorish, which now provided the mysterious and exotic, and which tended to be 'rather dark' too.[142]

But love for the quaint does not by itself completely explain why darkness turned from being threatening and disquieting to precisely the opposite: something that promised mildness and restfulness. Importantly, there were some rooms where relative darkness made more sense and could be regarded as normal. A new room type in which subdued lighting was preferred was the boudoir, which in some ways paralleled the secretiveness of the 'Gothic' interior; but at the same time it was a room that served an everyday use. The French-influenced Polish-Prussian illustrator Daniel Chodowiecki, working in the last quarter of the 18th century, adapted the subject of the dark interior to include aspects of everyday life, drawing individuals (mostly female) and families: 'wonderful groups in light and shade'.[143] His scenes found an echo in Georg Friedrich Kersting's images of solitary individuals at work in their homes in the evening or at night, with their careful depiction of artificial lighting. Significantly, Kersting had demystified the night, turning into normal, calculable darkness.[144] Whether romantic or not, artificial lighting, cheap and easy to regulate, banished much fear of the dark. As a corollary, the very light-coloured room began to go out of fashion; white walls and ceilings were considered 'crude'. Robert Adam had already banned them, and by 1830 pure white on buildings had been forbidden in Munich as harmful to the eyes.[145] Haweis thought that 'in a white room one can scarcely distinguish form and texture'. Designers were of course mindful of the obvious criticism that could be levelled at dark interiors: namely that they lacked an appearance of health and cleanliness. Of one particular 'crude white' ceiling, Lewis F. Day quipped: 'It looks so clean, even when it is not, that it makes all else look dirty, even though it may be clean.'[146]

Crucial in the formulation of a new meaning for subdued light were the universally legitimized sociological concepts of the comfortable home and family life. Every dweller – certainly every head of the family – who goes out to work all day was entitled to a period of rest, leisure or reflection upon their return.[147] The mellowness of eventide was a favourite topic in Romantic and post-Romantic popular poetry. Naturally, the contemplative element in all this principally concerned the individual, but it could influence communal situations, too: for the dining room, 'a room in which convivial conversation, wines and viands are consumed, the colour should never be white'.[148] In the 1850s the novelist Wilkie Collins complained bitterly of an uncomfortable experience in a modern room: 'all glared at you … There was no look of shadow, shelter, secrecy, or retirement in any one nook or corner of these four gaudy walls' – a complaint reminiscent of John Ruskin's vitriolic attack on the modernity of the interior in William Holman's Hunt's painting *The Awakening Conscience*. Darkness – or mellowness – and comfort concurred perfectly.[149]

From about 1870 onwards the psychology of subdued light, even of the 'lighted cavern',[150] appeared obvious. For Falke, light should be reduced 'for physical and mental reasons', and, according to Havard, any evenly lit room would soon be 'tiring'.[151] In 1869 Lucae wrote that rooms without deep shadows were like someone continuously giving the 'same conventional smile', and could never produce 'the homely poetic chiaroscuro' that 'evokes in us the feeling of comfort'.[152] Blanc rhapsodized about 'tranquillity … the shadows that favour dreaming, the silent shadows'. Furthermore, some even claimed that darkness could emanate warmth. For

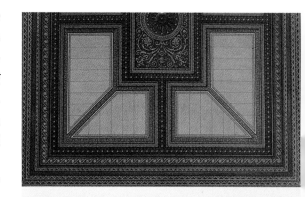

above Ceiling and wall designs, most probably for a dining room; by Gropius & Schmieden architects, Berlin, 1877.

left Georg Friedrich Kersting, *Man Reading by Lamplight* (1814).

opposite 'Mrs. Vanderbilt's Boudoir', designed by the Herter Brothers for William H. Vanderbilt's house, New York, *c.* 1881–82. Here, precious objects serve to catch the light (see also pp. 110, 115).

Falke, the relatively dark Renaissance interior was much 'warmer' in its effect than the 'modern' bright room. Luthmer recommends that bedrooms should be 'in a rather darker tone', since it makes them 'more comfortable'. Rooms by the renowned Mainz furnishing firm of Bembé & Co. come out as the most consistently dark: in a text written by their chief designer, Carl Behr, in 1881, the epithet 'warm' is much repeated.[153]

The manipulation of light

The origins of the 19th-century fascination with darkness could be found way back in the history of art. It had two aspects: first, the meaning of darkness, and second, the methods by which it could be represented in fine art. In the latter context, darkness by itself had no function: it appeared merely as the absence of light. Likewise, it is not darkness that a designer 'manages' in a room, but light. Painters strove to depict convincing light sources within their works, an effect that was most successful when the rest of the painting was quite dark.[154] In architecture, the contrast between light and dark had acquired a dynamic of its own during the

'A boudoir in the Renaissance style' by Bembé & Co., Mainz, 1881. This reproduction, from *The Builder*, somewhat exaggerates the darkness.

One of the few English illustrations to show a truly dark interior: a hallway from Mrs J. E. Panton's article 'Artistic Homes, and How to Make Them' (London, 1887).

later 18th century: designers had adopted the technique of geometric sciagraphy to render shadows in their interiors accurately, a prominent example being the Adam brothers' publication of their own buildings from 1773.[155]

Within real interiors, the control of light was now one of the designer's main responsibilities. This involved a gradual move away from the passive acceptance of light as it came in through large, regularly spaced windows. By the middle of the century English architects, in particular Pugin, had started a revolution in the shape and placement of windows. They did this primarily because of major changes in the type of exterior that was preferred: the even arrangement of frequent window openings was no longer in favour. Instead, designers preferred long stretches of solid wall and openings of different shapes and sizes. Besides, it was argued that windows should vary according to room usage. The question was asked: what character, based upon its function, should a room exhibit, and what kind of window opening best corresponds with that character?[156] On the whole, designers did not mind the fact that the total area occupied by windows was now much reduced. From the 1870s, the reintroduction of Georgian-type glazing bars in the upper half of the Anglo-American sash window provided a subtle method of restricting or breaking up direct light from outside. Occasionally a note of caution enters the discussion: rooms giving onto narrow streets ought to be made light, but where there was enough daylight or artificial light, Falke advised that one should be 'unafraid of light or dark and let artistic concerns have an effect'. Twelve years later, in 1883, he wrote: 'Unity of light is the main requirement in a picture … and it is the same for an artistic room.'[157]

Interior by the architects Ihne & Stegmüller, Berlin, 1879. This was the type of room criticized by Falke and Havard for the 'unsightly glare' of its large windows.

As noted at the very beginning of the century, curtains constituted an important element in the design of a room and were often used in conjunction with another 19th-century innovation, window blinds.[158] Although on the whole rooms were still becoming lighter during the first half of the 19th century, the bulk and diversity of curtains was also on the increase. Yet large windows posed a major design problem inside a room: they were felt to be bland interruptions in the décor, unfilled holes, a 'glaring mass of light' or of 'hard, sharp sunlight'. In the dining room, it was 'better to shut the sunshine out altogether'.[159] The purpose and appearance of curtains were much discussed. Their role was to soften the contours of the windows, to effect 'the transition, the interface with the wall … to break with their soft flow the sharp architectural lines of the window'.[160] But they also helped vary the light in a room. As we have seen above, Havard explicitly states that lighting which is evenly distributed over all objects in a room will 'have a tiring effect on us'.[161] Instead, light must be 'carefully directed'.[162] In most cases there ought to be only one light source: 'the light falls in a broad, self-contained mass and becomes more effective through contrast with its surroundings, constituting an artistic element'. The bay window or oriel was a preferred light source, as were windows set deep in a niche in the wall. In some of his most elaborate theories of the interior, Havard writes of the 'point of light', and of the way one appreciates 'a principal mass of light and a dominating mass of darkness'. Furthermore, he suggested that in a room with two windows, one should actively control the light, pulling the curtains wherever necessary. Luthmer hated the regular distribution of windows, and windows on opposite walls caused 'a hopeless situation: wall them up'. Blanc, like Havard, praises 'a managed light … entering through a single opening, and not interfered with by another light source'.[163] The main Anglo-American critics were not quite so discerning. Christopher Dresser,

'Gradual coloration, an example to imitate' (*above left*); and 'decoration with an abrupt change of coloration, to be condemned' (*above*): both from Henry Havard's *L'Art dans la maison* (1884). Havard makes absolutely sure that his readers know which is right and which is wrong by placing the words underneath each picture. The issue here is one of tone: an interior must not consist of a number of separate, flat, evenly lit or evenly shaded surfaces, but should be united through a continuous gradation of tone.

somewhat paradoxically, suggests: 'If it can be had, I like much window-space, to let in the light, but the walls I prefer of darkish hue.'[164] Mrs Haweis is even more puzzling: 'The most beautiful rooms are usually dark in colour with large windows through which plenteous sunlight streams.' In any case she, too, affirms the value of 'fine lights and shadows' – 'a pretty effect of light is worth half a dozen extra ornaments'. Moreover, contrary to established wisdom, she goes on to say that dark walls contribute to an appearance of size, while white walls make the room look smaller; even a white ceiling makes the 'room look lower'.[165] Mrs Spofford's summary gives us a choice between 'lights and splendid effects … or soft glooms and shadows'.[166]

The effect of bottle-glass windows: 'How unfinished and cold a room can be without coloured glass lowering the light' – advice from the furnishing firm Schäffer & Walcker, Berlin, 1890. An earlier comment on the same issue – that of controlling light – reads: 'the windows … are fitted with designs or bottle glass … in order to lend the room a poetic twilight, the coloured shine of an old room' (Vienna, 1872).

An alternative to the careful gradation of tones was to introduce a sharp contrast of light and dark, as in this dining room at Wilhelmstrasse 71, Berlin, by Friebus & Lange (1878).

opposite Léon Feuchère, design for a smoking room, Paris, *c.* 1857. Feuchère was known chiefly for his stage designs.

Such careful considerations of the effects of lighting were relevant for the whole room. In the previous chapter we dealt with the seemingly freer placement and grouping of objects; a major factor in achieving a successful arrangement was how they appeared in sharp or fleeting light: writers mentioned 'bodies in light', or light 'refracted by contrast and reflection'. For Mrs Haweis, it was clear that 'in a white room one can scarcely distinguish form and texture'.[167] Havard's analysis of these phenomena was more elaborate: the 'intensity of light manifests itself not only in the degree of brightness with which it hits the projecting parts of an object, but also in the degree of darkness enveloping those parts that remain in shadow'.[168] Here we return once more to the question of materials and the characteristic way in which they respond to light, such as the shiny surfaces of silk or the soft gleam of French polish on wood. Blanc goes into ecstasies over the fall of light on textiles: 'with a doubling of light, the fabric will regain in its prominent parts the effect it looses through the mass of shadows in its grooves'.[169] Shiny wooden floors were also a popular option. Dark backgrounds were viewed as advantageous in the way they help pictures and people 'come out' better. As a whole, 'a room has to surge from the dark into the light as it does in nature'. Yet the new movement for dark ceilings clearly ran against this old recipe; Falke, having cited it, then voices his doubts. However, he also warns against the opposite, floors that are too light.[170] Picturesqueness now came to include a heightened sensitivity towards the effects of light in paintings and in fiction, as can be sensed, for instance, in the work of Henry James.

Sharp contrasts of light and dark had their opposite: diffuse light. The later 19th century saw soft light as a distinct formal category. Havard maintained that an evenly lit room would cause fatigue, but this did not apply to rooms with a low light. Here, evenness could be highly desirable – a quality best expressed by the word 'tone'. Charles Blanc wrote of 'the restfulness … that comes from a softer light'.[171] This meant that the light curtains that appeared in the earlier 19th century were not superseded by heavy drapes, but only supplemented by them: 'The see-through curtains have the important task of diffusing the light that comes into the room and thus moderating it' (Luthmer).[172] In the end, all lighting effects were integrated carefully with the composition of the room as a whole; for Blanc, 'restfulness' also results from well-ordered furniture and the articulation of the wall, and even, he advises his readers, from simply being tidy. 'I like the whole tone of the room', wrote an American critic.[173]

Lastly, it is probable that artificial light played an important, though an indirect, role in the taste for dark interiors: simply put, it helped allay our fear of the dark and our sense of being so heavily dependent on natural light. With 'artificial light, one may operate as one likes', claimed one critic.[174] On the whole, however, discussions on the subject of lighting were dominated by technology and economics (mentioned briefly in the Introduction), even if candlesticks and lamps were also important vehicles for ornamentation.[175] The concept of manipulating artificial light sources for decorative purposes gained ground only slowly. Falke advocated an 'artistic' handling of lighting 'where, during the evening, artificial sources are the main providers of light', but did not go into much detail.[176] When electric light came in (very slowly) from the early 1880s, it was praised for revealing natural colours ('pure white light, natural colours'). At the same time gaslight was often declared to be unsuitable for living rooms, mainly on health grounds but also for aesthetic reasons. We are asked to improve on the 'old central gas chandelier … by placing two candles on mantels and arranging the gas bracket with saucer globes a little lower than the étagère mirrors, so that the position of light might harmonize with the general arrangement of the furniture'. Candles maintained their popularity: twenty candles 'carefully spread over the room' could give an assembled group of friends 'a more solemn and festive effect than the gaslight with the "patent burner"'.[177] In Continental Europe, the family congregating around a table in a corner of a modest room, illuminated by a main light hanging from the ceiling, became a favourite image, somewhat paralleling the family congregated around the fireplace in Anglo-Saxon countries.[178]

How widespread was this liking for fairly dark or shadowy rooms? It appears to have been popular above all in Central Europe, and also to a lesser extent in the United States. In spite of their heavy theorizing, the French did not seem to subscribe all that strongly to the practice. Although the new 'Art' faction in England was opposed to whiteness, it did not like extremes of darkness either, and nor, it seems, did architect-designers like Norman Shaw. English critics remained equivocal: '"Do you wish the room light or dark?"', Dresser purports to quote a decorator. In America, Eugene Gardner drew and wrote about both light and moderately dark rooms, but Mrs Church broke with a firmly established convention when she demanded a well-lit dining room: 'sunlight, sunlight, sunlight'.[179] By the 1880s, the new 'refine-ment' in England had already begun to shape rooms that showed an unpicturesque evenness of tone and a lightness of form. In Munich, Gabriel von Seidl was turning towards the use of lighter woods, and his porte-parole, Georg Hirth, complained about the heavy curtain and its 'senseless darkening'.[180]

As discussed above, one of the sources – perhaps the most important source – for the dark domestic interior was fine art painting. There was certainly a lot of dark painting around in those decades, and Rembrandt's work and reputation loomed larger than ever.[181] And yet an equally powerful movement was on the rise – that of *plein air* painting – which embodied the exact opposite and had soon ousted most of the older preferences for the picturesque. The Germans reacted particularly strongly against their culture of the 'braune Sosse'. The dark domestic interior was violently condemned, and the psychological qualities that were associated with it began to be ridiculed. Ultimately, light and dark could not convey meanings beyond a general psychological impact. The search for more specific cultural meanings is what the next chapter will explore.

Salon from the Munich Exhibition of 1888, designed by Otto Dorn from Lahr (Baden). The control of light in a room had become one of the most important of the designer's tasks. To convey shades of light and dark effortlessly was a challenge that photography was only just beginning to meet. In this case, it was made possible by the light shining into the room from behind the photographer.

V

Character

Jean Pape, design for a *Trinkstube*, or drinking den, in the German Renaissance style, Dresden, 1888 (see p. 229).

Rooms and styles

To provide a room with a theme that spoke of something beyond the domestic realm was nothing new. But this kind of room, by its very definition, had to be exceptional: a private chapel, for example, or a room in an 18th-century palace designed to house a collection of ceramics. To create rooms of a special character for the ordinary dwelling was one of the major new preoccupations of 19th-century design. This brings one back to the question asked at the beginning of this book: can a poetic home be both special and ordinary? Throughout, this discussion has had an upward trajectory, from the perceived lowliness of the trades to the more elevated language of 'design', then on to intellectual discussions on the subject of the home and the work of bona fide artists and artistic-minded designers. This chapter will bring in many eminent members of the architectural profession and even touch on aristocratic dwellings. At the same time, many 19th-century policies of design stressed the value of 'simplicity', to which we shall also return from time to time.

When something or someone is described as 'having character', this can refer both to strength of expression and to individuality, which in turn implies diversity. The word 'character' was foregrounded more and more during the course of the 18th century, especially in French architectural discourse. But in spite of its force, it is also rather vague, and betrays a reluctance to define forms clearly. In its desire for a convincing systematization of forms and their meaning, the 19th century took to the word 'style'. At its most basic level, it means the same as 'character'; what it lacks in impact, it gains in clarity. Among the various systems for codifying artefacts, the 19th-century concept of 'style' must be rated as one of the most successful, and it operates almost like biological taxonomy. 'Classical' or 'Gothic', for instance, were widely known terms, attached to clearly distinguishable forms that pointed to rich historical and geographical backgrounds.[1]

Yet the term 'style', like 'character', in fact has two meanings. Before the later 18th century, 'possessing style' was simply synonymous with possessing artistic quality – a meaning that still persists today. There was furniture, and there was furniture 'de style', for example.[2] For centuries, only one style could constitute 'style' – that is, the 'right' kind of décor – and that was the classical. Then, by 1800, other styles began to be seen as possessing at least an interesting 'character' – one may cite here Goethe's overview: 'partly harmonious' (the classical styles); 'partly characteristic' (some other styles); and also 'often disharmonious' (the outlandish styles).[3] Character and individuality have an in-built trend to multiplicity. Many theorists and historians of the 1830s–50s saw it as their task to describe all these styles in detail, and then to rate them as of strictly equal value. Loudon and Downing provided illustrations of large villas in which they scrupulously applied different styles to the same plan and elevation, both externally and internally. Under the catchword 'historicism', 20th-century

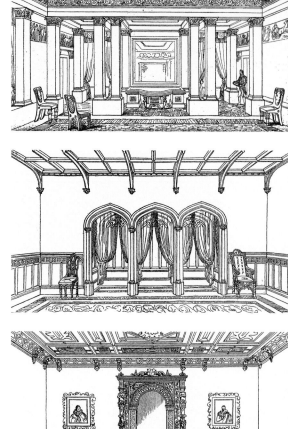

The emphasis on stylistic diversity: three plates from Martin Kimbel's *Der decorative Ausbau* (1870s; *left*); and a dining room in the 'Grecian, Tudor and Elizabethan' styles from John Claudius Loudon's *Encyclopaedia* (1833; *above*). Loudon's view was that the same architectural shell could be decorated successfully in at least three very different ways. By the 1870s, however, his basic set of styles had given way to a much wider and more sophisticated range of labels. Martin Kimbel's designs offer an anteroom in 'Néo-Grec', a library in 'Romanesque Gothic', and a salon in a fanciful mixture of Louis styles.

Dining room in 16th-century Italian Renaissance style at Villa Siemens, Berlin-Charlottenburg, by Richard Lucae, 1870s (*right*); and a 'cabinet in the Rococo style' by Anton Pössenbacher and Josef Wagner for the Munich Exhibition, 1888 (*below*). Italian Renaissance and Rococo were the period's two most frequently used styles.

Those who wanted a change from the endless repetition of classical décor or from cheaper and often flimsy-looking Rococo furnishings could resort to something entirely different: interiors inspired by the Near or Far East. Over time, however, these European versions of outlandish styles changed very considerably.

opposite 'Boudoir turc' in the Hôtel Beauharnais, Paris, *c.* 1810. This early example of complete Near Eastern décor shows meticulously detailed and unusual ornamentation on all surfaces.

right Orientalizing room in Paris, *c.* 1890. By the end of the century, the Oriental style was conceived as combining softness, comfort and informality, with objects seemingly spread around at random.

art historians assumed that the old styles were simply there, ready to be picked up and copied. But what needs to be stressed is the amount of study that went into finding and analysing examples of these 'learned styles'.[4] For the manufacturer, each 'new' style (that is, each newly discovered old style) 'required new schooling for the assistants'.[5] For much of the century the trade could appear quite ignorant, proffering mongrel labels such as 'style Roco-Louis-Grec'.[6] But publishers of pattern books gradually started to label their images historically and to arrange them chronologically, with some examples actually claiming to contain examples 'in all styles' – which could amount to some twenty or more labels. Occasionally the trade attempted to demonstrate its probity and originality by using additional terms such as 'moderne' or 'fantaisie'.[7]

Thus the first method of addressing the question of style was to set all styles neatly side by side. But by 1840 an alternative had emerged, mainly among the neo-Gothicists, which affirmed that one historical style could be applicable to all designs – an approach usually named revivalism. Gothic Revivalists like Pugin and Viollet-le-Duc made enormous efforts to provide detailed histories or theories, or both, for the style. Somewhat later, after mid-century, yet another attitude had developed: a belief in the serious mixing of many styles, called eclecticism. It is these two modes, revivalism and eclecticism, that will concern us most in this chapter.

What complicates matters is the way style labels vary in their applicability, especially in the field of interior decoration. Within the context of this book, such labels were clearest and most useful when they were used to describe architectural features and wooden furnishings. The latter, for example, could mostly be associated with Gothic or the Renaissance; heavy textiles usually spoke of the Italian Renaissance; and a house painter might be expected to be familiar with the 'Pompeian' style. But it was more difficult to link other materials, such as glass or metal, to a historical style. As a rule, domestic interiors displayed a style less forcefully than the exterior. Naturally, some of the richest houses did demonstrate strong and consistently applied style preferences, both outside and inside, but the overwhelming majority of more modest interiors used watered-down versions of the classical, about which there was comparatively little discussion during most of the 19th century. By 1870–80, the main 'art at home' writers were openly reluctant to discuss the issue. Richard Lucae, considering the issues of space and light in 1869, professed to avoid it: 'I purposely did not mention style.'[8]

The question of style has not thus far received much attention here; instead, discussion has centred on the new interest in textures, production techniques and abstract, formal elements of design. The argument must now proceed in the opposite direction. It must be recognized that historical style is something that can be discerned in (or read into) most, if not all, arte-facts. Notwithstanding the focus on form, space and light in Lucae's article, his own interiors were thoroughly characterized by the architectural elements of the Italian Renaissance. Style and form have been central themes in art history ever since this period of the 19th century: art historians of the 20th century borrowed from architectural discussions of the 1870s and 1880s, so that today 'form' is commonly understood as something abstract, while 'style' is now more tied to issues of meaning.

Another reason why Lucae wanted to sideline the question of style was that he tried to look beyond small-scale décor, beyond the smaller details of a room. Again, 'style' or 'diversity of styles' seemed linked above all to the multiplicity of decorative motifs. It was the apparent randomness of much décor, and the facile throwing-around of labels, that appeared so arbitrary to the serious revivalists and, later, to all modernists. What follows is a consideration of the intense meanings that can be conveyed by form and décor, which includes the smallest decorative details of a room as well as its overall feel.

Renaissance, Rococo, Oriental

The designer's wish to experiment with a diversity of styles could, and should, coincide with the user's desire to impart a different character to each of the common rooms in a dwelling. 'Every room should be furnished in a style not inconsistent with the use for which it is set apart', wrote Mrs Parkes in 1825.[9] It is very doubtful that she was referring here to the fully developed panoply of historical styles; what she probably had in mind was a generalized differentiation of character – darker and more serious, light and colourful, etc. In rich houses, décor could be further distinguished through the inclusion of diverse figurative work: 'the ballroom [decorated] with musicians, the bathroom with naked figures, the dining room with the delights of the kitchen'.[10] From about mid-century 'style' took over: within one house we meet a salon in the Louis XV style, a dining room in Henri II, a living room in the German Renaissance, smoking-room Japanese, and a bathroom in 'the English manner'.[11] Contrast was clearly the watchword in the new villas of Strasbourg in 1890.

The most commonly opposed styles were a sober version of classical and the Rococo. A frequently used label from about mid-century onwards was 'Renaissance', applied to the classical forms of the 16th and 17th centuries. The term was first coined in France in the 1820s and 1830s,[12] although it exited little discussion – in stark contrast to all the new writing about Gothic. Classical forms suited mainly the 'serious' side of the house – the dining room and the study, for example – while the Rococo seemed appropriate for the salon and for rooms assigned to women. The term 'Rococo' was used widely from the middle of the century, but in fact the style was revived in several 'waves': in 1830s–50s Vienna, this mode of interior décor became known as 'Blondelscher Stil' (after the French 18th-century writer J.-F. Blondel) and was later dubbed 'Second Rococo', while a 'Third Rococo' arrived in the 1880s and 1890s.[13] Naturally, everybody knew that these styles were Parisian, but since France was the centre of fashion anyway, the French aspect was not usually given prominence. The 'Louis' labels were always current, and France took them up again decisively when the 'French' 18th century was in vogue (to be discussed below). The Rococo of the 19th century was, moreover, a style largely generated by the interior decoration trades; it seems that architects were rarely involved. From the 1860s to 1880s the English applied arts reformers, and also Falke, condemned it as decadent whenever they could.[14] All in all, in terms of validity of expression for the producer as well for the user – it was one of the most potent conveyors of 'elegance' in one's immediate material environment – the Rococo was perhaps the most successful and most commonly used style. In addition, after the 18th century it was perhaps the only one to be employed almost exclusively for the home. It has remained popular across the world into the 21st century.

More sharply drawn was the contrast between home-grown Western styles and 'exotic' styles, which were always clearly recognizable. The use of Eastern styles in the West has quite a long history, beginning with the 'Chinese' modes of the late 17th century, continuing with early 19th-century 'Moorish' or 'Indian' styles, and consolidating itself from about 1830 under the general label 'Oriental'. The significance of Orientalism for the 19th-century domestic interior lay in the fact that it was employed only rarely for other types of building (occasionally for public baths and for synagogues); even in a domestic context it was used rarely for exteriors and infrequently for whole interiors. Essentially it was restricted to the boudoir and the smoking room, rooms that were both markedly gender-specific, evoking the image either of the harem or of the tobacco-smoker.[15] To many, the Oriental style convincingly marked out a sphere of intense privacy and intimacy: 'rooms [are] devoted exclusively to comfortable resting and to cosy chatting, under a lowered light from a hanging lamp'.[16]

More than most others, the Oriental style was flexible in the way it could be realized. Full Oriental décor could be immensely elaborate and controlled, and it was usually found only in the richest homes, but later in the century a sense of 'Oriental comfort' could be derived also from the informal display of cheaper loose textiles. By the 1870s the market was flooded with Oriental or Orientalizing metalwork, which could conjure up a hint of exotic atmosphere in any of the living rooms. In contrast to the Gothic and the classical, the Oriental was not considered a 'high' artistic style – or, rather, the distinction between 'high' and vernacular was not made. Neither did it appear to need heavy theorizing, which perhaps also helped its spread. The Arab and Indian Oriental styles were finally joined by Japonisme, whose influence on décor was mainly visible in graphic artworks, certain flower motifs, and precious ceramics and their colours. Examples of Japanese décor being extended over a whole room were somewhat rarer.[17]

All in all, whatever the atmosphere these options could evoke, the Renaissance, Rococo and Oriental styles did not require much commitment to, or personal identification with, a particular culture on the part of the Western user – the classical Italian Renaissance least of all. 'Style', it was claimed at the beginning, was a manner of labelling forms that made them appear highly specific and rich in meaning. Some designers and their spokespersons were working

'Interior in the Japanese Style' by Reinhardt Freiherr von Seydlitz, Munich, 1886. The main attraction of the 'Japanese' interior was a particular kind of linearity that could lead to a high degree of integration.

opposite 'Japon', from Henry Havard's *Dictionnaire de l'ameublement* of 1887–89.

eagerly on a set of styles that sent out a stronger message, but that also appeared convincing to many and usable in the home as a whole.

Revivalism: the romantic castle interior

In its early days, Gothic Revivalism benefited from a group of immensely determined patrons – figures such as Horace Walpole, Friedrich Wilhelm IV of Prussia and Sir Walter Scott, who created highly idiosyncratic interiors by using a comprehensive system of 'historical poetics'.[18] One reason for their existence was their owners' activity as private collectors, particularly of non-Classical artefacts such as medieval and Renaissance armour. Innumerable smaller residences in the Gothic style soon followed. In Paris, one of the most spectacular collections – that belonging to Alexandre Du Sommerard – became Europe's first major museum of medieval and Renaissance applied arts in 1843. The Musée de Cluny, as it became known, may also be considered one of the first public museums of material culture; moreover, it marked the beginning of 'period rooms' – the practice of arranging objects and wall décor from one period into a unified ensemble. A decade or so later, Victor Hugo fitted out his home-in-exile, Hauteville House in Guernsey, with remarkably complete interiors by reusing old panelling and carving on all its walls.[19] Many medieval and exotic paraphernalia then found their way into the ordinary 'poetic home', even if this popularized ideal no longer corresponded to the exceptional character of the 'romantic interior'.

With the eclipse of classicism after Napoleon I, there was a readiness to experiment with styles also in many French interiors. Gothic Revival painting led to the Troubadour style in art and to the often extremely elaborate *style cathédrale* in furnishings.[20] In mid-1830s France, as in

Britain, enthusiasm for the Middle Ages began to lose some of its exclusivity, and designers turned towards the 16th century and what was held to be a proper national Renaissance style under the vigorous patronage of Henri II. 'Henri Deux' became one of the 'serious' modes of furnishing, most suitable for the dining room. It was easily recognizable, with its square out-lines, well-ordered sets of low-backed chairs, richly turned legs, wooden panelling, heavy curtains, sparsely handled leather upholstery and a darkish atmosphere overall. But the Henri II

The Romantic interior in France and its derivatives: Princess Marie's salon in the Tuileries, Paris, in a painting by Prosper Lafaye (1842; *above*), and a Parisian dining room in the Henri II style (*c.* 1880; *below*). Following Britain's lead, France came up with its own Romantic interiors from the 1820s, whether in the Gothic style or in a romanticized Renaissance. After mid-century these were consolidated into an internationally accepted French Northern Renaissance style, but one that lacked the revivalist fervour of the Old English and Altdeutsch movements. In France, Henri II itself was now largely restricted to dining rooms.

style had very few academic spokespersons and, unlike its 'old' English and German neo-Renaissance equivalents, it was not connected to the deeply felt impulse of the incipient neo-vernacular movements. Neither did it enjoy a close association with the concept of 'vieille France'. Henri II furniture itself remained in the sphere of the trade, although during the late 1860s it was produced by some of the trade's most distinguished members – Fourdinois, for example, with his immensely admired figurative carvings.[21] It was effectively the *ancien régime* that embodied a really 'French' choice – the styles of the 18th century, to be discussed nearer the end of this chapter.

By the mid-19th century, the key protagonists of the Gothic Revival were the architect-theorists themselves: the indefatigable Pugin, Viollet-le-Duc and Georg Gottlob Ungewitter. All of them were also active in the design of domestic furnishings, but their influence was spread principally through their writings, polemics, theories and the illustrations they drew and published. They defended themselves staunchly against the champions of other styles; out went the liberal outlook of Loudon and Downing and the idea of stylistic diversity inside the home. With his sharp, commonsensical rationalist tone, and with his plea for 'truth' in planning and in the treatment of materials, Pugin made the greatest impact. Viollet-le-Duc conducted intensive research into medieval objects of all kinds and created a particular way of explaining form through practical use, although this did not lead him to recommend unambiguously a French medieval style for contemporary environments. Ungewitter's vigorous illustrations spread a picturesque take on Gothic – perhaps rather too picturesque, and certainly too expensive for 'normal' consumption.[22] The greatest impetus for a themed home would come in the 1860s and 1870s from a younger group of architects and critics.

Dining room, Paris, *c.* 1890: a late example of the French Renaissance style, but here more sober and vernacularized.

Distant yet familiar: national and vernacular revivals

No more treatises, no more strict rules! The generation of designers that followed Pugin, Viollet-le-Duc and the advocate of the Italian Renaissance, Semper, could perhaps be forgiven for laying aside the severe architectural and moral exhortations, the thousands of pages of theories and the precisely detailed illustrations of old churches. Surely this was not the way to design the everyday home. Many members of this younger generation, such as Philip Webb, Norman Shaw and Gabriel von Seidl, hardly published a word.

And yet these designers did remain faithful to a revivalist spirit, to the basic values of the Gothic Revival, proclaiming their profound convictions in everything they did, both intense and relaxed at the same time. In essence, the doctrine of 'truth to materials' moved towards an ever greater appreciation of the colour, and especially the textures, of materials for their own sake. But this did not mean that all connotations, all meanings were abandoned. On the contrary, the importance of meaning if anything grew, but it was a different kind of meaning that was being sought. The new trend departed from the earlier revivalist adherence to one chosen style and instead embraced the eclectic. The mighty terms 'Gothic' and 'classical' lost something of their appeal: the new names for old styles now indicated a greater vagueness but also a much deeper love. This vagueness primarily resulted from the period of architectural history that now attracted most attention – the 16th and 17th centuries – which came between late Gothic and the purer classical or Renaissance styles and thus constituted a transitional period of 'mixed styles' in itself. But the relationship between a style, any style, and a particular nation or a region was now much stronger, which lent it legitimacy. A style – a way of ornamenting, building and crafting – was now held to be a direct result of geography and the perceived general character of a people. There was now a greater emphasis on geographical diversity and multiplicity throughout Europe, and thus also a move away from the old universalism of design.

Key to this new movement was the fact that designers were looking at a 'lower' level of artefact. Architectural analysis had so far been applied almost exclusively to the world of 'high' style and décor. Now less accomplished examples of décor could also be found attractive, if at first only because they appeared curious or quaint. Increasingly, elements like the wooden surfaces inside a peasant hut or the rougher textures and 'simple' colours of some textiles could be appreciated aesthetically, as well as being taken as manifestations of regional peasant cultures. As Teresa Jabłońska said of Stanisław Witkiewicz, who led the revival of a wooden 'Old Polish' style from the late 1880s, 'the artist established the choice of forms … while the critic and the theorist established a moral framework of values, as "signs of the people"'.[23] In some cases, as with Witkiewicz and William Morris, the two agents – artist and guru – were one and the same person.

Whatever definitions of beauty were current, these newly discovered forms could attract as much attention as any element of high style evident in buildings or in the works of the established applied arts. By the end of the century, the principal agreed term for this type of material was 'folk art'. For the period under discussion here, however – the 1860s to the 1880s – a comprehensive label was still lacking; the clearest designation – 'vernacular' or, strictly speaking, 'vernacular revival' – was as yet rarely used.[24] A key value was 'simplicity'; like 'atmosphere', it was a vague and generalized quality that was held to be created unconsciously. However, it would be naive to disregard the sophistication that underpinned the new appreciation of the 'simple old' and any 'vernacular' design. In the words of one young English architect, it was all the result of 'observation … sensitiveness to the most subtile [*sic*] and infinitesimal relations of form and colour'.[25]

It seemed axiomatic that all folk art was 'old', and yet it is important to point out the new elements in this appreciation of oldness. Previously, the antiquarian and romantic 'old' had to be something rarefied, something that had to be searched out in antiquity or in the deep, dark and distant Middle Ages.[26] The object was then studied with great care, for clues as to date and authorship. Anything else old – common oldness – was not worth noticing; even in Dickens's work, the sense of a bad or humdrum oldness still prevailed. Now both the new stress on the vernacular and new studies of the architecture of more recent centuries meant that the old could be found much more widely: design appreciation was catching up, one might say, with the Wordsworthian view of the ordinary. By the same token, for any given vernacular artefact there might be very little to be said in terms of precise dating and history. Authenticity and meaning now resided in materiality rather than in anything bookish.

In 1874 the young and eager architect-designer Basil Champneys visited some old towns on the Sussex coast, where he found 'homely scenes' that contained a 'mystery of atmosphere and distance'; and yet 'an hour's drive will at any time take you to the nearest railway station and two hours to London'. If we wanted to enjoy the towns' 'sense of the ... quiet', all we had to do was try to adopt a 'sense of personal identification with the physical conditions of the soil'.[27] Likewise, when the poet Karl Gerok published a lavish edition of the Proverbs in 1885, whose illustrations transported the world of the Old Testament into Altdeutsch surroundings and dress (see p. 227), he wrote that this was done to 'in order to bring [it] nearer to us, in a homely [*heimathlich*] fashion, without obliterating a certain scent of distant lands'.[28] In the 1850s Ungewitter had already pointed out that 'even today' one could easily find chairmakers in the country who 'unconsciously' practised the rules of old Gothic.[29] The past was something that had to have been forgotten in order to be found again, although the process of finding grew progressively easier.

The political and other ideological aspects of nationalism can hardly be touched on here.[30] Although much of what follows here was connected with the self-assertiveness of both newer and older nation states, the discussion also considers larger groupings (such as 'Germanic') and smaller ones (the regions). 'National' or 'regional' in this context means that a label has been attached to a form, and that this form is held to be of aesthetic value. By the later 1880s the new vernacularism was tied in with the 19th century's campaign for design reform – the Arts and Crafts movement – and it became a signifier of advanced good taste.[31] Seemingly no old artefact could ever demonstrate bad taste.[32] Of critical importance was the vernacular revivalists' conception of the home – or 'the house and home', or the house in the landscape – as it had been in the olden days and as it would be in the future. Much later on, this trend was described in Britain as the 'Domestic Revival' – the second word still echoing the great moral crusades of the Gothicists. The account that follows considers the attempts to recapture national and regional 'oldness' in new designs, but ultimately the main concern of the 'love of the old' would be to preserve it wherever possible (see Chapter VI).

In the 1870s one could still appropriate the old in a number of quite different ways. One could assemble, with great diligence, a large collection of objects in diverse styles and coordinate their display, as happened at the World's Fairs and subsequently in museums (see p. 289).[33] Alternatively, one could evoke the 'old' by collecting objects of many diverse kinds, usually of a high degree of curiosity and uniqueness, and display them in an unordered, picturesque and atmospheric fashion (see p. 186). A third approach was rather different: it involved the look of a worn surface, which appeared the surest sign of great age. For the British in particular, it was, and is, often enough to catch no more than a glimpse – though the effect is intense – of a battered old wall or a scrappy piece of old furniture to get a comprehensive sense of that oldness. Old-looking surfaces, colours and textures could therefore be spread all over a room to create the atmosphere or character of antiquity. This chapter begins by considering the second method: the assembly of old curios. But slowly the third approach gained in importance, because it was crucial in the rediscovery of the common 'old', the vernacular. It could easily be applied to one's own surroundings. Champneys's 'homely scenes' and Gerok's sense of the 'heimatlich' testify to the immense power, as well as the flexibility, of the notion of the 'old home', which may comprise a whole country, a landscape or a town-scape, or a house or the corner of a room.

Old English I

The idea that one should cherish everything old would become a most pervasive attitude in England. But the fact that there was no early definition of what constituted 'Old English', combined with the almost complete lack of a discourse surrounding interior decoration, hardly made for a clear or vigorous start. 'The interiors of rooms, a subject rarely entered', wrote Henry Shaw in 1839; his brief *Specimens of Ancient Furniture*, which had appeared three years earlier, offers a short miscellany of English work and an equally patchy text, but is hardly comparable with contemporary research in many other fields of antiquity.[34] And yet, although by 1820 hardly any new homes had been built in a serious Old English style, by 1900 virtually all new detached houses in England were designed in something that could be called 'Old English'.

It should be emphasized at the outset that, more than any other European country, Britain was proud of its pre-classical heritage. By the 1820s and 1830s country houses of the new Gothic castle-type were being joined rapidly by examples in the Late Tudor, Elizabethan or Jacobean styles. These labels can all be taken as synonymous with 'Old English', although they did not, as yet, signify much of a vernacular element. As for the origin of the term 'Old English' within a design context,[35] it seems that the words were foregrounded pointedly during

A 17th-century staircase at Godinton, Kent. Henry Shaw wrote of the 'rude terminal figures' of the Old English style that exhibited a 'good cheer inseparable from the domestic establishment of a large mansion' (*Details of Elizabethan Architecture*, 1839).

Fireplaces from 16th- and 17th-century houses in London and Norwich, illustrated in C. J. Richardson's *Architectural Remains of the Reigns of Elizabeth and James I* (1840).

Fireplace in the 17th-century gatehouse of Kenilworth, Warwickshire; from Joseph Nash's celebrated *The Mansions of England in the Olden Time* (1849). Nash's view was that life in 16th- and 17th-century England had been both romantic and relaxed.

the early decades of the century, when English royalty was very keen to buy 'Old French' – i.e. pre-Revolutionary – furnishings for Carlton House in London and for Windsor Castle.

Until mid-century, oldness could still have negative connotations, which were probably quite widespread. Illustrators frequently drew old urban quarters in a dilapidated state, and where interiors were included, they signified the abject state of the poor and their dwellings.[36] The occasional pieces of furniture that appear in the pattern books from about 1810 seem to have been included mainly on account of their strangeness. On the other hand, an old building set in a landscape or a park could look equally unkempt, but would be appreciated precisely because of its old appearance. Architectural illustrators such as P. F. Robinson, who was working in the 1820s, ennobled buildings by showing their rough external textures, occasionally labelling them as 'Old English'.[37]

Inside, oldness had a somewhat different starting point, deriving from the 'romantic interiors' of the mock castles and halls mentioned above. Since old objects of craftsmanship are themselves utterly diverse, their display also seemed more random – a fact that, alongside their generally dark surroundings, distinguishes such interiors from the equally fulsome but tidier cabinets of curiosities of previous centuries. Probably most striking were the late medieval or Renaissance suits of armour. To amass and display armour had long been a custom in rulers' houses – a reminder of the family's past heroic deeds. With the arrival of Romanticism, the focus switched to a general nostalgia for past chivalrous warfare and to systematic research; now a suit of armour could constitute a trophy for a private or museum collector. A lively international trade in armour served the likes of Sir Walter Scott and Sir Samuel Rush Meyrick. The display of arms, often grouped with hunting trophies and heraldry, carried over into many lesser romanticized interiors and flourished belatedly in the Altdeutsch movement of the 1870s and 1880s.[38]

From here, a kind of contemplation of the past began to emerge from which the ordinary public was no longer entirely excluded. Peter Mandler has refocused attention on the 'Olden Times' movement, which projected a vision of 'Merrie Olde England' onto the life of 16th- and 17th-century county houses; it was popularized in illustrated publications and through the opening of more houses to the public. Reading about the olden times and seeing their relics became a pleasurable pastime. The image of medieval seriousness and seclusion was expanded into one of conviviality, even boisterousness, in which all classes belonging to an estate could take part. Life could be quite casual, even coarse; in any case, a good time was always had by all – or so it was believed. In the 1840s Merrie Olde England found its own illustrator, Joseph Nash, who determined the image of the English country house for decades and was noted even outside Britain. Nash's drawings cover the 16th and earlier 17th centuries, and he included both grand and not so grand houses. He took great care to render signs of age on surfaces, yet his interiors are mostly bright, straight-angled, high and spacious, so that they did not conflict with the contemporary conception of the interior. As for the apparent casualness of the users' lifestyles, it is possible that Nash was inspired by the prevailing fashion among the middle and upper classes for the 'lived-in' look (see the following chapter). Altogether, the old interiors exuded a 'genial warmth' and were full of 'creature comforts'. Nash presented a more carefully balanced combination of the distant old with the acceptable and familiar 'modern' look than any of his predecessors.[39]

On occasion, voices cautiously recommended these English styles for general use. Loudon placed Elizabethan side by side with Grecian and Gothic in his 1833 *Encyclopedia*. In 1839,

Feering House, Essex, 17th century, from Samuel Carter Hall's *The Baronial Halls and Picturesque Edifices of England* (1848). Here we see a close-knit family in a manor house, a notch or two down from the grandest country dwellings; the ornamentation is correspondingly coarser.

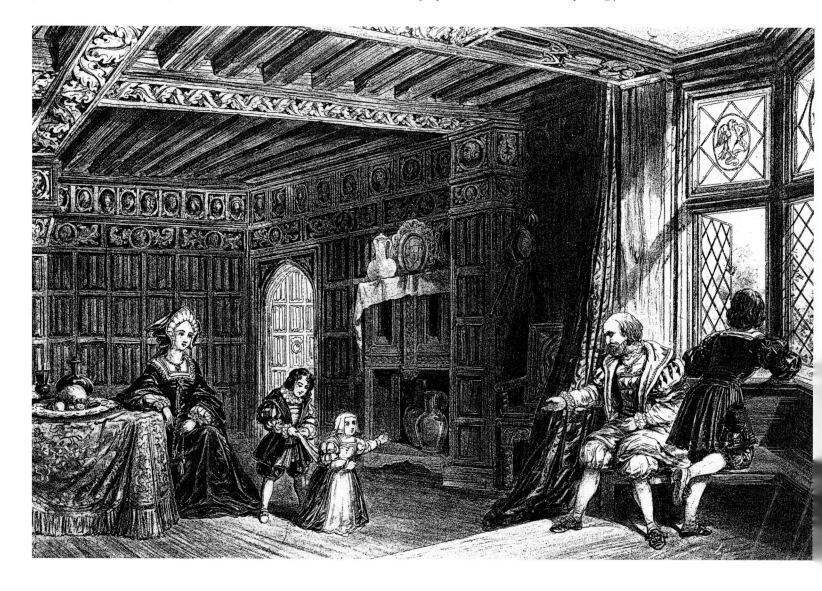

Thame Park, Oxfordshire, 16th century, from
T. H. Turner and J. H. Parker, *Some Account of
Domestic Architecture in England* (1859). Wall-
panelling was the most recognizable feature
of medium-sized Old English interiors.

Wainscoting from A. W. N. Pugin, *The True Principles
of Pointed or Christian Architecture* (1841).

Shaw maintained that these were 'ruder times' and that old furniture could be 'coarsely carved';[40] but he also wrote that 'however beautiful the elegant simplicity of Grecian forms, [they are] not of themselves sufficient for the effect that should be given to the interior of an English residence'.[41] Another antiquarian, T. F. Hunt, advocated old furniture for 'splendour' but still maintained that 'modern furniture' was more conducive to 'commodiousness'.[42] In 1840, one decorator noted that 'the picturesque and fantastic forms of the Elizabethan style [have] found many admirers'.[43] Interest in English Tudor architecture also led critics to look at lesser country houses and to extol certain features of their interiors, such as wooden ceilings and linenfold panelling; strictly speaking, the latter belonged to Gothic, but nobody would have wanted to exclude it from the 'Old English' label. During the 1850s the books of anti-quarians T. H. Turner and John Henry Parker were full of factual detail about medieval houses large and small.[44] More common than complete new interiors in the Old English style were the restoration and refitting of older interiors. The library and dining room at Charlecote, with their wooden panelling, 'Elizabethan' flock wallpaper, elaborate plaster ceilings and antique furniture, constitute a quieter version of the Old English atmosphere, while the interiors of Knebworth, from 1843, demonstrate a more dramatic, chivalrous and 'Gothic' interpretation.

Andrew Jackson Downing, 'Antique Apartment – Elizabethan Style', 1850. Downing's image is deliberately blurred in order to convey an impression of age.

In Scotland, a parallel 'Scots Baronial' style likewise sought to provide a complete formula for the elaborate house.[45]

More daring statements about Old England came from across the Atlantic, in the work of Andrew Jackson Downing: 'oaken wainscot … curiously carved furniture and fixtures … when harmoniously complete … seem to transport one back to a past age'.[46] In his main work of 1850, he included an image of an interior that had been deliberately made fuzzy in order to look old: 'Elizabethan … [a] style addressed to the feelings and capable of wonderfully varied expression … from the most grotesque and whimsical to the boldly picturesque and curiously beautiful … especially for domestic architecture'. But he goes on to call it a 'most dangerous style for any but an architect of great taste and judgement to handle'. A more widely acceptable version of Old English interior design had to wait another generation. Between the 1840s to the 1860s, 'English' to most people still meant Gothic, a style associated with churches rather than with houses.[47]

Altdeutsch I

As far as major groups of stereotypes were concerned, *Altdeutsch* ('Old German') was on the side of Old English, since both were in opposition to 'French' elegance and 'Italian' serenity and perfection. That said, Altdeutsch continued for longer and enjoyed a stronger and more comprehensive significance than its English counterpart, partly because the opposition to Frenchness continued much longer in Germany than in England. Altdeutsch meant old-fashioned and coarse, but also honest and straightforward. Liberal progressives could see in it negative traits such as immobility and a lack of politeness, while the Romantics were likely to praise the 'German' qualities of 'seriousness and feeling'.[48] Architecturally, Altdeutsch was firmly linked to the Middle Ages, that is to Gothic. Until the 1850s Germans believed that the Gothic style had been invented in Germany. Confusingly, however, when they adopted the English mode of landscaped gardens, the Germans also imported, as did most of Europe, the English castellated style for the medievalizing country house – although any accompanying chivalrous paraphernalia were always 'German'.[49] Altdeutsch, moreover, differed from Old English in that it applied not only to the old nobility, but also to old town burghers. The place where olden times had seemingly stood still was Nuremberg. Celebrated for its great artists

Peter Vischer and Albrecht Dürer, it was the city as a whole that visitors were most fascinated with.[50] In 1868 Old Nuremberg received an accolade, cherished the world over, when it featured as a backdrop to Richard Wagner's opera *Die Meistersinger*. The trend for precise historical detail on the stage was subsequently taken up by the Meiningen theatre company, which spread the image of Altdeutsch widely.[51]

Until the 1860s the domestic interior played only a minor role in all this. To surround oneself, in one's modern dwelling, with objects reminiscent of the rough or whimsical Middle Ages would not as yet appeal to many. Nuremberg's principal architect in the 1830s, Carl Alexander von Heideloff, promoted his neo-Gothic furniture as 'Altdeutsch',[52] but by the 1850s this link was questioned, and the next group of major German Gothicists, including Ungewitter, no longer stressed the Germanness of their Gothic designs. Nonetheless, Nuremberg continued to deal in Altdeutsch furnishings, especially the firm of Fleischmann.[53] Increasingly, support came from an institution for which Nuremberg seemed the ideal location: the Germanisches Nationalmuseum. Its main task, apart from acquiring all kinds of 'German' works of art, was defined in 1856 as showing 'living conditions in German history in the context of practical necessities'.[54] Many of the museum's objects were in fact bought cheaply, even at flea markets. These efforts in Nuremberg lacked the analytical precision of

The 'Lutherzimmer' – a design for the Veste Coburg, Thuringia, by the Nuremberg architect Carl Alexander von Heideloff, early 1840s. The lack of pointed arches here indicates a secularized, Altdeutsch type of Gothic.

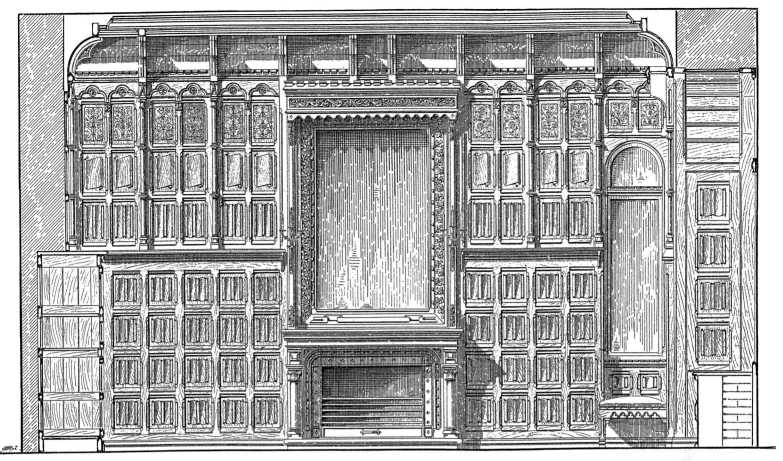

Design for a wall with fireplace for the Villa Laporte, Hanover, by Eduard Oppler, 1869. Wooden panelling and linenfold patterns were cherished throughout Northern Europe.

contemporary French endeavours, but they made up for it in their diversity. They also paved the way for an understanding of more mundane objects as quaint or vernacular, and from the 1870s the museum began to acquire peasant implements. The 'old room in the museum' now became an important issue. From the idea of assembling objects according to the period in which they were made, as at the Musée de Cluny in Paris, one progressed to the notion that a room in a museum should represent a specific interior, displaying related objects – say a kitchen or a living room. It was then a short step to the concept of transporting a complete old interior from its original site and re-erecting it within a museum building. These last two kinds of exhibit started in Nuremberg in the 1870s and 1880s.[55] A further example of the imitation of old domestic rooms could be found in the Salzburg Museum, arranged from the early 1870s.[56] The third type of exhibit only really made sense where complete wooden panelling existed, which narrowed the choice down to two main candidates (a very unlikely pair indeed): Parisian interiors of the 18th century, and the Alpine or North European 'peasant interior'.

Furthermore, the Germans cherished a number of 'monuments' connected with personalities both fictional and real, all of which were widely venerated and strongly characterized as 'German'. One of the most intriguing episodes in Goethe's *Faust* concerns the bashful Margarete (Gretchen), about to fall victim to the scheming Faust; in the 1820s Schinkel provided the most effective early stage set for the drama, fitting it out with numerous period details.[57] Martin Luther, too, loomed large in the German psyche. There cannot be many people who lived so long ago about whom so much is known – not only about his intellectual and political but also his personal life. There were in fact two rooms associated with Luther, neatly representing the two kinds of poetic interior discussed so far: the secluded study for the recluse (Luther's room in the Wartburg) and a room for the happy family man (his *Wohnzimmer* in Wittenberg).[58] In Nuremberg Dürer's house, too, had become a museum early in the 19th century, and in the 1870s had its rooms newly fitted out with old objects to evoke the atmosphere of the period. Whereas Luther's rooms could hardly be called attractive in terms of art, their interest deriving solely from the association with their famous occupant, Dürer's

Certain characters from the Renaissance period –
historical and fictional – loomed large in German
culture. 'Gretchen's room' (*above*) is a stage set
for Goethe's *Faust* designed in the 1820s by Karl
Friedrich Schinkel, while *Martin Luther and his
Family* (*left*), an anonymous engraving of *c.* 1825,
is an early example of a much-reprised scene.

Albrecht Dürer's 'workroom' – part of the Albrecht-Dürer-Haus in Nuremberg – was refitted from the 1870s. Perhaps the principal change shown by later Altdeutsch interiors was a move towards a warmer atmosphere – certainly when one compares them to Schinkel's design (*opposite*).

Room described as a 'study/drinking den/hunting room', from the Museum Carolino Augusteum, Salzburg. It was fitted out with old furniture and objects by the museum's director, the painter Jost Schiffmann, in 1871.

house came closer to works of interior design – the aim was 'to arrange it as faithfully as possible as an old German house'[59] – serving as an example of Riehl's 'das ganze Haus' and even reflecting Richter's whimsical visions of an Old Germany.

Altdeutsch as German neo-Renaissance

The years 1870–71 brought colossal changes for Germany, in particular unification under the Prussian king as the German Kaiser (Austria was excluded). This resolution fostered massive growth in the private economy and in public works. In the field of architecture and the applied arts, all this manifested itself very straightforwardly in the sheer volume of décor. But many were not satisfied: they felt that this expression of newly found confidence should be more specific, that is should signify a combination of new vigour with old German values. German academic research in history had been famed for some time; now it was directed to serve a very particular purpose. What whimsical antiquarians ('Raritätenkrämerei') had dug out of the past now appeared in splendour in paintings, illustrated books and sculptures, or as wall decorations on a grandiose scale. On the most basic level, there was a patriotic rush simply to label everything as German: Luther was a particularly German thinker; the family had always been a particularly German institution; and Luther's happy home and family life was a German phenomenon a fortiori.[60]

But the old tension between the positive traits of Altdeutsch and its negative, or at least its satirized, elements still had to be overcome. Its main virtues – faithfulness (*Treue*), solidity (*Solidität*) and *Gemüthlichkeit* – were evoked more than ever before, but so too was coarseness (*Derbheit*).[61] (The latter would be newly evaluated during the more strictly vernacular phase of Altdeutsch, to which we will come below.) For those who were inventing stereotypes at this point, the most important aim was to rid the image of Old Germany of any dustiness. A curious paradox was now entertained: the 'old as new'. Altdeutsch meant a 'healthy viewpoint … fresh imagination'; it was 'full of life … warmth of life, freshness of life'.[62] An English critic writing in 1879 tried to get across the atmosphere of Old Nuremberg, the *Meistersinger* and Hans Sachs and friends in particular, mentioning 'the poet of handworkers', 'cautious burghers' and their 'simplicity, force and homely humour'. Writing at the peak of the realist movement, this Englishman could even characterize such old figures as 'unromantic'.[63] To consider the distant past in terms of youthfulness seemed altogether a remarkable move. As a vision of the past it was indeed complete, paralleling that of Merrie Olde England; and in a domestic context, its major quality was once again 'warmth'. By the mid-1880s, however, some younger critics felt that there was too much 'German' vigour (the rejection of Altdeutsch will be outlined briefly below).

What should be the style for the new German movement? The answer was by no means straightforward. It could hardly be elaborate churchy Gothic. What offered itself, as in Britain, was the period immediately following the Middle Ages. 'Deutsche Renaissance' was the new catchphrase, powerful but flexible at the same time. Strictly speaking, this label covered only the period from about 1520 to 1618, when the Thirty Years' War broke out. But it was also extended back in time to include late Gothic and also Dürer and Old Nuremberg, thus absorbing what had so far been cherished as 'Altdeutsch'. In turn, 'Altdeutsch' could without too much forcing be extended to cover the period of the 'Deutsche Renaissance', so one meets the quite unlikely-sounding combination 'Altdeutsche Renaissance'.[64] All this was treated as a revelation, since before 1870 virtually nothing had been published on post-medieval German architecture.[65] The Germans also noted with some satisfaction that French and English commentators concurred with their definitions of Altdeutsch and German Renaissance, certainly in terms of the applied arts of the 16th century.[66] Much later on, architectural historians doubted the validity of the label 'German Renaissance', since the

'I'd love my four-poster more than anything, if only there weren't those large scrolls at the foot end' – a satire on the fashion for German Renaissance by Lothar Meggendorfer, 1879. Meggendorfer, who later became world-famous for his children's pop-up books, trained as a painter at the Munich Academy. In his early years, he drew for Munich's satirical journal *Fliegende Blätter*, and at the same time belonged briefly to the Munich applied arts coterie, designing the very furniture and interiors he lampooned (see also pp. 266, 309).

'German house, German land' – the frontispiece of an article on detached family dwellings from the Berlin architectural journal *Deutsche Bauzeitung* (1896).

Renaissance style had really originated (leaving Italy aside) in the Low Countries. Certainly, when one looked at the simpler manifestations of the Northern Renaissance it was hard to spot national variations.

The key to understanding this new revival was the way the old art appeared tied in with the society of its time. The Germany of the 16th century was thought to have been immensely prosperous and successful. In socio-political terms, the style of the period was understood as 'genuinely bourgeois'. The German Renaissance and its revival represented 'a general flowering of art that embraced all of life' in an 'unconsciously' practised national style.[67] As with the contemporary Queen Anne style in England, new research into Germany's Renaissance architecture produced much antiquarian description and copious illustrations, but virtually no theory.[68] Wilhelm Lübke, Germany's busiest architectural historian, wrote of an abundance of 'original ability, even naive genius, individual freedom', 'freshness' and a 'familiar warmth and liveliness' – notions clearly related to Michelet's and Burckhardt's view of the Italian Renaissance as an epoch of freely acting personalities, but here fitted into a more domestic framework.[69] It was recognized that the decorative vocabulary of the German Renaissance was Italian in origin, but such problems were brushed aside with the help of a few little metaphors: Italian art was 'beautiful and noble', while German art was 'gemütlich'; in Italy 'one lives like a god', but in Germany 'like a human being'.[70] Soon designers and their spokespersons confessed their satisfaction that the style had succeeded, that German art 'surprisingly quickly found its way into this manner, which comes from the heart'. Now, at last, Germanness

Exhibition of heraldry and associated Altdeutsch paraphernalia, Berlin, 1882.

appeared convincing when compared against other nationalities: critics proclaimed that there was now 'a quite pronounced German style, as there is an English and a French taste'.[71]

The Altdeutsch Renaissance now became the style for much domestic design, if somewhat by default at first: churches still tended to be Gothic, and public buildings of the highest rank demonstrated the Italian Renaissance style or, increasingly, neo-Baroque. German Renaissance, on the other hand, was used for a great many *Landschlösser* (smaller country houses), innumerable villas and even for blocks of flats. Such buildings usually adopted a 'Flemish gable' (to use a convenient English expression) – a stepped gable, often ornamented with scrolls, which at the time was considered credibly Altdeutsch, since its form dated back to before the Renaissance. Logic or precision in stylistic terms was not a priority; much more important was the fact that such signs were becoming commonly recognized. The other most important element on the exterior was timber framing or half-timbering, as in England – the clearest sign of common oldness, and one that referred to the Middle Ages as well as to the Renaissance periods.

More than elsewhere – and certainly much more than the earlier Old English revival – the new German national mode was adopted as a style for domestic interiors. Many authors on

Advertisement for arms and armour in papier mâché, for use in interior decorating. By the Nuremberg firm of Fleischmann, 1866.

'In praise of the virtuous woman', from the Book of Proverbs: the world of the Old Testament transferred to an Altdeutsch city. Illustration by Ludwig von Kramer, Munich, 1885.

art in the home were converts, writing of the 'unfathomable magic' of the Altdeutsch room,[72] 'that incomparable and complete impression of artistically ennobled comfort'.[73] Initially, it manifested itself most obviously in a greater quantity of furniture, which itself became much more bulky with Renaissance architectural motifs. In more elaborate rooms this style extended to wall panelling and wooden ceilings.

In the living room, Altdeutsch essentially consisted of a number of prominent objects, most of them belonging to the Gothic end of Altdeutsch. From the earlier 'Romantic' style, interior decorators borrowed suits of armour (already discussed in the context of Old English). These items had been faked for a very long time, but now they were reproduced on a large scale, using modern materials such as zinc and even papier-mâché. For the Germans, armour had an extended meaning: the heavily armed *Raubritter*, the roving, thieving knight, was believed to be a particularly German phenomenon of the Middle Ages. Moreover, German researchers were proud to discover that many celebrated examples of body armour in Western European collections were not Italian but of South German manufacture.[74]

More specifically German was the *Lüsterweibchen*, a type of chandelier in the shape of a mermaid originally based on a drawing by Dürer. It represented a combination of highly desirable elements: Nuremberg; authenticity; a design by the most celebrated German artist; and a link between fine art and applied art, between common use and the academic museum world – a cherished principle of the applied arts reform movement.[75] Particular types of chair were likewise employed in Altdeutsch interiors; as in the rest of Europe, some designs, such as the *Lutherstuhl*, carried special historical meaning.[76] Also common was the spinning wheel – 'an antiquarian ornament … the opposite of the nervous haste and the egalitarian elegance of the present'[77] – although this was a nostalgia shared by many Western countries. From the sphere of fine art came another prominent object: the easel, which formed part of the 'atelier' fashion discussed in Chapter III.

German designers and manufacturers rediscovered the large, ornamented *Kachelofen* – the tiled Renaissance stove – which soon replaced stoves in black iron or modish white ('French') ceramic. It was a square-shaped object with lively surface relief, mostly coloured dark green. Apart from providing a source of heat, the stove could function as a poeticized object. Its ceramic construction often included a seat (*Ofensitz*), which could either serve as a place for individual reveries (a *Schmollwinkel*) – particularly for the old – or help create a feeling of close companionship ('innige Gemeinschaft'). Historians of architecture and material culture traced the stove's 'poetically significant role' back to early Germanic times, or even beyond.[78]

Apart from these major items of furnishing, there were lesser objects that corresponded more closely to other Western collectables; in each case, however, their German origin was assumed or demonstrated.[79] Germany possessed the equivalents of Renaissance ceramics from France: their Rhenish *Steingut* (stoneware), for example, had always been recognized internationally. Leather upholstery and its appeal for practitioners of the Renaissance revival have already been mentioned. Much textile work – embroidery, lacework or trimmings – had strong claims to be a German artform closely associated with 'German' femininity (see p. 56).[80] Lastly, coloured glass had a decisive effect on the room as a whole. Although it enjoyed popularity across the West, in Germany it was valued more highly: bottle glass (*Butzenscheibe*) became Altdeutsch's unmistakable trademark (see p. 195), to the extent that the term *Butzenscheiben-romantik* has lasted into the 21st century.[81]

The Altdeutsch interior could be further enhanced by its occupants appearing in Old German dress and matching jewelry. In this respect, the Altdeutsch room mirrored the English Aesthetic interior, whose inhabitants liked to wear 'Anglo-Japanese' dresses. Possibly the German style was an even more rounded *Gesamtkunstwerk*, in that men, too, were often shown in Renaissance dress, at least in new images that conjured up the past. Although centred on the

Kneipstube, or drinking den, by Phillip Niederhöfer, Frankfurt, 1882. *Kneipe*, a colloquial term for a tavern, became a label for a type of room in large houses or hotels that was devoted to social drinking. Practically all drinking habits and venues now served as national, regional or local emblems.

Drinking den by Jean Pape, Dresden, 1887.

home, the Altdeutsch style was also employed elsewhere – especially in pageants, public festivities and other kinds of entertainment. Here, the Germans were enjoying something similar to the spirit of 'Merrie Olde England', at a time when British design was becoming less interested in it. The beer cellar formed an ideal vehicle for period style, and larger houses and hotels often contained a counterpart in the *Kneipstube*, or 'drinking den'.

To fill a room with such meaning-loaded paraphernalia clearly constituted one of the high points of later 19th-century domestic design. The users as well as the trades wanted to show that they were taking part in a wider cultural discourse. But it also represents a turning point. New definitions of the happy home from the late 1870s onwards in fact resulted in a concentration on those elements that were considered especially homelike. This will become clearer when we consider the more decidedly 'primitive' phase of the national and vernacular revivals, which would also bring an end to the type of vigorous Altdeutsch interior seen so far. The whole concept of the 'old' interior was to change, from an assembly of prominent objects to something that pervaded the room as a whole, its colours and its textures.

During the 1860s, 1870s and 1880s, the ways in which major European countries amassed objects in the home were noticeably different. In a previous discussion on the display of objects, we noted how, in the early 19th century, a well-known repertoire of classical allegories would be distributed in a regular fashion within the room's overall architectural design – works of sculpture displayed in niches, for example. This was replaced by a preference for an irregular, picturesque massing of often unusual objects. In France, this principally involved the picturesque arrangement of rather similar items, whereas England developed a sensitivity towards colour and textural effects that led to more ordered

Dining room for a villa in Kronberg, Germany, by Aage von Kauffmann, mid-1880s. The interior contains most of the usual Altdeutsch or German Renaissance paraphernalia but less wooden décor than usual, all of which lends it a certain restlessness.

arrangements, but in both cases the individual object was of less significance. In Germany, however, it was the presence of larger and highly individualized objects that crowded in on the spectator.

The old Low Countries

This section covers two countries that differed in the 19th century but had belonged together in the past, when their 'old' styles had been current – hence the rather awkward title. Despite their small size, Belgium and the Netherlands were both important centres for the Northern Renaissance revival and for 'art for the home' in general. Yet the vicissitudes involved in marking out a new national Renaissance were considerable, and the two countries emerged with rather different discourses surrounding very much the same forms.[82]

Belgium saw itself as the most stable, liberal, bourgeois–progressive state in Continental Europe, a view attributable to its recent foundation in 1830, when it liberated itself from many centuries of foreign domination. There followed an intense search for a precise historical pedigree, in which art played a leading role. As it happened, artists that were known throughout Europe had lived in what was now Belgium – figures such as Rubens and Jan van Eyck.[83] By the middle of the 19th century a number of young Belgian history painters also achieved Europe-wide fame; perhaps the most celebrated was Hendrik Leys, from Antwerp, who also tried his hand at interior decoration in a style that was non-Classical but not yet Flemish Renaissance. But any attempts to establish a national style ran straight into Belgium's most fundamental problem: its division into two language groups. The great art of the past belonged to only one region, Flanders, while the other half – French-speaking Wallonia – appeared to have little history in this respect. On the other hand, 19th-century Flanders was seen as economically and culturally inferior: Belgium as a whole was dominated by the French language, by French classical culture and by Parisian fashion. This state of affairs applied to Belgium's public and domestic architecture, and to its art manufactures, right through the 19th century.

Another division that ran through Belgian public life was that between the secular state and ultramontane Roman Catholicism. The first group preferred a French classical style, while the second was served by a strict neo-Gothic influenced by Pugin. But in the 1870s a liberal faction – mainly the Brussels *grande bourgeoisie* – began to adopt a third style, that of the Flemish

Renaissance. The mode practised in the great period of the 'free' Flemish cities – from the 15th into the 17th centuries – was now declared the national style of Belgium – ironically mainly by francophone patrons. It was a secular style suitable for both town and country houses, as well as municipal, but not state or ecclesiastical, buildings. Thus neatly described, the style appeared convincing and soon appeared in many better-class suburbs. It was instantly recognizable, with steep gables that contrasted sharply with the straight roof lines of classical French-derived architecture.[84]

Architectural debates began to consider the style from the 1840s; they saw it as something of a curiosity, as had happened with its English counterpart.[85] Its development followed a familiar route: the style was assigned, followed by demands for individuality and picturesqueness and the condemnation of all classicisms as monotonous, and with it came sideswipes against French cultural dominance.[86] At the same time architects emphasized the intrinsic qualities of building materials, especially regional ones and above all 'Flemish' brick. The style's international success was confirmed when Belgium's pavilion at the 1878 Exposition Universelle in Paris was widely praised.[87] In Antwerp, the Flemish capital, the discourse sounded slightly different, with an emphasis on liveliness ('so liveable … healthy'[88]). Thus Antwerp offered a touch of the vernacular and perhaps a small link to emerging notions of a Flemish folk culture, while the francophone liberals in Brussels kept to their interpretation of the *style flamand*, or *Renaissance flamande*, as the Belgian national manner. Some writers in Brussels did feel inclined to intersperse their texts with hearty inscriptions in Flemish, of the kind familiar in other Germanic countries, stressing their intranslatability into the 'prudish French language'.[89] Altogether, though, Belgian architectural writings on this topic did not achieve great depth. More important were the new illustrated works on old buildings, which demonstrated a quality hardly matched elsewhere.[90]

So was the *style flamand* a 19th-century style with a clear meaning, or at least one that was widely supported? Certainly, when one compared it to its Dutch counterpart. Dutch and Flemish architecture and applied arts of the 16th and 17th centuries had not differed greatly; although their golden ages had not coincided, in the 19th century both performed a very similar function in their countries' collective memories. Until the later 19th century the Netherlands, like Belgium, was enamoured of all fashions French – rationalist Neoclassicism as well as neo-Rococo. From the 1850s the country also harboured a vocal Roman Catholic faction that espoused the Gothic Revival, at odds with Protestant anti-medievalism. Since it possessed what Belgium was aspiring to create – a strong sense of a unified nation – the kingdom of the Netherlands seemed an ideal breeding ground for a national design style. Indeed, there was much enthusiastic talk of an 'Oud-Hollandsch' style, or a 'Nederlands' Renaissance.[91] In practice, however, exactly how it should be used in new designs proved problematic.

Part of the difficulty lay in distinguishing clearly between the various Northern Renaissance styles – Flemish, Dutch and German. Indeed, some Flemish and Dutch researchers claimed that much German work had been created or inspired by Old Netherlandish designers. Moreover, the old Low Countries produced their best art over quite a long period, from the early 16th to the mid-17th century, during which styles changed considerably. This seemed to create more problems for the Dutch than for the Belgians. Two aspects of Dutch history in particular hindered the formulation of a 'national' art: the country's Calvinist tradition, which supposedly lacked a strong artistic impulse, and the inter-national outlook of the Netherlands, which had prevented it from asserting itself culturally as a nation. Further reasons lay within the architectural discourse itself. Whereas Belgium perhaps devoted too little critical attention to architecture, the Dutch wrote copiously on the subject. By the 1870s and 1880s the Netherlands was smaller and less wealthy than Belgium, but its arenas for architectural discussion were many. Arising from the division between Catholic and Protestant, a bitter debate took place over the style of the Netherlands' two most prestigious public buildings of these decades: the Rijksmuseum and the Central Station, both in Amsterdam. The Protestants objected to the fact that they were being designed by the Catholic Gothicist P. J. H. Cuypers, although Cuypers's patrons – the Dutch government – claimed it was simplistic to associate these buildings' architectural rationalism with churchy medievalism.[92]

This impasse was but a symptom of a more fundamental division that underlies much of what is discussed in this chapter – the division between an architectural design practice that legitimized itself through professional and rationally conducted analyses of the architecture of the past, and the search for, and love of, the picturesque old, in which universalized rationalist meanings are replaced by particularized and (to put it briefly) sentimentalized meanings. As we have seen, the rediscoverers of the German Renaissance and the Queen Anne Revivalists in mid-1870s England had also turned away from theory, but some Dutch writers did try to compromise by looking for rationalist elements within the 'Oud-Hollandschen Bouwstijl'.[93] In any case, by the 1870s and 1880s most Dutch street façades showed at least some random elements of the Northern Renaissance. The 'Oud Hollandsch' style was also promoted fairly confidently in discussions – led mostly by architectural critics – surrounding the nascent Dutch applied arts reform movement.[94] Here, the argument ran that, more than the artist-individual, it was 'the people' who had created the major styles of the past.

There was a new unbounded enthusiasm for actual old buildings, and writers urged everyone to celebrate this heritage. The vogue for wood engravings, now common in all journals, reduced buildings to mere snapshots of gables and details, as if seen in passing. But however vague these images may appear, they always very clearly convey signs of age, of wear, imprinted on the buildings' surfaces. As long as their attention was being devoted to old buildings and not to the question of a new architecture, critics could enthuse freely: 'the charming Oud-Nederlandsche Renaissance …'.[95]

The home in Belgium

It has been assumed that domestic interiors in Belgium were made to correspond, at least to some extent, with the new kind of exterior. In this area, too, a lively local discourse was lacking.[96] There was hardly any 'art in the home' literature, of the type that had been produced so copiously in Germany and England; and until the 1880s Belgium, like France, lacked a true state-backed applied arts reform movement.[97] The Belgians no doubt relied on recent French publications. It is known that some prominent architects, including Henri Bayaert, Jules-Jacques van Ysendyck and Émile Janlet, were involved in designing grand domestic interiors in a Flemish style, but very few were published at the time. In Antwerp, the critic Max Rooses created richly furnished interiors for the Plantin-Moretus Museum in the 1880s, mostly using old pieces.[98] While a prominent example of the Old Flemish style, the Winders house in Antwerp, demonstrates a complex picturesque interior with screened partitions, the few published illustrations of new designs invariably stick to the old flat-wall elevations beloved of architects and the trade.[99] Belgian furniture-making, especially the large-scale manufacture at Mechelen, now also tended towards the Northern Renaissance style, employing lots of old oak, although this could hardly be called a Flemish or Belgian speciality.[100] Occasionally writers mention other kinds of décor that could be taken as more or less 'old Low Country': 'oak furniture, copper household ware, porcelain and glass, stained glass, coloured tiles, fabrics for covering the walls', etc. The revival of the large fireplace, the 'cheminée flamande', also attracted some attention.[101] As for the true 'antique', Belgium, like France, underwent a long

The dining room at 'De Passer', the architect Jean-Jacques Winders's own house in Antwerp, c. 1883 (the stained glass is later).

period of overlap in which imitations were tolerated at the same time as genuine antiques were insisted upon. The production of furniture in Mechelen in the 'antieke stijl' appeared to be acceptable for many decades, whereas the 1882 Exposition Nationale in Brussels stressed that all objects on show were originals.[102]

The lack of a general discourse in Belgium on art in the home was more than compensated for by the publicity given to one architect's undertaking: Charle-Albert's Château Flamand (or Vlaams Huis) in Boitsfort, near Brussels. On account of its singularity, one might be tempted to compare it with other idiosyncratic homes of architects or artists from the same period. But Charle-Albert, who styled himself an 'architecte décorateur', was not particularly wealthy, and this, his own house, was his life's work, occupying him from 1868 to 1889. On the whole, he emphasized not artistic individuality but faithfulness to the national art from the past, intending the house to function as an art historical narrative; room by room, it 'progressed' from the early 16th to the early 17th century, the time of the beloved Rubens.[103] It thus sums up the whole of the Belgian movement, celebrating the 'ancien et glorieux style flamand' but designed by a Belgian patriot and member of the 'bourgeoisie libérale francophone' (as Benoît Mihaïl has pointed out).

The dining room of the Château Flamand (Vlaams Huis) at Boitsfort, near Brussels – a large villa that the decorator Charle-Albert built and furnished for himself between 1868 and 1889.

All accounts maintain that right from the start, the interior of the Château Flamand, in its elaboration and diversity, was regarded as more important than the exterior. Charle-Albert took pains to underline the function of the house as a family home, applying what he saw as the practical virtues of the old style. Most descriptions of the house consisted simply of a long list of objects. Much is made of Charle-Albert's control of all elements 'down to the fire-tongs and the matchbox', as well as his devotion to the individual material qualities of oak, ebony and copper. Moreover, it was claimed that most of the décor had been made 'locally'; even though a plethora of objects had come from overseas, principally from the Orient ('the luxuries of overseas nations'), they could be considered in national terms by reference to the 'ancient commerce of Flanders'. As far as old work was concerned, Charle-Albert professed a dislike for bric-a-brac. He also sided with the older faction who preferred the elaborate restoration of objects rather than with the new group who insisted on mere preservation. Indeed, he did not eschew some blatant imitations, such as wall paintings that resembled tapestries. As regards the house's unity of interior design, comments varied. A German critic wrote in 1887 that 'an effect of space cannot be found anywhere', whereas Brussels's own architectural journal, *L'Emulation*, reported that 'no object shines to the detriment of another; all is executed after careful consideration with a talent that makes M. Charle-Albert an artist'. As if to make up for the lack of official concern in

Belgium for the applied arts, Charle-Albert opened his house to the public at the time of the great national Cinquantenaire celebrations in 1880, viewing it as a museum and even as a school for the nation.[104]

The home in the Netherlands

One is tempted to begin a discussion of the 'home' in the Netherlands with one of the 19th century's favourite stereotypes – the strong sense of homeliness in Germanic nations and the lack of it in Romance countries. Certainly the Dutch thought that their own *huiselijkheid* ('homeliness') at least rivalled that of other countries, a fact borne out by the considerable number of words that refer to 'comfort' and 'cosiness' in the home.[105] By the early 19th century the connection between family home and sense of nationhood appeared well established. In the sphere of art, too, the importance of the home was evident from many paintings of the Golden Age. But it seems that writers did not as yet see a link between home ideology and design; as elsewhere, a programme of 'art of the house' took a long time to develop.[106]

Like almost all other Europeans, the Dutch faithfully followed the French styles, which by the middle and latter part of the 19th century meant Rococo and Louis XVI. From about 1870 architects-cum-applied art reformers attempted to publish some of their own designs, emphasizing the need for them to contribute to the 'interieur' and condemning the decorators' French styles.[107] They claimed that 'making a room comfortable is an important component of architecture'.[108] This process might involve 'small rooms' and 'pretty corners'; there was some discussion of wainscoting ('kamerbetimmeringen'),[109] but surprisingly little of the fireplace. The Oud Hollandsch style was recommended as ensuring a 'warm feeling of domestic enjoyment'.[110] The first widely publicized building in this manner was the small palace of Oud Wassenaar, built by Constantijn Muysken between 1876 and 1879. The main rooms, especially the dining room (*eetkamer*), were distinguished by their heavy oak panelling. However, when the architect was asked to define the style of the house, he appeared to find this an altogether cumbersome question and made it clear that he considered it simply a comfortable 'modern building'. But then he relented: 'Oh heavens! It is actually a building in the "Old Dutch Style."'[111]

Uniquely among the 'old' movements in the West, the Dutch reformers went on record as saying that the Oud Hollandsch-style interior would probably not lead very far. In a report on applied arts reform, three adherents stated that the greater part of the Dutch public wanted 'light and air' above all; they would not want to live in 'small rooms' with small windows and 'bare, dark-coloured timbers': there was 'no sociability in mystical twilight'.[112] The least these reformers could expect was a turn away from naturalistic ('French') flower décor.

In 1884 the first Dutch book appeared in which a substantial chapter was devoted to the art of the home. Written by Carel Vosmaer, an author and critic, it was entitled *De kunst in het daaglijksch leven* ('Art in Daily Life') and was largely an adaptation of L. F. Day's *Everyday Art* of 1882, although the chapters on the domestic interior were written by Vosmaer and aimed explicitly at his Dutch audience. The book cleverly mixed firm advice with a chatty tone, but was serious about its main aim – to eradicate what Vosmaer (or, rather, Day) saw as the gap between art and practicality. After briefly mentioning homeliness as a special Dutch virtue, Vosmaer comes to the question of the Oud Hollandsch style. He hardly recommends it; in fact, his main love was for the Classical, in literature and in art. (As an anti-medievalist, he had also objected to the style adopted for the Rijksmuseum.) He writes that a national style is not really such a pressing issue, that all modern designers are eclectic. Vosmaer then cites lightness as the most important quality of any domestic interior: he does not approve of the new fashion for darkness, although he does recommend wainscoting. Like Charle-Albert, he

Elevation of the dining room at Oud Wassenaar by Constantijn Muysken, 1876–79.

is happy to use many imported objects, especially from Asia.[113] Two years later, the architect J. B. Kam published a longer but less incisive book in which he acknowledges his predecessors from other countries but is lukewarm about the Dutch style.[114]

With their relative darkness and massive furnishings, interiors like those at Wassenaar were indeed very different from the normally bright Dutch rooms. It was not clear from a more careful study of historical interiors in the Low Countries exactly what the ideal 'old Dutch' interior should be like. Dark, heavy timbering was more reminiscent of the South Netherlandish and German Renaissance of the 16th century, and was thus adopted by the Belgians in their revival, yet the interiors celebrated in Dutch paintings of the later 17th century did not look heavy at all. In 19th-century Dutch paintings of history and genre scenes, one can indeed distinguish between three kinds of interiors: the quiet, gently and evenly lit 17th-century room, peopled by virtuous workers; the darkish, heavily furnished Renaissance room, used by richer people; and the equally dark but coarsely furnished room of the lower classes.[115] This confusion reflected the situation in architecture at large – the feeling that old native buildings, admired as they may have been, did not necessarily offer the best style for new buildings.

Meanwhile people had grown fascinated with old objects and old interiors. For a long time Amsterdam had been a centre of the antiques market. By the later 19th century a good piece of old Delft was deemed to be worth its weight in gold, and it was noticed how foreign collectors and 'the ferreting antique dealer'[116] were sweeping up what was still available. During the 1860s ordinary, domestic objects from the past came into view. *Oude Tijd*, a pioneering journal that appeared from 1869 onwards, included stories and pictures and declared that the 'the olden times were merrier than ours … they lived fresher lives, more vigorously'. 'Old' did not necessarily mean 'unreadable parchments in an emaciated hand' – much the same attitude that the Germans were trying to foster towards their own Golden Age.[117]

In the mid-1870s the Dutch began an ambitious series of exhibitions arranged around old objects. Artefacts were no longer assembled according to type of object, but combined in room settings. At one such show in Amsterdam in 1876, the Netherlands' most noted and controversial architect, P. J. H. Cuypers, devised a number of rooms that served as a 'picturesque revelation of life in Amsterdam in earlier and later times'.[118] 'Picturesque' here meant an informal, almost casual arrangement of diverse objects – somewhat in the manner of the contemporary artist's studio. Two years later, at the Paris Exposition Universelle of 1878, the Netherlands attracted a great deal of attention with its carefully arranged 'Hindelooper Kamer' (to be discussed later in the context of the international vernacular revivals).[119]

The highpoint of the diorama-like room – the presentation of a complete interior – was the display of several 'kamers' at the Amsterdam World's Fair of 1883. The show's principal aim was to demonstrate a modern Netherlands to the world, yet a section entitled 'Retrospek-tieve Kunst' included four elaborately fitted-out 'old' rooms. Art, history and life were closely interwoven. Essentially the display was arranged by David van der Kellen junior, a painter and a director of a history museum who claimed to have been inspired by Dutch 17th-century painters, Gerrit Dou in particular. Visitors nicknamed the main room the 'Kamer van Jan Steen'.

Remarkably, we can read a most detailed interpretation of this 'retrospective' display by the young Hendrik Petrus Berlage, the Netherlands' most eminent architect-to-be, to which can be added comments by the Belgian critic Théophile Fumière and those of van der Kellen himself. For Fumière, the old rooms constituted the most 'original' part of the whole exhibition. For Berlage, they are, first of all, the work of an 'artist' and not of the fashionable trade. But, in accordance with the Gothic Revival ideals of Pugin and Ruskin, the high art aspect is matched by a close attention to the crafts, to the materials, predominantly oak. The heavy wooden ceiling shows that everything is 'true'. Berlage branches out into a history of oak, which, he claims, was introduced into the home during the Renaissance. He then vastly extends these historical considerations by citing his teacher, Gottfried Semper, and takes the reader right back to the Germanic tribes related in Tacitus, and their love of home and of the hearth, 'the flickering fire … exuding the whole of Germanic poetry'.

A '17th-century tavern' from the Amsterdam International Fair, 1883. The room's 'nationality' and position in the social hierarchy provoked much debate.

RETROSPECTIVE · KVNST

TAVERNE · VIT · DE · XVIIᵉ · EEVW

But this issue of comfort also needed to be addressed in a modern context. Berlage admonishes all those who, having become used to soft upholstery, complained that straight Renaissance furniture lacked the vital quality of comfort, reminding them that we normally sit on our chairs, not try to sleep on them. The furniture historian Barbara Laan has also pointed to comfort as a crucial issue and described how this quality was transferred from the realm of personal experience to the objects themselves – a trait visible in Berlage's account when he writes: 'the cupboard is, among the items of furniture, the epitome of homeliness'. It was then a short step to drawing conclusions about the objects' users: just as the wooden items on display in the bedroom were 'all of a piece', so were the people of those times – at least for the rooms' organizer, David van der Kellen. This effect of unity – the 'cachet de poésie' – was further enhanced by careful lighting: the interior was 'lit in the most effective fashion … with its background illuminated and the rest in happy half-shade … which successfully revives an epoch in which goodheartedness and frankness were greatly in favour'. For Fumière, the illusion of an old room was 'complete'.

Finally, Berlage once more asks the question: what is the Oud Hollandsch style? He avoids listing individual elements and goes directly to the central issue of the 'comfortable' ('gemakkelijk') room: it was impossible to define such a 'genuinely Dutch word', yet everybody knew what it meant. It was not enough just to collect a number of beautiful objects: one must also add a certain 'je ne sais pas quoi', so that one could say of a room, 'Isn't it comfy here?'.

Yet this model of the 'complete' domestic interior raised further problems. The main room in the Amsterdam exhibition was described as a 'taverne' – that is to say, part of an inn. But which class were its users supposed to belong to? The quality of the painterly or picturesque (in Dutch, *schilderachtig*) – 'the naive and intimate character that accounts for the great charm of old dwellings' – requires that there should be at least a little disorder, but if the room were full of drinkers (it was, after all, dubbed the 'Kamer van Jan Steen'), it would most likely belong to the world of the lower classes. This would not accord at all well with the very considerable wealth of materials and workmanship on display, nor with the room's height (over 3 metres, or 10 feet), and certainly not with the idea of the secluded, middle-class moral home. Thus, in the final analysis, the issue of the 'vernacular' was left unclear.[120]

In summing up the trends of the domestic interior in the Low Countries until the early 1890s, one may still leave aside the folk aspect. In Belgium, as in France, 'folk' culture as such hardly played a role. The *style flamand* overlapped only slightly with the incipient Flemish nationalist folk movement. The Dutch were most anxious to discuss their national architectural style at the highest levels, even though the 'old Dutch' feeling for domestic comfort could include a touch of folksy atmosphere. But it seems that a thorough-going Oud Hollandsch style for the better class of domestic interior never really gained the recognition that Old English, Altdeutsch and Bavarian Alpine were enjoying in their respective countries. Neither, however, did Belgium and the Netherlands experience anything like Germany's later rejection of its neo-Renaissance style. In the Netherlands, Berlage's introduction of bare brick walls and hard, straight woodwork from the mid-1890s expunged the picturesqueness of the previous decades, thus creating a sharper, 'cleaner' kind of Dutchness.[121] In Belgium, some architects preferred to design individualized detached houses that largely followed the English Arts and Crafts model.[122] Yet, on a basic level, fitting out one's home in a Dutch or Flemish manner presented no problems whatsoever: one simply bought and displayed a number of old, or old-looking, objects.

'Interior of Old English Cottage', from *The Penny Magazine* (1839).

Old English II

The ideal cottage

Around 1880, a client based in London who was relatively affluent and interested in design faced an array of style choices for his home. Rich but light 'French' elegance could still be had, but this style was totally pushed out by the often heavy and even purposely crude Eastlake–Talbert work, and less violently opposed by heavy and ornate 'Jacobean' design. All of these options in turn contrasted with the fashion for 'Oriental' casualness. There was also the Aesthetic liking for gentle, thin frameworks, flat surfaces and subtle colours, and a taste for the newest Adam and Sheraton revivals.[123] Several of these models could carry the label 'Old

Fisherman's Fireside by Henry Robert Robertson, reproduced in the *Art Journal* (1874). The quiet peasant in his or her small, tidy cottage – or, in this case, the fisherman's family home – constituted a new type of image of rural life. Much propagated by the painters of the Cranbrook colony, such representations superseded the old conception of peasant life as coarse and disorganized.

English'. From the mid-1880s some English vernacular revivals were consolidated into the Arts and Crafts movement. In 1900, Hermann Muthesius lavished praise on this development: 'England has achieved an art of building the home that is completely national, founded on the old art of its people [*Volkskunst*].'[124] Subsequent art historians, including Nikolaus Pevsner, distilled a modernist 'functionalist' essence out of these 19th-century styles, greatly under-emphasizing their Old English aspect, while the most recent interpretations have turned once again to Englishness but also emphasized the role of the artist and the artistic.

All the new Western trends shared the conviction that a good home need not – even should not – be obviously wealthy. Smallness could be an asset. During the 19th century it was the 'English country cottage' that emerged as the country's most cherished type of domestic environment. Since it formed part of the picturesque English landscape, its Englishness needed no explanation, and neither did the notion that country life in general was somehow attractive. When these houses became associated with the pastoral idyll, fortified by a new Wordsworthian claim to 'simplicity', they embodied 'a poetical idea of peace and happiness which is inexpressible', according to the writers William and Anna Mary Howitt.[125]

However, cottage life and the cottage interior still remained largely within the spheres of fine art and literature. 'What can the cottage have to do with art, except as part of a picture' or a poem? For town-dwelling lovers of picturesque scenery, the rough interior of a farmer's cottage would be the part that they could least imagine in their own abode. The turning point was a change in general perception – the adoption, one might say, of a modern view: the cottage-dwellers were now seen as industrious, and the inside, although bare, was also clean. Novelists and painters presented the 'cottiers' in a state of virtuous and happy domesticity; the furniture may have been rough and un-designed, but it was sturdy. These representations thereby jettisoned a crucial element of the Dutch tradition, that of the coarseness of rural folk.[126] Now rustic interiors were 'underwritten … by the rhetorical category of the pastoral', as Thad Logan has written, and thus may fall outside the traditional class hierarchy that applied to decoration.[127] This conception was somewhat reversed when the 'enthusiastic admirers of the poetry of poverty' teamed up with those who cherished the lived-in look of the lesser 'Merrie Olde English' country house or manor house. The values of sturdiness, independence, picturesqueness, oldness and Englishness reinforced one another. 'We Englishmen are proud, and justly proud of the stately homes and the cottage homes of our land', wrote one critic in 1894.[128]

Some of this appreciation of primitive-looking solidity was owed to the Gothic Revival. Pugin's disciples had experimented with versions of the country cottage since the later 1840s, producing village parsonages and schools that sported bare stone or brick walls and steeply pitched roofs, though virtually nothing is known of their interiors. Nonetheless, the painter colleagues of High Victorian Gothic architects – especially Dante Gabriel Rossetti, in his pastels and drawings of the 1850s – squeezed romances into small, cramped rooms, so as to catch, in Alistair Grieve's words, the 'heartbeat and minutiae of medieval daily life'.[129] Some of these images were based on German late medieval woodcuts, and perhaps even on Ludwig Richter's work. Moreover, Rossetti transferred the roughness of the cottagey exterior to the rudely hewn, decidedly unpolished, but also carefully shaped woodwork inside. A more relaxed medievalism can be found in the *Gesamtkunstwerk* of William Morris's Red House of 1859. Here, a suburban villa was given a moderately cottagey exterior, complemented by an oriel window of the type familiar from Nuremberg. Its interior, especially the fitted furnishings, received the fullest attention of the architect, Philip Webb, and of the artists Burne-Jones and Morris himself.[130]

Naturally these rarefied and personalized efforts as yet had little influence on trends in interior design. Morris himself did not find real repose in Red House and soon moved back to

Fireplace at Vallance House, Farnham Royal, Berkshire, by William Eden Nesfield, late 1860s – one of the first inglenooks.

inner London. A seemingly happy Old England country primitivism was practised in the 1850s and 1860s by another group of artists who had settled a little further away from London (while of course not rupturing their metropolitan connections), in Cranbrook, Kent, among them Thomas Webster and John Calcott Horsley. Vernacular life inside the cottage was one of their most frequent themes – not only in the distant past, but in the present as well. According to a critic in 1860, Cranbrook 'once was and still is Happy Old England'.[131]

Living room at Willesley, near Cranbrook, designed by Richard Norman Shaw for the painter John Callcott Horsley (1864–69).

'Elizabethan dining room', designed by D. Murray, 1872.

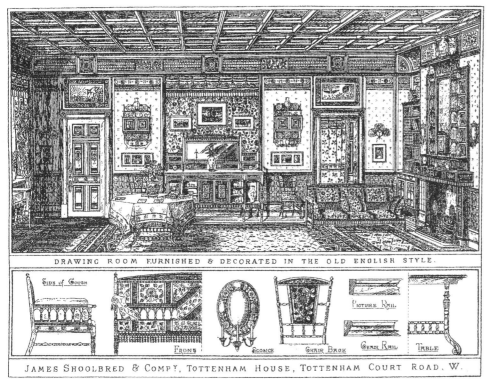

DRAWING ROOM FURNISHED & DECORATED IN THE OLD ENGLISH STYLE.

JAMES SHOOLBRED & COMP?, TOTTENHAM HOUSE, TOTTENHAM COURT ROAD, W.

Drawing room in the 'Old English Style', from *Designs of furniture … specially designed for James Shoolbred & Compy., Tottenham Court Road* (*c.* 1876).

Interior at Messrs M. B. Forster & Sons, North Woolwich, by the architect Thomas Harris, 1874. By the 1870s, English architectural journals featured many such views of whole interiors. The illustrators often tried hard to make the furnishings look as if they were old.

above 'An Old English Manor House' by Basil Champneys. His 1883 article on Ightham Mote, Kent (14th–17th centuries) is rich in nostalgia.

above right Hall Place, Leigh, Kent, by George Devey, 1872.

In the 1860s there was a decisive transition: the 'old cottage' manner was now applied to smaller country houses and large suburban dwellings. 'For transferring the style from cottage to country house, the [Cranbrook] painters themselves are in large part responsible', claims Andrew Saint.[132] They worked in collaboration with Richard Norman Shaw, whom they had commissioned as architect. Timber framing or half-timbering was a key element in these houses. Derived from cottage and manor houses, it had previously been confined to dwellings of a lowly status. It now became a standard feature for domestic architecture and was usually labelled 'Tudor', and for many it formed the leitmotif of Old English. Much less is known about the interiors at Cranbrook, although Willesley, built by Shaw for John Callcott Horsley between 1864 and 1869, still shows what would become the main ingredients of the Old English room: wooden ceiling beams, completely panelled walls and small-pane leaded windows.

Commentators on domestic architecture and furnishings extrapolated from these images for the wider socio-political context. They seized on the nationalist element, taking explicit sideswipes at other nations: 'old England, as distinguished from a new colony or an upstart republic'; 'the English manor house is in better keeping than … the Italian villa'. They preferred furniture made 'by a British village carpenter to a span-new cabinet from Paris shining in French polish', claiming that 'thus our nationality enters into domestic life and gives colour to the domestic arts'.[133] English stereotyping of the French could be every bit as acerbic as that heard in Germany: the 'art of the salon' was said to be 'rich, luxurious and coldly intellectual … indifferent as to truth of principle'.[134] After the nationalist argument for spreading the style came the socio-political one: 'All English, all our own … old manor farm houses, scattered over the length and breadth of our land'.[135] The vernacular, the 'old', was now considered available to, and beneficial to, the whole of society, and there was no longer anything particularly rarefied about Old English. By the 1870s 'dear Old English' was influencing the wider design reform movement. The publications of Talbert and Eastlake in the late 1860s had been key. Both authors helped to regularize the earlier crudeness and quaintness of Elizabethan furniture through the application of High Victorian heaviness and flat surfaces, although neither provided much lead for the appearance of complete 'cottagey' interiors.

Dining room at The Poplars, Avenue Road, London, by John McKean Brydon, 1874. The room is avant-garde, at least in its rejection of what was then considered elegant.

Underlying much of the new ethos was a love of materials for their own sake, which meant a liking for picturesquely rough surfaces. One critic thought that 'Pre-Raphaelites have done much to increase our regard for minute and honest workmanship' through their meticulous rendering of surfaces.[136] Old English was increasingly held to be a matter of craftsmanship. 'English habits and English tastes have always inclined to the use of homely rather than stately materials', claimed another writer in 1881.[137] Wood played a significant role; local wood was of course preferred, and 'English oak' in particular. The term 'old oak' crops up in the 1830s (not only in Britain, of course), and Loudon deals cautiously with oak wainscot – although, in reality, much of the woods used in 'English' wainscoting were imported. The love of timber manifested itself in two ways: in the massiveness discussed above, but also in a kind of myopia: 'a bit of grained oak may cultivate the eye in some measure unconsciously …'.[138] A growing antipathy to mechanization resulted in the feeling that 'modern machine made woodwork [gives] a sense of hopelessness … never-changing precision; … we may search for some flaw, some mistake, we can find none'. In sum, the new appreciation of roughness or simplicity was based on 'sensitiveness to the most subtile [*sic*] and infinitesimal relations of form and colour' (Basil Champneys).[139] Oldness was now created through a certain atmosphere, through the use of colours and textures rather than by surrounding oneself with many antique implements.

But could the rough and homely also be comfortable? In the debates about comfort the opposition is clearly modern France: Eastlake goes on the attack, maintaining that luxury and comfort 'should not be confounded … glaring chintzes, elaborate wallpapers, French polish … represent considerable expense and a certain order of luxury, but assuredly not comfort'; likewise, 'elegant', curved furniture was no good for ordinary daily use, being 'essentially effeminate'. He strongly approves of the straight lines of 17th-century settees at Knole, which were illustrated again and again. Modern French comfort is even seen as 'selfish' when its aim is 'to make personal ease the sole thought of home'. E. W. Godwin, designer of rectilinear furniture, sneered at the 'piggish laziness' of those who used curved and upholstered furniture.[140] For 'country life', Eastlake recommended 'the common wooden settle which forms so comfortable and snug-looking a seat by rustic hearths', while Walter Crane suggested that in old houses we look for 'romance' rather than modern 'comfort and convenience'.[141] 'Comfort' was thus separated into the purely physical and into something that also needed to be appreciated mentally. It all differed considerably from the earlier Old English trend, which had sought out the old lore of chivalry and merry-making. Now there was a need for quietness: Basil Champneys had called for 'a quiet corner', and William Morris would radicalize the issue by quitting the modern age altogether in order to create an 'epoch of rest'.[142]

The 18th-century revival

To greatly complicate matters, by the mid-1870s there was another major shift in formal and symbolic preferences. Until the 1850s and 1860s, the 'old' had been associated with the picturesque, with mystery, even with grime; it still spoke of a distant past. By 1870 a more subtle interpretation of the 'old' had come to the fore: it was seen as mellow rather than grimy, and it was not rare but ubiquitous. To understand fully the immensely complex developments in English domestic design that took place the 1870s, one would also have to consider the Aesthetic Movement. In its ethereal high artiness, it appeared the very opposite of jolly neo-vernacular comfort. But the designs of Morris, Webb and their adherents from the 1860s combined a neo-vernacular mellowness with high art seriousness, too – which accounts for Morris's immense success.[143] It was chiefly young architects who burst onto the scene around 1874 with a reinterpretation of an 'English' style: 'Queen Anne', which constituted one of the most intriguing and most original of all 19th-century revivals. It appeared, from the start, almost wholly contradictory. 'Why it has been called "Queen Anne" is more than any one can tell', wrote J. M. Brydon, a young pupil of Richard Norman

The 'Corridor' (hall) at Lowther Lodge, London, by Richard Norman Shaw, 1872–75.

The Corridor,
Lowther Lodge,
Kensington, London.
R. Norman Shaw. R.A.
Architect.

The 1870s saw a new fascination with the English 18th century and with 'Queen Anne' in particular, as in this children's book illustrated by J. G. Sowerby and Thomas Crane in 1881.

Shaw. Certainly 'Queen Anne' was 'all English, all our own';[144] it did not matter in the slightest that the whole vocabulary had come from abroad, from Classical Italy, the Netherlands or even France, because it had become vernacularized – a 'builder's' style. In contrast to 'Elizabethan' and 'Tudor', names supposed to mark periods in English history that were considered politically important, 'Queen Anne' referred to an era of lesser significance; but again, that hardly mattered, and in any case this new praise was extended to cover much of the 18th century, which would soon be given the much vaguer label 'Georgian'.

This new approach to 18th-century design was, like previous Old English movements, closely connected to trends in literature, notably W. M. Thackeray's tales of the period.[145] As Stephen Bann has argued, it all contained an element of satire and irony. A notion of Merrie Olde England was still present but was less emphatic. 'Nobody cared very much' in those days, claimed the *Cornhill Magazine* in 1878: 'they took things very easily' – a view of the 18th century that showed some parallels with current French ways of appreciating their *ancien régime*. The meaning of 'old' had shifted, from describing the medieval to encompassing the 17th century, and now the gap between the past and the present had been narrowed even further. The 18th century was 'so near to us and yet so far from us'. Because of that nearness, there was no need for 'a poet or novelist' to explain it,

Polly put the kettle on
Polly put the kettle on,
Polly put the kettle on,
We'll all have tea.
Sukey take it off again,
Sukey take it off again,
Sukey take it off again,
They're all gone away.

above Illustration from Kate Greenaway's
Mother Goose (1881). This cottage interior exhibits
the lightness of the Aesthetic Movement and
of the 18th-century classical style. It is furnished
with William Morris's vernacularized classical
'Sussex' chairs.

above right Dining room fireplace at Manor Farm,
by Basil Champneys – the architect's own home
(1884). The illustration is by T. Raffles Davison.

'John Gilpin was a citizen of credit and renown',
from William Cowper's *The Diverting History of
John Gilpin* (1782), here illustrated by Randolph
Caldecott, 1878.

'The fireplace of the model sitting room' from the 'Artizan's model dwelling', New Art Museum, Queen's Park, Manchester, 1884. A review in the *Cabinet Maker* credits the room to 'Mr. William Morris and his coadjutor Mr. W. A. S. Benson'.

as it had been necessary for the distant Elizabethan age: now 'every man can do [it] himself'.[146]

What was so attractive and so English about the style? Initially, the breaking of classical rules, especially those governing proportions, gave the style a certain 'quaintness'. Queen Anne Revival included both exteriors and interiors, although still far less was said about the latter: 'The interiors of our houses are now perfect studies compared to what they were ten or fifteen years ago'; 'Now the internal fittings of our houses are carefully designed and admirably worked out', etc.[147] Some architects publicly recorded their designs of profiles for all the interior divisions, such as dado and picture rails (see pp. 112, 113) and even sash windows (p. 183). White woodwork was employed extensively. From the 1880s a general brightness meant that the contributions of the individual trades, such the upholsterer or painter, were less obvious, and in many interiors by Shaw, for instance, the impact of patterned wallpaper was greatly reduced. All in all, the revival had 'brought with it a strong homeliness of feeling'.[148] Furniture styles from the 18th century formed an important and recognizable element. The name of Thomas Chippendale came up frequently: earlier Gothicists had disliked his work, but by the 1880s it became axiomatic that English furniture workmanship in the 18th century had been the best that ever existed, and there was a conviction that 'a multitude of modern comforts' was owed to this 18th-century master.[149]

Yet the era of Old English heaviness was not entirely over. The 19th century's view of the previous century was no doubt influenced by caricatures. According to Thackeray, 18th-century people had all been 'fat', and gentle satires on 'John Bull's' life and taste painted him as 'square' and as 'sound' as, for example, his dining room chairs; indeed, it was left a little unclear whether this archetypical Englishman had lived in the 18th century or had survived into the 1870s.[150] There must, of course, have been just as many thin people in the 18th century – especially when one considers the ever present fashion for extremely delicate seating.

Old English consolidated

In 1900, Hermann Muthesius commented on an English national domestic architecture that was accepted by all. What he does not make explicit is that this was limited to his favourite type of dwelling, the freestanding house. It was the one area in which Old English – albeit in very diverse forms – could be said to rule completely. One of the most important contributions of the Queen Anne movement had been to extend the notion of Old English so that it belonged to the town as well as to the country. However, where the vast majority of urban and suburban dwellings were concerned, the question of a national English style is far from clear-cut. One must always bear in mind that clients came from a very wide range of class and wealth. The very first examples of the Old English revival discussed earlier were larger country houses, and the innovative homes constructed in the 1860s were designed for the artistic elite by an elite of (younger) architects. This circle claimed – and publicized – an ascendancy in all matters of interior design, and in 1888 they once again tried to enter the limelight by setting up the Arts and Crafts Exhibition Society. At the same time their efforts were being matched by the trades, who had also begun to organize themselves in terms of publicity (see Chapter I).

On the whole, it is not hard to find praise for Old English designs, and yet the label itself was not used greatly by designers or manufacturers. For most, the 'old' in Britain was no longer anything exceptional, to be uncovered, but instead was a self-evident term that comprised everything from the Tudor period to the designs of Chippendale and even of Sheraton. 'Tudor' was mentioned least of all in the writings, since it might appear too monastic (neo-Gothic was at a low ebb generally in the later decades), and 'Elizabethan', too, was used less frequently than in the earlier days of Old English. The style that was mentioned most often was Jacobean, especially in connection with the dining room. Its most prominent manifestations were the richly appointed houses of London architects George & Peto. Further down the scale, innumerable examples of turned or knobbly legs were easily produced. 'Serviceable and sensible … no style … can eclipse our home-grown Jacobean', wrote J. W. Benn, champion of the upper- middle and middle-middle market. 'Queen Anne' remained a very widely used label, as ever imprecisely: a 'warm, comfortable and stately style'. 'Georgian' cropped up around the mid-1880s, although it was at first applied to lighter interiors in late 18th-century style.[151] 'Quaint', an epithet used occasionally throughout the texts, became a popular description among traders in the 1890s.

After 1890 the gap between what was characterized as 'refined' – using the most delicate 18th-century forms – and the coarsest examples of the vernacular revival widened once more. The country cottage – or, more precisely, the small 'yeoman's house' – was now regarded as a thoroughly desirable dwelling: 'never coarse, though often rude enough, sweet, natural and unaffected, an art of peasants', demonstrating 'tidiness' and 'white walls' (Morris).[152] The trend towards a rougher appearance, first evident in the 1860s, became stronger once again. The Arts and Crafts movement, with its own particular sense of the material, moved away from flat, planed wood and turned Jacobean legs, away from the mid-Victorian sense of flat walls, towards a feel for the thickness of a wall both inside and out. In this way it mirrored contemporary vernacular revivals on the Continent, which also veered away from wood – a material that had been favoured for so long. Ever more earthy characterizations of the home emerged, such as the 'honest English homestead' described by Benn.[153] This duality, of the most 'primitive' and the most elegant, can be exemplified by the cottage kitchen, now often without servants, enjoyed by middle-class and upper middle-class householders as their country holiday home, precisely as a contrast to their urban dwelling. Kate Greenaway's illustrations occupied a clever middle ground between gentility and a cottagey atmosphere.[154] A more literal return to the half-timbered cottage or small Tudor manor house was demonstrated in the work of Baillie Scott

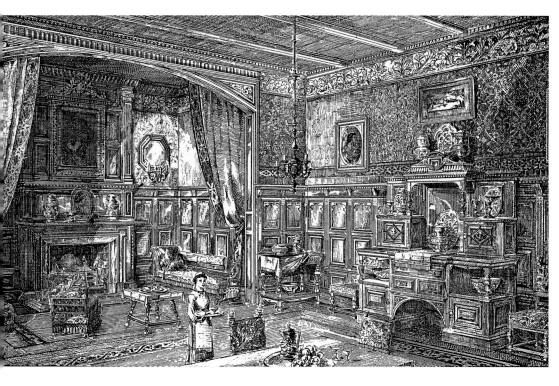

A 'Jacobean' dining room (*left*); a boudoir in a 'refined' manner (*below*) that was just beginning to assume the label 'Georgian' (the wood was painted 'ivory white'); and an inglenook for a dining room in a rougher cottage or manor-house style (*opposite*). All three interiors were published in the *Cabinet Maker* in the 1880s. Although somewhat below the level of the elite designs represented so far, they conveniently illustrate the major trends within the Old English movement.

and Crouch & Butler in the 1890s, in which, finally, the interior of a detached house was given the same attention as the exterior, if not more.[155]

What largely ceased in England was the discussion about 'style' in domestic design – in contrast to Scotland and Ireland, which at that time were discovering their own national and

vernacular styles. The process of gradually discovering the old was coming to an end, and effectively stopped after the term 'Regency' had been added to the other labels early in the 20th century. In contrast to the situation in other countries, where the debates about national styles were sometimes tortuous, the national validity of any of the 'English' styles, with or without the prefix 'old', never seemed in doubt.

Old Colonial

The American domestic interior up to the early 1870s can be seen as a distant disciple of European design, whereas by 1880 America was producing probably a greater variety of interiors than anywhere else; these included all the 'French' styles, heavy German or Northern Renaissance work and the most sophisticated Orientalist furnishings. But these years also demonstrated a new sense of independence from the old Continent, even though it was prompted by a new close familiarity with the latest English designs. Eastlake's quest for 'truth' and its manifestation in his heavy, squarish wooden furniture made the deepest impression. As we have seen, there was a flood of American articles and books on the interior from 1875 onwards. Soon after, a sense of an 'American Renaissance' took hold – part of a new cultural self-confidence in a period that would soon be dubbed the 'Gilded Age'. To the surprise of many, the nation was now held to have achieved a 'taste' of its own. It led to undertakings of the greatest splendour, novelty and artistic refinement, such as the decorating work of the Herter Brothers and of Tiffany (see pp. 153, 191). All this coincided with a new architectural and artistic independence adopted by certain architects in Boston and New York, many of whom had been closely involved in interior design from the start.[156]

Precisely at this time, the mid-1870s, the immense fascination with the 'old' – with anything that reminded them of the American past – became an overriding issue here, too. The most direct way of 'capturing' the past was to gather actual old objects that held a special significance for the history and customs of the country. According to the historian of material culture Kenneth Ames, 'the processes of the colonial [are] … deeply grounded in objects'. In Europe, such a desire for old objects usually led to the collection of diverse art treasures; in America, it appears that fewer objects were preferred, each of which then gained in significance.[157] At first, original items from past American kitchens were exhibited at fairs, most notably in Philadelphia in 1876. 'Old' in this context implied both an appearance

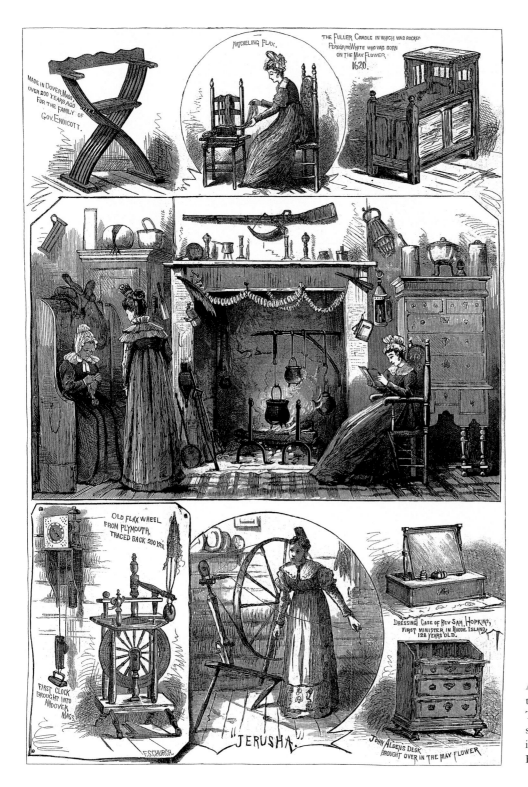

An 'Old Time New England Farmhouse', from the Centennial Exhibition, Philadelphia, 1876. This interior includes artefacts of special significance to the American 'Old Colonial' style, including the spinning wheel, and – in contrast to Britain – clearly stresses non-aristocratic virtues.

of age and a reflection of former virtuousness, reinforced by women in antique costume preparing old-fashioned dishes in a huge fireplace. From these *tableaux vivants* stemmed the first attempts to construct period interiors in American museums. Most significantly, and of interest to every home, was a classification of chair types, among which the legend of the 'Mayflower Chair' was the most persistent. Next in order of the significance they embodied were the grandfather clock, the guns over the mantelpiece, and numerous types of textile that represented the rhetoric surrounding the 'American woman'. The ultimate symbol of woman's work was the spinning wheel: it stood for active domesticity, as well as tying in with the politics of the 'Daughters of the American Revolution'.[158] It should be noted that in both these respects – the preference for single significant objects as well as for the complete old room – the American revival followed Central European rather than English trends.

An 18th-century New England interior, sketched by Arthur Little, Boston, in 1877. A new liking for the patina of age led architects and antiquarians to prize even apparently quite unprepossessing interiors.

Yet to revive the 'old look' for a whole house and all its rooms was a project of quite a different order. The English influence remained crucial, and there was now a phase of intense toing and froing between England and America – even if, according to Vincent Scully, it lasted only until 1880.[159] Needless to say, the issue under question was the proper expression of an American domestic architecture. What was 'American' about a given style? Could it be similar to English work and yet at the same time distinct?

Some earlier American houses in an English Gothic style had evoked some of the old atmosphere ('the view … across the lawn is exceedingly English'[160]). Americans were then much impressed with the timber-framed buildings in manor-house style that English exhibitors displayed in Philadelphia in 1876.[161] But during the years that followed it was the Queen Anne Revival that inspired most. 'Hitherto … in choice of style we have been cosmopolitan … [with] no conscious influence from local antiquarianism. It so happens that the Georgian [i.e. Queen Anne] revival in England refers back to a period which coincided with much of our earlier colonial history … thus at last we also are led to look for models of style nearer home.' Put simply, this meant that the Queen Anne style, which had just been established as properly English, was now declared, on account of the colonial period, to be an American style, too. The identification of work as 'old' and 'national' suddenly appeared very straightforward – in fact more so than in any other country so far discussed. In this context 'colonial' definitely referred to an American period of the past. Just as the English had declared the Continental origins of their classical styles as irrelevant to their own national significance, the Americans now disregarded – or at least bracketed – the English origins of 'their' style. They too now adopted the methods of appreciating the 'good old' times – in their case the 'good old Colony Times'.[162] Naturally, some of these values may reflect more perennial American concerns – especially agriculturalism, which Downing had celebrated in relation to domesticity, although for him it had not explicitly included they quality of oldness.

What helped establish a national style in New England, as in England itself, was that intensive search for the old: seeing distance in something relatively close by, as Champneys had experienced on his visit to the Sussex coast. During the 1870s New Yorkers quite suddenly began to discover older towns in their neighbourhood, even though the dates of the 'colonial'

'Hall of the Warner House', an 18th-century interior illustrated in T. B. Aldrich's 'An Old Town by the Sea', *Harper's New Monthly Magazine* (1874).

Hall and staircase of a Connecticut house, designed by Charles A. Gifford, 1886. When closely grouped, the main staircase and the fireplace form a kind of pivot within the house, even though the sense of enclosure provided by individual rooms has been lost.

period were now stretched to about 1830 or even later. This era already seemed very distant because it predated the modern urban age, to which observers felt they most decidedly belonged. One significant factor underlying this vision of the past was its completeness: landscape, riverscape, townscape, streets, houses, interiors, furniture, dress, and the character of the people. Portsmouth in New Hampshire was described as 'a very old town … . What a slumberous, delightful, lazy place it is!' In the end, there was no real need to worry about precise dates. In *The House Beautiful* (1877), Clarence Cook admires most of the objects he has seen because of their general age. The 'old time' residences, 'mostly square white houses', were illustrated frequently, in casual, vignette-like wood engravings that made them appear smaller than they probably were and that also reinforced their connection with their surroundings – a technique soon used by illustrators in the *American Architect* for new work, too. When they were new, these old houses were 'undoubtedly commonplace enough'; however, 'time and association with a major figure who once lived there have given them a quaintness and a significance

Sunset Hall, Lawrence, Long Island, by Lamb & Rich, 1883.

Stair hall from the Metcalfe House, Buffalo, New York, by McKim, Mead & White, c. 1886. It is now displayed in the Metropolitan Museum of Art, New York.

which now make their architecture a question of secondary importance.'[163] The term 'quaint' was used more in America than back in England; it could refer to a 'flavour of the past' or just to picturesqueness, but also to much more, such as 'individuality and inventiveness'.[164] The architectural elite soon published photographs of old cottages with commentaries: 'covered with grey moss and lichen, their colour effect was beautiful'.[165]

Through a type of Puritan introspection,[166] it was an easy step to combine the notion of the home with the oldness of these houses: 'abodes of peace …'.[167] It now all seemed 'cozy and convivial … the domestic scenes, the low ceilings, wainscot panels … the upright hall clock … the straight-backed mahogany chairs … the small window-panes often set in cedar wood, the green painted floors, the snug and sunny window seats, the broad hall and easy staircase, the high mantels and vast chimney, the quaint sideboard'. One critic, writing about Portsmouth, found that 'The halls are wide and deep after a gone-by fashion, with handsome staircases set at an angle, and not standing nearly upright [as in] modern houses.' Many also analysed the basic shape of the rooms: 'the rooms are not large, yet they seem to be extremely spacious …

the first assignable cause seems to be the low ceilings (about eight feet) which not only give an air of coziness but increase the breadth of the rooms'. The fireplaces 'live amid wainscoting, nestle in elliptical arched nooks, [we] warm ourselves beneath the high mantels at blazing wood fires'. Soon we read that 'Of the interior there is no need for words … we all know and like them'[168] Here, too, comfort was redefined: it could be found in a wooden bench just as much as in modern sprung seating.[169]

According to Scully, the American neo-Colonial style was firmly established by the late 1870s. By the mid-1880s, the work of many architects, like McKim, Mead & White, was viewed as entirely 'American'.[170] What particularly distinguished this revival was that it appeared to consist of one style and not, as in England or Germany, several styles that coexisted. In reality, though, the Americans did combine two quite distinct spheres: the 18th-century vernacularized classical and the small wooden peasant cottage from the 17th century. It was the image of the latter, recalling the homes of the first settlers, that lent so much backing to the rhetoric of the 'virtuous colonial'.

From the late 1870s there follows one of the best-known chapters of 19th-century architectural history. A large number of highly elaborate and astonishingly varied houses emerged in New England and beyond, both in suburban and out-of-town settings, which were later grouped under the term 'shingle style'. Of course, they were also modern homes in that they incorporated the latest technology – by that time the Americans prided themselves on having overtaken Europe in all aspects of modern convenience – and were normally reached by railroad.[171] At the same time, their external covering of shingles, and the resulting lack of conventional ornament, certainly invited a comparison with older cottages. On the other hand, their complex picturesque planning and massing, derived to some extent from Shaw's Old English Tudor, had very little to do with the original American colonial square-box plan. One important element borrowed from the older houses was the relative low height of the ceilings, which gave 'breadth and dignity'.[172] It was as if breadth had taken over from height as the sign of distinction. A further important element in the floorplan of these new houses was the central hall, which ultimately went back to the 'traditional' medieval English country house. As in some of Shaw's new houses, the hall now served as the main

'An Occidental Interior' by C. W. Clark, 1888. This extreme example of primitivism was also held to be the most genuinely 'American' kind of dwelling.

family room.[173] But the main trend in America was towards a completely open-plan interior in which individual rooms began to loose their distinctness and the central staircase was directly linked to the hall. The visual focus here was the fireplace, of which more in the next section.

The dominant element within these interiors was far and away the wood itself, both the complex framework and the diversely treated surfaces. Writers advised that the colour of the wood should generally be 'warm', suggesting 'the raw new tones of lighter woods which the purists now affect', such as a 'light golden yellow'[174] – quite in contrast to European preferences for dark old oak, yet akin to the light pine Alpine interiors discussed below. With their careful integration of plan, construction and décor both inside and outside – especially as shown in the wide-angled black-and-white photographs and lively sketches of the time – these houses blur the distinction between interior décor and interior design. Many of the effects designed by the trades, such as wallpaper, stencilling or complex drapes, appear to have lost out in importance. In the end, however, a comment from a non-architectural journal sums up the normality of routine Old Colonial at the end of the century: 'All Yankee people … have in their houses one or two apartments in the old colonial style with four walls of dark oak, massive rafters, huge fireplaces … reproduction furniture and the occasional spinning wheel.'[175]

By the later 1880s the vernacular, cottage-style element had begun to abate and a more 'correct' classical Colonial was favoured; décor turned subtly but decisively away from the vernacular towards the 'refined', as with the English revivals of Chippendale and Sheraton. Even the earliest analyses of the style affirmed that Colonial meant the very 'absence of vulgarity and eccentricity'. Essentially, the old interiors spoke of 'dignity', 'simplicity' and 'refinement'.[176] Eccentricity could, in fact, be expressed in a new type of interior – the rough log cabin – but this alternative was limited to the holiday home.[177] By the mid-1890s, designers once more felt the urge to employ classical European forms in the domestic interior. The most respected of the handbooks, published by Edith Wharton and Ogden Codman in 1897, expurgated virtually everything that this section has discussed. Picturesqueness was replaced by a pervasive sense of order, in which objects were not just 'old' but had to be proper antiques. The book even claimed that the very term 'Colonial style' made no sense at all. Once created, however, a style label can last for a long time.[178]

The old fireside

The most striking new design object of the Anglo-American domestic revival was the chimney-piece. Did not absolutely every house in those countries rely on a fireplace, and was it not the oldest distinctive feature in any dwelling? That is exactly why it formed an essential component of the new national 'old homes' rhetoric. The simple purpose of the fire was to warm the room, but there was no such thing as a 'simple' purpose: in fact, at times one gets the impression that the efficient warming of a room was now the least important of the fireplace's functions. The science of heating and ventilation was progressing rapidly, and it affirmed what had been realized a century before, that the English type of fireplace was the most inefficient kind of warming ever devised. Even the argument that it provided for good ventilation was found to be misleading. In the new Old English or Old Colonial houses the fireplace became largely a poetic installation.[179] All this was due to the new rhetoric of the designers, poets and social policy-makers. It was meant to provide a sense of domestic magic for the users, while designers seized their chance to produce endless variations of form and décor – by far their most individualistic design solutions in the home.

The dichotomy between science and old habits had been highlighted for a long time. The open fire, Benjamin Franklin had already argued, does not and cannot heat a room properly. His successor in these matters, Count Rumford, devised new shapes for the fireplace opening that improved the situation a little. Subsequent technical treatises complained more and more vociferously about the waste: it was claimed that 80 to 90 per cent of heat was lost through the chimney.[180]

Decoratively speaking, the fireplace had been losing importance from the later 18th century onwards.[181] In tightly squeezed, deep terraced houses the chimney breasts always projected into the room, whereas in larger freestanding houses this was avoided more and more, and the fireplace constituted a mere hole in the wall, often quite small and low. As most other features of the medium-sized house grew richer and more varied during the Victorian period, so of course did the fireplace. The surround itself was now executed in non-combustible materials on account of safety concerns. In addition, the metal parts of the fireplace were highly polished in order to avoid or to counter the messy look of the fire. A much greater variety of shapes and materials was now available, and advances in glass production meant that large mirrors began to appear over the mantelpieces of many houses.

Before the advent of new fashions in design in the 1860s and 1870s, historians in several countries had dealt more generally with the venerable subject of the domestic fire, citing Greek, Roman and Germanic myths and eulogizing the hearth as the centre of the house – indeed of all culture – comparing it to a church altar. The revival of the large enclosed ceramic stove in Altdeutsch and Old Alpine interiors has already been mentioned. However, by about 1890 the Germans began to imitate Anglo-Saxon open fireplaces. French custom was divided between stoves and fireplaces. Havard saw the hearth as a Northern feature and sings its praises, writing of 'elements of gaiety, the flickering flame … allowing us to stir it'.[182] Many French and Belgian architects now celebrated the large – even giant – fireplaces of olden times.

The Anglo-Saxon revival of the old fireplace formed part of the Old English movement. The ideal of the 'old cottage' fireplace was a relatively large recess – very large in comparison with its surroundings – in which there was often space to sit. More specifically, the 'open fireplace' was a fire that was not contained in a grate. The Americans adopted this image, reviving it in the 'colonial kitchens' mentioned above. Here, too, discussions tended to bypass the problems of technical inefficiency so as to embrace fully the moral, social and design discourses of the home. Already Franklin and Rumford had tempered their technical critiques by referring to the appearance of a fire as 'pleasant'; and later on the English writer Frederick Edwards, in his exhaustive technical book on the subject, felt obliged to stress the 'national custom', even the 'national interest', of cherishing the open

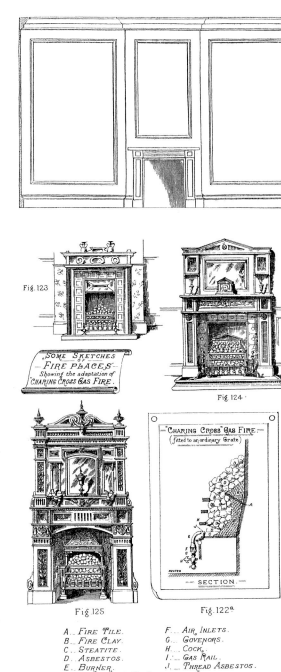

top Wall elevation with fireplace, from J. C. Loudon's *Encyclopedia of Cottage, Farm and Villa Architecture and Furniture* (1833). The early 19th century marks the nadir of fireplace design.

above Illustrations of imitation coal fires, from William T. Sugg's *The Domestic Uses of Coal Gas, as Applied to Cooking, Heating and Ventilation* (1884).

'Warmth is Beauty' – the title given to this rather casual image by Eugene Clarence Gardner in *The House that Jill Built*, one of his chatty advice books on home design (1882).

'Large Ventilating Fireplace in Medieval Style' –
the cover of the second edition of J. Pickering
Putnam's *The Open Fireplace in all Ages* (1882).
The idea is certainly romantic, if perhaps not
what one might call comfortable.

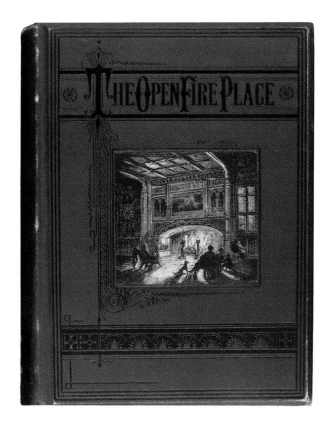

below Design for chimney-piece by Bernard Smith,
London, 1882.

below right American fireplace, 1881. Unusually,
the chimney flue is shown within the room.

fire. Designers and the writers who were associated with them were usually more
forceful, combining classical and medieval, Christian and secular rhetoric in their analyses:
they discussed 'the good old English circle around the fire', describing 'the hearth … the deity
of the home' as the place where 'so many tender memories of early days are centred'. It
was the 'sanctum sanctorum of home', and evoked the 'lares and penates of a loving
worship'.[183] A crucial element in this rhetoric was the way that everybody was considered

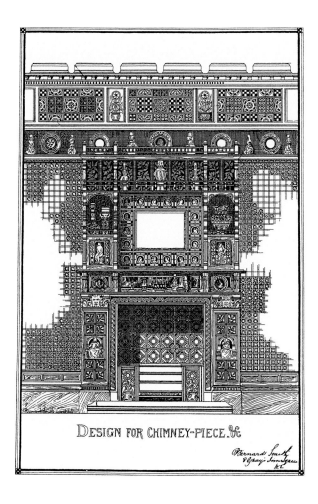

equal in front of the domestic fire. A prominent fireplace could be found in the old castle as well as in the old cottage, although in reality the new type of designer fireplace could only be afforded by the better-off. Illustrations of low-life scenes showed that, for the poor, the open fire had another main function: to give light. 'One might with only slight exaggeration claim that the firelight illuminates virtually every positive page in Victorian novels' (Tristram).[184]

What prompted a new attitude to the design of the fireplace was basically a greater sensitivity towards the relationship between its use and its materials, between how something worked and how it was seen or felt to work – all part of the more acute sense of the visual and tactile effects of materials that have been alluded to so many times in this book. Instead of the usual small grate with burning coals, people now preferred the larger and livelier fire that wooden logs provided. Mid-Victorian fireplace designs were now strongly disliked. The cold feel of the marble now appeared to contradict the whole purpose of heating; it was described as 'cold and uncongenial to the eye and to the touch'. Thus wooden fire surrounds came into fashion again for large houses. The 'sprucely polished but utterly heartless grate of a modern drawing room' (Eastlake) was disliked, too. 'The brass fender has a warmer and more attractive tint in firelight than the glitter of steel', wrote a critic.[185] In the United States, interest in the fireplace reached a high point with the widely

Hooded fireplace complete with window, by Henry J. Sheldon, Chicago, 1877. The design is somewhat mysterious, since there appears to be no room for the flue. Perhaps the whole was a mock installation?

'Oak Library at Southsea', Portsmouth, by Alfred Hudson, 1877 – perhaps the most 'architectural' fireplace of the period.

An early photograph of dining room inglenook at Willesley, Cranbrook, designed by Richard Norman Shaw, 1864–69.

publicized *Open Fireplace in all Ages* by J. Pickering Putnam (1880), who again emphasized all its practical disadvantages, now with the benefit of an extensive scientific discourse. On the other hand, Putnam was also fascinated with the historical panorama of fire surrounds, especially the giant hoods of the old French palaces.[186]

Architects now felt free to apply their full powers of design to the fire, with its 'friendly warmth … the immediate centre of attraction'; 'no part of the interior … offers so broad a

Fireplace in the study of the architect Henry Hobson Richardson, Boston, 1884. This room was a kind of inner sanctum within the extensive complex of offices used by Richardson's firm.

Private Study and Library.

A 'room decoration' by John Howard & Sons, London, shown at the Paris Exposition Universelle, 1878. Perhaps the most elaborate of all inglenooks, it was never published in England.

field for the exercise of the taste and skills of the designer as the open fireplace and chimney piece'. It 'can hardly be too highly decorated', since 'generally it is the one and only structural feature of any room'.[187] The main decorative feature of smaller examples was the overmantel – a series of shelves to hold the increasing number of collectables, which replaced the long-standing custom of the overmantel mirror. Looking back in 1900, Hermann Muthesius found a variety of arrangement that was almost 'unlimited', which he essentially attributed to the 'new art movement'.[188] In North America, a number of very different styles of fire surround emerged: the massive hood, which had more of a Continental than an English origin; coved projections; overmantels with pictures; or the frank display of the flue above the mantelpieces.

From the simple hole in the wall developed the type of fireplace in which walls could be extended into the room on both sides, thus creating a special niche; this was called an

A further elaboration on the inglenook: a 'fireplace in the house of an engineer in New York', 1885.

above The hall fireplace in Harold Ainsworth Peto's own house in London, by George & Peto, 1884.

above right 'Corner of a Boudoir' by Messrs Geo. Dobie & Son, shown at the Edinburgh International Exhibition, 1886.

Inglenook from the children's book *At Home Again*, by Eliza Keary (1886).

inglenook. It was in some ways an answer to the German *Erker*, a small space separated off the main room. Benches were placed on either side of the fire and often lit by small windows. In terms of planning it was an 'old' feature – held to be an 'old peasant form'[189] – since it presupposed that the chimney was situated on the outer walls and not, as with all classical country and town houses, inside the structure. The first examples of the inglenook seem to have occurred quite suddenly, in Nesfield's and Shaw's small country houses of the mid-1860s.[190] They then became particularly popular for dining rooms and billiard rooms.

In America, lavish detached houses departed from the English models in locating the fireplace in the centre of the house – partly a result of the need for a stone or brick core in the middle of an otherwise all-wooden construction. The main fireplace was now invariably connected to the great hall. One may argue, though, that in these wide, open spaces – now also heated by modern systems and lit from many sources – the rationale for reviving the open fire as the main focal point of a room (if not the whole interior) had been somewhat forgotten. The poetic link between physical necessity and visual attractiveness had been lost, even if inefficiency was still ignored in favour of poetic appeal.

Old Alpine and Bavarian (Altdeutsch II)

The most convincing, and probably the most enduring, style for 'old' interiors was the Alpine peasant theme, which emerged in Central Europe in the late 1870s. But the origin of this revival is unusually complex, involving several states and regions. It had started in the later 18th century with the revival of the 'Swiss' Alpine mountain house. After 1870 Bavaria quite suddenly took the lead in the cultivation of everything Alpine; Bavarianism, in turn, was partly integrated into the earlier Altdeutsch movement. The new style was a product of several groups: tourists in search of the picturesque; conservation-minded folklorists; the artists who illustrated it; and architect-designers. It was a Munich coterie of artists, decorative designers and architects (chiefly Gabriel von Seidl), together with Georg Hirth, effectively their spokesperson, who established the new Alpine and sub-Alpine revival style. Within this movement the domestic interior played the key role, fully in step with the 'art in the home' movement. Like the later English 'cottage style', Alpine Bavarianism was a revival of the vernacular, but as filtered through the eyes of the art and design world.

Alpine

The cultural manifestations of the Alpine region occupy a special place in this account of vernacular and folk revivals, since in fact they preceded all other such movements. Until the

Illustration from Eugen Napoleon Neureuther's *Baierische Gebirgslieder* ('Bavarian Mountain Songs'), published in 1834 – an early conception of the Alpine cottage used to frame a titillating, folksy narrative.

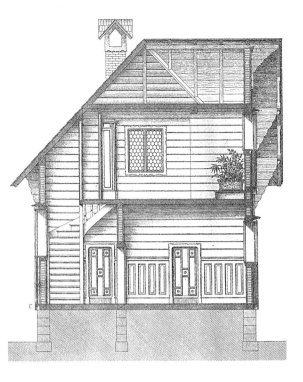

Contrasting interpretations of the Alpine: a 'maison tyrolienne', designed with an exact regard for constructional effectiveness for the Paris Exposition of 1867 (*above*); and a farmhouse interior, painted by the Tyrolean Franz von Defregger, *c*. 1880 (*above right*), that shows a rough, earthy view of the Alpine peasant's environment.

Furniture by the Munich architect-designer August Töpfer from the early 1860s. The 'Brettstuhl' – a chair essentially made of two boards – became an emblem of peasant and Alpine regional furniture.

18th century the Alps were seen as ugly and threatening, but now – through the well-documented efforts of poets, painters and tourists from many countries – they represented both the awe-inspiring Sublime and a picturesque rural idyll. Initially, the term 'Alpine' was associated principally with Switzerland, and the image of a small and intrepid yet peaceful and liberty-conscious nation gave the concept a special socio-political impetus.[191] Later on, an increasingly used synonym for all Alpine manifestations was 'Tyrolean'.[192] Within this context, the Alpine peasant house became the first seriously studied building of the vernacular type. The way in which it seemed to grow out of its environment, almost literally, led to an early appreciation of its materials and to praises of the textural effects of stone and wood, for instance from John Ruskin in the 1830s.[193] Crucially, 'Alpine house' also appeared exportable as a style of décor. From about 1820 onwards, *Schweizerhaus*, 'Swiss cottage' and *chalet suisse* were common enough descriptions throughout Europe, especially in resort towns. However, as in the case of the beloved 'English cottage', few early admirers of the picturesque Alpine chalet would have ventured inside. As with the peasant genre in painting, it was believed that this class of people lived in grimy surroundings. Tourism did help a little, in that exhausted walkers began to appreciate the rough comforts offered inside the mountain hut or shelter (the *Sennhütte*). At the Vienna Fair of 1873, just such a little hut, fitted out as an eatery, was apparently very popular.[194]

As with the translation of style from cottage to manor house in England, an upward trajectory can be applied to Alpine and most European farmhouses, too: wooden interiors from the 16th to the 18th centuries were found in minor country houses and even in many townhouses in southern Central Europe.[195] In 1862 Falke praised the all-wooden interiors he had seen in Nuremberg and the 'infinitely warm impression' they gave. These rooms were now increasingly preserved, such as the extremely elaborate Seidenhof in Zurich. One early attempt at re-creating such an interior was the Rütlistube near Luzern, in 1868: the site commemorated the establishment of the Swiss nation, even though the room was designed in a mainstream neo-Gothic style.[196]

One object in all these interiors stood out: the ubiquitous and evocative *Brettstuhl* (to cite but one of its many names), a chair made up from boards. In many parts of Europe it became a prominent feature of almost any peasant genre scene, while at the same time preserving a

The preferred interpretation of the Alpine cottage interior from the late 1870s onwards was synonymous with the appearance of vigorously textured pine or fir wood in light, clean colours. In Lothar Meggendorfer's view of a room in a 16th- or 17th-century farmhouse in the Tyrol, these vernacular elements are combined with a modicum of Altdeutsch décor (see also Meggendorfer's illustrations on pp. 224, 309).

specific Alpine feeling. By the 1870s it had become a collector's item as well.[197] A few designers of the incipient applied arts reform movements also took an interest in this kind of furniture and emphasized the way it was a cheap country product. A set of a table and chairs from southern Bavaria, showing an 'an extremely homely and liveable character', was published in several countries, labelled as either 'Swiss' or 'Tyrolean'.[198]

The Bavarian Alpine style in Munich

By the 1860s and 1870s the Swiss style had become routine for villas of all sizes in most Western countries. This very ubiquity made nonsense of any attempt to identify the 'Swiss' peasant house as strictly regional, at a time when the movement to discover 'primitive' folk characteristics had begun in earnest. The Austria-Hungarians and the Scandinavians were familiarizing themselves with *Hausindustrie* or *Hauskunst* – what was later called 'folk art', of the type already mentioned in relation to the Netherlands. However, most local manufacture in the Alps, especially its woodcarving, was already aimed at the export and tourist markets; the new *Hauskunst* apostles, especially Falke, thought it far too naturalistic and sentimentalized.[199]

In a way, the definition of Alpine peasant culture had to start all over again. This time, however, it had a centre: Munich, the capital of Bavaria, which in fact had appropriated elements of Alpine style from other countries. For instance, it was while the Tyrolean painter Franz von Defregger was based at the Munich Akademie that he publicized his home region, with its tough people and archaic-looking houses; and it was Munich artists and architects who discovered and promoted Tyrolean, and even some Swiss, vernacular interiors.[200] In actual fact, Bavaria's share of the Alps is small, and yet its folkloric image – the Lederhosen and other paraphernalia – soon became so well known that even today it symbolizes Bavarian culture, and even German culture, all over the world.

'Germany', by contrast, was a region full of cultural and political dilemmas. The overt nationalism of the new united German Empire and attempts to connect it to a 'German Renaissance' have been dealt with above. Conscious of lagging behind Britain and France in terms of wealth and modern industry, Germany did not want to display any kind of vernacular work at the World's Fairs of the 1870s and 1880s. At the same time, it was made up of a number of smaller regional cultures – far more so than other European countries of comparable size – and the Germans felt a strong desire to investigate these aspects of their make-up. Such localized research invariably tended towards the folkloristic. The Germans now began a process that slightly later, in about 1900, would be termed 'the discovery of the

Heimat': the exploration of one's home region, including one's ancestral home, resulting in a loving regard for everything considered 'traditional' in that region. These sentiments did not have to be explained or proven; nevertheless, empirical studies demonstrated strong differences between artefacts from different localities.[201] A case in point was the 'deutsche Bauernhaus', or 'old farmhouse' (a new term): it was considered to exhibit marked regional variations but at the same time provided a more generalized image of a house with a huge protective roof, whether it was called 'North German', 'Black Forest' or 'Alpine'.[202]

At the heart of the movement in Bavaria was its peculiar relationship with Germany – the relationship between an old established region and a new state. Of course, Bavaria had always been part of the loose federation that had constituted 'Germany'. But it joined the new German Empire under Prussian rule only reluctantly. After 1871, Bavarians began to cultivate their dialect, customs, beer and foul-mouthed but harmless jokes all the more assiduously. The Bavarians called the Prussians humourless upstarts, and were loved all the more for it. North Germans marvelled at 'the apparently sorrow-free zest for life of the German South'.[203] The Bavarian Alps became Germany's top tourist destination. The region was thus the new Germany's 'other', but one that was located within the country itself, fulfilling a role as Germany's vernacular group. Perhaps uniquely among European countries, this 'other' was not an Orientalist one; its folksy image was created and supported both within the Bavarian region and by outsiders. Furthermore, because Bavaria formed part of a newly created state, its regionalism, its 'nationalism', appeared entirely non-political.

Preliminary design for a bedroom in Ludwig II's Neuschwanstein, by Peter Herwegen, 1869. A late manifestation of rich but delicate neo-Gothic, it conjures up a world of remoteness.

Frontispiece of the *Zeitschrift des Kunstgewerbevereins in München* ('Journal of the Munich Applied Arts Society'), 1878, drawn by Rudolf von Seitz. A retrospective section at the great Munich 1876 Art and Applied Arts Exhibition bore the title 'The Works of our Fathers' – a rhetorical invocation of old German art. The Munich designers now aimed to create a sense of immediacy for a vigorous, newly revived style that could be applied comprehensively to all aspects of design.

Something similar applied to the relationship between the capital city and its hinterland. Normally, as in Paris or Vienna, the 'primitive' people's art in the 'country' was defined as such not by its producers but by connoisseurs who had often travelled a long way to find it. Yet Munich's most celebrated painters of those decades – Karl Theodor von Piloty, Hans Makart, Franz von Lenbach – all had their roots in the region, and the designers who contributed so much to the local style – Lorenz Gedon, Rudolf von Seitz and Gabriel von Seidl – were ur-Münchners themselves. There was, furthermore, a strong connection between the city and its hinterland. Bavarianism was an important element of artistic life and creativity in Munich itself. The tourists who arrived there before travelling into the Alps were already in Bavaria, in 'Urbayern'.[204] There was nothing more quintessentially Bavarian (and vernacular) than the Munich Bierkellers, all created by the young Munich designers.[205]

All this was in no way detrimental to Munich's reputation as Central Europe's major art city, the 'Kunststadt'. The teaching of its academy was second only to Paris; Ludwig I's patronage of all the arts, especially architecture, was admired throughout Europe; and many found Ludwig II's more private and lavish artistic projects awe-inspiring at the very least. Furthermore, artists in Munich were known for their active self-representation and for their bohemian leanings. The city enjoyed an international avant-garde image for many decades, which was itself often linked with a sophisticated appreciation of a folk culture. Kandinsky's paintings of the early 1900s formed the last and most celebrated combination of these two strands.[206]

As elsewhere, the painters in Munich were most influential in producing novel interpretations of the land and its 'original' inhabitants. The 1870s witnessed a turn away from the dramatic and burlesque representations of mountain life. The work of the younger painters such as Wilhelm Leibl and Karl Haider, and also of Bavarian writers like Herman Schmid, no longer emphasized the complex picturesqueness and drama of life in the Alps, but focused much more on its 'uniformity, cleanliness [and] exactness'. One of the early writers on ancient pan-Germanism had remarked that 'the basic relationships in the life of the old Germans are simple and quiet', and Beavington Atkinson, an acute observer of German painting, wrote: 'repose and contemplation … find poetry, like Wordsworth, in the untrodden paths of nature'.[207] So much for the images of the old Germanic warrior or the roving medieval knight, beloved of the Altdeutsch movement thus far; indeed, they soon dropped out of fashion.

In contrast to its schools of painting, Munich's architecture and applied arts appeared somewhat directionless in 1870: Ludwig II's medievalist and French fantasies, the Italianesque neo-Renaissance style and even the new 'Swiss' houses in the Bavarian Alps revealed nothing of a *genius loci*.[208] Then, in 1873, the sculptor and decorator Lorenz Gedon created a spectacular façade for the Schack-Galerie, a private collector's residence; labelled 'German Renaissance', it was immediately hailed as the pioneering building.[209] Munich now also employed the 'Altdeutsch label', in a way stealing it from Nuremberg. That city's great epic, Richard Wagner's *Die Meistersinger*, was indeed first performed in Munich, and its sets and costumes were produced by Munich artists.[210] By the late 1870s architects were simplifying and coarsening the external features of buildings, Seidl first of all. The most important type of structure to which this applied was the Bierhalle or Bierkeller – a masterstroke of stereotyping that declared a 'Merrie Olde England' kind of harmless banter to be typically (Upper) Bavarian and thus Alpine, too. After a decade or more this style, which never acquired an actual name (the label 'Bavarian' was used only rarely), found adherents throughout Germany. Clearly, many parallels with the London Queen Anne Revival can be drawn.[211]

Within the decorative arts, the situation was more complex. Munich lacked both a wealthy manufacturing scene and decisive state support for applied arts reform enjoyed by other cities. But, true to its image as a 'city of art', Munich fostered work that was firmly artist-led, at the same time demanding that these artist-designed objects should include all the implements of daily life.[212] In 1876 Munich celebrated itself and the new German state with a huge, and hugely successful, art and applied arts exhibition. The whole exhibition employed a highly innovative mode of display. Thus far, exhibits had been ordered according to their 'class', but hundreds of clocks or stoves in one place had led to fatigue in the viewer. Now different kinds of art objects, both fine and applied, were grouped together in rooms or room units in order to create a context and a unity of meaning and space, 'preparing [the visitor's] feelings and perceptions'. It was all provided by the same team of architects and artists, who shared a common vision and an agreed starting point. The exhibition also contained a section of old German artworks of all kinds that was cleverly entitled 'Unserer Väter Werke' ('The Works of our Fathers'). Their extremely high quality was intended to persuade visitors that such levels could be, or were, achieved in new German work, too – which was generally still held to be inferior to French and English production.[213]

A new concept of the artist working in the applied arts was emerging. Painters and sculptors no longer condescended to devise the occasional work of 'décor', but demonstrated an all-roundness and a new sense of their involvement in life and society – particularly in the realm of stage sets, exhibitions, and pageants and festivals of every kind, as well as in the stage-settings of their own living rooms and ateliers. Critics lavished considerable praise on the work of the multi-talented Lorenz Gedon and of the father-and-son team of Franz and Rudolf von Seitz, which included their own domestic interiors.[214] Only an artist-designer could be entrusted with the task of combining the calculated with the improvised. An artist-designer trained in the fine arts was in any case more likely to be interested in 'content', in motifs that told a story, than the more run-of-the-mill low-ranked *dessinateur* who churned out schematic décor for a manufacturer. This situation contrasted with the more architecturally controlled approach to the applied arts that pertained in other centres, especially Vienna. In Munich, the idea was that all decoration should demonstrate the utmost liveliness, 'a free kind of verve', and even an improvisatory streak; the artist should be 'working fast', even at the risk of being accused of superficiality. The *Makartbouquet* – a seemingly improvised arrangement of mainly dried flowers and leaves, mentioned in Chapter III – typified this approach. Contemporaries likened this freedom and verve to the step from the Renaissance to the livelier Baroque, with the rediscovery of Bavarian Rococo just round the corner. Munich art as a whole seemed to possess a new kind of artistic hedonism. 'We need an art that makes us feel good', opined one writer in 1876.[215] The basic aims of art in Munich appeared quite clear. As in other major centres, painting served two aims: on the one hand, it appealed to a demand for realistic or spiritual content, and on the other hand, much 'realistic' painting could now also be seen as 'colouristic', in a quite abstract sense.[216] The applied arts and architecture were understood in the same way. One the one hand the meaningful motifs present within décor tell a story, while on the other hand artists were arriving at a new appreciation of pure materiality, and that of wood in particular, including Alpine pine and other conifers ('very beautiful juicy brown colours'). 'Warmth' was now one of these timbers' most desirable qualities.[217] Friedrich Pecht, Munich's main art critic, discerned the same attributes in Defregger's pictures, describing how 'warmth and deep ideal zest' were allied to the 'greatest realistic truth'.[218]

After the mid-1870s, critics began to formulate a clearer picture of the interior. Since the displays in the 1876 exhibition had successfully integrated diverse items, critics now suggested that 'the enclosed space allows for architectural unity, a richly articulated work of art in itself', helped by an element that is 'completely owed to the Germans, atmosphere [*Stimmung*]'.[219] What should be remembered about the Munich art movement as a whole is that the cultivation of a design style that reflected the *genius loci* of Munich and Bavaria was taken as seriously as any other task in art. Painting catered for it, architecture had begun to follow it, and now applied arts décor fully embraced 'folk' motifs. A local, vernacular character was thought especially appropriate for all spheres of daily life, and that, too, required as comprehensive an artistic effort as possible.

The 'Seidlzimmer'

What was required now was a designed domestic space that reflected all these considerations and that would serve as an example for all to see. In fact, there was just such a work at the 1876 Munich exhibition: known straightaway after the name of its designer, Gabriel von Seidl, it was immediately illustrated and commented upon widely – something that constituted a novelty in itself.[220]

The 'Seidlzimmer' appeared effortlessly to combine most of the qualities outlined so far. It belonged definitively to the German Renaissance. It could also be labelled 'Altdeutsch', 'Bavarian', or at any rate 'Alpine': 'In the Alpine region … people feel enclosed in a lively,

Gabriel von Seidl's room at the Munich Art and Applied Arts Exhibition, 1876, known as the 'Seidlzimmer' – the most frequently illustrated German room of the decade. The interior contained numerous colour accents: fresh-looking timberwork, a dark green stove, red embroidery on the linens, variously coloured ceramics and white walls.

homely way … in a house that that belongs to them [i.e. as inhabitants of the region]'. Many critics described the room as 'bürgerlich', but it was also characterized as 'peasant', and most agreed that this 'favourite of the visitors' was not a rich person's interior. Others wrote of its 'delightful simplicity' and asserted 'that the effect [of an interior] is now based more on harmony than on splendour'. Its space appeared unified yet also informal. Some picked up on its contrived nature: with the calculated display of 'a well-used, dog-eared chronicle', the room 'appears to be staged for the painter of a genre painting'; 'a poet could not have written about it more beautifully'. Once more we encounter that paradoxical juxtaposition of old and new: the

Wall painting by Otto Hupp, *c.* 1881, in a villa by Gabriel von Seidl (destroyed). This joyful and naive scheme for a nursery is one of the earliest examples of décor aimed specifically at children.

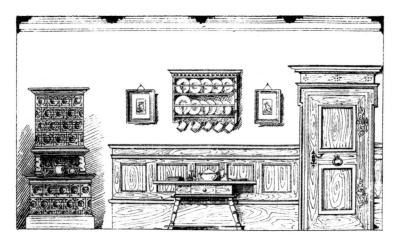 

Seidlzimmer was the type of room in which ancestors had enjoyed their lives 'in youthful fresh-ness'. Even more important was the impression of comfort that Seidl's design conveyed. The whole panoply of German terms was brought in: 'das Heimliche' (homely), 'das Gemütliche' (cosy), 'Behaglichkeit' (comfort), 'Traulichkeit' (cosiness), 'Wohnlichkeit' (liveableness) – all of which resulted in a 'warm, saturated tone' that was described as 'so very cosy, so poetic'. Such terms could just as readily be applied to individual furnishings, such as the stove, 'a fresh and life-warming comrade'.[221]

For some years, from the late 1870s, Seidl belonged to the firm of Kunsthandwerk Seitz & Seidl, about which very little is known, but which must have been a rather friendly, informal concern. Although Seidl went on to design many prestigious public buildings, this partnership was on record as having designed a fret-sawed plate rack for the kitchen that could hardly have cost more than a few Marks. Seidl's 'peasant' forms were clean and his rooms were spacious – not crude, musty or oppressive as in some Northern European images of old peasant interiors. As an architect, he aimed for a greater precision of line and surface, distancing himself some-what from his Munich artist-designer-decorator friends and their improvisatory outlook.[222] The love of the appearance of timber and clean, bare boards, whether they were labelled Altdeutsch, Tyrolean or Bavarian, spread throughout the 1880s.[223]

Georg Hirth

Although notoriously non-literate, the Munich designers found a congenial spokesperson in a writer from Protestant Thuringia. Georg Hirth, whose mother had come from France, was to become one of the most colourful figures in the late 19th-century art world – the chief instiga-tor of the avant-garde Munich Secession of 1892–93, and in 1896 the founder of the journal *Jugend*, and thus of Jugendstil itself, Germany's version of Art Nouveau. Hirth does not fit the mould of the typical writer on the applied arts of the time; he was not an architect, nor a patron

Four sketches for a utility room, by Gabriel von Seidl, *c.* 1879. Although Hirth never writes explicitly about Seidl in his book, he does illustrate a number of his projects.

of contemporary art, nor an erudite art historian like Havard. He was not a museum official or taste-overseer like Falke (although he was a collector), and neither did he act as a direct spokesperson for commerce like Mothes. He did, however, have something of the theorist about him, in the manner of Charles Blanc, coupled with the lighter-toned journalism of his English contemporaries. Hirth's actual profession, if it can be narrowed down to just one, was proprietor of a printing works and a Munich liberal newspaper (today's *Süddeutsche Zeitung*). He comes across chiefly as a campaigner, in this respect similar to William Morris. But there was one huge difference: Hirth was thoroughly liberal in his political and cultural outlook. His major achievement was to found publications that were perceived to be of high quality and astonishingly cheap at the same time, especially when one bears in mind the comparatively high cost of illustrated publications. His lavish book on the home interior cost 14 Marks, while large pattern books might retail for up to 80 Marks.[224] Hirth was passionately interested in printing and along with William Morris is regarded as one of the founders of the 'art of the book' (or *Buchkunst*) movement, which encouraged a return to early Renaissance forms and to the strong black tones of early woodcuts (see p. 46). Hirth did not at all subscribe to the contemporary trend for rich chromolithographic colouring, but cleverly (and cheaply) inserted single-colour backgrounds in gentle tones.[225]

To call Hirth's book – *Das deutsche Zimmer der Renaissance: Anregungen zur häuslichen Kunstpflege* ('The German Room of the Renaissance: Hints for the Domestic Cultivation of Art') – a manifesto would be going too far. It can, however, be seen as providing a platform for the Munich group, with its numerous prominent illustrations of Seidl's designs and theoretical underpinnings of his work and that of many other contemporary designers.[226] Hirth does not come across as too dogmatic a supporter of the Altdeutsch Renaissance revival. His greatest delight lies in the small woodcuts of Dürer and especially those of Holbein, but late Raphael and Flemish Mannerism are never unwelcome. What was peculiarly German in all this? Hirth's nebulous arguments here are much like to those of the Queen Anne Revivalists: he writes of 'our unconscious and loving taking-up of the Renaissance'. What the style achieves for the interior is made to sound very basic: 'Yes, I do think that … these models – I name only the sap-green oven with the golden-brown wall of timber, the deep-blue stoneware jug with the tablecloth embroidered in red – would have to be invented as a kind of natural necessity if they did not exist already.'[227]

The principal subject of Hirth's book is, arguably, the user of the house, but the main addressee (one must conclude) is the designer, who is offered an explanation of how the user reacts to certain forms. In that respect Hirth differs from Falke, who largely dictates 'taste' to both users and designers. Indeed, Hirth comes closer to the new user-friendliness of Anglo-American texts and to French works with their emphasis on the user's psyche. Falke, writing in the 1870s, still subscribes to a strong sense of hierarchy: the richer the home, the more artistic it will appear. But Hirth maintains that 'between "high" and "low" art, inasmuch as it concerns the décor of our dwellings, there is no difference *in principle*'. A rich room can be comfortable, but a cheaper interior can also present 'a cosy [*gemütlich*], simple, beautiful, heart-warming homeliness'. As he stresses at the end of his introduction, 'beauty does not acknowledge a person's status'.[228] Seidl's neo-vernacular art and his (by conventional standards) rough designs cannot be considered inferior. Consequently, Hirth does not explicitly acknowledge 'folk art', the vernacular, as a real issue either.

Hirth's view of the recipient is not bound up in the practical question of how room functions should be distinguished – a key topic in most books on the home. Nor is he concerned, like Falke, with evaluating works of fine art in the home. Instead, he sees the dweller as someone whose psychological and physical sensibilities lead him or her react in certain ways to the forms and colours of the complete interior. Hirth, who became increasingly interested in physics and medicine, applies a strict scientific reasoning to this question: in a room where 'the parts by themselves or as a whole claim our attention, we may speak of their activities or … their functions'. These functions may be divided into those that belong to the realm of physical necessity, and those that satisfy 'our sense of humour and of beauty, our pleasures of imagination and symbolism, and finally our aesthetic dogmas'.[229] In brief: that forms within the domestic interior affect the user both physically and psychologically is held to be a scientific truth. Hirth here borrows from von Helmholtz's work in cognitive science, as well as from Semper's new understanding of the history and nature of materials.

The heart of Hirth's book is its longest chapter, 'Die Farbe' ('Colour'; already referred to briefly in Chapter III). It begins with an ample discourse on the science of colour, based on the standard sources. The argument then centres on the physiology of the eye and on the eye's psychological and physiological 'requirements'. Its preference for certain colour contrasts is mainly a result of these requirements – as a matter of 'purely physiological satisfaction'. The aim is 'to get to the stage where the eye no longer demands anything more but is resting in enjoyment'. It was the old Germans' love of the forest and their need for warmth that principally informed their 'art in the home' ('häusliche Kunst'). Hirth's main colour choice is brown: he chides Goethe for calling it 'dirty', and Chevreul for not showing it in his charts – in any event not 'the golden glowing colours of, for instance, Hungarian ash'. Hirth's 'principle of brown' conjures up a picture of autumn light; it creates a 'warm, lush colour atmosphere … [of] browns, brownish reds and greens, greenish and brownish yellows, and finally the yellow-white tones, all mixed colours in which the "warm" rays predominate'.[230] His assessment of the colour effects of the beloved German forest thus differs from other, more commonly held views that tended to evoke elaborate fairytale qualities, as in a comment on the Seidlzimmer claiming that the 'life' of a tree could be transferred to a beam in a house, and thus 'would become the spirit of the house, sometimes protecting, sometimes more mischievous'.[231]

In conjunction with colour and its effects on the user, Hirth goes on to discuss further the textural qualities of materials. He elaborates on the neo-Gothic doctrine of 'truth to materials', introducing ideas from the latest areas of psychological research. For him, any kind of smooth, uniform colouring, any kind of oil paint on wood or shiny polish, is to be avoided. Basing himself once more on von Helmholtz's highly scientific observations, Hirth writes: 'considered purely in physiological terms, the demand for an interruption of colours can be fulfilled through the merest perceptible change in appearance, that is, as soon as we focus our eyes on certain points'. Thus 'the more we use natural surfaces for decoration', the better; 'a noble material even tolerates faulty colouring'. We love the 'annual rings, medullary rays and the pattern of the wood'.[232] Hirth then briefly but vigorously defends the choice of white walls over panelling, a new element in Seidl's work that was initially disliked by most: he approves of its 'rough rendering, which provides the smallest of resting places for our roaming glances'.[233]

In an earlier section Hirth touches on the psychology of décor – the effect of lines on the user, for instance – which would feature also in Havard's book. But his experimental theorizing was more advanced than Havard's generalized psychological observations. Furthermore, Hirth was considering a type of design that could completely exclude the representational and the symbolic: he talks of 'massive wooden constructions' that 'in their forceful reality exclude any kind of symbolic illusions'.[234] With his preference for light brown, Hirth was also a very early pioneer in the rejection of the dramatically darkened room.[235] Thus, in the end, in spite of his talk of Germanness and the Munich–Bavarian origins of certain forms, Hirth does not care much for geographical or historical specificity. We have already moved beyond the themed interior. Even oldness is no longer attracts much attention. Instead, design is radically reduced to that favourite 19th-century catchphrase for the fine arts, 'form and colour'.

The end of Altdeutsch

'If we are not mistaken, we have, at this moment, reached the point where the word "Altdeutsch" is no longer music to our ears.' This astonishing statement was made by Luthmer in 1885. Thus far we have noted a great deal of similarity between all the movements that sought to appropriate the 'old'. As we look back over a century later, we can see that they had all discovered something enduring. But Germany was the exception. Barely a dozen years after the inception of 'their' Altdeutsch Renaissance, the Germans had already begun to tire of the style. It seems critics took fright at the movement's success, having once commented on its great popularity. To an extent, this was due to the way in which taste gurus like Julius Lessing and Alfred Lichtwark assumed an ever greater role and produced ever sharper commentary, constantly reinforcing the moralist, anti-commercial, reformist tenor of their messages.[236] Moreover, the perennial question of 'style' – that is, of a national style – appeared more difficult to resolve in Germany than anywhere else. Georg Hirth, who had preached the restful home, was himself the most restless of men, advocating ever more styles for the interior. By 1870 Germany had already adopted and discarded neo-Gothic in favour of neo-Renaissance, and would soon work its way through neo-Baroque, neo-Romanesque, and even neo-Neoclassicism and neo-Biedermeier. Besides, some critics openly questioned the very suitability of a national style. A woman writer in Berlin agreed that the Germans wanted to be patriotic – of course they did – but this need not extend to the shape of their sofas.[237] The basic problem with styles was that a desire for more meaning was always accompanied by an unease about surfeit of meaning. In addition, the conviction that arose in the 1880s that 'old' should actually mean old, and not just an imitation of it, appears to have hit the Germans harder than, say, the French.

Seitz & Seidl, design for a hunting room, 1887. Here, the Alpine Bavarian style comes close to a 'countrified' version of Rococo, resulting in an unusually unthreatening hunting room.

Design for a living room by H. Kirchmayr, a designer from the Tyrol working in Munich, 1885. The Alpine/Altdeutsch room has here reverted to a slightly earlier type, full of lively Altdeutsch paraphernalia (compare pp. 225ff.).

As far as the Alpine and Bavarian styles were concerned, they had already begun to sever their ties to Altdeutsch. Gabriel von Seidl's own work went from strength to strength, although his championing of timber was soon much curtailed by the discovery of the 'Bavarian' Rococo and its coloured décor on whitewashed walls. By the 1890s, the severe, gloomy and unrefined 'old' was being expunged from the image of healthy Alpine life. For the Bavarians, dropping the Altdeutsch label did not present a problem: on the contrary, they now had a style all of their own. Indeed, they no longer felt any real need to stress the 'old'; the design label 'altbayrisch' never caught on, and everything was simply and self-evidently 'bayerisch'. Endlessly reproduced, it became one of the most stable versions of regionalism in the West. And so did the Seidl–Hirth kind of interior: harmless, slanted towards recreation and a holiday atmosphere, and referencing 'Alpine' or 'peasant' in whatever measure seemed desirable.

Ultimately, all discussions of German nationalism raise the issue of the 'Sonderweg' – the question of the deeper origins of Germany's political problems in the 20th century. Most often, all manifestations of German nationalism are thrown into one pot and held to be equally

A 'Tyrolean Peasant Room', from the *Illustrierte Frauenzeitung* ('Illustrated Women's Magazine'), Berlin, 1896. Here, it is the ornamentation of the objects that is in the peasant style, not the room as a whole.

responsible. In the context of this chapter on 19th-century German art, one may draw some distinctions, however. First, there was an older kind of a 'noisy' patriotism, of a kind shared by many countries, that was fascinated with the concept of medieval people as warriors, for example. Second, there was a more purist (and in some ways modernist) notion that valued *Volk*, tradition, roots, *Heimat*, simplicity, etc., and which took hold in the 1890s (only marginally dealt with here). Lastly, there were types of European regionalism that reached beyond borders: groupings such as 'Nordic', which linked northern Germany with Scandinavia, and 'Alpine', which included Germany, Austria, Switzerland and other countries, which one may see as something quite separate from 'German'. However, this Alpine regionalism could also demonstrate a strong tendency towards conservatism and agrarianism, which during the 1920s and 1930s helped to nurture pan-German racism in Bavaria and Austria. By contrast, the first and oldest trend, patriotism, was the one least likely to produce anti-urbanism and racism. Ultimately, one has to bear in mind that all three kinds of nationalism could be, and were, used by 20th-century Fascism.[238]

French 18th-century revival

In considering the neo-vernacular style, how should one approach France – the country that for centuries had been responsible for most of the high styles of furnishing? The Henri II interiors mentioned earlier to some extent corresponded to neo-Elizabethan or neo-Jacobean styles, but one could only call them 'national', and certainly not vernacular. A vague *chalet suisse* style could be found on the exterior of many French villas, and from about 1880 onwards the half-timbered Normandy style was popular, although little attention was paid to the characteristics of Normandy interiors; but otherwise there is little evidence of regional vernacular revivals. Neither did there seem to be a generally recognized image of a French peasant hut. From the end of the century France did go on to develop a number of regionalist and vernacular styles, but they remained regionalist in the sense of being limited to their areas and always contrasting with the styles produced in the great centres.[239]

How, then, did France address the issue of a proper national style? France's Grand Siècle – the 17th century of Louis XIV – appeared too grand for a revival in the more common homes of the 19th century. 'Rococo' furniture, as we saw, was produced in most, if not all, countries of the West. Its 19th-century makers were aware that the style ultimately derived from Paris, but choosing the Rococo did not necessarily equate with choosing the latest Paris fashion, as had certainly been the case with Empire or 'Néo-Grec', even if those styles arguably contained few elements that could be called French. It was earlier 19th-century English collectors and traders who used the label 'Old French' for the Louis styles, which meant much the same as what the Viennese called their 'Blondelscher Stil',[240] but these terms did not last for long and would have made no sense to the French themselves. In any case, during the 19th century all style labels developed precise meanings only very slowly.

It was the polyphony of exhibits at the World's Fairs that enabled 'French' design to emerge as such, when it was displayed next to that of other countries. In London in 1851 one could still see work in the Rococo style by non-French producers alongside French-made products. By 1867 that was less likely. In the exhibitions of the 1870s, English furniture was making a major impact with forms that nobody had previously seen, and which certainly the French saw as very English. At the same time the Germans were proclaiming their own 'Deutsche Renaissance'. The national styles of furnishing seemed to exemplify the old stereotypes – 'French elegance', 'German forcefulness', and 'English puritanism' resulting in 'gauntness' – more clearly than ever before.[241] Moreover, one of the results of the applied arts reform movements, first in London and then in Vienna, was the declaration of most French work as in 'bad taste'. Falke in particular hated the Rococo and thought it vulgar.

Scenery for *Une Fille du Régent* ('The Regent's Daughter'), a drama by Alexandre Dumas père set in 1719; it was painted by Philastre et Cambon, Paris, 1846. From the 1820s onwards many stage designers were just as attentive to period décor as genre painters.

Drawing room in the Château de Ferrières, near Paris, built for the Rothschild family in the 1850s. The interior reflects the 'Louis' styles, although here one might well ask 'Louis Who?'

Two interiors, in the Louis XV and Louis XVI styles respectively, adapted by Paul Lacroix in 1878 from 18th-century illustrations. The domesticity of the fireside scene, however, fits more neatly with 19th-century notions of the cosy home.

Commercially, all this seemed to be paying off, and France's export monopoly was threatened. To complicate matters, from the 1880s the Viennese and the Bavarians began to promote their own regional variations on the 18th century, their own Rococo.[242] Of course, the French had long been aware of foreign imitations of their styles, but these were now declared as inferior and retardataire.[243]

The key question, clearly, is whether a national 18th-century revival occurred, or whether we should just see a continuation of French and international trade fashions. 'Rococo' was a relatively new word, in general currency only by the 1840s, from which point on it was also used internationally.[244] For France itself, the 'Louis' labels were of much greater significance. But the revaluation of the 18th-century styles that began around 1880 certainly did not arrive with a fanfare: there was no zealousness about it, little connection with the design reform movements, and few ruthless promoters. Perhaps only the Goncourt brothers come close to that definition; their main activity, alongside the nurturing of literature, was to collect all the fine and applied arts of the 18th century – the 'siècle de joli' – constantly expressing their love of that period and seeing it as a totality. The brothers fervently believed in that 'old' society, holding their own in contempt. Apart from the art of Japan, they disliked or professed disinterest in all other styles, be they ancient Greek, medieval, Renaissance or 19th-century eclectic.[245]

It was natural that writers should look for greater historical precision. Traders, too, increasingly applied the 'Louis' labels. By now the two main modes – Louis XV and Louis XVI – appeared as clearly differentiated styles but maintained a peaceful coexistence. The former was better known, but the latter was just as important in the creation of unified interiors. Yet precise historical labelling was not sufficient in itself. A revival, by definition, had to be preceded by periods of neglect. Certainly for the Neoclassical architects, Rococo was the style that had had to be eradicated completely; 18th-century taste, wrote Percier and Fontaine, was 'mean' and 'false'. But soon the situation switched around. After 1850, it was the turn of Napoleon's Empire style to be condemned, as the 'very falsest period of the decorative arts the world has yet seen'; the painter David spread 'boredom' and 'an icy wind'.[246]

Under the definition outlined in this chapter, revivals could hardly be created by the trades, and it is not possible here to evaluate properly the Rococo forms of French manufacturers from the 1830s and 1840s. By 1863 Hippolyte Destailleur, one of France's most recognized architects and designers, fervently praised 18th-century design and production and regretted its break-up under the Revolution. Destailleur worked for the new imperial court of Napoleon III, and the Empress Eugénie herself now harked back to the 18th century and to Louis XVI in particular, resulting in some of those interiors being dubbed 'Louis Seize Impératrice'.[247] Crucial for patrons of the 1850s and 1860s was the connection between an old piece of furniture and its original owner, especially when it evoked the tragic figures of late 18th-century royalty, above all Marie-Antoinette, executed at the hands of the Revolutionaries.[248] Critics sought a more comprehensive understanding of old objects within their historical context[249] – the type of intensive research that the Gothicists, above all Viollet-le-Duc, had undertaken for 'their' period.

At this point, politics rather than history became the burning issue. Anyone taking a passionate interest in the design of the *ancien régime* during the 19th century – especially during the early years of the Third Republic, from 1871 onwards – first had to clarify his or her own position towards monarchist, pre-republican times. Some asked how anyone could find anything to praise among all the 'the bad manners of the 18th century'?[250] The historian Hippolyte Taine considered this problem in terms of the distant/close-by conundrum, mirroring what the English said about their 18th century: on one hand, the total collapse of the *ancien régime* in the Revolution represented a 'terrible and productive crisis', but, on the other, the world of the 18th century was still very close to our own; their thinking and even their 'informal conversation' could be reconstructed so that 'one becomes almost a contemporary'.[251] Quite subtle historical constructions were also put forward on the subject of patronage, succinctly analysed recently by Debora Silverman. The fact that art in the 18th century had been aristocratic posed no problems if one despised the new bourgeoisie anyway, as the Goncourts did. But the political mainstream would rather look to the rise of the bourgeoisie and argue that the modern non-aristocratic collector could be seen as the legitimate successor to the old aristocrats. Should all this be regretted as having led to an 'unfortunate democratizing of the ideal'? No – it should serve to 'make the manufacturers more aristocratic'.[252]

More significant than such political issues, however, were general perceptions regarding the 18th-century lifestyle. What for moralists amounted to depravity, many others – especially the art world – found highly, if often titillatingly, attractive. Everything seemed easy in that period: 'delicate' and 'playful', with a 'seductive grace'. They never had anything to do in those days and amused themselves continuously. This behaviour was expressed in the 18th century's appearance of 'finesse, distinction' or simply 'refinement'. The general *savoir vivre* likewise extended to what were imagined to have been the intensely private spheres of the 18th-century home; the key word here was intimacy, which led to informality and to a 'douceur de vivre', as shown in the 'softly poetic' illustrations of Boucher or Fragonard. One saw a 'smile in the forms, [and] warmth' – the latter, as we have seen, a key quality in all 19th-century perceptions of national and vernacular pasts.[253] These aspects of comfort were summed up by the boudoir and by smaller objects, especially the highly differentiated items of furniture used by women. To French intellectuals like Arsène Housaye and Théophile Gautier, the 18th century seemed altogether dominated by women.[254] As with all revivals, the celebrated period in question was held to have been largely homogeneous, and in spite of its sophistication it was considered to have lacked pretence. Havard believed that 'everything [our ancestors] had in their houses was of

A corner of Edmond de Goncourt's dining room, Paris, *c.* 1880.

one kind, was in harmony … They were a people who had a character of their own and wished their houses to fit them'. There were no commercial pressures, either ('there was no fashion') – the careful distinction between 'style' and 'fashion', and contempt for the latter, being a notable feature of 19th-century revivals.[255]

In the end, whatever the moral basis for all those 18th-century comforts, they were felt to be eminently suitable for the stress-conscious period that followed. The special importance of the French 18th century lay in its devotion to the domestic sphere. Socializing took place happened largely in the salons – ten hours a day, according to Taine.[256] 'The magnificence of the nation [could be seen] especially inside the houses', and this 'passion for furnishings increased incessantly'. The art of the *mobilier* was *the* art form of the period and, lest anyone had forgotten about the concept of unity of design, this period excelled in it, too; Havard praised its 'unity of conception and totality of execution'.[257] Havard's illustrations include a great number of 18th-century rooms, mostly rendered with great subtlety, taking their cue from the sketches of Boucher or Watteau and thus differing considerably from the 18th century's own, usually very precise, representations of interiors. Other countries to some extent confirmed the new French position: the earlier English, Dutch and Austrian condemnations of the Rococo had helped, if only by default. But by the 1880s the British and Americans took to collecting French art avidly. 'The XVIII century, that essentially French century, when France was more French than its has even been before or since', wrote the New York *Decorator and Furnisher* in 1884.[258]

Documentary research into the period, as well as the republishing of old illustrations, proceeded rapidly, especially from the 1880s (it should be remembered that few of the applied

One of many late 19th-century versions of 'Louis XV': a freely coloured design for a bedroom by Adrien Simoneton, *c.* 1893.

arts had so far benefited from thorough historical investigation).[259] An important advance was the display of old objects in their own right in publications and in exhibitions, alongside the trades' vaguer imitations ('in the style of …').

Most significant in this process of revaluation was a new kind of attention to workmanship. Hitherto, this had been a matter for the craftsman and the manufacturer. For the client, the high cost of décor would guarantee a high level of workmanship in accordance with the customs of the trade. What has to be remembered once more is the connoisseurs' and critics' new interest in the surface qualities of materials. The problems of French craftsmanship came to a head in the 1880s for other reasons, too: economic depression, strikes, weakened exports, the renewed reputation of English work and, as in other countries, a broadening of the market, with more and cheaper imitations being produced. In fact, the Henri II style had contributed to a method of furniture production in which parts could be made relatively easily and assembled quickly.[260] To complicate matters even further, all this was now also tied in with France's belated adoption of applied arts reform. Increasingly from the 1870s, state and corporate agencies advocated new ways to educate the craftsperson and the manufacturer, in which the perceived quality of indigenous 18th-century work served as the principal model.[261]

In a lament of 1883, we read of the decline and underemployment of those craftsmen who produce the most dextrous work, the 'meuble placqué' – pieces that were curved, veneered and generally delicate. Charles Mayet takes us to a workshop where the 'little manufacturer', with his 'mediterranean vivacity … lively eyes and few words', shows us 'all the delicious fantasies of veneered furniture'. This kind of work, the master craftsman claimed, can be done only in Paris. It is a 'product of the spirit of our race'; it bears 'the imprint of the feelings and passions of its time' and demonstrates 'originality and personality'. Simply put, 18th-century furniture was best. Another writer maintains that 'from a technical point of view nothing surpasses the perfection of the Cressent [masters]'. Naturally, the craftsman quoted above believes in the continuity of 'the great traditions'. The solution to the trades' problems was to support 'the clients who have taste', and to return to, or adhere to, 18th-century styles and modes of working. In this respect the French had joined the English and the Americans: 18th-century furniture was simply unsurpassed. After France's defeat in the Franco-Prussian War in 1871, voices praising the nation were given more weight in all fields of culture, accompanied by the notion that these values were long-lived: one should always be 'infinitely respectful of … the eternal masters'. Thus important elements of neo-vernacularism were present in France – a local, Parisian, element ('Parisianisme') and the way in which the craftsman and his work ethos were closely connected to the whole range of qualities outlined above.[262] Here, too, the beloved historical period was declared to be distant, irretrievably lost, only for its revival to be advocated all the more fervently.

Large interior furnished with delicate objects in the 18th- and 19th-century cabinetmakers' tradition. From the *Album Général de l'Ameublement Parisien*, c. 1890.

An art historian's new appreciation of restraint, as observed in the apartments of Marie-Antoinette in the Petit Trianon, Versailles, created from the mid-1770s. Drawn by 'Mangonnot' (Charles Monginot?); from Henry Havard's *Dictionnaire de l'ameublement et de la décoration depuis le XIIIe siècle* (1887–89).

'The style of Louis XV was coming back in force', claims a modern critic, and yet one hesitates to call it programmed revival. This was in sharp contrast to the situation in Britain, where ambitious designers excelled within the English neo-vernacular modes. The terminology itself – a French equivalent to 'Old English' or 'Altdeutsch' – was lacking. The Parisian designers who were making a modest name for themselves with independent publications – Eugène Prignot, M. Bajot, Félix Lenoir or E. Maincent, for instance – did not want to tie themselves

down too precisely to any particular style. The contribution of the Goncourt brothers, important though it was, may be called passive – certainly as far as their own house was concerned, where the interiors were those of a collector rather than a designer. At the cheaper end of the market, there were still plenty of trade publications that featured the delicate versions of the Louis styles familiar from the early to mid-19th century. One may consider this sphere of production as precisely the one that never changed – the stratum that the revival was so eager to characterize as 'tradition'.[263] In its lesser versions, Rococo furniture was found in almost unlimited quantities.

On the other hand, expensive new work in the 1890s tended to be increasingly restrained, paralleling the turn to a more 'refined' 18th century 'Adamesque' in Britain and America. This is where the Louis XVI style played a special role, but it was not dominant. Ultimately, the movement's influence was greatly enhanced through the acquisition of 'antiques'. As everywhere in the West, slightly faded surfaces were an asset, and interiors were united overall by their common mellow tone. But how many of these 'antiques' were imitations or fakes, made at some later point within the 'great tradition', will never be known. In the end, the existence of this 'tradition' renders the definition of the movement as a 'revival' doubtful; the near–far conundrum, in which a revival sought to revitalize 'a living tradition', can probably never be solved.

A European round-up

By the 1880s, every person in Europe was found to belong to a nation or ethnic group. Of course, one should remember the absolute continuity of applied arts at the highest level across Western Europe until late into the century, since for the very rich the distance to Paris or London never really mattered. Until the middle of the 19th century, a number of cities like Vienna, St Petersburg, Madrid, Milan and Mainz may be seen as subsidiary centres. The previous two chapters, concentrating on issues of design shared by all, did not deal with the geography of design and production, and many of these lesser centres – and indeed their countries – were not even mentioned. This chapter, by contrast, is organized by country. The geographical scope of the term 'Western' has been reduced here: in 1869 the Larousse *Grand Dictionnaire universel du XIXe siècle* may have exaggerated somewhat by claiming that 'comfort' was 'born with the people of the North',[264] but it seemed evident that Southern Europe had little to offer, at least to others, on the questions of homeliness and the design specificity of the 'domestic' sphere. The flourishing national and vernacular 'Old Russian' revival in domestic design lies altogether beyond the scope of this book, although the question must be asked whether Russia's extreme anti-Western stance was *sui generis* or whether it can be compared to the anti-Westernism, or at least anti-Parisianism, of the Altdeutsch or even the Old English revival movements. From the time of the 1867 Paris exhibition onwards, the 'Russian style' became widely known; it was seen by some as close to Oriental, but many others thought it also belonged in the context of the new Northern, Eastern and east Central European folk revivals, to be discussed below.[265] The far north of Europe, on the other hand, most closely resembled Britain and Central Europe in its concern for the national and the vernacular, as well as for specifically domestic styles, even if a definition of what was typically 'Scandinavian' remained unclear.

One should be careful to distinguish between those countries that formulated strong regional design policies and those that, for complex political reasons, did not. The situation was most complex in Central Europe. The new Germany's Altdeutsch Renaissance style, as we have seen, was largely based in the south, leaving the middle and northern parts of the country to find their own regional vernacular forms, very few of which emerged before the later 1890s. The situation in the region immediately to the east – the lands of the (German) Austrians, the Czechs, the Hungarians and the Poles (meaning the southernmost part of divided Poland), all

Opposite
left New signs of restraint also from the trade. What comes across above all is the trade's particular product, in this case chairs. From the *Album Général d'Ameublement Parisien, c.* 1890.

right Illustration by the architect E. Guillaume, published in 1889, showing a new emphasis on tone (see also pp. 194–99). The style of rendering, based on photography or etching, has a unifying effect on the interior and provides a look both of casualness and of greater substance.

under the Austro-Hungarian double crown – was even more complicated. In the Austrian-controlled region, the official government line was that there should be no 'national' style for the German-speaking parts.[266] When German and Austrian publications on the applied arts spread to Scandinavia and Southern Europe, the designs they included were hardly understood as specifically German or Austrian. On the other hand, the many localized revivals of smaller ethnic and regional peasant cultures in the Empire (e.g. in the Bukovina region) were sanctioned and even supported, even though they were directed strictly from the centres (that is, mostly from Vienna). Yet the major nationalities within the Austrian Empire – the Poles and the Czechs – were not encouraged to formulate a national style, since the central government and the elite of Vienna lived in fear of national uprisings – also the reason why Falke and his colleagues in Vienna remained such staunch internationalists against any notion of a 'German' style. No specifically Polish, Czech or Hungarian style emerged before 1890. The 'Polish' Tatra style, later one of the strongest national-vernacular modes anywhere (see below), began as a highly localized movement in the far (Austrian) south of Poland. One should note that neither the Czech lands, nor Poland, Hungary or, for that matter, Austria or Germany, made a distinct impression at the Paris fairs from 1867 to 1889, in contrast to the strong presence of the Dutch, Scandinavian and Russian 'folk' styles.

The Renaissances

Rather than just listing country after country, this summary account considers general shared trends. As was noted at the beginning of this section, it was the Renaissance, or rather its many variations, that seemed to lend themselves to the formulation of national styles in most of the countries dealt with so far, though one should remember that the term 'Renaissance' was itself a construct of 19th-century historians.

One might think that Italy should be given pride of place in any discussion of the Renaissance. The classical style, in its widest sense, remained dominant in Italy throughout the century, although, like the rest of Europe, Italy imported most style models from Paris. From the 1820s on, after centuries of neglect, the ancient craftsmanship of Tuscany seemed to be revitalized, especially woodcarving and inlay. In the 1860s and 1870s these traditions of excellence were connected to a new rhetoric of *italianità* ('Italianness') and to a sense of patriotism for the newly united country and its king. But in the end, according to the researches of Ornella Selvafolta and Rosanna Pavoni, little appears to have been written about specifically Italian interior design either inside or outside the country. The excellence of Italy's original Renaissance art was recognized internationally, and the Italians benefited greatly from foreign historians, including Jules Michelet, Jacob Burckhardt and even Falke. On the whole, there was no real need to 'discover' a style, and there was no question of reviving any kind of curious vernacular.[267] Spain, in contrast, and more especially one of its provinces, Catalonia, developed a totally anti-classical architectural and applied arts regionalism during in the 1880s. It was influenced by Orientalism with a Spanish slant (the *Mudéjar* style), and by a Viollet-le-Duc-inspired attention to the textural effects of materials, which were exuberantly displayed. However, there appeared to be no special emphasis on domesticity. Altogether, the question of a specifically South European domesticity must be left aside here; northerners noted the relative lack of wood and textiles.

Scandinavians, too, were keen on their versions of the Renaissance style, especially the Swedes. As in England, its local phases were closely associated with the country's politics and the names of its rulers. For Sweden, the Renaissance had marked a period of independence, from the early 16th century onwards, and the zenith of Swedish power during the 17th century. Its revival first appeared with the refitting of some royal palaces, notably Ulriksdal, in the late 1850s. In the 1870s and 1880s, a rich version of the Renaissance found its way into many lesser interiors, but around 1890 the style was considered rather too German after all. Instead, the Swedes adopted a lighter blend of Louis XVI and Neoclassical, mirroring the trend for refinement seen elsewhere, and duly named after their own Gustavus IV.[268] Denmark had far more splendid buildings of the original Northern – i.e. Flemish – Renaissance to its credit than Sweden, and in the 1870s and 1880s named its revival after the much-loved king of that period, Christian IV, but the style seemed to find less favour in interiors than its Swedish, let alone its German, equivalents.[269] In eastern Central Europe, Kraków initiated a more modest revival of Poland's 'Golden Age', although it hardly applied to domestic décor, while Hungary was in the unique position of having missed out on a Northern Renaissance phase altogether, on account of Turkish occupation during the 16th and 17th centuries. Closer to southern Germany and Austria were the cautious attempts to formulate a Czech national style, notably in the somewhat vernacularized Renaissance architecture and furniture of Antonín Wiehl, designing from the 1870s.[270]

International vernacular revivalism

In the early days of Altdeutsch and Old English the term 'vernacular' was mentioned only from time to time. When it came to the later stages of Old English and its Dutch equivalent, discussion had to be widened to include it. Bavarian or Old Alpine most definitely constituted a vernacular revival (the roots of this pan-European movement in the revival of 'Alpine' styles have already been emphasized). By the 1870s, vernacularism – later called 'folk art' – had emerged as one of the most vigorous and most innovative trends in many countries.

In most parts of Europe (Britain being the major exception) peasants constituted a strictly defined social group. They were held to be persons of substance and independence, even if

The Netherlands' 'Hindelooper Kamer' as first exhibited at the Paris Exposition Universelle, 1878. In the late 19th century this interior became the best known of all North European 'peasant' rooms and was re-created frequently.

A view of peasant life as clean and orderly: the interior of an old 'Saxon' farmhouse from Transylvania (formerly Hungary, now Romania), exhibited at the Vienna World's Fair in 1873.

their holding was very small. A homogeneous peasantry could be seen as the equivalent of the old bourgeoisie in the towns. From the late 18th century the notion of the peasant idyll exhibited strong moralistic undertones, influenced by the ideas of Rousseau and Diderot, and thus the image of the peasant proceeded from old Netherlandish burlesque to one of utmost seriousness and steadfastness. The great virtues of peasant life were rooted in the two aspects of place and time: in their natural, healthy environment and in their ancientness, which predated the foundation of European nations and went back to the pre-medieval Nordic–Germanic, Central Germanic or Slavic tribes. Like the idyll of the old bourgeois gradually accumulating realist detail, the poetry of peasant life, too, was worked into countless painted rural genre scenes – the *Bauernroman* ('rustic novel') and *Dorfgeschichte* ('village tale'), for instance.[271]

A 17th-century peasant interior from Sjælland, Denmark, as published in 1888. The image emphasizes the room's patina of age and its primeval coarseness.

Crucially, interest extended beyond the existence of the visible past to what was still being produced. Modern economists were fascinated by what they saw as the remnants of an archaic, self-sufficient form of peasant manufacture – labelled *Hausindustrie* or *Hauskunst* in German, or *hemslöjd* in Swedish – especially of ornamental textiles. At the same time, those of a contemporary mercantilist outlook wanted to help the peasants sell more goods. The applied arts reform movement, discussed in Chapter II, sought to spread recognized 'taste' – essentially the Renaissance style of décor – to all classes and to the most distant parts in the country. This initiative was now put into a quandary: the old, unreformed peasant work increasingly appeared so attractive that the reform movement was effectively obliged to turn into its opposite: a movement for the preservation of peasant crafts. Jakob von Falke, the chief organizer of the applied art museums and of teaching in Austria, must himself have gone through a process of conversion, since he added a love of 'primitive' forms to his love of the Renaissance. By 1880 Falke was the main expert in all matters of *Hausindustrie* for most parts of Europe.[272]

Distant yet available: this general European rediscovery of the old folk object took place at the Paris Exposition Universelle in 1867. In the Vienna Fair of 1873, folk objects arrived in 'crate after crate of further deliveries' (Lessing).[273] Each product bore a precise geographical label, yet they all appeared very similar, especially in the case of textile work. As Falke remarked, they showed 'hardly ever the same patterns, but the same style'.[274] An international network of knowledge of folk styles developed, which reached from Serbia to Norway and from Russia to Italy. By the late 1870s the enthusiasm for peasant textile work had become as strong as that for 'Oriental' work. Indeed, love for the latter might have been the trigger for the appreciation of European peasant work, with its flat, abstracted decoration and strong

The 'North Friesian Room', designed and made by the firm of Heinrich Sauermann, Flensburg, Schleswig-Holstein, 1888.

colours. Also similar to Orientalism was the way in which the vernacular could be evaluated only by researchers and collectors from the capital cities, while its producers played virtually no role in the formulation of the new discourse. As yet, however, decorators in Berlin or Vienna were not creating whole interiors in the folk style, as they had done with types of Orientalism. Although he supported the display of individual folk items, Falke never wanted to combine his new concern for folk styles with his concern for systematized interior décor, and he disapproved of the Munich Alpine movement.[275]

From the temporary world capital, Paris, the major exhibits were taken back to their own countries and installed either in further exhibitions or permanently in museums. Here, far from the major centres, they were firmly designated as belonging to their different 'nationalities'. From classifying the objects individually, the experts proceeded towards more comprehensive settings, and here the home interior provided an obvious context. What is needed is more detailed historical research into the whole practice of exhibiting complete domestic interiors, commercial as well as ethnic, at fairs as well as in museums. To provide the 'correct' historical setting for objects had been the aim of many collectors and subsequently of museums – first the Musée de Cluny in Paris and then, from the early 1870s, the Germanisches National-museum in Nuremberg and the Salzburg Museum (see p. 223). At the World's Fairs from 1867 onwards, both the commercial displays and the folk exhibits showed a new completeness in their arrangement. In 1876, Seidl's room in Munich cleverly combined both. Exhibitions teemed with *tableaux vivants*, comprising European folk elements and displays from overseas colonies. The trend towards make-believe went one step further with the erection of whole peasant houses, for which the Vienna World's Fair of 1873 became particularly well known. The Scandinavians headed the movement for folk interiors. The Stockholm researcher Artur Hazelius had already created a series of diorama-like scenes at the 1867 Paris Exposition. Folk dress shown on life-sized mannequins, peasant interiors and national history were merged effectively. Hazelius went on to organize permanent displays in the Skandinaviska-Etnografiska Samlingen in Stockholm, which opened in 1873; it gradually included more and more actual interiors and even, later on, whole farmhouses. Stockholm's Nordiska Museet and its open-air Skansen section became a spectacular example of a national museum of material culture. All this coincided with a vigorous new concern for art in the home (*konsten i hemmet*) that was directly inspired by Falke's *Die Kunst im Hause*.[276]

The Swedes' endeavours were closely followed by the Dutch, who produced one of the best-known room settings of the time, the 'Hindelooper Kamer'. It attracted attention as one of the main Dutch exhibits in Paris in 1878 but in fact represented the small northern province of Friesland, which claimed its own culture within the Netherlands. As with the 'Kamer van Jan Steen' in Amsterdam, the issue of class was highly ambiguous here, too. Clearly, it presented a 'primitive', 'folk' appearance, yet this kind of room had originally belonged to an urbanized, albeit provincial, elite of shipping entrepreneurs. The Delft tiles, carved oak furniture, copper pots and exotic ceramics had hardly been the typical belongings of the poorer 'folk'. On the other hand, these rooms did appear crowded and inelegant – that was partly why they were cherished. During the next decades many museums, including some in Germany, acquired and installed their own versions of the Hindelooper Kamer.[277]

For many decades the Danes had also sought what they saw as the poetry, quiet cosiness and curious décor of peasant homes. For the Paris Exposition of 1878 they put together an interior known as the 'Amager Stue' ('Amager Room'). As with the Hindelooper Kamer, one could actually enter the room and not just look in from outside, as with Hazelius's early displays. Bernhard Olsen, Denmark's own Hazelius and an organizer of entertainments (at one time he had been in charge of Copenhagen's famed Tivoli Gardens), rushed together a number of peasant rooms for a trade exhibition in 1879 and soon afterwards set up the

Old interiors at the Exhibition of Art Industries, Copenhagen, 1879.

Dansk Folkmuseum in Copenhagen, which was largely grouped in rooms of all periods. Like the Hindelooper Kamer, the Danish peasant rooms were richly furnished and also gave the impression of being low and crowded.[278] Just south of the border, in Germany, the Flensburg furniture manufacturer and collector Heinrich Sauermann began to show his 'Nordfriesische Zimmer' ('North Friesian Room') in the 1880s, although his version of the vernacular is much richer.[279]

Reflecting on the folk art (or *Volkskunst*) movement so far, we should bear in mind that its main instigator, Falke, had studiously avoided a link between his theories of art in the home and his discussions of *Hauskunst*. Hence, although they enriched contemporary knowledge of old household artefacts to a very considerable extent, neither the Austro-Hungarian nor the Scandinavian movements had thus far produced a complete, revived 'peasant' interior in the way that the Munich movement had done.

All the more significant was one small-scale movement that offered conceptions of the whole house in a highly individual style. It was created almost single-handedly, through both texts and illustrations, by the Polish artist and critic Stanisław Witkiewicz, and was dubbed the 'styl zakopiański'. It, too, fell within Falke's Austrian orbit. In contrast to the Scandinavian

Stanisław Witkiewicz's Villa Koliba at Zakopane, Tatra Mountains, Poland, 1891–93: (*above*) 'Gnatkoski's Room', with furniture designed by Witkiewicz's disciple Wojciech Brzega, early 1900s; (*right*) the 'Highlanders' Chamber' or Hall. A painter, designer and writer, Witkiewicz insisted on the comprehensive study of peasant life and all of its material culture (see also overleaf).

'From the Tatras': four drawings by Stanisław Witkiewicz, 1888–89.

movements, what happened in the southern Polish mountain resort of Zakopane hardly attracted international attention, even if the Warsawian Witkiewicz himself was well versed in contemporary art movements, travelling widely and receiving first-hand knowledge of the Old Russian style as well as news of the art world in Munich. In Zakopane, Witkiewicz did find two preconditions that favoured a new style: the new taste for Alpine tourism and an Austrian regional craft school, which together encouraged an interest in local styles from the late 1870s onwards. But from 1886 Witkiewicz firmly rejected both the prevailing 'Swiss' (or, in his words, 'Tyrolean Viennese') wooden chalet style and the school's attempts to 'civilize' local peasant forms in its furniture designs. For him, the foreign experts from Vienna could not be trusted to recognize the national or the vernacular. Witkiewicz was able, in fact, to build on an older notion of the small manor house with its rural surroundings as a manifestation of the virtues of a lost 'Old Poland'. His Zakopane style now offered a comprehensive, highly integrated programme for a vernacular revival, ranging from the atmosphere of the landscape and the folk dress and manners of the old inhabitants to the heavy, wooden construction of the house itself, with its low roof, external and internal details in wood, its big ceramic stove and smaller objects of daily use, including all the kitchen implements. From 1889 onwards Witkiewicz designed items of furniture in this new style, and soon a whole house complete with all its furnishings: the Villa Koliba in Zakopane. As elsewhere, much discussion and many drawings were devoted to the construction and external details of this neo-vernacular building, but very little to the interior as such. But then the character of the interior was simply the result of the construction; the same beams visible on the outside were visible inside, only with a smoother finish. The concept of the vernacular home, the peasant house, was a concept of the whole house.[280]

Naturally, all the ambiguities of the neo-vernacular remained. First, there was the dilemma of a style that emerged from a 'genuine folk' background but that was recognized as such only by an urban, avant-garde artist and intellectual – even if Witkiewicz was trying to counter it through his close and deeply sympathetic study of the 'local characters'. The style, deriving from the 'primitive' peasants, was then adapted for the houses of intellectuals and even the rich. Second, what was claimed to originate from a small region with very specific conditions was then widened to serve as the 'national' style for a large country in its entirety. Last of all was the problem of the style's international nature: the close resemblance of all those wooden 'peasant' forms stretching from Moscow to Munich or Oslo and beyond.

Old Nordic

'Old' has never been a static term; on the contrary, it showed a very considerable range of meanings. While few of the newly cherished peasant interiors actually stretched back before the 16th century, 'Old Nordic' was supposed to date back to pre-Christian times. One may

The Villa Edward Cederlund on Storholmen, Stockholm, by Magnus Isaeus, 1874. Here, the 'Old Nordic' wooden framework has accommodated the more modern concern for white walls and ceilings.

easily see it as the most impressive movement of its kind, not least because of the ways in which later German Romanticism – and Richard Wagner above all – set up a generalized 'Germanic North' as the counterpart to the Classical cultures of the Mediterranean. The literary and artistic credentials of the Old Nordic movement could not have been better, but it was also located much more precisely in terms of geography and climate than the other concepts of the 'old', exhibiting darkness and coldness – a pure Sublime if ever there was one.[281]

In terms of architecture and material culture, the homelands of Old Nordic were progressively narrowed to the monuments in Scandinavia and more particularly to Norway's wooden churches. Their medieval décor influenced the first applications of the Nordic style in the applied arts in the the first half of the 19th century, which took the form of interlacing patterns and filigree work in jewelry and soon also in wood, and which was usually called *Dragestil* ('dragon style'). During the 1850s and 1860s researchers began to pay attention also to houses in the countryside. Although one of the tenets of the Nordic style from the start had been a fusion of high culture and that of the 'ordinary folk', now the notion of a more specifically Nordic peasant culture came to the fore. The revived interlace décor had been characterized mainly by its delicacy, but now certain forms of peasant material culture were appreciated for their wooden bulkiness. As with all vernacular revivals of those decades – the 1860s to the 1880s – the Romantics' search for other-worldliness and a distant past evolved into a stress on the lively presence of a peasant culture, which even showed 'force and courage'.[282] In practice, however, as Jens Christian Eldal has shown, it is extremely difficult to distinguish between 19th-century wooden houses built within a vaguely defined local tradition or in a watered-down *chalet suisse* style, and those that display a specifically Scandinavian–Nordic revival

Interior near Trondheim, by A. Schirmer, 1881–83. There is no compromise here between traditional style and modern comfort: this Norwegian interior is clad only in 'primitive' boarding, lacking the Northern Renaissance décor on display in, for instance, the 'North Friesian Room' on p. 289.

'Norwegian carved lintels', from the *Art Journal* (1877).

style. Inside better-class houses, the forgoing of common white plastered walls and ceilings in order to show the dark timbers must rate as one of the clearest signs of a commitment to the vernacular.[283]

It was intellectuals and designers from 1870s Stockholm who tried to promote the notion of a poetic Nordic home: the art historian Lorenz Dietrichson, Artur Hazelius, the patron Carl Curman and the painter August Malmström. For them, the subject of a Nordic décor itself was of the highest importance. In 1871 Malmström produced his Nordic chair designs – a very early case of an established painter publicizing his work in the applied arts for everyday surroundings under the special banner of a national style. The main products of this movement were suburban villas and a group of dwellings in the seaside resort of Lysekil in western Sweden, whose unusual exteriors borrowed some forms from the very distinctive Swedish House shown in Paris at the 1867 Exposition Universelle. More remarkably, the interiors of these houses were now treated with the same importance as the exteriors. The villas' main living rooms presented a balanced combination of light walls and dark wooden battens, of Renaissance and Nordic décor.

Did all these elements really form a convincing theme for the Scandinavian home? Sweden's most favoured interior style was still the (North European) Renaissance. The country's foray into the Nordic in the 1870s in a way backfired, since the Norwegians claimed it as theirs, and by the 1880s the Swedes had virtually stopped using the Dragon style. At the same time, the quasi-official support for the revival of Swedish folk motifs, especially in textile work, did seem to constitute something particularly Swedish, even if the forms themselves resembled folk textile work from all over Europe. Are recent Swedish art historians right when they claim that Sweden normally turns abroad for models? The fact is that, over the following decades, the complex architectural discourses that took place in Sweden, as in Germany, showed a number of 'national' styles competing with each other.[284]

It was Norway that profited most from the model of the dark wooden building for both exteriors and interiors, and from the continued use of the Dragon style. 'Old Nordic', a putative Scandinavia-wide style from the remote past, had now become narrowed down to 'Old Norwegian' ('Gamle Norsk'). In those decades Norway was eagerly awaiting its complete independence from Sweden, which it achieved in 1905. Tourists were arriving in large numbers, and everything 'Nordic' was exported, particularly to northern Germany.[285]

And yet, in terms of interior design, the days of the severe, dark Nordic style were numbered. By the late 1880s two internationally trained Swedish painters, Anders Zorn and Carl Larsson, settled for the summer in the country's most celebrated folksy region, Dalarna. Zorn was still attracted by the dark Northern world, but the Paris-influenced *plein-air* painters Carl and Karin Larsson virtually eliminated darkness altogether: they removed all dark wood, dragons and interlace from their art; they brightened up the colours, to some extent influenced by gentler versions of the Empire style, and possibly by recent children's books from England; and they began to create one of the most comprehensively integrated and serenely poetic homes ever, soon to be widely publicized internationally.[286] In Norway, the painter Gerhard Munthe also turned towards a lighter touch, while new artists' and architects' homes in Finland from the 1890s onwards combined white walls with dark wood and a new kind of heavy stonework. Here, at least, some impression of a primeval world was preserved. But elsewhere in the North the old Nordic darkness had miraculously turned into a new 'northern light'.

Denmark practised the Nordic style rather less fervently, mainly in metalwork, although it continued to discuss its applications until the late 1880s. This style still played a vital role in the large Nordic Exhibition in Copenhagen in 1888. But by the 1880s Denmark had also begun to practise an architectural nationalism of its own in an attempt to escape altogether from outside influences. As a result, it turned away from the style debate per se and seemed reluctant to follow any kind of specific décor, be it Nordic or 'peasant'. By the late 1880s critics were using the term 'Almuestil' – a word that could refer to peasant décor as well to the world of country folk in general. In the 1850s one already finds major architects looking to the ubiquitous 'traditional' Danish house, which was small, of only one storey, and had a massive roof and plain geometric gables. The Danish liking for the old home ('gamle hjem') manifested itself in what was called 'the little Danish house' ('det lille danske hus'). This theme formed a vital component of the work of Denmark's most prominent and most nationally minded architect, Martin Nyrop. However, very little indeed was said about the interiors. The comparatively small windows, placed high up near the ceiling and subdivided into small panes, and the exposed ceiling beams were prominent features of the style.[287] This new restraint in Sweden and Denmark, and especially the clarity of the vernacularized early 19th-century classical, also pointed in the direction of the latest Anglo-American taste for refinement, as well as forward to Central Europe's love affair with Biedermeier.

One may conclude that a unified Nordic style never got off the ground. It never became quite clear whether the Scandinavian countries preferred a common formula, their own national and vernacular revivals – which were often hard to distinguish – or a style imported from outside the region. At the same time, the countries all shared a succession of trends: neo-Renaissance, Nordic, peasant primitivism, and the neo-Neoclassical revival. These styles produced some notable conceptions of the small detached house as a whole, but seemingly less in the way of interiors that could be used in any kind of dwelling. In the end, vernacularism seemed to limit the sphere of the 'poetic home' to one's second or holiday home.

This summary ends before the arrival of a new, stronger phase in national and vernacular design. Up to the early 1890s, only a few major centres had fostered an influential revival. A new style, even a revival of the vernacular, had to develop a certain 'critical mass'; it needed to come from the shared discourses of established designers, historians, critics and patrons. By definition, there could only be few of these centres. Less important centres of design simply had to follow suit, meaning that they were subjected to many diverse trends, as the example of Sweden has shown. Ten years later, by the beginning of the 20th century, the geography of architecture and design innovation had changed drastically. Now there could be a general acknowledgment across the West of exciting designs that came from the remotest areas, such as Finland and Transylvania. The ever more vocal supporters of each type of vernacular were convinced of the utter uniqueness of their style, and the folkloristic and anthropological study of peasant objects started in earnest. The dominance of the old major centres, certainly that of Paris, was now receding. Instead, 'quaint' vernacular had developed into an outright primitivism which, miraculously, was also taken as reformist and 'progressive'.

A poetics of interior design?

In these last two chapters, the meaning of 'poetic' has undergone a number of permutations. Initially, we traced the way in which a 'poetic home' and its users was constructed in literature and in the visual arts. We then saw how the overall arrangement of an interior was devised by designers in order to encourage certain pleasurable psychological states. The last and longest section investigated yet another contribution of the 19th century to interior design: the creation of references to past cultures that served to enhance further the effect of an interior.

Few can doubt the success of the 19th-century image of poetic home life in literature, painting and the graphic arts, backed up as it was by old moral and religious values and new socio-political concerns. How exactly could all this translate into the material elements that made up the actual home – the rooms that were used on a daily basis? Much 19th-century literature on the home did contain strong visual components. One of the most important was the

The 'White House', a summer villa by Martin Nyrop, Copenhagen, 1891. No Nordic darkness here.

image of seclusion, which manifested itself in small rooms and enclosures and, often enough, in relative darkness, all of which was a recipe for physical and psychological comfort. These concerns certainly found their way into the work of designers. And yet the usefulness of a small, darkish room was limited for practical reasons – a drawback to which books and pictures did not have to pay too much notice.

More comprehensive was the discussion of a *genius loci* and the way in which, combined with notions of age, it was translated into design. It dealt with geographical multiplicity and diversity, and a wider cultural context had to be sketched out in each case. Within these movements – which comprised socio-political rhetoric, literature, painting and architecture – nostalgic designs for domestic interiors were not delineated as clearly as their external architectural equivalents, but they were important on account of their ubiquity, since they could be found in any apartment in any modern town.

A running theme of the very last section was the notion of distance from, as well as closeness to, the historical artefact. One is fascinated by the old as something that had been forgotten, and yet one tries to identify with it, almost as if it were part of one's own ancestry, and certainly as part of the shared history of one's group or country. At this point it was decided that the old could still be reached quite easily after all, and even reinstated. A great variety of objects could be brought into a room: pictures could be displayed on the walls, souvenirs placed on the mantelpiece, and collections of many kinds put on show. But 'design' entails something different: to devise a comprehensive theme or a 'style' – a term so familiar in the architecture and applied arts of the 19th century. The search for styles and their accurate, or at least convincing, identification was a major preoccupation for most designers and critics.

How successful were these styles, these themed interiors? Crucial, as mentioned earlier, was the question of how firmly each label stuck. A quite unexpected ranking of revivals has emerged. The least confident were the Dutch, quite unassured of the suitability of a thoroughgoing Old Dutch style for their ordinary domestic interiors. At the opposite end of the scale we can probably place ever-confident North America, which to this day fondly admires, and reuses, almost everything from its early history. It is closely followed by France, full of self-assurance. After that come the seemingly uncomplicated Bavarian, Polish and Belgian–Flemish revivals, which at least remained undisputed once they had become established. Finally, there were the two countries that conducted the most searching and also the most wide-ranging debates on 'style': England and Germany. As far as the outcome of the movements discussed here are concerned, these two countries' respective positions were, and still

are, very much opposed. England, confident in knowing its tangible, reusable heritage, is often so confident that its does not need to stress a national meaning, whereas Germany seems to possess very little of it, or simply denies its existence.

One problem in discussing 'style' was the precision of the label. A style depends on detail: the more 'correct' details that can be assembled, the more convincing, or at least the more informed, the whole will come across. But all this could well result in a surfeit of meaning, leading to unfamiliarity, even to distance.[288] Few could be expected to follow slavishly the prescriptions of academically investigated décor in their ordinary dwellings. The identification of style can come close to taxonomic rigidity, and a reaction set in. Critics and designers began to look to a less exacting analysis of details, hence the turn towards the vernacular; it was seen as 'primitive', 'simple', relaxing and full of warmth, and therefore all the more expressive. One conviction was universal among producers and users alike: that the 'olden times' represented a utopia, where life was in balance and at one with its décor. The revived vernacular thus required a different kind of vocabulary from that of 'style' – one that was related less to décor and more to materials and their textures and colours. These effects, in turn, were considered particularly suitable for the look of the home. A generalized character rather than a rigid set of values was what these themes of national or regional antiquity helped to achieve.

Ultimately, however, it would be hard to guess the number of 19th-century dwellers who actually wanted to acquire such a model home. Social historians and art historians alike tend to see 'the Victorians' and 'the Victorian home' as following these agendas very closely. But very probably, as is the case today, clients and users demonstrated a wide range of attitudes towards the choice of a domestic interior, from the most intense desire for specific meanings to total and utter indifference. The next chapter will touch on these complex issues.

Carl Larsson's 'The Flower Window', an illustration of Lilla Hyttnäs, his family's home at Sundborn, Dalarna, Sweden, *c.* 1894. The image comes from the Larssons' book *Ett Hem* ('A Home') of 1899. Larsson has expunged all sense of Nordic darkness and 'primitive' wooden forms, replacing them with furnishings in a sub-classical, Gustavian style that would soon be given the label 'Biedermeier'.

opposite Laurits Regner Tuxen's *The Coffee is Poured* (1906) – a view of the artist's house in Skagen, Denmark, built in 1902.

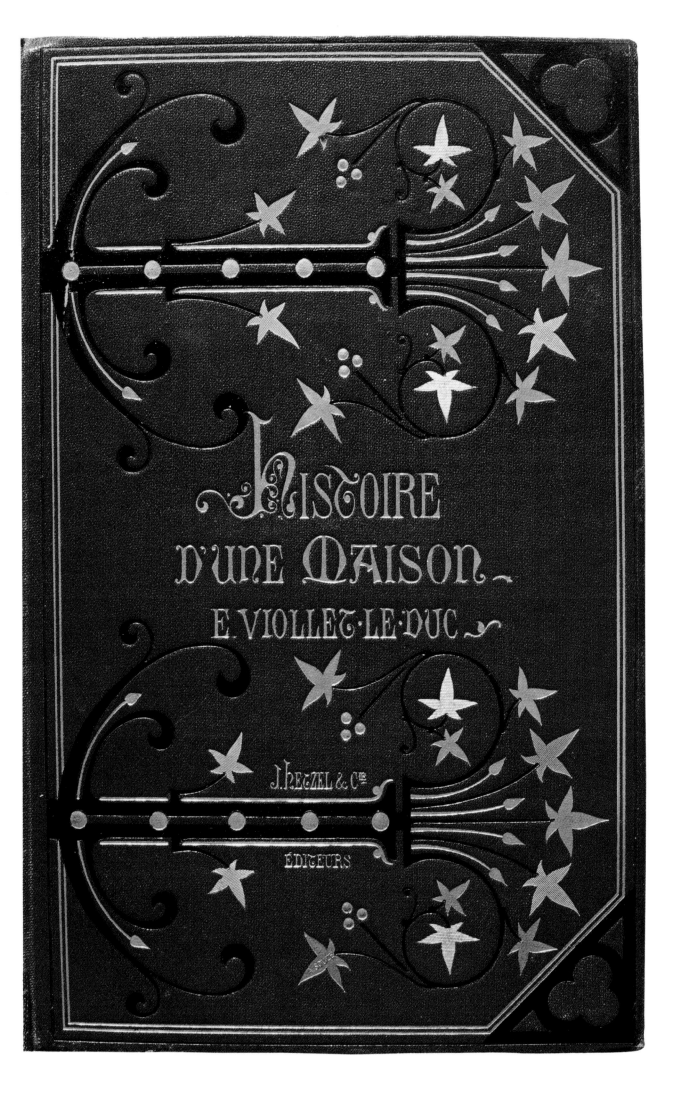

Histoire d'une Maison

E. Viollet-le-Duc

J. Hetzel & Cⁱᵉ

ÉDITEURS

VI

A Disparate Legacy

Viollet-le-Duc opens and closes his *Histoire d'une maison* of 1874 with the image of solid metal hinges on its cover. The book recounts in great detail the planning and construction of a house that is both sober and stately. The cover's ornamentation reflects the conspicuous metal hinges that reached across the whole door in Gothic Revival designs (in classical doors they were hidden away) – a favourite way of conveying impressions of comfort and security.

By the 1880s, the sort of modern dwelling that we might still expect to find today was being built in vast numbers. It was light and airy, it had the most recent technical conveniences installed and it was fitted out with ample décor and a good number of artworks. An ever greater number of traders were now involved, and by the early 1890s their marketing sounded thoroughly sophisticated. 'In addition to the "many", one may acquire even "more"', but only when everything is unified or put 'in its proper place'; if this rule is observed, there can never be 'too much' – one notices overloading or 'too much' only 'when the arrangement is inept'.[1]

Chapter IV introduced those figures who provided new meanings for the interior, all of whom, from about the middle of the century onwards, came from beyond the sphere of the trade. These new agents were architects or consultant designers who were closely connected to critics, theorists and art historians. Thus, from about 1870 in England, and in Germany somewhat later, the role of the trades seemed to have been eclipsed. Their contribution was even condemned in artistic circles – a situation that pertained for much of the 20th century. Only very occasionally would the trades try to get their own back, for instance when Williams Benn, a trade journal editor and journalist, offered 'a cabinet-maker's view' and noted deficiencies in a 'working class' interior designed by William Morris. But Benn, who greatly distrusted Morris's socialism, was concerned above all with impracticalities, in this instance finding fault with a small washstand. He was thus also speaking out on behalf of another agent: the user of the dwelling.[2]

Enter the real user

Thus far, the users of the home have been considered in relation to the way they were idealized by writers, artists and designers. But can one pinpoint the 'real' users? From the 16th century to the present day, there is no shortage of statements by literati or academics to the effect that a home reflects the character of its user.[3] As such this conclusion means little; it may simply indicate that a certain character of an interior has been chosen by the user, by the client, and that the producer, the designer or the shops were able to fulfil the user's desires. It does not really question the notion that the chief agent in the creation of the interior is still the designer or the producer. By the middle of the 19th century the plans devised by some architects reach a high point of complexity, for instance in Robert Kerr's country house plans that feature a dozen or so living rooms that seem literally to parcel up their occupiers' lives. Ostensibly the designer served the user. But did the user always behave as the architect prescribed?

What was now emerging was the idea that users could display a strong independence in their influence on the interior. By the 1820s the English upper classes were already cultivating what was dubbed the 'lived-in look'; numerous pictures show unnamed individuals, usually young ladies, apparently unobserved, sitting in their richly appointed drawing rooms, occupied in leisure activities or just relaxing (see pp. 191, 197). In the United States we note a multifunctional use of the parlour, formal as well as relaxed; the rocking chair became a home-grown

Interior in the Viennese home of Franz Joseph Karl, Herzog von Reichstadt; gouache by Johann Nepomuk Hoechle, 1818.

symbol for the latter. The way the new English home design books of the 1870s appeared to take the user's side, adopting a journalistic and non-technical style of writing, was a crucial step forward. Their authors, mostly women, recommended a new independence from the diktats of the trade, and although they still contained plenty of (usually gentle) prescriptions on the subject of taste, little remained of the heavy preaching of the South Kensington design manuals.[4] In architectural illustration the trend towards informality reached a peak in the work of T. Raffles Davison in the 1880s (see p. 165). One significant, though not always explicitly worded, attack on the trade – evident particularly in the first half of the 20th century – was the condemnation of the formal and heavily decorated but unused parlour in the smaller home, which seemed to epitomize the bad influence of the decoration industry.[5] In France, the situation was subtly different: there was an even greater emphasis on freedom and on intimacy, but only in rooms that were designated as suitable for them.[6] Whereas the discussion in England and Germany continued under the assumption that private and less private rooms were thoroughly opposed and even irreconcilably different, French thinking simply accepted a seamless gradation from the almost public grand salon to the personalized intimacy of the study, the boudoir or the bedroom.

The polemics against the 'shopman' (Eastlake's term) soon widened into an attack on 'fashion' generally and all the frequent changes it supposedly encouraged: simply disregard it, was Mrs Haweis's advice. It could occasionally culminate in absolute-sounding statements, such as 'our furniture is intended for us, and not for our furniture', or 'nobody can make a thorough home for anybody but himself'. Taste is defined as a personal matter, even as a subconscious one : 'by incessant contact with certain forms and certain colours … it works away steadily and unconsciously'.[7] In early 1880s Britain, there was a limited revival of amateur craftwork – paradoxically at exactly the time when women were being urged to abandon certain textile crafts because they looked amateurish and whimsical. The new literature preached 'do-it-yourself' not so that the practitioner could reach professional competence, but so that they could achieve whatever they felt like. The 'art in the home' discourse was diversifying yet further.[8]

By the late 1870s the United States already possessed a more diverse literature on the domestic interior than any other country. One of the trends here, too, was to address the 'amateur', which meant not so much the amateur artist at home as users generally (examples were Eugene Gardner's writings and the journal *The Art Amateur*). The most extraordinary text of the genre was published by America's premier art critic, Clarence Cook, in 1877, rather plainly entitled *The House Beautiful*. It is not a book for anyone who wants clear facts, recipes, any kind of precision about 'form and colour', or explanations of the splendours of history, all of which could conveniently be found in Mrs Spofford's writings the following year. Instead, Cook presented a long, gentle and always interesting ramble on the subject of the house, inviting one to cherish the look of this little corner, that intriguing passage, and any object in the home, even if its intrinsic value may not seem immediately apparent. There is no high art celebration, there is no demand for the education of universal taste.[9] Most importantly, although the book seems to give hardly any rules on how one may achieve unity of interior design or décor, a pervasive sense of the unity of this particular home does come across – of a kind that could, by extension, apply to anyone's dwelling. The illustrations are hardly spectacular (see p. 312), but on closer inspection they correspond exactly to the text. For Cook, the charm of this kind of home lies in something very specific: the look of the old, of the 'antique'.

In the late 1880s the Germans began to notice the new traits in British discourses on the home: 'the Englishman wants to live in his own world, by himself, undisturbed and not disturbing others'.[10] Cornelius Gurlitt's *Im Bürgerhause: Plaudereien über Kunst, Kunstgewerbe und Wohnungs-Ausstattung* ('In the Bourgeois Home: Chats about Art, the Applied Arts and

'Turn of the Year', an illustration from the *Illustrierte Frauenzeitung*, 1895. How many people desired poeticized interiors for their homes? In the images opposite and right, it seems that the occupants cared very little about any specific historical style of décor. The Viennese gouache demonstrates a straightforward way of showing a room and its users. But this picture of a New Year celebration in Munich, painted at the end of the century after two or more decades of a concerted campaign to poeticize all homes, perhaps tells of a carefully devised indifference. The by then ubiquitous Northern Renaissance chairs upholstered in leather and the equally common Rococo-style clock clearly do not go together; furthermore, there is no sense at all of a *genius loci*.

Furnishing the Dwelling'; 1888), actually written in England, urged 'the right to an independent formulation of taste'. It was opposed to the influence of all other agents: the 'architects and decorators', the 'German art philosophy' and even the art historian.[11] By the mid-1890s we come close to 20th-century definitions of lifestyle: 'our habits' and 'our way of life … form the basis of the design of our house'.[12]

From this point on, the users' agency could be traced even further – well beyond the confines of this book. One should remember, though, that throughout these chapters a 'poetic' home has meant a 'happy' home. Gurlitt, on the other hand, hints at the way in which presentations of home should serve also 'to present life in its imperfections'; he is no doubt thinking of the new trend of Naturalism in Norwegian, French and German literature. Its authors were often diametrically opposed to the idealism of the 'happy' home, as well as to the realist genre picture's mass of entertaining details. Academics in the 20th century focused on what they saw as highly problematic notions of home living, sometimes borrowing Freud's psychoanalytical tools and taking special note of wordplays on 'Heim' such as 'heimlich' ('homely', but also

Three late 19th-century versions of the familiar motif of the young lady sitting near a window: 'Industriousness' by A. Brunner, 1888 (*left*); 'Great-Grandmother's Treasures' by Hans Fechner, 1888 (*opposite left*); and 'At Work' by W. Auberlen, 1887 (*opposite right*). As a late example of Altdeutsch stage-setting, 'Industriousness' is almost overloaded with significant detail: spatial complexity, allegory, historically 'exact' costume, but also issues relating to gender and class. By contrast the third illustration, 'At Work', does not make special reference to the issue of class. The furnishings indicate a low social class, but one that is 'normal' rather than explicit and picturesque poverty. The chair appears old-fashioned rather than old, and room's only decoration are real, local flowers – the only type of floral décor, or indeed of any décor, worth having, according to William Morris and Alfred Lichtwark. 'Great-Grandmother's Treasures', however, falls between the two: a thoroughly old-fashioned room, but one with little sense of historical fiction and no apparent allegorical content. This scene emphasizes that the 'old' may be something personal or related to one's immediate family. All three illustrations are taken from the popular journal *Die Gartenlaube*.

'secretive') and 'unheimlich' ('uncanny'). They followed this up by considering further constructions of the self in relation to the object and within space.[13] Others investigated the home users of the past and the present within the new discipline of the history of the everyday.[14] The 19th-century 'poetic home', in which art and social aspects appeared always happily united, would now seem a utopian impossibility.

The rise of designer power

The writers' new criticism of the trade was meant not only to provide moral support for the users, but also to make room for the agency of the artist. In a trenchant analysis of the status of the ornamentist and designer in 1890, Cornelius Gurlitt demanded that their contribution should be fully recognized, employing a Nietzschean kind of rhetoric: 'the artist who has the force to carry all before him, whose overpowering force of will *compels* the crowds to accept his designs as beautiful …'.[15] Likewise, an earlier architect-critic had lavished praise on the Munich Seidlzimmer of 1876: 'the inspired breath of the inventor floats through the room and, even with all its simplicity, exerts its magical effect on the onlooker'.[16] Such high-flown characterizations of design were as yet rare, and the designers' names that usually appeared in tiny script under the left-hand corner of the illustrations (prefaced by 'entworfen von' or 'dessiné par') did not normally become well known, certainly not in Continental Europe.

In England, Bruce Talbert pioneered the publication of a designer's work by the designer himself, in his case issuing a collection of designs for mostly imaginary interiors. Christopher

Dresser published his own decorative patterns in the same way. In the 1880s figures including E. W. Godwin, Robert Edis, Lewis F. Day, Walter Crane and Moyr Smith produced books and articles that featured examples of their own work, but these publications were not yet meant to foreground the designers as artistic individuals. The Aesthetic Movement, for its part, encouraged a sense of artistic autonomy in design, for example in the way painters and illustrators such as Whistler took charge of the interior décor in their own homes. Morris never really published pictures of his designs as part of his general writings, presumably because they might have looked like advertisements for his firm, which would have been inappropriate. By the mid-1880s Morris's designs were nevertheless very widely known under his name and, combined with the effect of his fundamentalist writings, could convince the world that his style of designing was a superior one.

It is not until the mid-1890s that we can speak of a new type of monograph on a designer's work, complete with pictures. Insignificant though this may at first sound, it did represent a revolutionary step in the development of agency: the design of this or that object or interior was considered not as an example of a well-designed dining room in the latest fashion or of the 'right' style, but first and foremost as having been devised by this or that name. It was this kind of article in the spectacularly successful art journal *The Studio* that made the international careers of Voysey, Baillie Scott and others from the mid-1890s. In the United States it all still hinged on the architects' influence and on professional publications, but in 1886, upon the death of the country's premier architect, H. H. Richardson, the art journal *The Art Amateur* described him an 'interior designer' – possibly the first time that term had been used so prominently.[17] Likewise in Germany a new concept of *Raumschöpfung* ('space-creation') or *Raumkunst* ('space art') raised the status of all kinds of interior design from around 1900.[18]

What fell by the wayside, however, was the 'home'. Neither the interior designer nor the *Raumkünstler* would now publish their work under the label 'home', let alone employ references to the 'cosy home' or the 'poetic home'. In Central Europe, *gemütlich* became a non-word in high architectural circles. The houses of Baillie Scott and Voysey from the mid-1890s still included a notion of quaintness and comfort, but it was no longer present in the work of avant-garde masters like Henry van de Velde or Peter Behrens. As was mentioned in Chapter II, in connection with the development of journals just before 1900, 'art' and 'the home' appeared to part company. Interiors by top designers were bracketed with high art, the 'homely interior' from now on belonged to the middle and lower classes, and the concept of 'art at home' in a way returns to one of its starting points: home advice literature.[19]

By about 1880 writers had become aware of the possibility of conflict between the designer and the user. Later on, this situation was poignantly captured in a well-known satire from the radical and ever-sceptic Adolf Loos: the owner of a fashionable home is visited one day by his designer, who tells him off in no uncertain terms for ruining his artistic interior by wearing the wrong kind of slippers. Two decades earlier, the manufacturer and decorator Bembé had complained about the 'process of destruction' that took place when owners arranged various presents they had received in their new interiors. The ever astute and ever friendly-sounding Georg Hirth remarked in 1880: 'If you ask the educated occupant why he has done it all like that, you will not get the answer "because the German Renaissance requires it to be exactly in this way and no other", but "because that is how it delights me, because it goes together and because it's beautiful, pleasant, cosy and cheerful."' Nevertheless, Hirth seeks to reinforce the designer's autonomy, or rather that of the chosen historical style: 'we may emphasize that the whole [room] is built according to the principles and to the form and colour harmony of the German Renaissance'.[20] In the final analysis, however, one may view the independence of both users and artists as the sign of a general push for a greater subjectivity and independence of will.[21]

The technically up-to-date household …

In 1888 Gurlitt adopted another radical position with regard to all objects in the house. He claimed that one's home should contain only three kinds of object: first, proper works of fine art; second, real antiques; and third, items of furnishing that serve no decorative purpose.[22] Taken to a radical conclusion – which of course Gurlitt himself was far from presenting in his appraisal of all aspects of domestic art and décor – this philosophy would exclude the vast majority of objects cited in the present book, anything that serves the practical and the artful in combination, and of course anything newly fashioned in an old style.

Gurlitt's third category of object comes close to what was later described as 'functional'. A section in Hermann Muthesius's *Das englische Haus* is devoted to those parts of the home that supposedly lie beyond 'fluctuating feelings and art fashions'.[23] It deals with climatic conditions and with the utilitarian and practical considerations of planning and building, ending with all matters to do with water. It should be remembered that most of these concerns were far from new – indeed, the further one goes back, the more likely treatises on building and on houses in particular are to consider practical matters only. What was new was simply the amount of technology, the number of novel appliances.

The present book has not done justice to the decorative history of home conveniences, except for the Anglo-American fireplace, where we noted the decisive victory of the decorative (or, to be precise, of decorative-cum-psychological considerations) over the practical. Separate bathrooms were found initially only in some of the most lavish houses, where they would be highly decorated as a matter of course – first in the manner of Roman bathhouses, then perhaps in a tiled Oriental style. In the 1880s and 1890s, following changes in the definition

The kitchen of a large Hamburg house, 1893. The room shows a new concern for 'hygienic' whiteness; almost all utensils have been banished into the cupboards.

A kitchen design that combines (vaguely) peasant forms with new hygienic whiteness; by F. Kiefhaber, Magdeburg, 1894.

Design for a kitchen by K. Spaeth, 1893; from the same issue of *Innendekoration* as the Hamburg kitchen on p. 307. There was now a choice in kitchen design: between the demonstratively 'modern' and hygienic, and old-style disguise.

Kitchen design by Lothar Meggendorfer, Munich, late 1870s. Meggendorfer has combined an Old Alpine/Bavarian 'peasant' image with the naive drawing style he used for children's books. One may call the result a unified 'design' in the modern sense of the word, in contrast to the other kitchens shown here, which were either purged of décor or stuffed with it.

of comfort, 'warmer' materials like timber and fabric were sought. But the latest English bathrooms illustrated by Hermann Muthesius were devoid of wood: he claims that the new 'scientifically orientated' desire for cleanliness was also beginning to drive out upholstery and any kind of 'textile-enveloped cosiness'.[24]

Likewise, the kitchens of larger houses could carry a certain measure of décor, even if it consisted only of the mass display of ornamented crockery or polished metal pots, which helped to contrast the main kitchen area with the purely utilitarian character of adjacent smaller service rooms – especially the scullery. On average, however, the kitchens – which could be found in every dwelling, unlike bathrooms – were treated as a place without comfort or décor. This conception was reinforced also by new considerations of health, which might recommend that the kitchen face 'to the north or the north-east' for ventilation purposes. Yet ornament did begin to creep into even the smallest kitchens, on the edges of the main cupboard or dresser, say (see p. 23). The Germans maintained that their *bürgerliche Hausfrau* spent more time here than her middle-class English equivalent.[25] If there was a cook, he or she deserved a somewhat better environment than the cleaning personnel. One of the attractions of the old 'primitive' house was its large welcoming kitchen with a big stove – an image familiar from so many old Netherlandish paintings and now reaffirmed by the real old 'peasant' kitchen. Morris, too, proclaimed a soft spot for the clean (in his case white) country cottage kitchen.[26] Thus one could construct a history of the 'poetic kitchen'.

Peasant cleanliness was one way of imagining the ideal kitchen; but another kitchen aesthetic ('Aesthetik der Küche', in Luthmer's words) that had also evolved by the mid-1890s meant no décor, no colour at all: it promised 'the possibility of the most absolute cleanliness … tiles for the whole room … a radical guarantee of cleanliness', preferably white glazed tiles ('Porzellantafeln'). The proud, rather ritualistic décor of the earlier well-appointed kitchen – the displayed pots and pans – was now shut away in cupboards. It was the smooth, shiny surfaces and the overall whiteness that constituted the element of display within this increasingly rigorous taste for coordination.[27]

… and the authentic antique

An earlier chapter considered the artistic object and its display. Most of these objects showed a style from the past, regardless of whether they were old or new. Here, however, we are concerned with 'real' antiques, whose primary appeal resided in their age. Terms like *bibelots*, bric-a-brac, knick-knacks and *Nippes* all referred to the old kind of 'collecting'. Owning a proper antique, however, came to mean something different: it was a completely serious matter, as demonstrated by the word itself, which harked back to Classical antiquity. It did not necessarily mean showing off a plethora of objects; but the display of one single object (or possibly a matching pair), preferably before a neutral background, could be quite sufficient.

What lent authority to the antique object was the determination of its precise age and origin – the kind of historical knowledge that one might expect to find in a museum. It was a trend that is evidenced by an increase in the number of books on the history of the applied arts. Antiquarian precision had been an ideal for a long time, but its application to old objects in the home happened only very gradually; as always, the applied arts, including furniture, lagged behind architectural studies. Histories of furniture, of furniture styles, began very modestly in the 1830s in England. Most publications showing furniture mixed old and new indiscriminately until the 1870s and 1880s. For more thorough surveys of authentic antiques, France had to wait until the 1880s and Havard's *Dictionnaire*, and England until the early 1890s.[28]

Aside from the antiquarian history of an object, its materiality now also attracted close scrutiny. Very slowly, an attitude developed that we have since taken for granted: an item is old only if its *material* is old, if it has definitely not been renewed. This is clearly related to the growing appreciation of textures and their diversity, as well as an increasing dislike of the perfect, the shiny and thus the new appearance of objects. Somewhat paradoxically, it was precisely the damaged, worn and thus incomplete materiality of an old object that was valued most. Soon the double function of the worn surface was firmly established: it was appreciated as picturesque, and it served as a guarantee of genuineness, of authenticity. The term 'patina' began to appear with greater frequency around this time.[29] Of course, the association was far from failsafe: the fakers were never far behind.

This crucial change in the notion of the 'antique' occurred in the 1870s. Earlier collectors of bric-a-brac and other *objets* looked for rare items of distant origin – a desire that could be amply satisfied with medieval as well as Oriental objects. In the case of the latter (at least when they came from the Near Orient), age and authenticity were not so important, unlike with European antiques. But from the 1870s there arose a desire for the local 'old' – a fundamental element of the 'distant-yet-familiar' conundrum discussed in Chapter V. The vernacular revival brought many objects to attention that were in fact near at hand – including ordinary domestic items that could be used daily in the domestic interior.[30] The acquisition of antiques now overlapped with buying second-hand to a much greater extent. The first of the famed 'Art at Home' series of books began with an onslaught on the furniture trade by presenting an old piece and by telling the story of how the client bought it. This object was given the provocative caption 'Smith's Sideboard', implying that antiques were no longer just for the privileged. In the 1870s London already had 'several thousand homes filled' with antiques, and we even read that 'the art of furnishing must for the present moment be closely connected with the judicious buying of old furniture'.[31]

In New York, Clarence Cook stated simply that 'the pleasure of "picking up things" is in my humble opinion the only way to furnish a home'.[32] In France, collecting and museology were as developed as in Britain, and the expectation that objects should be genuine was probably just as high. It was taken for granted by the Goncourts, for example – although, in the case of the works of fine art that interested them most, authenticity had been prized for a long time. By the 1880s wider circles of collectors were demanding absolute authenticity for all pre-19th century furniture. This expectation was greatly reinforced by a group of plutocratic collectors from Britain and soon from the United States, who required full guarantees in the form of provenances stretching back to an object's first owner and to its maker. Partly driven by this desire for proven authenticity, prices for the best 18th-century work went sky-high; relatively speaking, they have probably not been matched since.[33] However, what France appeared to lack was any kind of influential movement to bring the antique or second-hand piece into the ordinary home, which in England and the United States had resulted from the taste for 'vernacular' objects. In Central Europe private collecting appears to have been less well developed. Munich, however, resembled London quite closely, for instance in the way the great theorist and supporter of the Munich design school Georg Hirth claimed that his own home contained 'not a single piece of modern furniture'. What consolidated this view, in the mid-1880s, was an opinion from on high, as in France. Julius Lessing, director of the Berlin Kunstgewerbemuseum, hammered home the point that you cannot imitate the old: any imitation will always turn out to be just that, and will always be recognizable as an object from the period in which it was made. Lessing then hints at the special value of a piece that has been guaranteed as old, outlining a position that was soon theorized further by the noted Viennese art historian Alois Riegl, with his emphasis on 'Alterswert' – 'the value of age'.[34]

Of course, there never was a closed world of the absolute authentic antique. On the contrary, the increasingly sophisticated manufacture of old-looking objects gave rise to ever greater ambiguity. This could involve the fabrication of 'old' surfaces – hence the verbs 'patiner' in French and 'patinieren' in German, which during the middle and latter parts of the century were employed completely openly, just like the imitative processes outlined at the beginning of Chapter III. Metals – especially bronze – were oxidized, and textiles such as velvet were deliberately faded. Most easily manipulated was wood: the methods by which it could be made to deceive were numerous, ranging from the widespread use of old wood from lesser objects to make up better pieces, to the drilling of artificial wormholes. More respectable was 'vieux chêne' or 'old oak' – a standard classification from the 1830s onwards – in which the wood was left in a rougher state, a method that contrasted with the usual high polish.[35]

Both the business of open and covert fakery and repeated warnings from some manufacturers and the big shops (who feared the competition presented by second-hand buying) can be taken as proof of how seriously the notion of the authentic was taken. On the other hand, professional dealing in old objects was as old as collecting itself. The 'old curiosity shops' in London – immortalized by Dickens, who himself still subscribed to the notion that the everyday old object could not be attractive – were notorious. By the latter part of the century shops had responded to changes in demand and divided themselves into the high-class antique shop, guaranteeing authenticity, and the rest of the second-hand trade. Production occupied a vast sliding scale, from an admitted copy of a particular old work (which even the circles of plutocrats mentioned above were not immune to buying), to the still faithful but more generic imitations of old pieces known as 'reproduction', down to the ordinary 'in-the-style-of' articles.[36]

Antiques and the unity of interior design

In Chapter III, the assembly of large numbers of objects was treated as a way of unifying the impression given by a room. The use of individual antique objects is less likely to give the same effect. However, many antique dealers were acting just like normal furnishing shops, as decorators adding to and 'completing' any interior. Some architects like Richard Norman Shaw helped their clients to buy antiques and, conversely, some shops fitted themselves out to look like old homes.[37]

But the 1870s antiques movement in England and Clarence Cook in New York were aiming for more than the casual unity to be found in an arrangement of bric-a-brac. The old provided a feeling of completeness, of comfort, even of 'companionship'; Mrs Haweis wrote how 'good old work is so good, that you require but a few pieces, and it always harmonises with itself'. Havard, thinking mainly of the French 18th century, nostalgically tells his readers that there were never any problems harmonizing the interiors of the past. The bothers Goncourt despised the work of the modern decorator altogether: 'an upholsterer's dream, without a piece of the past', they sneered in connection with one of Paris's most celebrated new interiors, the Hôtel Païva.[38] Soon the Germans and Austrians also joined in: Falke maintained that it was the 'reconciling patina' that allowed stylistically different objects to be easily combined.[39] At the very top of the hierarchy of antique buying was the acquisition of an old room in its entirety. The special case of the 'period room', according to Bruno Pons, emerged in the 1860s in France; this was on account of a particular type of French 18th-century interior décor known as a *boiserie*, in which the room was completely panelled in wood. British and American collectors and museums bought up the panels, re-erected them more or less faithfully, and wherever possible filled the rooms with authentic objects.[40]

The trend of the 1890s for brighter interiors resulted in more white walls, against which the old objects stood out; this also meant that they had to be selected with greater care, and to some exent there was anti-picturesque return to strict order. By the early 1890s the Austrian commentator on the applied arts Bruno Bucher summed up the prevailing attitude by distinguishing clearly between objects in the old style and original antiques: 'the old is no longer valued in the way its serves as a model, but rather is appreciated for its own sake'.[41]

below left 'Smith's Sideboard' reads the caption underneath the frontispiece of W. H. Loftie's *A Plea for Art in the House* (1876). The author praises all buyers of second-hand furniture who then adapt pieces for their own homes.

below 'Why, this is Spode!', from Clarence Cook's *The House Beautiful* (1877). Cook satirizes the small-time collector, but what he really wants to show is the quiet, friendly look of authenticity that pervades the whole house.

Georg Hirth's own living room in Munich –
'in the character of the German Renaissance,
1580–1620' – from the later 1870s. The designer
of this interior, one of the most important of
the period, is unknown; however, much of the
furnishing is likely to have been antique, the
panelling in particular.

Memory

When one contrasts the plutocrat assembling whole antique interiors with the lesser
customers' pride in whatever he or she could find, one sees the emergence of two very distinct
notions of authenticity. For the big collector, authenticity is guaranteed by professional
experts, while the small collector relies on his or her personal conviction that an otherwise
unauthenticated object is 'genuinely old'. The latter trend accompanied a new sense that
middling and lesser homes should above all display the taste of the user: 'We do not want to
be reminded of the factory or the shop', said Hirth. We read that 'the upholsterers ruled'
earlier on, but 'now houses are furnished by their owners'.[42]

During the last decades of the 19th century, we note the development of the notion of
'Heimat' or 'heritage', in which everyone supposedly became conscious of the age of his or
her own region or town ('Vieux Paris', 'Alt Wien', and so on). But was that matched by a
personalization of the antique in the domestic interior? In 1874, a hawkish Friedrich
Nietzsche had nothing but contempt for those who appropriated 'rotten' and 'outmoded'
objects to serve the 'homely nest', desired by the 'preserving and venerating soul'.[43] But in
1884 the moderately well-known Munich academic Max Haushofer examined this question in
remarkable detail in his article 'Die Poesie unseres Hausraths' ('The Poetry of our Household
Objects'). For Haushofer, poetry in the house is intimately linked to personal memory and
thus to the individual user: 'for the grown-up person, the poetic content of furnishings
resides only in the form of memory'. In a formidably detailed analysis that is both factual and

romanticized, Haushofer addresses himself explicitly to the inside of the dwelling. 'Poetry' lies in a great number of movable objects, so the author concentrates on objects of common use ('Hausrath'). He offers a comprehensive list: the oven or fireplace and its related implements, the bed, the table, the cupboard, the seating furniture, and curtains and carpets, followed by smaller objects such as the clock, the lamp, the mirror, the key, the spinning wheel and the cradle. Haushofer conjures up meanings from 'tales, dreams and daydreaming' that emerge in the evening or at night – not, of course, under a modern lamp, but by the light of the old fireplace or a 'pine torch'. The big old-fashioned key, for instance, can be seen as 'the key to a secret', whereby family tales can be interwoven with fairytales. All objects function within 'an extensive network of relationships'. For children, Haushofer maintains, 'these objects have a creative effect on their imagination, and where [the household] contains artefacts, forms and effects that cannot be understood by the child's brain, it acquires a fairytale life'.[44]

Gurlitt, too, begins his book of 1888 by considering the memories that might be conjured up by one's parents' or grandparents' home – 'the quiet, fairytale-like atmosphere of the room'. In any case, it seemed that one's parents' furniture could always be easily located: 'Go to the junk room and enjoy the memories …'; 'Domestic furniture is perhaps the most subtle recorder of the varied changes which come over the fancies and fortunes of people.' Lady Barker muses that, when fitting out a room for one's daughter, one remembers 'bygone girl days'. Authors frequently now also harked back (usually without bothering about the details) to the *lares* and *penates* – the spirits of the ancestors and the protecting house gods of the Romans.[45] Yet again, nothing could surpass the open fire in helping to produce memories. Clarence Cook focuses his long book on the home's user himself: 'let his sparkling eye roam over [the flames] in the twilight as he recalls a thousand memories of the days that are no more.'[46] New furnishings, according to German contemporary, 'say nothing'.[47]

An immense gulf had opened up. There was the 'new', which stood for the impersonal, and there was the cherished 'old', which developed from decoration in a recognized historical style, via an individual's buying and collecting to an individualized and a completely personalized sphere. Quite possibly, this very juxtaposition was the 19th century's most influential legacy for domestic design.

Interiority: poetic house or poetic room?

'To say that a room looks like a picture is considered a high meed of praise … but there is no reason … why a whole house should not be a poem.' So wrote Ella Rodman Church in her little home decoration advice manual of 1881.[48] The present book has attempted to apply the characterization 'poetic' to the domestic interior, following the words and images of the period itself. The interiors it features were very rarely identified by the type of dwelling for which they were intended – apartments or villas, or, in the case of England, detached houses or tightly squeezed terraced houses. Haushofer was most explicit on this issue: 'All advice that aims to make our existence more beautiful is only of good use if it takes into consideration the rented apartment.'[49] In an 1896 book on lesser kinds of dwellings, one French critic states explicitly that 'an apartment resembles a poem'.[50]

Undeniably, though, most of the eminent architectural writers of the 19th century concentrated not on the apartment, the flat, but on the larger, strongly individualized house: the indefatigable Loudon; the circumspect Downing; the elaborately factual Kerr; the sociologist Riehl, with his 'whole house'; Daly, France's premier architectural publicist; and of course Viollet-le-Duc,[51] Ungewitter and many more after them. Perhaps the most strident demonstration of the universal validity of the individual house was the housing reformers' conviction that even workers' families needed small houses rather than flats.[52] Another type

The beginning of the end of poetic interiority?
Two trends dominated 19th-century housing:
the ever increasing size and density of towns, and
the desire for access to light and air. A plethora
of balconies, bay windows and oriels seemed
to provide the best of both worlds. With many
Anglo-American suburban terraced houses (*right*;
in Washington, D.C., built 1884), there did indeed
appear to be the opportunity for lively interchange
between exterior and interior. In Continental
Europe, however, the desire for openness resulted
in a new dislike for large blocks of flats, with or
without balconies (*above*: Berlin flats of the 1890s,
photographed in 1962). We have noted the way
the artful and poetic home had come to mean
something entirely secluded, inward-looking, so
that it could be enjoyed even when it was quite
dark. In effect, much of this book has dealt with
the urban apartment. The insistence on happiness
that accompanied the secluded interior can be
understood as an escape from modern urban
life, but it must in turn have contributed to the
indifference towards, or the dislike of, the urban
street. In the 1890s, the complexities of the
interior–exterior relationship came to a head.
The condemnation of urban density, uniformity
and 'darkness' – in fact, of just about everything
the city stood for – swelled to a massive chorus.
To live in an open, natural setting was the new
ideal. Millions, including everyone in the street
shown here, were now held to be living in squalor.
By 1900, the condemnation of the 'dark' city finally
hit the secluded interior as well.

of affirmation of individuality were the wholly exceptional houses that artist-architects built and fitted out for themselves: one thinks of William Burges or, later on, Henry van de Velde and Franz Stuck. This movement peaked perhaps in Hermann Muthesius's massive work of 1904, *Das englische Haus*. Since it deals primarily with the largest, most complex kinds of house, its correct title (and also that of its predecessor, *Das englische Haus* by Robert Dohme, published in 1888) should have been *Das englische Landhaus*, covering both a house in the country and a country house. But by that stage, the simple word 'house' was carrying an enormous weight of meaning, pushing aside the other poetically charged terms of the 19th century that were used throughout the West, 'villa', 'cottage' and 'chalet'.[53]

The detached house was undoubtedly the work of the architect, while books on art inside the house were written by different kinds of authors, mainly from the sphere of the applied arts. Chapter II stressed the cooperation of a large number of agents in 'art in the house', but now we begin to note an element of rivalry. One German architectural critic in 1896 wrote proudly of the 'recent project of the art of architecture that has perhaps found its most intimate and spiritualized expression in the single-family house'.[54] By the later 1890s, such a medium-sized house could be a most complex organism. A new fashion was for one room to open into another, chiefly via a central hall that contained the central fireplace and gave access to the main staircase. The earlier trend for opening the house onto the garden also intensified. The ideal had become 'the whole house', including its garden. By the end of the century such detached houses were built in large numbers in the suburbs of most Western cities. Their plans and exteriors appeared highly individual, and their décor was full of style and character.

For most Anglo-Americans this could become a reality in their new low-density suburbs, even if for the general run of houses the poetic element was rather small.[55] But matters in Continental Europe were very different. By the turn of the 20th century only between 12.5 and 25 per cent of the population lived in detached houses in medium-sized towns, and as few as 6 per cent could afford to do so in very large towns. In the early 20th century Berlin was dubbed 'the largest rent-barrack city in the world' – a reference to the city's enormous new apartment blocks. The restlessness of the population was then a frequent subject of discussions in Germany, and writers identified a new 'Nomadenklasse', to which the interior decorating trade tried to respond by advertising its supply of movable décor.[56] All this anti-urbanism soon made designers forget about the origins of the smart urban flat as the *piano nobile* or *bel étage* of an urban palace. Critics or historians no longer wanted to know that the well-appointed apartments in central Paris or along the Vienna Ringstrasse, and countless lesser dwellings with their ornamented façades that gave out onto the wider streets of the late 19th century, were remnants of that old urban pattern. As a result, the apartment in a mansion block and the freestanding house were now perceived as vastly different. It hardly needs stating which solution early modernism preferred.

With the ascendancy of the word 'house', and soon 'housing', the much-loved 19th-century term 'home' was beginning to lose its cachet, certainly for the most prestigious designers, who now avoided the term altogether. The literature on the house interior reverted from 'art in the house' books back to manuals full of practical and moral advice for the home, addressed to those classes who could not afford the art-filled villa in splendid suburban isolation. In the 20th century the notion of the 'happy home' did not seem entirely lacking in validity, but it did sound simplistic to most. It was a concept that involved a strict division between the outside world and an inside. All this was soon mistrusted as something that could lead to isolation. For the 19th century it was precisely this interiority, achieved through careful design, that ensured an 'apartment resembles a poem'[57] – 'apartment' being synonymous with 'flat', and with the individual room itself.

Select Bibliography

A list of relevant journals is provided at the beginning of the Notes.

ACKERMANN
The Repository of Arts, Literature, Commerce, Manufactures, Fashions and Politics, London: Rudolph Ackermann, 1809–28; selection in P. Agius (ed.), *Ackermann's Regency Furniture and Interiors*, Ramsbury: Crowood, 1984

ADAM
Robert Adam and James Adam, *The Works in Architecture of Robert and James Adam*, London: the authors, 1773–78 and 1822; new edn London: Batsford, 1880, repr. London: Academy Editions, 1975

AMES
Kenneth L. Ames, *Death in the Dining Room and Other Tales of Victorian Culture*, Philadelphia: Temple University Press, 1992

ARTISTIC HOUSES
[Anon.], *Artistic Houses: being a Series of Interior Views of a Number of the Most Beautiful and Celebrated Homes in the United States*, 2 vols., New York: Appleton, 1883[–84]; repr. as *The Opulent Interiors of the Gilded Age: All 203 Photographs from 'Artistic Houses'*, new text by S. McQuillin et al., New York: Dover, 1987

AUSLANDER
Leora Auslander, *Taste and Power: Furnishing Modern France*, Berkeley: University of California Press, 1996

AUSSTELLUNGS-BERICHT
C. T. Richter and General Direktion der Weltausstellung (eds), *Officieller Ausstellungs-Bericht* [also known as *Wiener Ausstellungs-Bericht*] of the Vienna World Fair, 1873, Vienna: K.u.k. Hof- und Staatsdruckerei, 1874; vols. here numbered after the sections ('Gruppe') of the exhibition

AYNSLEY & GRANT
Jeremy Aynsley and Charlotte Grant (eds), *Imagining Interiors: Representing the Domestic Interior since the Renaissance*, London: V&A, 2006

BANHAM
Joanna Banham, S. Macdonald and J. Porter, *Victorian Interior Design*, London: Cassell, 1991

BANN
Stephen Bann, *The Clothing of Clio: A Study of the Representation of History in Nineteenth-Century Britain and France*, Cambridge University Press, 1984

BEAUTY
Dorren Bulger Burkee et al., *In Pursuit of Beauty: Americans and the Aesthetic Movement*, exh. cat. Metropolitan Museum of Art, New York/Rizzoli, 1986

BENJAMIN
Walter Benjamin, 'Das Interieur, die Spur', in *Das Passagen-Werk. Aufzeichnungen und Materialien.* (W. Benjamin, *Gesammelte Schriften*, Frankfurt am Main: Suhrkamp, 1991, vol. 5, part 1); trans. H. Eiland and K. McLaughlin as *The Arcades Project*, Cambridge, MA: Belknap Press, 1999

BERGAU
R. Bergau, *Über Einrichtung und Ausstattung der Wohnung*, Nuremberg: Vortrag Gewerbemuseum Nürnberg, 1873

BISKY
Jens Bisky, *Poesie der Baukunst. Architekturästhetik von Winckelmann bis Boisserée*, Weimar: Böhlau, 2000

BLANC
Charles Blanc, *Grammaire des arts décoratifs: Décoration intérieure de la maison*, Paris: Renouard, 1882; 2nd edn 1885

BLANCHARD
Mary Warner Blanchard, *Oscar Wilde's America: Counterculture in the Gilded Age*, New Haven and London: Yale University Press, 1998

BRISTOW 1996a
Ian C. Bristow, *Architectural Colour in British Interiors 1615–1840*, New Haven and London: Yale University Press, 1996

BRISTOW 1996b
Ian C. Bristow, *Interior House-Painting: Colours and Technology 1615–1840*, New Haven and London: Yale University Press, 1996

BRÖNNER 1978
Wolfgang Brönner, 'Farbige Architektur- und Architekturdekoration des Historismus', *Deutsche Kunst und Denkmalpflege,* vol. 36 (Jan.–Feb. 1978), 57–68

BRÖNNER 1994
Wolfgang Brönner, *Die bürgerliche Villa in Deutschland 1830–1890*, 2nd edn, Worms: Wernersche, 1994

CALDER
Jenni Calder, *The Victorian Home*, London: Batsford, 1977

CHEVREUL
Michel-Eugène Chevreul, *De la Loi du contraste simultané des couleurs et ses applications*, Paris: Pitois-Levrault, 1839; trans. C. Martel as *The Principles of Harmony and Contrast of Colours and their Applications to the Arts*, London: Longman, 1854 [used here; see Ch. III, n. 198]

COHEN
Deborah Cohen, *Household Gods: The British and Their Possessions*, New Haven and London: Yale University Press, 2006

COOK
Clarence Cook, *The House Beautiful: Essays on Beds and Tables, Stools and Candlesticks*, New York: Scribner, 1877; 2nd edn 1882, repr. New York: Dover, 1995

COOPER, H. J.
H. J. Cooper, *The Art of Furnishing on Rational and Aesthetic Principles*, London: H. S. King, 1876

COOPER, J.
Jeremy Cooper, *Victorian and Edwardian Furniture and Interiors*, London: Thames & Hudson, 1987

COOPER, N.
Nicholas Cooper, *The Opulent Eye: Late Victorian and Edwardian Taste in Interior Design*, London: Architectural Press, 1976

CORNFORTH
John Cornforth, *English Interiors 1790–1848: The Quest for Comfort*, London: Barrie & Jenkins, 1978

CROWLEY
John E. Crowley, *The Invention of Comfort: Sensibilities and Design in Early Modern Britain and Early America*, Baltimore: Johns Hopkins University Press, 2000

CRYSTAL PALACE
The Crystal Palace Exhibition, London 1851, London: Virtue, 1851, repr. New York: Dover, 1970 [*Art Journal*, special issue]

DALY
César Daly, *L'Architecture privée au XIXème siècle. Troisième série: Décorations intérieures peintes*, Paris: Ducher, 1877; abridged edn *Interior Design Motifs of the 19th Century*, London: Bracken 1988

DAVIDOFF & HALL
Leonore Davidoff and Catherine Hall, *Family Fortunes, Men and Women of the English Middle Class 1780–1850*, London: Hutchinson, 1987

DAY
Lewis Forman Day, *Everyday Art: Short Essays on the Arts not Fine*, London: Batsford, 1882

DOHME
Robert Dohme, *Das englische Haus. Eine kultur- und baugeschichtliche Skizze*, Braunschweig: Westermann, 1888

DOWNING
Andrew Jackson Downing, *The Architecture of Country Houses*, New York: Appleton, 1850; repr. New York: Dover, 1969

DRESSER 1873
Christopher Dresser, *Principles of Decorative Design*, London, 1873; repr. London: Academy Editions, 1973

DRESSER 1876
Christopher Dresser, *Studies in Design*, London: Cassell, 1876; repr. London: Studio Editions, 1988

EASTLAKE
Charles L. Eastlake, *Hints on Household Taste in Furniture, Upholstery and Other Details*, London: Longman, 1868; 4th edn 1878 [used here], repr. New York: Dover, 1969 [see Ch. II, n. 70]

EDIS
Robert W. Edis, *Decoration and Furniture of Town Houses*, London: Kegan Paul, 1881; repr. Wakefield: E. P. Publishing, 1972

EDWARDS
Clive Edwards, *Turning Houses into Homes: A History of the Retailing and Consumption of Domestic Furnishings*, Aldershot: Ashgate, 2005

EID
Joanna Banham (ed.), *Encyclopedia of Interior Design*, 2 vols., London: Fitzroy Dearborn, 1997

ELEB & BLANCHARD
Monique Eleb-Vidal and Anne Debarre-Blanchard, *Architecture de la vie privée: Maison et mentalités XVII–XIXe siècles*, Brussels: Archives d'Architecture Moderne, 1989

FALKE 1862
Jakob Falke, 'Die Kunst im Hause und im Gewerbe', part viii: 'Die Wohnung …', *Westermanns Illustrierte Deutsche Monatshefte*, vol. 6 (March 1862), 664–80

FALKE 1871
Jakob (von) Falke, *Die Kunst im Hause. Geschichtliche und kritisch-ästhetische Studien über die Decoration und Ausstattung der Wohnung*, Vienna: Gerold, 1871 [see Ch. II, nn. 65, 83; Ch. V, nn. 270, 276]

FALKE 1883
Jakob von Falke, *Die Kunst im Hause*, 5th edn, Vienna: Gerold, 1883

FOLNESICS
Josef Folnesics, *Innenräume und Hausrat der Empire- und Biedermeierzeit in Österreich Ungarn*, Vienna: Schroll, 1904

GARNIER-AUDIGER
A. Garnier-Audiger, *Manual du tapissier, décorateur et marchand de meubles*, Paris: Roret 1830

GARRETT
Rhoda and Agnes Garrett, *Suggestions for House Decoration*, Art at Home series, London: Macmillan, 1876

GEIST
Johann Friedrich Geist and Klaus Kürvers, *Das Berliner Mietshaus*, 3 vols., Munich: Prestel, 1984; used here: vol. 2: *1862–1945*

GEUL
Albert Geul, *Die Anlage der Wohngebäude mit besonderer Rücksicht auf das städtische Wohn- und Miethaus*, Stuttgart: Weise, 1868; 2nd edn Leipzig: Gebhardt, 1885

GERE
Charlotte Gere, *Nineteenth-Century Decoration: The Art of the Interior*, London: Weidenfeld and Nicholson, 1989

GIEDION
Siegfried Giedion, *Mechanization Takes Command: A Contribution to Anonymous History*, New York: Oxford University Press, 1948; new edn New York: Norton, 1969

GIROUARD 1977
Mark Girouard, *Sweetness and Light: The Queen Anne Movement 1860–1900*, Oxford: Clarendon, 1977

GIROUARD 1979
Mark Girouard, *The Victorian Country House*, revised edn, New Haven and London: Yale University Press, 1979

GL 1864
A. v. St., 'Die Poesie unserer vier Wände. Der kleine oder häusliche, der gelehrte, der gemüthliche und der elegante Comfort', *Die Gartenlaube* (1864), 599–603

GODWIN 1877
William Watt, *Art Furniture from Designs by E. W. Godwin and Others*, London: Batsford, 1877; repr. New York: Garland, 1978

GODWIN *Ar*
E. W. Godwin, 'My Chambers and What I Did to Them', *Architect*, 1 July 1876, 4–5; 8 July 1876, 18–19; 'My House "in" London', 15 July 1876, 33–34; 22 July 1876, 45–46; 29 July 1876, 58–59; 5 Aug. 1876, 72–73; 12 Aug. 1876, 86–87; 19 Aug. 1876, 112–113; 'From the Home Top', 26 July 1876, 112–13, etc.

GOETHE
Johann Wolfgang von Goethe, *Zur Farbenlehre*, Tübingen: Cotta, 1810; *Theory of Colours*, trans. C. L. Eastlake, London: Murray, 1840; R. Matthaei (ed.), *Goethe's Colour Theory*, London: Studio Vista, 1971

GRIER
Katherine C. Grier, *Culture and Comfort: Parlor-Making and Middle-Class Identity 1850–1930*, Washington, D.C.: Smithsonian Institution, 1997; revised edn of *Culture and Comfort: People, Parlors and Upholstery 1850–1930*, Rochester, NY: The Strong Museum, 1988

GUICHARD
Ernest Guichard, *De l'Ameublement et de la décoration intérieure de nos appartements*, Paris: Sevigné Frères, 1866; 2nd edn Paris: Rouveyre, 1880

GURLITT
Cornelius Gurlitt, *Im Bürgerhause. Plaudereien über Kunst, Kunstgewerbe und Wohnungs-Ausstattung*, Dresden: Gilbers, 1888

HAAFF
Rainer Haaff, *Gründerzeit. Möbel und Wohnkultur*, Westheim am Rhein: Verlag Haaff, 1992

HANDLIN
David Handlin, *The American Home* (Boston, MA: Little, Brown, 1979).

HAUSHOFER
Max Haushofer, 'Die Poesie unseres Hausraths', *Zeitschrift des Bayerischen Kunstgewerbevereins München* (1884), 57–60, 69–72

HAVARD 1884
Henry Havard, *L'Art dans la maison: Grammaire de l'ameublement*, Paris: Rouveyre, 1884 [see Ch. II, n. 85]

HAVARD *Dict.*
Henry Havard, *Dictionnaire de l'ameublement et de la décoration depuis le XIIIe siècle jusqu'à nos jours*, 4 vols., Paris: Quantin, 1887–89

HAWEIS
Mrs H. R. [Eliza] Haweis, *The Art of Decoration*, London: Chatto & Windus, 1881; new edn 1889, repr. London: Garland, 1977

HAY
David Ramsay Hay, *The Laws of Harmonious Colouring Adapted to Interior Decorations*, 5th edn Edinburgh: Blackwoods, 1844 [original edn Edinburgh: D. Lizars, 1828; see Ch. III, n. 199]

HEGEL
Georg Wilhelm Friedrich Hegel, *Vorlesungen über die Ästhetik* (1835); edn use. in G. W. F. Hegel, *Werke* (Frankfurt am Main: Suhrkamp, 1970), vols. 13–15

HENRICI
Karl Henrici, 'Betrachtungen über die Grundlagen zu behaglicher Einrichtung', in K. Henrici, *Abhandlungen aus dem Gebiete der Architektur*, Munich: Callwey, n.d. [*c*. 1906], 1–35 [originally pub. as issue no. 56 of *Deutsche Zeit- und Streitfragen* (1889)]

HESSEMER
F. M. Hessemer, *Arabische und Alt-italienische Bau-Verzierungen*, Berlin: Reimer, 1842; repr. without text as *Historic Designs and Patterns in Color from Arabic and Italian Sources*, New York: Dover, 1990

HIMMELHEBER
Georg Himmelheber, *Klassizismus/Historismus/Jugendstil*, vol. 3 of H. Kreisel (ed.), *Die Kunst des deutschen Möbels*, Munich: Beck, 1973

HIRTH
Georg Hirth, *Das deutsche Zimmer der Renaissance. Anregungen zur häuslichen Kunstpflege*, Munich: Hirth, 1879–80 [see Ch. V, n. 226]

HOLLY
H. Hudson Holly, 'Modern Dwellings: Their Construction, Decoration and Furniture': 'II: Color Decoration', *Harper's*, vol. 53 (June 1876), 49–64; 'III: Furniture', *Harper's*, vol. 53 (July 1876), 217–26; 'IV: Furniture', *Harper's*, vol. 53 (Aug. 1876), 354–63

HÖLZ
Christoph Hölz (ed.), *Interieurs der Goethezeit. Klassizismus, Empire, Biedermeier*, Augsburg: Battenberg, 1999

HOME 1853
[Anon.], *How to Furnish a House and Make it a Home*, The Economic Library V, London: Groombridge, n.d. [*c*. 1853]

HOPE
Thomas Hope, *Household Furniture and Interior Decoration Executed from Designs by Thomas Hope*, London: Longman, 1807; repr. New York: Dover, 1971

HUG
Friedrich Hug, *Anleitung zur geschmackvollen*

Einrichtung unserer Wohnung, Bern: Büchler, 1889

JERVIS
Simon Jervis, 'Cottage, Farm and Villa Furniture', *Burlington Magazine*, vol. 117, Dec. 1975, 848–59

JOY
Edward T. Joy, *A Pictorial Dictionary of British 19th-Century Furniture Design*, Woodbridge: Antique Collectors' Club, 1977

KENT *AM*
J. J. Kent, 'The Dwelling Rooms of a House', *Architectural Magazine*, vol. 2 (1835): 'The Dining Room', 228–33; 'The Dining Room, cont.', 275–81; 'The Drawing Room', 348–58; 'The Library', 404–7

KERR
Robert Kerr, *The Gentleman's House, or How to Plan English Residences*, London: Murray, 1864; 3rd edn 1871, repr. New York: Johnson, 1972

KIMBEL
Martin Kimbel, *Der decorative Ausbau*, Dresden: Gilbers, instalments, n.d. [1872–73; 1874–81; 1876–81]

LAURENT
Stéphane Laurent, *Les Arts appliqués en France: Genèse d'un enseignement*, Paris: Comité des Travaux Historiques et Scientifiques, 1999

LAXTON'S
Laxton's Price Book for Architects, Builders, Engineers and Contractors, 77th edn, London: Kelly, 1894

LE CAMUS
Nicolas Le Camus de Mézières, *Le Génie de l'architecture, ou l'analogie de cet art avec nos sensations*, Paris: Morin, 1780; repr. Geneva: Minkoff, 1972

LEHNERT
Georg Lehnert, *Illustrierte Geschichte des Kunstgewerbes*, vol. 2, Berlin: Oldenbourg, n.d. [1907]

LERIS-LAFFARGUE
Janine Leris-Laffargue, *Restauration Louis-Philippe*, Le Mobilier Français, Paris: Massin, 1994

LOGAN
Thad Logan, *The Victorian Parlour*, Cambridge University Press, 2001

LONG
Helen Long, *The Edwardian House: The Middle-Class Home in Britain 1880–1914*, Manchester University Press, 1993

LOUDON
John Claudius Loudon, *An Encyclopedia of Cottage, Farm and Villa Architecture and Furniture*, London: Longman, 1833; new edn with additions, 1842, repr. Fairfield, IA: Merrymeeting Archives LCC, 2002

LOYER
François Loyer, *Paris XIXe siècle: L'immeuble et la rue*, Paris: Hazan, 1987; trans. Charles Lynn Clark as *Paris Nineteenth Century: Architecture and Urbanism*, New York: Abbeville, 1988

LUCAE
Richard Lucae, 'Über die Macht des Raumes in der Baukunst', *Zeitschrift für Bauwesen*, vol. 19 (1869), 293–306

LUTHMER 1884a
Ferdinand Luthmer, *Werkbuch des Tapezierers. Eine praktische Darstellung*, Berlin: Spemann, 1884–86

LUTHMER 1884b
Ferdinand Luthmer, *Malerische Innenräume moderner Wohnungen in Aufnahmen nach der Natur*, Frankfurt am Main: Keller, 1884

LUTHMER 1892
Ferdinand Luthmer, 'Unser Haus', *Spemanns Schatzkästlein der guten Rats*, 6th edn, Stuttgart: Spemann, 1892, 1–98; very similar text in 4th edn, 1888, 1–107

LUTHMER 1897
Ferdinand Luthmer, *Werkbuch des Dekorateurs*, Stuttgart: Spemann, 1897

MANDLER
Peter Mandler, *The Fall and Rise of the Stately Home*, New Haven and London: Yale University Press, 1997

MARCUS
Sharon Marcus, *Apartment Stories: City and Home in Nineteenth-Century Paris and London*, Berkeley: University of California Press, 1999

MENNEKES
Ralf Mennekes, *Die Renaissance der deutschen Renaissance*, Petersberg: Imhof, 2005

MORLEY
John Morley, *Regency Design 1790–1840*, London: Zwemmer, 1993

MORRIS
William Morris, *Hopes and Fears for Art*, London: Ellis and White, 1882

MOTHES
Oscar Mothes, *Unser Heim im Schmucke der Kunst*, Leipzig: Schloemp, 1879; 2nd expanded edn 1882

MUTHESIUS, H.
Hermann Muthesius, *Das englische Haus*, 3 vols., Berlin: Wasmuth, 1904–5: vol. 3: *Der Innenraum des englischen Hauses*; 2nd edn 1908, repr. Berlin: Mann, 1999; *The English House*, trans. Janet Seligman and ed. D. Sharp, London: BSP Professional Books, 1987 [abridged]; complete trans. by D. Sharp, London: F. Lincoln, 2007.

MUTHESIUS, S.
Stefan Muthesius, *Das englische Vorbild. Eine Studie zu den deutschen Reformbewegungen in Architektur, Wohnbau und Kunstgewerbe im späteren 19. Jahrhundert*, Munich: Prestel, 1974

NOUVEL-KAMMERER
Odile Nouvel-Kammerer, *Napoléon III, Années 1880*, Le Mobilier Français, Paris: Massin, 1996

OTTILLINGER
Eva B. Ottillinger and L. Hanzl, *Kaiserliche Interieurs. Die Wohnkultur der Wiener Hofes im 19. Jahrhundert und die Wiener Kunstgewerbereform*, Vienna: Böhlau, 1997

OTTOMEYER
Hans Ottomeyer (ed.), *Biedermeiers Glück und Ende 1815–1848*, Munich: Hugendubel, 1987

PAOLINI
Claudio Paolini, Alessandra Ponte and Ornella Selvafolta, *Il bello ritrovato: Gusto, ambienti, mobili dell'ottocento*, Novara: Agostini, 1990

PAPE
Jean Pape, *Musterzimmer, Vollständige Decorationen für bürgerliche und herrschaftliche Wohnunge in Form und Farbe*, Dresden: Gilbers, 1887; 2nd edn 1890

PARDAILHÉ-GALABRUN
Annik Pardailhé-Galabrun, *La Naissance de l'intime: 3000 Foyers parisiens XVIIe–XVIIIe siècles*, Paris: Presses Universitaires de France, 1988; trans. Jocelyn Phelps as *The Birth of Intimacy: Privacy and Domestic Life in Early Modern Paris*, Oxford: Polity, 1991

PARKES
Mrs William Parkes, *Domestic Duties, or Instructions to Young Married Ladies on the Management of their Households*, London: Longman, 1825; 5th edn 1841

PERCIER & FONTAINE
Charles Percier and Pierre-François-Léonard Fontaine, *Receuil de décorations intérieures comprenant tout ce qui a rapport à l'ameublement*, Paris: the authors, 1801–12; expanded edn Venice, 1843, repr. Farnborough: Gregg, 1971

PEVSNER
Nikolaus Pevsner, *Studies in Art, Architecture and Design*, 2 vols, London: Thames & Hudson, 1968

PIEŃKOS
Andrzej Pieńkos, *Dom Sztuki. Siedziby artystów w nowoczesnej kulturze europejskiej* ('The House of Art: Artists' Residences in European Culture') [mainly 19th century], Warsaw: Wydawnictwa Uniwersytetu Warszawskeigo, 2005

POE
Edgar Allan Poe, 'Philosophy of Furniture', *Burton's Gentleman's Magazine,* May 1840, 243–45; repr. in *Collected Works of Edgar Allan Poe*, Cambridge, MA: 1978, vol. 2, 494–504

PONS
Bruno Pons, *French Period Rooms 1650–1800: Rebuilt in England, France, and the Americas*, trans. Ann Sautier-Greening, Dijon: Faton, 1995

PRAZ
Mario Praz, *La filosofia dell'arredamento: I mutamenti nel gusto della decorazione interna attraverso i secoli dall'antica Roma ai nostri tempi*, Milan: Longanesi, 1964; trans. as *An Illustrated History of Interior Decoration from Pompeii to Art Nouveau*, William Weaver, London: Thames & Hudson, 1964

RENAISSANCE
G. Ulrich Grossmann and Petra Krutisch (eds), *Renaissance Der [der Renaissance]. Ein bürgerlicher Kunststil im 19. Jahrhundert*, 8 vols., Weserrenaissance-Museum Schloss Brake/Munich: Deutscher Kunstverlag, 1992

REULECKE
Jürgen Reulecke (ed.), *Geschichte des Wohnens 1800–1918. Das bürgerliche Zeitalter*, Stuttgart: Deutsche Verlags Anstalt, 1997

RICE
Charles Rice, *The Emergence of the Interior: Architecture, Modernity, Domesticity*, London: Routledge, 2007

RIEHL
Wilhelm Heinrich Riehl, *Die Familie*, Stuttgart: Cotta, 1855; 3rd edn 1855 [used here; thereafter the text changes with each edn: see Ch. IV, n. 58]

RIS-PAQUOT
Ris-Paquot [pseudonym of Oscar Edmont], *Le Livre de la femme d'intérieur: Table, couture, ménage, hygiène*, Paris: H. Laurens, n.d. [c. 1892]

ROMBERG
Andreas Romberg, *Dekorationen innerer Räume*, Munich: Fischer, 1834

RYBCZYNSKI
Witold Rybczynski, *Home: A Short History of an Idea*, London: Heinemann, 1988

SAINT
Andrew Saint, *Richard Norman Shaw*, New Haven and London: Yale University Press, 1976

SCULLY
Vincent J. Scully, *The Shingle Style: Architectural Theory and Design from Richardson to the Origins of Wright*, New Haven and London: Yale University Press, 1955; revised edn *The Shingle and Stick Style*, 1971

SECOND EMPIRE
L'Art en France sous le Second Empire, exh. cat. Grand Palais, Paris/Editions RMN, 1979

SEMPER
Gottfried Semper, *Der Stil in den technischen und tektonischen Künsten, oder praktische Aesthetik*, 2 vols., Frankfurt am Main: Verlag für Kunst und Wissenschaft, 1860–63; 2nd edn Munich: Bruckmann, 1878–79; trans. H. Mallgrave and

M. Robinson as *Style in the Technical and Tectonic Arts or Practical Aesthetic*, Los Angeles, CA: Getty, 2004

SIDLAUSKAS
Susan Sidlauskas, *Body, Place, and Self in Nineteenth-Century Painting*, Cambridge University Press, 2000

SIEBEL
Ernst Siebel, *Der grossbürgerliche Salon 1850–1918. Geselligkeit und Wohnkultur*, Berlin: Reimer, 1999

SILVERMAN
Debora L. Silverman, *L'Art Nouveau en France: Politique, psychologie et style fin de siècle*, Paris: Flammarion, 1994; translated from *Art Nouveau in Fin-de-Siècle France: Politics, Psychology, and Style*, Berkeley: University of California Press, 1989

SMITH
George Smith, *Collection of Designs for Household Furniture and Interior Decoration*, London: J. Taylor, 1808, repr. New York: Praeger, 1970; also repr. in J. Harris (ed.), *Regency Furniture: Furniture Designs from Contemporary Sourcebooks 1803–1826*, London: Tiranti, 1961

SNODIN & HOWARD
'Ornament and the Domestic Interior', in Michael Snodin and Maurice Howard, *Ornament: A Social History since 1450*, New Haven and London: Yale University Press, 1996

SPOFFORD
Harriet Prescott Spofford, *Art Decoration Applied to Furniture*, New York: Harper's, 1878

STERNBERGER
Dolf Sternberger, *Panorama oder Ansichten vom 19. Jahrhundert*, Hamburg: Claassen, 1938; 3rd edn 1955

STIEGEL
Achim S. Stiegel, *Berliner Möbelkunst vom Ende des 18. bis zur Mitte des 19. Jahrhunderts*, Munich: Deutscher Kunstverlag, 2003

TALBERT
Bruce J. Talbert, *Gothic Forms Applied to Furniture, Metal Work and Decoration for Domestic Purposes*, Bristol: Birbeck, 1867; repr. Farnborough: Gregg, 1971

TAYLOR
Mark Taylor and Julieanna Preston (eds), *Intimus:*

Interior Design Theory Reader, Chichester: Wiley, 2006

THORNTON
Peter Thornton, *Authentic Décor: The Domestic Interior 1620–1920*, London: Weidenfeld and Nicholson, 1984 [also pub. in many other languages]

TRISTRAM
Philippa Tristram, *Living Space in Fact and Fiction*, London: Routledge, 1989

VAN VOORST TOT VOORST
J. M. W. van Voorst tot Voorst, *Tussen Biedermeier en Berlage: Meubel en Interieur in Nederland 1835–1895*, Amsterdam: De Bataavsche Leeuw, 1992

VIOLLET-LE-DUC
Eugène-Emmanuel Viollet-le-Duc, *Dictionnaire raisonné du mobilier français de l'époque carolingienne à la renaissance*, 6 vols., Paris: Bance, 1858–75: used here vol. 1 (1855–57)

WAINWRIGHT
Clive Wainwright, *The Romantic Interior: The British Collector at Home 1750–1850*, New Haven and London: Yale University Press, 1989

WALSH
J. H. Walsh, *A Manual of Domestic Economy, Suited to Families Spending from 100 to 1000 Pounds a Year*, London: Routledge, 1856 [see Ch. III, n. 46]

WEISMANN
Anabella Weismann, *Froh erfülle Deine Pflicht! Die Entwicklung des modernen Hausfrauenleitbildes im Spiegel trivialer Massenmedien in der Zeit zwischen Reichsgründung und Weltwirtschaftskrise*, Berlin: Schelzky & Jeep, 1989

WERNER
Peter Werner, *Pompeji und die Wanddekoration der Goethezeit*, Munich: Fink, 1970

WITT-DÖRRING
Christian Witt-Dörring (ed.), *Bürgersinn und Aufbegehren. Biedermeier und Vormärz in Wien 1815–1848*, exh. cat. Historisches Museum, Vienna/Jugend und Volk, 1988

YAPP
George Wagstaffe Yapp, *Art Industry: Furniture, Upholstery, and House-Decoration*, London: Virtue, n.d., c.1879, repr. Farnborough: Gregg, 1972

Notes

ABBREVIATIONS

AA	*Art Amateur* (New York)
ABZ	*Allgemeine Bauzeitung* (Vienna)
AJ	*Art Journal* (London)
AM	*Architectural Magazine* (London)
AmA	*American Architect and Building News* (Boston, MA)
Ar	*Architect* (London)
AR	*Architektonische Rundschau* (Stuttgart)
B	*The Builder* (London)
BfK	*Blätter für Kunstgewerbe* (Vienna)
BN	*Building News* (London)
BrA	*The British Architect and Northern Engineer* (London/Manchester)
ChM	*Cornhill Magazine* (London)
CM	*Cabinet Maker* (London)
DB	*Deutsche Bauzeitung* (Berlin)
DF	*Decorator and Furnisher* (New York)
EH	*Eigen Haard* (Haarlem)
FG	*Furniture Gazette* (London)
FH	*Furniture History* (London)
Gh	*Gewerbehalle* (Stuttgart)
Gl	*Die Gartenlaube* (Leipzig)
Harper's	*Harper's New Monthly Magazine* (New York)
Id	*Innendekoration* (Darmstadt)
IFz	*Illustrierte Frauenzeitung* (Berlin)
JDH	*Journal of Design History* (Oxford)
KAS	*Kunst + Architektur in der Schweiz* (Berne)
MA	*Magazine of Art* (London)
MoA	*Moniteur des Architectes* (Paris)
MH	*Monuments Historiques* (Paris)
RAD	*Revue des Arts Décoratifs* (Paris)
RGA	*Revue Générale de l'Architecture et des Travaux Publics* (Paris)
WP	*Winterthur Portfolio* (Wilmington, DE)
ZBKM	*Zeitschrift des Bayerischen Kunstgewerbevereins zu München* (until 1868 *Zeitschrift des Vereins zur Ausbildung der Gewerke*) (Munich)

For abbreviations of books, please refer to the Bibliography.

These notes cover various topics, sometimes within a single entry. A change in topic is signalled by a §.

PREFACE

Sources and methods

1 See Thornton, Intr.. Photos: G. Benker, *Bürgerliches Wohnen. Städtische Wohnkultur in Mitteleuropa von der Gotik bis zum Jugendstil* (Munich: Callwey, 1984), 8.

2 On issues of 'historical reality', see e.g. M. Forkel, *Wohnen im 'Stil' des Historismus* (Museumsdorf Cloppenburg, 1996), 36–37. For scepticism as regards taking advice books as 'evidence': G. Lees-Maffei, 'Studying Advice …', *JDH*, vol. 16, no. 1 (2003), 1–14; cf. Eleb & Blanchard, 11–15. For a contrasting view: 'each aspect of the house and of the running of it conformed to rules': A. St George, *The Descent of Manners: Etiquette, Rules and the Victorians* (London: Chatto & Windus, 1993), 104.

3 See e.g. Rice, 130–31.

4 Most recently J. Styles and A. Vickery (eds), *Gender, Taste and Material Culture in Britain and North America 1700–1830* (New Haven and London: Yale University Press, 2006).

5 Cf. such statements at their simplest, e.g. 'taste (i.e. judgments of what is desirable) …': M. Harvey et al., *Between Demand and Consumption: A Framework for Research*, CRIC Discussion Paper No. 40 (Manchester University and UMIST, 2001), 56.

Scope

6 To cite statistics relating to the social classes would appear of limited use here. No precise answers can be expected for the questions: Who was prepared to spend what proportion of his or her income on furnishings? How much secondhand furniture was available (and wanted) when the expansion of urban populations was at its strongest? (There were 21,644 new dwellings in Berlin in 1890: Geist, 332.) The range with which this book is concerned lies somewhere between the furnishings available in Germany in 1883 at a cost of 330 Marks (then £17) for the 'only room' of an 'orderly but most modest' working-class family, and a complete new living room for 700 Marks (£65, still considered 'low cost'): 'Konkurrenzen', *Illustrierte Schreinerzeitung*, vol. 1, no. 2 (1883), 8. £17 would have represented more than 8 weeks' earnings for the average worker living on £2 a week, and 80–90% of the population did not earn more. Cf. Walsh: the income bracket at which his book (1856) is aimed begins at £100 p.a. (see also Ch. II, n. 46).

The West

7 Exceptions are Thornton, who considers countries together, and Paolini et al., who keep them strictly apart.

8 Spreading ideas: Thornton, 9; cf. Lehnert.

9 M. North, *Genuss und Glück des Lebens. Kulturkonsum im Zeitalter der Aufklärung* (Cologne: Böhlau, 2003), 217ff.; see also Ch. II, n. 88 for German and Austrian influence.

10 W. F. Exner, *Der Aussteller und die Ausstellungen* (Weimar: Voigt, 1866); E. Findling, *Historical Dictionary of World's Fairs and Expositions* (n.p.: Greenwood, 1990).

INTRODUCTION

Modernity

1 H. Repton, *Fragments on the Theory of Landscape Gardening, including some Remarks on Grecian and Gothic Architecture* (London: Taylor, 1816; repr. New York: Garland, 1982), 36.

2 Bedrooms, newly combining factors of hygiene, privacy and décor: e.g. *EID*, 116–17; Barker (see below, Ch. II, n. 140); Geul 1885, 8–9; P. Diebie, *Ethnologie de la chambre à coucher* (Paris: Grasset, 1987).

3 'hohe, freie Räume unserer heutigen Wohnungen': W. Hamm, *Ordnung und Schönheit am häuslichen Herd. Haushaltungskunst und Gesundheitspflege für deutsche Frauen* (Jena: Costenoble, 1887), 210, cf. 150.

4 Havard *Dict.*, vol. 1, 110.

5 In mid-19th century Britain (probably occupying a middling position in Europe), *c.* 66% of households had more than five people, 22% had ten or more: Davidoff & Hall, 319–20.

6 For Mothes's reception rooms, see the present book, pp. 18, 19, 156, 157, 168; those not included are the 'Vestibül', 'Gesellschaftssaal' (room for large gatherings), 'Jagdsaal' (hunting room) and library. See also Mothes's 2nd edn (1882); Kerr. § J. F. Blondel, *Cours d'architecture ou traité de la décoration, distribution et construction des bâtiments*, 9 vols. (Paris: Desaint, 1771–77): see vols. 2, 5, 8, 9; cf. Le Camus, 86–88; Eleb & Blanchard; A. Hauser, 'Die Formierung des bürgerlichen Interieurs', and D. Lüthi, 'Le langage du plan, distribution intérieure …', both *KAS*, vol. 55, no. 2 (2004), 6–13, 61–67. By 1900 half of all dwellings in Berlin had two rooms or fewer; in England the average dwelling had two to four (smallish) rooms. § A room's furnishings give it 'the stamp of its purpose' ('den Stempel seiner Bestimmung'): F. Ebhardt, *Der gute Ton in allen Lebenslagen* (Leipzig: Klinkhardt, 1898), 6. Separate access to each room came more slowly: cf. E. Asmus, *Wie Europa baut und wohnt. Vergleichende Darstellung von Typen eingebauter Wohnhäuser* ['urban dwellings'] *der Hauptstädte Europas* (Hamburg: Strumper, 1883).

7 On the dining room: *EID*, 377–80; 'warm, rich, substantial': Hay, 32 (1828 edn, 21; 1836 edn, 27); Loftie (see below, Ch. II, n. 75), 140; R. Rich, '"Designing the Dinner Party": Advice on Dining and Décor in London and Paris 1860–1914', in K. Grover (ed.), *Dining in America c. 1850–1900* (University of Massachusetts Press, 1987). According to one writer in 1879, the idea that dining rooms were introduced to Germany only from *c.* 1865 needed further exploration: 'Deutschlands grosse Industrie-Werkstätten', *Gl* (1879), 44–46 (46).

8 *salon*: Eleb & Blanchard; I. Eleb with A. Debarre, *L'Invention de l'habitation moderne: Paris 1880–1914* (Paris: Hazan / Brussels: Archives d'Architecture Moderne, 1995). 'Drawing room': J. Kinchin in *EID*, 388–92; according to Loudon, 650, the independent landowner has a drawing room, the farmer a drawing room or a parlour. For the United States: Grier. For the German *Salon/Empfangszimmer*: Siebel. 'French furnishing' ('französische Hauseinrichtung') in Germany: Luthmer 1897, 197.

9 'les parties en quelque sorte extérieure, le salon, la salle à manger, l'antichambre, le vestibule': Blanc, 223–24; see also Havard at his most elliptical: 'solemnité légèrement cérémonieuse': Havard 1884, 317. Germans insisted that small middle-class (*bürgerliche*) dwellings needed at least one room that did not serve domestic purposes ('häuslichen Zwecken im eigenen Sinne'): Geul, 11 (1885 edn, 23).

10 'confort', 'mot de création essentiellement récente': Havard *Dict.*, vol. 1, 961; the French held that the English took this word from them and that the French took it back: see 'confortable' in Larousse, *Grand Dictionnaire universel du XIXe siècle*, vol. 4 (1869), 915; 'elegance allied to that useful and sweet convenience [*commodité*] which the English call *comfortable*': Garnier-Audiger, 92. No linear progression of 'comfort': Crowley. Cf. Rybczynski; Morley, 357–58; Giedion; J. P. Goubert, *Du Luxe au confort* (series: *Modernité XIX–XX siècle*; n.p.: Belin, 1988); cf. Arbeitskreis für Hausforschung, *Jahrbuch für Hausforschung und Historische Ausstattung*, 2004 (Marburg: Jonas).

11 W. Walton, *France at the Crystal Palace: Bourgeois Taste and Artisan Manufacture in the 19th Century* (Berkeley: University of California Press, 1992), 15.

12 'Le moindre des petits bourgeois de nos jours est cent fois plus commodement installé, que les plus grands seigneurs des siècles passés': Havard 1884, 269–70.

13 'gewissermassen eine künstlich zusammengesetzte Maschine für alle häuslichen Lebensverrichtungen': Hessemer, 20; cf. 'Sanitär, Sittlich ['moral'], Schönheit ['beauty'], Sicherheit ['security']': A. Wolf, *Der bauliche Comfort des Wohnhauses* (Prague: Dominicus, 1882), review in *Zeitschrift für Baukunde*, vol. 5 (Munich, 1882), 184.

14 A. W. Fuller and W. A. Wheeler, *Artistic Homes in City and Country* (Boston, MA: Ticknor, 1891), Intr.; cf. M. Alsberg, *Die gesunde Wohnung* (Berlin, 1882).

15 Blanc, 186.

16 Argand lamps appeared from the late 18th century, and kerosene lamps were widespread by the 1870s. 'Today's light in every little drawing room is such as hardly a nobleman could then [i.e. 40 years before] procure': 'The Cost of Living', *ChM*, vol. 31 (1875), 412–21 (415). Gas was widespread after *c.* 1850, and electricity slowly gained ground after 1880: W. Schivelbusch, *Lichtblicke. Zur Generation der künstlichen Helligkeit im 19. Jahrhundert* (Munich: Hanser, 1983) / *Disenchanted Night: The Industrialization of Light in the Nineteenth Century* (Berkeley: University of California Press, 1988); cf. M. Ierley, *The Comforts of Home: The American House and the Evolution of Modern Convenience* (New York: Three Rivers, 1999); A. Rüegg (ed.), *Swiss Furniture and Interiors in the 20th Century* (Basel: Birkhäuser, 2002), 44ff.

17 Home security: W. Howitt, *The Rural Life of England* (London: Longman, 1844; repr. Shannon: Irish University Press, 1971), 139; Gardner, 1878 (see below, Ch. II, n. 83), 112; 1885 edn, 398. Locks: Giedion, 56ff. Smells: A. Corbin, *Le Miasme et la jonquille* (Paris: Montaigne, 1982) / *The Foul and the Fragrant: Odour and the French Social Imagination* (London: Picador, 1984). For seating upholstery, see the present book, p. 85; for early ergonomics, see Havard, 68ff.

18 'The further …' ('plus la civilisation s'est avancé, plus le meuble devient somptueux'): F. Roger, *Exposition du travail, Palais de l'Industrie: Histoire du siège à travers les âges* (Paris: Châtelus, 1891), 9–10; cf. K. Frey, 'Distribution et décoration intérieure', *KAS*, vol. 55 (2004), 14–19. § 'poverty-stricken …' ('kahle Nüchternheit und hässliche Farblosigkeit'): Carl Müller & Comp., *Complette Einrichtungen* (sales cat., Berlin, 1894), 46. § 'a splendid house …': [Anon.], *Untersuchungen in den Charakter der Gebäude. Über die Verbindung der Baukunst mit den schönen Künsten* (Dessau, 1785 / Leipzig, 1788), quoted in Bisky, 105. § 'elegant …' : Crace, 'Decoration' (Ch. II, n. 251). § 'pour le confort …': Centre National de la Recherche Scientifique (CNRS), *Trésor de la Langue Française* (Paris: Gallimard, 1992); cf. Grier; C. J. Berry, *The Idea of Luxury: A Conceptual and Historical Investigation* (Cambridge University Press, 1994).

19 Dwellings and class: T. Nipperdey, *Deutsche Geschichte 1866–1918* (Munich: Beck, 1990), 144; S. Muthesius, *The English Terraced House* (New Haven and London: Yale University Press, 1984), Ch. 17; cf. 'the progress of civilisation has constantly a tendency to make articles of convenience become objects of luxury': H. Shaw, *Specimens of Ancient Furniture* (London: Pickering, 1836), 1; 'L'art crée les types, les beaux modèles, l'industrie les multiple par la fabrication': 'L'Art de la chambre', *L'Art Moderne* (Brussels), 24 May 1885, 166–67.

20 F. Eulenburg, *Kosten der Lebenshaltung in deutschen Grossstädten* (*Schriften des Vereins für Socialpoliitk*, vol. 145, Munich, 1914), 55.

21 Geist, 124. Did the increased desire for luxury in France result in a reduced birth rate? See T. Zeldin, *France*

1848–1945 (Oxford University Press, 1973–77), vol. 2, 420–431; 'The Cost of Living', *ChM*, vol. 31, Jan.–June 1875, 412–421 (419). Modest people chose a modest new dwelling at first, but became more ambitious when they compared themselves to others: Deutsche Bauzeitung, *Deutsches Bauhandbuch*, vol. 2: 2nd half-volume of *Baukunde des Architekten* (Berlin: Toeche, 1884), part 2, 201–2.

Anti-modernity

22 For plans and room uses, see Ch. IV.

23 According to Falke, new windows were a 'technischer Triumph', yet users now preferred darker rooms: Falke 1883, 281; see also Ch. IV, 'Darkness'.

24 For French 'bourgeoisie', see Auslander. Daly explicitly excluded large palaces: C. Daly, *L'Architecture privée au XIXème siècle (2e série), Nouvelles Maisons de Paris …* (Paris: Librairie Générale d'Architecture, 1872), 1; cf. H. Lipstadt, 'Housing the Bourgeosie: César Daly and the Ideal Home', *Oppositions*, vol. 8 (1977), 34–47; Loyer. However, see the many contradictory statements, e.g.: 'Manières bourgeoises ont certes le charme de la simplicité' (Victor Hugo on King Louis-Philippe, 1846), quoted in A. Martin-Fugier, *La Vie élégante ou la formation de Tout-Paris 1815–1848* (Paris: Fayard, 1990), 77; and yet 'l'industriel et le commerçant … s'allaièrent à la noblesse sous Louis-Philippe': J. Verdellet, *L'Art pratique du tapissier* (Paris, 1871), 7. Cf. Havard's claim that the need or desire for luxury had spread with 'republican equality': F. Luthmer, 'Eine französische Kunst im Hause' (review of Havard 1884), *Deutsche Tischlerzeitung*, vol. 13 (1886), 318ff. § For German 'burghers': J. Kocka (ed.), *Bürger und Bürgerlichkeit im 19. Jahrhundert* (Göttingen: Vandenhoek, 1987); Brönner 1994; A. Hufschmidt, '"Zwischen Luxus und Schundwaare". Überlegungen zur bürgerlichen Wohnung der zweiten Hälfte des 19. Jahrhundert', *Renaissance*, vol. 6, 95–111; W. Brönner, 'Schichtenspezifische Wohnkultur. Die bürgerliche Wohnung des Historismus', in E. Mai et al. (eds), *Kunstpolitik und Kunstförderung im Kaiserreich* (Berlin: Mann, 1982), 361–78; Reulecke, 174. Cf. the progression in 'fein' (smart), 'vornehm' (noble), 'räpresentativ' (distinguished/elevated): Nipperdey, *Deutsche Geschichte 1866–1918* (above, n. 19), 129. Cf. W. G. Breckman, 'Disciplining Consumption: The Debate about Luxury in Wilhemine Germany 1890–1914', *Journal of Social History*, vol. 24 (1990–91), 485–505. Older *Bürgerliche Baukunst* was also synonymous with *Civilbaukunst*, i.e. mundane types of building and all housing. § For the British 'middle classes': 'middle-class domesticity': Davidoff & Hall, 184. Loudon's belief was that décor can and should be available to all: 274. London houses were classed I–IV – a steep gradation of sizes but class labels were rarely used overtly. However, at any level some words such as 'genteel' could be used with an upward trajectory. The 1870s 'Art at Home' series was to be used 'only for the decoration and the furnishing of middle-class houses … people of moderate means': Garrett, 6; cf. E. Ferry, '"Decorators may be Compared to Doctors": An analysis of Rhoda and Agnes Garrett's *Suggestions for House Decoration*', *JDH*, vol. 16, no. 1 (2003), 15–34. More general demands for modesty could be expressed as e.g. warnings against 'French "trumpery"': 'French Taste and English', *B*, 12 Sept. 1863, 649–50; see Cohen.

25 Geist, 469; cf. Geul, 1868 and 1885. Pape divides his rooms into 'bürgerliche' and 'herrschaftliche': Pape; cf. Werle's 'vornehme Haus' and 'Bürgerheim' (see below, Ch. II, n. 87); but neither Pape's nor Werle's designs show much actual difference between 'noble' and 'bürgerlich'.

26 'Bieder' normally means conventional and 'petit-bourgeois'; from mid-century a slightly ridiculed character, the 'Biedermeier', appeared in fiction. By 1900 use of the term implied a sense of endearment and a new evaluation of people and objects of the 1820s to the 1840s as 'simple' and 'naive'; it was also linked to *bürgerlich* values in general, and corresponded to other primitivisms of the late 19th and early 20th centuries. Furniture was now the chief bearer of the so-called *Biedermeierstil*. But H. Ottomeyer in Munich and C. Witt-Dörring in Vienna have long stressed that most known Biedermeier furniture was made for the nobility and for the rich, hardly ever for the broader middle classes, let alone the lower bourgeois strata; it constituted cheaper, and regionally diverse, versions of the Paris Empire style (with additional English influence). Thus the chief meaning of Biedermeier furniture in its own time ('elegant', etc.) was the very opposite of *bieder* or naïve: Ottomeyer, Witt-Dörring; cf. Himmelheber; Paolini, 283–93; Stiegel, 26–28; Hölz; H. Ottomeyer et al., *Biedermeier. Die Erfindung der Einfachkeit / The Invention of Simplicity* (exh. cat. Milwaukee / Ostfildern: Hatje Cantz, 2006). § 'Regency', used from *c.* 1910 for British furnishings between *c.* 1810 and the 1840s, is a less problematic term, but like 'Biedermeier' initially marked the 'good' (even the 'best') period before the onset of the 'bad' 19th century.

27 'im Masshalten und Wahrbleiben beruht ewig allein die wahre Vornehmheit': Henrici, 21; cf. 'pure and elegant simplicity of Greek ornament … appreciable only by the more highly cultivated tastes': C. F. Bielefeld, *On the Use of the Improved Papier Maché in Furniture, in the Interior Decoration of Buildings …* (London: publ. by author, 1840).

28 'suffrage universelle …': H. Penon, *Le Mobilier des siècles passés* (Paris: Libr. Centrale des Beaux Arts, n.d. [1882]), 83; cf. Nouvel-Kammerer, 86–87; 'cet amour de la montre': C. Daly, 'Maisons de Paris', *RGA*, 1852, 396–402 (399). Scepticism about 'mass' production: J. Lessing, *Handarbeit* (*Volkswirtschaftliche Zeitfragen*, year 9, no. 67) (Berlin: Simion, 1887); 'Belle Époque' etc: cf. Ch. III, 'Refinement'.

29 Once issues of class and décor had become problematized from a socio-political standpoint, the debate never stopped. Well-known sociologists, including Thorstein Veblen and Pierre Bourdieu, essentially argued that the main motivation underlying consumers' complex selection of goods or kinds of décor was an attempt to manipulate class appearance. This meant a departure from the simpler, 'traditional' concept of goods and décor reflecting actual status.

30 R. Baarsen et al., *'De Lelijke Tijd'. Pronkstukken van de Nederlandse Interieurkunst 1835–1895* (exh. cat. Amsterdam: Rijksmuseum, 1995). The work is, however, hardly condemnatory.

31 C. Asendorf, *Batterien der Lebenskraft. Zur Geschichte der Dinge und ihrer Wahrnehmung im 19. Jahrhundert* (Giessen: Anabas, 1984) / *Batteries of Life: On the History of Things and their Perception in Modernity* (Berkeley: University of California Press, 1993); cf. H. Heynen and G. Baydar (eds), *Negotiating Domesticity* (London: Routledge, 2005); 'Kitsch' issue of *Home Cultures*, vol. 3, 3 Nov. 2006; Z. Sternhell, *Les anti-Lumières: Du XVIIIe siècle au guerre froide* (Paris: Fayard, 2006).

I A POETIC EVERYDAY HOME?

1 'Les sujets stériles sont ceux d'habitations: on ne parvient les faire distinguer que par un peu plus ou moins des richesses: mais il est difficile d'y introduire la poésie de l'architecture': E. L. Boullée, *Architecture, essai sur l'art* (*c.* 1788), trans. and ed. H. Rosenau as *Boullée's Treatise on Architecture* (London: Tiranti, 1953), 68; see also J.-M. Pérouse de Montclos (ed.), *Etienne-Louis Boullée: Architecture, essai sur l'art* (Paris: Hermann, 1968). Cf. W. Szambien, *Symétrie, goût, charactère: Théorie et terminologie de l'architecture à l'âge classique, 1550–1800* (Paris: Picard, 1986); K. Barck et al. (eds), *Ästhetische Grundbegriffe*, 7 vols. (Stuttgart: Metzler, 2000–2005); Bisky. See also B. Hanson, *Architects and the 'Building World' from Chambers to Ruskin: Constructing Authority* (Cambridge University Press, 2003); A. Pérez-Gómez, *Built upon Love: Architectural Longing after Ethics and Aesthetics* (Cambridge, MA: MIT Press, 2006); W. Kemp, 'Beziehungsspiele. Versuch einer Gattungspoetik des Interieurs', in *Kemp-Reader* (Berlin: Deutscher Kunstverlag, 2006), 123–43.

2 'un appartement rassemble à un poème': H. de Noussanne, *Le Goût dans l'ameublement* (Paris: Firmin Didot, 1896), 7.

Poetics

3 See 'Tyrolese House-Mottoes', *ChM*, vol. 28, July–Dec. 1873, 575–82; J. Lessing, 'Sprüche auf altdeutschen Leinendecken', *IFz*, vol. 4 (1877), 302–3 (with bibliography).

4 See Hope, 25; R. Guilding, *Marble Mania: Sculpture Galleries in England 1640–1840* (London: Soane Museum, 2001); M. Droth, 'Private Views: Statuettes in the English Domestic Interior 1900', in U. Szulakowska (ed.), *Power and Persuasion: Sculpture in its Rhetorical Context* (Warsaw: IS PAN, 2004), 125–41. Cf. [A. Benn], 'Among Painters and Poets', *CM*, Nov. 1887, 113–17. For painting: *Decoration in Painting* … (Ch. II, n. 88); H. E. Smith, 'Decorative Paintings in the Domestic Interior in England and Wales, *c.* 1850–1890' (diss., University of London, 1980; printed 1984); Brönner 1994.

5 *The Concise Oxford Dictionary* (Oxford University Press, 1999).

6 Sidlauskas, 20; Rice, 121.

7 C. C. L. Hirschfeld, *Theorie der Gartenkunst* (Leipzig, 1775); partially trans. by L. B. Parshall (ed.), *Theory of Gardening Art* (Philadelphia: University of Pennsylvania Press, 2001); Bisky 87, 92–93; J. D. Hunt, *The Picturesque Garden in Europe* (London: Thames & Hudson, 2003).

8 W. Wordsworth, Preface to *Lyrical Ballads* (1800). See Wordsworth, *Poetical Works* (Oxford University Press, 1904), 734.

9 'das Äussere … *muss* in die Gestalt der Gewöhnlichkeit, des empirisch Menschlichen eintreten. … Diese Heimatlichkeit im Gewöhnlichen ist es, durch welche die romantische Kunst von aussen her zutraulich anlockt': Hegel, Part II, 3rd sect., Ch. 1, Intr. (vol. 14, 145–46); cf. D. Solkin, *Painting Out of the Ordinary … in Early 19th-Century Britain* (New Haven and London: Yale University Press, 2008).

10 Davidoff & Hall, 147.

11 'als Herrin über die Gemüther … brachte [die Frau] die Poesie in das Leben … diese ihrer Wesenheit entsprechende Stellung … wonach sie die Hälfte des menschlichen Lebens, das Gemüth und die Häuslichkeit auf sich nimmt, pflegt und vertritt': J. [von] Falke, *Die ritterliche Gesellschaft im Zeitalter des Frauentums* (Berlin: Brigl & Lobeck, 1862), 72. For early use of 'poetic' in the context of décor more generally, see books by Claude-Aimé Chenavard from the 1830–40s: M. H. Calvignac, 'C.-A. Chenavard …', *Histoire de l'Art*, vol. 13, no. 4, May 1991, 41–53.

12 'das Poesie …': J. Falke, *Die Kunstindustrie auf der Wiener Weltausstellung* (Vienna, 1873), 132; cf. *Gl* 1864. § 'homely …': 'Quam Delecta: Japanese Decoration versus "the flat geometric"', *B*, 7 Nov. 1863, 798–99. § 'The continuous …' ('die anhaltend freudigen Gefühle sicheren Behagens, die tiefere künstlerische Poesie der Häuslichkeit'): Hirth, 73. § E., 'The Perfect House', *AJ* (1877), 207–8. Cf. 'whatever poetry of art or of culture there is in us will manifest itself in the fittings and accessories of the with-drawing room': Cooper, H. J., 11–12. § 'Grâce … foyer domestique … sous prétexte qu'elles sont de pures illusions, il faudrait également renoncer la poésie': Blanc 487. § G. Bachelard, *La Poétique de l'espace* (Paris: Presses Universitaires, 1957) / *The Poetics of Space* (Boston, MA: Beacon, 2nd edn 1994) / *Die Poetik des Raumes* (Munich: Hanser, 1960).

13 Cf. *Volksliteratur*. H. Bausinger, *Formen der 'Volkspoesie'* (Berlin: E. Schmidt, 1968, 1985). On the *Poesiealbum* and adolescents, see *Der Souvenir. Erinnerungen in Dingen von der Reliquie zum Andenken* (exh. cat. Frankfurt am Main: Museum für Angewandte Kunst, 2006).

14 In an early satirizing of what was to be called 'bad taste', Falke points to a carpet with 'three knights leaving the city gates' ('drei Ritter zum Tore hinaus'): Falke 1862, 665. Cf. H. Lorm, who states that in poorer times poetry meant longing for things, whereas in affluent times 'poetry … would only be treated as an empty cliché' ('die Poesie selbst nur als Phrase behandelt werden könnte'): *Der Abend zu Hause … in Wissenschaft und Leben* (Berlin: Hofmann, 1881), 307.

15 *Trivialliteratur*. J. Imorde, 'Zur Säkularisierung religiöser Empfindsamkeit', *KAS*, vol. 55, no. 4 (2004), 237–41; H. and H. Schlaffer, *Studien zum ästhetischen Historismus* (Frankfurt am Main: Suhrkamp, 1975).

Poetry, decoration, design and art

16 'ein Jahr lang auf dem Toilettentisch zu liegen': G. Freytag, 'Luxus und Schönheit im modernen Leben. Die Anlage von Hausbibliotheken', *Die Grenzboten*, vol. 11, no. 2 (1852), 102–9, quoted in M. Bucher et al. (eds), *Realismus und Gründerzeit. Manifeste und Dokumente zur deutschen Literatur 1848–1880* (Stuttgart: Metzler, 1975), vol. 2, 627.

17 'l'attrait sublime de la poésie': Boullée (above, n. 1), 97; cf. 34, 44, etc.

18 'design': for France, see Laurent. Germans did not import the term until later in the 20th century: cf. *Entwerfer*, 'designer', and *entworfen von*, 'designed by'. For some 19th-century uses of 'design' in a near-20th century sense: 'the furniture of any room requires to be in unison with architectural fittings, and to attain this it is necessary to have the designs made expressly for the apartment': Talbert, Intr.; 'well-designed furniture [not] necessarily expensive': Eastlake, 283; 'self-restraint is necessary in all good design': H. Van Brunt, 'Studies in Interior Decoration VIII', *AmA*, 5 May 1877, 139. High Modernism vastly expanded on the concept of 'design', especially its aesthetic and 'purely functional' aspects, adding the notion of the 'designer' as the prime agent; art historians (e.g. N. Pevsner) followed suit. But the 20th century was also dominated by the term's subdivision into the more mundane 'graphic design', 'product design', 'interior design', etc. Late Modernist and postmodern trends have since placed more emphasis on the

consumers' input (cf. 'Preface'). In this book, the use of 'design' is eclectic, encompassing: (i) the Renaissance-to-Modernism sense of overall control, implying also, as with 'architecture', a built-in distinctiveness; (ii) the factual sense of 'a design', i.e. a drawing for something; (iii) a combination of (i) and (ii) as the conception and pictorial representation of a whole interior. Cf. G. Meikle, 'A World History of Design', *JDH*, vol. 18 (2005), 235–44; C. McDermott, *Design: The Key Concepts* (London: Routledge 2007); Mark Taylor and J. Preston (eds), *Intimus: Interior Design Theory Reader* (Chichester: Wiley, 2006).

19 For *Stimmung*, see Chapter IV.

20 'German Art in … Furnishing', *FG*, 1 Jan. 1887, 6–8.

21 'das Haus … eine menschliche … noch nicht künstlerische Erfindung': Hegel, Part III, 2nd Sect., Ch. 1, pt. 2 (vol. 14, 366).

II ART IN THE HOME: A NEW DISCOURSE

The trades

1 *Post Office Directory of the Cabinet, Furniture and Upholstery Trades* (London: Kelly, 1877). § E. B. Ottillinger, 'The "Kaiser Salon" [at the 3rd Gewerbe Ausstellung,Vienna]. Beginnings of the Rococo Revival in Vienna', *FH*, vol. 36 (1991), 137–48. § Louis XV's 'bureau du roi' for Ludwig II, 1874–75 (by Anton Pössenbacher): S. Sangl, 'Princely Writing Tables and the "Third Rococo" in Bavaria', *FH*, vol. 29 (1993), 184–200 (190). For trades and techniques in France to the early 19th century, see J. Feray, *Architecture intérieure et décoration en France des origines à 1875* (Paris: Berger Levrault, 1988).

2 'we may justly state …' ('künstlerischen Ausstattung der Wohnung'): F. Fischbach, *Album für Wohnungsdekorationen* (Hanau: Fischbach, n.d. [*c.* 1872]), Vorwort; cf. 'No undertaking seems too gigantic': Yapp, 52; 'the union of science and practice in our tradesmen and manufacturers': D. R. Hay, 'The Laws of Harmonious Colouring …', *AM*, vol. 3 (1836), 226–30 (226).

3 Elegance: Szambien (Ch. I, n. 1); cf. P. E. Knabe, *Schlüsselbegriffe des kunsttheoretischen Denkens in Frankreich … bis zum Ende der Aufklärung* (Düsseldorf: Schwann, 1972). The use of 'elegant' 'increased dramatically in the 1790s': Crowley, 228. Cf. an advert for the shop Chez Boin in Paris: 'le bizarre, le pur, l'élégant': *La Mode*, Oct.–Nov. 1835, 275, quoted in B. Dragic, *Le Décor intérieur de la maison française à l'époque romantique 1828–48* (thesis, University of Paris, 1963, Libr. INHA, Paris), 112. 'Elegance' was also extended to the lifestyle of the 'élégant', or dandy: see H. de Balzac, 'Traité de la vie élégante', first publ. in *La Mode*, 1830, reprinted as part of 'Pathologie de la Vie Sociale': Balzac, *Romans et Contes*, vol. 25 (Paris: Les Bibliophiles, 1973), 323–34; cf. 'the old-fashioned word "elegant"': Balfour in *MA* (1884) (Ch. V, n. 249). See also M. Berg and H. Clifford (eds), *Consumers and Luxury: Consumer Culture in Europe 1650–1850* (Manchester University Press, 1999); Grier, 156.

4 Parkes 193. According to Adam Smith, dress fashions changed every year, and furniture fashions every five to six years: see Berg and Clifford (above, n. 3), Intr., Ch. 1; M. North (Preface, n. 9). But for a slower speed of fashions in some regions, see B. Post, 'Schreibmöbel der Bremer Tischler aus der ersten Hälfte des 19. Jh.' (diss., University of Münster, 1995).

5 V. Teirich, *Die moderne Richtung in der Bronze- und Möbelindustrie* … [on the Paris 1867 exh.] (Vienna: Beck'sche, 1868); cf. Himmelheber, 316 etc.

6 On early craft knowledge being inaccessible to outsiders, cf. 'studying the secrets of the craft' ('main d'oeuvre'): Havard 1884, viii. Housepainters were not used to written 'exchanges': review of Hay, *Edinburgh Review*, Oct. 1843, reprinted in Hay, Appendix 9. The firm of Bembé stated that by *c.* 1865 the greater number ('Mehrzahl') of German manufacturers still worked almost entirely without any models or drawings: see Behr, *Entwicklung* (below, n. 69), 5.

7 Cf. [N. E.] Roret, *Manuels* … (Paris: Roret, 1827–); *Schauplatz der Künste und Handwerke* (Weimar: Voigt, 1817; later *Neuer Schauplatz der Künste*); *Weale's Rudimentary Series* (London: Weale, 1854–).

8 *Journal des Dames et des Modes* (Paris, 1796–1839. See also P. Cornu (ed.), *Meubles et objets du goût 1796–1830. 678 Documents tirés des Journaux des Modes* (Paris: Libr. Arts Décoratifs, n.d. [*c.* 1914]); G. Kleinert, *Le Journal des Dames et Modes* … (Stuttgart: Thorbecke, 2001); *Journal des Luxus und der Moden* (Weimar: F. J. Bertuch, 1786–1827); C. Bertuch (ed.), *Musterblätter für Schreiner, Tapezierer etc. Arbeiten … aus Journal des Luxus und der Moden* (Weimar: Bertuch, 1807); [J. G.] Grohmann, *Ideenmagazin für Liebhaber von Gärten / Recueil des Idées Nouvelles pour la Décoration* (Leipzig: Baumgärtner, 1796–); *Wiener Modenzeitung und Zeitschrift für Kunst, schöne Literatur und Theater* (Vienna, 1816–44; title changes). See also C. Witt-Dörring; Ackermann.

9 Pattern books: [Anon.], *Verzeichnis von 1000 Mustervorlagenwerken Deutschlands und des Auslandes für Kunstgewerbe und Kunstindustrie in neuester Zeit* (Dresden: A. Dieckmann, 1886; copy Kunstbibliothek Berlin); Himmelheber; G. Himmelheber, *Deutsche Möbelvorlagen 1800–1900* (Munich: Beck, 1988); D. Schneider-Henn, *Ornament und Dekoration. Vorlagenwerke und Motivsammlungen des 19. und 20 Jh.* (Munich: Prestel, 1997); M. Nungasser, J. Brand and B. Evers, *Ornamentale Vorlagenwerke des 19. Jh.* (Berlin: Kunstbibliothek – SMPK, 2000); C. Grund, *Deutschsprachige Vorlagenwerke des 19. Jh. zur Neuromanik und Neugotik*, vol. 2 (Wiesbaden: Harrassowitz, 1997). See also G. Zinnkann, *Mainzer Möbelschreiner der ersten Hälfte des 19. Jh.* (Frankfurt am Main: Kramer, 1985); A.-L. Hübner, 'Zur Verbürgerlichung preussischer Wohnkultur. Schloss Charlottenhof und Berliner Interieurs der ersten Hälfte des 19. Jh.' (diss., Technische Universität Berlin, 1997). For France, there is no comprehensive list so far, but see J.-P. Garric et al., *La Construction savante: Les Avatars de la littérature technique* (Paris: Picard, 2007); S. Laurent, *Figures de l'ornement* (Paris: Massin, 2005); K. L. Ames, 'Designed in France … Transmission of French Style to America', *WP*, vol. 12 (1977), 103–14. See below, n. 87, 'Folio volumes and journals'. § On décor more generally, see S-S. Tzeng, *Imitation und Originalität des Ornamentdesigns. Studien zur Entwicklung der kunstgewerblichen Musterbücher von 1750 bis 1900* (Munich: Scaneg, 1994). In England: H. Batsford, 'Reference Books on Ornament and the Decorative Arts', *BN*, 21 Jan. 1898, 89–90; Joy; S. Durant, *A Survey of Decoration since 1830* (London: Macdonald, 1986).

10 Costs: [F. Nauert], 'Welche Aufgaben hat eine Fachzeitschrift III', *Die Mappe, Zeitschrift für dekorative Gewerbe* (Leipzig), vol. 2, no. 18, 15 Sept. 1882, 205–8 (207).

11 One journal's ethos: 'The *Furniture Worker* … is published for the trade (not by the trade) …': *Furniture Worker* [Cincinatti], 25 Dec. 1893, Intr.; cf. n. 88, below.

12 For firms' publications in London, see Joy; Edwards; C. & R. Light (London): see the present book, p. 20. See also the new type of comprehensive illustrated exhibition reports, e.g. *Crystal Palace*.

13 Textile *dessinateur*: see M. Schoeser, '"Shewey and Full of Work"', in M. B. Rose (ed.), *The Lancashire Cotton Industry … since 1700* (Lancashire County Books, 1996), 186–205. '[It is] the design [i.e. the ornamentation] that sells the carpet in nine cases out of ten': 'Brussels Tapestry and Carpets', *FG*, 9 Feb. 1878, 74. Cf. E. Didron, *Exposition Universelle … Rapport d'ensemble sur les arts décoratifs* (Paris: Imprimerie Nationale, 1882), 195–205; M. Digby Wyatt (with J. Dieterle), *The Arts of Decoration at the International Exhibition at Paris, 1867* (London: priv. circul., 1868); C. Gurlitt, *Die deutsche Musterzeichnerkunst und ihre Geschichte* (Darmstadt: Koch, 1890), contains much on Paris. F. Fischbach, studying in Berlin 1858–62, was told he was too German ('zu deutsch') to become a good *dessinateur*: *Ornamente der Gewebe* (Hanau: Alberti, n.d. [*c.* 1883]), viii–x. See also M. de Ferrière le Vayer, *Christofle. Deux siècles d'aventure industrielle 1793–1993* (Paris: Le Onde, 1995).

14 V. Champier, 'Les artistes de l'industrie: Constant Sevin', *RAD*, vol. 9 (1888–89), 161–76 (164).

15 'Designers such as Bruce J. Talbert, Owen W. Davis, the Craces, Walter Hensman, Christopher Gill …': J. Benn, 'Furniture at Royal Academy …', *CM*, June 1887, 309.

The decorator

16 S. Eriksen, *Early Neo-Classicism in France* (London: Faber, 1974); C. Sargentson, *Merchants and Luxury Markets: The Marchands Merciers of Eighteenth-Century Paris* (London: V&A, 1996).

17 C. Edwards, 'Seddon's …', *Apollo*, vol. 65 (1957), 177–81. § *Wiener Modenzeitung* (above, n. 8): Witt-Dörring. § C. Edwards, 'Jackson & Graham …', *FH* (1998), 238–63; E. Joy, 'The royal Furniture Makers 1837–1887 … Holland & Sons', *Burlington Magazine*, vol. 111, Nov. 1969, 677 87. § Fourdinois: I. Vetois and Y. Badetz, '… La Maison Fourdinois en 1860', *MH*, no. 190, Nov.–Dec. 1993, 30–35. S. Laurent, 'Jules Verchère, dessinateur d'ameublement', *Revista de História da Arte e Arqueologia*, vol. 2 (1996), 139–48. On designers and decorators: F. Bracquemont ('peintre et graveur'), *Du Dessin et de la couleur* (Paris: Charpentier, 1885), 139, 194, 256. § L. Frankel (ed.), *Herter Brothers: Furniture and Interiors for a Gilded Age* (exh. cat. New York: Metropolitan Museum, 1994–95); Earl Shin [E. Strahan], *Mr. Vanderbilt's House and Collection* (Boston, MA: Barvie, 1883–84); see also Kimbel and Cabus in *Beauty*, 446–47; for Kimbel in Germany, see Zinnkann (above, n. 9). § *Liberty's 1875–1975* (exh. cat. London: V&A, 1975).

18 'tapissier … couturière … modiste de l'appartement': *La Mode Illustrée et Journal de Famille*, vol. 9, 1868, 390–91.

19 Ottillinger, '"Kaiser Salon"' (above, n. 1) 137–48. § Haweis, 51. Cf. 'upholstery' in *EID*, 1322–24; *Second Empire*, 104; 'the decorator and more often the upholsterer': Havard, *Décoration* (below, n. 85), 135; the 'tapissier … façonne et met en place les tableaux, les cuivres': 'Tapissier', in *La Grande Encyclopédie* (Paris: Societé … Grande Encyclopédie, 1887–1902), vol. 30, 928; Giedion, 364–65. See also 'architectural upholsterers': M. Edgeworth, *The Absentee* (London, 1812), 13, quoted in Edwards, 104–6.

20 L. F. Day, 'The Relation of the Architect to the Decorator', *BrA*, 16 March 1883, 125–26; cf. the contradictory remark, probably made by an architect, that there is 'no intermediary grade between the painter (the better ones of which we call decorator) and the fully educated professional artist': 'Correspondence', *BN*, 23 March 1866, 193; cf. Blanc 223.

21 M. Aldrich (ed.), *The Craces: Royal Decorators 1768–1899* (London: Murray, 1990).

22 Haweis, 51.

23 'The decorators [Penon in Paris and Jackson & Graham in London] supply everything': J. Lessing, *Berichte von der Pariser Weltausstellung 1878* (Berlin: Wasmuth, 1878), 141. § 'manages to link': J. Lessing, *Das Kunstgewerbe auf der Wiener Weltausstellung* (Berlin: Wasmuth, 1874), 42.

24 'one fixed mind': *FG*, vol. 4, 24 July 1875, 79. § 'Connoissance aprofondie du style', 'goût personel': 'Tapissier' in *Grande Encyclopédie* (above, n. 19), 928. § 'Skilful …' ('décorateur habile … le jeux des rideaux ou des stores, l'éclairage'): Havard, *Décoration* (below, n. 85), 134. § 'Dexterity' ('Fingerfertigkeit, Kunstgeschmack, gutes Augenmass'): K. Kuntze, 'Das Leipziger Tapezierergewerbe', in: *Untersuchungen über die Lage des Handwerks in Deutschland* (*Schriften des Vereins für Socialpolitik*, vol. 56, Leipzig, 1896), 359.

25 'a celebrated …': Yapp, pl. 40; 'of the decorative painters and draughtsmen … the first place must be given to Herrn Prignot': F. Lieb, 'Musterzeichnungen und Decorationsmalerei', *Ausstellungs-Bericht* (46) 46; '[Prignot] architecte déorateur': Havard 1884, ix. Prignot also worked for Jackson & Graham in London: see S. Jervis, *Penguin Dictionary of Design and Designers* (Harmondsworth: Penguin, 1984), 392. Prignot's papers are in the Musée d'Orsay, Paris.

26 E. Crawford, *Enterprising Women: The Garretts and their Circle* (London: Francis Boutle, 2002); E. Ferry, '"Decorators"' (Introduction, n. 26).

27 Havard 1884, 38.

28 Laxton's, 415. § *Post Office Directory* (above, n. 1) of 1877 lists 27 London 'Interior Decorators', mostly the large firms such as Collinson & Lock, Cotier, Edgington, Jackson & Graham, Maple & Co., Morant Boyd & Blandford, Shoolbred, Trollope, etc. According to Lessing, Germany is behind in all this, but not Vienna: see above, n. 23, but also the earlier K. L. Mattaey, *Neues Ideenmagazin für Luxus, Ameublement und Draperien: ein Musterbuch für Tapezier, Decorateur, Meubleurs* … (Weimar: Voigt, 1841). See also below, n. 42.

The architect

29 On Adam, see below, Ch. III, 'Plaster'.

30 Downing, 364.

31 Le Camus, 164ff.

32 W. Nerdinger and W. Oechslin (eds), *Gottfried Semper 1803–1879* (Munich: Prestel, 2003); M. Hvattum, *Gottfried Semper and the Problem of Historicism* (Cambridge University Press, 2004); H. F. Mallgrave, *Gottfried Semper* (New Haven and London: Yale University Press, 1996); cf. P. Goessel and G. Leuthäuser (eds), *Villenarchitektur in Dresden* (Cologne: Taschen, 1991).

33 Vienna: R. Wagner-Rieger and M. Reissberger, *Theophil von Hansen* (*Wiener Ringstrasse* series, Wiesbaden: Steiner, 1980); cf. J. Storck, *Einfache Möbel im Character der Renaissance* (Vienna: Technik / Kunst, 1875). See also D. Klemme and H. Frantz, *Alexis de Chateauneuf* (exh. cat. Hamburg: Museum für Kunst und Gewerbe, 2000).

34 Percier & Fontaine, Foreword: 'l'art de décorer …': 18;

closeness to architecture: 15; the 'ensemble' and 'rapport intime' between construction and decoration: 15; 'réformer les pratiques de l'ameublement moderne': 4. Nevertheless, the long list of objects on the title page also implies a pattern-book like use by the trades; cf. Percier & Fontaine, *Innendekorationen, Möbel und Geräte* (Berlin: Wasmuth, 1888, 1898).

35 D. Watkin, *Thomas Hope and the Neo-Classical Idea* (London: Murray, 1968); D. Watkin and P. Hewat-Jaboor, *Thomas Hope: Regency Designer* (New Haven and London: Yale University Press, 2008); D. Watkin, *Sir John Soane …, The Royal Academy Lectures* (Cambridge University Press, 1996); cf. Morley, 282. § J. Sievers, *Die Arbeiten für Prinz Wilhelm von Preussen* (Berlin: Deutscher Kunstverlag, 1955; part of P. O. Rave, *Karl Friedrich Schinkel: Lebenswerk* ['*Schinkelwerk*'], 1941–); K. F. Schinkel, *Vorbilder für Fabrikanten und Handwerker* (Berlin: Königliche Technische Deputation für Gewerbe, 1821–, 2nd edn Berlin 1863); B. Hedinger and J. Berger (eds), *Karl Friedrich Schinkel, Möbel und Interieur* (Berlin: Deutscher Kunstverlag, 2002); cf. F. Tietze, 'Die Innendekorationen J. H. Stracks 1805–1880' (diss., Technische Universität Berlin, 1999). See also E. Börsch-Supan, *Berliner Baukunst nach Schinkel 1840–1870* (Munich: Prestel, 1977).

36 For the view that upholsterers disregard principles and that décor should be provided by 'l'artiste': Le Camus, 113. Against vulgar imitations and rapid changes of fashion: Percier & Fontaine, 12; ' entirely ignorant … only fraught with a few wretched ideas and trivial conceits … borrowed from the worst models of the degraded French school of the middle of the last century': Hope, 1. With 'industry' and the 'plodding artisan', Hope contrasts the 'professor of the more liberal arts, the draughtsman, the modeller, the painter and the sculptor … the arts of design': Hope, 4.

37 A. von Buttlar, *Leo von Klenze* (Munich: Beck, 1999); W. Nerdinger (ed.), *Leo von Klenze* (Munich: Prestel, 2000); G. Hojer, *Die Prunkappartements Ludwigs I. im Königsbau der Münchner Residenz* (Munich: Bayerische Verwaltung der Staatlichen Schlösser, 1992).

38 See Victor Ruprich-Robert, 'Le premier des décorateurs, c'est l'architecte', *RGA* (1862), 263–271.

39 J. M. Brydon, 'A few more words about "Queen Anne"', *AmA*, 6 Oct. 1877, 320–22 (322). § Eastlake 1869, Pref.; cf. C. L. Eastlake, *A History of the Gothic Revival* (London: Longmans, 1872; repr. Leicester University Press 1970), 344; cf. Saint, 257.

40 H. G. Clarke,'Richardson as an interior designer', *AA*, Aug. 1887, 62–64.

41 H. W. and A. Arrowsmith, *The House Decorator and Painter's Guide* (London: Kelly, 1840), iii–iv.

42 R. Eitelberger, 'Kunstgewerbliche Zeitfragen', *BfK* (1876), 41–44 etc. (43); cf. K., 'Der Architekt und das Kunstgewerbe. Die architektonische Innen-Dekoration als Unterrichtsgegenstand', *DB*, 10 Dec. 1887, 589–94. But cf. the opposite demand: architects must liven up designs to compete with the new decorators: G. Davioud, 'Décorations intérieures', *RGA* (1869), 283–84.

43 H. Roberts, *For the King's Pleasure: The Furnishing and Decoration of George IV's Apartments at Windsor Castle* (London: Royal Collection, 2001), 26; Morley, 229–30.

44 L. F. Day, 'The Relation of the Architect to the Decorator', *BrA*, 16 March 1883, 125–26; same title but other writers, *BrA*, 16 Feb. – 6 April 1883. Cf. J. W. Benn, *CM*, Aug. 1884, 21–23, June 1887, 309; cf. Kerr, 111.

Books and periodicals

An impetus from below: home and architectural advice books

45 Parkes; [Anon.], *A New System of Practical Economy founded on modern Discoveries* (London: Colburn, 1825). For Germany, see Henriette Davidis from the 1850s (e.g. Ch. III, n. 158); E. F. Celnart, *Nouveau Manuel complet de l'economie domestique*, 3rd edn (Paris: Roret 1837). § D. Attar, *Bibliography of Household Books Published in Britain 1800–1914* (London: Prospect, 1987); S. Verk, *Geschmacksache. Kochbücher aus dem Museum für Volkskunde* (Berlin, 1995); I. Richartz, *Oikos. Haus und Haushalt. Usprung und Geschichte der Haushaltsökonomie* (Göttingen: VandenHoek & Rupprecht, 1991); I. Wiedemann, *Herrin im Hause. Durch Koch- und Haushaltsbücher zur bürgerlichen Hausfrau* (Pfaffenweiler: Centaurus, 1993).

46 Walsh's 3rd edition (1879) gives £150–1,500.

47 Catherine Beecher, *Treatise on Domestic Economy for the Use of Young Ladies* (Boston, MA: Marsh, 1841; new edn K. K. Sklar (ed.), New York: Schocken 1977), greatly enlarged as C. E. Beecher and H. Beecher Stowe, *The American Woman's Home or Principles of Domestic Science* (New York: Ford, 1869; repr. New Brunswick: Rutgers University Press, 2002); cf. Grier, 108.

48 *Godey's Lady's Book / Ladies' American Magazine* (Philadelphia 1840–93); Mrs. C. Jones and H. T. Williams, *Household Elegancies: Suggestions in Household Art and Tasteful Home Decorations* (New York: H. T. Williams, 1879).

49 Loudon, 1039. On the trades: [J.C. Loudon], 'Introduction', *AM*, vol. 1 (1834), 6ff.

50 Downing, 263; cf. K. L. Ames, 'Downing and the Rationalisation of Interior Design', in G. B. Tatum and E. B. MacDougall (eds), *Prophet with Honor: The Career of Andrew Jackson Downing 1815–1852* (Philadelphia: Dumbarton Oaks Center Studies, 1989), 191–217; A. Schuyler, *Apostle of Taste: A. J. Downing* (Baltimore, MA: Johns Hopkins University Press, 1976).

51 H. Long, *Victorian Houses and their Details: The Role of Publications* (London: Architectural Press, 2002).

Applied arts and reform

52 On hierarchies: N. Pevsner, *Academies of Art, Past and Present* (Cambridge University Press, 1940; repr. New York: DaCapo, 1973); H. Waentig, *Wirtschaft und Kunst* (Jena: Fischer, 1909); S. Muthesius, 'Handwerk/Kunsthandwerk …', *JDH*, vol. 11, no. 1 (1998), 85–95; and, more broadly, M. Schwarzer, *German Architectural Theory and the Search for Modern Identity* (Cambridge University Press, 1995).

53 A. Burton, *Vision and Accident: The Story of the Victoria and Albert Museum* (London: V&A, 1999); A. M. Baker, *A Grand Design: The Start of the Victoria and Albert Museum* (London: V&A, 1997); S. Gronert, 'The Best Patterns at the Cheapest Rate', *Studien zum englischen Design im 19. Jahrhundert* (thesis, University of Cologne, 1989); B. Mundt, *Die deutschen Kunstgewerbemuseen im 19. Jahrhundert* (Munich: Prestel, 1974); G. Fliedl, *Kunst und Lehre am Beginn der Moderne* (Salzburg: Residenz, 1986); Y. Brunhammer, *Le Beau dans l'utile: Un musée pour les arts décoratifs* (Paris: Gallimard, 1992); Laurent; U. Leben et al., *Histoire de l'École Nationale Supérieure des Arts Décoratifs 1766–1941* (Paris: École Nationale …, 2004).

54 See 'Line and Surface' in the present book, pp. 143–45.

55 'Berufsaesthetiker': C. T. Richter, 'Das bürgerliche Wohnhaus', *Ausstellungs-Bericht* (19) 4; cf. 'taste professionals' (Auslander).

56 For the view that the reform of the art industry was of world historical importance: 'Kunstgwerbe', in *Meyers Konversationslexikon*, 3rd edn (Leipzig: Bibliographisches Institut, 1874–78), vol. 10, 446–47.

A flood of new texts

57 'hatte [man] keine Vorstellung, dass in dem Hausgeräth ein Kunstsinn sich erweisen sollte', referring back to *c.* 1850: Otto Baehr, *Aus meinem Leben* (Kassel: Doll, 1898), quoted in M. Freudenthal, *Gestaltwandel der … Hauswirtschaft zwischen 1760 und 1910* (Berlin: Ullstein, 1986), 35.

58 Cf. Baudelaire's translation 'Philosophie de l'ameublement', first publ. in *Magazin des Familles*, autumn 1852, and *Le Monde Literaire*, 1853; Hessemer, 20–28.

59 É. Guichard, 'architecte et décorateur': see Laurent; cf. 'on furnishing and interior decoration per se very little … has been written': 'Furniture and Interior Decoration' (review of Guichard), *AJ* (1867), 228–29. See also the earlier Garnier-Audiger, and Mme E. Rémond's articles in *La Mode Illustrée: Journal de la Famille*, 1860s.

60 A. Scheffers, *Architektonische Formenschule*, 3rd pt.: *Bauformen und Farben … Ausstattung des Inneren …* (Leipzig: Seemann, 1868; 3rd edn renamed as *Bauformen zur Ausbildung des Inneren*, Leipzig: Gebhardt, 1880).

61 Viollet-le-Duc, 426ff.; see Ch. IV, n. 20; Falke 1871, 54, 81, 88; cf. Nuremberg, Ch. V, n. 54.

62 'the furnishing …' ('Wohnräume … Ernährer und Erzieher'): 'Die Zimmereinrichtungen auf der Berliner Gewerbeausstellung', *Kunst und Gewerbe*, no. 41 (1879), 323. § 'only when it finds' ('ein Gemeingut des ganzen Volkes … am Herd des Hauses eine Heimstätte findet'): W. Sonntag, 'Die Kunst im Hause', *Gl* (1879), 20. § 'fast laws': Loftie, *Dining Room* (below, n. 75), viii.

63 Falke noted this very early on: 'We thus criticise ourselves and others'; J. Falke, *Über Kunstgewerbe* (Vienna: Hof- und Staatsdruckerei, 1860), 72.

64 Falke was ennobled as von Falke in 1873; Ottillinger; E. B. Ottillinger, 'Jakob von Falke (1825–1897) und die Theorie des Kunstgewerbes', *Wiener Jahrbuch für Kunstgeschichte* (1989), 205–23.

65 Cf. J. Falke, 'Über Kunstgewerbe …', *Wiener Zeitung*, July 1860; Falke, *Kunstgewerbe* (above, n. 63); Falke 1862; Falke: lst edn 1871, edns 1872, 1877, 4th edn 1881 (illustrated like the American edn; below, n. 83), 5th edn 1883, 6th edn 1897; Swedish: see Ch. V, n. 276; Hungarian: Ch. V, n. 270.

66 'Gefässe und Geräte sind einzelne selbstständige Individuen … bilden erst in ihrer Vereinigung ein volles Kunstwerk, die menschliche Wohnung': Falke 1862, 664.

67 'die Sprache des Schönen, das schönste Glück … jener Nektar, welche Minerva ihrem Liebling Prometeus vom Himmel herabbrachte … und hat dadurch Antheil erhalten an dem schönsten Glück, der Kunst': Falke 1871, 324; cf. A. Schwarz, *Brevier der Kunst in Haus und Leben* (Leipzig: Spamer, 1877).

68 'Haus und Wohnung sollen künstlerisch geschmückt sein, aber schwerlich ein Kunstwerk im höchsten, im monumentalen Sinne sein': Falke 1871, 173. See also Falke's earlier demands for beauty in the house, not the palace: *Wiener Zeitung*, 27 July 1860, 3017.

69 Luthmer, architect-trained director of the Kunstgewerbemuseum in Frankfurt am Main: obituary, *DB*, 5 Feb. 1921, 59–60. § German and Austrian books (all short): Bergau; Hug; Henrici; Carl Behr, *Die Entwicklung der Möbelindustrie in Deutschland während der letzten 10 Jahre* (Mainz: Bembé, 1880); C. Behr, *Über Dekoration und Möblierung unserer Wohnungen* (Mainz: Pickarts, 1881); J[osef] Stockbauer, *Die Kunst im Hause* (Leipzig: Schloemp, 1881); Friedrich Fischbach, *Die künstlerische Austattung der bürgerlichen Wohnung* (Basel: Schwabe, 1883).

70 For all figures in England, see *Beauty*. § Charles Locke Eastlake (nephew of painter Charles Lock Eastlake, non-practising architect and art administrator): 2nd edn 1869, 3rd edn 1872, 4th edn 1878; see J. Gloag, Intr., in 1978 repr.; [Eastlake], 'The Fashion of Furniture', *ChM*, vol. 9, March 1864, 337–49; also articles in *The Queen* and *London Review*. For the US edn, see below, n. 83. See also J. M. Crook, Intr. to Eastlake, *Gothic Revival* (above, n. 39).

71 'the ordinary and uneducated professional decorator': Eastlake, 194. § *Athenaeum*, no. 2144, 28 Nov. 1868, 713–14.

72 Bruce J. Talbert was a pupil of architect G. E. Street. See Talbert; B. J. Talbert, *Examples of Ancient and Modern Furniture: Metalwork, Tapestries, Decorations, etc.* (London: Batsford, 1876).

73 See Godwin *Ar*; 'Edward W. Godwin' (obituary), *BrA*, 15 Oct. 1886, 347–48. Bibliography in S. Weber-Soros (ed.), *E. W. Godwin, Aesthetic Movement Architect and Designer*, 197ff.; see also S. Weber-Soros, *The Secular Furniture of E. W. Godwin* (both New Haven and London: Yale University Press, 1999).

74 Dresser 1873; Dresser 1876; W. Halen, *Christopher Dresser* (Oxford: Phaidon, 1990).

75 'Art at Home' series (all London: Macmillan): W. J. Loftie, *A Plea for Art in the House* (1876); 'the prudence of making collections … To lead people to think for themselves … what is suitable, comfortable, and useful … what is beautiful in the highest and wisest sense of the word': Loftie, *Plea*, vii–viii; Garrett; Mrs Orrinsmith, *The Drawing Room* (1877); Mrs W. J. Loftie, *The Dining Room* (1878); Lady Barker, *The Bedroom and Boudoir* (1878); E. R. Glaister, *Needlework* (1880); C. G. Leland, *Minor Arts* (1880) and others; see Ferry (Introduction, n. 26). Reviews: '"Art at Home"', *B*, 9 Dec. 1876, 1188–89; '"The Drawing Room"', *B*, 1 Dec. 1877, 1241–42; E. W. Godwin, 'To our Readers', *BrA*, vol. 9, Jan. 1878, 1; 'In the *Art at Home* Series …', *BrA*, vol. 9, Feb. 1878, 64.

76 Also by Haweis: *The Art of Beauty* [on dress and furnishings] (London: Chatto & Windus, 1878); *Beautiful Houses: being a description of certain well-known artistic houses* (London: Sampson Low, 1882); *The Art of Housekeeping* (London: Sampson Low, n.d. [*c.* 1889–90]); cf. Cohen; J. A. Neiswander, 'Liberalism, Nationalism and the Middle-Class Interior: The Literature on Domestic Decor in England 1870–1914' (diss., University of London, Westfield Coll., 1988). § See Edis; Day. § J. E. Panton, *From Kitchen to Garret* (London: Ward Downey, 1888, 7th edn 1890); J. E. Panton, *Nooks and Corners* (London: Ward Downey, 1889). § Other sources in England: 'Furniture and Decoration', *BN*, 1869–70; Conway, *Harper's* (below, n. 81); Cooper, H. J.; William Morris, 'Making the best of it', written *c.* 1879: Morris, 114–48; Oetzmann & Co., *Hints on House Furnishings and Decoration* (London, 1871, not seen); William Young, *Town and Country Mansions and Suburban Houses* (London: Spon, 1879); T. Knight & Son Decorators and Builders [designs by J. D. Sedding], *Suggestions for House Decoration* (London: priv. circul., 1880); [Anon.], *Artists' Homes or How to Furnish with Taste* (London: Ward Lock, n.d.

[*c.* 1881]); H. W. Batley, *A Series of Studies for Domestic Furniture, Decorations, etc.* (London: Sampson Low, 1883); S. Foster Murphy (ed.), *Our Homes, and How to Make them Healthy* (London: Cassell, 1883); Fred Miller, *Interior Decoration* (London: Wyman, n.d. [*c.* 1885]); J. Moyr Smith, *Ornamental Interiors* (London: Crosby Lockwood, 1887); Maurice B. Adams, *Examples of Old English Houses and Furniture* (London: Batsford, 1888).

77 C. Harvey and J. Press, *William Morris: Design and Enterprise in Victorian Britain* (Manchester University Press, 1991); Godwin 1877; J. M. Conway, *Travels in South Kensington with Notes on Decorative Art and Architecture in England* (London: Trubner, 1882). See also W. Hamilton, *The Aesthetic Movement* (London: Reeves and Turner 1882; repr. New York: AMS Press, 1971); L. Lambourne, *The Aesthetic Movement* (London: Phaidon, 1996). A. Anderson, '"Doing As We Like": Grant Allen, Harry Quilter and Aesthetic Dogma', *JDH*, vol. 18, April 2005, 335–55; A. Anderson, 'At Home with Oscar …', *The Wildean*, no. 24, Jan. 2004, 1–25; J. Freedman, *Professions of Taste: Henry James, British Aestheticism …* (Stanford University Press, 1990); Blanchard. See also Ch.V, n. 123.

78 'humble': 'every woman could … produce work which, humble as it might be, was indeed art': L. F. Day, 'The Woman's Part in Domestic Decoration', *MA* (1881), 457–65 (457); Day; J. M. Hansen, *Lewis Foreman Day. Unity in Design* (Woodbridge: Antique Collectors' Club, 2007). § On refinement, see Oscar Wilde, 'The House Beautiful' (Dublin lecture), *FG*, 8 Dec. 1883, 397–99; Ch. III, n. 276. § Morris: see above, n. 76. § L. F. Day: 'the cheapest, if not necessarily the nastiest thing to be had in the way of carpets; our instinctive distrust of that word "Art" was well founded': 'Decoration …', *AJ* (1893), 85–88.

79 For earlier in the US, see C. Hoover Voorsanger and J. K. Howat (eds), *Art and the Empire City: New York 1825–1861* (New York: Metropolitan Museum / New Haven and London: Yale University Press, 2000). For the 1870s–1880s, see: M. Johnson, 'The Artful Interior', in *Beauty*, 110–41; Blanchard; Grier; Ames; *WP*; M. G. Humphreys, 'The Progress of American Decorative Art', *AJ* (1884).

80 C. L. Eastlake, *Hints …*, ed. with notes by Charles C. Perkins (Boston, MA: Osgood 1872); there were seven American edns 1872–83. Scully, 29; Mary Jean Smith, *Eastlake's Influence in American Furniture* (exh. cat. Yonkers, NY: Hudson River Museum, 1994). For Mrs Spofford, Eastlake meant 'a movement' as was 'seldom if ever before effected by a single person': Spofford, 153.

81 M. D. Conway, 'Decorative Art and Architecture in England', *Harper's*, vol. 49 (1874), 617–32, 777–89; vol. 50 (1874), 40–49.

82 Holly's articles were reprinted in H. Hudson Holly, *Modern Dwellings in Town and City* (New York: Harper's, 1878). § Four 'Appletons' Home Books' (all New York: Appletons): Ella Rodman Church, *How to Furnish a Home* (1881); A. F. Oakey, *Building a Home* (1881); E. W. Babcock, *Household Hints* (1881); Janet E. Ruutz-Rees, *Home Occupations* (1883). § F. H. Norton, *Illustrated Historical Register of the Centennial Exhibition* [i.e. Philadelphia, 1876, and the Exposition Universelle, 1878] (New York: American News Co., 1879). § H. Van Brunt, 'Studies in Interior Decoration', *AmA*, Feb.–June 1877.

83 Harriet Prescott Spofford: [unsigned; see *Beauty*, 468], 'Medieval Furniture', *Harper's*, vol. 53 (1876), 809–29; 'Furniture … Renaissance', vol. 54 (1877), 633–54; 'Elizabethan and Later English Furniture', vol. 56 (1877), 18–33. § Eugene Clarence Gardner, *Homes and How to Make Them* (Boston, MA: Osgood, 1874); *Illustrated Homes, a Series of Papers describing real Houses and real People* (Boston, MA: Osgood, 1875); *Home Interiors* (Boston, MA: Osgood, 1878); *The House that Jill Built, after Jack's had Proved a Failure: A Book on Home Architecture* (Springfield, MA: Adams, 1882); and *Homes and All About Them* (contains: *Homes and How to Make Them, Home Interiors, and Illustrated Homes* (Boston, MA: Osgood, 1885). § J. Falke, *Art in the House* (German 3rd edn with ills), with notes by Charles C. Perkins (Boston, MA: Prang, 1879); see review in *Art Journal* (New York edn), vol. 5, 1879, 113. § Cook; C. Cook, 'Beds and Tables …', *Scribners Monthly*, vol. 12, June 1875; vol. 14, May 1877. See also J. A. Weiss, 'Clarence Cook: His Critical Writings' (diss., Johns Hopkins University, Baltimore, MA, 1976). § Oscar Wilde, 'House Decoration' [US lecture, 1882], in O. Wilde, *The Complete Works* (New York: Gigelow Brown, 1908), vol. 'Miscellanies', 281–90; Blanchard. § Other books in the US: Charles Wyllis Elliott, *The Book of American Interiors* (Boston, MA: Osgood, 1876); C. W. Elliott, 'Household Art', *Art Journal* (New York edn), vol. 2, 1876; C. Cook, *What Shall We Do With Our Walls* (New York: Warren Fuller, 1881); Constance Cary Harrington, *Woman's Handiwork in Modern Homes* (New York: Scribner, 1881); A. C. Varney, *Our Homes and their Adornment* (Detroit: Chilton, 1882); Mrs T. W. Dewing, *Beauty in the Household* (New York: Harper's, 1882); Albert W. Fuller, *Artistic Homes in City and Country* (Boston, MA: Osgood, 1882, 5th edn Boston, MA: Ticknor, 1891); *Artistic Houses*; Arnold W. Brummer and T. Tyron, *Interior Decoration* (New York: Comstock, 1887); Agnes Bailey Ormsbee, *House Comfortable* (New York, 1892); Candace Wheeler (ed.), *Household Art* (New York: Harper's, 1893).

84 Blanc was quite explicit on this: 'je ne sais rien' [referring to bookbinding]: Blanc, 419. See M. Song, *The Art Theories of Charles Blanc 1813–1882* (Ann Arbor: University of Michigan, 1984); cf. R. Froissart-Pezone, *Les Arts dans tout: Les arts décoratifs en France et l'utopie d'un art nouveau* (Paris: CNRS, 2004); Silverman.

85 'uncontested authority': P. Rémond, 'Une existence au service des arts: H. Havard (1838–1921)', *Annales de Bourgogne*, vol. 70 (1998), 281–92 (285); *L'Art dans la maison*, much reduced edn in 2 vols. (Paris: Rouveyre, 1887); see reviews at Ch. V, n. 255, and Ch. VI, n. 31. See also: H. Havard, *Les Arts de l'ameublement: La décoration*, 3rd edn (Paris: Delagrave, n.d. [*c.* 1890]); H. Havard, *Les Arts de l'ameublement: Les styles* (Paris: Delagrave, n.d. [*c.* 1890]). § 'harmonie …': Havard 1884, 318; 'le bon sens contrôlé par le bon goût': Havard 1884, 242. § France, other books: Guichard; Mme la Comtesse de Bassanville, *L'Art de bien tenir une Maison* (Paris: Broussons, 1878); Emile Cardon, *L'Art au foyer domestique: La décoration de l'appartement* (Paris: Renouard, 1884); J. Boussard, *L'Art de bâtir sa maison* (Paris: Imprimeries Réunies, n.d. [1887]); C. L. Magne, *L'Art dans l'habitat moderne* (Paris: Firmin Didot, 1887); Ris-Paquot; O. E. Ris-Paquot, *L'Art de bâtir, meubler et entretenir sa maison* (Paris: Laurens, n.d. [1880s]); P. Bichet, *L'Art de bien être chez soi* (Paris: Marpon, 1890); de Noussanne (see Ch. I, n. 2).

86 See A. Lichtwark, *Makartbouquet und Blumenstrauss* (Hamburg: O. Meissner, 1892).

Folio volumes and journals

87 Folio volumes from the later 19th century contain many whole interiors. Many dates are taken from general bibliographies or are conjectural: almost all works were published in instalments, whose numbering is often opaque. § From France and Belgium (NB: the publisher Claesen was based at Liège/Paris/Berlin): Serials: *Le Garde-Meuble*, 1839–1900 (ed. Desiré Guilmard, from 1883 E. Maincent, Paris), monthly sheets; unrelated [?] to the Garde Meuble, the French state's repository of furnishings; *L'Ameublement: Deuxième partie du Journal de Garde Meuble. Recueil des dessins. Sièges, meubles, tentures genre simple* (dates similar to above); Daly; E. Prignot, *L'Architecture, la décoration, l'ameublement* (Claesen, n.d. [early 1870s]); *L'Ameublement moderne par MM. Prignot, Liénard, Coignet, F. Lenoir* (Claesen, n.d. [*c.* 1876]); G. Félix Lenoir ['Professeur de Dessin Décoratif'], *Décors de fenêtres et de lits: Ensembles d'intérieurs et dispositions diverses … par G. F. Lenoir* (Paris, 1879; Engl. edn London, 1890); M. Bajot, *Intérieures d'appartements meublés vue en perpective … reproduit en phototypie des dessins de l'auteur* (Claesen, n.d. [*c.* 1880]); T. Villeneuve, *Intérieurs d'appartemenes de haut style: Vues en perspective d'après des Frères Gueret* (Paris: A.Guerinet, n.d. [*c.* 1880]); T. Merlin, *Ameublement pratique de tous styles composés et dessinés* (Claesen, n.d., *c.* 1882); E. Prignot, *La Tenture moderne* (Claesen, n.d. [*c.* 1883]); D. Guilmard, *La Petite Décoration, menuiserie décorative …* (Paris: Garde Meuble, n.d. [*c.* 1885]); E. Maincent, *La Disposition des appartements: Intérieures complets* (Paris: Garde Meuble, n.d. [*c.* 1886]); *Album Général de l'Ameublement Parisien* (Paris: Imprimerie Camis, n.d. [*c.* 1890]); P. Planat, *Décoration d'intérieures* (Paris: Dujardin, 1888–89), repr. as *French Decorative Designs* (New York: Dover, 2006); P. Planat, *Habitations particuliers, hôtels privés* (Paris: Dujardin, n.d. [*c.* 1890]); G. Rémon, *Möbel im Empirestil* (Berlin: Wasmuth, 1894); *Die Tapezierkunst. Vorlagen für Dekoration und Möblierung* (mostly by G. Rémon) (Berlin: Wasmuth, 1895; copy Stadtbibliothek Trier); A. Simoneton, *La Décoration intérieure* (Paris: Librairie Construction Aulanier, 1893–95); E. Foussier, *Bibliothèque de l'ameublement: L'Appartment français à la fin du XIX s.* (Dourdan, Seine-et-Oise: Thézard, n.d. [*c.* 1896]). § For England, see the few folio volumes of Batley, Seddon, Young Adams (above, n. 75). § Not many were produced in the US: see above, n. 83, and *Artistic Houses*. In Germany and Austria: see J. Rennert, *Das Wohnhaus in Deutschland im Historismus. Bibliographischer Querschnitt von Vorlagewerken 1830–1910. Teil 1, Innenarchitektur, Möblierung und Ornamentik* (*Schriftenreihe der Fachhochschule Lippe*, vol. 8; Fachhochschule Lippe: Lemgo, 1992); M. Kimbel, *Der decorative Ausbau* (Dresden: Gilbers, n.d. [*c.* 1871, 1876, 1880]); N. Hofmann, *Renaissance Möbel und Decoration* (Berlin: Nicolai, n.d. [1876/81]); [Anon.], *Musterbuch für Möbeltischler* (Stuttgart: Engelhorn, n.d. [1881–82]; plates from *Gh*); F. Schwenke, *Ausgeführte Möbel und Zimmereinrichtungen der Gegenwart* (Berlin: Wasmuth, vol. 1 1881, vol. 2 1884; repr. Hanover: Schaefer, 1985), also publ. as *Designs for Decorative Furniture and Modern Chamber Arrangement* (London: Southeran, 1882, not seen); K. Schaupert, *Zimmereinrichtungen* (Weimar: Voigt, 1881); L. Caspar, *Deutsche Kunst- und Prachtmöbel neuester Zeit* (Frankfurt am Main: Keller, 1884); P. Niederhöfer, *Frankfurter Möbel=Bazar* (Frankfurt am Main: Eigenverlag, series 1–5, 1881–86); H. Kolb and T. Seubert, *Mustersammlung für Tapezierer* (Stuttgart: Wittwer, 1885–88); A. Lambert and E. Stahl, *Das Möbel. Ein Musterbuch stilvoller Möbel aus allen Ländern* (Stuttgart: J. Hoffmann, 1886–89); Pape; J. Pape, *Die Wohnungsausstattung der Gegenwart* (Dresden: Winter, 1889); A. and L. Streitenfeld, *Ausstattung vornehmer Wohnräume* (Berlin: Claesen, 1888ff.); H. Werle, *Das vornehme deutsche Haus* (Darmstadt: Koch, 1896); H. Werle, *Ein malerisches Bürgerheim* (Darmstadt: Koch, 1897). See also under 'Wood', Ch. III, n. 113. § Photographic volumes: [Anon.] *Cojen der Berliner Gewerbeausstellung im Jahre 1879* (Berlin: Wasmuth, 1880); C. Lipsius, *Sammlung Moderner Zimmerarbeiten* (Dresden: Gilbert, 1880–81); R. Eitelberger and A. Décsey, *Wohnungseinrichtungen der elektrischen Ausstellung Wien 1883* (Vienna: 1884); Luthmer 1884b, 2nd edn 1885 and ff.; H. Rückwardt, *Innen Architektur und Dekorationen der Neuzeit* (Berlin: Rückwardt, 1884); R. Schumann, *Das Zimmer der Gegenwart* (Leipzig: Hessling, n.d. [1885–87]); Niederösterreichischer Gewerbeverein (Vienna), *Möbel auf der Jubiläumskunstgewerbeausstellung Wien 1888* (Vienna: Scholl, 1888); W. Kick, *Dekorationen und Möbel deutsch-nationalen-Kunstgewerbeausstellung München 1888* (Stuttgart: Engelhorn, 1889); P. Naumann, *Möbel und Zimmer auf der deutsch-nationalen Kunstgewerbeausstellung München 1888* (Dresden: Gilbers, 1889); [Anon.], *Traute Wohnräume, Sammlung moderner Innenräume aller Art* (Berlin: Wasmuth, 1892. See also above, nn. 10, 11, 33, 41; Ch. III, n. 113.

88 Applied arts journals: *L'Art pour tous* [sheets of old works] (Paris: 1861–78); *RAD* 1880– ; *Journal of Design and Manufacture* (London: 1849–52); *ZBKM*; *BfK*; *Kunsthandwerk* (Stuttgart 1874–76); *Kunst und Gewerbe* (Nuremberg/ Weimar: 1867–87); *Kunstgewerbeblatt* (Berlin: 1885–). Most ambitious was the *Gh* (eds W. Baeumer, J. Schorn; Stuttgart: 1863–) and its foreign language versions (many dates unknown): *The Workshop: A Monthly Journal devoted to Progress of the Useful Arts* (eds W. Baeumer and J. Schorn; New York, London, 1863–72); thereafter as *The Art Workman, Monthly Journal of Design for the Artist, Artificer and Manufacturer* (1873–84); *Magasin des Arts et de l'Industrie: Organe du progrès …* (n.p.: Cagnon, late 1860s); *Guide per le arti e mestieri …* (Bologna: Wenk 1869– ; Milan: Hoepli, 1871–); *Kunst en Industrie. Verzameling von Modellen voor alle Takken van Nijverheid* (ed. J.Schnorr, 1870–83). § Journals, slanted towards interior decoration: In France: *Album d'ameublement journal de la décoration intérieure: Seul Organ …* (1881[?]–91). In England: *The Decorator's Assistant Weekly Journal of Painting, Sculpture and Popular Science* (ed. W. Gibbs, 1847–48); *The Decorator* (1864–); *The Cabinet Maker & Journal of Designs for the use of Upholsterers etc.* (London: Spon, 1868); *FG* (1870– ; new series 1873–); *The House Furnisher and Decorators', Upholsterers' and Cabinet-makers' Monthly Journal* (1871–73); *The Cabinet and Upholstery Advertiser* (1877–); *The House Decorator & School of Handicraft. Painters, Plumbers, Gas Fitters, Brass and Wireworkers, Builders, Carpenters, etc.* (1880–); *The Artist and Journal of Home Culture* (1880–); *Decoration in Painting, Sculpture and Art Manufacture* (n.p.: Sampson Low, 1880–); *CM*; *Amateur Work Illustrated* (P. Hasluck, 1881– ; see Ch. VI, n. 8). In the US: *Appletons' Journal of Literature, Science, and Art* (New York: 1876, 1877ff.); *The Art Worker* (New York: O'Kane, 1878–); *The Art Interchange: A Household Journal* (New York: 1878–); *AA*; *DF*; *Ladies' Home Journal* (1895–), see J. Scanlon, *Inarticulate Longings: The Ladies' Home Journal* (New York: Routledge, 1995). In Germany and Austria: see S. Muthesius, 'Communications between Traders, Users and Artists. … German Language Serial Publications on Domestic Interior Decoration in the 19th Century', *JDH*,

vol. 18, no. 1 (2005), 7–20. Trades: *Deutsche Tischlerzeitung*, (Berlin: 1874–1930); *Illustrierte Schreinerzeitung* (ed. Ferdinand Luthmer, Berlin–Stuttgart: 1883–85); *Deutsches Malerjournal* (Berlin–Stuttgart: 1876–94); *Deutsche Tapeziererzeitung* (Berlin: 1882–1942). More specifically on interiors: *Deutsche Möbelindustrie-Zeitung. Centralorgan für Austsattung, Möblierung und Dekoration der Wohnräume. Fachzeitschrift für Möbelfabrikanten und Kunsttischler, Tapezierer etc.* (ed. W. Schmidt, Berlin, 1879–80, not located); *IFz* (cf. Ch. V, n. 80); *Der Bazaar. Illustrierte Damenzeitung* (Berlin: 1855–).

89 *Innendekoration: Fachblatt für Innendekoration insbesondere der Möbel, Teppich, Tapeten* ... ; from year 2 (1891) *Illustrierte Kunstgewerbliche Zeitschrift für Innendekoration zur Ausschmückung und Einrichtung der Wohnräume.* See [A. Koch], 'An unsere geehrten Leser ...', *Id*, vol. 2, Jan. 1891, 1. Early on, the journal had a print run of 15,000 copies: see S. Randa, *Alexander Koch, Publizist und Verleger* (Worms: Werner, 1990).

Shops and exhibitions

90 Commerce in London: see Edwards; Berg and Clifford (above, n. 3); S. Muthesius,"'We do not understand what is meant by a 'Company' designing": Design versus Commerce in 19th-century English Furniture', *JDH*, vol. 5, no. 2 (1992), 113–20. See also 'furniture': Ch. III, n. 91.

91 'O heiliger Falke, Grossinquisitor aller Industriellen': F. Pecht, *Aus dem Münchner Glaspalast* (Stuttgart, 1876), 231.

92 'art': see Day (above, n. 78). Cf. the late 19th-century German term *Kunst-Tischlerei* ('art-cabinetmaking').

93 Falke 1883, 283; cf. 'The commercial element that is so often complained of by modern artists has proved a powerful assistant in the development of art industries': 'A Trial Balance of Decoration', *Harper's*, vol. 64 (1882), 734–40 (734).

94 For restraint advocated by a shop, see Schäffer & Walcker, *Der Zimmerschmuck für ein behagliches Heim* (sales cat., Berlin: Wasmuth, 1890), 13.

95 Advertisement, *BN*, 27 April 1866, iii.

96 '... without the trouble and inconvenience of going to different houses': advertisement for Jackson & Graham in *The London Post Office Directory*, quoted in C. Edwards, 'Jackson ...' (above, n. 17), 240.

97 'stilistische Einheit': Falke 1862, 675; cf. J. Falke, *Die Kunstindustrie auf der Ausstellung zu Dublin* [exh. not identified] (Vienna: K. K. Österreichisches Museum, 1865), 13.

98 'middling consumers' ('Musterzimmer ... Einheitlichkeit ... eine Selbstverständlichkeit'): A. Schwab, 'Der Einfluss der Konsumption auf die Möbelindustrie und Möbelhandel in Deutschland' (diss., University of Heidelberg, 1914), 59–60, 63–71. § 'bazaar': Schäffer & Walcker (above, n. 94), 13; cf. Carl Müller (Introduction, n. 18); cf. Amalie Baisch, *Ins eigene Heim. Ein Buch für erwachsene Mädchen und junge Frauen*, 3rd edn (Stuttgart: Deutsche Verlagsanstalt, 1893), 52 . § 'un musée': advertisement for the Societé Anonyme d'Ameublement, 26 Avenue de l'Opéra, in F. G. Dumas (ed.), *Catalogue Illustré du Salon*, 4th Year (Paris: 1882), 295. Cf. 'The Establishment of a New York Decorator' (J. P. McHugh & Co.), *FD*, vol. 16 (1890), 7–9.

99 See, for example, *Designs of furniture illustrative of cabinet furniture and interior decoration, specially designed for James Shoolbred & Compy., Tottenham Court Road* (London: 1876 edn); Carl Müller (Introduction, n. 18); C. & R. Light, see the present book, pp. 20–21.

100 D. Guilmard (& A. Dauvergne), *Le Garde-meuble: Album de l'exposition de l'industie 1844* (Paris: Guilmard, 1844; cf. n. 87 above), 9; Ottillinger, '"Kaiser Salon"' (above, n. 1).

101 'all manifestations': Lessing, *Wien* (above, n. 23), 25. § 'Gallery': A. Ebeling, *Die Wunder der Pariser Weltausstellung* (Cologne: Bachem, 1867), 306–39; cf. J. Mesnard, *Les Merveilles de l'Exposition de 1867*, 2 vols. (Paris: Lahure, 1867–68).

102 'parfaite': A. Luchet, *L'Art industriel à l'Exposition de 1867* (Paris: Lacroix, 1868), 138–39; costs: C. Daly, 'L'Exposition Universelle de 1867', *RGA*, 1868, 25–27.

103 'von einer Hand entworfen ... Ausführung durch einen Kopf leiten' (referring to designs by Storck and Teirich): Lehnert, 555; cf. ill. on p. 13 of the present book. § 'etwas ganz neues': 'Die Ausstellung vollständiger, künstlerisch concipierter Zimmer', K. K. Öterreichisches Museum für Kunst und Industrie(ed.), *Ausstellung Österreichisches Kunstgewerbe 1871–1872* (*Fachmännische Berichte*, Vienna: Gerold, 1872), 40–45 (41), no ill.

104 See H. Frauberger, *Die Leipziger Gewerbeausstellung 1879* (Leipzig: Scholtze, 1879); cf. the exhibitions in Munich 1888 and Vienna 1888 (list of folio albums, above).

The purchaser

105 Dumas, *Salon* (above, n. 98), 295.

106 'for stock' ('auf Verkauf'): F. Luthmer, 'Die Innere Austattung ...': *Deutsche Tischler Zeitung*, vol. 13 (1886), 282–83. § 'the purchaser ...' : K. Kuntze, 'Das Leipziger Tapeziergewerbe', in *Schriften des Vereins für Sozialpolitik*, vol. 56 (subseries *Lage des Handwerks in Deutschland*) (Leipzig, 1896), 357–87 (378). § 'What do the people want and care for in domestic art? For what they insist upon they will assuredly get': Haweis, 20. § D. Handlin, *The American Home* (Boston, MA: Little, Brown, 1979), 428. § Reference to H. James, *The Golden Bowl* (1904) in J.-C. Agnew, 'The House of Fiction: Domestic Interiors and the Commodity Aesthetic', in S. J. Bronner (ed.), *Consuming Visions: Accumulation and Display of Goods in America 1880–1920* (New York: Norton, 1989), 133–180 (152). § 'Die Kauflust ...' 'is the gauge [*Gradmesser*] for the styles of the present': R. Mielke, *Die Münchener Kunstgewerbe-Ausstellung* (Berlin: Claesen, 1889), 28. Cf. 'the self-conscious consumer' from late 18th century: Crowley, 291–92; Edwards, 66ff.; C. Gurlitt, 'Wie entstehen Moden ...', *GI* (1889), 674–78 (678).

107 Consumption studies: see e.g. Grier, Ames, Logan and Siebel. § Edwards, 3–11, 53–55, 167ff., 248ff.

Women and interior décor

108 Vicomtesse Nacla, *Le Boudoir: Conseils d'élégance* (Paris: Flammarion, 1896), 213. 'Ladies' played a considerable role in choosing interior features: Kent *AM*, 232; cf. I. Bryden and J. Floyd, *Domestic Space: Reading the Nineteenth-Century Interior* (Manchester University Press, 1999); E. Darling, *Women and the Making of Built-up Space in England, 1870–1950* (Aldershot: Ashgate, 2007).

109 'versed in ...': W. Mitford, *Principles of Design in Architecture*, 2nd edn (London, n.d. [1824]), 253, quoted in Jervis, 859. § 'Ladies are ...': 'Mr. Eastlake on Taste', *BN*, 19 March 1869, 260–61; cf. Eastlake, 14–15; 'capricious, uneducated, and frequently feminine tastes': 'Interior Decoration: The Drawing Room', *BN*, 5 Feb. 1869, 120.

110 G. Simmel, 'Bruchstücke aus einer Psychologie der Frauen' (1904), in G. Simmel, *Schriften zur Philosophie und Soziologie der Geschlechter* (Frankfurt am Main: Suhrkamp, 1985), 177–82.

111 J. C. Loudon, *A Treatise on Farming, Improving and Managing Country Residences* (London: Longman, 1806), vol. 1, 38–39, quoted in Davidoff & Hall, 191.

112 See *Deutsches Bauhandbuch* (Introduction, n. 21), 104, 111; Blanc, 226.

113 On poetry, humanity, morality: C. Oeser, *Briefe an eine Jungfrau über die Hauptgegenstände der Ästhetik*, 24th edn (ed. A. W. Grube, Leipzig: Brandstätter, 1883), 626–27; cf. 'the useful paired with the enjoyable, the good with the beautiful' ('zum Nützlichen das Angenehme, zum Guten das Schöne'): Louise Otto, *Der Genius des Hauses* (Vienna: Hartleben, 1869), 91–110, quoted in G. Häentzschel, *Bildung und Kultur bürgerlicher Frauen 1850–1918*, *Quellendokumentation* ... (Tübingen: Niemeyer, 1986), 344; cf. pp. 160ff.

114 Falke 1871, 341–74; cf. Stockbauer (Ch. II, n. 69), 32ff.; Edwards 163ff. § 'comprehensive view' ('vorzugsweise ein solcher Gesammtblick, das Gefühl für die Harmonie, die Empfänglichkeit für künstlerische Wirkung'): Falke 1871, 371; cf. Frau Isa von der Lütt, *Die elegante Hausfrau* (Stuttgart: Deutsche Verlagsanstalt, 1892).

115 'sentiment décoratif inné chez l'autre sexe': du Seigneur (Ch. IV, n. 73), 221–23. § 'monotonie engendrée par sa banalité': Ris-Paquot, 292; cf. Ch. III, n. 165. Cf. Auslander, 220–24, 292–95.

116 'unzähliges Gerät des häuslichen Lebens': A. von Zahn, 'Häusliche Kunstarbeiten', *Daheim*, vol. 1b, no. 30 (1865), 440–43 (442); cf. A. von Zahn, *Musterbuch häuslicher Kunstarbeiten* (Leizpig: Wiegand, 1865); F. Lipperheide (ed.), *Häusliche Kunst* (Berlin: Lipperheide, 1896); Celnart, above, n. 45; *Cassells Household Guide: A Complete Encyclopedia of Domestic and Social Economy*, 4 vols. (London, n.d. [1870]).

117 Embroidery: R. Parker and G. Pollock, *Old Mistresses: Women, Art, Ideology* (London: Women's Press, 1996). See also above, n. 78.

118 For the new stress on elegance out of the house: Baronesse Blanche Staffe, *Usages du monde: Règles du savoir-vivre dans la societé moderne* (Paris: Havard, n.d. [*c.* 1889]; repr. Paris: Les Editions, 1990); Lütt (above, n. 117).

The dynamics of the illustration

119 Gere, 60.

120 See S. Schultze (ed.), *Innenleben. Die Kunst des Interieurs. Vermeer bis Kabakov* (exh. cat. Frankfurt am Main: Städel-Museum / Stuttgart: Hatje-Cantz, 1998); F. Borzello, *At Home: The Domestic Interior in Art* (London: Thames & Hudson, 2006); C. Saumarez Smith, *Eighteenth-Century Decoration and Design and the Domestic Interior in England* (London: Weidenfeld & Nicholson, 1993, repr. as *The Rise of Design in the Domestic Interior in 18th-Century England* (London: Pimlico, 2000); Sidlauskas.

121 Architectural drawing: G. Stamp, *The Great Perspectivists* (London: Royal Institute of British Architects 1982); E. Blau and E. Kaufman (eds), *Architecture and its Images: Four Centuries of Architectural Representation* (Montreal: Centre Canadien d'Architecture, 1989); Long, *Houses* (above, n. 51), 36–37.

122 On chronicle or 'Biedermeier' (cf. Introduction, n. 26) views of interiors: Thornton, 217; C. Gere (ed. J. Focarino), *Nineteenth-Century Interiors: An Album of Watercolours* (London: Thames & Hudson, 1992); Cornforth, 13–18; S. Lasdun, *The Victorians at Home* (London: Weidenfeld & Nicholson, 1981); C. Davidson, *The World of Mary Ellen Best* (London: Chatto & Windus, 1985); *Wohnen in Berlin. Berliner Innenräume der Vergangenheit* (exh. cat. Berlin-Museum, 1970); H. Börsch-Supan, *Marmorsaal und Blaues Zimmer* (Berlin: Mann, 1976); H. Ottomeyer (ed.), *Das Wittelsbacher Album. Interieurs königlicher Wohn- und Festräume 1799–1848* (Munich: Prestel, 1979); *Biedermeier in Wien 1815–1848. Sein und Schein einer Bürgeridylle* (Mainz: Zabern, 1990); *Mein Blauer Salon. Zimmerbilder der Biedermeierzeit* (exh. cat. Nuremberg: Germanisches Nationalmuseum, 1995); Hessische Hausstiftung Schloss Fasanerie Fulda, *Interieurs der Biedermeierzeit. Zimmeraquarelle aus fürstlichen Schlössern ...* (Petersberg: Imhof, 2004); J.-P. Babelon and R. Hurel (eds), *Le Parisien chez lui au XIXe siècle* (exh. cat. Paris: Archives Nationales, 1975); *Second Empire*, 108–10; Mayhew. See also the more amateurish illustrations in N. Whittock, *The Decorative Painters and Glazier's Guide* (London: Taylor Hinton, 1827, 2nd edn 1841).

123 L. Jacobus, 'On "Whether a man could see before him and behind him ...": The role of drawing in the design of interior space in England *c.* 1600–1880', *Architectural History*, vol. 31 (1988), 148–165; cf. Maincent (above, n. 87); R. Evans, *Translations from Drawing to Building and other Essays* (London: Architectural Association, 1997); Luthmer 1884a, 246ff.

124 On illustrated books generally, see 'Les Arts du Livre', in Mairie de Paris (ed.), *La France de 1886: Centenaire de la Bibliothèque Forney* (exh. cat. Paris: Bibl. Forney, 1986), 128–32; R. Timm (ed.), *Die Kunst der Illustration. Deutsche Buchillustrationen des 19. Jh.* (exh. cat. Wolfenbüttel: Herzog August Bibliothek / Weinheim: *Acta Humaniora* VCH, 1986); R. Palmer and T. Frangenberg (eds), *The Rise of the Image: Essays on the History of the Illustrated Art Book* (Aldershot: Ashgate, 2003). § On printing: L. Jacoby, 'Kupfer- und Stahlstichdruck', and C. Greve, 'Lithographie und Chromographie', both *Ausstellungs-Bericht* (20; 33); G. Brindson and G. Wakeman, *Printmaking and Picture Printing* (Oxford: Plough, 1984); E. Rebel, *Druckgrafik. Geschichte. Fachbegriffe* (Stuttgart: Reclam, 2003); Long, *Houses* (above, n. 51), 36–37, 125. See also R. Pfnor, e.g. *Architecture, décoration et ameublement époque Louis XVI* (Paris: Morel, 1865).

125 Falke 4th edn (1881) contains 8 colour reproductions, 54 'Licht-und Tondruck' (heliogravures) and 219 woodcuts; cf. Falke 1883 edn, 'Foreword'.

126 See J. Crary, *Techniques of the Observer: On Vision and Modernity in the Nineteenth Century* (Cambridge, MA: MIT Press, 1990); D. Arnold and S. Bending, *Tracing Architecture: The Aesthetics of Antiquarianism* (Oxford: Blackwell, 2002).

127 Davison, 'unrivalled draughtsmanship': J. W. Benn, 'At the Royal Academy', *CM*, *June* 1887, 308–14 (312); 'Davison', in C. G. Harper, *English Pen Artists of Today* (London: Percival, 1892), 103–7 . Cf. George du Maurier's caricatures in *Punch*; also a new sketchiness in G. Félix Lenoir's works (above, n. 87), as well as a new peephole stiffness, e.g. Lothar Meggendorfer's images on pp. 266, 309 of the present book.

128 W. Searle, *The Tasteful Interlude: American Interiors through the Camara's Eye, 1860–1917* (New York: Praeger, 1975); F. Stille, 'Häusliche Photos in bürgerlichen Wohnräumen', *Fotogeschichte*, vol. 1 (1981), 33–44; Grier. See also Eugène Atget's photographs in Paris.

129 See photographic volumes above, n. 87. Cf. 'lebenswahrer und lebensvolle Wiedergabe ... der ganzen reizvollen Wahrheit': Caspar (above, n. 87), Intr.; 'New lenses free from distortion': 'Photographing furniture', *FG*, vol. 5, 18 March 1876, 171–72; Rice, 76ff.; Lighting: 'wait until high summer': [Text: J. Lessing], *Das Speisezimmer und andere Festgaben dargebracht ... dem Kronprinzen und der Kronprinzessin* (Berlin: Wasmuth, 1886), Preface; but there was much

artificial lighting in US: see *Artists' Houses*.
130 Sometimes photographs were used as the basis for chromolithographs: see the present book, pp. 134, 191.
131 See 'photolitho': Talbert 1868, Intr.; Eastlake, 2nd edn 1869, 'Foreword'. 'Phototipie': E. Prignot, *L'Architecture* (above, n. 87); cf. review of M. Kimbel (above, n. 87) in *BfK*, vol. 1 (1872), 20; P. A. Frijlink, 'Lichtdrukken …', *Bouwkundig Tijdschrift*, vol. 10 (1890), 2–5.
132 E.g. the 'Stil Werle': Werle, *Vornehme Haus* (above, n. 87), publisher's remarks.

III THE UNIFIED INTERIOR: FROM DECORATION TO DESIGN

Competing materials
1 I. Ware, *A Complete Body of Architecture* (London: Shipton, 1756), 469.
2 Falke 1862, 665. Gilding could be shiny, matte or burnished for a 'very pale old gold' surface: R. H. Pratt, 'The Parlor', *DF*, vol. 4, June 1884, 86. Gilding was 2 to 3 times the price of the most expensive colour: Laxton's, 418; Bristow 1996b, xi, 89. Cf. the Palais Liechtenstein, Vienna (1840s): Ottillinger, 288ff. § Loudon (i.e. in his journal, *AM*); 'gaudy …': Kent *AM*, 351; 'gilt sham …': Hamilton (Ch. II, n. 77), 126, 127; Garnier-Audiger, 152.
3 'grössten Täuschung': 'durchaus zu vermeiden und die hölzernen Fussböden nicht als solche, sondern in einer Art Mosaik auszuführen; er war nun durch diese Bestimmungen auf eine Dekoration im Sinne höherer Kunst angewiesen, wobei er jedoch der Character eines heiteren Wohnhauses nicht aus den Augen verlieren durfte:' [L. von Klenze], *Die Dekoration der inneren Räume des Königsbaus zu München* (Vienna: Allgemeine Bauzeitung, 1842) (4 pages). Also publ. in *ABZ*, vol. 4 (1839), 9–16, without the passage cited; see also Klenze (Ch. II, n. 37).
4 Friedrich Peters, Berlin, 'Klempnerei und Fabrik gestanzter Zinkornamente' [title not known] (sales cat., n.d. [*c.* 1876], copy Instytut Historii Sztuki, Uniwersytet Jagielloński, Krakow); Schäffer & Walcker (Ch. II, n. 94).
5 Emile Meron, *Papiers Vitraux: Vitrauphanie Parisienne* (sales cat. [Paris], n.d. [*c.* 1895], copy Cambridge University Library).
6 An early view: 'toutes sortes de falsification … prostituées aux emplois les plus vulgaires': Percier & Fontaine, 12; but cf. Fischbach, *Wohnung* (Ch. II, n. 69), 24, still in favour of graining in 1883. See also M. Wagner et al. (eds), *Material in Kunst und Alltag* (Berlin: Akademie Verlag, 2002); § 'noble fabrics …' ('vornehme Leute, vornehme Stoffe, keine Surrogate'): Luthmer 1884a, 44. § 'every material' ('zijn stijl en behandeling'): L.Vosmaer (Ch. V, n. 113), 135. For all aspects of materials early on in England, see Morley.

Plaster
7 Loudon, 272, 274. § 'rosette': G. Freytag, *Erinnerungen aus meinem Leben* (Greiz: Deutscher Bücherbund, 1926), 64, quoted in Wiedemann (Ch. II, n. 45), 76. § 'every décor' ('naturgemäss'): Luthmer 1884a, 32.
8 Hay, 59; Loudon, 272, 277; Muthesius, H., 93. M. Woelfer, *Gründliche und Kunstgemässe Anweisung zur Stukkatur-, Tüncher- und Cementierarbeit* (see *Schauplatz*, Ch. II, n. 7), vol. 77, 1835; F. Fink, *Der Tüncher, Stubenmaler, Stukkator und Gypser* (Leipzig: Spamer, 1866); G. Steinhausen, *Zimmerwände* (Weimar: Voigt, 1881, 1885); F. Theilmann and F. Schulze, *Über das Stukkaturhandwerk* (*Schriften zur deutschen Handwerkskunst*, Berlin: Metzner, 1934); M. Lebrun, *Nouveau Manuel du mouleur* (Paris: Roret, 1838).
9 E. G. Beard, *Craftsmen and Interior Decoration in England 1660–1820* (Edinburgh: Bartholomew, 1981).
10 'Adam brought …': G. T. Robinson, 'A Glimpse of its History', in W. Millar (ed.), *Plastering Plain and Decorative*, 2nd edn (London: Batsford, 1899), 22. § 'the plasterers' methods' ('ohne jede künstlerische Schulung'): Luthmer 1897, 103. § '"Centre Flowers"': Godwin *Ar*, 58; cf. 'cheap material, easily wrought, the more the worse …': E. Gardner, *Homes* 1874 (Ch. II, n. 83), 198.
11 On substitutes: Bielefeld (Introduction, n. 27), 4–7; a 'beggar's luxury' ('Bettelluxus'): F. Luthmer, 'Holz und Gips', *Illustrierte Schreinerzeitung*, vol. 2, no. 1 (1884), 1–2; Long, 184–85; Loyer, 194–95.
12 J. Banham, 'W. Crane and the Decoration of the Artist's Interior', in Greg Smith and S. Hyde (eds), *Walter Crane 1845–1915* (London: Hutton, 1989), 47–58; cf. Girouard 1979, 356ff.; 'Rococo-Dekorationen', *BfK* (1885), 43.
13 Millar (above, n. 10), 240.

Paint
14 *Maler*, *peintre*, *peintre-décorateur*, painter, etc. compared to the low-status *Tüncher*, *Anstreicher*, *badigeonneur* and whitewasher; see Geist, 252. Whistler was jokingly referred to as 'merely a housepainter': 'History of the Week', *John Bull*, vol. 30, Nov. 1878, 773, quoted in D. M. Bendix, *Diabolical Designs: Painting, Interiors, and Exhibitions of James McNeill Whistler* (Washington, D.C.: Smithsonian, 1995), 34. Painters hardly figured in the World's Fairs, but see Lieb (Ch. II, n. 25).
15 For whitewash (*blanc de chaux*, *Kalkfarbe*; *lait de chaux*, *Milchfarbe*; *détrempe*, etc.): 'Anstrich' in Meyer (Ch. II, n. 56), vol. 1, 682–83; Laxton's, 410, 414. § On methods: Loudon, 274–79; D. R. Hay, 'On the comparative Advantages of Painting and Papering …', *AM*, vol. 2 (1835), 362–65; M. E. James, *How to Decorate our Ceilings, Walls and Floors* (London: Bell & Sons, 1883); J. W. Facey jun., *Elementary Decoration … as applied to the interior and exterior decoration of dwelling-houses*, 2nd edn (London: Crosby Lockwood, 1889); J. F. Watin, *Art du peintre, doreur et vernisseur*, 2nd edn Paris 1773 (many 19th-century edns, Paris: Roret); Fink (above, n. 8); L. Bregnhøi, 'Handbooks for Housepainters in Denmark in the 19th Century' [also on German works], *Zeitschrift für Kunsttechnologie und Konservierung*, vol. 17, no. 1 (2003), 105–15; H. Hillig, *Um die Zukunft der Dekorationsmalerei* (Stuttgart: Steinkopf, 1907); H. Hillig, *Geschichte der Dekorationsmalerei* (Hamburg: Hilligs, 1911). § Stencilling (*Patronenmalerei*, *peintre au patron*), see W. Hering, *Die angewandte oder praktische Ästhetik oder die Theorie der dekorativen Architektur* (Leizpig: Scholtz, n.d. [1873]), 261; G. G. Ungewitter, *Entwürfe für gotische Ornamente … Decken und Wände* (Leipzig: Romberg, 1854); M. Digby Wyatt, 'Report on Paperhangings' in *Report on the Paris Exhibition 1867* (London, 1867); Edis, 174–75.
16 Graining (*masern*, *veiner*): see Bristow 1996a; cf. A. Vallance, 'The Furnishing and Decoration of the House II', *AJ* (1892), 45–49 (46). § On painted skies: Bristow 1996a, 163; Bristow 1996b, 141.
17 Klenze and Munich: see caption p. 67; cf. R. Wiegmann, *Malerei der Alten in ihrer Anwendung und Technik, insbesondere als Dekorationsmalerei* (Hannover, 1836); Werner.
18 W. von Zahn, *Die schönsten Ornamente und merkwürdigsten Gemälde aus Pompeji / Les plus beaux ornements … de Pompéi*, 3 vols. (Berlin: Reimer, 1828–59); Werner; M. G. Zimmermann, 'Schinkels farbige Innendekoration', *Wasmuths Monatshefte für Baukunst*, vol. 1 (1914), 110–17; J. Schönwalder, 'Pompeianische Wandmalerei' in Hölz, 134–57. Cf. J. Miziołek, *Villa Laurentiana: Arcydzieło Epoki Stanisławowskiej* [early Neoclassical painting scheme] (Warsaw: Biblioteka Narodowa, 2007).
19 Also called the '3rd style of Pompeii', it showed more vigorous drawing and more unusual colouring, e.g. in the Maison Pompéienne, Paris, 1856: see *Alfred Normand* (exh. cat. Paris: Musée des Arts Décoratifs, 1979).
20 See Ch. I, n. 4; Edis, 83ff.
21 'Those gaudy paper-hangings which impinge the most obtrusive rays in all their vigour, or those carpets where the preponderance of bright yellow and red attracts the eye': Hay, 25 (1836 edn, 20). § On the painter's task: Hay, 32 (1836 edn, 26). § 'perfect harmony' ('harmonische Gesamtwirkung'), 'lighter …' ('heller oder dunkler, freundlicher oder ernster'): F. Fink (above, n. 15), 290.
22 'One is tempted' ('Fast möchte man versucht werden, der üppigen Gestaltungskraft der Textilbranche Mässigung anzuraten … Decke, Wände und Fussboden in einfachen, ruhigen Tönen gehalten, hingegen die Möbel farbigen Schmuck erhielten'). Cf. 'Pinewood … of an repulsive red or dirty brown should be treated with cosy wood colours and corresponding varnish and given coloured décor' ('Kiefernholz … ein widerliches Rot oder ein schmutziges Braun zeigen, müsste in traulicher Holzfarbe mit entsprechenden Lasuren und farbigen Ornamenten [bemalt werden]': 'Über farbige Bemalung der Möbel', *Der Dekorationsmaler*, no. 2, 15 Jan. 1888, 9–10. § Godwin's white walls: see Soros, *Godwin Aesthetic* (Ch. II, n. 73), 187, 188; cf. D. M. Bendix, 'Whistler as Interior Designer', *Apollo*, vol. 143 (Jan. 1996), 31–38.

Wallpaper
23 C. Lynn, *Wallpaper in America: From the Seventeenth Century to World War I* (New York: Norton, 1980), 178. In England and France: L. Hoskins (ed.), *The Papered Wall: History, Pattern, Technique* (London: Thames & Hudson, 1994). England: G. Saunders, *Wallpaper in Interior Decoration* (London: V&A, 2002); C. Velut, 'Between Invention and Production: The Role of Design in the Manufacture of Wallpaper in France and England at the Turn of the Nineteenth Century', *JDH*, vol. 17, no. 1 (2004), 55–69. See also the Musée du Papier Peint, Rixheim, Alsace. For Germany and Austria: H. Olligs (ed.), *Tapeten. Ihre Geschichte bis zur Gegenwart*, 2 vols. (Braunschweig: Klinkhart & Biermann, 1970); Staatliche Schlösser, Burgen und Gärten Sachsen / Landesamt für Denkmalpflege Sachsen, *Papiertapeten* (Dresden: Sandstein, 2004); S. Forge, *Victorian Splendour, Australian Interior Decoration 1837–1901* (Melbourne: Oxford University Press, 1981).
24 Havard 1884, 217; cf. 'l'avènement de la démocratie coïncidait … participer le grand nombre aux bienfaits de l'industrie humaine': Blanc, 58.
25 Cf. the French *papier peint*; the German *Tapete* and Dutch *tapijt* derive from textiles (French *tapis*, 'carpet', and *tapisserie*, 'tapestry').
26 On technology, see Hoskins (above, n. 23), 132ff.; Edis, 69, 144. Britain produced *c.* 1,200,000 rolls in 1834, 5,500,000 in 1851, and 32,000,000 in 1874. France used machines from England from the 1850s: M. Vachon, *Les Arts et les industries du papier en France, 1871–1894* (Paris: Imprimeries Unies, 1894).
27 'a simple …' ('einfache Bürgerwohnung'): Lehnert, 447. § 'cold …' ('kalt und unbehaglich'): [Anon.], *Das häusliche Glück. Vollständiger Haushaltungsunterricht und Anweisung … für Arbeiterfrauen*, 11th edn (München-Gladbach: Riffarth, 1882; repr. Munich: Rogner & Bernhard, 1975), 48. § Cook, *Walls* (Ch. II, n. 83), 7, 8, quoted in Lynn (above, n. 23), 406. Cf. papering and painting 'self-done': *Home* 1853, 76–78; 'so simple an operation': M. E. James (above, n. 15), 9.
28 Textile-effect: Hoskins (above, n. 23), 25, 66, 74; Lynn (above, n. 23), 143, 261. Cf. Luthmer 1884a; Luthmer 1892, 68; C. E. Clerget's wallpapers in Fleury Chavant (ed.), *Le Dessinateur des papiers peints* (Paris, 1837, 1838); C. E. Clerget, 'Papiers peints', *RGA* (1855), 392–402, 454–63. On flock paper, or *Velourtapete*: Muthesius, H., 102; A. Fix, 'Tapezierarbeiten und Decoration', *Ausstellungs-Bericht* (44); L. Bodenschatz, *Ausschmückung und Einrichtung der Wohnräume … Wahl der Tapeten* (Darmstadt: Koch, 1888).
29 O. Nouvel-Kammerer, *Papiers peints panoramiques* (Paris: Flammarion, 1990; English edn *French Scenic Wallpapers*, 2000); *Second Empire*, 124ff.; *EID*, 1364; cf. E. Börsch-Supan, *Der Innenraum als Garten* (Berlin: Hessling, 1967). § Imitation of wood: L. Bodenschatz (above, n. 28), 19.
30 Hoskins (above, n. 23), 157ff.; W. F. Exner, 'Tapeten und Buntpapiere', *Ausstellungs-Bericht* (53).
31 Staatliche Schlösser, Burgen … Sachsen, *Ledertapeten* (Dresden: Sandstein, 2004); see below, n. 77.
32 R. Parsons, *From Floor to Ceiling* (pamphlet on Lincrusta; Spelthorne Museum, 1997); 'Relief Decorations' in *EID*, 1043–45; J. Mönich, 'Embossed Wall Coverings', in M. Auer et al. (eds), *The Interiors: Handbook for Historic Buildings II* (Washington, D.C.: Historic Preservation Education Foundation, 1993).
33 Zinc: Long, 139–41; see above, n. 4.
34 Tiffany: see below, n. 278.
35 'constituent' ('l'élément constitutif de l'industrie du papier peint, c'est la fleur … Transporter à l'intérieur de nos habitations un peu des charmes de la nature et un reflet de dehors, est un de nos plus grands besoins'): Mesnard (Ch. II, n. 101), 53–54; see below, n. 120.
36 Loudon, 279; cf. Wyatt, 'Paperhangings' (above, n. 15), 4.
37 Flatness: see the present book, pp. 144–45; Clerget (above, n. 28). Some claimed that you would never hang a repeat of the same picture on a wall (an accusation aimed at repeat patterns on wallpapers): Falke 1862, 672. Cf. Ottillinger.
38 Jeffrey & Co: *EID*, 652–55. § £200 (4,000 Marks): Dohme, 56.
39 Edis, 69.
40 On quiet patterns: Oakey (Ch. II, n. 82), 82; but cf. strong designs: Chevreul, 248; Morris, 144ff.; Muthesius, H., 89.
41 See e.g. Mayhew, 208–10.
42 'cheaper papers': 'The Establishment of a New York Decorator,' *DF*, vol. 16 (1890), 7–9 (9). § 'healthy …': *Das häusliche Glück* (above, n. 27), 48.
43 G. T. Robinson, 'The Year's Advance in Art Manufacture VIII: Wallpapers', *AJ* (1883), 353–56. Prices *c.* 1900 ranged from 6*s.* to 75*s* a roll: Muthesius, H., 102–3.
44 Quoted in Clerget, *RGA* (above, n. 28), 458–60.
45 'the pattern …' ('Muster bedeutungslos, Gesamteindruck wichtig'): Falke, quoted in Hug, 14. § On the impression of colour ('Farbstimmung') and precision of design more and more given up: Dohme, 55. § Uniformity: Olligs (above,

n. 23), 87–90; see also F. Fischbach, *Beitrag zur Geschichte der Tapeten-Industrie* (Darmstadt: Koch, 1889). § 'overpapered': Godwin *Ar*, 19.

Textiles

46 D. Jenkins (ed.), *The Cambridge History of Western Textiles* (Cambridge University Press, 2003); M. Schoeser, *Silk* (New Haven and London: Yale University Press, 2007); F. Fischbach, *Geschichte der Textilkunst … Ornamente der Gewebe* (Hanau: Albert, 1883); M. Duport-Auberville, *Art industriel d'ornement des tissus* (Paris: Ducher, 1877); Witt-Dörring, 114ff.; Ottomeyer, 379ff.; Grier. On France: e.g. Loudon, 338. 'Germany behind': G. Buss, 'Ein Rückblick auf die Ausstellung der Wollenindustrie zu Leipzig', *GI* (1880), 735. Cf. C. Edwards, *Encyclopedia of Furnishing Textiles, Floor Coverings and Home Furnishing Practices 1200–1950* (London: Lund Humphries, 2007).

47 Edwards, 27–29.

48 'Fingerfertigkeit, Kunstgeschmack und gutes Augenmass': Kuntze (Ch. II, n. 106), 359.

49 Lehnert, 444. Cf. also imitation lace for curtains, such as Nottingham manufactures and Swiss white work. Cf. Grier, Ch. 5.

Materiality

50 'solide Pracht': J. von Falke, 'Plüsch Studie', *IFz*, 16 June 1884, 189–90 ; cf. the chapter on textiles in J. Falke, *Ästhetik des Kunstgewerbes. Handbuch …* (Stuttgart: Spemann, 1883). See also F. de' Marinis, *Velvet: History, Techniques, Fashions* (Milan: Idea Books, 1993).

51 Prices: W. F. Exner, 'Tapeten und Buntpapier', *Ausstellungs-Bericht* (53). § On cotton: *Home* 1853, 119; Luthmer 1884a, 9. § Mungo: H. Grothe, *Technologie der Gespinstfaser* (Berlin: Springer, 1875), 429; Luthmer 1884a, 6. § Jute: Luthmer 1884a, 14.

52 'Drapery is …': *Home* 1853, 118. 'Japanese and Medieval decorators hung upon their walls the best they could; if partly for warmth, for beauty also … they made their warmth beautiful': [H. P. Spofford], Medieval Furniture', *Harper's*, vol .53 (1876), 809–29 (818). § 'the feeling …' ('Berührung mit der Haut erzeugten Empfindung'): Luthmer 1884a, 4.

53 Patterns were 'numberless': *Home* 1853, 13. § 'meaningless' ('gleichgültigem Muster') patterns for curtains and carpets: Bergau, 19, 26. For illustrations of décor, see Yapp.

54 'gorgeous …': 'Exhibition of Textile Fabrics', *AJ* (1870) 106. Cf. 'serving far more as models [*mustergültiger*] than ours …': J. Falke, *Die Kunstindustrie der Gegenwart. Studien auf der Pariser Weltausstellung 1867* (Leipzig: Quant und Handel, 1868), 252. § 'away from …': Lessing, *Kunstgewerbe Wien* (Ch. II, n. 23), 16.

Flat coverings

55 For a brief overview, see Harvey and Press (Ch. II, n. 77), 96; cf. Chevreul 1854; Walsh; Blanc, 118–34; Muthesius, H., 121–22. There was little change between 1780 and 1820: Thornton, 155.

56 *Wachstuch*, *toile cirée*. In the 19th century this was a cheap method. In the 1860s came the English invention of linoleum, whose décor imitated other flooring materials: C. D. Edwards, 'Floorcloth and Linoleum', *Textile History*, vol. 27, no. 2 (1996), 148–71; S. Sarin,'The Floorcloth and Other Floor Coverings in the London Domestic Interior 1700–1800', *JDH*, vol. 18, no. 2 (2005), 133–46.

57 Walsh, 179. § On the increasing use of carpets: 'Teppich', in Meyer (Ch. II, n. 56), vol. 15, 34–35.

58 Kent *AM*, 232; Meyer (above, n. 57).

59 '[and are] most perfect in colour fabric and design': Haweis, *Art of Beauty* (Ch. II, n. 76), 251–52.

Stretched coverings

60 On silk and colour: *EID*, 1273. § According to Mothes, silk plush had a 'fascinating shine' ('bezaubernden Schimmer'): Mothes, 2nd edn 1882, 35.

61 E.g. 'the seats covered with embossed damasked satin like the curtains': Kent *AM*, 355; for 'uni', see below (n. 208).

62 The term 'French stuffed': Ackermann (vol. 1, no. 4, July 1810), 46, 53. On seating: C. D. Edwards, *Victorian Furniture: Technology and Design* (Manchester University Press, 1993); E. S. Cooke Jr. et al., *Upholstery in America and Europe from the Seventeenth Century to World War I* (New York: Norton, 1987); Ames, 184ff.; Havard *Dict.* I, 951; Witt-Dörring, 379; Grier; Siebel, 144ff. § On tufting: 'La garniture capitonnée est plus douce et plus gracieuse à l'oeil': H. Lacroix, *Nouveau Manuel complet du tapissier et décorateur* (Paris: Roret, 1901), 42. A European view of the American rocking chair as 'sybaritic': Falke 1862, 676, cf. p. 33.

Hanging fabrics and the all-textile room

63 'hermetically …': 'Moeurs Parisiennes', *L'Illustration Journal Universel*, 14/21 Feb. 1851, 112; cf. 'Drapery' in *EID*, 335–39. On the use of curtains: Walsh 183. Colour preservation: *Home* 1853, 119.

64 'infinite variety' ('dans la manière d'ajuster les draperies'): M. Santi, *Modèles de meuble et de décorations pour l'ameublement* (Paris: Bance, 1828), 2. § On curtains: Cornu (Ch. II, n. 8); Ackermann; T. Pasquier, *Dessin d'ameublement* (Paris: author, n.d. [*c.* 1830]), 183; C. Muidebled, *Le Pandore du tapissier de 1837* (n.p. [Paris]: n.d. [1837]); S. J. Dornsife, 'Design Sources for Nineteenth-Century Window Hangings', *WP*, vol. 10 (1975), 69–99; F. Collard, 'Curtains up' (Regency-period draperies), *Country Life*, 20 April 1989, 194–97; A. Westman, 'Festoon Window Curtains in Neo-Classical England', *FH*, vol. 29 (1993), 81–86. On 'extraordinary' festoons: R. Bidlingmaier, *Das Residenzpalais in Kassel. Der Architekt J.C. Bromeis* (Regensburg: Schnell & Steiner, 2000).

65 For portières, see *Deutsches Bauhandbuch* (Introduction, n. 21), 108. Dressing-up furniture: Logan, 135.

66 On tent rooms: Morley, 268–71; O. Nouvel-Kammerer, *Symbols of Power: Napoleon and the Art of the Empire Style, 1800–1815* (exh. cat. St Louis Art Museum etc. / New York: Abrams, 2007). See Schinkel's design *c.* 1830 in the Schloss Charlottenhof, Potsdam.

67 Smith, 29–30, pl. 151.

68 See e.g. Luthmer 1884a, 131–34 (partly after Verdellet); Grier, 57.

69 Lessing, *Pariser Weltausstellung* (Ch. II, n. 23), 143; Luthmer 1884a, 84.

70 G. Doy, *Drapery: Classicism and Barbarism in Visual Culture* (London: Tauris, 2002), 230.

71 'the judicious …': Mrs Merrifield, 'The Harmony of Colours as exemplified in the Exhibition', p. iii of a section near the end of *Crystal Palace*.

72 J. Verdellet, *Manuel géométrique du tapissier*, 2 vols., text and plates (Paris: author, 1851; 2nd edn Paris: Morel, 1862–64; 3rd edn Paris: author, 1877); J. Verdellet, *L'Art pratique du tapissier*, 1st–3rd series (Paris: author, 1871–75); Luthmer 1884a. For the view that, earlier on, much art had been displayed in the ordering of folds, whereas the 'modern upholsterer' was freer artistically and the fabric taken as a whole and arranged *in situ*: Luthmer 1892, 72.

73 'materiality …' ('Das stoffliche der Gewebe'): Falke, *Ästhetik* (above, n. 51), 438. § 'optical effect …': Falke 1883, 297–98. Cf. smoother fabric ('glatter', 'uni'): Luthmer 1884a, 15.

74 'one usually …' ('man gibt meist zuviel auf die Konturen der Vorhänge; doch nicht durch die Konturen, sondern durch die Falten und Farben des Stoffes sollen sie wirken'): Bergau, 19.

75 'crumpled' ('knittrig '), 'suppleness and softness' ('Schmiegsamkeit und Weichheit'): Luthmer 1884a, 4–5. § 'massive …' ('Mässigen, grossen runden Wurf im grossen Stil'): Falke, *Ästhetik* (above, n. 51), 439; 'moderne … Renaissance': Luthmer 1884a, 157.

76 Prignot, *Architecture* (Ch. II, n. 87); cf. E. Plasky, *La Tenture artistique* (Brussels/Lyon: Claesen, n.d. [early 1890s]); Foussier (Ch. II, n. 87).

77 See above, n. 31; also *Deutsches Bauhandbuch* (Introduction, n. 21), 104; Luthmer 1884a, 70ff.; Whistler's Peacock Room: L. Merrill, *The Peacock Room …* (Washington, D.C.: Freer Gallery of Art / New Haven and London: Yale University Press, 1998).

78 'What an air …': *Home* 1853, 118; cf. Loudon, 338–41. Cf. also the use of different sets of textiles for winter and summer: Garnier-Audiger 96–97. § 'the upholsterer surpasses …' ('le tapissier l'emporte sur l'ébéniste'): H. de Balzac, quoted in J. Guichardet, *Balzac 'archéologue' de Paris* (Paris: Sedes, 1986), 294. § 'textile will prevail … it will harmoniously supplement [*harmonisch ergänzen*] the wooden décor and the free painting ('freie Malerei')': F. Fischbach, 'Bedeutung der Stickereimaschinen': *Leipziger Monatsschrift für Textilindustrie*, vol. 1, no. 2 (1886), 70. § 'The art of … cotton satin draped in picturesque folds': Luthmer 1884a, 235.

79 Feray (Ch. II, n. 1), 349.

80 'barbaric opulence' ('barabarische Pracht … nur Wert der Stoffe'): G. Waagen, *Kunstwerk und Künstler England und Paris*, vol. 1 (Berlin: Nikolai, 1837), 4–5. Cf. Le Camus, 113; Eastlake, 54; Dresser 1873, 69. § 'death of …' ('la mort de l'art et du goût'): du Seigneur (Ch. IV, n. 73), 197–99.

81 Ris-Paquot, 292. On dust and delicate furnishings: Godwin *Ar*, 5; 'heavy wool curtains retaining the effluvia …': G. Wheeler, *A Practical Handbook of Useful Information on All Points Connected with Hiring, Buying, or Building a House*, 2nd edn (London, 1872), 216.

Wood

82 Sculpture: *Crystal Palace*; Nouvel–Kammerer; *Second Empire*, 134; 'Le mobilier national et ses manufactures', *MH*, no. 190, Nov.–Dec. 1993; Ames 62.

83 See Ch. VI.

Timber and its industry

84 'On Furniture Woods', *BN*, 16 April 1869, 339; Havard 1884, 48ff., 103–4. Britain imported almost all its timber.

85 Sheraton: *EID*, 1168.

86 For relative costs, see Walsh, 162; cf. 'The Furniture Trade', in C. M. Depew (ed.), *1795–1895: One Hundred Years of American Commerce*, vol. 2 (New York: Haynes, 1895), 628–32.Cf. the disparaging comment 'Mahagoni Gerümpel' ('junk'): 'Die Wohnung des "kleinen Mannes"', *Illustrierte Schreiner Zeitung*, vol. 2, no. 8 (1884), 16.

87 Oak, 'not polished': E. B. Lamb, 'Villa in the Norman Style', *AM*, vol. 2 (1834), 333–51 (339); see also Jervis. § 'Oaken panelling … admirable construction and cleanliness': Haweis, 34. § Oak thought to have a 'rather cold look': Walsh, 214; cf. N. D. G. James, *Oak: A British History* (Macclesfield: Bollington, 2003). § 'so-called old oak' ('vieux chêne'): Staffe (Ch. II, n. 121), 362–65; cf. Nouvel-Kammerer, 76, 77.

88 Hungarian ash: *Illustrierte Schreiner Zeitung*, vol. 1, no. 1 (1883), 3; Talbert, 4. Cf. walnut: Lütt (Ch. II, n. 117), 26.

89 'Deal … humble material': E. Gaskell, *Mary Barton* (1848), Chapter II, quoted in Calder, 78; cf. the description 'beautiful fir wood' ('schönes Tannenholz'), and if one wanted to go higher, one could use pitch pine: Niederhöfer (Ch. II, n. 87), 3rd series 1882, pl. 47. Cf. 'pitch pin' in L. d'Alq, *Les Secrets du cabinet de toilette* (Paris, 1881), 9;. For the 'knots' and 'cheapness' of American pitch pine, 'of late so familiar', see *FG*, vol. 7, 17 March 1877, 161; 'goldgelbes Kiefernholz': Luthmer 1892, 86. Morris was for oak but against deal, calling 'its natural colour poor': Morris, 137–38.

90 'carpentry …': *Möbel Franken* (Ch. V, n. 52), 96.

91 On the vast scale of industry in Paris: P. du Maroussem, *La Question ouvrière*, vol. 2: *Ebenistes …* (Paris: Rousseau, 1892), 26–27. § Production in the US grew 2½-fold between 1860 and 1870: K. L. Ames, 'Grand Rapids Furniture', *WP*, vol. 10 (1975), 23–50. § Berlin: 'good average …': 'Zimmereinrichtungen, Berliner' (Ch. II, n. 62), 324; P. Voigt, *Das Tischlergewerbe in Berlin* (series: *Schriften des Vereins für Socialpolitik*, vol. 65 [= vol. 4 of its sub-series *Untersuchungen zur Lage des Handwerks in Deutschland*]; Leipzig, 1895), 325–498; L. Maass, *Der Einfluss der Maschine auf das Schreinergerwerbe* (Stuttgart, 1901); J. Seidel, *Möbelherstellung und Möbelhandel 1850–1914* (*Veröffentlichungen Volkskunst …*, vol. 21; Würzburg, 1986); Stiegel.

92 For machinery and division of labour in the upper range of production, see C. D. Edwards, *Victorian Furniture Technology and Design* (Manchester University Press, 1993), 170 etc.; M. J. Ettema, 'Technological Innovation and Design Economics in Furniture': *WP*, vol. 16 (1981), 196–223; R. Allwood, 'Machine Carving of the late 1840s … Patent Wood Carving Co.', *FH*, vol. 32, 1996, 90–103. On Bembé, see Zinnkann (Ch. II, n. 9); Himmelheber, 197.

A new materiality

93 'For our furniture makers': [Anon.; J. Hungerford Pollen?], 'Woodwork VIII', *BN*, 12 March 1875, 282–83. Cf. 'Practical Hints on Furniture', *BN*, 20 June 1873, 697–98; J. Hungerford Pollen, *Ancient and Modern Furniture in the South Kensington Museum* (London: Science and Art Dept. of the Comm. of the Council on Education, 1874); Edwards, *Technology* (above, n. 91), 75–77; Bristow 1996b, 119ff. For France, see the list of Roret's manuals. M. C. Preller, 'Fassung oder Beize … Möbel des deutschen Klassizismus', *Weltkunst*, Nov. 1999, 2438–41 (info. S. Michalski). See also Grier, 156.

94 On 'truth to materials': see above, n. 6; Pugin (below, n. 164); Ungewitter: see Ch. V, n. 22. Cf. Luthmer 1884a, 25.

95 'painted in …': *AM*, Kent, 232.

96 'polishing, finishing …': 'Something more on Furniture', *B*, 10 Oct. 1874, 840–42; cf. Eastlake, 106; § 'broader play of light and shade which this rougher execution allows … [against] the smooth surfaces and the sharp edges of modern work': J. H. Pollen, 'Ancient and Modern Furniture', *B*, 5 Sept. 1874, 739–91 (extract from J. H. Pollen, *Ancient …*

(above, n. 93)). § Unpainted wood lasting longer: *Laxton's*, 409.

97 'mockery ...' ('spottet der Struktur des Holzes'): Falke 1871, 273. § 'natural "vein"': Eastlake, 43. § Talbert, Intr. § 'woodenness" ('Hölzern'): 'Aus der Fachliteratur', *D* (1873), 362; cf. E.Gardner, *Homes 1874* (Ch. II, n. 83), 179. § 'sugary ...' ('süssliche minutiöse Ausführung [vs.] derb'): Frauberger (Ch. II, n. 104), 38. See also a new Ruskinian reaction regarding workmanship: 'hopelessness' and 'never-ending precision' (on the Morrison interior, see below, n. 251): M. RIBA, 'Mr. Eastlake on Taste', *BN*, 19 March 1869, 260–61.

98 'light and wooden': 'Art Furniture' (review of *Art Furniture*), *BN*, 24 Aug. 1877, 174. Cf. 'perhaps more suited to a proper use of wood in design than any other modern furniture we have seen': [Anon.], 'Edward W. Godwin', *BrAr*, 15 Oct. 1886, 347–48. See also G. T. Robinson, 'Cabinetmakers' Art', *AJ* (1884), 373–76 (373); Schaupert (Ch. II, n. 87).

99 'demands a relative elasticity' ('Le bois ... exige une élasticité relative et une température voisine de celle du corps humain'): Didron (Ch. II, n. 13), 202; cf. Havard 1884, 46–47.

Furniture and the room

100 'careful adjustment of solid and void' (said here about façades): E. W. Godwin, 'The Ex-Classic Style called "Queen Anne"', *BN*, 16 April 1875, 441–42.

101 Spofford, 217.

102 On minimal amounts of furniture: Witt-Dörring, 379; Ottomeyer, 114; Thornton, 147.

103 On furnishing 'en suite': Eriksen (Ch. II, n. 16), 136; cf. Grier 175ff., 188; Loudon. § Cf. the new terms for furnishing: *ameublement*, *Möblierung* and *Einrichtung*: H. G. Ehrlich, *Lebenskunst und Kunstleben* (Berlin, 1884), 213; Teirich, *Richtung* (Ch. II, n. 5), 108; cf. Witt-Dörring, 380–86; Auslander, 330–31; E. U. Leben, *Bernard Molitor (1755–1833). Leben und Werk eines Pariser Kunsttischlers* (University of Bonn, 1989); R. Haaff, *Louis-Philippe-Möbel. Bürgerliche Möbel des Historismus* (Stuttgart: Arnoldsche, 2004); J. Bahns, *Zwischen Biedermeier und Jugendstil. Möbel des Historismus* (Munich: Keyser, 1987); Forkel (Preface, n. 1); J. Krawczyk, *Meble jako przedmioty użytkowej i zabytki* ('Furniture as useful object and as art object') (Toruń: Uniwersytet M. Kopernik, 2006).

104 The habit of buying items individually came from America: Luthmer 1897, 138; cf. Siebel, 13.

105 *meubles de parade*: Blanc, 182; *Paradestellung*: Sonntag (Ch. II, n. 62), 18.

106 On the sideboard: G. T. Robinson, 'Our Household Furniture ... The Dining Room and its Furniture ... the Sideboard', *AJ* (1881), 89–92 and 153–56. In 1841 'sideboard' was seemingly a new term: Hunt (Ch. V, n. 42), 122; Ames, 49ff. Cf. 'Armoire', Viollet-le-Duc, 1–18; Frankel, *Herter* (Ch. II, n. 16); Talbert; Yapp, several illus.: *AJ* (1871), 22, 70; 'Dining room furniture', *FG*, 11 (1878), 283–84; Loftie, *Dining Room* (Ch. II, n. 75); Joy, 426–80. The fashion subsided quickly: 'buffet, made simple in design ...': Edis, 115; in the US, 'simple old dresser in place of the heavy and elaborate sideboard ... useless ... clumsy': 'The Decoration of our Houses V. The dining room', *AmA*, vol. 8, no. 1 (1883), 64–65.

107 On the sofa/settee: Himmelheber; cf. 'Dorsal' in Viollet-le-Duc, 96.

The all-wooden room

108 For 'fitments', see W. Morris's Red House, from 1859 onwards; Talbert; 'wall furniture' as a term owed to Eastlake: 'Furniture and decoration', *BN*, 22 Jan. 1869, 76–77; Godwin *Ar*, 20 Aug. 1870; 'fitments' [by Jackson & Graham]: 'Health Exhibition', *CM*, July 1884, 1–6 (3), and *CM* Aug 1884, 21–25 (22); '"fitments" introduced by Mr. Edis': Mrs Panton, 'Artistic Homes ...', *The Lady* [*Lady's World*], 1887, 412–13; Saint, 172ff..; Oakey (Ch. II, n. 82), 80; Long. See also the inglenook, e.g. p. 262.

109 Panelling or wainscoting, known elsewhere as *(Ver)täfelung*, *lambris(sage)* or *boiserie*. Early use: see Morley, 276–78; W. Papworth, 'An Attempt to Determine the Periods ... when Fir, Deal ... were introduced', *Papers Read at the Royal Institute of British Architects Session 1857–8* [London] 1858, 1–8. Cf. 'whole wainscoting not only gives warmth and protection from damp, but its rational explanation lies also in the intention of showing people who meet in a panelled room that this object has been accomplished': Chevreul, 259, also 154, 246; Loyer, 192f.

110 S. Giedion, *Spätbarocker und romantischer Klassizismus* (Munich: Bruckmann, 1922), 94.

111 Havard 1884, 50–51.

112 Thiollet: see caption p. 99.

113 'the whole room ...' ('das ganze Zimmer aus einem Gusse'): Falke 1862, 673. Cf. Luthmer 1884b, 16; Luthmer 1892, 70, 78; the 'Furniture' part of the 'Gesamtdekoration': *Illustrierte Schreinerzeitung*, vol. 2 (1884) (in 'Stimmen der Presse'); J. Lessing, 'Zimmertäfelungen', *IFz*, vol. 12 (1885), 65–66; Luthmer 1897, 132–33. See also folio volumes by R. Schumann, Kimbel, Hofmann, Schwenke, Schaupert (Ch. II, n. 87); also A. Huber, *Die Arbeiten des Bautischlers* (Berlin: Claesen, 1888–96); H. Issel, *Wandtäfelungen und Holzdecken* (Leipzig: Scholtze, n.d. [1889]); E. Oppler (ed. F. Schorbach), *Architektonische Entwürfe* (Halle: Knapp, 1884); A. Huber, *Allerlei Schreinerwerk* (Berlin: Claesen 1887–89). An early example of a wooden interior was at Villa Seebach, Dresden, by Hermann Nicolai; it contained wainscoting and furniture in oak, giving an impression of 'affluence' ('wohlhabend') and a 'feeling of great comfort' ('Gefühl grosser Behaglichkeit'): *ABZ*, vol. 9 (1844), 1010–13 and plates; cf. Geist, 471. See also G. T. Robinson, 'Our Household Furniture ... The Dining Room Wall', *AJ* (1881), 201–4; Muthesius, H., 95ff.

114 Luthmer claimed that there should be no curtains where the window jambs were integrated into the 'artful woodwork', which in the olden days would not have appeared naked: Luthmer 1884a, 159; Luthmer 1884b, 15.

115 'wainscoted walls ...': Bergau, 20. Cf. Viollet-le-Duc's articles 'Plafond', 'Menuiserie', in E. E. Viollet-le-Duc, *Dictionnaire raisonné de l'architecture française du XIe au XVIe siècle* (Paris: Morel, 1854–68), vol. 7, 203ff. and vol. 6, 357–59.

116 P. Nickl (ed.), *Parkett, Historische Holzfussböden* (Munich: Klinkhardt & Biermann, 1995); Thornton, 153. New machinery and imitations: Yapp, 2; Folnesics, 7; *Wiener Weltausstellung ... Katalog Ausstellung deutschen Reichs* (Berlin: Hofbuchdruckerei, 1873), 340; Edis, 40ff. Cf. wooden floors (i.e. wide boards): e.g. 'oak floors of the "good old times of England"': 'French Taste and English', *B*, 12 Sept. 1863, 649–50.

117 'Carpenters, Joiners and Cabinet Makers, feeling a desire to hold their pre-eminence, have solicited for works of superior character, both as regards elucidation of principles and ornamental embellishments': [Anon.], *Practical Carpentry, Joinery and Cabinetmaking* (London: Kelly, 1840), Preface. § 'not much sympathy ...': 'Working Drawings', *FG*, vol. 3, 3 April 1875, 431–33. § [J. W. Benn], 'Some Old English Fireplaces' ("Old London" Exhibition)', *CM*, Sept. 1885, 57–61 (57).

118 Cf.: 'coloured fittings ... connect the interior ... such as ceilings, walls and carpets harmonically ..., produced less by furniture than by the other technical arts, which thanks to the applied arts movement [*kunstgewerblichen Bestrebungen*] have developed very much more favourably than the techniques of furniture production [*Möbeltechnik*]': 'Farbige Bemalung der Möbel', *Der Dekorationsmaler*, no. 2, 15 Jan. 1888, 10.

Objects and their display

Products

119 On cheap pictures: Loudon, 352–53; not wanted or needed: B. Koehler, 'Erfindung des Boudoirs im 18. Jh. ...', *KAS*, vol. 55, 4 (2004), 227–36. Also sceptical were: Hay, 28; Dresser 1873, 100, 108; Cooper, H. J., 71; Haweis ('ugly gold frame'): 217; see also Day, 214–248; Bergau, 18. There was a strict distinction between a picture on a wall and an element of décor: the latter could not be 'the representation of an absent object but a beautiful object in itself': 'L'emploi des couleurs...', *L'Art Moderne* (Brussels), vol. 7, 7 Aug. 1887, 253–54.

120 See e.g. *Fleurs de Lyon 1807–1917* (exh. cat. Lyon: Musée des Beaux Arts, 1982); Beecher (Ch. II, n. 47); Gilberte, 'La Plante d'appartement: Son histoire ...', *RAD*, vol. 12 (1891–92), 170–79; Morris, 123–28. Cf. Lichtwark (Ch. II, n. 86).

121 On metal, see e.g. *Second Empire*, 158ff.; A. Jacquemart, *Histoire du mobilier* (much on metal) (Paris: Hachette, 1876) / *A History of Furniture* (London: Chapman & Hall, 1878); M. Koch, 'Bijoutier, joaillier, orfèvre ...', in Bayerisches Nationalmuseum, Munich, *Pariser Schmuck vom Zweiten Kaiserreich zur Belle Époque* (Munich, 1989), 11–35. In Paris, the production of bronzes in the 1850s involved 11,000 workers, and half was for export: Dr Huber, 'Die deutsche Renaissance und der Weltmarkt', *Deutsche Tischler Zeitung*, vol. 13, 6 Feb. 1886, 43–44; *Crystal Palace*; Yapp; cf. S. Blondel, *Grammaire de la curiosité: L'Art intime et le goût en France* (Paris: Marpon/Flammarion, 1884).

122 On electroplate: S. Bury, *Victorian Electroplate* (London: Hamlyn, 1971); Christofle (Ch. II, n. 13); cf. Eva Schmidt, *Der preussische Eisenkunstguss* (Berlin: Mann, 1981). See also *zincs d'art*, *Zinkguss* (above, nn. 4, 33); *Second Empire*, 156ff.; W. Walton (Introduction, n. 11), 143ff.; Lehnert.

123 Lehnert, 468.

124 'dignity of life ...' ('La dignité de la vie s'étend à un plus grand nombre'): Blanc, 336.

125 *Second Empire*, 157; *Christofle* (Ch. II, n. 13).

126 Blanc, 293; § 'glint': 'Some Oriental Brass Work. I', *MA* (1885), 56–58. § 'glaring ...' ('grelle Schein'): W. Lübke, *Bericht über die ... allgemeine Ausstellung zu Paris* (Stuttgart: Ebner / Seubert, 1867), 63.

127 Blanc, 250–77. Cf. e.g. P. Noever, *J. L. Lobmeyr. Tradition und Innovation. Gläser ...* (Munich: Prestel, 2006).

128 On ceramics, see e.g. H. J. McCormick and H. Ottomeyer, *Vasemania: Neoclassical Form and Ornament in Europe* (exh. cat. New York: Bard Graduate Center / New Haven and London: Yale University Press 2004); Blanc, 338–416. § 'blue and white': J. D. Crace, 'Household Taste', *B*, 4 Mar. 1882, 243–45 (245).

Meaning

129 Cf. 'furniture painted in white gloss decorated with gold, Chinese silk ... the fireplace white marble, decorated with large medallions of painted porcelain framed with mouldings of gold ... aimed at the German middle class' ('deutschen Mittelstand' [*sic*]): 'Zimmereinrichtungen', *Frauenzeitung für Hauswesen, weibliche Arbeiten und Moden,* year 1, no. 19, 1 Oct. 1852, 80.

130 In France, works of 'pure art' ('reine Kunst') fulfilled a decorative aim: Falke, *Dublin* (Ch. II, n. 97), 7; cf. Munich in Ch. V, p. 270. § 'le sentiment et la possession du beau': Blanc, 332; cf. Falke, 'art' (Ch. II, nn. 67, 68); Intr.

131 'rapport ...': Blanc, 135; cf. Havard 1884, 248; S. Melville (ed.), *The Lure of the Object* (New Haven and London: Yale University Press, 2005). § 'which favours ...' ('objets variés et nombreux ... qui favorisent la liberté de son esprit'): Blanc, 137. Objects in the drawing room help 'while away the listless hour': Parkes, 194. § 'The salon ...' ('Zwiegespräche ... künstlerisch durchgeführtes'), Bergau, 24–25. Cf.: 'a socialising influence in the household art ... that not only furnishes subjects for conservation but which inspires a certain social feeling': *American Crockery and Glass Journal*, 6 March 1879, 26, quoted in Blanchard, 270.

132 'une garniture de parade' (here made of glass): Blanc, 397.

133 'Trifles ...': Spofford, 65; 'lovely outline ...': Spofford, 224–25; 'they go very far ...': Spofford, 225; cf. 'Drawing Room Oddments', *CM*, Feb. 1889, 203–5. § 'The little nothings ...' ('les petits riens qui sont la joie des yeux et l'agrément de la maison'): de Noussanne (Ch. I, n. 2), 10. Cf. R. G. Saisselin, *Bricacabracomania: The Bourgeois and the Bibelot* (London: Thames & Hudson, 1990) / *Le Bourgeois et le Bibelot* (Paris: Albin Michel, 1984); M. Vernes, 'Divagation intérieure: Le décor fin de siècle', *MH*, no. 195, March 1995, 11–18; S. Stewart, *On Longing: Narratives of the Miniature, the Gigantic, the Souvenir, the Collection* (Durham, NC and London: Duke University Press, 1993).

134 *Nippes*: German, *c.* 1760, after the French *nippe*, meaning female dressing-up. *Nippsachen* appeared before mid-century: F. Kluge and A. Götze, *Etymologisches Wörterbuch* (Berlin: de Gruyter, 1951 edn); cf. Ch. II, n. 17.

135 'bric à brac ...': Major H. Byng Hall, *The Adventure of a Bric à Brac Hunter* (London: Thisley, 1868), 3.

136 Galanteriewaren: *Ausstellungs-Bericht* (2nd edn; 47).

137 On applied art theories of the 19th and 20th centuries, see M. O. Fernandez, *Ornament und Moderne* (Berlin: Reimer, 2003). An early observer of such fetishization was Dr W. Hamm, who claimed that more attention was given to the linen than to the children, and that the aim of existence was seen in the keeping of shiny crockery: *Ordnung und Schönheit am häuslichen Herd ...* (Jena: Costenoble, 1887), 172–73; cf. 'Furniture & Decoration', *BN*, 27 Feb. 1874, 223. See also Ames; Logan. On the wider context: M. Csikszentmihalyi, *The Meaning of Things: Domestic Symbol and the Self* (Cambridge University Press, 1981); T. Dant, *Material Culture and the Social World* (Buckingham: Open University Press, 1999), 40–59.

Mass display

138 See 'Tapissier' in *Grande Encyclopédie* (Introduction, n. 10).

139 On the interference of clients, see Ch. VI, 'Designer power'.

140 'hundreds ...' ('sogenante "Nippsachen"'): Schäffer &

Walcker (Ch. II, n. 94), 22.

141 On display: Morley, 325–26; Thornton, 74–75; Thornton, *Seventeenth Century* (above, n. 62), 248ff. § Nanking ware: E. B. Shuldham, 'Old Nanking Blue', *AJ* (1877), 302–4 (204).

142 Wainwright; see also the present book, pp. 186–87.

143 'an artist needs …' ('un artiste … a besoin d'être entouré des objets variés et nombreux, qui favorisent la liberté de son esprit et qui la provoquent par l'inattendu de leurs rapprochements, par l'étrangeté de leurs contrastes'): Blanc, 137. § On ateliers, see B. Langer, *Das Münchner Künstleratelier des Historismus* (Dachau: Bayerland, 1992); B. Schnabel, *Künstlerleben 1850–1910* (Luzern: Bucher, 1978); E. Mongi-Vollmer, *Das Atelier des Malers. Die Diskurse eines Raumes in der zweiten Hälfte des 19. Jh.* (Berlin: Lukas, 2004); G. Walkley, *Artists' Houses in London 1764–1914* (Aldershot: Scholar, 1994). For the US: *Art Journal* (New York edn), vol. 3 (1877); *DF*, vol. 8 (1886). For Paris: *L'Illustration Journal Universel*, Jan.–June 1886 (info. Louise Campbell).

144 'the right instinct …' ('Den richtigen Instinkt für den Zusammenhang der Erscheinungen'): Lichtwark (Ch. II, n. 86), 21. Cf. Schäffer & Walcker (Ch. II, n. 94), 146–48; F. Minkus, 'Atelierstil', *Id* (1895), 9–10.

145 'Ordentlich …': 'Wie die Frauen ihre Salons einrichten sollen' (taken 'from the French by Emile de Girardin)', *Frauenzeitung für Hauswesen, weibliche Arbeiten und Moden*, vol. 1, 15 March 1852, 27–28. § Bergau, 24.

146 G. Godwin, *Town Swamps and Social Bridges* (London: Routledge, 1859, repr. Leicester University Press, 1972), 18–19 with illus.; R. Edis, 'Internal Decoration', in Foster Murphy (Ch. II, n. 76), 300–72 (347); 'Garnitures de cheminée', *EID*, 474–75.

147 'the vitrine …': L. M., 'Zimmer-Einrichtung in englischem Geschmack', *Frauenzeitung* (above, n. 45), vol. 8, 15 Nov. 1859, 175.

148 On tables, etc.: Blanc, 164. Corner cabinets: Loudon 299, 301. 'To Talbert also belongs the honour of making china cabinets popular on the wall and floors of reception rooms': J. Benn, 'The Talbert Sketches', *CM*, Jan. 1883, 127. Overdoors: Long, 120. § 'corner potpourri': Church (Ch. II, n. 82), 14; cf. Joy, 412ff.; 'The Philosophy of Drawing Rooms', *ChM*, vol. 41, Jan.–June 1880, 312–26 (324–25); M. Graef, *Renaissance Geräte und Galanteriestücke* (Weimar: Voigt, 1888).

149 'for the purpose …': 'Some Fine Furniture', *B*, 29 March 1873, 240–41. § 'a large amount': Shoolbred (Ch. II, n. 99), prelim. remarks.

150 Spofford, 321.

151 Lamb, 'Norman Style' (Ch. III, n. 87), 337–38.

152 See S. Bellenger and F. Hamon (eds), *Félix Duban 1798–1870: Les couleurs de l'architecte* (Paris: Gallimard-Electa, 1996).

153 According to Havard, the assembly of vases, bowls, statuettes etc., always pleasant and picturesque, casts 'over the furnishings a living and brilliant note': Havard 1884, 201. 'In order to be logical, all decoration … either has to take as its point of departure fixed from décor … or it must result from mobile décor': Havard 1884, 247. § 'accidental …': Havard, *Décoration* (Ch. II, n. 85), 133.

154 'things … should find themselves *at home* and not … "placed"': Godwin 1877, v. § Wilde: quoted in 'The Establishment of a New York Decorator', *DF*, vol. 16 (1890), 7–9 (no source given). § 'picturesque' ('malerische'): Luthmer 1897, 50–51. § 'désordre': Havard 1884, 317, here restricted to 'appartements intimes'. Cf. 'L'apparence du beaux désordre qui est un effet d'art': E. Raymond, 'Ameublement', *La Mode Illustré*, vol. 17 (1876), 295, quoted in van Voorst tot Voorst, 31; J. B. Laurens, *Études théoriques et pratiques sur le beau pittoresque dans les arts du dessin* (Paris, 1856), 24–25, points to Joshua Reynolds (*Discours on Art* (no. 8, 1797). § 'people always go to the prettiest and brightest part of the room, by instinct': Haweis, 10.

155 knick-knacks: L. F. Day, 'How to Decorate a Room', *MA* (1881), 182–86 (184). § 'not infrequently …' ('nicht selten wird schon durch ein einziges solches Stück die harmonische Gesamtwirking eines Zimmers gestört'): Lütt (Ch. II, n. 118), 35–36. See also B. Bucher, 'Styl im Zimmer', *BfK* (1880), 1–4.

156 'a good arrangement …': Bergau, 23–24; see also Edis, 212–16. § 'little precious objects …' ('diese kleinen Prunkgreräthe sind Glanz-und Lichtpunkte des Zimmers'), Behr, *Dekoration* (Ch. II, n. 69) 31. § 'merciless …': R. M. Watson, *The Art of the Home* (London: Bell, 1897), 6. § 'china, glass': Cook, 105–6; cf. Bergau, 23; Luthmer 1897, 50–52.

157 For early critiques: Parkes, 194 (written in 1825); Cook, 98; see Grier, 65. Avoid 'sogenante ['so-called'] "Horreurs"': Lütt (Ch. II, n. 118), 42.

Upkeep

158 Cf. Corbin (Introduction, n. 17); M. Frey, *Der reinliche Bürger* (Göttingen: Vandenhoek und Rupprecht, 1997). This section only deals with the cleaning methods of the living rooms. Methods are held to have been 'uniform in Britain': C. Davidson, *A Woman's Work is Never Done: A History of Housework in the British Isles 1650–1950* (London: Chatto & Windus, 1982), 121. On chemicals, from laboriously mixed at home to ready-made: Davidson, 117ff. § All housework planned: see e.g. H. Davidis, *Die Jungfrau*, 2nd edn (Leipzig: Seemann, 1863). For home advice books in general, see Ch.II, n. 45.

159 On the rearrangement of cleaned furnishings, see Grier, Ch. 2.

160 P. Horn, *The Rise and Fall of the Victorian Servant* (Stroud: Sutton, 2004). § On routines, see e.g. Frau Erna Grauenhorst, *Katechismus für das feine Haus- und Stubenmädchen*, 1897/98 edn ('200,000 Exemplare') (Berlin: Selbstverlag); Celnart (Ch. II, n. 45), 161–72.

161 'the art of …' ('zartes Blau … Mull Vorhang … die Kunst der Wäscherin'): Luthmer 1884b, 10.

162 Rooms for best: Ebhardt claimed that one must have a room to protect the 'better pieces of furniture': Ebhardt (Introduction, n. 6), 7. § For the antimacassar ((Möbel)-Schoner or, in French, housse), see 'Protective Coverings' in *EID*, 1003–5.

163 For whiteness, absolute ('unbedingte') purity and simplicity, see J. W. von Goethe,'Versuch, die Elemente der Farbenlehre zu entdecken' [*c.* 1794], para. 6, first publ. in *Goethes Werke*, ed. S. Kalischer (Berlin: Hempel, n.d. [*c.* 1878]), vol. 35, 52. § 'cleanliness …', *Journal du Lycée des Arts*, 1795, quoted in Hoskins (above, n. 23), 57. Cf. 'pure, clean, strict order everywhere [leads to] the comfortable and agreeable': *Häusliche Glück* (above, n. 27), 28.

164 A. K., 'Praktische Erfahrung über [chemische] Reinigung feinerer Gewebe und Stoffe', *Deutsche Tapeten Zeitung*, vol. 5, no. 2, 10 Jan. 1887, 2; St George (Preface, n. 2), 8. Some fabrics were thought to be easier to clean: 'French Furniture of the Olden Times', *B*, 22 Aug. 1863, 593–96 (594). Fast colours were few in number: Hug, 28.

165 'It is the manner …' ('se révèle le génie da la femme dans ce veritable travail d'art'): Ris-Paquot, 335.

166 'methodical cleaning …' ('nettoyage méthodique et raisonné'): Ris-Paquot, 327. § Staffe (Ch. II, n. 121), 246. § Uneven floors required less cleaning …while 'polished floors [require] constant care': Oakey (Ch. II, n. 82), 74. § Walsh, 165.

167 As Calder notes, the user was advised to eliminate all signs of the hard work necessary to maintain cleanliness: Calder, 28. On the awkwardness of cleaning: M. J. Loftie, *Comfort in the Home* (London: Leadenhall Press, 1895), 80.

168 Pugin, for example, wrote of dust and vermin in curtains: A. W. N. Pugin, *The True Principles of Pointed or Christian Architecture* (London: Bohn, 1841), 25. § 'Who is …' ('Wer putzt hier Staub?'): Lichtwark (Ch. II, n. 86), 20. § Godwin *Ar*, 45–46.

Colour

Materials

169 Dresser 1873, 31.

170 Bristow 1996a and 1996b; Brönner 1978; F. Jaennicke, *Farbenharmonie mit besonderer Rücksicht auf gleichzeitigen Kontrast … Dekoration, Kunst, Kostüm und Toilette*, 3rd edn (Stuttgart, 1902); 'Farbe', in O. Schmitt (ed.), *Reallexikon zur deutschen Kunstgeschichte*, vol. 6 (Munich: Druckenmüller, 1973) and vol. 7 (Munich: Beck, 1981); J. Gage, *Colour and Culture: Practice and Meaning from Antiquity to Abstraction* (London: Thames & Hudson, 1993); J. Gage, *Colour and Meaning: Art, Science and Symbolism* (London: Thames & Hudson, 1999); F. Roy Osborne, *Books on Colour 1500–2000* (2,500 titles in English and other European languages) (n.p.: Universal Publishing, 2004).

171 Laxton's, 409, 414. § The cost of 1lb of red pigment was 5*s.* or 3*d.*: Laxton's, 414; Cf. Bristow 1996a, 98ff.; Bristow 1996b.

172 Bristow 1996a, 24.

173 F. Delamare and B. Guineau, *Colour: Making and Using Dyes and Pigments* (London: Thames & Hudson, 2000); 'Printed Textiles' in *EID*, 1002; S. Lowengard, 'Colour and colour making in the eighteenth century', in Berg and Clifford (Ch. II, n. 3), 103–19. Cf. 'Die Farben und ihre Bereitung', in F. Luckenbacher et al., *Buch der Erfindungen, Gewerbe und Industrien*, 7th edn (Leipzig: Spamer, 1877), vol. 4, 547–76 . § On dying textiles: D. Jenkins (ed.), *The Cambridge History of Western Textiles* (Cambridge University Press, 2003), vol. 2, 766; cf. A. Peez, 'Baumwolle und Baumwollewaren', *Ausstellungs-Bericht* (53), 23ff.

174 'Tar colours …' ('Theerfarben beherrschen …'): 'Färberei' in Meyer (Ch. II, n. 56), vol. 6, 1874, 525–30 (530); cf. Lehnert, 445–46, 485. § 'Ultramarin synthèse' in 1826; 'green arsenic' in 1830s; and mauve, the first coal-tar dye, in England in 1857.

175 Yapp, 65. § 'complete choice' for textiles: Falke 1883, 296. § 'purchased ready …': E. A. Davidson, *A Practical Manual of House Painting, Graining, Marbling and Sign-Writing* (London: Lockwood, 1875), ix, 41ff.

Early use

176 'Introduction', *AM*, vol. 1 (1834), 1–12 (7).

177 Ware (above, n. 1), 469.

178 Bristow 1996a, 158.

179 For France, see Pardailhé-Galabrun, 170.

180 On Adam, see Bristow 1996a, 99; Bristow 1996b, 144–45.

181 'distempered …': G. Freytag, *Erinnerungen aus meinem Leben* (Greiz, 1926), 64, quoted in Wiedemann (Ch.II, n. 45), 76. § 'the chief vehicle …': Thornton, 141; cf. Bristow 1996a, 205ff. Cf. 'Colour is the luxury of the common home, without cost, yet priceless as sunshine and air': 'A Study for a Country House', *AA*, vol. 5, no. 9 (1881), 76–80 (77); 'pure, forceful, saturated colours': G. Wagner, *Die Ästhetik der Baukunst* (Dresden: Arnoldsche, 1838), 10ff., quoted in Brönner 1978, 58. § 'colour is the main …': Hug, 7; cf. Guichard; E .L. R., 'Vom ornamentalen Farbenkontur', *DB*, 18 Oct. 1867, 407–8; 'On the Use and Abuse of Ornament and Colour', *BN*, 17 June 1870, 456–57, *BN*, 24 June 1870, 468; Spofford 235. § G. Aitchison, 'On Colour as Applied to Architecture', *Papers Read: Royal Institute of British Architects, Session 1857–8* (London, 1858), 47–60 (47). § 'carpets …': Walsh, 179.

182 Ottillinger, '"Kaiser Salon"' (Ch. II, n. 1), 143; cf. 'uni', below, n. 208.

183 'Royal red': de' Marinis (above, n. 50), 55. § On crimson: Smith 1808, xii. § On *Königsblau*: Brönner 1978, 60.

184 On Windsor, see Roberts, *King's Pleasure* (Ch. II, n. 43). A ladies' journal of 1852 mentions three guest rooms, in blue, green and 'lila' (pale violet): 'Zimmereinrichtungen', *Frauenzeitung für Hauswesen gewerbliche Arbeiten und Moden*, no. 19, 1 Oct. 1852, 80; cf. Guichardet, *Balzac* (above, n. 78), 291; John Soane's alterative schemes for the dining room of Taymouth Castle, Perthshire, 1808; Bristow 1996a, 194ff.

185 For draperies, see above, nn. 46, 47. Cf. 'Curtains', *EID*, 332–36; Davidson, *Mary Ellen Best* (Ch. II, n. 122).

186 Ribbons: Witt-Dörring, 379.

187 'colours as …': Smith, xii; cf. Muthesius, H., 71. According to Folnesics, there were no rules in early 19th-century Vienna: Folnesics, 3. § Hope, 15, on his own interiors. § S. Wettstein and R. Fontana, 'Farbkonzepte? Beispiele farbiger Innenräume in vier Bürgerhäusern des 19. Jh.', *KAS*, vol. 55, 2 (2004), 34–40.

188 For the *Prachtsaal*, see Hering (above, n. 15), 266; on white: Bristow 1996a, 144ff.; Bristow 1996b, 142ff. The kind of statement that 'Form provides significance and meaning [*Bedeutsamkeit, Gehalt*]' while colour provides 'expression of feelings [*Empfindung*]' – Hessemer, 32 – could still mean that line or form was valued above colour. One should also remember Goethe, for whom lively colours were for 'wild nations, uneducated people, children': Goethe, para. 135. Later conceptions of white (i.e. off-white) as 'vornhem' (smart, elegant) and 'Gebrochenheit' (muted) suggest that strong multicolouring was still considered vulgar: M. Schasler, *Die Farbenwelt* (Berlin: Habel, 1883), 9–10. § T. H. Vanherman, *Every Man His Own House-Painter and Colour-Man* (London: Setchell, 1827), argued that light rooms seemed larger: quoted in Bristow 1996a, 200. See also Ch. IV, 'From colour to tone'.

189 'French white': Bristow 1996a, 144ff.

190 'plain white …' ('Ein schlichtes weisses Leichentuch … kalte Nüchternheit'), Issel, *Wandtäfelung* (Ch. II, n. 87), 5. George Gilbert Scott considered it 'quaker-like': *Remarks on Secular and Domestic Architecture* (London: Murray, 1857), 73.

History and science

191 For the 'new' polychromy, defended by Klenze, Cockerell, Hittorf, Schinkel, Semper and others, see D. van Zanten, *The*

Architectural Polychromy of the 1830s (New York: Garland, 1977); Werner, 158. See also C. J. Walker, 'British Architectural Polychromy 1840–1870' (diss., University of London, 2002).

192 Pompeii a popular model for the 'middle classes' (*c.* 1766): R. Alex, 'F. W. von Erdmannsdorff', in *F. W. von Erdmannsdorff* (exh. cat. Schloss Wörlitz, 1986), 6, quoted in Hölz, 140. § 'no lack of unity' ('Einheit … mit *einer* Farbe rein angestrichen'): J. W. von Goethe, 'Zahns Ornamente und Gemälde', review, 1830, of Zahn, *Pompeji* (above, n. 18), taken here from *Goethes Werke* (Berlin: Hempel, n.d. [*c.* 1880]), vol. 28, 604–18 (610). See also Wiegmann (above, n. 17).

193 Stained glass: see the present book, p. 184. For strong colours in earlier neo-Gothic interiors, see Fonthill Abbey; Bristow 1996a, 185; Bellenger and Hamon, *Duban* (above, n. 152).

194 J. Morley, *The Making of the Brighton Pavilion* (London: Sotheby's/Philip Wilson, 1984); cf. Villa Berg, Stuttgart (1850s; by C. L. Zanth).

195 On colour science, see J. Gage (above, n. 170).

196 Goethe, paras 801f.; cf. para. 763 etc.; Conway (Ch. II, n. 77), 154–59. On Goethe's own house in Weimar, *c.* 1782: A. Beyer, 'Weimarer Kulissen', in Hölz, 19–49. Brief comments by on complementarity: para. 808, paras 806, 813.

197 G. Field, *Chromatography, or an Essay on the Analogy and Harmony of Colours* (London: Newman, 1817).

198 Michel-Eugène Chevreul, *De la loi du contraste simultané des couleurs et l'assortiment des objets colorés … ses applications* (Paris: Pitois Levrault, 1839, and many later edns). Further books by Chevreul and their translations: *Die Farbenharmonie in ihrer Anwendung …* (Stuttgart: Neff, 1840); *Théorie des effets optiques que présentent les étoffes de soie* (Paris: Firmin Didot, 1846); *The Principles of Harmony and Contrast of Colours and their Application to the Arts*, trans. C. Martel (London: Longman, 1854; used here); *The Laws of Colour and their Application to the Arts*, trans. J. Spanton (London: Routledge, 1857, shortened); *Des Couleurs et de leurs applications à l'aide des cercles chronomatiques* (Paris: Baillière 1864); *Harmony of Contrast of Colours and their Application to the Arts*, after the 1854 English edition, ed. F. Birren, incomplete (New York: Reinhold 1967). See also E. Guichard, *La Grammaire de la couleur: 765 planches*, 3 vols. (Paris, 1882). § 'apparent brightness …': Chevreul, 37–38.

199 D. R. Hay, *On the Laws of Harmonious Colouring Adapted to House Painting* (Edinburgh: Lizards, 1828), 2nd edn 1829, 3rd edn 1836, 4th edn 1838, 5th edn 1844, 6th edn 1847; the title keeps changing somewhat, here mostly quoted from the 5th edn (see Bibliography). See also D. R. Hay ('Decorative Painter to her Majesty, Edinburgh'), *The Principles of Beauty in Colouring* (Edinburgh: Blackie, 1845); D. R. Hay, *Die Gesetze der Farbenharmonie, vorzüglich für die Zwecke der Haus-, Stuben- und Dekorationsmalerei* (see *Schauplatz*, Ch. II, n. 7), vol. 172, 1848; D. R. Hay, *Die Lehre von der Harmonie der Farben*, 3rd edn (*Schauplatz*, Ch. II, n. 7), 1881. Hay's main stipulations can be found at the following places: 1828 edn, 18ff.; 1836 edn, 23ff.; 1844 edn, 28ff. See also I. Gow, *The Scottish Interior: Georgian and Victorian Décor* (Edinburgh University Press, 1992).

200 Loudon, 1014–16; Downing, 400ff.; *Home* 1853, 88–89; 'Dr. [*sic*] Hay …', in Facey (above, n. 15), 29. Cf. Merrifield in *Crystal Palace*.

201 O. Jones obituary, *Ar*, vol. 11 (1874), 236ff.; O. Jones, *The Grammar of Ornament* (London: Day, 1856; many reprints) / *Grammatik der Ornamente* (Leipzig: Dürr, 1865); Jones, influenced by Chevreul and Field, stipulated that colours should be kep flat and separate, but he wrote little on interiors as such: see n. 251 below. § For more on colour and décor: A. Leimgrub, 'Die Farbgebung in ihrer praktischen Anwendung auf die Gewerbe', *Gb*, vols. 1, 2 (1863), etc.; G. Schreiber, *Das technische Zeichnen, praktische Anleitung für Architekten, Maler, Techniker und Bauhandwerker*, Part 3: *Die Farbenlehre* (Leipzig: Spamer, 1868); J. Thiele, *Die Farbenlehre als Hilfswissenschaft für Künstler und Industrielle …* (Berlin: Nicolaische, 1873); W. von Bezold, *Die Farbenlehre im Hinblick auf Kunst und Kunstgewerbe* (Braunschweig, 1874); W. von Bezold, *The Theory of Colour in its Relation to Art Industry* (Boston, MA: Prang, 1876); W. Lübke, 'Zur künstlerischen Farbenlehre', *Gb*, vol. 5 (1867) 1–4; E. Brücke, *Physiologie der Farben für die Zwecke der Kunstgewerbe*, 2nd edn (Leipzig: Hirzel, 1887); Schasler (above, n. 188). Probably the most fruitful for interiors are A. Scheffers (Ch. II, n. 60) and Ogden N. Rood, *Modern Chromatics with Application to Art and Industry* (London: Kegan Paul, 1879).

202 'une science …': Guichard, 26. § 'the linking …': G. Schreiber (above, n. 201), 121.

203 'insecurely groping …' ('Unsicher tastender Stümper'): Hirth, 33. § H. von Helmholtz, *Handbuch der physiologischen Optik* (Leipzig, 1867). § Hirth, 33; on 'spatial effects', 57. Following von Helmholtz, Hirth wrote of 'pure physiological satisfactions … the eye does not demand anything else, but rests, enjoying itself': Hirth, 43.

204 'fashionable colours …' ('sog. Modefarben'): Goethe, para. 845; cf. Hay, 35ff.; 'Instead of pure colour, a so-called fashionable colour': Luthmer 1884a, 20.

205 'That colour could be seen as capable of transposition between paint and fabric in this way argues again that these were seen as related within an abstract concept rather than, as in previous years, a quality related to cost and technological means': Bristow 1996a, 188ff., 194. In other words, from early to mid-century onwards, colour choice could overrule the choice of materials.

206 Quoted in 'The Colours and Forms of Room Decorations', *B*, 23 Aug. 1845, 406–7.

207 On the order of choosing colours: Hug, 10; Hay, 31 (1836 edn, 26). When it came to coordinating the colours, the curtains should be same colour as the seats, and their trimmings ('bordures') the colour of the hangings. If the hangings were neutral, the curtains should be the same colour as the seats or the colour of the hangings: see F. Goupil, *Manuel général de l'ornement décoratif* (Paris: Le Bailly, n. d., *c.* 1862), 44.

208 See Poe. § For 'uni', see Walsh, 183; Hering (above, n. 15), 262–63. Against 'uni': see Ottomeyer, 114. Luthmer claimed that, although some liked it, its effect was monotonous: Luthmer 1884a, 2–3; cf. 'monotonie désespérante': Havard 1884, 246 etc.

209 'yellow …': Goethe, para. 810, cf. para. 845. 'Complementaries' was a relatively new term, used by Count Rumford in 1794: Gage, *Colour and Culture* (above, n. 170), 172. See also Soane's colour at Taymout (above, n. 184). For Goethe *avant la lettre*, see Vanherman (above, n. 188), 41–43. § Some suggested contrasts: light salmon and cold green; light plum and white straw; delicate pink and light green; light cinnamon brown and light grey; dark red and warm green: Whittock (Ch. II, n. 125), 132–33. Also blue and white-yellow; green and blue-white; white and any colour, etc.: W. Butcher, *Smith's Art of House-Painting improved by Wm. Butcher* (London: R. Holmes Laurie, 1821), 20; cf. Hay, 20, 38ff. By the 1880s, we read that it was not necessary that 'the painter devotes a great deal of time to an attempt to match the colour[s] in … corresponding tints … The true artists instead of matching … would at once ascertain the most appropriate corresponding colour …, producing the harmony needed': Facey, *Elementary Decoration* (above, n. 15), 2.

210 'predominance': Hay, 28, 29 (1836 edn, 23; 1828 edn, 18). 'parts of equal strength': Hay, 30 (1828 edn, 21; 1836 edn, 24).

211 'With walnut …': 'Interior Decoration: The Drawing room', *BN*, 12 Feb. 1869, 143; cf. J. Gregory Crace, 'On Colour', *B*, 30 Nov. 1867, 874–75; *B*, 7 Dec. 1867, 888–89.

212 Gage, *Colour and Culture* (above, n. 170), 175.

Eclipse

213 'colour scales' ('Unsere abstrakten Farbscalen'), 'undefinable' ('undefinierbare'), 'deeply harmonic …' ('tiefe harmonische Naturfarbe'): Semper, vol. 1, 195, 191, 46; cf. Eastlake, 129–30.

214 Ruskin, quoted in Haweis, 237–38 (cf. J. Ruskin, *The Two Paths*, 1859). § J. Gregory Crace, 'On Colour', *B*, 30 Nov. 1867, 874–75.

215 'infinite realm …' ('Das unendliche Reich von Tinten und Tönen … Gefühl'): Falke, *Ästhetik* (above, n. 51), 167, 169; cf. the very negative review of the 1881 German edn of Hay (above, n. 199), probably by Falke, in *BfK*, vol. 10 (1881), 12. § According to Havard, practice was much less rigorous than the rules: 'couleur' in Havard *Dict.*, vol. 1, 1005. There is very little in Lucae, Bergau, Cook, Blanc: 83–84, 226–27; Edis is indifferent: 205, 210; Morris on colour in the room reads awkwardly: Morris, 138–144; see also Harvey and Press (Ch. II, n. 77), 98, 216. Luthmer mentions the 'physics of colour', which we want to deal with as little as possible: Luthmer 1884a, 17; cf. 'more decisive colours with natural materials' ('entschiedenere Farben an natürlichen Materialen'): Luthmer 1884b, 11–12.

216 Luthmer 1884b, 10; Mrs Haweis gave mixed advice: 11–13, 23, 215ff., 365ff.

217 'colours of the house painter': Hay, 25 (1836 edn, 20); 'degree of warmth': Hay, 30 (1836 edn, 25).

218 Church (Ch. II, n. 82), 47–48. § 'restrained tones …' ('Gedämpfte Töne'): Luthmer 1884b, 12; Brönner 1978, 58–60. See also Hirth below, p. 274; Daly; Niederhöfer (Ch. II, n. 87). § 'excremental' ('kotig'): Goethe, para. 771.

219 'chaude et profonde … rouge … granat', contrasting with 'nuance fine et froide, vert clair, bleu …': Havard 1884, 348. § 'luminous colour': 'French Home Life. No. iii: Furniture', *Blackwood's Edinburgh Magazine* vol. 111, Jan. 1872, 30–46 (35). In the mid-1880s even 'third-rate furnishing' in London abandoned bright colours: [J. W. Benn], 'At the Royal Academy', *CM*, June 1887, 308–14 (308).

220 'untried eye': Conway (Ch. II, n. 77), 170. Cf. 'To guard against gold, white, and the three primaries': E. W. Godwin, 'The Sister Arts in Relation to Architecture', *B*, 29 March 1862, 200–1. § 'shrill white' ('tache criarde des blancs'): Cardon (Ch. II, 85), 47. § Luthmer objected to those 'anaemic furnishings' ('bleichsüchtigen Einrichtungen') of the 1830s and 1840s: Luthmer 1884b, 10. § 'the paler tints': 'French Home Life' (above, n. 219), 31.

221 'against white …': Luthmer 1884, 28.

222 On white becoming important for the 'Queen Anne Leute ['people']': Dohme, 27. Cf. Morris: 'sanded floor, whitewashed wall': 'The Prospect of Architecture in Civilisation', in Morris, 214. For white walls and white frieze in Berlin, cf. the architect Hans Grisebach; in Munich, see Seidl and Hirth (Ch. V, n. 234).

223 'Chocoladensauce': A. Lichtwark, 'Teppichausstellung Berlin Gewerbemuseum', *Gegenwart*, vol. 26 (1884), 30–31. § Aniline dyes: 'in spite of their brightness they are raw and cold': Lucy Crane, *Art and the Formation of Taste* (London: Macmillan, 1882), 112. § Dohme, 27. § 'today one aims …' ('heutige Bestrebungen der Farbfreudigkeit'): Werle, *Bürgerheim* (Ch. II, n. 87), text for pl. 3.

224 'When it comes to …' ('Quant à la couleur des draperies et des sièges, elle dépend à vous … Madame'): de Noussanne (Ch. I, n. 2), 155.

225 'natural colours' ('Naturfarben'): Semper (above, n. 213). § Lübke, 'Farbenlehre' (above, n. 201), 4; Jones and Dresser called the Oriental colour effects 'bloom'. § 'simple …' ('einfache Farben'): Lessing, *Wien* (Ch. II, n. 23), 33.

Form

226 'Unity …': Percier & Fontaine, quoted in Havard 1884, 305–6; cf. Hope; Smith; Hay; Downing, 377; Thornton, 89; 'J.-F. Blondel' in *EID*, 151.

227 C. H. Terne, *Form und Farbe und ihre hohe Bedeutung für die Industrie* (Chemnitz: Gewerbeblatt Sachsen, 1839), 14, here on the effect of furniture when seen alongside clothes. See also Léon Feuchère, *L'Art industriel: Recueil de dispositions et de décorations intérieures* (Paris: Goupil, n.d. [1842–49]); 'Le principe fondamental est l'accord et l'uniformité': Balzac, 'Vie élégante' (Ch. II, n. 3), 332.

228 'the great luxury …' ('le grand luxe d'appartement c'est l'ensemble'): C. Aubert, 'Moeurs Parisiennes', *L'Illustration*, 17–24 Jan. 1851, 112. § 'in order to …' ('le detail le plus infime jusqu'à l'objet formant le clé de l'oeuvre soient conçus dans la même série de pensées'): Bracquemont (Ch. II, n. 17), 200. § Luthmer 1892, 95–97; cf. '" in keeping" … a term readily understood though not easily defined': Walsh, 212.

229 E. Harris, *The Genius of Robert Adam* (New Haven and London: Yale University Press, 2001); Muthesius, H., 41ff.

230 '… by the higher class of architects, nor has it formed the subject of any graphic work': J. Britton, *The Union of Architecture, Sculpture, and Painting …* (London, 1827), quoted in Cornforth, 18; cf. Garnier-Audiger, 92. § 'taken for granted' ('heute eine Selbstverständlichkeit'): Schwab (above, n. 98), 59.

231 Thornton, *Seventeenth Century* (above, n. 62), 6; cf. D. Church, 'Curtains', in *EID*, 332–33. § Havard 1884, 8; cf. 'une progression logique': Havard 1884, 240.

232 [J. C. Loudon], 'On those Principles of Composition in Architecture …', *AM*, vol. 1 (1834), 249–55 (249); 'guides in the general composition of lines and forms, whether of nature or of art': [J. C. Loudon], 'Introduction', *AM*, vol. 1 (1834), 9.

233 On 'form': Terne (above, n. 227); 'the principle[s] of volume, form, stability, colour, variety … general harmony': Chevreul, 382ff. § 'noticed by our …' ('Dem kundigen Auge bemerkbar … wie schon gesagt, nicht historischer Stil'): Falke 1871, 181. Cf. 'form and colour': Godwin 1877, 'Foreword'. See also the new content-less 'form' of Wölfflinian art history. For the widest remit: D. Burdorf, *Poetik der Form* (Stuttgart: Metzler, 2001).

234 'a painting presents an illustration of reality, decoration a play of forms and colours' ('Spiel von Formen und Farben'):

Hessemer, 25. § 'artistic harmony …' ('zwei Momenten … Farbe'): Bergau, 9. § 'unity in …' ('die Einheit in Form und Farbe'): Sonntag (Ch. II, n. 62), 18.

235 'A room is like a picture; it must be composed with equal skill and forethought, but unlike a picture, the arrangement must revolve around to a point which is never stationary, always in motion': Haweis, 10. § 'harmonisches Gesamtbild': Fischbach, *Ausstattung* (Ch. II, n. 69), 3.

236 On symmetry, see Folnesics; also, as a rather late advocate, H. Fawcett: *Art in Everything* (London: Holsten, 1882), 55.

237 'the delimited …' ('der begrenzte geschlossene Raum'): Falke 1871, 171, 199ff; cf. Falke 1862, 664.

238 'anything that hinder': Luthmer 1884b, 14. § 'quiet …': Bergau, 13. Cf. Oakey (Ch. II, n. 82), 73–74.

239 Ceilings painted like blue sky: Thornton, 150–51; Bristow 1996b, 141; Hay, 65.

240 Scott (above, n. 190), 60, 82–84; cf. Bergau, 20; J. Hugerford Pollen, 'Ceilings and Walls', *MA* (1886), 228–32; Haweis, 229–34. § Falke 1862, 669; Falke 1871, 236ff.. § Dresser 1873, 75–83 (75); cf. *Beauty*, 134. § On heaviness, see Semper, vol. 1, 61; on its psychological effect: Havard *Dict.*, 303.

Line and surface

241 Downing, 406.

242 For the skirting-board (*Scheuerleiste*, *antébois*, *plinthe*), see Muthesius, H., 98. The dado gives 'apparent stability to the wall by making its lower portion dark': Dresser 1873, 85. On friezes, see R. H. Pratt, 'The Parlor', *DF*, vol. 4, June 1884, 86; Falke 1862, 672–73. § On early panels: Morley, 255–56; Smith, 1808; Werner, 100, 121.

243 The height of the dado in 1835 was between 2 ft 3 in. and 2 ft 9 in. (69–84 cm): Kent *AM*, 229; cf. Loudon, 1017, 1095; Smith, 27; Bristow 1996a, 212. § 'dado movement': 'English Progress reviewed by a Foreign Critic', *The Artist and Journal of Home Culture*, vol. 1, Oct. 1882, 302–4 (302). See also Eastlake, 52, 123; 'Interior Decoration', *BN*, 8 Jan. 1869, 39; *BN*, 22 Jan. 1869, 76–77. 'in the dado style': Garrett, 56; cf. Muthesius, H., 98.

244 Morris, 1883, quoted in Harvey and Press (Ch. II, 77), 81; Morris on horizontals: L. F. Day, 'A Kensington Interior', *AJ*, 1893, 139–44, (141); cf. J. D. Crace, '"Household Taste"', *B*, 4 March 1882, 243–45. § Cook, *Walls* (Ch. II, n. 83), 30. Cf. 'sometimes a mere line introduced here and there to define the construction': Eastlake, 130, here on High Victorian Gothic architecture, with its strong horizontal bands in stone or brick ('constructional polychromy').§ Dado out of fashion: Dohme, 56.

245 'simple lines' ('lignes simples, des contours pures, des formes correctes remplacèrent le mixtiligne, le contourné et l'irregulier'): Percier & Fontaine, 4; cf. Bisky, 109. Strongly linear illustrations: J. Britton, *Graphic Illustrations … of Toddington, Gloucestershire* (London: author, 1840); C. A. Chenavard, *Recueil de dessins de tapis, tapisseries et d'autres objets (*Paris: Leconte, 1833, 1836, 1845). § According to Hope, 'The mode … best calculated to render … the chastity and the play of their contour, is in mere outlines': Hope, 12.

246 J. Benn, 'Old English Woodwork', *CM*, July 1888, 11.

247 Col. Edis, 'Internal Decoration', in Foster Murphy (Ch. II, n. 76), pp. 300–72 (336). § 'Ligne envelopante': Ruprich-Robert (Ch. II, n. 38), 270. § 'Linienführung': Bucher, 'Styl' (above, n. 155), 1; cf. Luthmer 1884a, 247ff. § 'lineal harmony': [J. W. Benn], 'The Morrisean Furnishings … Manchester', *CM*, Jan. 1885, 121–25 (124).

248 Haweis, 149, cf. p. 203. Many earlier critics considered curved lines 'more graceful': e.g. *Home* 1853, 109–10; Poe, 499. § 'lovely lines': Whistler to F. R. Leyland in 1876, quoted in Bendix (above, n. 15), 130; cf. 'Working Drawings', *FG*, vol. 3, March–April 1875, 431–32.

249 E. H. Van Brunt, *Greek Lines and other Architectural Essays* (Boston/Cambridge, MA: Riverside Press, 1893), 7. Cf. 'lignes architecturales': E. Guichard, 'Classe 14 Meubles du Luxe', in M. Chevalier (ed.), *Rapports du Jury International, Exposition Universelle Paris 1867*, vol. 3 (Paris: Imprimerie Administrative / Dupont, 1868), 5–20 (6); Havard 1884, 276ff.; cf. also 'Une décoration est toujours une combinaison de lignes, de couleurs': Ruprich-Robert, 'Décorateurs' (Ch. II, n. 38), 269. For others, edgings and trimmings ('Borten') mark out the surfaces' proportions ('Flächenverhältnisse'): Fischbach, *Ausstattung* (Ch. II, n. 69), 20

250 'the entirely flat …' ('Die Hauptерfordernis ist die ganz plane Darstellung der Fläche'): Anon., 'Überblick … bildenden Künste … München 1834', *Kunstblatt* [part of *Mogenblatt für gebildete Stände*, Stuttgart], Year 28 (1834), no. 102, 405–7.

251 On 'South Kensington flatness': B. W. Keyser, 'Ornament as Idea: Indirect Imitation of Nature in the Design Reform Movement', *JDH*, vol. 11, no. 2 (1998), 127–41. Cf. J. G. Crace, 'On the Decoration of Some of the Buildings at Munich', *Proceedings of the Royal Institute of British Architects* (1850–51), 7 (Crace was in Munich in 1843); Jones, *Grammar* (above, n. 201); G. A. Davies, *Y Llaw Broffwydol: Owen Jones, Pensaer 1809–1874* (Talybont: Ceredigion Ylolfa, 2004, not seen); C. A. Hrvol Flores, *Owen Jones: Design, Ornament, Architecture, and Theory* (New York: Rizzoli, 2006); 'Treasure Houses of Art I' (Alfred Morrison's London interiors by O. Jones), *MA* (1879), 140–44; cf. Conway (Ch. II, n. 77), 154–59. § Flat décor: Crace (Ch. II, 21); Haweis, 222ff. In the US: Gardner (Ch. II, n. 83); Mayhew; Lynn, *Wallpaper* (above, n. 23), 405. In Austria: Ottillinger, 80–90.

252 'all decorative work': Dresser 1874, 6, 22.

253 'walls form …' ('Wände nur einen Teil bilden, nur den Hintergrund der Bewohner ausmachen, und für sich keine Selbsständigkeit haben'): Falke 1862, 672. § 'simple patterns' ('ziemlich einfach'): *Fachmännische Berichte* (Ch. II, n. 103); Bergau, 15.

254 'tapezierte …' ('Zimmer, nichts weiter als eine austapezierte Kiste'): Fischbach, *Ausstattung* (Ch. II, 69), 20; cf. the boxy room 'on the floor of which is placed furniture and whose walls are hung with pictures': Werle, *Bürgerheim* (Ch. II, n. 87), text for pl. 12. Stockbauer wrote of paper being glued on like the insides of a cigar-box, and of the lonely painted-on ceiling rosette: Ch. II, n. 69, 16.

Picturesqueness

255 See generally: D. Marshall, *The Frame of Art: Fictions of Aesthetic Experience* (Baltimore, MA: Johns Hopkins University Press, 2005); J. Macarthur, *The Picturesque* (London: Routledge, 2007); 'Malerisch/Pittoresk' in Barck, vol. 3 (Ch. I, n. 1); Parks (Ch. I, n. 6). § 'Picturesque': used in Eastlake 116, 121, 177; Garrett, 43, 46. § Havard 1884, 296; cf. Laurens, *Pittoresque* (above, n. 154). § L.Trzeschtik, 'Das malerische in der Architektur', *ABZ* (1877), 81–85; cf. the view that picturesque is popular (and thus likely to be of no academic value): T. 'Salzburger' (Ch. V, n. 56). § Holland: C. van Eck (Ch. V, n. 93).

Mass

256 On mass, see Szambien (Ch. I, n. 1). § 'The harmony …' ('l'harmonie de l'ensemble … d'où émanent les grandes masses qui donnent et décident le charactère'): Le Camus, 105. § Reynolds: see above, n. 154; walls: see the present book, p. 181.

257 Falke 1862, 680. § Spofford, 217.

258 'Plastisch': see e.g. Stockbauer (Ch. II, n. 69), 29.

259 'Space': H. F. Mallgrave and E. Ikonomou, *Empathy, Form, Space: Problems in German Esthetics 1873–1893* (Santa Monica, CA: Getty, 1994); S. Muthesius, 'Przestrzeń Neobarokowa i Przestrzeń Historików Sztuki' ['New German concepts of space before 1900'], in *Kwartalnik Architektury i Urbanistyki* (1991), vol. 36, 23–44; cf. Hirth, occasionally: 'edelstes Raumgefühl' (of the Renaissance), *ZBKM* (1879), 36. Lucae's conception of 'space' mainly means 'Form, Licht, Farbe, Masstab'. Cf. Godwin (Ch. II, n. 73); Sidlauskas, 17.

260 Height (here a simplified paraphrase): Havard 1884, 347. § On size, see 'elbow room': Kerr, 74; 'spacious effect': Moyr Smith (Ch. II, n. 76), 84. § Loudon (in his *AM)*, Kent *AM*, 349; cf. Downing, 396; 'Salon 6 m long, 4.5 m deep, 3.8 m high': Luthmer 1884b, 6; 'The most universally recognised rule for determining the height of a room is the sum of half the width and the square root of the length': [Anon.; E. Gardner?], 'Hints on Domestic Decoration', *Harper's*, vol. 68, March 1884, 579–89 (579).

261 'zierlich': Lessing, *Paris* (Ch. II, n. 23), 146–47.

262 See the chapter 'Masstab' ('scale') in Luthmer 1897, 31–39.

263 Godwin *Ar*, 112; see also Muthesius, H., 90.

264 'one does not …' ('überrascht und erfreut jedesmal ein Anblick, der uns auf Augenblicke entgegentritt'): *Deutsches Bauhandbuch* (Introduction, n. 21), 106. § 'We much prefer …': Cooper, H. J., 74. § 'create as animated a picture …' ('ein möglichst bewegtes Bild zu schaffen') 'revived by a warmth that does [one] good' ('eine wohltuende Wärme empfängt'): Hug, 18.

265 F. Brochier in *AR*, *Id*; W. Felix (Vienna) in Hirth, 183, 184; Hermann Kirchmayr (Munich/Innsbruck) in *AR*; also Otto Fritzsche in *Id* 1890.

266 'vistas …' ('freie Durchblicke … nicht … Zellen für grundverschieden fühlende Einsiedler'): Werle, *vornehme Haus* (Ch. II, n. 87), Foreword; cf. G. G. Ungewitter: below, Ch. IV, n. 22.

267 Halls: see the present book, pp. 253ff.; cf. Ebe & Benda [architects], 'Das altdeutsche Dreifenster-Wohnhaus … Diele': *DB*, 2 Oct. 1880, 425–26; *DB*, 9 Oct. 1880, 436–38, 446.

268 Spofford, 217; cf. Blanchard, 109. § 'Symmetry the arch enemy …': O. Mothes, 'Das Bespannen von Tapetenthüren', *Deutsche Tapezierer Zeitung*, 10 Jan. 1887, 3. § 'poetry …': Church (Ch. II, n. 82), 14, 15; cf. Wheeler's view that 'Corners … have great capabilities': Ch. II, n. 83, 185.

269 E.g. when one steps into a bow window: Luthmer 1884a, 7.

270 Bay windows: see the present book, pp. 171ff. § Long, 170–75.

271 *EID*, 1146–47; J. W. Adams, *Decorative Folding Screens in the West from 1600 to the Present Day* (London: Thames & Hudson, 1982); Joy, 406–7; H. Jordan, 'Europäische Paravents. Beiträge zu ihrer Entstehung und Geschichte' (diss., University of Cologne, 1989); Blanc, 233. They 'suggest a change of scene or purpose': 'The Decoration of Our Homes iv', *AA*, vol. 8, Jan. 1883, 64–65.

272 'standardized furnishing' ('schablonenhafte Ausstattung'): C. Graef, 'Kunstgewerbliches', *IFz*, 29 Jan. 1883, 48–49.

273 'La décoration comme la nature a horreur du vide': Havard 1884, 262. The *horror vacui* 'stares us in the face' ('starrt uns an') and demands the livening up of the surface: Falke 1862 667.

274 'must be furnished …' ('salons … trop meublés … l'apparance de beau désordre qui est un effet de l'art'): E. Raymond, 'Ameublement', *La Mode Illustrée*, vol. 17 (1876), 295, quoted in van Voorst tot Voorst, 31.

275 Spofford, 217, 224, 231 etc. § 'principles of organic …' ('Grundsätze organischen Bildens'): Scheffers (Ch. II, n. 60), 261 (see also 1st edn of 1868). § 'variety …' ('La varieté dans l'unité'): Havard 1884, 246. Cf. 'the salt of all artistic compositions is the opposition [*Gegensatz*] and its resolution': Luthmer 1884a, 3.

The new 'refinement'

276 O. Wilde, 'The House Beautiful' (Dublin lecture), *FG*, 8 Dec. 1883, 397–99. See also, on E. W. Godwin's furniture: 'good proportion and refined simplicity … erring sometimes in … over-elegance': 'Edward W. Godwin' (obituary), *BrA*, 15 Oct. 1886, 347–48; cf. Grier 154ff. Cf. the earlier mention of 'Lighter elegancies which modern refinement has introduced': Loudon, 909.

277 'constructiveness': E. Balfour, 'Sheraton's Furniture', *MA* (1883), 190–96 (193, 194). Cf. the ephemeral-looking illustrations in J. A. Heaton, *Furniture and Decoration in England during the 18th Century* (London: Bumpus, 1882); E. Harris, 'Adams in the Family: Wright and Mansfield …', *FH* (1996), 141–57; J. H. V. Dyer archive (furniture and interior designers, *c.* 1822–1904) now at the V&A, London. See also anti-picturesque voices, e.g. Balfour, 'Sheraton's …' (above), 190; but also the ridiculing of thin furniture in Haweis, 54; cf. Cooper, N.; J. Mordaunt Crook, *The Rise of the Nouveau Riches: Style and Status in Victorian and Edwardian Architecture* (London: Murray, 1999).

278 Tiffany: 'A Trial Balance of Decoration', *Harper's*, vol. 64, April 1882, 734–40; Margaret Hunt, 'The Progress of American Decorative Art', *AJ* (1884), 25–28, 69–73; [Anon.], *The Art of Louis Tiffany* (Garden City, NY: 1914); *Beauty*, 120ff.; Blanchard, 59, 98, 112–13; A. Duncan, *Louis Comfort Tiffany* (Woodbridge: Antique Collectors' Club, 2004); M. A. Johnson, *Louis Comfort Tiffany* (London: Scala, 2005); Frankel, *Herter* (Ch. II, n. 16); A. Peck and C. Irish, *Candace Wheeler: Art and Enterprise in American Design 1875–1900* (New York: Metropolitan Museum / New Haven and London: Yale University Press, 2000); see also Ch.V, n. 178.

279 See U. Bode (ed.), *Paris Belle Époque 1880–1914* (exh. cat. Essen: Villa Hügel / Recklinghausen: Bongers, 1994); Silverman.

280 On 'Englishness' in general: S. Muthesius; G. C. Krause, *Möbel im modernen englischen Style* (Berlin: Claesen, 1887–88). See also C. Graff, 'Der Anglo Japanische Stil des 19. Jahrhunderts', *Österreichische Monatsschrift für den Orient*, 15 Feb. 1885, 39–41; *Id*; Luthmer 1892, 95 (1888 edn, 103). § On neo-Baroque and neo-Rococo, for big interiors ('grosse Innenräume'): F. Ewerbeck, 'Niederländische Städtebilder', *DB*, (1887), 517–23 (517); cf. V. Feldhahn, 'Das Palais Bourgeois in Wien', *Österreichische Zeitschrift für Kunst und Denkmalpflege*, vol. 56, no. 2 (2003), 285–96.

281 Morris, 214.

IV ATMOSPHERE

Enter the imagined user

1 'House' versus 'home': see e.g. H. Jones,'Homes of the Town Poor', *ChM*, vol. 42, Jul.–Dec. 1880, 452–62.

2 'le lecteur dit peut-être: … laissez aux menusiers le soin de corroyer, d'assembler leurs bois … La félicité des humains ne tient pas à si peu! … Cela contribue au confort de l'âme d'être entouré des objets bien conçus': Blanc, 185.

3 On the outside world: 'The struggle between outdoor temptations and home joys … one of the great social difficulties of our time': 'French Home Life' (Ch. III, n. 219), 34. See also J. Habermas, *The Structural Transformation of the Public Sphere* (Cambridge: Polity, 1989; orig. German edn 1965). Cf. 'A castle against the demon of revolution': Revd Baldwin Brown, 'The Domestic Character of Englishmen', *Evangelical Magazine*, vol. 10, new series (1868), 583–87. § 'One of the most …' ('brennendsten socialwissenschaftlichen Fragen … Das Wohnhaus, die Wohnung … Ausdruck … Einfluss'): C. T. Richter, 'Das bürgerliche Wohnhaus', *Ausstellungs-Bericht* (19) 1.

4 'the nineteenth century …' ('Das neunzehnte Jahrhundert war wie kein anderes wohnsüchtig'): Benjamin, para. I 4, 4, p. 292. § On the zenith of home idea, 1850s–60s: Thornton 216. Design for the home flourished in the 1870s and 1880s: see St George (Preface, n. 2), 85; cf. 'American residentiality' in T. J. Schlereth, *American Home Life 1880–1930* (Knoxville: University of Tennessee Press, 1991), 2; Rybczynski; Reulecke.

5 On the rise of illustrations, see Weismann 241ff.; B .E. Maidment, *Reading Popular Prints 1790–1870* (Manchester University Press, 1996). See also Ch. II, n. 134.

Privacy

6 *Gl* 1864 lists four kinds of comfort: (i) 'The small or domestic comfort', for man and wife in the lower middle-class household; parsimony and cleanliness reign. (ii) 'learned comfort': the book-filled, untidy study of the male. (iii) 'cosy comfort': the home of the whimsical old lady, crowded with mementoes. (iv) 'elegant comfort': luxury and décor, but seemingly not addressing the practical use of the room at all.

7 'a way of …' ('l'outillage de la vie privée'): E. Bonnafé, *Le Meuble en France au XVIe siècle* (Paris: Librarie de l'Art, 1887), 19.

8 P. Aries, *L'Enfant et la vie familiale sous l'ancien régime* (Paris: Plon, 1960), 450. On the processes of separating out 'private' activities and necessities within the house, see N. Elias, *The Civilizing Process* (Oxford: Blackwell, 2000; orig. German edn Basel: 1939). Cf. Kerr; Davidoff & Hall, 156. § 'rooms for individual …': Richter (above, n. 3), 11.

9 H. Jones (above, n. 1), 455 .

Gendered rooms: the boudoir and the study

10 'By the end …': Edwards, 97; cf. J. Kinchin, 'Interiors: Nineteenth-Century Essays on the "Masculine" and the "Feminine" Room', in P. Kirkham (ed.), *The Gendered Object* (Manchester University Press, 1996), 12–29.

11 Havard *Dict.*, vol. 1, 362–69; Vicomtesse Nacla, *Le Boudoir: Conseils d'élégance* (Paris: Flammarion, n.d. [*c.* 1890]); J. von Falke, 'Das Boudoir', in *Aus alter und neuer Zeit. Neue Studien* … (Berlin: Verein deutsche Literatur, 1895), 181–91; *EID*, 166–68; E. Lilly, 'The Name of the Boudoir', *Journal of the Society of Architectural Historians* [US], vol. 53, no. 2 (1994), 193–98; B. Koehler, 'Die Erfindung des Boudoirs im 18. Jahrhundert', *KAS*, vol. 55, no. 4 (2004), 227–36; P. Prange, *Das Paradies im Boudoir. Glanz und Elend der erotischen Libertinage* (Marburg: Hitzeroth, 1990); Pardailhé-Galabrun; Eleb & Blanchard, 58, 184–185, 236ff., 261ff., 284; Siebel 93ff.; A. K. Rossberg, 'Frauenzimmer. Tradition des Boudoirs im 20 Jh.' (diss., University of Vienna, 1994, not seen). See also C. de Noëlle Guibert, *Portrait de Sarah Bernhardt* (Paris: Bibliothèque Nationale, 2000).

12 'le luxe, la molesse et le goût … mystérieux': Le Camus, 116.

13 'Poesie des Boudoirs … ein traulicher Winkel … kleines Nestchen': Mothes, 16–18.

14 See Kerr, 114–15; Barker, *Bedroom* (Ch. II, n. 75). There is very little here on intimacy and secrecy; see Haweis, 269–70.

15 'One gets away …' ('s'éloigner de tout son domestique'): Le Camus, 82, 161. § 'study': in French, it was known as the *étude* or *cabinet Monsieur*, and in German *Studierzimmer* or *Herrenzimmer*. § On untidiness: *Gl* 1864; Blanc, 137. § On 19th-century masculinity and design: M. Girouard, *The Return to Camelot:Chivalry and the English Gentleman* (New Haven and London: Yale University Press, 1981); Davidson (Ch. III, n. 158), 181, 188; Siebel, 97; and, earlier, Kent *AM*, 404–7. § 'library solemn and grave': Hay, 32–34 (1836 edn, 27); Bristow 1996a, 203. Images frequently showed the sober rooms of important male occupants, e.g. Kaiser Franz I in Vienna, painted by S. Decker, in his 'Arbeitszimmer', 1826, ill. in Ottillinger). Cf. 'le cabinet du maître … renferme un certain je ne sais quoi qui y règne qui est facile de reconnaître': Bassanville (Ch. II, n. 85), 66; see also below, n. 19.

16 Mothes, 29; cf. Luthmer 1897, 220ff. Mothes lists only two rooms for women: the boudoir and the *Damenzimmer.*

Idylls unlimited

17 A real boudoir, 'as a place for a woman's purely spiritual life' ('als Stätte für ein rein seelisches Frauenleben'), only really functions when material means are present in unlimited quantities: Mothes, 17.

18 For solitude, see J. G. Zimmermann, *Über die Einsamkeit. Auszüge* … (Leipzig, 1784–85; repr. Zurich: Tanner & Staehelin, 1982), 82. 'Einsamkeit' here includes domesticity ('Häuslichkeit').

19 On St Jerome, see Rybczynski, Ch. 2. Cf. also the designer's cell in A. W. Pugin, *Contrasts* … (1836; reprints).

20 See R. Wedewer and J. C. Jensen (eds), *Die Idylle. Eine Bildform im Wandel zwischen Hoffnung und Wirklichkeit 1750–1930* (Cologne: DuMont, 1986); I. Feuerlicht, 'Analyse des Idyllischen', *Psychoanalytische Bewegung*, vol. 5 (1933), 167–86. Cf. also the Zurich poet and artist Salomon Gessner, e.g his *Idyllen* (Leipzig, 1760); Köhler (above, n. 11).

21 See early Gothic authors such as Anne Radcliffe, Horace Walpole, etc.. M. Lévy, *Le Roman 'Gothique' anglais 1764–1824* (Toulouse, 1968); P. Morrison, 'Enclosed in Openness: Northhanger Abbey and the Domestic Carceral', *Texas Studies in Literature and Language*, vol. 33, no. 1 (1991), 1–23; 'The Gothic is the motor that truly drives the action': A Milbank, 'The Victorian Gothic in English Novels and Stories', in E. Hogle (ed.), *The Cambridge Companion to Gothic Fiction* (Cambridge University Press, 2002), 156. A. Taubenböck, *Die binäre Raumstruktur der Gothic Novel, 18.–20. Jh.* (Munich: Fink, 2002).

22 'mixture …' ('Vermischung von Madgalene und Pompadour'): F. T. Fischer, *Kritische Gänge*, (Tübingen, 1844), vol. 1, 187–88, quoted in J. Imorde, 'Zur Säkularisierung religiöser Empfindsamkeit', *KAS*, vol. 55, no. 4 (2004), 237–43 (241).

23 For 'Kämmerlein', see Imorde (above, n. 22); [ed. L. Grodecki], *Le Gothique retrouvé avant Viollet-le-Duc* (exh. cat. Paris: Hotel de Sully, 1979–80); E. Sainty (ed.), *Romance and Chivalry: History and Literature Reflected in Early 19th-Century French Painting* (exh. cat. New York: Matthiesen Gallery, 1996–97).

24 F. H. Lehr, *Die Blütezeit Romantischer Bildkunst. Franz Pforr* (Marburg University, 1924); K. Kaiser (ed.), *Klassizismus und Romantik in Deutschland … Sammlung Georg Schäfer, Schweinfurt* (exh. cat. Nuremberg: Germanisches Nationalmuseum, 1966), 85–87; S. Fastert, *Die Entdeckung des Mittelalters. Geschichtsrezeption in der nazarenischen Malerei des 19. Jh.* (Berlin: Deutscher Kunstverlag, 2000).

25 'Happiness …' ('In der Stille wohnt das Glück'): H. Davidis, *Die Jungfrau* (Bielefeld: Velhagen & Klasing, 1857), 203. On advice books, see Ch. II, n. 45.

26 See Falke, *Die ritterliche Gesellschaft* (Ch. I, n. 10); cf. Viollet-le-Duc.

27 J. H. Campe, for instance, referred to the spouse and mother as the 'wise directress of the inner household' ('weise Vorsteherin des inneren Hauswesens'): *Väterlicher Rath für meine Tochter* … (Braunschweig, 1789), 14ff., quoted in K. Schlegel-Matthies, *Im Haus und am Herd. Studien zur Geschichte des Alltags* (Stuttgart: Steiner, 1995), 24. Cf. 'combine the beautiful, the mental and the useful into a harmonious whole' ('das Notwendige mit dem Schönen, das Geistige mit dem Materiellen zu einem harmonischen Ganzen zu verbinden'): L. B., *Die Frauen und ihr Beruf. Ein Buch der weiblichen Erziehung* (Frankfurt am Main, 1856), Preface; G. Haentzschel, *Bildung und Kultur bürgerlicher Frauen 1850–1918* ((Tübingen: Niemeyer, 1986), 352; E. Spickernagel, 'Die Macht des Innenraumes. Verhältnis … Frauerolle Biedermeierzeit', *Kritische Berichte*, vol. 13, no. 3 (1985); 'La charité, l'ordre … l'élégance, le savoir faire': Bassanville (Ch. II, n. 85), 2. For a Fourrierist counter-emphasis on the wider social group, see A. Fremy, *Les Moeurs de notre temps* (Paris: Librarie Nouvelle, 1861); Coventry Patmore, *The Angel in the House* (London: Parker, 1854); Davidoff & Hall; Calder, 115; G. Wright, *Moralism and the Model Home: Domestic Architecture and the Cultural Conflict in Chicago 1873–1912* (University of Chicago Press, 1980). For a broader discussion, see 'The Production of Women, Real and Imaginary', in G. Fraisse and M. Perrot (eds), *A History of Women in the West*, vol. 4 (Cambridge, MA: Belknap/Harvard University Press, 1993) 121ff., 185ff.

Domesticity

Literature and illustration

28 D. I. Kertzer and M. Barbagli (eds), *The History of the European Family*, vol. 2: *Family Life in the Long Nineteenth Century 1789–1913* (New Haven and London: Yale University Press, 2002); M. Perrot, *From the Fire of the Revolution to the Great War*, vol. 4 of P. Aries and G. Duby (eds), *A History of Private Life* (Cambridge, MA: Belknap/Harvard University Press, 1987–94); A. Adams, *Architecture in the Family Way. Doctors, Houses and Women 1870–1900* (Montreal: McGill-Queen's University Press, 1996); Davidoff & Hall. For smaller tracts, see e.g. [Anon.], *Homes: Homely and Happy* (London: The Religious Tract Society, 1874); Eleb & Blanchard; Eleb with Debarre (Intr., n. 8); M. Eleb-Vidal and A. Debarre-Blanchard (eds), *La Maison: Espaces et intimités* (conference in Paris, 1975); P. G. F. Le Play, *La Réforme sociale en France* (Paris: Plon, 1864); F. le Play, *L'Organisation de la famille* (Paris, 1871). See also 'Familie', in O. Brunner et al. (eds), *Geschichtliche Grundbegriffe*, vol. 2 (Stuttgart: Klett, 1975), 253–301 (285–89); T. G. von Hippel, *Über die Ehe* (Berlin: Voss 1774, repr. Stuttgart: Deutsche Verlagsanstalt, 1972); K. P. Moritz, 'Häusliche Glückseligkeit', in *Abhandlungen* (1785–93), in K. P. Moritz, *Schriften zur Ästhetik und Poetik* (Tübingen: Niemeyer, 1962), 33–35; A. Freybe, *Das deutsche Haus und seine Sitte* (Gütersloh: Bertelsmann, 1892); K. Dorenwell, 1885, 1893: see the present book, p. 32; Reulecke; A. Linke, *Sprachkultur im Bürgertum … Mentalitätsgeschichte des 19. Jh.* (Stuttgart: Metzler, 1996). Philosophers and social and political scientists argued about the emotional and erotic ties behind poetic images of married life (underlined by the Romantics) as opposed to the material ties and legal restrictions of the martital contract.

29 On children in the home, see e.g. F. Stamm, 'Der Pavillion des kleinen Kindes', *Ausstellungs-Bericht* (1); Davidoff & Hall 343ff.; *Vater Mutter Kind* (exh. cat. Munich: Stadtmuseum, 1987–88). For England as a model: Muthesius, H., 234; below, n. 64.

30 On the aged, see T. Küpper, *Das inszenierte Alter. Seniorität als literarisches Programm 1750–1850* (Würzburg: Königshausens, 2004).

31 'Der Einzelne, die Lust des Genusses seiner Einzelheit suchend, findet sie in der Familie': G. W. F. Hegel, *Phänomenologie des Geistes* (1807), Chapter VI: 'Der Geist', Section A (Frankfurt am Main: Suhrkamp, 1970), 339.

32 Goethe recommended avoiding 'das gemeine Wirkliche' ('common reality') – i.e. the ordinary domestic room – on stage. Quoted in A. Bosselt, 'Das Zimmer auf der Bühne. Die Gestaltung des Innenraumes von der Kulissenbühne der klassischen Zeit bis zum Naturalismus' (diss., Kiel University, 1927), 25.

33 'The definition of living space continues to be of more importance than its detail'; and most of the earlier Gothic novels contain much description of landscape but little of interiors: Tristram, 12. Cf. S. Watkins, *Jane Austen's Town and Country Style* (London: Thames & Hudson, 1990).

34 A. Hauffen, *Das deutsche Haus in der Poesie*, Sammlung gemeinnütziger Vorträge, no. 163 (Prague: Deutscher Verein zur Verbreitung gemeinnütziger Künste, 1892).

35 See L. Hautecoeur, *Les Peintres de la vie familiale* (Paris: Éditions Galerie Charpentier, 1945); A. Lorenz, *Das deutsche Familienbild in der Malerei des 19. Jahrhunderts* (Darmstadt: Wissenschaftliche Buchgesellschaft, 1985); P. Pacey, *Family Art* (Cambridge: Polity, 1989). § D. Chodowiecki, *Kupfersammlung zu J. B. Basedows Elementarwerk / Recueil d'estampes relatives au manuel élémentaire* (Berlin/Dessau, 1774; repr. as *J. B. Basedows Elementarwerk*, ed. T. Fritsch (Leipzig: Wiegandt, 1909). See also Chodowiecki in Hippel (above, n. 28); W. Geismeier, *Daniel Chodowiecki* (Leipzig: Seemann, 1993); M. Ehler, *D. N. Chodowiecki: Le petit maître als grosser Illustrator* (Berlin: Lukas, 2003).

36 For 'chronicle' pictures, see Ch. II, n. 122.

37 See R. Rand, *Intimate Encounters: Love and Domesticity in Eighteenth-Century France* (Hood Museum of Art, Dartmouth College, NH / Princeton University Press, 1997); D. de

Chapeaurouge, 'Das Milieu als Porträt', *Wallraff-Richartz Jahrbuch*, vol. 22 (1960), 137–69.
38 'complete happiness' ('das Vollglück der Beschränkung'): Jean Paul [Johann Paul Friedrich Richter], *Vorschule der Ästhetik* (1804), in *Jean Pauls Werke* (Leipzig/Wien: Bibliographisches Institut, *c*. 1905, vol. 4), para. 73.
39 F. Armstrong. *Dickens and the Concept of Home* (Ann Arbor: University of Michigan, 1990). On Dickens's sentiment-laden but modest establishments: Calder, 15; Tristram, 213ff.. See also R. L. Pattern, *George Cruikshank's Life, Times and Art*, 2 vols. (London: Lutterworth, 1992); C. Walters, *Commodity Culture in Dickens's 'Household Words': The Social Life of Goods* (Aldershot: Ashgate, 2008).
40 W. Stubbe (ed.), *Das Ludwig Richter Album: Sämtliche Holzschnitte*, 2 vols. (Munich: Rogner & Bernhard, 1971); H. Damisch, *Ludwig Richter 1803–1884* (Berlin: Mann, 2003); G. Spitzer and U. Bischoff (eds), *Ludwig Richter* (exh. cat. Staatliche Kunstsammlungen Dresden, 2003); J. Beavington Atkinson, 'L. Richter', *AJ* (1885), 173–76.
41 'German' ('Deutsch und einfach ['modest'], sinnig ['apt'], wahr ['true']'): C. Gurlitt, *Die deutsche Kunst seit 1800* (Berlin: Bondi, 1924), 127. § 'depths …' ('die Tiefe des Gemüts, Innigkeit und Wahrheit der Empfindungen'): *Deutsches Museum – Zeitschrift für Literatur, Kunst und öffentliches Leben*, vol. 12, Jan.–June 1862, 834–35. Cf. 'Verinnerlichung ['interiorization'] des deutschen Familienlebens': Oppermann, 'Ludwig Richter', *Daheim*, vol. 5 (1868–69), 166–69; 'harmlos sinnige Humor': G. Treu, *Zum Gedächtnis L. Richters* (Dresden: Zahn & Jaensch, 1884), 14; H. Kg.,'Ludwig Richter', *GI* (1862), 116–18. § 'Poetic beauties' ('poetische Schönheiten'): L. Richter, *Lebenserinnerungen eines deutschen Malers* (Leipzig: Diederichs, 1944), 443. § 'Richter's spitzes': J. Erler, *Ludwig Richter der Maler des deutschen Hauses* (Leipzig: Sigismund & Volkening, 1898), 101. § On wood engraving, see Richter, *Lebenserinnerungen* (above), 397ff.
42 On the vignette, see W. Busch, *Die notwendige Arabeske. Wirklichkeitsaneignung und Stilisierung in der deutschen Kunst des 19. Jh.* (Berlin: Mann, 1985).
43 'like a case' ('die Wohnung als Futteral'): Benjamin, para. I 4, 4, p. 292.
44 'kleinste Hütte': Erler (above, n. 41), 85.
45 'city poet …': [Anon.], 'English Rural Poetry', *ChM*, vol. 25, Jan.–June 1872, 164–76 (164).
46 On genre painting and the realistic idyll, see Wedewer (above, n. 20), 21; M. Cowling, *Victorian Figurative Painting: Domestic Life and the Contemporary Social Scene* (London: Papadakis, 2000); G. P. Weisberg, *Redefining Genre: French and American Painting 1850–1900* (Washington, D.C.: Trust Museum, 1995); B. Gaethgens (ed.), *Genremalerei* (Darmstadt: Wissenschaftliche Buchgesellschaft, 2003).
47 'unity …' ('Einheit der Stimmung … gewisser geschichtlicher Faden'): Julian Schmidt, *Geschichte der deutschen Literatur seit Lessings Tod*, 4th edn (Leipzig, 1858), vol. 3, 372, quoted in E. Seybold, *Das Genrebild in der deutschen Literatur* (Stuttgart: Kohlhammer, 1967), 192.
48 'advance …' ('Beschreibungsempirismus'): F. Sengle, *Biedermeierzeit, Deutsche Literatur … 1815–1848*, vol. 1 (Stuttgart: Metzler, 1971), 1008.
49 'those people …' ('comparses un peu incolorés'): Guichardet (Ch. III, n. 78), 296, cf. 300, 314.
50 On the stage: Bosselt (above, n. 32); U. Harten, *Die Bühnenentwürfe* (Rave, *Schinkelwerk* [Ch. III, n. 35]), vol. 17 (Munich/Berlin: Deutscher Kunstverlag, 2000); J. Zukowsky (ed.), *Karl Friedrich Schinkel: The Drama of Architecture* (exh. cat. Art Institute of Chicago / Tübingen: Wasmuth, 1994); B. Daniels, *Le Décor de théâtre à l'époque romantique* (Paris: Bibliothèque Nationale, 2003).
51 'A series of livened-up pictures' ('belebten Bildern') by 'Maler Schmid in Rom' [not traced]: Mothes, 8.
52 See K. Belgum, *Interior Meaning: Design of the Bourgeois Home in the Realist Novel* [on Germany] (New York: Lang, 1991); for Zola, see Marcus; Auslander 270ff.
53 'the ordinary …' ('das Gewöhnlichste mit dem Zauberschein der Poesie zu umleuchten'): Hauffen (above, n. 34), 19.

Family rooms

54 'la maison, le vêtement de la famille': C. Daly, *L'Architecture privée aux XIXème siècle sous Napoléon III*, vol. 1 (Paris: Marcel, 1864), 10.
55 Brönner 1994, 37.
56 For 'living room' and 'sitting room', see Kerr, 99–103. Living room: see R. N. Shaw in Bedford Park, late 1870s: Saint, 203ff.; see also Day, 203, 204. § *petit salon*, often assuming the roles of the former boudoir or the *cabinet*: de Noussanne (Ch. I, n. 2), 149. Cf. also the separate 'family wing' in some large country houses: Girouard 1979.
57 'for the daily …' ('Hausgenossen … den besten Platz im Hause … dem Familienleben seine alte Innigkeit bewahren … schönen und bequemen Raum'): Luthmer 1892, 84; cf. Stiegel, 571. See also Geul; Geist; Reulecke, 354–57. Mothes's 'Wohnzimmer' appears inferior to his *Salon*, but he quotes Riehl: see following note.
58 See 'Das ganze Haus' in Riehl, 142–62. Cf. Richter's frontispiece to W. H. Riehl, *Hausmusik* (Stuttgart: Cotta, 1855). See also W. H. Riehl, *Die bürgerliche Gesellschaft*, ed. P. Steinbach (Berlin: Ullstein, 1970); W. H. Riehl, *The Natural History of the German People* trans. (somewhat freely) and ed. D. J. Diephouse (Lampeter: Edwin Mellen, 1990), 259–354.
59 'The family house …' ('Das Familienhaus und die echte Sitte des Hauses bedingen sich gegenseitig'): Riehl, 245. On the main rooms: Riehl, 223. On the *Salon* versus the *Familienzimmer*: Riehl, 217–18. Not the English hall: W. H. Riehl, *Die Familie*, 9th edn (Stuttgart: Cotta, 1882), 250. On the hearth ('häusliche Herd'): Riehl, 204. 'image of German unity' ('Bild der deutschen Einheit'): Riehl, 219–220. 'the idyll' ('Das Idyll vom deutsche Hause'): Riehl, vii. 'The real …' ('Die echte bonne société ist das zum Freundeskreis erweiterte Haus'): Riehl, *Die Familie* (above), 250, also quoted in Luthmer 1892, 94 (1888 edn, 103).
60 [Anon.], 'German domestic architecture', *B*, 17 Sept. 1853, 598 ('from *German Quarterly*'); [Anon.: C. Daly], 'De l'architecture civile moderne', *RGA* (1854), 323–31 ('from *Revue Trimestrielle Allemande*'). Cf. 'Maison', in Viollet-le-Duc, *Dictionnaire raisonné de l'architecture* (Ch. III, 115), vol. 6, 272.
61 Luthmer saw English room use as part of English nature ('englisches Wesen'), intended as a compromise between the luxury and formality ('Förmlichkeit') of society and the informal comfort of intimate domesticity ('Häuslichkeit'): Luthmer 1892, 95 (1888 edn, 103).
62 'pattern of use …' ('Benutzungsprogram'): Luthmer 1897, 216. According to Geul, the *Wohnzimmer* was as a rule used by the woman of the house and by friends in the evening; in smaller dwellings it also served as the dining room: Geul 1868, 5 (1885 edn, 7). See also Brönner 1994, 55–56.
63 'simple and rough' ('einfach und derb'): Muthesius, H., 230.
64 Girouard 1977, 139ff.; P. Dewan, *The House as Setting: Symbol and Structural Motif in Children's Literature* (Lewiston, NY: Mellen Press, 2004); Colin White, *The World of the Nursery* (London: Herbert Press, 1984); K. Calvert, 'Children in the House, 1890–1930', in T. J. Schlereth (ed.), *American Home Life 1880–1930* (Knoxville: University of Tennessee Press, 1991), 75–93. Illustrations of children's rooms are apparently rare before *c*. 1890: see Mothes, 'Kinderschlafzimmer', *Illustrierte Schreinerzeitung*, vol.1, no. 5 (1883), 9–10. See also K. Doderer and H. Müller, *Das Bilderbuch* (Weinheim/Basel: Beltz, 1973).

Poeticization through design

Comfort

65 'objective architectural …' ('architektonischen objektiven Eindruck … subjektive Empfindung'): Lucae, 295. He writes also of the 'scale of experience that space can elicit in us' ('die Scala von Emfindungen die der Raum in uns hervorbingen kann').
66 'splendid company …' ('für eine glänzende Gesellschaft … strahlender Räume', 'modern und elegant', 'ein behaglich wohliges Nest … warm still gemütlich'): Falke 1862, 664–65; see also Lucae, 293. For the room's varied uses – talking, listening, reading, etc. – see Perrot, *Private Life* (above, n. 28), vol. 4, 536–37.
67 'fixed carpet, tiling, soft and warm underfoot, avoiding the noise of footsteps' ('tapis et carrelages inaltérables, doux et chaux aux pieds, empêchant le bruit des pas'): Maincent (Ch. II, n. 23), pl. 1; 'silent door spring': advertisement in *Laxton's*, xv. § 'happy …' ('glückliche, vornehme Ruhe'), here in a Rococo room: F. Luthmer, 'Die Möbel- und Zimmereinrichtungen', in P. von Salvisberg (ed.), *Chronik der deutsch-nationalen Kunstgewerbe Ausstellung München* (Munich: Monatshefte, 1888), 198–205 (204).
68 '*Gemütlichkeit* or splendour' ('Gemüthlichkeit oder Glanz'): Falke 1871, 170. All practical matters are carefully excluded from his book, although he frequently mentions the lack of comfort in the Middle Ages.
69 *GI* 1864.
70 See M. Billinge, 'A Time and Place for Everything: An Essay on Re-creation and the Victorians', *Journal of Historical Geography*, vol. 22, no. 5 (1996), 443–59.
71 Hegel: see above, n. 31.
72 'culte du moi': Silverman, 82ff.; Eleb & Blanchard; Marcus, 161ff.; in fiction, see e.g. J.-K. Huysmans, *A Rebours* (Paris, 1884). According to Blanc, 85, a certain luxury has a moral aim, inspiring 'l'amour du chez soi' in everybody.
73 M. du Seigneur, 'L'art d'être artiste chez soi', *La Construction Moderne*, 5 Feb. 1887, 197–99; 19. Feb. 1887, 221–23 (198).
74 'fleeting moments …' ('Moments fugitifs, sans doute … mais de ces minutes se compose le menu de la vie; ces moments sont les trois quarts de l'existence': Blanc, 230. Cf. Silverman, 102ff., on J. M. Charcot's psychological theories of interiority. There are mild echoes in Luthmer 1892, 67. See also Blanchard, 121, 136.
75 Unconsciouly effects ('unbewusst'): Luthmer 1897, 44; see also Reulecke, 183; Logan, 96–97; A. Vidler, *The Architecture of the Uncanny* (Cambridge, MA: MIT Press, 1992).

'Gemütlichkeit' and 'Stimmung'

76 'home': see G. T. Robinson, 'Our Household Furniture' [introduction to series], *AJ* (1881), 21–26 (22); J. Rykwert, 'House and Home' [on etymology], *Social Research*, vol. 58, no. 1 (1991), 51–61.
77 'old Saxon': A. C. Varney, *Our Homes and their Adornments* (Detroit: Chilton, 1883), v. § *Das Heim*: W. Kuhberg, *Verschollenes Sprachgut*, Frankfurter Quellen … zur germanischen und romanischen Philologie, vol. 4 (Hildesheim: Gerstenberg, 1973), 50.
78 'homely' in its original sense: see 'homely: adv. einfach … schlicht, hässlich, bäuerisch' ('simple, ugly, peasanty'), in Flügel–Schmidt–Tanger, *Dictionary of the English and German Languages* (London: Asher & Co., 1896), 331. *Heimlich*, the German version of 'homely', mutated into 'secretive', while *heimisch* refers to the region where one 'belongs'.
79 There was no German word for 'interior', 'Interieur' being used instead.
80 'Die Gemüthlichkeit', in Stockbauer (Ch. II, n. 69), 2.
81 On the word 'home' in France, borrowed from the English in 1816, see Auslander, 221; Marcus, 136ff. In 1887, Bonnafé claimed that the French loved 'le home' more than the English, even though the word was theirs: Bonnafé (above, n. 7), 19. Cf. 'foyer', which usually means the fireplace but was also extended to the (smaller) home as a whole: Cardon (Ch. II, n. 85).
82 On *confort* and 'comfort', see Introduction, n. 10.
83 On *Gemütlich* or *Gemüthlich*, see: the *Zeitschrift für deutsche Wortforschung*, ed. F. Kluge, vol. 5 (1903–4), 99; vol. 13 (1911–12), 111; 'die Stimmung geselligen Genusses': Meyer (Ch. II, n. 56), vol. 7 (1876), 581; J. S. Ersch and J. G. Gruber (eds), *Allgemeine Encyclopedie der Wissenschaften und Künste*, 57th part [vol.] (Leipzig: Brockhaus, 1853), 308–21. Later writers, e.g. Walter Benjamin (see above, n. 4), were sceptical, yet a recent anthropological study fully accepts the old perceptions ('kleine, gemütvolle häusliche Welt'): see H. Bausinger, *Typisch deutsch. Wie Deutsch sind die Deutschen?* (Munich: Beck, 2000), 64. See also Mennekes, 326ff.; R. Haussmann and K. Schulte (eds) with Weissenhof-Institut Stuttgart, *Gemütlichkeit* (Munich: Aries, 1996). On uses of the interior, see G. Gilloch, *Myth and Metropolis: Walter Benjamin and the City* (Cambridge: Polity, 1996), 70–78.
84 *Stimmung* / space: cf. 'The power that space [i.e. a room] exercises upon us …' ('Die Macht, welche der Raum auf unser Gefühl ausübt'). 'Every room has a certain character, and influences … our mood and our feelings …; its proportions, its form and its lighting … influences our thoughts like a musician with the sequence of its tones and its rhythm' ('jeder dieser Räume … hat einen bestimmten Charakter, und wirkt diesem Charakter entsprechend auf unsere Stimmung, unser Gefühl ein … in seinen Verhältnissen, seiner Form und Beleuchtung … beeinflusst unsere Gedanken und Stimmungen in ähnlicher Weise wie der Musiker durch die Folge seiner Töne und den Rhythmus'): Luthmer 1884b, 5. § On 'space', see also Ch. III, n. 259. For a broader view of *Stimmung* around 1800, in the 'period of sensitivity' ('Empfindsmakeit', i.e. Romanticism), see K. Trübner, *Trübners deutsches Wörterbuch* (Berlin: Gruyter, 1939–57), 598–600. Cf. also Schinkel: 'Stimmungsbilder … Seelenzustände' ('pictures of mood … state of mind') [here on stage design], quoted in Rave, *Schinkelwerk* (Ch. III, n. 35), vol. 1, 79ff., and in Zukowsky (above, n. 50). For Gurlitt, in the late 19th century, *Stimmung* was the catchword of painters ('Die "Stimmung" wurde das Stichwort der Maler'): Gurlitt, 84. See also A. Riegl, 'Die Stimmung als Inhalt der modernen Kunst' (1899), in

A. Riegl, *Essays zur Kunstgeschichte* (Augsburg/Vienna: B. Filser, 1929), 28–42; Praz, 53ff.; Rybczynski, 43ff.

85 'there may be ...' ('es kann Stimmungen der Seele geben ... [die] in einer unbeschreiblichen Analogie mit dem Zimmer stehen; ... die Stimmung und Rührung unserer Seele sehr oft von den Gegenständen, die uns umgeben, abhängt') – a comment on designs for wall décor in the 'Etruscan' and 'Pompeian' styles: Grohmann (Ch. II, n. 8), no. 5, cahier 18, pl. vii, and no. 1, cahier 19 (1797), quoted in Hölz, 142–44.

86 'produced through ...' ('durch die Ausstattung ... einen bestimmten Character zu verleihen, zum Ausdruck einer Stimmung zu machen ... der süss träumerischen Ruhe und Abspannung'): J. Lessing 'Pariser Briefe No. 4', *National Zeitung*, 13 July 1867.

87 Haweis, 370.

88 'Light ...' ('Das Licht [ist] die Seele des Raumes. Die Farbe dagegen wird ihm noch eine spezifische Stimmung geben. Sie wird uns vor allen Dingen lyrisch berühren und also besonders unser Gemüth in Anspruch nehmen'): Lucae, 304.

89 'to give the room ...' ('Einem ... Zimmer jenen poetischen Reiz, jenen unbewussten fesselnden Zauber zu geben, den wir im Bilde als Stimmung bezeichnen'): Falke 1871, 224. See also: 'gibt ... dem Gemach ... poetische Stimmmung': Falke 1883, 288.

90 'The total harmonic ...('die harmonische Gesamtwirkung ... das, was im Wohnräume den darin weilenden unbewusst sammelnd, beruhigend und anheimelnd berührt'): Lütt (Ch. II, n. 118), 35–36. Cf. 'the sensation that we call "a home feeling"': Spofford, 234; 'completeness of the home ... provision of mental as well as the physical wants': Wheeler, *Household Art* (Ch. II, n. 83), 14.

Inside/outside

91 'domestic bliss ...' ('häusliche Glückseligkeit; Blick auf die Natur'): K. P. Moritz (above, n. 24); cf. Repton (Intr., n. 1), 31–32.

92 'more pleasant ...' ('angenehmere und unterhaltendere Aussicht'): A. Geul 1868, 5; the same words occur in the 1888 edn, 8, but with the omission of 'angenehmere'. Cf. Stiegel, 257. See also light and simple bourgeois interiors with large window panes: *Gl* 1864, 600. According to Henrici, 7–8, being smart and modern demanded light and air, but rooms could be uncomfortably large.

93 'show order ...': *Home* 1853, 118. Good façades: Havard 1884, 243; cf. home's 'contradictions with the external world': Hessemer, 2; Silverman, 82ff. See also Benjamin: 'The space of life as a whole [*Lebensraum*] was expanding and at the same time getting smaller': Benjamin, para. J 67a, 5, p. 440. Camillo Sitte also turned towards the cosy old street or square: see *Der Städtebau nach seinen künstlerishen Grundsätzen* (Vienna, 1889).

94 'as a rule ...': Eastlake, 41. Cf. the view that there was 'no external architectural beauty in London': Conway (Ch. II, n. 77), 154. § For apartments in Paris, see the pre-1850 sections through Parisian flats (ill. pp. 16–17). According to Marcus, there was later an absolute separation between street and interior.

95 'There is no need ...' ('der schönen Aussicht bedarf die Wohnung nicht, denn all ihr Reiz muss nach innen gehen'): Falke 1862, 680. § 'ladies sat there' ('Hier sassen Damen, sehend und ungesehen'): Falke 1883, 279–80.

96 Oscar Wilde, 'The House Beautiful' (Dublin lecture), *FG*, 8 Dec. 1883, 397–99 (398).

97 Balconies: see the present book, p. 315.

98 Morris, 131, 117.

Tight enclosures

99 'Only those who, owing to a finely disposed susceptibility in that direction, can be called upon to create a space of a specific character – and the philosophers of art will know the factors which, in their combination, become what one calls effect or, as I permit myself to say, the power of space in architecture' ('Nur diejenigen, die vermöge einer nach dieser Richtung feiner organisierten Empfindung berufen sind, einen Raum von einem bestimmen Character zu schaffen – und die Kunstphilosophen – werden Factoren kennen müssen, welche in ihrer Vereinigung zu dem werden, was man Wirkung – oder wie ich mir zu sagen erlaubt habe – was man die Macht des Raumes in der Baukunst nennt!'): Lucae, 293–94.

100 'form and light' ('Form und Licht'): Lucae, 293–94.

101 'make my small room' ('Mein Zimmerlein zu einem Schatzkästgen machen'), letter from Goethe to J. G. Herder concerning paintings by J. W. H. Tischbein: *Goethes Werke* (Sophien Ausgabe: Weimar 1887–1920) Pt. IV, vol. 8, 109–110 (thanks to Michael Schläfer).

102 'What is being realized' ('C'est qu'on a realisé, à Paris, de commode, de mignon, de joli dans les petits espaces, par d'ingenieux arrangements intérieurs et une intelligente distribution, est inimaginable'): C. Daly, 'Maisons de Paris', *RGA* (1852), 396–402 (401), cf. Guichard 33.

103 C. Daly, 'Une Villa', *RGA* (1867), 155–58.

104 A. Jowers, *"On the Principles which should Govern the Decoration of a Suite of Apartments": An Essay to which the silver medal ... was awarded* (London: G. & J. W. Taylor, 1871), 23.

105 John D. Crace, 'Household Taste', *B*, 4 March 1882, 243–45 (244).

106 Muthesius, H., 90. § Godwin *Ar*, 112; see also Miller (Ch. II, n. 76), 11; A. Service, *Edwardian Interiors* (London: Barrie & Jenkins, 1982), 71, 96–97.

107 'only the horizontal ...' ('behaglich nur Horizontalismus; Raum muss gelagert sein ... Eindruck der Raumruhe, Wände nicht höher als breit'; 'Decke nicht zu hoch in der Luft schweben, dass man sich nicht mehr under ihrem Schutze fühlt'): Henrici, 7. Luthmer claimed that exaggerated height equalled coldness: Luthmer 1897, 30–31.

108 'Die Kunst liegt eben darin, ein möglichst bewegtes Bild zu schaffen, damit den Eintretenden eine wohltuende Wärme empfängt': Hug, 18.

109 'Bay windows ... making a cozy corner', Holly, 354. For the Germans, the *Erker* was a specifically German medieval feature: see Brönner 1994; Stiegel, 257. § 'Cosy corners': Long, 170–75.

110 Baisch (Ch. II, n. 98), 72. On the '(Zimmer-)Laube', see Luthmer 1884b, 16; Thornton, 229.

111 On coving, see Viollet-le-Duc, 96, 102. § 'canopy effect': Holly, 61.

112 'break up ...': 'Screens', *Furnisher and Decorator*, 2 Feb. 1891, 88–91. § 'add an air ...': Holly, 59.

113 'The eye demands ...' ('Das Auge verlangt Unterbrechen der glatten Fläche'): Luthmer, 1884, 21. Carl Müller suggested a compromise: stimulate the imagination, but remember that too much décor can be distracting: Müller (Introduction, n. 18), 43.

114 'Longues horizontalites apaisent notre esprit': Havard 1884, 251–61 (253). He refers to Humbert de Superville's experiments with facial expressions, demonstrated with simple lines: see J. Bolten (ed.), *Miscellanea Humbert de Superville* (Leiden: 1997), which contains an 'Essai sur les signes inconditionels dans l'art' (first publ. Leiden: Hoek, 1827). See also Luthmer 1897, 38–39; Sidlauskas. § 'Parallelismus ... trägt den Charakter des Freundschaftlichen': Henrici, 8.

115 On empathy, see Ch. III, n. 259. § 'the explicit ...' ('Sinnbild des Abgeschlossenseins'): Scheffers (Ch. II, n. 60), 72.

116 Henrici, 7, etc.

117 'we do not ...' ('ungemüthliches Raummoment ... Wir fühlen uns dann zwischen ihnen nicht heimisch. Wir haben nirgends den Rücken gedeckt und es ist uns zumuthe, als könnten wir in jedem Augenblicke von allen Seiten einen Überfall erwarten'): Lucae, 297.

118 On windows: 'es fehlt diesen dann ein fühlbarer Abschluss': Henrici, 21. § 'Geborgensein': Henrici, 23. § 'activity' ('Aktivität'): a window is there not just to let in light, but can also play 'a more significant role', thus being raised from passivity to 'an effective activity': Henrici, 22.

The new darkened interior

Light

119 'Blaze of light and colour': Arrowsmith (Ch. II, n. 41), 117–20. § 'without light ...' ('ohne Licht keine Heiterkeit'): Wiegmann (Ch. III, n. 17), 28; cf. 'cheerfulness, healthiness ... abundance of light': J. J. Kent, 'Further Observations on the Choice of a House', *AM*, vol. 1 (1834), 166–71 (166). On the desirability of bright, friendly rooms, see W. Baeumer, *Feier Geburstagsfestes Königs von Württemberg, Denkschrift ... über das bürgerliche Wohnhaus* (Stuttgart, 1862), 13; 'Gutes Licht': H. Schülke, *Gesunde Wohnungen* (Berlin: J. Springer, 1880), 9–27; 'cheerfulness a great blessing ... darkness and gloom [have a] depressing effect: [Anon.], 'The Influence of Light and Health': *The Family Economist*, vol. 2 (1849), 63–67. See also the later *Häusliche Glück* (Ch. III, n. 27), 23.

120 On mirrors: Le Camus, 116–17; Poe, 105; their expense: Stiegel, 571; Havard 1884, 303–5; S. Roche, *Spiegel* (Tübingen: Wasmuth, 1985); S. Roche et al., *Mirroirs* (Paris: Bibliothèque des Arts, 1986); 'Spiegel und Spiegelung', *Kritische Berichte*, vol. 32, no. 2 (2004). Mrs Haweis, as so often, is ambivalent: 'A good many mirrors and bright objects ... really [do] refract light by contrast and reflection': Haweis, 248–49.

121 'a large amount ...' ('die grosse gleichmässige Lichtmenge'): Luthmer 1884b, 9; see also Introduction.

122 Repton (Introduction, n. 1), 58.

From colour to tone

123 'Colour is the most ...': Wheeler (Ch. II, n. 83), 7. All colours inspire 'a deep feeling of inexpressible wellbeing' ('tiefes Gefühl des unaussprechlichen Behagens'): Goethe, para. 759. According to Goethe, para. 762, a 'French writer' claimed that switching the colour of his furnishings from blue to crimson caused a change in his relationship with a woman. Vivid colour indicates uneducated people, however: Goethe, para.134.

124 'It is design ...' ('C'est le dessin qui donne la forme aux êtres, c'est la couleur qui leur donne la vie'): D. Diderot, *Essais sur la peinture* (Paris: 1765–66; repr. D. Diderot, *Oeuvres Esthétiques*, Paris: Garnier, 1959, 674); cf. Ch. III, n. 188.

125 'the pleasures ...' ('Lust an der Farbe'): Semper, vol. 1, 189. § 'effect of colour ...' ('koloristische Wirkung im praktischen Leben'): Lübke, 'Farbenlehre' (Ch. III, n. 201), 1; cf. 'happiness in life' ('Lebensglück'): Schasler (Ch. III, n. 188), 7; C. W. Dempsey, 'Advanced Art', *MA* (1882), 358–59.

126 'yellow...' ('Gelb, Rothgelb (Orange), Gelbroth (Mennig Zinnober): sie stimmen regsam, lebhaft, strebend'): Goethe, para.764. § 'warm ...' ('warm und behaglich'): para.768. § 'Rein blau ... weit, leer und kalt': para.783. § On the colour green: 'the eye and the mind rest on something simple' ('ruht das Auge und das Gemüt auf ... einem Einfachen'), para.802. Cf. Pardailhé-Galabrun, Engl. edn, 171.

127 'gay', etc., all 'according to the general sentiment': 'The decorator must confine himself to neither a vivid, sombre, warm, nor cold style of colouring': Hay, 24–25 (1836 edn, 19); cf. Luthmer 1884a, 25ff. § For main recommendations, see Hay, 32–33 (1836 edn, 26–29), also in Loudon, 1015; but see also Loudon, 909–10.

128 'warm': Bristow 1996a, 200. For Goethe, principally the light colours were 'warm', such as 'red-yellow': Goethe para, 773. 'The apartments of town houses require to be all more or less warm in their tone': *Home* 1853, 120; 'the forceful and energetic colouring of the Middle Ages and the Renaissance ... decisively darker but at the same time also much warmer' ('das kräftige und energischere Kolorit'), Falke, *Dublin* (Ch. II, n. 97), 12. Cf. 'a darkish warm tint' (in the dining room): E. B. Lamb, 'Design for a Villa in the Style of the 13th c.', *AM*, vol. 2 (1835), 257–75 (264). The scientist E. Brücke denied the effects of colour on one's psychological state: see Ch. III, n. 201, 2nd edn, 181. § 'tendency towards red': Luthmer 1884a, 25; see also Brönner 1978.

129 See J. Cheshire, *Stained Glass and the Victorian Gothic Revival* (Manchester University Press, 2004). See also Whittock (Ch. II, n. 125); Haweis, 242ff.

130 See Boussard (Ch. II, n. 85), 405; Luthmer 1884b, 10. § 'where the view ...': Luthmer, 'Unser Haus', 1888 edn, 76–77; cf. *EID*, 1214.

131 'nothing ...' ('Nichts, Nüchternheit, Alltäglichkeit ... verleiht Poesie dem Gemache, gibt ihm Weihe, Leben und Wärme, Schimmer der Verklärung'): Falke 1883, 282–84.

132 'cathedral glass': Long, 128–29; Meron (Ch. III, n. 5). Cf. 'subdued light ... casement of green bottle-bottoms': [Anon.], 'Furniture and Decoration', *BN*, 27 Feb. 1874, 223. Cf. also T. Jeckyll's yellow glass in the Peacock Room: Merrill (Ch. II, n. 78), 167ff; 'a certain coloured substantiality' ('Körperlichkeit'): J. Lessing, 'Glasmalerei in der Wohnung', *IFz*, 31 May 1880, 214; 'a specific texture of glass' ('eigenthümliche Glas-Textur'): Luthmer 1884b, 10.

The changing meaning of darkness

133 According to Havard, painters know more about chiaroscuro than decorators, but he sees their tasks as almost identical: Havard 1884, 296.

134 Photography: see the present book, p. 62.

135 See B. Borchardt-Birbaumer, *Imago Noctis. Die Nacht in der Kunst des Abendlandes vom alten Orient bis zum Zeitalter des Barock* (Wien: Böhlau, 2003), 742; M .C. Ramirez, *Das Helldunkel in der italienischen Kunsttheorie des 15. und 16. Jhs. .... Notturno* (Münster: LIT, 2000); M. Rzepinska, 'Tenebrism in Baroque Painting', Artibus et Historiae, vol. 7, no. 13 (1986), 91–112; A. Blühm and L. Lippincott, *Light! The Industrial Age 1750–1900* (exh. cat. Amsterdam: Van Gogh Museum / London: Thames & Hudson, 2000); J. J .L. Whiteley, 'Light

and Shade in French Neo-Classicism', *Burlington Magazine*, vol. 117, no. 12 (1975), 768–73; A. Roger Ekirch, *At Day's Close: A History of Nighttime* [before 1789] (London: Weidenfeld & Nicholson, 2005).
136 'well-managed darkness': E. Burke, *A Philosophical Enquiry into the Origin of our Ideas of the Sublime and the Beautiful* [first publ. 1756], Part II, sect. xiv ff.; see also Part IV, sect. viii ff.
137 'tied …' ('collées aux architectures'): Lévy, *Roman 'Gothique'* (above, n. 21), 262, 266. Cf. 'The Gothic is the motor that truly drives the action': Hogle (above, n. 21), 156.
138 For Beckford, Scott and the Troubadour style, see Wainwright; Bann. For Dickens, see Hogle (above, n. 21), 156; Tristram, 23.
139 de Musset: J .R. Dakyns, *The Middle Ages in French Literature 1851–1900* (Oxford University Press, 1973), 11, 18, 24. § On Charcot, see Silverman, 99ff.
140 'domesticity': Downing, 383; 'home-like': Downing, 387–88.
141 Lehr, *Franz Pforr* (above, n. 24).
142 M. E. James (Ch. III, n. 15), 75.
143 'wonderful groups' ('herrliche Gruppen'): quoted in Geismeier (above, n. 35), 73. Cf. the late 18th-century illustrations of dark interiors by J.-B. Isabey, in the Coll. B. Houthakker, Amsterdam: Praz 198–99.
144 H. Gärtner, *Georg Friedrich Kersting* (Leipzig: Seemann, 1988).
145 For white on the exterior of buildings, see the *Reallexikon* (Ch. III, n. 170), vol. 7, 416.
146 'in a white room': Haweis, *Art of Beauty* (Ch. II, n. 76), 228. § 'It looks so clean.': L. F. Day, 'How to Decorate a Room', *MA* (1881), 182–86 (183).
147 On evening atmosphere, see *Home* 1853. Cf. the German 'Feierabend': literally a celebration of evening, it has come to mean the end of the working day. See also Ohlsen (Ch. V, n. 281).
148 Holly, *Modern Dwellings* (Ch. II, 82), 164, quoted in Blanchard 124; cf. E. B. Lamb, '13th c' (above, n. 128).
149 W. Collins, *Basil*, Chapter 10 (1852; repr. Oxford University Press, 1990, 61). § W. H. Hunt, *The Awakening Conscience*, 1854 (London, Tate); J. Ruskin, 'Letter to *The Times*, 25 May 1854', in E. T. Cook (eds) and A. Wedderburn, *Complete Works of John Ruskin* (London: Allen & Unwin, 1903–12), vol. 12, 333–35.
150 Mennekes, 329ff.. See also B. Köhler, 'Between Industry and Craft: the Interior', in Rüegg (Introduction, n. 16), 33–53.
151 'physical …' ('aus physischen oder gemüthlichen Gründen'): Falke 1883, 277. § 'tiring' ('nous fatiguer'): Havard 1884, 296.
152 'conventional smile' ('Heimliche poetische Helldunkel … erweckt in uns ein Gefühl der Behaglichkeit … tiefe Schatten … poetische Wirkung … ein immer gleiches konventionelles Lächeln'): Lucae, 296.
153 'tranquillité … Les ombres … propices à la rêverie, des ombres silencieuses': Blanc, 136–37. § Falke, *Dublin* (Ch. II, 97), 12. § 'rather darker tone …' ('Eher dunklen warmen Ton … Raum behaglicher'): Luthmer 1892, 89. § Behr: 'really stylish and warmly furnished' ('recht stylvoll und warm einrichten'); 'a comforting [*beruhigend*] and warm effect'; 'the atmospheric [*stimmungsvollen*] warmth of the whole': Behr, *Dekoration* (Ch. II, n. 69), 4, 27, 41. Additionally, according to Blanc, 226, subdued light served 'the woman whose beauty, even though unfaded, is in need of mystery'.

The manipulation of light

154 Ramirez (above, n. 135), 241.
155 Cf. 18th-century scenography and G. B. Piranesi's etchings of Rome. On the two 18th-century modes of representing shadow – precise and blurred – see M. Baxendall, *Shadows and the Enlightenment* (New Haven and London: Yale University Press, 1995). Cf. Reynolds, *Discourses*, no. viii (1797); Ackermann; Stamp (Ch. II, n. 124); K. Niehr, *Gotikbilder–Gotiktheorien. Studien zur Wahrnehmung und Erforschung mittelaterlicher Architektur in Deutschland zwischen 1750 und 1850* (Berlin: Mann 1999); F. Gilly and F. Frick, *Schloss Marienburg in Preussen* (Berlin, 1803; repr. Düsseldorf: Galtgarben, 1965).
156 On the character of rooms, see Henrici, 15. Cf. W. White, 'On Windows in Domestic Architecture', *The Ecclesiologist*, vol. 17 (1856), 319–30; *EID*, 336; 'Windows and their treatment', *BN*, 29 Nov. 1878, 555–57.
157 'unafraid …' ('furchtlos und unbekümmert um Hell oder Dunkel allein die künstlerischen Rücksichten obwalten lassen'): Falke 1871, 225. Cf. 'Das Fenster und seine Dekoration. Glasgemälde und Vorhänge', in Falke 1883, 275–301 (4th edn 1882, 319–51). § 'Unity …' ('Einheit des Lichtes ist die Hauptbedingung für ein Bild … sie ist es auch für ein künstlerisches Gemach'): Falke 1883, 278.
158 On blinds: Long, 124–28.
159 'glaring mass' ('unausgefülltes Loch … die grelle, farblose Lichtmasse tut unseren Augen weh'): Falke 1883, 281. § 'hard, sharp sunlight' ('das scharfe Sonnenlicht'): Behr, *Entwicklung* (Ch. II, n. 69), 18. § 'better to shut …': Church (Ch. II, 82), 43, but see also below, n. 179.
160 'the transition …' ('den Übergang, die Verbindung mit der Wand herzustellen'; 'Durch ihren weichen Fluss die scharfen architektonischen Linien des Fensters zu brechen'): Falke 1883, 282, 290, cf. 278. Cf. F. Collard, 'Curtains Up', *Country Life*, 20 April 1989, 194–97; *EID*, 332–39.
161 'have a tiring effect' ('ne tarderait pas à nous fatiguer'): Havard 1884, 296.
162 'carefully directed' ('savamment ménagée'): Guichard, 24.
163 'the light falls …' ('Das Licht fällt in einer breiten geschlossenen Masse ein und steigert sich selber durch die Kontraste seiner Umgebung zu einem künstlerischen Moment'): Lucae, 296. § 'point of light' ('point de lumière'): Havard 1884, 294; 'principal mass …' ('qu'on puisse constater l'existence d'une masse claire principale, et d'une masse sombre dominante'): Havard 1884, 297. § On drawing the curtains: Havard 1884, 297. § 'hopeless' ('rettungslos … zumauern'): Luthmer 1897, 82. § 'managed light …' ('une lumière ménagée … entrant par une ouverture unique, et non combattu par d'autres lumières'): Blanc, 136–37.
164 Dresser 1876, 12.
165 'most beautiful rooms': Haweis, 221; 'lights': Haweis, 200; 'pretty effect': Haweis, 213–14; 'white walls … greatly diminish the size of the room, as a white ceiling diminishes its height. A dark wall adds size because the eye cannot exactly measure the distance at which the wall stands': Haweis, 217.
166 Spofford, 233.
167 'bodies in light' ('Körper … im Licht)': Henrici, 13. § 'refracted': Haweis, 248–49.
168 'intensity of light' ('l'intensité plus ou moins grande de l'éclairage se traduit non seulement par le degré de clarté qui frappe les saillies d'un objet, mais encore par l'obscurité plus ou moins opaque qui enveloppe les partis restées dans l'ombre': Havard, *Décoration* (Ch. II, n. 85), 138.
169 'doubling of light …' ('Le tissu retrouvera ainsi par un redoublement de lumière, dans les parties saillantes, ce qu'il doit perdre d'éclat par la somme des ombres, logées dans les parties creuses': Blanc, 91.
170 'come out': Falke 1871, 224; cf. Hug, 10. § 'a room has to …': Falke 1871, 202–4. Cf. Havard 1884, 292.
171 'restfulness' ('la tranquillité qui résulte sous une lumière plus douce'): Blanc, 136.
172 'see-through curtains …' ('die durchsichtigen Vorhänge … Licht zu zerstreuen und dadurch zu mildern'): Luthmer 1884a, 28. Cf. 'fill the whole room with a soft light': Luthmer 1884b, 10.
173 Blanc, 136. § 'I like …': Frank T. Robinson, 'Boston Artists' Studios', No. III, *DF*, vol. vi, April 1885, 17–19.
174 'artificial light …' ('nach Belieben operieren'): Henrici, 15. Cf. Mennekes, 333–34; T. Rees, *Theatre Lighting in the Age of Gas* (London: Society for Theatre Research, 1978); 'Illuminotecnica' ('Theatre Lighting'), in *Enciclopedia dello Spettacolo*, vol. VI, (Rome: Maschere, 1959).
175 See C. Cohn, 'Lampen und Beleuchtungsapparate', in 'Waffen, Metallwaren Lampen …,' *Ausstellungs-Bericht* (44), 45–48.
176 Falke 1871, 225.
177 'pure white light': R. Hammond [of Hammond Electric Light Co.], *The Electric Light in Our Homes* (London: Warne, 1884), 93; Luthmer 1897, 86ff. Cf. 'Elektisches Licht- und Kunstgewerbe', *BfK* (1883), 1–2; L. Bell, *The Art of Illumination* (New York: McGraw Hill, 1902); Schivelbusch (Introduction, n. 16). § 'Old central gas …': G. A. [Grant Allen], 'The Philosophy of the Drawing-Room', *ChM*, vol. 41, Jan.–June 1880, 312–26 (321). § 'carefully spread …' ('Sinnig im Raume verteilt … eine weihevollere, festlichere Wirkung … "Patentbrenner"'): Henrici, 14.
178 See I. Ehrensperger, 'Im Lichtkreis der Petroleumlampe', *KAS*, vol. 55, no. 2, (2004), 54–60.
179 Dresser 1876, 38. § 'sunlight': Church, 46. But see also above, n. 159.
180 'senseless darkening' ('sinnlose Dunkelmacherei'): Hirth, 82. See also Henrici, 14; Falke 1862, 680; 'Lichtdurchströmte ['flooded through with light'] Wohnungen': M. Haushofer, 'Kunstgewerbliches', *IFz*, 1 July 1886, 228. Can we draw a parallel between the fashion for dark rooms and modern 'pictures of a dispiriting and morbid character'? asked the editor of *FD*, Nov. 1882, 41.
181 See. J. Burckhardt, 'Zwei elementare Grossmächte: Licht und Luft', in 'Rembrandt' (1877). repr. in J. Burckhardt, *Vorträge 1844–1887* (Basel, 1918), 130–50.

V CHARACTER

Rooms and styles

1 On styles: W. Szambien (Ch. I, n. 1); P. Collins, *Changing Ideals in Modern Architecture 1750–1950* (London: Faber, 1965); J. M. Crook, *The Dilemma of Style: Architectural Ideas from the Picturesque to Post-Modern* (London: Murray, 1987); H. U .Gumprecht et al. (eds), *Stil. Geschichte und Funktionen eines kulturwissenschaftlichen Diskurselements* (Frankfurt am Main: Suhrkamp, 1986); Bisky; Himmelheber. Cf. 'The architectonic value [of an interior] is based principally on style': [Anon.], *Unsere Frauen und ihr Heim …* (Darmstadt: Koch, 1892), 11.
2 E.g. 'garniture des sièges' and 'garniture des sièges de style': H. Lacroix (Ch. III, n. 62), Chs. vi and vii.
3 'partly harmonious …' ('Teils harmonisch, teils characteristisch, oft auch unharmonisch'): Goethe, para. 758b.
4 Paolini, 31.
5 Dr Huber, 'Die deutsche Renaissance und der Weltmarkt', *Deutsche Tischler Zeitung*, 27 Feb. 1886, 66.
6 Comte (below, n. 94), 21.
7 'in all styles': see e.g. A. Chenavard, *Album de l'ornementiste … dans tous les genres et tout les styles* (Paris, 1836); G. Umé, *L'Art décoratif, modèles … de tout les styles et de tout les époques* (Paris, 1862); Timms and Webb, *Select Furniture in All Styles* (London: Furniture Press, n.d. [1890]); see also D. Guilmard, *La Connaissance des styles de l'ornementation* (Paris: Garde Meuble, 1853). § 'Salon Genre Moderne …', Maincent (Ch. II, n. 87); 'style fantaisie', *La Mode Illlustrée*, vol. 7 (1866), 69–70; vol. 8 (1867), 295.
8 'I purposely did not mention style because it merely serves to shift the major formal components around': Lucae, 294. For the relative indifference to 'style' in domestic architecture in the 1860s, see Kerr.

Renaissance, Rococo, Oriental

9 Parkes, 191.
10 'the ballroom …' ('musizierenden Gestalten, nackte Figuren … Küchengenüsse'): Hessemer, 27.
11 See Architekten- und Ingenieur-Verein, *Strassburg und seine Bauten* (Strasbourg, 1894), 557, 560. Cf. J. Castex et al., *Lecture d'une ville: Versailles* (Paris: Moniteur, 1980), 209, 224.
12 See W. Krause, H. Laudel and W. Nerdinger (eds), *Neo-Renaissance … Zweites Historismus Symposium Bad Muskau* (Dresden: Verlag der Kunst, 2001).
13 See K. Ireland, *Cythera Regained? The Rococo Revival in European Literature and the Arts* (Fairleigh, NJ: Dickinson University Press, 2006) (with thanks to Ken Ireland); M. Eberle, 'Zur politischen und gesellschaftlichen Bedeutung des Neorokoko … in Stuttgart', in A. Kreul (ed.), *Barock als Aufgabe* (Wiesbaden: Harrassowitz, 2005), 125–44; Sangl, 'Princely Writing Tables' (Ch. III, n. 1); S. Sangl, *Biedermeier to Bauhaus* (n.p.: Lincolns, 2000), 123–27; M. Zweig (ed.), *Zweites Rokoko. Innenräume und Hausrat in Wien um 1830–1860* (Vienna: Schroll, 1924); E. Götz, 'Zweites Rokoko um 1840', in K.-H. Klingenburg (ed.), *Historismus* (Leipzig: Seemann, 1985); G. Pazaurek, *Dreierlei Rokoko* (exh. cat. Stuttgart: Landesgewerbemuseum, 1909); Ottillinger, '"Kaiser Salon"' (Ch. II, n. 1). See also F. Kugler, *Handbuch der Kunstgeschichte*, 3rd edn, vol. 1 (Stuttgart: Ebner & Seubert, 1856), 605; Semper, vol. 1, 333, who claimed to have initiated the word 'Rococo'; for the 1870s in the Netherlands, rooms in 'Louis XIII, XIV, XV, XVI', see J. M. W. van Voorst tot Voorst, in *Haagse Meubelmakers … 19e Eeuw* (exh. cat. The Hague: Gemeentemuseum, 1974), 24. A watered-down Louis XIX/XV style was called 'Old French' in London in the 1820s–40s: J. Yorke, *Lancaster House: London's Grandest Town House* (London: Merrell, 2001).
14 'overloaded bombast, artificiality, of a faded youth' ('überladener Bombast … Künstelei und Verziertheit einer verblühten Judend'): J. Falke, *Paris* (Ch. II. n. 54), 88–89; cf. Falke 1871, 162–63.
15 'Oriental' label: A. L. Macfie, *Orientalism* (London: Longmans, 2002); *EID*, 908–11; S. Koppelkam, *Der*

imaginäre Orient. Bauten des 18. und 19. Jahrhunderts in Europa (Berlin: Ernst, 1987); Morley, 336ff.

16 'rooms devoted …' ('behaglichen Ausruhen … gemütlichen Geplauder … mildes gedämpftes Licht'): Lübke (Ch. III, n. 201), 1–4; Oriental smoking rooms 'not so rare': Luthmer 1884a, 186; Ottillinger, 133–34.

17 On Japanese décor: A. Humbert, *Le Japon illustré* (Paris: Hachette, 1870); S. B. Morse, *Japanese Homes and their Surroundings* (Boston, MA: Ticknow, 1886; repr. New York: Dover, 1961); J. Brinckmann, *Kunst und Handwerk in Japan* (Berlin, 1889); J. Converse Brown, *The Japanese Taste and its Role in American Houses* (diss., University of Madison, 1987); *Le Japonisme* (exh. cat. Paris: Grand Palais, 1988); T. Watanabe, *High Victorian Japonisme* (Bern: Lang, 1991); G. P. Weisberg, *Japonisme: An Annotated Bibliography* (New York: Garland, 1991); Silverman, 136ff.

Revivalism: the romantic castle interior

18 On the fashion for 'castles': M. Walter and J. Coignart, *Dream Palaces: Romantic Castles in Europe* (New York: Vendome Press, 2004); Wainwright; Girouard 1979; *Friedrich Wilhelm IV. Künstler und König* (exh. cat. Potsdam: Sanssouci, 1995); Niehr (Ch. IV, n. 155); R. Wagner-Rieger and W. Krause (eds), *Historismus und Schlossbau* (Munich: Prestel, 1975); A. Ley, *Die Villa als Burg* (Munich: Callwey, 1981); J. Vybíral, *Století dědiců a zakladatelů: Architektura jižních Čech období historismu* [on Czech historicist castles] (Prague: Argo, 1999); J. Cavalier, *American Castles* (New York: Barnes, 1973). § 'historical poetics': Bann, 3.

19 C. Charles, *Victor Hugo, visions d'intérieurs: Du meuble au décor* (Paris: Musées Nationaux, 2003).

20 See Grodecki, *Gothique* (Ch. IV, n. 23); F. Pupil, *Le Style Troubadour* (Nancy: Presses Universitaires, 1985).

21 J.-M. Leniaud, 'Néo-Renaissance et style Henri II au XIXe siècle', in H. Oursel and J. Fritsch (eds), *Henri II et les arts* (Paris: École du Louvre, 1997), 319–36; Bonnafé (Ch. IV, n. 7); K. L. Ames, *Renaissance Revival Furniture in America* (Ann Arbor: University of Michigan, 1991). With thanks also to Anne Dion.

22 See Pugin (Ch. III, n. 168; Ch. IV, n. 19); M. L. Charlesworth, *The Gothic Revival: Literary Sources …* (Mountfield: Helm Information, 2002); C. Brooks, *The Gothic Revival* (London: Phaidon, 1999); S. Muthesius, *The High Victorian Movement in Architecture 1850–1870* (London: Routledge, 1972). Viollet-le-Duc: *Dictionnaire raisonné de l'architecture* (Ch. III, n. 115); *Entretiens sur l'architecture* (1863); *Histoire de l'habitation humaine depuis les temps préhistoriques jusqu'à nos jours* (1875); *Histoire d'une maison* (Paris: Bibliothèque d'Éducation, n.d. [1874]). Cf. J.-M. Leniaud, *Viollet-le-Duc ou les délires du système* (Paris: Menges, 1994); see the present book, p. 161; Niehr (Ch. IV, n. 155); Bisky; K. David-Sirocko, *Georg Gottlob Ungewitter und die malerische Neugotik* (Petersberg: Imhof, 1997); Semper, especially vol. 1, *Textile Kunst,* and vol. 2, Ch. 'Zimmerei'; see also Ch. II, n. 32.

Distant yet familiar: national and vernacular revivals

23 'the choice of forms …' ('wyboru formy … i wsparł moralnie … "cechami plemionymi"'), Jabłońska, *'Koliba'* (Ch. V, n. 280), 11.

24 'vernacular' [its meaning still close to 'national']: 'The unity of our Vernacular …', review of A. J. Bicknell, *Specimen Book of One Hundred Architectural Designs* (New York, 1878), in *AmA* (1878), 5, quoted in Scully, 63. Cf. 'Vernacular …': E. W. Godwin, 'The Ex-Classic Style', *BN*, 16 April 1875, 441–42.

25 B. Champneys, 'Winchelsea, Rye and the Romney Marsh', *Portfolio*, vol. 5 (1874), 9–13.

26 'Only from a distance, only separated from all commonness, only as something past, can the old world be appreciated by us': J. W. von Goethe, quoting W. von Humboldt, quoted in W. Rehm, *Griechentum und Goethezeit*, 3rd edn (Munich, 1952), 6.

27 Champneys, 'Winchelsea' (above, n. 25).

28 'in order to …' ('Uns heimathlich näher zu rücken, ohne dass doch ein gewisser idealer Duft der Ferne verwischt wird'): L. von Kramer with K. Gerok, *Das Lob des tugendsamen Weibes, Sprüche Salomonis 31* (Munich: Stroefer, n.d. [1885]; repr. Dortmund: Harenberg, 1977), Preface.

29 G. G. Ungewitter, *Entwürfe zu Gotischen Möbeln*, 2nd edn (Glogau: 1855; repr. in Engl. 1858), Preface.

30 Examples of chauvinism and racism: for Champneys, attention devoted to foreign splendours often 'blunts' our 'sense of the genuine charm of … native architecture' (above, n. 25); Riehl condemns the modern (i.e. the Renaissance–classical) urban street; 'by their very nature commercial streets had to become Jewish streets [*Judengassen*]': Riehl, 241.

31 After more than a hundred years of proselytizing, the Arts and Crafts movement is still held to have created something 'better' than the 19th-century design out of which it grew: cf. K. Livingstone and L. Parry (eds), *International Arts and Crafts* (exh. cat. London: V&A, 2005); *EID*, 838–41; W. Kaplan, *The Arts & Crafts Movement* (London: Thames & Hudson, 2004).

32 The 'old' had not appeared in Austen: see Tristram, 124; Dickens on pp. 162–64. Cf. J. Ruskin, *The Seven Lamps of Architecture* (1849). Riehl, 224, claims that old houses are 'transfigured in a poetical light' ('in dichterischem Schimmer verklärt'), whereas a new building 'leaves us cold' ('uns kalt lässt'). See also Stewart (Ch. III, n. 133), 161–71; S. Muthesius, 'Old English, Altdeutsch. Some 19th-Century Appropriations of a "Homely" Past', *Rocznik Historii Sztuki* (Warsaw), vol. 30 (2005), 259–84; S. Muthesius, 'Verjüngung durch Verehrung des Alten', in *Grenzen überwindend: Festschrift für Adam S. Labuda* (Berlin: Lukas, 2006), 144–54.

33 Paris 1878: see 'Rue des Nations' in *Art Journal Illustrated Catalogue of the Paris International Exhibition 1878* (London, 1878); cf. also the present book, p. 288.

Old English I

34 H. Shaw, *Details of Elizabethan Architecture* (London: Pickering, 1839), 4; see also H. Shaw [and S. R. Meyrick], *Specimens of Ancient Furniture drawn from existing authorities* (London: Pickering, 1836); C. Wainwright, 'Specimens of Ancient Furniture', *Connoisseur*, vol. 184 (1973), 105–13. Cf. C. J. Richardson, *Architectural Remains of the Reigns of Elizabeth and James I* (London: author, 1840); P. F. Robinson, *Vitruvius Britannicus*, 5 vols. (London, 1833–44); C. J. Richardson, *Studies from Old English Mansions: Their Furniture, Gold and Silver Plate, etc.*, 4 vols. (London: McLean 1841–48). Early vagueness of terminology: Ackermann states that furniture 'called "Gothic" … really should be "old German"': Ackermann, pl. 102, p. 120 (2nd series: vol. 7 [1819] pl. 21, p. 246); M. Girouard, 'Attitudes to Elizabethan Architecture, 1600–1900', in J. Summerson (ed.), *Concerning Architecture … Essays Presented to Nikolaus Pevsner* (Harmondsworth: Penguin, 1968), 13–27; Cornforth, 14, 20; Gere, 47; Jervis; E. T. Joy, 'A Source of Victorian Romanticism: George Bullock', *Country Life*, 29 Aug. 1968, 507–8; V. Glenn, 'G. Bullock, R. Bridgens and J. Watt's Regency Furnishing', *FH*, vol. 15 (1979), 54–67; C. Wainwright, *George Bullock: Cabinet Maker* (London: Murray, 1988); Morley, 274–79, 327–30, 391ff; M. Westgarth, *Emergence* (Ch. IV, n. 36).

35 'Old English': 'origin unknown': Wainwright, 2.

36 For 'bad' old buildings, see e.g. *Penny Magazine* in the 1830s, and *B* in the 1840s–50s.

37 'Old English … peculiarly picturesque': P. F. Robinson, *Designs for Ornamental Villas*, 3rd edn (London, 1830), 1.

38 On the armoury, see Wainwright, 60–64, 205, 242; Smith, vii; S. R. Meyrick, *A Critical Enquiry into Ancient Armour* (London: Jennings, 1824) [Meyrick's house was Goodrich Court, Herefordshire]. Cf. S. Jervis, 'Antler Horn Furniture', *Victoria and Albert Museum Yearbook*, 1972, 87–100; R. Strong, *And When Did You Last See Your Father? The Victorian Painter and British History* (London: Thames & Hudson, 1978).

39 J. Nash, *The Mansions of England in the Olden Time* (London: M'Lean, 1839–1849; rev. edn London: Southern, 1869–72); *Altengliche Herrensitze* [after 1st edn] (Berlin: Hessling, 1899–1900). Cf. S. C. Hall, *The Baronial Halls and Picturesque Edifices of England*, 2 vols. (London, 1848); S. C. Hall, 'The Stately Homes of England', series in *AJ* (1869); Mandler, 40ff.; Tristram, 131. § 'creature comforts': Nash (above), vol. 4 (1849), 1–2.

40 Shaw, *Details* (above, n. 35), 38.

41 Shaw, *Specimens* (above, n. 35), 26.

42 'splendour': T. F. Hunt, *Exemplars of Tudor Architecture Adapted to Modern Habitations* (London: Bohn, 1841), 106.

43 Bielefeld (Introduction, n. 27), 3, 5.

44 Books mainly by T. Hudson Turner (with John Henry Parker): (i) 'By the editor of the Glossary of Architecture', *Some Account of Domestic Architecture in England. From Edward I to Richard II* (Oxford: Parker, 1853); (ii) 'By the editor …' (as above), *Some Account of Domestic Architecture in England. From Richard II to Henry VIII* (Oxford: Parker, 1859); (iii) these texts repr. in [Anon.], *Our English Home: Its Early History and Progress* (Oxford: Parker, 1861); (iv) new edn of *Our English Home: Its Early History and Progress* (Oxford: Parker, 1876). Cf. T. Wright, 'The Domestic Manners of the English', *AJ* (1851), 13–14; *AJ* (1854), 365–67.

45 See I. Gow, 'Mary Queen of Scots meets C. R. Mackintosh: Some Problems … of the Scotch Baronial Revival Interior', *FH*, vol. 32 (1996), 1–32. The author concludes that there is no proper 'Scots Baronial' interior. See also Gow, *Scottish Interior* (Ch. III, n. 199).

46 A. J. Downing, *Cottage Residences* (New York: Putnam, 1842), quoted in A. P. Kenney and L. J. Workman, 'Ruins, Romance and Reality: Medievalism in Anglo-American Imagination and Taste 1750–1840', *WP*, vol. 10 (1975), 131–63 (160).

47 Downing, 391. Cf. the Jacobethan interiors of *c.* 1850 at Gawthorpe Hall, Padiham, Lancashire, by C. Barry, ill. in A. and A. Gore, *The History of English Interiors* (Oxford: Phaidon, 1991), 128–29.

Altdeutsch I

48 H. Möller, 'Altdeutsch. Ideologie, Stereotyp, Verhalten', *Hessische Blätter für Volkskunde*, vol. 57 (1966), 9–30. § 'seriousness and feeling' ('Ernst und Innerlichkeit'): Hessemer, 21. Cf. S. Brunsiek, *Auf dem Weg der alten Kunst. Der 'altdeutsche Stil' in der Buchillustration des 19. Jh.* (Marburg: Jonas, 1994); S. A. Crane, *Collecting and Historical Consciousness in Early 19th-Century Germany* (Ithaka, NY: Cornell University Press, 2000).

49 Wagner-Rieger and Krause, *Historismus* (above, n. 18).

50 M. Brix, *Nürnberg und Lübeck im 19. Jh.* (Munich: Prestel, 1981); N. Götz, *Um Neugotik und Nürnberger Stil* (*Nürnberger Forschungen* vol. 23, 1981).

51 D. Petzet, *Die Richard-Wagner-Bühne König Ludwigs II. München, Bayreuth* (Munich: Prestel, 1970); Mennekes, 92–98. § J. Osborne, *The Meiningen Court Theatre* (Cambridge: University Press, 1988).

52 C. Heideloff, *Ornamentik des Mittelalters*, vol. 1 (Nuremberg: Geigers, 1843–52); U. Boeck, K. A. von Heideloff, *Mitteilungen des Vereins Geschichte Nürnbergs*, vol. 48 (1958); I. Bauer (ed.), *Möbel aus Franken. Oberflächen und Hintergründe* (exh. cat. Nuremberg: Germanisches Nationalmuseum, 1991).

53 C. W. Fleischmann, *Plastische Kunstanstalt Nürnberg* (sale catalogue, Nuremberg, *c.* 1867, copy Germanisches Nationalmuseum library); Mennekes, 77–84.

54 'living conditions …' ('die Lebensumstände der deutschen Vorzeit in gewissem Zusammenhang mit praktischer Notwendigkeit' [mostly exhibited in the 'Frauenhalle']: [Anon.], *Kunst- und Altertumssammlung des Germanischen Nationalmuseums zu Nürnberg* (Nuremberg, 1856), Vorerinnerung; B. Deneke and R. Kahsnitz (eds), *Das Germanische Nationalmuseum in Nürnberg 1852–1977* (Munich: Deutscher Kunstverlag, 1978), 761–62.

55 B. Deneke and R. Kahsnitz (eds), *Das Kunst und kulturgeschichtliche Museum im 19. Jahrhundert* (Munich: Prestel, 1977); Bauer, *Möbel aus Franken* (above, n. 52). Cf. C. A. Harrer, *Das ältere bayerische Nationalmuseum … München* (Munich: Tudur, 1993); Bann. See also the present book, p. 144.

56 *Führer durch die Sammlungen de Städtischen Museums Carolino-Augsteum in Salzburg* (Salzburg, n.d. [*c.* 1900]); *Jahresberichte des Städtischen Museums … 1872–1883*; T. [V. Teirich?], 'Das Salzburger Museum', *BfK*, vol. 4 (1875), 11–12; C. Normand, *Musées européens: Chambres et décorations intérieures en styles anciens* (Paris: Bureau de la Revue, 1895); see ills in Hirth, 73, 109, 168 (thanks to Dr K. Ehrenfellner). See also the enormous collection of old objects of all kinds in the Paris Exposition of 1867 ('Histoire du travail'): C. de Linas, *L'Histoire du travail à l'Exposition universelle de 1867* (Arras: Didron, 1868).

57 On Schinkel, see Harten, Zukowsky (both Ch. IV, n. 50).

58 See E. S. Laube and K.-H. Fix, *Lutherinszenierung und Reformationserinnerung* (Leipzig: Evangelische Verlagsanstalt, 2002); Mennekes, 260.

59 'to arrange …': A. Essenwein (1874), quoted from documents in the *Acta Albrecht Dürer Haus 1871–1874* (Stadtarchiv Nuremberg), repr. in Stadt Nürnberg et al., *Hundert Jahre Albrecht-Dürer-Haus-Stiftung* (exh. cat. Nuremberg: 1976), 19, 32; see also photos in the library of the Museé des Arts Décoratifs, Paris (section on 19th-century interiors). Cf. P. Vaisse, *Reître ou chevalier: Dürer et l'idéologie allemande* (Paris: Passerelles, 2006).

Altdeutsch as German neo-Renaissance

60 For German art and its institutions generally, see R. Lenman, *Artists and Society in Germany 1850–1914*

(Manchester University Press, 1997). Cf. P. Paret, *Art as History: Episodes in the Culture and Politics of 19th-Century Germany* (Princeton University Press: 1988). For architectural and applied art theory: Schwarzer (Ch. II, n. 52). For nationalisms in art, see e.g. W. Lübke, *Die moderne französische Kunst* (Stuttgart: Weise, 1872). § 'Raritätenkrämerei': A. H. Horawitz, *Gustav Freytag als Dichter und Historiker* (Wien: Becksche, 1871), 33.

61 *Derbheit*: 'das bürgerlich derbe, solide': Luthmer 1892, 44. Again, the word 'bürgerlich' should be used with caution (cf. Introduction), since the style was used very successfully in many new lavish country seats: see Brönner 1994; Mennekes.

62 'healthy …' ('gesunde Anschauungen … frische Phantasie'): 'Deutschlands grosse Industrie-Werkstätten', *Gl* (1879), 44–47 (45). § 'full of life …' ('lebensvoll, lebenswarm, lebensfrisch'): Stockbauer (Ch. II, n. 69), 4. Cf. 'warmth': Horawitz (above, n. 60), 33.

63 M. W. M.-C., 'Hans Sachs and the Mastersong', *ChM*, vol. 40, Jul.–Dec.1879, 475–92: 'simplicity': 486; 'poet', 475; 'cautious burghers': 487; 'unromantic': 475.

64 New catchword: Fischbach, *Ausstattung* (Ch. II, n. 69), 6. Cf. 'electrifying effect' ('elektrisierende Wirkung'): O. Wagner, *Moderne Architektur*, 2nd edn (Vienna, 1898), 35–36. Cf. Mennekes; *Renaissance*; Brönner 1994; A. Bartetzky, *Die Baumeister der 'Deutschen Renaissance'. Ein Mythos der Kunstgeschichte?* (Beucha: Sax, 2004). § 'altdeutsche Renaissance': Lipsius (Ch. II, n. 87).

65 See A. Stüler and et al. (eds), *Das Schloss zu Schwerin* (Berlin: Ernst & Korn, 1869), esp. the foreword on 'Northern Renaissance Style'.

66 See 'Albert Dürer …', *BN*, 2 May 1873, 504; J. Hinton, 'Pugin and Dürer …, True Principles', *Journal of the Pugin Society*, vol. 3, no. 1 (2004), 7–17. Many 'old German towns' were ill. by W. H. Brewer, *B*, in the 1870s and 1880s. 'The German race has never been remarkable for … the highest qualities of art … Their merit lay in depth of feeling and an elevated tone of truth and morality': J. J. Stevenson, *House Architecture*, 2 vols. (London: Macmillan, 1880) vol. 1, 278. R. Pfnor, *Monographie du Château de Heidelberg* (Paris: Morel, 1859). However, new German work was considered of low quality: P. Rouaix, *Dictionnaire des arts décoratifs* (Paris: Librairie Illustrée, n.d. [*c.* 1886]), 41.

67 'genuinely …' ('echt bürgerlich'): Luthmer 1884b, 5. On large, ornate houses: W. Brönner, *Die Villa Cahn. Ein 'deutsches Haus' am Rhein* (Köln: Bachem, 1991). § 'a general flowering …' ('Allgemein das ganze Leben umspannende Kunstblüte'): W. Lübke, 'Das Kunstgewerbe und die Architektur', *BfK* (1872), 1–3. § 'unconsciously … without theoretical motivation … artists who followed that unconscious drive' ('unbewussten Triebe'): F. Pecht, 'deutsche Renaissancestil': *ZGVM* (1879), 49–53 (49).

68 K. Weissbach and E. Lottermoser, *Architektonische Motive … Renaissance* (Leipzig, 1868); A. Ortwein, *Deutsche Renaissance. Eine Sammlung … Architektur, Dekoration und Kunstgewerbe*, vol. 1 (Leipzig: Seemann, n.d. [1871]).

69 'an abundance …' ('fülle origineller Kraft, ja naive Genialität, individuelle Freiheit … Frische … anheimelnde Wärme und Lebendigkeit'): W. Lübke, *Geschichte der deutschen Renaissance* (vol. 5 of *Geschichte der Baukunst*, originally ed. F .Kugler; Stuttgart: Ebner & Seubert, 1873), 967–68; 2nd edn 1882, Foreword. On the term 'Renaissance', see above, n. 12.

70 'one lives …' ('Im italienischen Palaste lebt sichs wie wie ein Gott, im deutschen Patrizierhause wie ein Mensch'): Stockbauer (Ch. II, n. 69), 6.

71 'surprisingly quickly' ('aus dem Herzen kommend'): Luthmer 1892, 17; cf. Luthmer 1884b. See also under 'Reichsstil' in E. Neumeier, *Schmuck und Weiblichkeit in der Kaiserzeit* (Berlin: Reimer, 2000), 251. § 'a German trait …' ('ganz ausgesprochen deutsche Richtung'): C. Graff, in *IFz* (1882), 301.

72 'unfathomable …' ('unfassbaren Zauber'): Stockbauer (Ch. II, n. 69), 6; cf. Lehnert, 557.

73 'that incomparable …' ('jenen unvergleichlichen Gesamteindruck künstlerisch geadelten häuslichen Behagens'): Lübke, *Renaissance* (above, n. 69), 224. § Cf. Lübke on the Renaissance interior, who sees the furnishings as integral parts of the architectural composition ('Integrierende Teile der architektonischen Raumgliederung'): W. Lübke, *Renaissance* (above, n. 69), 93.

74 See G. Fincke, *Abbildungen und Beschreibungen von alten Waffen und Rüstungen* (adapted from L. Meyrick [above, n. 38], Berlin: Fincke, 1836); F. A. K. von Specht, *Geschichte der Waffen … aus alten Zeiten*, 3 vols. (Leipzig, 1869–77). Cf. the trope of the *Landsknecht* or mercenary soldier: Mennekes, 255.

75 See M. Bach, *Musterbuch für Zeichner, Lithographen, Graveure und Kunstgewerbe* (Carlsruhe: Veith, n.d. [1873–76]), pl. 56; Stockbauer (Ch. II, n. 69), 7.

76 For the *Lutherstuhl*, see e.g. *Id* (1893), 55, 64.

77 'The highly poetic spinning wheel [*das hochpoetische Spinnrad*] had become a collectors' ornament … the sewing machine, its very opposite, wholly representing the nervous haste and the egalitarian [*nivellierende*] elegance of the present', Haushofer, 71; now spinning wheels were produced 'over-delicate and breakable [*überzierlich und gebrechlich*]': Bucher, *München* (below, n. 213), 35.

78 'innige Gemeinschaft': Lübke saw the stove as a representation of 'basic family life', serving a 'poetically important role': W. Lübke, 'Über alte Öfen in der Schweiz', 2nd edn, bound with *Mitteilungen der Antiquarischen Gesellschaft Zürich*, vols. 14–15 (Zurich, 1861–66), 161–71. See also Semper vol. 2, 335; 'Schweizer Öfen', *BfK* (1881), 21–23. § *Schmollwinkel*: Stockbauer (Ch. II, n. 69), 8, 17.

79 On varied objects as *altdeutsch*, see *IFz in the* 1880s; M. Graef, *Renaissance Geräte und Galanteriestücke … im jetzigen Renaissance Stil* (Weimar: Voigt, 1888); M. Graef, *Altdeutsche und gotische Zimmermöbel* (Weimar: Voigt, 1895).

80 In addition to 'male' elements of Altdeutsch, there was a distinctive style of period dress for women, in opposition to 'French' fashion. On dress in relation to home décor, see Bergau, 24; Frieda Lipperheide, cover article in *Die Modenwelt* (part of *IFz*), vol. 6, no. 1, 1 Oct. 1870; E. Neumeier (above, n. 71); A. Rasche, *Die Kultur der Kleider* [on F. Lipperheide, editor of *IFz*] (Berlin: SMPK, 1999); Mennekes, 300ff. See the present book, p. 56.

81 *Butzenscheibe*: Lehnert, 571; also the present book, pp. 177, 195. Cf. 'Butzenscheibenlyrik' in W. Kohlschmidt (ed.), *Reallexikon der deutschen Literaturgeschichte* (Berlin: Gruyter, 1958).

The old Low Countries

82 For views from outside, see F. Narjoux, *Notes de voyage d'un architecte dans le Nord-Ouest de l'Europe* (Paris, 1876); trans. J. Peto as *Notes and Sketches of an Architect …* (London: Sampson Low, 1876); M. Vachon, *Rapports sur les musées et les écoles d'art industriel* (Paris: Quantin, 1888); and the German authors F. Ewerbeck and G. Galland. See also the notes below.

83 P. Verbraeken, *Na & naar Van Dyck: De romantische recuperatie in de 19e Eeuw* (Antwerp: Hessenhuis, 1999).

84 J. Vandenbreeden and F. Dierkens-Aubry, *The 19th Century in Belgium: Architecture and Design* (Tielt: Lannoo, 1994), also French, Dutch edns. § B. Mihaïl, 'Un movement culturel libéral à Bruxelles … la "Néo-Renaissance"', *Revue Belge de Philologie et d'Histoire*, vol. 76, no. 4 (1998), 979–1019 (with thanks to B. Mihaïl); A. E. Willis, *The Flemish Renaissance Revival in Belgian Architecture 1830–1930* (Ann Arbor: University of Michigan, 1984; with thanks to A. Willis); I. Bertels, 'Expressing Local Specificity: The Flemish Renaissance Revival,' *Architectural History*, vol. 50, (2007), 149–170; C. Buls, 'Revue de l'architecture en Belgique', *Journal of the Royal Institute of British Architects*, 3rd series, vol. 4 (1897), 445–53. A Dutch view on Flemish architecture: 'rich and forceful [*krachtig*] relief, heavy, even plump, profiles': E. Gugel, *Geschiedenis van de Bouwstijlen in de Hoofdtijdperken der Architektuur* (Arnhem: Quint, 1886), 859. See also C. H. Buls, 'Histoire de l'architecture', in E. van Bemmel (ed.), *Patria Belgica* (Brussels, 1873–75), vol. 3, 576–612 ; [A. Trappeniers], *Du nationalisme dans les Beaux-Arts considéré au point de vue du progrès* [pamphlet] (Brussels: 1877; copy Antwerp Library).

85 J.-P. Cluysenaar, *Maisons de campagne, châteaux, fermes … en Belgique* (Brussels: J van der Kalk, 1859); cf. 'formes bizarres' [of a fireplace], *L'Emulation*, vol. 1, suppl. no. 4 (1874), 27; J. M. Ryssens de Lauw, *De bouwkunde in België … 25 voorgevels ontworpen in de smaak van de Vlaamsche Bouwkunst de 16de eeuw / Architecture en Belgique …* (Liège: Claesen, 1878).

86 E.g. 'instead of being pulled in tow [*se trainer sottement à la remorque*] by the fashion of Paris': A. Schoy, *Histoire de l'influence italienne sur l'architecture des Pays Bas* (Brussels: Hayez, 1879), 155.

87 'La Belgique pouvait revendiquer un style autochtone': A. Schoy on the Belgian Pavilion by E. Janlet, in E. Frédérix (ed.), *La Belgique à l'Exposition Universelle de 1878*, vol. 2, 239, quoted in A. E. Willis (above, n. 84), 142. § A. Trappeniers, 'Les matériaux de construction …', *Revue de Belgique* vol. 31 (1879), 97–105 (104).

88 M. Rooses, *Over Stijl in de Bouwkunst* [pamphlet] (Antwerp, 22 July 1888).

89 G. Lagye, 'Le Castel de Boitsfort', *La Fédération Artistique*, vol. 3 (1874–75), 214–17 (216).

90 E.g. J. J. van Ysendyck, *Documents classés de l'art dans les Pays Bas du Xième au XVIIIième siècle* (Antwerp, 1880–89). See also L. Verpoest, 'Hans Vredeman de Vries en de Belgische architectuur in de 19e. Eeuw', in H. Borggrefe et al. (eds), *Tussen Stadspaleizen en Luchtkastelen* (Amsterdam: Ludion Gent, 2002), 375–81 .

91 'Netherlandish', 'Dutch' and 'Hollands[ch]' are here treated as synonymous.

92 On the Netherlands generally, see B. Bley, *Vom Staat zur Nation. Zur Rolle der Kunst bei der Herausbildung eines niederländischen Nationalbewusstseins im langen 19. Jahrhundert* (Münster: LIT, 2004). § Architecture: A. van der Woud, *The Art of Building, From Classicism to Modernity: The Dutch Architectural Debate 1840–1900* (Aldershot: Ashgate, 2001); R. Stenvert, 'Die Wiederentdeckung der Renaissance in der niederländischen Architekur', in *Renaissance*, vol. 3, 113–37; M. Brekelmans, 'Analyses van gebouwen van G. van Arkel … en H. P. Berlage', *Tweemaandelijks Tijdschrift voor Monumentenzorg* (KNOB), vol. 88, no. 1 (1989), 21–41; C. van Eck et al. (eds), *Het Schilderachtige. Studies … in de Nederlandsche kunsttheorie en architektuur 1650–1900* (Amsterdam: Architectura & Natura Pers, 1994); V. de Stuers, *Holland op zijn smalst* [1873], ed. M. Beck (Bussum: De Haan, 1975), 36–119.

93 'Zoo-genaamden "Oud-Hollandschen Bouwstijl"', *Bouwkundig Weekblad*, vol. 1–2, 13 April 1882, 269–70; W. van Leeuwen, 'Rationeel en schilderachtig. Isaac Gosschalk en … de Neorenaissance in Nederland', *Archis*, Feb. 1987, 30–39 (36).

94 On the Dutch applied arts: A. Martis, 'Het ontstaan van het kunstnijverheidsonderwijs in Nederland', *Nederlands Kunsthistorisch Jaarboek*, vol. 30 (1973), 79–159; J. R. de Kruyff, P. N. Muller, E. Gugel and D. van der Kellen jr, *De Nederlandsche Kunstnijverheid in verband met den internationalen wedstijd* (Amsterdam, 1876); A. le Comte, *Binnen- en Buitenlandsch Kunst-Nijverheid* (Amsterdam: Brinkman, 1877); J. R. de Kruyff et al., *Rapport der Rijkscommissie … naar de Toestand der Nederlandsche Kunstnijverheid* (The Hague, 1878); M. Vachon (above, n. 81).

95 'the charming …' ('de bekoorlijke'): *De Opmerker*, vol. 18, 2 June 1883, 235.

The home in Belgium

96 On interiors, see A. E. Willis (above, n. 84), 76ff.; W. van Leeuwen and R. van de Weijer, 'De "fortune critique" van het binnenhuis. Het negentien-eeuwse interieur', in A. Bergmans, J. de Maeyer et al. (eds), *Neo Stijlen in de 19. Eeuw* (Leuven: Universitaire Pers, 2002), 77–98; J. Vandenbreeden (above, n. 84).

97 B. Mihaïl, 'Exposition des arts décoratifs de Bruxelles en 1874 et la néo-Renaissance flamande', in C. Leblanc (ed.), *Les Arts décoratifs en Belgique au XIXe siècle* (Brussels: Musées Royaux d'Art et d'Histoire, 2004), 55–65. Cf. G. DeCock-Rutsaert, *La Menuiserie au XIXe siècle* (Ghent: Dick, 1873); T. Fumière, *Les Arts décoratifs à l'exposition du Cinquantenaire Belge* (Brussels: Guyot, 1880); *L'Emulation* (1874–); *Revue de l'architecture en Belgique* (1882); T. Fumière, *Amsterdam* (below, n. 120); P. Wytsman, *Interieurs et mobiliers de styles anciens* (Brussels: Wytsman, 1898).

98 Plantin-Moretus Museum: see e.g. *CM*, April 1886, 262, 265; H. Billung, 'Museum Plantin …', *Kunst und Gewerbe*, vol. 15 (1881), 257–73, 289–95. Cf. L. DeClercq,'Max Rooses Inspirator van de Neo-Vlaamse Renaissance', *Bulletin van der Antwerpse Vereniging voor Bodem- en Grotonderzoek*, vol. 2, April–May 1990, 37–44.

99 H. Stynen and I. van der Avoirt, 'Dit huis is De Passer genaamd', *De Woonstede door de eeuwen heen / Maisons d'hier et d'aujourd'hui*, vol. 19 (1987), 2–25; H. Stynen and I. van der Avoirt, '"Kunst brengt Gunst"'. Jean-Jacques Winders (1849–1936) en de Neo-Vlaamse Renaissance', *Monumenten en Landschappen (M&L)*, vol. 5, no. 6, Nov.-Dec. 1986, 6–26; A. E. Willis, '… J.-J. Winders and the Flemish Renaissance Revival', *Bulletin van der Antwerpse Vereniging voor Bodem- en Grotonderzoek* vol. 1, no. 2 (1988), 35–49.

100 On Mechelen, see H. De Nijn(ed.), *Het Mechelse Meubel*, 3 vols. (Mechelen: Stedelijke Musea, 2000).

101 M. Rooses, 'Over Stijl in de Bouwkunst,' *De Vlaamse School*, vol. 36 (1890), 180–85 (185). § On the fireplace, see e.g. 'Old Flemish fireplace', *BN* illus., 1 March 1872; *L'Emulation*, vol. 1, April 1874, pl. 15.

102 'antieke stijl': De Nijn (above, n. 100), 21. § All originals: C. de Roddaz, *L'Art ancien à l'Exposition Nationale Belge* (Brussels/Paris: Rozez, 1882).

103 Charle-Albert (real name: Albert Joseph Charle) was called 'the most noted "peintre décorateur, architecte décorateur" in Brussels': J. Stübben, 'Von Berlin nach Brüssel', *DB*, 25 Dec. 1880, 556; see also notes by E. Oppler in his *Die Kunst im Gewerbe* (Hanover), vols. 4–7 (1875–78); Willis (above, n. 84) 85ff.. The house, south of Brussels, is now ruined. See T. L. Lanceot and B. Mihaïl, *Charle-Albert, Maître du romantisme Belge* (Louvain la Neuve: Tabize, 2004).

104 'ancien et glorieux style flamand': 'La maison flamande de Charle-Albert', *L'Art Moderne*, vol. 7 (1887), 154–55. § 'bourgeoisie libérale': Lanceot and Mihaïl (above, n. 103), 8. § On the importance of the interior: G. Lagye, 'La Maison flamande de Boitsfort', *Couronnement de l'oeuvre de Charle-Albert* (Brussel: Verteneuil, 1887), repr. in Lancelot and Mihaïl (above, n. 103), 44–55 (46). § As a family home: Lancelot and Mihaïl (above, n. 103), 47; cf. G Lagye, 'Castel de Boitsfort' (above, n. 89), 214–17. § 'bis hinab zur Feuerzange und Zündhölzschachtel alles künstlerisch durchgebildet': J. Stübben (above, n. 103), 554; Willis (above, n. 84), 87. § made 'locally': Lancelot and Mihaïl (above, n. 103), 47. § 'commerce de Flandres': G. Lagye in Lancelot and Mihaïl (above, n. 103), 47. § Antiques: Lagye, 'Castel de Boitsfort' (above, n. 89), 215. § 'greater effect of space …' ('eine grössere Raumwirkung ist nirgendwo erzielt'): J. Stübben (above, n. 103), 554. § 'no object …' ('aucun objet ne brille au détriment d'un autre, tout est fait dans une juste pondération avec un goût et un talent qui fait de M. Charle-Albert un artiste': G. Lagye, 'Excursion au Château de M. Albert à Boitsfort', *L'Emulation*, vol. 3 (1877), 11–13. § Exposition 1880: see Lanceot and Mihaïl (above, n. 103), 56ff.

The home in the Netherlands

105 The words 'gemakkelijk', 'gemoedelijk'and 'gezellig': see E. J. Krol, *De smaak der natie. Opvattingen over huiselijkheid in de Noord-Nederlandsche poëzie van 1800–1840* (Hilversum, 1997). See also M. Westermann, '*Wooncultuur* in the Netherlands: A Historiography in Progress', *Nederlands Kunsthistorisch Jaarboek*, vol. 51 (2000), 7–35; Van Voorst tot Voorst; J. M. W. van Voorst tot Voorst, *Meubles in Nederland 1840–1900*, 2 vols. (Lochem: Tijdstroom, 1979); R. Baarsen et al., *Pronkstukken van Nederlandse interieurkunst 1835–1895* (Amsterdam: Rijksmuseum, 1995); B. Laan (ed.), *Achter gesloten deuren. Bronnen voor interieur-historisch Onderzoek 1800–1950* (Rotterdam: 010, 2000); F. van Burkom et al.(eds), *Vier eeuwen leven in toen. Nederlands Interieur in beeld* (Zwolle: Waanders, 2001); C. W. Fink, *Het Nederlandse interieur in beeld 1600–1900* (Zwolle: Waanders, 2001).

106 See G. D. J. Schotel, *Het oud-hollandsche huis-gezin der seventiende eeuw* (Haarlem: Kruseman, 1868).

107 For anti-Rococo views, see Kruyff, *De Nederlandsche Kunstnijverheid* (above, n. 94), 21–22.

108 'making a room …' ('eene kamer schoon, angenaam en gesellig te maken, een belangrijk onderdeel der bouwkunst': J. Kok, 'Kamerbetimmeringen en inrichtingen', *Bouwkundig Tijdschrift*, vol. 4 (1884), 42–43. Cf. 'De Bouwmeester is de beste decorateur', *Bouwkundige Bijdragen* (Amsterdam), vol. 14 (1865), 43 (after Rupprich-Robert; see Ch. II, n. 38).

109 'small rooms': see Kruyff, *De Nederlandsche Kunstnijverheid* (above, n. 94), 65. § 'pretty …' ('moje …'): Kam (below, n. 114), quoted in van Voorst to Voorst, 299. § On wainscoting: E. Gugel, *Geschiedenis van de bouwstijlen in de hooftijdperken der architektuur* (Arnhem: Nijhoff, 1869), 549. § On fireplaces: C. Vosmaer (below, n. 113), 156–57.

110 'warm feeling …' ('Zekere warme gevoel van huiselijke genot'): E. Gugel, 'Kastel Oud Wassenaar', *EH* (1880), 56–58; cf. Voorst tot Voorst, 301.

111 'O hemel!! dus een gebouw in "Oud Hollandschen Stijl".' Muyskens elaborates further: 'No, esteemed reader', it is a style loved by some, hated by others; not Gothic, not Greek, but a modern building with 'modern comfort … shall we admit here that the "the building is in the Renaissance style"?': *Bouwkundig Tijdschrift*, vol. 1 (1881), 1–2.

112 'light and air' ('Het vindt geen gezelligheid in een mystisch schemerlicht'): Kruyff, *Rapport* (above, n. 94), 10.

113 E. C. Vosmaer, *De kunst in het daaglijksch leven. Vrij naar het Engelsch van Lewis Foreman Day* (The Hague: Nijhoff, 1884; 2nd edn 1886) § On 'homeliness' ('huislijkheid'): 119; eclectics: 24; Oud Hollandsch style too dark: 145, 147; on light: 155ff.; darkness: 162; wainscoting: 138, 158; Eastern porcelain ('niets schoner'): 151.

114 J. B. Kam, *De Versiering van onze woning* (Haarlem: Bohn, 1886; 2nd edn 1898); cf. Day, Blanc, Falke.

115 On paintings: *EH* (1875ff.); H. Kraan, 'Le Goût de la Hollande', in J. Sillevis et al. (eds), *L'École de la Haye* (exh. cat. Paris: Grand Palais, 1983), 115–24.

116 Old Delft: Kruyff, *Rapport* (above, n. 94), 9. § 'ferreting …' ('snuffelende antiquiteten handelaar'): Comte (above, n. 94), 22.

117 'the olden times …' ('de oude tijd was veel vrolijker van aard dan onze is'). According to J. Ter Gouw, the olden times did not necessarily look like a 'skeleton in an opened grave' ('een geraamte bij een ingestorte graftombe'), or a pale ghost with 'unreadable parchments in his emaciated hand' ('met onleesbare pergamenten in de dorre hand'). 'No! He lives, he looks fresher and more forceful than the younger generations' ('Neen! hij leeft, en ziet er frisscher en krachtiger uit dan 't jonger geslacht over 't algemeen'): J. Ter Gouw, 'Voorrede', *Oude Tijd*, vol. 3 (1871), iii–iv.

118 'picturesque …' ('schilderachtige openbaring van het Amsterdamsche leven van vroeger en later tijd'): J. A. Alberdingk Thijm, 'Historische Tentoonstelling van Amsterdam', *EH* (1876), 212–16, 222–24 (224).

119 Hindelooper Kamer: see the present book, p. 287.

120 H. P. Berlage, 'De Retrospektieve Kunst', *Bouwkundig Tijdschrift*, vol. 4 (1883), 777–88; D. van der Kellen, jr, 'De "retrospective kunst" op de Internationale Tentoonstelling in 1883 te Amsterdam', *EH* (1884), 17–20; T. Fumière, *L'Exposition d'Amsterdam et la Belgique aux Pays Bas* (Brussels, 1883), 34–39. § 'original' ('la partie vraiment originale'): Fumière, 34. § See Berlage on commercial décor: 'miserable whims' ('ellendigste modefratsen'): Berlage, 81; 'true' ('waar'): Berlage, 81. § 'whole of …' ('dit voorwerp vol poëzie … geheele germanische poëzie'): Berlage, 78. § On sitting/sleeping: Berlage, 81; cf. here B. Laan, 'Een schilderij in drie dimensies. De "Kamer van Jan Steen"', in van Eck, *Schilderachtige* (above, n. 92), 117–28 (126–27). § 'The cupboard …' ('De kast is onder de meubles het inbegrijp van huiselijkheit'): Berlage, 83. § 'Aren't we put into a serious mood by the rich yet modest woodwork of the chimney-piece, the cupboard, the bedstead and the door, as if it were all of a piece, just as the men of that period were also of a piece' ('hoe ernstig steemde ons de rijke en toch zedige betimmering van schoornsteen, kast, ledikant en deur, alles als war't uit een stuk, evenals de mannen van dien tijd uit een stuk waren'): D. van der Kellen, jr., 18. § 'lit in the most …': ('cet intérieur, eclairé de la plus heureuse façon, avec son arrière plan en lumière et le reste dans une heureuse pénombre, a un cachet de poésie, qui fait bien revivre une époque où la bonhomie et la franchise étaient grandement en faveur'): Fumière, 36; 'compléter l'illusion': Fumière, 35–36. § Cf. the definitely Dutch motif of 'flesschenpooten', or claw feet: Berlage, 80. § 'comfortable' ('een "gezellige" kamer … "Wat is hier gezellig"'): Berlage, 78. 'One can see that everything has been devised in the charming interior to give it the naïve and intimate character that accounts for the great charm of old dwellings' ('Tout, on le voit, a été étudié dans cet intérieur charmant pour lui donner ce cachet naïf et intime qui fait le grand charme des anciens demeures'): Fumière, 38. § On the Dutch folk movement, see DeJong, 1991 (below, n. 277).

121 On Berlage etc.: S. Polana, *H. P. Berlage: Opera Completa* (Milan, 1987); T. M. Eliëns, *H. P. Berlage. Ontwerpen voor het interieur* (exh. cat. The Hague: Gemeentemuseum / Waanders: Zwolle, 1998).

122 For the 'ideal' suburban home in Belgium from the 1880s, see A. F. Ogata, *Art Nouveau and the Social Vision of Modern Living* (Cambridge University Press, 2001).

Old English II

The ideal cottage

123 For books on Victorian and Arts and Crafts domestic décor and design, see Ch. II, nn. 70–77; n. 31 (above); and Ch. VI, n. 14. Three further works, of a very different kind, are: L. F. Day, 'Victorian Progress in Applied Design', *AJ* (1887), 184–202; C. Newton, *Victorian Design for the Home* (London: V&A, 1999); T. Keeble, *The Domestic Moment: Design, Taste and Identity in the Late Victorian Interior* (diss., Royal College of Arts, London, 2004). For earlier, see also J. Ayres, *The Domestic Interior: The British Tradition 1500–1850* (New Haven and London: Yale University Press, 2003).

124 'England has achieved …' ('was England bereits erreicht hat, eine vollkommen nationale auf der Grundlage der alten Volkskunst aufgebaute Hausbaukunst'): Muthesius, H., vol. 1, 209; cf. D. Crellin and I. Dungavell (eds), *Architecture and Englishness 1880–1914* ([London]: Society of Architectural Historians of Great Britain, 2006).

125 K. Sayer, *Country Cottages: A Cultural History* (Manchester University Press, 2000); C. Payne, *Rustic Simplicity: Scenes of Cottage Life in Nineteenth-Century British Art* (London: Lund Humphries, 1998); Crowley; Mandler, 26ff., 141ff. § W. Howitt (Introduction, n. 17), 411.

126 'What can art …': E. Goadby, 'Art in the Cottage', *AJ* (1879), 5–8. § Cf. 'The rural peasant life of honest poverty … an eye on comfort and cleanliness': 'Royal Academy and other Exhibitions', *Blackwoods Edinburgh Magazine*, vol. 88 (1860), 65–74 (70).

127 'sensory details are underwritten both by the concept of utility and by the rhetorical category of the pastoral … no admiration for rank and wealth, nor a lust for the superficial pleasures of the eye': T. Logan on George Elliot's *Daniel Deronda* (1876): see 'Decorating Domestic Space: Middle-Class Women and Victorian interiors', in V. D. Dickerson (ed.), *Keeping the Victorian House* (New York: Garland, 1995), 207–34 (228); cf. Cruickshank (Ch. IV, n. 40).

128 'enthusiastic admirers': [Anon], 'Cottager and Cottages', *ChM*, vol. 41, Jan.-June 1880, 683–98 (688). § 'We Englishmen …': 'The American House', *All the Year Round* [London], 6 Jan. 1894, 153–55 (153).

129 A. Grieve, 'The Content and Form of Furniture in Rossetti's Art of 1848–1858', *Journal of Pre-Raphaelite Studies*, no. 8, Fall 1999, 9–28 (11).

130 J. Marsh, *William Morris and the Red House* (London: National Trust, 2005); P. Todd, *William Morris and the Arts & Crafts Home* (London: Thames & Hudson, 2005).

131 'once was …': 'Royal Academy …', *Blackwoods Edinburgh Magazine*, vol. 88 (1860), 65–74 (70); cf. *The Cranbrook Colony* (exh. cat. Wolverhampton Art Gallery, 1977; repr. Maidstone, 1981); J. Dafforne,'The Works of Frederick Daniel Hardy', *AJ* (1875), 73–76.

132 Saint, 38.

133 'old England': 'The Arts in the Household', *Blackwoods Edinburgh Magazine*, vol. 105 (1869), 361–78 (368); cf. Eastlake, 6, 18, 34. See also 'The modern art revival is a national movement': Miller (Ch. II, n. 76), 3.

134 'art of the salon': J. Hungerford Pollen, 'Ancient and Modern Furniture', *B*, 5 Sept. 1874, 739–41 (740).

135 'All English …': J. M. Brydon, 'A few more words about "Queen Anne"', *AmA*, 6 Oct. 1877, 320–22. Cf. 'Domestic Architectural Style', *Ar*, 6 July 1878, 1–2; 'Old English … lend[s] itself very easily to modern requirements' [on Brydon's dining room in 'Poplar', Regent's Park, London]: *BN*, 19 Sept. 1873, 310; 'The Rustic Theory of Art', *Ar*, 14 April 1877, 239. See also Conway (Ch. II, n. 77), 217; M. B. Adams (Ch. II, n. 76); J. Allibone, *George Devey, Architect 1820–1886* (Cambridge: Lutterworth, 1991); S. W. Soros, *Thomas Jeckyll: Architect and Designer 1872–1881* (New Haven and London: Yale University Press, 2003), 172, 368.

136 'Pre-Raphaelites': Goadby (above, n. 126).

137 'English habits': W. Meynell, 'The Homes of Our Artists (Leighton)', *MA* (1881), 169–76 (176).

138 On oak, see 'English Wood … ', *BN*, 10 April 1885, 556–57; Jervis; Cornforth, 22; Robinson, 'Dining Room Wall' (Ch. III, n. 113). § 'a bit of …': Haweis, *Beauty* (Ch. II, n. 76), 227; cf. Ch. III, n. 87.

139 'modern machine …': [Anon], 'Treasure Houses of Art I' [Morrison interior; see also Ch. III, n. 251], *MA* (1879), 140–44 (141). § 'sensitiveness': Champneys (above, n. 25), 10.

140 Eastlake 201–2, 162ff. Knole illustrated 160. § On modern French comfort: G. R. R., 'Furniture and Decoration', *BN*, 27 Feb. 1874, 223–24. § 'piggish laziness': Godwin *Ar*, 86, here on bedrooms.

141 'Common wooden settle': Eastlake, 163. Cf. the view that German houses may lack 'what we English denominate *comfort*', yet still convey 'a picturesque and refined homeliness': Mrs Jameson, *Sketches of Germany* (Frankfurt am Main: C. Jügel, 1837), 260. § 'romance': W. Crane, 'The English Revival in Decorative Art', in W. Crane, *William Morris to Whistler* (London: Bell, 1911), 76–77.

142 Champneys: see above, n. 25. § W. Morris, *News from Nowhere* (1890).

The 18th-century revival

143 See Morris on 'refinement', p. 153 of the present book. See also earlier views on national Gothic: 'Our Gothic … was homely and sweet … French Gothic heavy': C. Everington, 'English versus French Gothic', *Ecclesiologist*, vol. 25 (1864), 332. Cf. similar discussions between Morris and Warrington Taylor, in Girouard 1977, 15. See also Morris's 1860s 'Sussex' ('Morris') chair and his Green Dining Room in the V&A, from 1865; R .N. Shaw, too,'blends roughness and refinement': Saint, 34.

144 J. M. Brydon, '"Queen Anne"' (above, n. 135); Girouard

1977; G. T. Robinson, 'Our Household Furniture', *AJ* (1881), 313–16 (315).
145 See Bann, Chapter 7.
146 'Nobody cared': T. E. Kebbel, 'The 18th c.', *ChM*, vol 38, July–Dec. 1878, 540–58 (542, 540).
147 J. M. Brydon (above, n. 135), 322.
148 Robinson (above, n. 76), 26.
149 See 'The Furniture Exhibition', *B*, 18 May 1878, 503; J. Beavington Atkinson, 'Gothic Furniture: Recent Revivals', *AJ* (1867), 25. On 'sound' joinery in the early Georgian era: Eastlake, 4; Muthesius, H., 87.
150 On fat people, see Kebbel (above, n. 146), 541; see also W. M. Thackeray's own (partly neo-Rococo) house: 'W. M. Thackeray', *Harper's*, vol. 49, Sept. 1874, 533–49. § 'John Bull's … square in his taste as in his seating furniture': 'John Bull's New House', *All the Year Round*, 2nd series, vol. 19 (1877–78), 5–10 (5). § Satires on thin furniture: see e.g. Haweis, 54.

Old English consolidated

151 George and Peto: see Cooper, N. § 'Serviceable and sensible': J. W. Benn, 'Some New Things in "Old London"', *CM*, vol. 6, June 1886, 308–12 (311). § 'warm, comfortable': J. W. Benn, 'At the Royal Academy', *CM*, vol. 7, June 1887, 308–14 (310). § On 'Georgian', see e.g. W. Timms, *CM*, vol. 5, May 1885, 223.
152 'never coarse': W. Morris, 'The Lesser Arts', in Morris, 1–37 (24); 'tidiness': quoted in A. Vallance, *William Morris: His Art, His Writings …* (London: Bell, 1897), 84.
153 'honest English': J. W. Benn, 'Furniture …"Arts and Crafts Exhibitions"', *CM*, vol. 9, Dec. 1888, 141–46 (143). See illustrations of old cottages by Myles Birkett Foster, Helen Allingham and others (very few of interiors).
154 H. Spielmann, 'Kate Greenaway', *MA* (1902), 118–122; I. Taylor, '*The Art of Kate Greenaway* (Exeter: Webb & Bower, 1991).
155 See M. H. Baillie Scott's early illustrations in *BN*, *The Studio*. Cf. J. D. Kornwolf, *M. H. Baillie Scott and the Arts and Crafts Movement* (Baltimore, MA: Johns Hopkins University Press), 1972. See also the present book, p. 9; A. Crawford, *C. R. Ashbee* (New Haven and London: Yale University Press, 1985).

Old Colonial

156 See Ch. II, nn. 79–83; Ch. III, n. 278; Girouard 1977, 209–33. By 1879 Eastlake was less influential: see e.g. 'The Union Club', *AA*, vol. 1, June 1879, 9–10. § Cf. *New York Sketchbook on Architecture*, 1874–76, followed by *AmA*.
157 K. Ames in Intr. to A. Axelrod (ed.), *The Colonial Revival in America* (New York: Norton, 1985), 9; W. B. Rhoads, 'The Colonial Revival and American Nationalism', *Journal of the Society of Architectural Historians*, vol. 35, no. 4, (1976), 239–54.
158 For kitchens at Philadelphia World's Fair 1876: R. Roth, 'The New England, or "Old Tyme", Kitchen Exhibitions at Nineteenth Century Fairs', in Axelrod (above, n. 157), 159–83; T .A. Denenberg, *Wallace Nutting and the Invention of Old America* (New Haven and London: Yale University Press, 2003); L. T. Ulrich, *The Age of Homespun Objects and Stories in the Creation of an American Myth* (New York: Knopf, 2006). § M. Y. Frye, 'The Beginnings of the Period Room in American Museums', in Axelrod (above, n. 157), 217–40; Denenberg (above). § On furniture: see the illustrations in 'A glimpse at "Seventy-Six"', *Harper's*, vol. 49, Jul. 1874, 230–45 (231); R. Roth,'The Colonial Revival and "Centennial Furniture"', *Art Quarterly*, vol. 27, no. 1 (1964), 58–78; K. A. Marling, *George Washington Slept Here: Colonial Revivals and American Culture 1876–1986* (Cambridge, MA: Harvard University Press, 1988); *EID*, 300. § C. Monkhouse, 'The Spinning Wheel as Artifact, Symbol …', in K. L. Ames (ed.), *Victorian Furniture*, vol. 8 of *Nineteenth Century* (Philadelphia: Victorian Society of America), 155–72; cf. above, n. 770.
159 Scully, 88.
160 Said about Rockwood House (mid-19th century), near Tarrytown, NY: [Anon], 'The Homes of America', *Art Journal* (New York edn), vol. 1 (1875), 369–70.
161 Cf. the British Commissioner's Residence at the Philadelphia Centennial Exhibition (des. T. Harris, 1876; see Scully, 19–21, ill. 14), in timber-framed 'Old English', confusingly also called 'Queen Anne' in the US.
162 'Hitherto …': 'Colonial Houses and their uses to Art' (review of A. Little, *Early New England Interiors*, Boston, MA: A. Williams, 1878), *AmA*, 12 Jan. 1878, 12–13; cf. Brydon (above, n. 135). § 'good old colony…': Holly, 864.
163 'a very old town': T. B. Aldrich, 'An Old Town by the Sea' [Portsmouth], *Harper's*, vol. 49, Nov. 1874, 632–50. § 'old time …': 'The Queen of Aquidneck' [Newport, RI], *Harper's*, vol. 49, Aug. 1874, 305–20. § 'mostly square …': *Harper's*, 'An Old Town' (above), 636–37. § 'undoubtedly commonplace': *Harper's*, 'An Old Town' (above), 643.
164 'flavour of the past', 'old work … picturesqueness … quaintness': Spofford, 157–58. § 'Furniture … Renaissance', *Harper's*, vol. 54, Nov. 1877, 633–54 (644).
165 'covered with …': 'Fairbanks house, Dedham MA', *AmA*, 26 Nov. 1881. Cf. G. W. Sheldon (ed.), *Artistic Country Seats* (New York: Appletons, 1886–87); repr. with new text by A. Lewis as *American Country Seats of the Golden Age* (New York: Dover, 1982), vol. 1, 177, quoted in Scully, 118.
166 'Puritan introspection': Axelrod (above, n. 158), 275–77; cf. D. E. Shi, *The Simple Life: Plain Living and High Thinking in American Culture* (New York: Oxford University Press, 1985); E. J. Lapsansky, *Quaker Aesthetics* (Philadelphia: Pennsylvania University Press, 2003).
167 'Graves of Newport', *Harper's*, vol. 39, Aug. 1869, 373–88 (375). Cf. 'old time festivities': L. Viele, 'The Knickerbockers of New York', *Harper's*, vol. 54, Dec. 1876, 33–43 (42).
168 'Cozy and convivial': 'Graves of Newport' (above), 382. § 'The halls …': *Harper's*, 'An Old Town' (above, n. 163), 634. § 'the rooms …': J. C. Cady, 'Dutch Farmhouses in New Jersey', *AmA* (1877), 401–2, quoted in Scully, 49. § 'live amid …', 'of the interior …': R. S. Peabody, 'Georgian Homes of New England', *AmA* (1877), 338–39, quoted in Scully, 44–45.
169 On comfort: 'the hardest and homeliest bench … made of oak plank [is] more comfortable and more respectable than many of the spring seats and hair cloth sofas and rocking chairs': W. H. Cleaveland et al., *Villa and Farm Cottage: The Requirements of American Village Homes* (New York: Backus, 1856), 133; cf. Grier for 'soft' comforts.
170 See Scully 54, 144, etc.
171 Convenience: Handlin; Ierley (Introduction, n. 16). § Railroad: Holly, 856.
172 'breadth and dignity': 'Accessories … of Home Decoration', *DF*, vol. 5, Oct. 1884, 14.
173 See e.g. Sherman House, Newport, 1874: Scully, 114; M. Meister (ed.), *H.H. Richardson* (Cambridge, MA: MIT Press, 1999). Scully, 99, characterized the interiors as 'spatial movements'.
174 'raw new tones': Elliott (Ch. II, n. 83), 73–74. § 'light golden yellow': R. Riordan, 'Artistic Homes … Montclair N.J.', *MA* (1886), 45–48.
175 'All Yankee people': [Anon.], 'Antiques made to Order', *Scientific American*, 15 Feb. 1890, 99.
176 'absence of vulgarity', 'dignity': R. S. Peabody, 'The Georgian Houses of New England', *AmA* (1878), 54–55, quoted in Scully, 60; cf. 'crispness of colonial woodworking': Scully, 63; 'simplicity and smallness of details … have increased the apparent size of the rooms': P. J. C. Cady, 'Some features of Dutch farmhouses of New Jersey', *AmA* (1877), 401–2, quoted in Scully, 49.
177 Cf. Frank Furness's log hut, built 1873, in *Artistic Houses*, 101. C. W. Clark wrote of 'barbaric comfort': 'An Occidental Interior', *DF*, vol. 13, Nov. 1888, 53–54. See also Mayhew 291–95; W. Barkside Maynard, 'Thoreau's House at Walden' [*c.* 1845], *Art Bulletin*, vol. 81, no. 2 (1999), 303–25.
178 Cf. 'The application of the word "Colonial" to pre-Revolutionary architecture and decoration has created a vague impression that there existed at that time an American architectural style. … "Colonial" architecture is simply a modest copy of Georgian models': Edith Wharton and Ogden Codman, jr., *The Decoration of Houses* (New York: Scribners / London: Batsford, 1898; reprints), 81–82. Compare earlier 'Biedermeier' problems, above, Ch. I, n. 26.

The old fireside

179 See Giedion; Crowley; Ierley (Introduction, n. 16), 27; L. Wright, *Home Fires Burning: The History of Domestic Heating and Cooking* (London: Routledge, 1964); H. J. Kauffman, *The American Fireplace* (New York: Galahead, 1972); G. Bachelard, *Fragment d'une poétique du feu* (Paris: Presses Universitaires, 1988; American edn Dallas Institute, 1990); G. B. Piranesi, *Diverse maniere d'adornare i cammini et ogni altra parte degli edifizi* (Paris: Firmin Didot, n.d. [1836]).
180 Britons argued, in defence, that coal was cheap and there were servants to do the work: see F. Edwards, jr., *Our Domestic Fireplaces* (London: Longmans Green, 1870). The US also used stoves of a Continental European kind.
181 Loudon says little on the fireplace: cf. 650, 652, 1017; ill. in Joy, 366–77.
182 'gaité …. la flamme pétillante nous permet de tisonner': Havard 1884, 310–12. French fireplaces generally small: Loyer, 182; cf. E. Peclet, *Traité de la chaleur*, 3rd edn (Paris: Masson, 1860). Blanc, 232, disliked stoves as 'gloomy' and 'German' ('lugubres, allemandes').
183 'pleasant': Rumford quoted in Ierley (Introduction, n. 16), 27. § 'national custom': Edwards (above, n. 181), 62; Davidson (Ch. III, n. 158), 100–101. § 'The good old …': Kerr, 101. § 'dignity …': Spofford, 233. § 'so many tender …': Holly, 57. § 'sanctum …', 'lares': G. T. Robinson (above, n. 76), 23, 24. Cf. the hearth's 'poetic attraction … images arise … of planning, of hoping, dreaming' ('poetischen Reiz … traulich flackerndes Kaminfeuer … liebe Bilder aus demselben aufsteigen, der Erinnerung, des Planens, Hoffens, Träumens'): Dohme, 35.
184 Tristram, 103.
185 'cold and uncongenial': 'Art Literature' (review of Cooper, H. J.), *The Artist Journal of Home Culture*, vol. 1, 15 Jan. 1880, 19–22 (20). § 'sprucely …': Eastlake, *Gothic Revival* (Ch. II n. 39), 344. 'brass fender': review of Orrinsmith (see Ch. II, n. 75) in *B*, 15 Dec. 1877, 1241–42.
186 J. Pickering Putnam, *The Open Fireplace in all Ages* (Boston, MA: Osgood, 1880; here 2nd edn 1882), Intr.
187 'friendly warmth …': Putnam (above, n. 186), Intr. § 'can hardly …': 'Chapter on Fireplaces', *MA* (1886), 187–91 (187).
188 'new art movement' ('Neue Kunstbewegung'): Muthesius, H., 128, cf. 137.
189 The inglenook an 'old peasant form' ('Altes Bauernmotiv'): Muthesius, H., 128. The etymology was unclear: 'such "ingle nooks" – deeply recessed fireplaces, forming a family gathering-place, a medievalism … this word "ingle" was one which never dare have ventured into polite society until long after Elizabeth's days': G. T. Robinson, 'Our Houshold Furniture … The Chimney-piece (cont.)', *AJ* (1881), 57–61 (61); M. Harper, 'Here to the Ingle Where True Hearts Mingle: The Revival of the Settle and the Ingle Nook by 19th-Century English Architects', *Journal of the Decorative Arts Society 1850–the present*, no. 12, n.d. [*c.* 1988], 10–17; cf. Saint, 116ff.; Girouard 1979; M. H. Baillie Scott, 'The Fireplace in the Suburban House', *The Studio*, vol. 6, Nov. 1895, 101–8.
190 W. E. Nesfield in *c.* 1864, and R .N. Shaw in the mid-1860s: Saint 33. Cf. Lord Armstrong's inglenook in Cragside (by R. N. Shaw), ill. in Girouard 1979, 299.

Old Alpine and Bavarian (Altdeutsch II)

Alpine

191 Cf. the comment 'No catastrophy without idyll, no idyll without catastrophy': Harald Szemann, quoted in S. Desarnaulds (ed.), *Le Chalet dans tous ses états* (Chêne Bourg/Genève: Georg, 1999), 61, 82. See also P. B. Bernard, *Rush to the Alps … Vacationing in Switzerland* (New York: Columbia University Press, 1978).
192 There was less emphasis on the 'Alpine' in Austria (but cf. *ABZ* (1843)). Tyrol's 'Alpine' movement came after that of Switzerland: see *Bayerisch-Tirolische G'schichten: … eine Nachbarschaft* (exh. cat. Festung Kufstein, 1993).
193 J. Ruskin, *The Poetry of Architecture* [i.e. on cottages in the Alps and in Britain] (first publ. under pseudonym Kata Pushin), *AM* (1837–38); E. Gladbach, *Der Schweizer Holzstyl* (Darmstadt: Koehler, 1868); Semper, vol. 2; cf. *E.-E. Viollet-le-Duc: Centenaire de la mort à Lausanne* (exh. cat. Lausanne: Musée historique de l'Ancien-Evêché, 1979); J. Gubler, *Nationalisme et internationalisme dans l'architecture moderne de la Suisse* (Lausanne: Age d'homme, 1975); E. Crettaz-Stürzel, *Heimatstil. Reformarchitektur in der Schweiz 1896–1914* (Frauenfeld: Huber, 2005).
194 Cf. the 'Swiss cottages' in parks in England, Prussia, etc., from *c.* 1810–60. Thereafter a generalized Alpine wooden décor was applied to larger villas in Europe (except Britain) and the US, even where there was a local tradition of wooden building, such as in Norway; see J.-M. Pérouse de Montclos, 'Le Chalet à la Suisse … modèle vernaculaire', *Architectura* 1987) 76–96; C. Norberg-Schulz, 'The "Swiss Style"', in (ed.) W. Blaser, *Fantasie in Holz / Fantasy in Wood* (Basel: Birkhäuser, 1987), 7–23; M. Imhof, *Historistisches Fachwerk … im 19. Jh. in Deutschland, Grossbritannien, Frankreich, Österreich, Schweiz, USA* (Bamberg: Bayerische Verlagsanstalt, 1996); Eldahl (below, n. 283). § 'Salzburger Sennhütte': *Illustrierte Zeitung* [Leipzig], 30 Aug. 1873, 152.
195 See S. Ziegler, *Holzvertäfelte Stuben der Renaissance zwischen*

Main und südlichem Alpenrand (Frankfurt am Main: Lang, 1995); 'Picturesque examples of Swiss Timberwork', *Ar*, 10 Jan 1874; M. Heyne, *Kunst im Hause* (Munich, 1881).

196 'infinitely warm ...' ('unendlich warmen Eindruck'): Falke 1862, 674. § On the Rütlistube (1868): H. Gasser, *Die Kunstdenkmäler des Kantons Uri* (Basel: Birkhäuser, 1986), vol. 2, 424–25. Cf. 'Renaissance Stube für die Pariser Weltausstellung 1878', *Die Eisenbahn*, vol. 8, 12 April 1878, 121–22 [no. ill.]; Rüegg (Introduction, n. 16); M. Bilfinger, 'In welchem Stil sollen wir einrichten ... Der Bund und die Räpresentation; die Innenaustattung', *KAS*, vol. 43, no. 4 (1996), 335–40.

197 *Brettstuhl*: cf. Renaissance chair types such as *stabelle*, *sgabello*, *escabeau*: Havard *Dict.*, vol. 2, 450–54; Rüegg (Introduction, n. 16), 54–55; K. Csilléry, 'Zur Geschichte des Brettstuhls', *Jahrbuch für Volkskunde*, Neue Folge, vol. 10 (1987), 217–40.

198 'extremely homely' ['wohnlich']... countrified character of the Bavarian Highlands': *Gb*, vol. 2 (1864), 31–32; also [Anon.], *Musterbuch* (Ch. II, n. 87), pl. 132. Cf. I. Bauer, 'Von "Tölzer Art" zur "Volkskunst"', *Zeitschrift für Bayerische Landesgeschichte*, vol. 60, no. 2 (1997), 803–18; Bauer, *Möbel aus Franken* (above, n. 52), 92–93. For later versions, see B. Kleindorfer-Marx, *Volkskunst als Stil. ... Franz Zell* (Regensburg: S. Röderer, 1996) § Illustrations of some 'Tölzer' furniture in Eastlake, 178 (also 1st edn 1868); see also Loftie, *Dining Room* (Ch. II, n. 75), 20; 'from Tyrol, Bavaria': Cook, 255; 'Swiss': *FG*, vol. 2, 2 Jan. 1875, 17.

The Bavarian Alpine style in Munich

199 Cf. 'the wildest and coarsest naturalism ... of carved Black Forest clocks and objects from the Tyrol': Falke, *Paris* (Ch. III, n. 54), 41.

200 Illustrated in Hirth; cf. H. E. von Berlepsch, 'Renaissance Interieurs in der Schweiz', *ZBKM* (1876), no. 1, 3–5.

201 *Heimat*: A. Schumann, *Heimatdenken. Regionales Bewusstsein in der deutschsprachigen Literatur 1815–1914* (Cologne: Böhlau, 2002). Cf. Riehl: 'Every real human thinks his own *Heimat* as the most beautiful in the whole world ... healthy, joyous, conscious of *Heimat* ['-Bewusstsein']: W. H. Riehl, *Volkskunde als Wissenschaft*, in *Wissenschaftliche Vorträge* (Braunschweig, 1858) 411–31 (431).

202 'Bauernhaus': Meyer (Ch. II, n. 56), in Supplement vol., 1878; K. J. Schröer, 'Das Bauernhaus', *Austellungs Bericht* (20); cf. S. Muthesius, 'The "Deutsches Bauernhaus"', in J. Purchla (ed.), *Vernacular Art in Central Europe* (Krakow: International Cultural Centre, 2001), 65–69 .

203 'the apparently ...': A. Hoffmann, 'Gabriel Seidl', *DB*, 3 May 1913, 326–28, 335–36 (336). Cf. J. Erichsen and E. Brockhoff (eds), *Bayern & Preussen & Bayerns Preussen. ... historische Beziehungen* (Munich: Haus der bayerischen Geschichte, 1999).

204 Bavarianism: I. Bauer (ed.), *Das Bayerische Nationalmuseum. Der Neubau an der Prinzregentenstrasse 1892–1900* (Munich: Hirmer, 2000); H. Bauer, *Mythos Bayern* [exhaustively pictorial] (exh. cat. Munich: Stadtmuseum, n.d. [2004]).

205 On the Bierkeller, see Pasinger Fabrik (ed.), *Wirtshäuser in München um 1900* (Munich: Buchendorfer, 1997), e.g. Gabriel Seidl's 'Deutsches Haus' in Munich, built 1880.

206 N. Götz and C. Schack-Simitzis (eds), *Die Prinzregentenzeit* (exh. cat. Munich: Stadtmuseum, 1988–89); M. Makela, *The Munich Secession: Art and Artists in Turn of the Century Munich* (Princeton University Press, 1990). Most informative on all aspects of late 19th-century Munich art is A.-C. Foulon, *De L'Art pour tous: Les éditions F. Bruckmann et leurs revues d'art dans Munich 'ville d'art' vers 1900* (Frankfurt am Main: P. Lang, 2002).

207 'uniformity ...' ('einförmig ... schlicht und einfach, Reinlichkeit und Genauigkeit'): H. Schmid, *Der Loder, Gesammelte Schriften*, vol. 29 (Leipzig: Keil, 1874), 12–13; cf. Karl Stieler, *Bilder aus Bayern. Ausgewählte Schriften* (Stuttgart: Bonz, 1908). § 'the basic ...' ('die Grundverhältnisse des altgermanischen Lebens sind einfach und ruhig'): K. Weinhold, *Altnordisches Leben* (Berlin: 1856; repr. Graz: Akademischer Verlag, 1977), 238. § 'Mountains, said to symbolize energy and action, have given place to plains and valleys which represent repose and contemplation': J. Beavington Atkinson, 'The Exhibition of German Art', *AJ* (1880), 304–7; cf. H. Ludwig et al., *Münchner Malerei im 19. Jh.* (Munich: Bruckmann, 1981–83).

208 Cf. 'Schweizerei' [building] in der Bleckenau, Poellattal, Upper Bavaria, by G .F. Ziebland, 1853–54: W. Nerdinger (ed.), *Zwischen Glaspalast und Maximilianeum. Architektur in Bayern zur Zeit Maximiians II 1848–1864* (exh. cat. Munich: Stadtmuseum, 1997); G. Schober, *Frühe Villen und Landhäuser am Starnberger See* (Waakirchen-Schaftlach: Orea, 1998).

209 B. Gedon, *Lorenz Gedon. Die Kunst des Schönen* (Munich: Nymphenburger, 1994); D. Bachmeier, *Gedon ... Leben und Werk* (diss., University of Munich, 1988).

210 On Wagner, see above, n. 51.

211 On beer, see above, n. 205.

212 C. Hölz (ed.), *Schön und gut. Positionen des Gestaltens seit 1850* [on Munich applied arts] (Munich: Zentralinstitut für Kunstgeschichte / Bayerischer Kunstgewebeverein, 2002); *ZBKM*; Münchner Kunstgewerbeverein [= Bayerischer Kunstgewerbeverein], *Festschrift zur Jubiläumsfeier* (Munich, 1876); L. Gmelin (ed.), *Festschrift zum fünfzigjährigen Jubiläum des Bayerischen Kunstgewerbevereins* (Munich: Oldenbourg, 1901).

213 'preparing feelings ...': J. von Schmädel, 'Zweck und Ziel ... der allgemeinen deutschen Kunst- und Kunstgewerbeausstellung [name of exhibition varies somewhat] in München', *ZBKM*, 1876, nos. 3–4, 1–4 (3). § 'directed ...': B. Bucher, *Die Kunst-Industrie auf der deutschen Ausstellung in München* (Vienna: Österreichisches Central-Comité, 1876), 9; S. Wieber, *Designing the Nation: Neo-Northern Renaissance Interiors and the Politics of Identity in Late Nineteenth-Century Germany 1876–1888* (diss., University of Chicago, 2004). For ateliers, see the present book, p. 117.

214 Gedon (see above, n. 209), and F. Seitz in *ZGVM* (1884).

215 'a free ...' ('Freier Schwung'): O. Mothes, 'Münchener Kunstgewerbeausstellung ...', [Romberg's] *Zeitschrift für praktische Baukunst*, vol. 76 (1876), 307–19 (315); cf. 'flotter Wurf': 'Die deutsch-nationale Kunstgewerbeausstellung München': *D* (1888), 314–15. § 'working fast' ('rasch arbeiten'): Lehnert, 475. Falke disliked it all: 'Die moderne Kunstindustrie ...', and G. Hirth [in reply]: 'Der Stil unserer Zeitschrift', *ZBKM* (1879), no. 2, 12–15. § 'We need an art ...' ('Wir brauchen eine Kunst bei welcher uns wohl wird'): M. Carriere in E. E. Eckstein (ed.), *Deutsche Dichterhalle* (Leipzig, 1876), 229–32, 275–81. For Munich generally, see: M. Bringmann, *Friedrich Pecht (1814–1903). Massstäbe der deutschen Kunstkritik 1850–1900* (Berlin: Mann, 1982); F. Pecht, *Geschichte der Münchner Kunst im 19. Jahrhundert* (Munich: Bruckmann, 1888); above, n. 206.

216 'koloristisch ...', i.e. painting was understood as 'purely physical'. See A. Bayersdorfer, 'Neue Kunstbestrebungen in München' (1874), in *A. Bayersdorfer[s] Leben und Schriften* (Munich: Bruckmann, 1902), 206–44 (238).

217 'very beautiful': W. F. Exner, *Holz als Rohstoff für das Kunstgewerbe* (Weimar: Voigt, 1869), 10. § On 'warmth' in Swiss houses: 'the wainscoting shows, like the boards of the floor and the ceiling, the natural colours of the wood in the warm reflective sunlight': Gladbach (above, n. 193), 23.

218 F. Pecht, *Aus dem Münchner Glaspalast Studien* [on the 1876 exhibition] (Stuttgart: Cotta, 1876), 73; cf. *Franz von Defregger und sein Kreis* [as 'Tiroler Landesausstellung', 1987], exh. cat. Museum Stadt Lienz, 1987.

219 'the enclosed space ...' ('abgeschlossener Raum ... eine Art von architektonischer Einheit bildet, ein reich gegliedertes Kunstwerk für sich'): F. Pecht, 'Koloristische Wirkungen im Kunstgewerbe', *ZBKM* (1880), nos. 3–4, 1–4 (1); on the exhibition: 'künstlerischen Totalwirkung eines Raumes': J. von Schmädel, 'Zweck und Ziel der ... Ausstellung München', *ZBKM* (1876), nos. 1–2, 1–4 (3). § 'completely owed': F. Pecht, 'Eröffnung ...Jahrgangs', *ZBKM* (1877), nos. 1–2, 1–6 (5); cf. Pecht, *Glaspalast* (above, n. 218), 191; F. Pecht, *Geschichte der Münchener Kunst im neunzehnten Jahrhundert* (Munich: Verlagsanstalt Kunst und Wissenschaft, 1888).

The 'Seidlzimmer'

220 The *Seidlzimmer*'s predecessors: cf. the 'wainscoted' ('holzvertäfelte') room by H. H. Schmidt & Sugg. in the Vienna Museum für Kunst und Industrie in 1871–72, which demonstrated a 'homely cosiness' ('anheimelnde Gemüthlichkeit') and warmth familiar from 'the old times in the German dwelling' ('Wohnung'): *Fachmännische Berichte* (Ch. II, n. 103), 40–45 (41), no illustration of whole interior known. See also L. Gedon's interiors *c.* 1872–75 for the Schloss Abtsee and Schloss Seehaus, Waginger See, Bavaria: Gedon (above, n. 209), 80–84. Cf. H. Ottomeyer, 'A Secret Designer: Hans Jehly and the Firm of Anton Pössenbacher', *FH*, vol. 27 (1991), 149–158; S. Muthesius, 'The "altdeutsche Zimmer", or Cosiness in Plain Pine: An 1870s Munich Contribution to the Definition of Interior Design', *JDH*, vol. 16, no. 4 (2003), 269–90; S. Wieber, 'Eduard Grützner's Villa and the German Renaissance', *Intellectual History Review*, vol. 2 (2007), 153–74.

221 'Altdeutsch': F. Pecht, *Glaspalast* (above, n. 218), 201; Bucher (above, n. 213), 17. § 'In the Alpine region ... people feel enclosed ... in a dwelling [*Gehäus*] that belongs to them ... in a lively, homely way [*lebhaft angeheimelt*]': S. Lichtenstein, 'Die deutsche Kunst ... Ausstellung München', *Zeitschrift für bildende Kunst*, vol. 11 (1876), 289–371, 331–38, 363–71 (290). § 'peasant' (Wohnstube in einem Bürger- oder Bauernhaus'): Bucher, *München* (above, n. 213), 17. § 'favourite of the visitors' ('das Lieblingsstück des Publikums'): L. Pfau, 'Die erste deutsche Ausstellung dekorativer Kunst', in L. Pfau, *Kunst und Kritik* (Stuttgart: Ebner, 1888), vol. 2, 356–82 (373). § 'delightful ...' ('reizende Einfachheit'): D. Duncker, *Über die Bedeutung der deutschen Ausstellung in München 1876* (Berlin: Duncker, 1876), 18. § 'that the effect ...' ('dass die Wirkung nunmehr mehr von der Harmonie als von der Pracht abhängt'): L. Pfau (above), 373. 'well-used ...' ('abgregriffene Chronik mit vielen Eselsohren'): Duncker (above), 18. § 'a poet ...' ('Wie es der Dichter nicht schöner schreiben kann': E. Oppler, 'Die Kunst- ... Ausstellung München', *Die Kunst im Gewerbe*, vol. 7, 1878, no. 6, 21–22. § 'to take us back to those times in which our forefathers in youthful freshness and modest aspirations enjoyed what was theirs': Duncker (above), 18. § 'das Heimliche ...': Bucher (above, n. 213), 17. § 'cosiness' ('Traulichkeit'), 'livableness ('Wohnlichkeit'), etc.: Oppler, above. § 'urgemütlich ... der satte warme Ton': Lichtenstein (above), 290. § 'a fresh ...' ('ein frischer lebenswarmer Kamerad') [on Altdeutsch ceramic stoves generally]: Hirth, 172. On women's work, see also K. A. Regnet, 'Die Frauenarbeit ... Ausstellung München', *IFz*, vol. 3, 2 Oct. 1876, 302–3.

222 On Seidl: Hirth, *ZBKM* from 1877, *IFz* in the 1880s; V. Hofer (ed.), *Gabriel von Seidl. Architekt und Naturschützer* (Kreuzlingen: Hugendubel, 2002), 37; G. Schickel, 'Der Architekt G. v. Seidl', in Bauer, *Nationalmuseum* (above, n. 204), 73–101. § The plate rack is illustrated in Hirth, 78, 179.

223 Alpine/Bavarian interiors: see *ZGVM*; cf. the room by H. Fickler, Dresden, *IFz*, 16 April 1883, 129; J. Lessing, 'Gotische Zimmereinrichtungen', *IFz*, 16 April 1885, 133–34; F. Paukert, *Die Zimmergotik in Deutsch-Tirol* (Leipzig: Seemann, 1892–94).

Georg Hirth

224 F. C. Endres, *G. Hirth, Ein deutscher Publicist* (Munich: Hirth, 1921); review of Hirth by F. Pecht in *Westermanns Monatshefte*, vol. 47 (1880), 765–69; cf. G. Hirth, *Aufgaben der Kunstpsychologie* (Hirth: Munich, 1891). See also G. Hirth, *Formenschatz der Renaissance* (Munich: Hirth, 1877–), publ. in French as *L'Art pratique: Recueil d'ornements ...* (Munich: Hirth, 1879–).

225 See Buch- und Kunstdruckerei Knorr & Hirth, *Rückblicke und Erinnerungen ...* (Munich: Knorr & Hirth, 1900).

226 Publ. 1879–80; 2nd edn 1881, 3rd edn: *Das deutsche Zimmer der Gotik und Renaissance, des Barock und Rococo und Zopfstils* [i.e. Louis XVI], 1886; 4th edn: *Das deutsche Zimmer vom Mittelalter bis zur Gegenwart ...*, 1899 (all Munich: Hirth). See also G. Hirth, 'Zimmereinrichtung im Renaissancegeschmack', *ZBKM* (1879), nos. 1–2, 33–41; G. Hirth, 'Deutsche Renaissance Einst und Jetzt', *ZBKM* (1879), nos. 1–2, 1–8.

227 'our unconscious ...' ('unbewusst liebevollen Anschluss an die Renaissance'): Hirth, 'Deutsche Renaissance' (above, n. 226), 4. § 'Yes ...' ('Ja, ich meine, diese Vorbilder – ich nenne nur den saftgrünen Ofen mit der goldbraunen Holzwand, den tiefblauen Steingutkrug mit der rotgestickten Tischdecke – müssten mit einer gewissen Naturnotwendigkeit auf's neue erfunden werden, wenn sie nicht schon da wären'): Hirth, 30.

228 'between "high" ...' ('zwischen "hoher" und "niederer" Kunst, insofern es sich um den Schmuck unserer Häuslichkeit handelt, eine *grundsätzliche* Unterscheidung nicht besteht'): Hirth, 100; cf. B. Bucher, 'Einfache Möbel', *BfK* (1878), 49–50. § 'a cosy, simple ...' ('einer gemüthlichen, einfach schönen herzerwärmenden Häuslichkeit'): Hirth, 30. § 'beauty ...' ('die Schöheit kennt kein Ansehen der Person'): Hirth, 9.

229 'the parts ...' ('Insofern die Teile für sich und als Ganzes unser Denken und Fühlen in Anspruch nehmen und auf uns "einwirken", können wir von *Tätigkeiten* derselben sprechen, oder wenn wir mehr die Aufgaben bezeichnen wollen, besser von ihren *Funktionen*'): Hirth, 145; cf. Henrici, the present book, p. 181. § 'our ... ('unserem Humor und Schönheitgefühl, unserer Illusionslust und Symbolik,

endlich unserer aesthetischen Dogmatik Genüge leistet'): Hirth, 145–46.

230 'purely physiological ...' ('rein physiologische Befriedigung', 'das Auge fordert nicht mehr, sondern ruht sich geniessend aus'): Hirth, 43. § 'dirty' ('schmutzig'): Hirth 40. § On Chevreul: 'golden ...' ('goldig leuchtenden feurigen Töne' [Hungarian ash]): Hirth, 45–46. § 'warm, lush ... ('warmen, saftvollen Farbenstimmungen ... die braunen, bräunlich rothen und grünen, die grünlich- und bräunlich gelben und endlich die gelblich-weissen Töne, lauter Mischfarben, in denen die "warmen" Strahlen überwiegend vertreten sind'): Hirth, 63.

231 German love of the forest: 'aus [dem] Stamm gezimmerten Hausbalken übersiedelt ... und zum Hausgeiste werden lässt, welcher bald als Schutzgeist, bald als neckender Kobold auftritt': Lichtenstein (above, n. 221), 290.

232 Avoid paint on wood, Hirth, 66. § 'considered purely ...' ('rein physiologisch betrachtet, wird die Forderung der farbigen Unterbrechung schon durch die kleinsten wahrnehmbaren Bilder erfüllt, d.h. sobald wir unsere beiden Augen auf bestimmte Punkte fest "einstellen"'): Hirth, 65. § 'the more we ...' ('Je mehr natürliche Oberflächen wir zur Dekoration verwenden ... ein edler Stoff erträgt sogar fehlerhafte Farbgebungen'): Hirth, 68. § 'annual rings ...' ('in den Jahresringen, Markstrahlen und Masern des Holzes'): Hirth, 65.

233 'rough rendering ...' ('Rohen Kalkbewurf oder sandigen Anstrich, der dem irrenden Blicke kleinste Ruhepunkte gönnt'): Hirth, 65, cf. 170.

234 'massive wooden ...' ('die massiven Holzkonstruktionen ... [die] in ihrer kraftvollen Realität jede sinnbildliche Illusion auszuschliessen scheinen'): Hirth, 153.

235 Darkness: see the present book, p. 198.

The end of Altdeutsch

236 'If we are not ...' ('Wenn uns nicht alles täuscht, so befinden wir uns gerade jetzt an der Stelle, wo das Wort "altdeutsch" aufhört, unseren Ohren Musik zu sein'): Luthmer 1884b, here 2nd edn 1885, 2. § Cf. A. Lichtwark, *Eine Auswahl aus seinen Schriften*, 2 vols. (Berlin: Cassirer 1917); *Die Gegenwart*, 1880s; [Anon.; by A. J. Langbehn], *Rembrandt als Erzieher von einem Deutschen*, 22nd edn (Leipzig: Hirschfeld 1890), 125, 189. J. Lessing, *Handarbeit* (Berlin: L. Simon, 1887); J. Lessing, *Unserer Väter Werke* (*Volkswirtschaftliche Zeitfragen*, vol. 11, nos. 82–83, 1889). Later, the all-wooden room was held to be specifically English (!): Muthesius, H., 98.

237 'Patriotism is good ... but our cupboards, window panes and stiff sofa backs do not need to preach it' ('Patriotismus ist ein gut Ding ... aber unsere Schränke, unsere Fensterscheiben und steifen Sofalehnen brauchen ihn doch nicht zu verkündigen'): Baisch (Ch. III, n. 98), 49.

238 'Sonderweg': G. Eley, *Reshaping the Right: Radical Nationalism and Political Change after Bismarck* (New Haven and London: Yale Univerity Press, 1980); O. Dann, *Nation und Nationalismus in Deuschland 1770–1990* (Munich: Beck, 1993). Cf. P.-K. Schuster (ed.), *Die 'Kunststadt' München 1937. Nationalsozialismus und 'Entartete Kunst'* (Munich: Prestel, 1987); A. Zinnecker, *Romantik Rokoko und Kamisol. Volkskunde auf dem Weg ins 3. Reich. Die Riehl Rezeption* (Münster: Waxmann, 1996).

French 18th-century revival

239 On later 19th-century French applied arts, see Ch. II, nn. 84, 87; Paolini; D. Alcouffe et al., *Les Arts décoratifs 1851–1900 à travers les Expositions Universelles* (Milan: Le Arti 1988). On regional and national aspects of the applied arts: D. Le Couédic, 'The Garden of Illusions' [on regionalism], in *National Identities*, vol. 8, 3 Sept. 2006, 225–34; A. Thomine, *Émile Vaudremer 1829–1914* (Paris: Picard, 2004); C. Hattendorff, *Die Suche nach der Nationaltradition in der französischen Malerei, Kunstliteratur und nationales Bewusstsein im 19. Jh.* (Freiburg im Breisgau: Rombach, 2004); C. Mignot, 'Le Néo-Normand', *MH*, no. 189, Sept.–Oct. 1993 (issue 'Le Régionalisme'), 52–64. On 'Gallo-Roman style', see Boussard (Ch. II, n. 85). See also Daly, who claimed that peasant houses ('chaumières') cannot be classified as art: C. Daly, *L'Architecture privée au XIXème siècle*, 2nd series (Paris: Ducker etc., 1872); cf. C. Garnier and A. Ammann, *L'Habitation humaine* [on the Paris 1889 fair] (Paris: Hachette, 1889).

240 'Old French' and 'Blondelscher Stil': see the present book, p. 207.

241 On the new English furniture in Paris 1878: 'sévérité apparente': Didron (Ch. II, n. 13), 202; on Collinson & Lock: 'an interesting physiognomy', but 'thin forms ... a purtanism mixed with morbid and childish naivity that do not at all suit our exuberant temperament' ('une physiognomie intéressante ... formes grêles ... puritanisme mélangée de naiveté morbide et enfantine qui ne conviendrait point à notre tempérament exubérant'): L. Gonse (ed.), *L'Art moderne à l'Exposition de 1878* (Paris: *Gazette des Beaux Arts*, 1879), vol., 1, 388–90.

242 For views against the Rococo, see the present book, p. 207. See also R. Redgrave, *Manual of Design* (London: Chapman & Hall, 1876), 91ff.

243 F. Roger, for example, thought them about fifty years out of date: *Exposition du travail, Palais de l'Industrie: Histoire du siège à travers les âges* (Paris: Châtelus, 1891), 31–33; German Rococo as 'ridiculous' ('ridicule et insupportable'): P. Lacroix, *XVIII siècle: Lettres, sciences et arts, France 1700–1789* (Paris: Firmin Didot, 1878), 466.

244 'Rococo': 'Promenades à travers Paris', *RGA* (1883), 253–58 (254).

245 'siècle de joli': quoted in P. Sabatier, *L'Esthétique des Goncourt* (Paris: Hachette, 1920), 471, 474; cf. E. Launay, 'Le dernier grenier ... E. de Goncourt', *MH*, no. 195, March 1995, 27–29. § Indifference to other styles: P. Sabatier (above), 43, 100, 465.

246 'mean ...' ('mesquin, faux'): Percier & Fontaine, 3. § 'very falsest ...': Yapp, xxxiv. § 'boredom ...' ('l'ennui ... vent glacé'): P. Mantz, 'Les Meubles du XVIIIe siècle', *RAD*, vol. 4 (1883–84), 313–25, 356–57, 377–89 (389), quoted in Silverman, 134, cf. 21.

247 On 'tous les Louis', see D. Linstrum,'France', in *EID*, 453–54; Pons; Guichardet, *Balzac* (Ch. III, n. 78), 287ff. § 'Percier & Fontaine broke brutally ... with the ancient French traditions': M. H. Destailleur, *Recueil d'estampes relatives à l'ornementation des ... XVIe, XVIIe et XVIIIe siècles* (Paris: Rapilly, 1863), Preface.

248 See Feray (Ch. II, n. 1), 348, 356; *Second Empire*; H. Lefuel, *Appartements privés de S.M. l'Impératrice au Palais des Tuileries* (Paris: Baudry, 1867); *MoA in the* 1850s; A. Dion-Tenenbaum, *Les Apartements Napoléon III au Musée du Louvre* (Paris: RMN, 1993).

249 The argument was that furniture reflected society: 'loi inexorable, le meuble a reflété exactement la société': 'French Furniture ...', anon. review of Union Centrale des Arts Décoratifs, *Les Arts du bois, des tissus et du papier* (Paris: Quantin, 1883) in *MA* (1884), 22–25.

250 'bad manners': Le Play (Ch. IV, n. 28), 187.

251 'terrible and productive crisis' ('crise terrible et féconde'): H. Taine, *Les Origines de la France contemporaine*, vol. 1: *Ancien Régime* (Paris, 1876), viii. § 'informal conversation' ('conversation familière'): Taine (above), ix; 'one becomes ...' ('on devient prèsque contemporain'): Taine (above), xii, cf. 190ff.

252 'unfortunate democratizing' ('démocratisation fâcheuse'): Penon (Introduction, n. 30), 93. § 'make the manufacturers ...' ('aristocratisation des producteurs'): L. de Fourcaud, 'Les Arts décoratifs au Salon de 1892', *RAD*, vol. 12 (1891–92), 329–30, quoted in Silverman, 167–68, cf. 123.

253 'delicate ...': H. Thirion, 'L'oeuvre de Clodion', *RAD*, vol. 5 (1884–85), 33–44 (36), quoted in Silverman, 131. § 'seductive grace' ('grâce séductrice'): V. Champier, 'La collection d'orfèvrerie de M. Paul Endel', *RAD*, vol. 4 (1883–84), 313ff. (387), quoted in Silverman, 132. § On 18th-century life: Taine (above, n. 251). § 'finesse': Didron (Ch. II, n. 13), 197; cf. E. Balfour, review of *Les Arts du bois* (above, n. 249) in *MA* (1884), 522–27. § 'douceur de vivre': Taine (above, n. 251), 196; cf. Silverman 32, 133. § 'softly poetic' ('poésie molle'): P. de Chennevières, in Preface of P. Ratouis de Limay, *A. T. Désfriches, sa vie* (Paris: Champion, 1907), vi–vii, xxv–xxviii, quoted in Silverman, 123. § 'smile ...' : P. Mantz, 'Les meubles du XVIIIe siècle', *RDA*, vol. 4 (1883–84), 313ff. (389).

254 Silverman, 26; cf. C. Duncan, *The Pursuit of Pleasure: The Rococo Revival in French Romantic Art* (New York: Garland, 1976); J. Seigel, *Bohemian Paris: Culture, Politics, and the Boundaries of Bourgeois Life 1830–1930* (New York: Viking, 1986). Cf. notions of the '18th-century boudoir', in e.g. Havard *Dict.*, vol. 1, 365; Ch. IV above.

255 'everything ... ': '"L'art dans la maison"' (review of Havard 1884), *AA*, Jan. 1884, 50–52. § 'La mode n'existait pas': Didron (Ch. II, n. 13), 5.

256 Socializing: Taine (above, n. 251), 194.

257 'The magnificence ...': Lacroix (above, n. 243), 474. § 'passion ...': Lacroix (above, n. 243), 462. § 'C'est le mobilier qui, cette fois, fournit la note vraie, charactéristique, dominante de l'époque': H. Havard, *L'Art à travers les moeurs* (Paris: Quantin, 1882), 346. § 'unity of conception' ('unité de conception et totalité d'execution'): Havard 1884, 8. Cf. Kugler, who very briefly mentions the 'so-called Rococo, a most convincing, firmly enclosed picturesque whole' ('fest geschlossenes malerisches Ganzes'): F. Kugler, *Handbuch der Kunstgeschichte*, 3rd edn (Stuttgart: Ebener & Seubert 1856), 605.

258 T. Child, 'An Artists' House', *DF*, vol. 4, June 1884, 98–100 (98). See also a recent and very different art historical view of the 18th century: 'consumption in its widest sense was not a matter of personal and private gratification, but a public act of social responsibility': K Scott, *The Rococo Interior* (New Haven and London: Yale University Press, 1999), 81.

259 Historical research in *RAD*; *Gazette des Beaux-Arts*; see Silverman.

260 'The Renaissance ... the straight line ... as an enemy' (i.e. furniture made of rectangular parts was considered inferior): C. Mayet, *La Crise industrielle de l'ameublement* (Paris: 1883), 39.

261 On reform, see Laurent; Brunhammer (Ch. II, n. 53); Silverman.

262 'little manufacturer ...' ('Petit fabricant, avec sa vivacité toute méridionale ... l'oeil vif, à la parole brève'; '[il] porte l'empreinte des sentiments et des passions de son époque ... originalité et personalité'; 'Les ébénistes étrangers sont incapables de fabriquer l'ébénisterie de luxe. Les mobiliers Louis XIV, Louis XV, Louis XVI, la marqueterie, toutes ces délicieuses fantaisies du meuble plaqué sont restés le privilège de la fabrication française ... Elle est encore restée sans rivale sur tous les marchés du monde; elle est en quelque sorte une émanation du génie de notre race ... aucune règle ne la régit. Elle est en quelque sorte l'expression de la destination du meuble': Mayet (above, n. 260), 40–41. § 'from a technical ...' ('rien ne surpasse ou point de vue technique'): A. de Champeaux, *Le Meuble* (Paris: Quantin, 1885), 130; cf. the view in 1825: 'au génie des artistes français ... l'art de l'ébénisteries doit les plus beaux perfectionneurs': F. N. Mellet, *L'Art du menuisier en meubles et de l'ébéniste* (Paris, 1825), xix–xx. § 'the great traditions' ('les grandes traditions'): Mayet (above), 8–9. § 'clients who have taste' (la clientèle du goût'): Mayet (above), 39. § 'Infiniment respectueux pour les maîtres éternels': Succession E. Lièvre, *Catalogues des meubles d'art ...* (Paris: Hôtel Drouot, 1887), Intr. § 'Parisianisme': J. Hoche, *Les Parisiens chez eux* (Paris: Dentu, 1883–84).

263 On the style of Louis XV: *Christofle* (Ch. II, n. 13), 280; Nouvel-Kammerer. See also English comments: 'Every rich person who dreams of luxury is obliged to return to the eighteenth-century productions or have them severely imitated': [Anon], 'French Homes of Today': *FG*, 21 July 1877, 37–38. Cf. 'The Furniture Renaissance in France', *B*, 28 Aug. 1875, 768–69; 'Parisian Household Taste': *B*, 14 July 1877, 699–700; 'French Furniture', *B*, 10 March 1883, 304–5; C. B. A.,'The Artist Workman and House Furniture', *BN*, 2 July 1883, 120; Zeldin (Introduction, n. 21), 420–31. § E.g. 'French upholsterers of today follow the glorious traditions without turning their back on the way of progress': F. Husson, *Artisans français: Les tapissiers. Étude historique* (Paris: 1905), Preface.

A European round-up

264 See 'confortable' in Larousse (Introduction, n. 10), vol. 4 (1869), 915–16.

265 Paolini; E. Kirichenko and M. M. Anikist, *The Russian Style: Russian Design and the Fine Arts 1750–1917* (New York: Abrams, 1991).

266 Cf. S. Muthesius, '"An der Spitze des Geschmacks dürfen wir keine nationalen Elemente erwarten". ... Universalismus und Nationalismus im Kunstgewerbe des 19. Jhs', in J. Purchla et al. (eds), *Nation, Style Modernism* (Krakow, 2006), 25–34; S. Muthesius, 'Nationalisme et internationalisme dans les arts appliqués et le folklore en Autriche-Hongrie et en Allemagne à la fin du XIXe siècle', in F. Chevalier, J.-Y. Andrieux et al. (eds), *Idée nationale et architecture en Europe 1860–1919* (Paris: PU Rennes, 2006), 79–86.

The Renaissances

267 Italy: see above, n. 12; Paolini; J. Wilton-Ely, *Piranesi as Architect and Designer* (New Haven and London: Yale

University Press, 1993); A. Buck and C. Vasoli (eds), *Il Rinascimento dell'Ottocento: Italia e Germania / Die Renaissance im 19. Jh. in Italien und Deutschland*, Annali dell'Instituto Storico Italo-Germanico, Trento, no. 3, 1989; O. Selvafolta, 'Decoro e arti applicate nelle riviste italiane dell'Ottocento', in C. Mozzarelli and R. Pavoni (eds), *Milano Fin de Siècle* (Milan: Guerini, 1991), 85–118; R. Pavoni, *Moda e sentimento dell'abitare* (Torino: Allemandi, 1992); R.Pavoni (ed.), *Reviving the Renaissance: The Use and Abuse of the Past in Nineteenth-Century Italian Art and Decoration* (Cambridge University Press, 1997); ICARO, *Progetti x l'arte: Arredi dell'Ottocento* (Modena: Artoli, 2002).

268 On the neo-Renaisance in Sweden: B. Grandien, *Drömmen om Renässansen*, Nordiska Museets Handlingar no. 93 (Stockholm, 1979); B. Grandien, *Drömmen om Medeltiden: Carl Georg Brunius*, Nordiska Museets Handlingar no. 82 (Stockholm, 1979); F. Lilljekvist, 'Det svenska rummet under Renässansen', *Meddelanden från Svenska slöjdföreningen* (1887), 70–90; F. Lilljekvist, 'Det svenska rummet under Barocktiden', *Meddelanden* (as above) (1889), 82–104; L. Loström, 'Gustaviansk stil', *Meddelanden* (as above) (1891), 58–77. See also below, nn. 276, 281, 284.

269 Neo-Renaissance in Denmark: see F. S. Neckelmann and F. Meldahl, *Denkmäler der Renaissance in Dänemark* (Berlin: Wasmuth, 1888); *Tidsskrift for Kunstindustri* 1888– ; M. Spies, *Klunketijd – en Kavalkade* (Copenhagen: Vinten, 1979); K. Millech, *Danske Arkitekturstrøminger 1850–1950* (Copenhagen: Østifternes Kreditforening, 1951); see also relevant notes below.

270 J. Kybálova, 'Kunstgewerbe und Wohnkultur', in F. Seibt (ed.), *Böhmen im 19.Jh.* (Frankfurt am Main: Propyläen, 1995), 319–46. See also P. Hanak (ed.), *Bürgerliche Wohnkultur des Fin de Siècle in Ungarn* (Vienna: Böhlau, 1994); J. von Falke, *A müvészet a ház ban: Falke munkája után irta* (Budapest, 1882; with thanks to J. Sisa).

International vernacular revivalism

271 Cf. 'peasants, tidy cottages, signs of … manners … gentleness of thought': 'French Home Life' (Ch. III, n. 219), 37; 'Bauer' in Meyer (Ch. II, n. 56), vol. 2 (1874), 686–91; Riehl; Riehl, *Volkskunde* (above, n. 201); Semper; R. Mielke, *Volkskunst* Magdeburg: Niemann, 1896). See also M. Bucher, *Realismus und Gründerzeit. Manifeste und Dokumente zur deutschen Literatur 1848–1880* (Stuttgart: Metzler, 1976); A.-M. Thiesse, *La Création des identités nationales en Europe XVII–XXe siècles* (Paris: Seuil, 1999).

272 J. von Falke, 'Die nationale Hausindustrie', in *Zur Cultur und Kunst, Studien* (Vienna: Gerold, 1878), 287–327; Falke, *Paris* (Ch. III, n. 54); C. T. Richter, 'Die Nationale Hausindustrie', *Ausstellungs-Bericht* (21); C. von Lützow, *Kunst und Kunstgewerbe auf der Wiener Weltausstellung 1873* (Leipzig: Seemann, 1875); G. Korff, 'Volkskunst und Primitivismus … um 1900', *Österreichische Zeitschrift für Volkskunde*, vol. 58, no. 97 (1994), 373–94; A. Moravánszky, *Competing Visions: Aesthetic Invention and Social Imagination in Central European Architecture 1867–1918* (Cambridge, MA: MIT Press, 1998); D. Crowley and L. Taylor, *The Lost Arts of Europe: The Haslemere Collection of European Peasant Art* (Haslemere Museum, Surrey: 1999); S. Muthesius, 'Alois Riegl. Volkskunst, Hausfleiss and Hausindustrie', in R. Woodfield (ed.), *Framing Formalism: Riegl's Work* (Amsterdam: G+B Arts, 2001), 135–50 .

273 'kistenweise': Lessing, *Wien* (Ch. II, n. 23), 225.

274 J. von Falke, 'Hausindustrie' (above, n. 272), 312.

275 Falke's view on Zakopane was that the Galician way could not form the basis ('Grundlage') of a modern furniture style ('modernen Möbel-Stil'), but could still constitute a pretty ('hübsche') variant for the better class of burgher's house: J.von Falke, 'Kunstgewerbliches Mobiliar aus Zakopane', *IFz*, 1 Jan. 1890, 8; for Falke on Munich, see above, n. 215.

276 A. Hazelius, *Ur de Nordiska Folkens lif* (Stockholm: Beijers, 1882); I. Bergman, *Artur Hazelius, Nordiska Museets och Skansens Skapare* (Stockholm, 1999). See also J. von Falke, *Konsten i hemmet* (Stockholm: Norstedt, 1876); Falke's articles in *Tidskrift för Hemmet*, vols. 16–19 (1874–77); J. Falke, 'Einige Bemerkungen über die Kunstindustrie in Schweden', *Mitteilungen des k.u. k. Österreichischen Museums für Kunst und Industrie*, vol. 6, no. 65, 15 Feb. 1871, 326–31; Frick (below, n. 284); L. Dietrichson, 'Den nordiska konstindustrien på Vereldutställingen i Wien 1873', *Tidskrift för Kunstindustri*, vol. 1 (1875–76), 203–8; Stavenow-Hidemark (below, nn. 282, 284, 286); S. Danielson, *Den goda smaken och samhällsnyttan. Om Handarbetets Vänner och den svenska hemslöjdsrörelsen*, Nordiska Museets Handlingar no. 111 (Stockholm, 1991).

277 S. O. Roosjen et al., *Merkwaardigheden van Hindeloopen* (Leeuwarden, 1855; new edn Hindeloopen: Hidde Nijland Stichtung, 1979); S. J. van der Molen, *De Hindelooper Wooncultuur. Interieur en kledertracht in het licht der archiven* (Bolsward: Osinga, 1967); A. de Jong and M. Skougaard, 'The Hindeloopen and the Amager Rooms', *Journal of the History of Collections*, vol. 5, no. 2 (1993), 165–78; A. De Jong, *De Dirigenten van de Herinering. Musealisiering en nationalisiering van de volkscultuur in Nederland 1815–1940* [on the Netherlands and beyond] (Nijmegen: SUN, 1991).

278 C. Nyrop, *Fra den Kunstindustrielle Udstilling* (Copenhagen: Schubothes, 1879); R. Mejborg, *Gamle danske Hjem i det 16de, 17de og 18de Århundrede* (Copenhagen: Roms, 1888); M. Zenius, *Genremaleri og Virklighed … billeder af Dalsgaard, Exner …* (Copenhagen, 1976); H. Rasmussen, *Bernard Olsen. Virke og Vaerker* (Copenhagen: Nationalmuseet, 1979).

279 [Anon.], *Heinrich Sauermann (1842–1904). Ein Flensburger Möbelfabrikant* (exh. cat. Flensburg Städtisches Museum, 1979); cf. U. Claassen, *Fischernetz, Tracht und Bauernstube. Imaginiertes Landleben in norddeutscher Malerei des 19. Jh.* (Neumünster: Wachholz, 1996).

280 Drawings by S. Witkiewicz in *Tygodnik Illustrowany*, vol. 12 (new series), 29 Dec. 1888, 404, 418; vol. 13, 26 Jan. 1889, 69; S. Witkiewicz, 'Drzwi Chaty Góralskiej w Zakopanem', *Wisła Miesięcznik geograficzno-etnograficzny*, vol. 2 (1888), 120–21; Falke, 'Zakopane' (above, n. 275); S. Witkiewicz, *Na Przełęczy. Wrażenia I. Obrazy z Tatr* (Warsaw: Gebethner & Wolf, 1891); L. Méyet, 'Kilka Słów o Szkołach Zawodowych w Zakopanem', *Wisła* (above), vol. 5 (1891), 249–77. Against 'tyrolsko-wiedeńska galanteria': S. Witkiewicz, 'Styl Zakopiański' (1891), *Pisma Tatrzańskie* (Krakow, 1963) vol. 2, 285; T. Jabłońska and Z. Moździerz, *'Koliba'. Pierwszy Dom w Stylu Zakopiańskim*, Wydawnictwa Muzeum Tatrzańskiego … vol. 20 (Zakopane, 1994); Z. Moździerz, *Dom 'Pod Jedlami' Pawlikowskich* (Zakopane, 2003); M. Omilanowska, 'Searching for a National Style in Polish Architecture at the End of the 19th and Beginning of the 20th Century', in N. Gordon-Bowe (ed.), *Art and the National Dream* (Dublin: Irish Academic Press, 1993), 99–117; D. Crowley, *National Style and Nation-State: Design in Poland from the Vernacular Revival to the International Style* (Manchester University Press, 1992); S. Muthesius, *Art, Architecture and Design in Poland 966–1980* (Königstein: Langewiesche, 1994). See also V. Mayer, 'Architektur und Folklorismus im 19. Jahrhundert am Beispiel von Böhmen und Mähren', in *Hausforschung* (Introduction, n. 10), 263–85. Hungary's first 'peasant' interiors appeared in country houses from around 1886: J. Sisa, *Kastélyépitészet és kastélykultúra magyarországon* [on later 19th-century Hungarian country houses] (Budapest: Vince Kiadó 2007; with thanks to J. Sisa).

Old Nordic

281 On Scandinavia and Nordic style generally (see also under Sweden and Denmark, above): A.-B. Skaug, 'Interior design: A neglected field of Scandinavian art history', *Scandinavian Journal of Design History*, vol. 3 (1993), 9–18; D. R. McFadden (ed.), *Scandinavian Modern Design 1880–1980* (exh. cat. New York: Cooper-Hewitt Museum / Abrams, 1982); B. Miller Lane, *National Romanticism and Modern Architecture in Germany and the Scandinavian Countries* (Cambridge University Press, 2000); B. Grandien, *Rönndruvans Glöd. Nygöticistiskt i tanke, konst och miljö under 1800–talet*, Nordiska Museets Handlingar no. 107 (Stockholm, 1987); N. Ohlsen, *Skandinavische Interieurmalerei zur Zeit C. Larssons* (Berlin: Reimer, 1999); B. Henningsen et al. (eds), *Skandinavien och Tyskland 1800–1914. Möten och Vänskapsband / Wahlverwandschaft Skandinavien und Deutschland 1800 bis 1914* (exh. cat. Berlin: Deutsches Historisches Museum, 1997).

282 'force and courage' ('kraft och mod'): recent words by E. E. Stavenow-Hidemark, in E.-L. Bengtsson et al., *Konsten 1845–1890* (Lund: Signum, 2000), 563. See also J. T. Ahlstrand (ed.), *Konsten 1890–1915* (Lund: Signum, 2001) – both vols. of series *Signums Svenska Konsthistoria.*

283 J. C. Eldal, *Historisme i tre. "Sveitserstil" byggeskikks-romatikk og nasjonal egenart i europeisk og norsk trearkitektur på 1800–tallet* (Oslo: Unversitetsforlaget, 1998); J. C. Eldal, *European Forms in the New Wooden Architecture imported into Norway* (Oslo: Norges Forskningsråd, 1995; with thanks to J. C. Eldal).

284 Sweden: see above, nn. 276, 282, and below, n. 286; G. Nordensvan, *Schwedische Kunst des 19. Jh.* (Leipzig, Seemann, 1904); G. Frick, *Svenska Slöjdföreningen och konstindustrin före 1905*, Nordiska Museets Handlingar no. 91 (Stockholm, 1978; with thanks to G. Frick); E. Stavenow-Hidemark, 'Hemmet som konstverk … på 1870– och 80–talen', *Fataburen. Nordiska Museets och Skansen, Årsbok* (1984), 129–48; A. Eggum (ed.), *Lorentz Dietrichson som Kunstpolitiker under Naturalismen frembrudd*, Kunst og Kultur vol. 64 (Oslo, 1981); L. Dietrichson, 'Om Skönhetssinnets Utveckling. Möbler … utkast af Professor Malmström', *Nordisk Tidskrift för Byggnadskonst och Slöjd*, vol. 1 (1871), 9–13, 21ff. See also the festive 'Höganloftsalen' in the Storstugan II villa (late 1870s), showing Nordic sagas by Malmström, in which users wore Nordic dress. § Cf. 'Sweden turns abroad', e.g. G. Frick (above), 194.

285 Norway: L. Dietrichson and H. Munthe, *Die Holzbaukunst Norwegens in Vergangenheit und Gegenwart* (Dresden: Kühtmann, 1893); S. Tschudi-Madsen, 'Dragestilen …', *Vestlandske Kunstindustrimuseum Årbok* (1949–50), 19–53; S. Tschudi-Madsen, 'Morris and Munthe', *Journal of the William Morris Society*, vol. 4 (1964), 34–40; A. Bøe, *Kunsthåndwerk 1870–1914*, in K. Berg (ed.), *Norges Kunsthistorie*, vol. 5 (Oslo: Gyldendal, 1982), 377ff.; cf. the series by R. T. Pritchett on Norway peasant culture in *AJ*, 1877, 1878.

286 C. and K. Larsson, *Ett Hem* (Stockholm: Bonniers, 1899); C. Larsson, *Das Haus in der Sonne* (Königstein: Langewiesche, 1913); C. Lengefeld, *Der Maler C. Larsson. Zur Rezeption C. Larssons im wilhelminischen Deutschland* (Heidelberg: Winter, 1913); M. Snodin and E. Stavenow-Hidemark (eds), *Carl and Karin Larsson: Creation of the Swedish Style* (London: V&A, 1997); cf. 'Delecarlia', *Harper's*, vol. 67, Sept. 1883.

287 Denmark: E. Hannover, 'Skandinavisches Kunstgewerbe auf der nordischen Ausstellung in Kopenhagen', *Kunstgewerbeblatt* (1888), 195–203. 'Almuestil': A. J. Råvad, 'En national stil', *Tidskrift for Kunstindustri* (1888), 25–33; Fru Emma Gad (ed.), *Vort Hjem*, 3 vols. (Copenhagen: Nordiske Forlag, 1903); L. Balslev-Jørgensen, *Danmarks Arkitektur. Enfamiliehuset* (Copenhagen: Gydlendal, 1979); E. Johannsen, '"Til pryd i alle de nordiske hjem". Omkring den "oldnordiske stil"', in *Kobstadmuseet 'Den gamle By' Årbog* (1983), 71–103.

A poetics of interior design?

288 Cf. Day's suggestion of avoiding a style for your interior that may make you feel 'uncomfortable': L. F. Day, 'Decorative Art IV', *MA* (1880), 355–59 (355).

VI A DISPARATE LEGACY

Enter the real user

1 'In addition …' ('"vielen" noch "immer mehr"', 'einheitliches Zusammenwirken … Überladensein, ein "Zuviel" fällt nur bei nicht geschickter Anordnung in die Augen'): Schäffer & Walcker (Ch. II, n. 94), 3.

2 Williams Benn mocks Morris: '"eventfulness of form"' and 'philosophical and socialistic mazes': [J. W. Benn], 'The Morrisian Furnishings … Manchester', *CM*, Jan. 1885, 121–25 (122, 125).

3 Snodin & Howard, 133; Pacey (Ch. IV, n. 35); Tristram, 237.

4 On the 'lived-in-kook': Cornforth, 12ff. Cf. Tristram, 185–87; Rybczynski, 84, 90, 93; A. and A. Gore (Ch. V, n. 47), 102ff. On the US: Ames; Grier. § English home books: see the 'Art at Home' series (Ch. II, n. 75); J. J. Stevenson, *House Architecture*, 2 vols. (London: Macmillan, 1880), vol. 2.

5 On the room 'for show', see Riehl, pp. 169–170. Cf. Anderson (Ch. II, n. 77). For Raymond Unwin, see J. Attfield, 'Bringing Modernity Home: Open Plan in the British Domestic Interior', in I. Cieraad (ed.), *At Home: An Anthropology of Domestic Space* (Syracuse University Press, 1999), 73–82.

6 Cf. the view that one should 'abandon oneself in the bedrooms': see 'La maison modèle … Études et types d'ameublement', *RAD*, vol. 3 (1882–83), 41; cf. Blanc, 137. For the atelier,

7 'shopman': Eastlake, 11, cf. 14, 15. § Haweis, 23–24. § 'our furniture …': E. Goadby, 'Furnishing a "Perfect House"', *AJ* (1877), 300–302. § 'nobody can make …': 'French Home Life' (Ch. III, n. 219), 30, 40. § 'works away … unconsciously' ('unbewusst auf sich wirken lässt'): Luthmer 1897, 44. Cf. Reulecke, 183.

8 [Paul Hasluck; 'ed. by author of *Every Man his own Mechanic*'], *Amateur Work Illustrated*, London, 1881–87; cf. Leland (Ch. II, n. 75).

9 Cook, 16.

10 Dohme, 28.

11 'the right …' ('recht auf selbsständige Ausgestaltung des

Geschmacks': Gurlitt, 1. § 'architects …' ('Architekten und Dekorateure'): Gurlitt, 4. § 'German art philosophy' ('deutsche Kunstphilophie'): Gurlitt, Foreword. The book was written at 'The Shrubbery, Winchmore Hill [London], 1887'.

12 'our habits' ('unsere Lebensgewohnheit … Lebensführung … wie sie der Gestaltung des Hauses zugrunde [liegen])': 'Deutsche Einfamilienhäuser', *DB*, 17 Oct. 1896, 528ff. (601).

13 'to present …' ('Unvollkommenheiten … darzustellen'): Gurlitt, 59; on Naturalism, see Ch. IV, n. 52. § S. Freud, 'Das Unheimliche' (1906; cf. Ch. IV, n. 78). Cf. A. Vidler, *The Architecture of the Uncanny* (Cambridge, MA: MIT Press, 1992); Logan, 96–97; S. McKellar and P. Sparke (eds), *Interior Design and Identity* (Manchester University Press, 2002). Cf. D. Fuss, *The Sense of an Interior: Four Writers and the Rooms that Shaped Them* [Dickinson, Freud, Keller, Proust] (New York & London: Routledge, 2004); F. Krämer, *Das unheimliche Heim. Zur Interieurmalerei um 1900* (Cologne: Böhlau, 2007);

14 H.-J. Teuteberg and C. Wischermann, *Wohnalltag in Deutschland 1850–1914* (Münster: Coppenrath, 1985); J. Flanders, *The Victorian House: Domestic Life from Childbirth to Deathbed* (London: Harper & Collins, 2002).

The rise of designer power

15 'the artist …' ('die fortreissende Kraft des Künstlers, dessen übermächtige Willenskraft die Menge *zwingt*, seine Entwurfe für schön hinzunehmen'): Gurlitt, *Musterzeichnerkunst* (Ch. II, n. 13), 16. Cf. F. Forster-Hahn (ed.), *Imagining Modern German Culture: 1889–1910* (Washington, D.C.: National Gallery of Art, 1996).

16 'The inspired …' ('Der geniale Hauch des Erfinders durchweht das Gemach und übte bei aller Einfachheit seine zauberhafte Wirkung auf den Beschauer aus'): Oppler, 'München' (Ch. V, n. 222), 21–22.

17 See Clarke, 'Richardson' (Ch. II, n. 40).

18 'Raumausstattung', 'Raumschöpfung': see Folnesics, 3. 'Raumkunst': see Lehnert, 551. Cf. W. Fred, *Die Wohnung und ihre Ausstattung* (Bielefeld: Velhagen & Klasing, 1903).

19 See the stark class and cultural contrast between, for example, (i) E. Hayck (ed.), *Moderne Kultur. Ein Handbuch der Lebensbildung und des guten Geschmacks*, vol. 1: *Die Häuslichkeit* (Stuttgart: Deutsche Verlagsanstalt, n.d. [1907]), chapter 'Kultur und Geschmack des Wohnens' by Modernist design critic Karl Scheffler, 149–268, which is culturally elevated, dealing mainly with fine art; and (ii) Luise Holle (ed.), *Im deutschen Hause. Ein Ratgeber und Helfer für das gesammte häusliche Leben der deutschen Famile* (Hanau: König, n.d. [1903]), with its modest, practical tone. Scheffler also warns against overvaluing art in the home: see Hayck (above), 214.

20 A. Loos, 'Von einem armen reichen Manne' (1900), in A. Loos, *Sämtliche Schriften* (Vienna: Herold, 1962). Cf. a similar point in Gurlitt, 55–57. § 'process of destruction' ('Vernichtungsprozess'): Behr, *Dekoration* (Ch. II, n. 69), 8–9; cf. Edis, 167. § '"that is how it delights me …"' ('"weil's mich so freut, weil's zusammen stimmt und weil's schön, nett, gemüthlich und lustig ist"'): Hirth, 31.

21 E.g. 'real beauty is natural' ('das wahrhaft Schöne ist unbefangen'): Gurlitt, 29.

The technically up-to-date household …

22 Gurlitt, 224–25.

23 'fluctuating feelings …' ('schwankenden Empfindungen und Kunstmoden'): Muthesius, H., vol. 2, 1.

24 'textile-enveloped …' ('stoffeingehüllte Gemütlichkeit'): Muthesius (above, n. 23), 235. Yet he still divides his consideration of the bathroom into technology (vol. 2) and décor (vol. 3, 235–40). Cf. 'Bad' in Meyer (Ch. II, n. 56), vol. 2 (1874), 376–81; H. Lachmeyer et al. (eds), *Das Bad* (Salzburg: Residenz, 1991).

25 On the direction of the kitchen, see 'Küche' in Meyer (Ch. II, n. 56), vol. 10 (1877), 416. § Housewives: Muthesius, H., vol. 2 (above, n. 23), 69.

26 'The kitchen in a country farmhouse is most commonly a pleasant and homelike place, the parlour dreary and useless': W. Morris, 'The Lesser Arts', in Morris, 32.

27 'the most absolute …' ('absoluteste Reinlichkeit … radikale Garantie der Sauberkeit'): F. Luthmer, 'Schmucke Küchen', *Id* (1893), 153–57; cf. J. Faulwasser, 'Neuere Hamburger Kücheneinrichtungen', *Id* (1893), 145–50. § 'Porzellantafeln': Meyer (above, n. 25). See also D. Southerton, 'Ordinary and Distinctive Kitchens', in J. Gronow and A. Wardle (eds), *Ordinary Consumption* (Reading: Harwood Press, 2001).

… and the authentic antique

28 See S. Muthesius, 'Why do we buy old furniture? Aspects of the authentic antique in Britain 1870–1910', *Art History*, vol. 11, no. 2 (June 1988), 231–53; S. Muthesius, '"Patina"': Aspects of the history of the kook of age in the late 19th century', *Zeitschrift für Kunsttechnologie und Konservierung*, vol. 17, no. 1 (2003), 138–42. § Old and new mixed: see e.g. *Gh* and *Kunsthandwerk*, 1870s. § Histories of furniture: see Jacquemart (Ch. III, n. 121), review in 'French and Continental Furniture', *B*, 1 March 1878, 207–8; G. T. Robinson, series in *AJ* (1883ff.); Hungerford Pollen (Ch. II, n. 93); F. Lichfield, *An Illustrated History of Furniture* (London, 1892). See also Semper; Falke; B. Bucher (below, n. 41).

29 On oldness and authenticity, see e.g. J. Ruskin, *The Seven Lamps of Architecture* (1849). § Patina: 'La consecration du temps et sa patine' [here on painting], E. and J. de Goncourt, *Journal* (Paris, 1956–59), entry for 19 April 1863.

30 A bucket, for example, made by a country carpenter: Eastlake, 168. See also Ungewitter, *Möbel* (Ch. V, n. 29).

31 'several thousand homes': Conway (Ch. II, n. 82), 787; Edwards, 73, 126ff., 140ff. § See the 'Art of Furnishing …', *ChM*, vol. 31, Jan.–June 1875, 535–47 (537).

32 Cook, 159–60; see also his 'protest' against new architecture: 'American Architecture', *North American Review*, Sept. 1882, 243–52; Scully, 70; E. Stillinger, *Antiquers …* (New York: Knopf, 1980).

33 Pons; J.-L. Gaillemin, *Antiquaires* (Paris: Assouline, 2000), 14–15; trans. as *The Finest Dealers in Paris* (London: Thames & Hudson, 2000); Silverman. § On prices: G. Reitlinger, *The Economics of Taste*, vol. 2: *The Rise and Fall of Objets d'Art Prices since 1750* (London: Barrie & Rockliff, 1963), 3, 6, 13.

34 'not a single …': letter from Lichtwark in Munich, 18 Sept. 1888, in A. Lichtwark, *Briefe an seine Familie* (Hamburg: Christiansen, 1972), 685 § Cf. J. Lessing, *Was ist altes Kunstgewerbe wert?*, Vortrag Volkswirtschaftliche Gesellschaft (Berlin: L. Simon, 1885); A. Riegl, 'Der moderne Denkmalkultus, sein Wesen, seine Entstehung' (1903), in A. Riegl, *Gesammelte Aufsätze* (Vienna/Augsburg: Filser, 1929), 144–93.

35 Lehnert, 457–58, 501; Blanc, 331ff.; Havard 1884, 138–40. On velvet, 'velours de Gênes', see Luthmer 1884a, 12.

36 On the trade, see Wainwright, 26, 35, 57–69; Gow, *Scottish Interior* (Ch. III, n. 199), 42; *The Antiquarian* (1871–73); *The Antiquary* (1880–1915); M. Westgarth, *The Emergence of the Antique and Curiosity Dealer 1815–1850: The Commodification of Historical Objects* (diss., University of Southampton, 2006). Cf. Sangl (Ch. III, n. 1).

Antiques and the unity of interior design

37 Trade helping clients: Wainwright, 26ff. § Shaw: Saint, 256.

38 'companionship', here in relation to carved furniture, new and old: see J. Hungerford Pollen, 'Carving and Furniture', *Journal of the Society of Arts*, 4 Sept. 1885, 983–88 (988). § 'good old work': Haweis, *Housekeeping* (Ch. II, n. 76), 31–32. § Havard claimed that our ancestors would have had furniture made to their pattern and not resorted to anything old: Havard 1884. '"Antique" would have sounded 'uncivil'. Thus everything was 'of one kind, was in harmony': [Anon.] '"L'art dans la maison"' [review of Havard 1884], *AA*, Jan. 1884, 50–52. § 'an upholsterer's …' ('un rêve de tapissier, sans un morceau de passé'): E. and J. de Goncourt, *Journal* (above, n. 29), entry for 31 May 1867.

39 'time has given it a reconciling patina [*versöhnende Patina*] that allows an easier combination of different elements and the stylistically diverse': Falke 1871, 245.

40 Pons; see the present book, p. 221.

41 'Das Alte wird nicht mehr nach seinem vorbildlichen Werte, sondern als solches geschätzt': B. Bucher, *Geschichte der technischen Künste*, vol. 3: *Möbel* (Stuttgart, 1893), 254; cf. 'Il ne faut demander au passé que le passé lui même': Ernest Renan, 1852, quoted in Dakyns (Ch. V, n. 39), 85.

Memory

42 'We do not want …': Hirth, 73–74. § 'the upholsterers ruled': [Anon.], 'The Art of Furnishing', *ChM*, vol. 31, Jan.–June 1875, 535–47 (535).

43 Bachelard: see Ch. I, n. 12. § Nietzsche: 'The small, the limited, the rotten and the outmoded [*das Beschränkte, das Morsche und Veraltete*] is rendered dignified and untouchable by the way the soul … preserves and venerates it, and takes up residence in those things and creates itself a homely nest': F. Nietzsche, 'Vom Nutzen und Nachteil der Historie für das Leben', in *Unzeitgemässe Betrachtungen* (first pub. 1874; Leipzig: Kröner, 1917, used here), 127.

44 'for the grown-up …' ('bei dem erwachsenen Menschen wirkt der poetische Gehalt seines Hausrathes nur in der Form der Erinnerung'): Haushofer, 59. § 'tales …' ('Erzählungen, Träumereien und Phantasien'): 70; § 'pine torch' ('Kienspan'): 71. § 'key' ('schlüssel'): 71. § 'network …' ('ein grosses Netz von Lebensbeziehungen'): 71. § 'these objects …' ('Eindruck, den der Hausrath auf die Phantasie des Kindes macht; und wo er Gegenstände, Formen und Wirkungen zeigt, die dem Kinderverstand unbegreiflich sind, gewinnt er ein märchenhaftes Leben'): 59.

45 'The quiet …' ('die stille, märchenhafte Stimmung eines Raumes'): Gurlitt, 1–2. § Parents' furniture: Bergau, 21. § 'junk room': Hug, 7. § 'Domestic furniture': G. T. Robinson, 'Cabinet Maker's Art', *AJ* (1884), 373–75 (373). § 'bygone girl days': Barker (Ch. II, n. 75), 31. § *Lares* and *penates*: G. W. F. Hegel, *Philosophie der Geschichte* (1822/31), here in *Hegel Werke*, vol. 11 (Frankfurt am Main: Suhrkamp, 1970), 75, quoted in O. Brunner et al. (eds), *Geschichtliche Gundbegriffe. Historisches Lexikon … Deutschland* (Stuttgart: Klett, 1975), 288–89. Cf. 'Hausgeister' in W. H. Riehl, *Die Familie*, 9th edn (Stuttgart, 1882), 285; Bachelard (Ch. I, n. 12).

46 'sparkling eye': Cook, 113.

47 'say nothing' ('nichtssagend') [here about kitchen utensils]: Sonntag (Ch. II, n. 62), 18.

Interiority: poetic house, poetic room

48 Church (Ch. II, n. 82), 5.

49 'All advice …' ('Verschönerung unseres häuslichen Daseins … Mietswohnung'); but then he contradicts himself: 'the human heart does not grow with a rented apartment, only with [one's own] property [*Eigentum*]': Haushofer, 58.

50 'un apartement resemble à un poème': de Noussanne (Ch. I, n. 2), 7–8.

51 'If there is a human artefact [*oeuvre humaine*] that gives an indication of [the state of] a civilization, then it is certainly the dwelling': E.-E. Viollet-le-Duc (and F. Narjoux), *Habitations modernes* (Paris: Morel, 1875), Intr.

52 See J. Ackermann, *The Villa* (London: Thames & Hudson, 1990); Brönner 1994; *MH*, no. 102 (1979); J.-P. Pérouse de Monclos, 'De la villa rustique d'Italie au pavillon de banlieue', *Revue de l'Art*, no. 32 (1976), 23–36. 'Villa' lost much of its cachet during the later 19th century. § 'cottage': see e.g. the 'Cottagenviertel' district in Vienna with villas from the 1870s § Swiss chalet: see the present book, pp. 264–65; cf. Österreichische Gesellschaft für Denkmal- und Ortsbildpflege, *Landhaus und Villa in Niederösterreich 1840–1914* (Wien: Böhlau, 1982); P. Bissegger, *Entre Arcadie et Panthéon: Grandes demeures néoclassiques aux environs de Rolle* (Lausanne: Bibliothèque Historique Vaudoise, 2001).

53 See G. Klette, *Das deutsche Familienhaus* (Leipzig: Knapp, 1878); Muthesius, S.; J. Rodríguez and G. Fehl, *Die Kleinwohnungsfrage … in Europa* (Hamburg: Christians, 1988); Ogata (Ch. V, n. 122); B. Miller Lane (Ch. V, n. 281).

54 'newer architectural …' ('neuere architektonische Kunstwerk, das im Einfamilienhaus vielleicht seinen intimsten und vergeistigsten Ausdruck gefunden hat'): 'Einfamilienhäuser' (above, n. 12), 528.

55 Open interiors: Saint; Scully; Brönner 1994; Muthesius, S.

56 'largest rent-barrack …' ('grösste Mietkasernenstadt der Welt'): H. Hegemann, *Das steinerne Berlin* (Berlin, 1930). § Moving home: in 1895, 31.5% of Berliners moved within a year or less: see D. Langewiesche, 'Wanderungs-bewegungen in der Hochindustrialisierungsperiode', *Vierteljahresschrift für Sozial- und Wirtschaftsgeschichte*, vol. 64 (1966), 11, quoted in Mennekes, 341. See also W. Sombart, *Luxus und Kapitalismus* (Munich: Duncker & Humbolt, 1913), trans. W. R. Dittmar as *Luxury and Capitalism* (Ann Arbor. MI: University of Michigan Press, 1967), 101, 107; P. King, *Private Dwelling: Contemplating the Use of Housing* (London: Routledge, 2004).

57 On 'apartment', see above, n. 50.

Sources of Illustrations

Illustrations are listed by page number.

1 *The Crystal Palace Exhibition, London 1851* (London: Virtue, 1851), 256 [*Art Journal* special issue].

2–3 From C. J. Richardson, *Architectural Remains of the Reigns of Elizabeth and James I* (London: author, 1840).

5 *Consult me* … . Publ. anonymously by the author of *Enquire Within* [Robert Kemp Philp] (Wakefield: W. Nicholson & Sons, 1866).

9 Hall for Carl St. Amory House, Bedford, not built; *Building News*, 10 May 1895.

10–11 T. Knight & Son, *Suggestions for House Decoration* (London, priv. circ., 1880).

13 'Wanddekoration', *Blätter für Kunstgewerbe* (1875), pl. iii.

14 E. Texier, *Tableau de Paris*, vol. 1 (Paris, 1852), 65.

15 Council of Hygiene and Public Health of the Citizens' Association of New York, *Report upon the Sanitary Condition of the City* (New York, 1865), 158.

16–17 *Moniteur des Architectes* (1861), pls 784–85.

18–19 Oskar Mothes, *Unser Heim im Schmucke der Kunst* (Leipzig: Schloemp, 1879). Anteroom p. 11; dining room 2nd edn (Leipzig: Schloemp, 1882), p. 13; salon p. 24; music room p. 15; 'ladies' room' p. 27; 'gentlemens' room' p. 29.

20–21 C. & R. Light, *Designs and Catalogue of Cabinet and Upholstery Furniture* (London, c. 1880).

21 Smithsonian Institution, Washington, D.C.

22 Max Schulz & Co. Möbelfabrik; [Anon.], *Cojen der Berliner Gewerbeaussetlung, 1879* (Berlin: Wasmuth, 1880), pl. 2.

23l & 23r 'Erkerzimmer' and 'Küche', from R. Schumann, *Das Zimmer der Gegenwart* (Leipzig: Hessling, n.d. [1885–87]).

25 'Die Wohnung', lithograph by Willi Baumeister, 1927.

26 *Spemanns Schatzkästlein des guten Rats*, 6th edn (Stuttgart: Spemann, 1892).

28 O. Speckter, 'Der Froschkönig', from the *Münchner Bilderbogen* (Munich: Braun und Schneider), vol. 9, no. 193 (1857).

29 Jakob and Wilhelm Grimm, *German Popular Stories translated from the Kinder und Haus Märchen* (London: C. Baldwyn, 1823).

30 Title page of 'Le Cachemire', from J. N. Bouilly, *Contes à ma fille*, vol. 1 (Paris: Rosa, 1814).

31 From J. P. Hebel, *Allemannische Gedichte* (Leipzig: Wiegand, 1851).

32 K. Dorenwell, *Das deutsche House im Schmucke der Poesie und Kunst*, 3rd edn (Wolffenbüttel: Zwissler, 1893).

33t From *The British Architect and Northern Engineer*, 25 Feb. 1887.

33b H. Havard, *L'Art dans la maison: Grammaire de l'ameublement* (Paris: Rouveyre, 1884), 70.

34 *Album Général d'Ameublement Parisien* (Paris: Camis, n.d [after 1890]).

37 G. Félix Lenoir, *Traité théorique et pratique du tapissier* (Paris: Juliot, n.d. [1886]).

38 G. G. Ungewitter, *Entwürfe zu Möbeln* (Leipzig: Romberg, 1851).

40 M. Kimbel, *Der decorative Ausbau* (Dresden: Gilbers, n.d. [this instalment c. 1880]).

42 C. G. Leland, *Minor Arts* (London: Macmillan, 1880).

43 Ella Rodman Church, *How to Furnish a Home* (New York: Appletons, 1881). Avery Architectural and Fine Art Library, Columbia University, New York.

46 Georg Hirth, *Das deutsche Zimmer der Renaissance. Anregungen zur häuslichen Kunstpflege* (Munich: Hirth, 1879–80).

49 H. Havard, *L'Art dans la maison* (Paris: Rouveyre, 1884).

50 *Cabinet Maker and Art Furnisher* (1885).

51t From *The Penny Magazine*, 28 Aug. 1841, 337.

51l W. & A. C. Russell & Co., stand at the Royal Jubilee Exhibition, Manchester, 1887, from the *Cabinet Maker*, July 1887.

51r *Art Journal* (1876), 365.

52t *American Architect and Building News*, 22 July 1876.

52–53 'Intérieur d'un magazin à Paris. Vitraux émaillés et objets de collection de M. Imberton', *Moniteur des Architectes* (1886), pl. 34.

53t Schäffer & Walcker, 'Der Zimmerschmuck für ein behagliches Heim' (sales catalogue, Berlin: Wasmuth, 1890), 60–61.

54 *Cabinet Maker* (1886), from a calendar for 1887.

55l Carl Müller & Co., sales catalogue (Berlin, 1894).

55r *The Decorator and Furnisher* (New York, 1883).

56 F. Lipperheide, *Muster altdeuscher Leinenstickerei* (Berlin: Lipperheide, 1888).

58 D. Diderot and J. le R. d'Alembert, *Grande Encyclopédie* (Paris, 1751–72), vol. 1 of plates (1762).

59 'Villa Environs Boulogne-sur-Mer, par P. Manguin'. *Revue Générale de l'Architecture et des Travaux Publics* (1867), pl. 43.

60 'Petit salon executé pour M. Duf… fils': H. Havard, *L'Art dans la maison* (Paris: Rouveyre, 1884), pl. 37.

61 H. Kolb and T. Seubert, *Mustersammlung für Tapezierer* (Stuttgart: Wittwer, 1885–88), pl. 41.

62 'Interieur d'Antichambre', in *Le Magazin de Meubles*, issue 3, subseries *Tentures*, no. 23 (Paris: V. Quetin, n.d. [1865]).

63 *The Decorator and Furnisher*, vol. 6, Apr. 1885, 19.

64 By 'M. Chafanjon, architecte'; C. Daly, *L'Architecture privée au XIX siècle (3e série), Décoration intérieure peinte* (Paris: Ducher, 1877), vol. 2, sect. 2, pl. 3.

66t H. Havard, *L'Art dans la maison* (Paris: Rouveyre, 1884), 241.

66b G. Lehnert, *Illustrierte Geschichte des Kunstgewerbes*, vol. 2 (Berlin: Oldenbourg, n.d. [1907]), 434.

67 Watercolour by F. Xaver Nachtmann, 1836; Pierpont Morgan Library, New York.

68 Villa Meissner, Leipzig, architect W. Cremer, exec. M. Bösenberg. *Architektonisches Skizzenbuch* (1882), no. 5, pl. 3.

69t John Claudius Loudon, *An Encyclopedia of Cottage, Farm and Villa Architecture and Furniture* (London: Longman, 1833), 274–76.

69b Messrs. Boucher & Cousland, architects, and J. Steel, plasterer; from W. Millar, *Plastering Plain and Decorative* (London: Batsford, 1899), 140.

70 From the C. A. Nölting House, Lübeck, 1835. Museum für Kunst und Gewerbe, Hamburg.

71 Wilhelm von Zahn, *Die schönsten Ornamente und merkwürdigsten Gemälde aus Pompeji, Herkulaneum und Stabiae* (Berlin: Reimer, 1828–59), vol. 2 (parts 1–5), no. 4 (1842), pl. 35. Villa excavated in 1833. For Goethe, see Ch. III, n. 192.

72 M. Rehsener, *Silhouetten zu Gregorovius' Euphorion* (Leipzig, 1882); reproduced in Jane E. Harrison, 'Pompeii in Black and White', *Magazine of Art* (1882), 101.

74 Victoria & Albert Museum, London, given by P. J. Gordon, Esq. E. 876-1982.

75t 'Panneau en papier peint … décor Louis XVI', from J. Mesnard, *Les Merveilles de l'exposition de 1867* (Paris: Lahure, 1867–68).

75l Klassik Stiftung, Weimar.

75r View of the Salon Princes Radziwill in Schloss Ruhberg (Kowary-Ciszyca, Silesia), after 1831. Hessische Hausstiftung, Museum Schloss Fasanerie, Eichenzell bei Fulda.

76 *Building News*, 11 Oct. 1872 and 8 May 1874.

77 Lewis Forman Day, *Everyday Art: Short Essays on the Arts not Fine* (London: Batsford, 1882), 217.

78 Photo Irvine Green.

79 Jean Pape, *Musterzimmer*, *Vollständige Decorationen für bürgerliche und herrschaftliche Wohnunge in Form und Farbe*, 2nd edn (Dresden: Gilbers, 1890), vol. 1, part 2.

80 J. Verdellet, *Manuel géométrique du tapissier* (Paris: author, 1851), pl. v.

81 *Album Général d'Ameublement Parisien* (Paris: Camis, n.d [after 1890]).

83 Queen Karoline's bedroom in the Residenz, Munich. Watercolour by Wilhelm Relfen, 1820. Wittelsbacher Ausgleichsfonds, Munich.

85 *Cabinet Maker*, Feb. 1889.

86t M. Santi, *Modèles des meubles et des décorations intérieures … dessinés par M. Santi* (Paris: Bance, 1828).

86b Watercolour, Victoria & Albert Museum, London, E 789-1970.

87 A. & L. Streitenfeld, *Ausstattung vornehmer Wohnräume* (Berlin: Claesen, 1888–).

88t Johann Andreas Romberg, *Dekorationen innerer Räumer* (Munich: Fischer, 1834), pl. 9.

88l 'Einseitiger Thürvorhang. Motiv nach Prignot', Ferdinand Luthmer, *Werkbuch des Tapezierers. Eine praktische Darstellung* (Berlin: Spemann, 1884–86), 139.

88r 'Thürvorhang im modernen Reniassancestil', Luthmer (as above), 163.

89 G. Félix Lenoir, *Traité théorique et pratique du tapissier* (Paris: Juliot, n.d. [1886])

90, 91 T. Pasquier, *Dessins d'ameublement* (Paris, n.d. [c. 1840]).

92 W. Kick, *Dekorationen und Möbel deutsch-nationalen-Kunstgewerbeausstellung München 1888* (Stuttgart: Engelhorn, 1889), pl. 3.

93t E. Maincent, *La Disposition des appartements: Intérieurs complets* (Paris: Garde Meuble, n.d. [c. 1886]), pl. 16.

93b *Gewerbehalle* (1880), pl. 64.

94t F. H. Norton, *Illustrated Historical Register of the Centennial Exhibition, Philadelphia, 1876, and of the Exposition Universelle, Paris, 1878* (New York: American News Co., 1879).

94b E. Prignot, *L'Architecture, la décoration, l'ameublement* (Claesen, n.d. [early 1870s]).

95 E. Foussier, *Bibliothèque d'ameublement* (Dourdan: Thézard, n.d. [c. 1896]).

96t *The British Architect and Northern Engineer*, 26 Jul. 1878.

96b Ernst Plassmann, *Designs for Furniture* (New York, 1877).

97t *Building News*, 24 Dec. 1868.

97b *Art Journal* (1879), 121.

98t Phillip Niederhöfer, *Frankfurter Möbelbazar*, 4th series (1884), pl. 72.

98b Photograph from a loose-leaf folder, *Ausstellung von A. Bembé in Mainz, Düsseldorf* (n.p.: n.d. [1880]), Darmstadt Technische Universitäts Bibliothek.

99 Thiollet et Roux, *Nouveau Recueil de menuiserie et de décorations intérieures et exterieures* (Paris: Bance Ainé, 1837), pl. 32.

100 *The Builder*, 4 Jul. 1885, xix.

101 *American Architect and Building News*, 15 Jan. 1876.

102 Executed by F. Wirth's Söhne, K. Hofebenisten, Stuttgart; *Gewerbehalle* (1880), 22.

103 Photo courtesy Mircea Hortopan.

104 From O. H. P. Silber (ed.), *Schloss Hummelshain* (Kattowitz, 1897), pl. 36.

106 Musée d'Orsay, Paris. Photo RMN/Hervé Lewandowski.

107 E. Keary with J. G. Sowerby and T. Crane, *At Home Again* (London: Marcus Ward, 1886).

108t Thomas Hope, *Household Furniture and Interior Decoration* (London: Longman, 1807), 22.

108b H. Havard, *L'Art dans la maison* (Paris: Rouveyre, 1884), 256; [Anon.], 'Principles governing the arrangement of movable decorating', *Decorator and Furnisher*, vol. 19, Feb. 1892, 185–86.

109 *Amateur Work Illustrated*, vol. 3 (1883), 380–81 (cabinet), and vol. 2 (1882), 441 (overdoors).

110 A. & L. Streitenfeld, *Ausstattung vornehmer Wohnräume* (Berlin: Claesen, 1888–).

111 O. H. P. Silber (ed.), *Schloss Hummelshain* (Kattowitz, 1897), 112–13.

112–13 *Building News*, 18 Jan. 1878. p. 112: *top* W. R. Lethaby, *bottom* J. O. Harris. p. 113: *top* W. K. Booth, *bottom* A. Marshall. Texts in *Building News*, 28 Dec. 1877, 664; 4 Jan. 1878, 23; 18 Jan. 1878, 5.

114t *Illustrierte Zeitung*, Leipzig, 27 Dec. 1873, 496.

114b Collection Maciet, Bibliothèque du Musée des Arts Décoratifs, Paris.

115 *L'Art Pour Tous* (1868–69), no. 224.

116 Ill. by W. Czerner, *Tygodnik Illustrowany* (Warsaw), vol. 2 (new series), 23. Jan. 1876, 416–17.

117 After photo by Carl Teufel; *Art Journal* (1890), 13.

118l & r *Innendekoration* (1893), 68–69.

119 P. Naumann, *Möbel und Zimmer auf der deutsch-nationalen Kunstgewerbeausstellung München 1888* (Dresden: Gilbers, 1889).

121 John Johnson Collection, Bodleian Library, Oxford; Oil and Candles box 2.

123 Jean Pape, *Musterzimmer, Vollständige Decorationen …*, 2nd edn (Dresden: Gilbers, 1890), vol. 1, part 1.

124 Watercolour by Franz Malek, 1836. Historisches Museum der Stadt Wien, Vienna.

125 Villa von Arnim, Sanssouci, Potsdam, 1864. *Architektonisches Skizzenbuch* (1864), no. 58, pl. 1.

126 *Journal für Bau- und Möbelschreiner, Tapezierer …* (1843), new series 1, no. 5.

127 Album Gräfin Clothilde von Wylich und Lottum, Bildarchiv, Germanisches Nationalmuseum, Nuremberg.

128 Salon in the Governor's Residence, Hermannstadt (now Sibiu, Romania), *c.* 1840. Watercolour. Private collection.

129 Carl Graeb, *Album von Schloss Babelsberg* (Potsdam: Riegel, 1853).

130 Watercolour by Jean Baptiste van Moer, *c.* 1860, Château de Compiegne. Photo RMN/Franck Raux.

131t *Decorator and Furnisher*, Jan. 1895.

131b J. W. Facey, *Practical House Decoration* (London: Crosby Lockwood, 1892), 21.

132t Library by C. Schnitzler, *Architektonisches Skizzenbuch* (1881), no. 6 , pl. 1.

132b Living room in the Schloss Gross Merzdorf (Marciszów), Silesia, by C. Grosser; *Architektonisches Skizzenbuch* (1877), no. 2, pl. 1.

133t & b Living room and dining room by Jean Pape, *Musterzimmer, Vollständige Decorationen …*, 2nd edn (Dresden: Gilbers, 1890), vol. 1, part 1, and vol. 2, part 3.

134l & r Designer unknown; Ferdinand Luthmer, *Malerische Innenräume moderner Wohnungen in Aufnahmen nach der Natur* (Frankfurt am Main: Keller, 1884), pls. 5, 6.

135 Museum of the City of New York. Photo Scott Hyde.

136t Jean Pape, *Musterzimmer* (as above), vol. 1, part 6.

136l Phillip Niederhöfer, *Frankfurter Möbelbazar*, 3rd series (1883), pl. 58.

136r Christopher Dresser, *Principles of Decorative Design* (London, 1873), pl. 2.

138 Charles Percier and Pierre-François-Léonard Fontaine, *Receuil de décorations intérieures …* (Paris: the authors, 1801–12), pl. 13.

138–39 Thomas Hope, *Household Furniture and Interior Decoration* (London: Longman, 1807), pl. 6.

139 'Spielzimmer', Johann Andreas Romberg, *Dekorationen innerer Räumer* (Munich: Fischer, 1834), pl. 32.

140l *Moniteur des Architectes*, vol. 54 (1859), pl. 642.

140r *Furniture Gazette*, 3 Apr. 1875, 432.

141t Bruce J. Talbert, *Gothic Forms Applied to Furniture …* (Bristol: Birbeck, 1867), pl. 11.

141b *American Architect and Building News*, 5 May 1877.

142tl H. Hudson Holly, 'Modern Dwellings': 'II: Color Decoration', *Harper's New Monthly Magazine*, vol. 53 (June 1876), 61.

142tr William Watt, *Art Furniture from Designs by E. W. Godwin and Others* (London: Batsford, 1877), pl. 2.

142bl & bc H. Havard, *L'Art dans la maison* (Paris: Rouveyre, 1884), 44, 45.

142br [Anon.; E. Gardner?], 'Hints on Domestic Decoration', *Harpers*, vol. 86, Mar. 1884, 579, 582.

143 J. W. Facey, *Practical House Decoration* (London: Crosby Lockwood, 1882), 50, 52, 53.

144, 145 Lewis Foreman Day, *Everyday Art: Short Essays on the Arts not Fine* (London: Batsford, 1882), 194–95.

146t *Decorator and Furnisher*, vol. 3, Dec 1883, 89.

146b E. Keary with J. G. Sowerby and T. Crane, *At Home Again* (London: Marcus Ward, 1886).

147tl *Garde Meuble*, subsection *Collection Tentures*, 175th instalment, no. 513 (*c.* 1867).

147tr C. & R. Light, *Designs and Catalogue of Cabinet and Upholstery Furniture* (London, *c.* 1880), pl. 178.

147b E. B. Lamb, 'Villa Norman Style', *Architectural Magazine*, vol. 1 (1834), 338.

148t 'Wiener Möbel Formen', *Wiener Zeitschrift für Kunst, Literatur, Theater und Mode*, no. 122, 11 Oct. 1834.

148b *Architektonische Rundschau* (1889), pl. 67.

149t 'Innenraum mit Gitter-Zierwerk nach amerikanischer Art, deutschen Verhältnissen angepasst. Original-Komposition von Hermann Werle', *Innendekoration* (1894), 124.

149c 'Inside the house of [the painter] Friedrich August Kaulbach in Munich, furnished by the fine and decorating artist Lorenz Gedon', later 1870s. Georg Hirth, *Das deutsche Zimmer der Renaissance* (Munich: Hirth, 1879–80), 113.

149bl 'Artistic Homes, and How to Make Them', *The Lady's World* [*The Lady*] (1887), 344–46.

149br H. Havard, *L'Art dans la maison* (Paris: Rouveyre, 1884), pl. 24,

150t A. Simoneton, *La Décoration intérieure* (Paris: Aulainier, 1893–95).

150b 'La chambre des paons', E. Maincent, *La Disposition des appartements* (Paris: Garde Meuble, n.d. [*c.* 1886]), pl. 16.

151t Ernst Wasmuth, *Die Tapezierkunst. Vorlagen für Dekoration* (Berlin: Wasmuth, 1895).

151b *The British Architect and Northern Engineer*, 3 Sep. 1880.

152 Photo by Bedford Lemere, no. 0828. National Monuments Record/English Heritage.

153 *Harpers*, vol. 64, Apr. 1882, 737.

154 Museum Georg Schäfer, Schweinfurt.

156, 157 Oskar Mothes, *Unser Heim im Schmucke der Kunst*, 2nd edn (Leipzig: Schloemp, 1879), pls. 16, 19.

158l Formerly Corcoran Gallery Washington, D.C.

158r Watts Gallery, Compton, Surrey.

159t Engraving by J. A. Darnstedt in W. G. Becker, *Das Seifersdorfer Tal* (Leipzig: Voss, 1792).

159b Museum Georg Schäfer, Schweinfurt.

160t Drawing in the Nationalgalerie, Berlin.

160b From the *Art Journal* (1885), 416–18.

161t 'Chambre de château au XIVe siècle', E.-E. Viollet-le-Duc, *Dictionnaire raisonné du mobilier français* (Paris: Bance, 1858–75): vol. 1 (1855–57), pl. 14 (p. 364).

161b Jean-Michel Moreau le Jeune, *The Delights of Motherhood* (1777).

162t *Family Economist*, vol. 2 (1849).

162b George Cruikshank, *The Bottle* (London: David Bogue, 1847), pls 1, 5.

163l & r 'Glückliche Menschen: 1. Im Schloss; 2. In der Hütte', after paintings by C. E. Böttcher, *Die Gartenlaube* (1867), 124–25, 253.

164l & r L. Richter, *Schillers Lied von der Glocke in Bildern von Ludwig Richter* (Leipzig: Wigand, 1857).

165bl The letter 'z', from O. Pletsch, *Die Kinderstube in 36 Bildern* (Hamburg, 1860).

165br Room 'fitted and furnished' by Kendal, Milne & Co., Manchester. *The British Architect and Northern Engineer*, 18 Dec. 1885.

166 Musée du Louvre, Paris. Photo RMN/Gérard Blot/Christian Jean.

167 Musée du Louvre, Paris. Photo RMN/Gérard Blot

168 Oskar Mothes, *Unser Heim im Schmucke der Kunst* (Leipzig: Schloemp, 1879), 23–24.

169 Phillip Niederhöfer, *Frankfurter Möbelbazar*, 4th series (1884), pl. 98.

171 H. Kolb and T. Seubert, *Mustersammlung für Tapezierer* (Stuttgart: Wittwer, 1885–88), pl. 6.

174 A. & L. Streitenfeld, *Ausstattung vornehmer Wohnräume* (Berlin: Claesen, 1888–).

176l Henry A. Page House, Montrose, NJ, from the *New York Sketchbook of Architecture*, vol. 3, Apr. 1876. Photo courtesy Avery Architectural and Fine Arts Library, Columbia University, New York.

176r 'Corner in a study designed and executed by G. Seidl', *Zeitschrift des Bayerischen Kunstgewerbevereins zu München* (1884), pl. 28.

177t Georg Hirth, *Das deutsche Zimmer der Renaissance* (Munich: Hirth, 1879–80), 77.

177l & r 'Canopied Settee at W. Reade-Revell's, Esq.' and 'Arkley House, Barnet', *The Lady's World* [*The Lady*] (1887), 381, 344.

178 Max Schulz & Co. Möbelfabrik: [Anon.], *Cojen der Berliner Gewerbeausstellung, 1879* (Berlin: Wasmuth, 1880), pl. 22.

179r & l G. G. Ungewitter, *Entwürfe zu Stadt- und Landhäusern* (Leipzig: Romberg, 1856), pl. 4.

179b H. Kolb and T. Seubert, *Mustersammlung für Tapezierer* (Stuttgart: Wittwer, 1885–88), pl. 16.

180t Leicester City Art Gallery, reproduced in the *Art Journal* (1877), 280.

180b 'Einiges über das Arrangement von Erker Ausbildungen', *Innendekoration* (1893), 129–33.

181tl A. Scheffers, *Bauformen und Farben … des Inneren*, part 3 of the *Architektonische Formenschule*, 3rd edn (Leipzig: Gebhardt, 1880), 72.

181tr Eugene Clarence Gardner, *Home Interiors* (Boston, MA: Osgood, 1878), 395.

181b Vienna apartment by K. Tietz, from L. Klasen, *Grundriss-Vorbilder von Wohn- und Geschäftshäusern* (Leipzig: Baumgartner, 1884), pl. 28. Apartment by R. N. Shaw from H. Muthesius, *Das englische Haus* (Berlin: Wasmuth, 1904), vol. 2, 158.

182tl F. Robinson, *Sketches for Ornamental Villas* (London: J. Carpenter, 1830).

182tr Photo: author.

182bl Wimbledon Common by E. J. May, *The British Architect and Northern Engineer*, 11 Dec. 1885.

182br Design for Parson's House, Moor Green, Nottingham, from *Building News*, 6 Mar. 1874.

183t Etching by Johann Michael Voltz, 1823.

183b Ackermann's *Repository of Arts* (London: Rudolph Ackermann, 1809–28), series 1, vol. 6 (Nov. 1811), pl. 27.

184 J. Storer, *A Description of Fonthill* (London: Clarke, 1812).

185 Engraving from J. G. Hertel, *Historiae et Allegoriae … Cesaris Ripae* (Augsburg, n.d. [*c.* 1758–60]).

186 Victoria & Albert Museum, London./V&A Images.

187tl E. B. Lamb, 'Design for a Villa in the Style of Architecture of the Thirteenth Century', *Architectural Magazine*, vol. 2 (1835), 263.

187tr Present whereabouts unknown. I am grateful for the help of Jane Wainwright and Abbotsford House.

187b After a watercolour by Waller Hugh Paton. Private collection.

188tl After a drawing by W. Ramberg, from W. G. Becker, *Taschenbuch zum geselligen Vergnügen*, ed. F. Kind (Leipzig: Voss & Leo, 1793–1830), vol. for 1815.

188tr *Art Journal* (1874), 300.

188bl Johann Christiaan Bendorp, *Liedjes van Matthias Claudius* (Leeuwarden: G. T. N. Suringar), 1833.

188br From Theodor Gottlieb von Hippel, *Über die Ehe* (Berlin, 1774).

190t *Architektonisches Skizzenbuch* (1877), no. 3, pl. 1.

190b Sammlung Oskar Reinhart, Winterthur.

191 E. Strahan, *Mr. Vanderbilt's House and Collection*, vol. 1 (Boston: G. Barrie, 1883–84), pl. 114.

192 Premiated at the Patent- and Musterschutz Ausstellung, Frankfurt am Main, 1881; from *The Builder*, 3 Nov. 1883.

193t *The Lady* [*Lady's World*] (1887), 241–42.

193b [Anon.], *Cojen der Berliner Gewerbeaussetllung, 1879* (Berlin: Wasmuth, 1880), pl. 17.

194 Henry Havard, *L'Art dans la maison* (1884), 292.

195 Schäffer & Walcker, 'Der Zimmerschmuck für ein behagliches Heim' (sales catalogue, Berlin: Wasmuth, 1890), 145.

196 L. Feuchère, *L'Art Industriel* (Paris: Goupil, n.d. [1850s]), part 1, pl. 68.

197 *Architektonisches Skizzenbuch* (1878), no. 2, pl. 1.

199 W. Kick, *Dekorationen und Möbel deutsch-nationalen-Kunstgewerbeausstellung München 1888* (Stuttgart: Engelhorn, 1889), pl. 12.

200 Jean Pape, *Musterzimmer, Vollständige Decorationen …*, 2nd edn (Dresden: Gilbers, 1890), vol. 1, part 4.

202l Martin Kimbel, *Der decorative Ausbau* (Dresden: Gilbers, n.d. [this instalment *c.* 1880]), pls 3, 39, 42.

202r John Claudius Loudon, *An Encyclopedia of Cottage, Farm and Villa Architecture and Furniture* (London: Longman, 1833), 1052, 1091, 1104.

203t bpk/Kunstbibliothek der Staatliche Museen zu Berlin.

203b P. Naumann, *Möbel und Zimmer auf der deutsch-nationalen Kunstgewerbeausstellung München 1888* (Dresden: Gilbers, 1889).

204 By kind permission of the German Embassy, Paris. Photo AKG Images/Erich Lessing.

205 *Album Général d'Ameublement Parisien* (Paris: Camis, n.d [after 1890]).

208 Henry Havard, *Dictionnaire de l'ameublement* (Paris: Quantin, 1887–89), vol. 3, pl. 5.

209 *Zeitschrift des Bayerischen Kunstgewerbevereins zu München* (1886), 4.

210t Musée National du Château de Versailles/Photo RMN.

210b T. Villeneuve, *Intérieurs d'appartements de haut style* (Paris: Guérinet, n.d. [*c.* 1880]).

211 *Album Général d'Ameublement Parisien* (Paris: Camis, n.d [after 1890]).

214t Henry Shaw, *Details of Elizabethan Architecture* (London: Pickering, 1839), pl. 40.

214b C. J. Richardson, *Architectural Remains of the Reigns of Elizabeth and James I* (London: author, 1840).

215 Joseph Nash, *The Mansions of England in the Olden Time* (London: M'Lean, 1849), vol. 4, pl. 13.

216 Drawn by S. W. Fairholt; from Samuel Carter Hall's *The Baronial Halls and Picturesque Edifices of England* (London, 1848), vol. 1.

217t T. H. Turner and J. H. Parker, *Some Account of Domestic Architecture in England* (1859).

217b A. W. N. Pugin, *The True Principles of Pointed or Christian Architecture* (London: Bohn, 1841).

218t Photo courtesy Country Life.

218b *The Crystal Palace Exhibition, London 1851* (London: Virtue, 1851), 256.

219 Andrew Jackson Downing, *The Architecture of Country Houses* (New York: Appletons, 1850), 390.

220 G. Rothbart (ed.), *Das Lutherzimmer …* (Nuremberg: Stein, 1845).

221 F. Schorbach, *Architektonische Entwürfe von Edwin Oppler* (Leipzig, 1885), 20.

222t Kupferstichkabinett, Berlin, SM 22 d 95.

222b Engraving by Peter Carl Geisler, published by Friedrich Campe, Nuremberg, *c.* 1825.

223t Late 19th-century photograph, from the Stadtarchiv Nürnberg.

223b 'Studier/Zunft/Jagdstube', from Georg Hirth, *Das deutsche Zimmer der Renaissance* (Munich: Hirth, 1879–80), 168.

224 'Der Renaissance-Fez', *Fliegende Blätter*, vol. 70, no. 1754 (n.d. [1879]), 72.

225 Article by A. Hoffmann in *Deutsche Bauzeitung*, 17 Oct. 1896, 528.

226 'Heraldische Ausstellung Berlin', *Illustrierte Frauenzeitung* (1882), 176.

227t P. Walter, 'Nachbildung von Waffen und Rüstungen aus der C .W. Fleischmannschen Papiermache-Fabrik zu Nürnberg'. From the Fleischmann papers in the library of the Germanisches Nationalmuseum, Nuremberg: *C. W. Fleischmann Nuernberg, Verkaufskatalog* (Nuremberg, n.d. [*c.* 1867]).

227b L. von Kramer and K. Gerok, *Lob des tugendsamen Weibes. Sprüche Salomonis* (Munich: Stroefer, n.d. [1885]), Proverb 30.

228 P. Niederhöfer, *Frankfurter Möbelbazar*, 2nd series (1882), pl. 33.

229 Jean Pape, *Musterzimmer, Vollständige Decorationen …*, 2nd edn (Dresden: Gilbers, 1890), vol. 1, part 4.

230 [Anon.], *Traute Wohnräume* (Berlin: Wasmuth, 1892).

233 Photo Bastin Evrard.

234 P. Wytsman, *Intérieurs et mobiliers de styles anciens* (Brussels: P. Wytsman, 1900 edn).

236 *Bouwkundig Tijdschrift*, vol. 1 (1881), pl. 13.

237 *Bouwkundig Tijdschrift*, vol. 4 (1884), pl. 46.

239t [Anon.], 'Domestic Architecture', *Penny Magazine*, 14 Sept. 1839, 356–57.

239b H. R. Robertson, 'Life on the Upper Thames', *Art Journal* (1874), 174–75.

241t C. L. Eastlake, *A History of the Gothic Revival* (London: Longmans, 1872), 345.

241b *Country Life*, vol. 150, 30 Aug. 1973, 554–57.

242t *The House Furnisher and Decorators', Upholsterers' and Cabinet-makers' Monthly Journal*, Oct. 1872, 136.

242c *Designs of furniture … specially designed for James Shoolbred & Compy., Tottenham Court Road* (London, n.d. [*c.* 1876]), pl. 5.

242b *Architect*, 7 Nov. 1874.

243l *Magazine of Art* (1883), 184–88.

243r *American Architect and Building News*, 24 Jul. 1880.

244 *Building News*, 19 Sept. 1874.

245 *American Architect and Building News*, 11 Mar. 1882.

246 J. G. Sowerby and Thomas Crane, *At Home* (London: M. Ward, 1881).

247tl Kate Greenaway, *Mother Goose* (London: Routledge, 1881), 25.

247tr *The British Architect and Northern Engineer*, 9 Jan. 1885.

247b Illustration by Randolph Caldecott, from William Cowper, *The Diverting History of John Gilpin* (London: Routledge, 1878).

248 *Cabinet Maker*, Jan. 1885.

250t 'Original design by C. Gill, furniture designer for the trade'; *Cabinet Maker*, Jul. 1882.

250b 'Corner of a Boudoir exhibited at the Health Exhibition by Messrs W. A. & S. Smee'; *Cabinet Maker*, Aug. 1884.

251 'Chimney Corner in Dining Room, Stonelands, Sussex'; *Cabinet Maker*, June 1887.

252 *Harper's Weekly*, 15 Jul. 1876.

253t A. Little, *Early New England Interiors* (Boston, MA: Williams 1878).

253b *Harper's New Monthly Magazine*, Nov. 1874.

254t *Art Amateur*, Mar. 1886, 89.

254b Sunset Hall, Lawrence, Long Island. *American Architect and Building News*, 2 Feb. 1884.

255 Photo courtesy Metropolitan Museum of Art, New York.

256 *Decorator and Furnisher*, vol. 13, Nov. 1888, 53.

258t John Claudius Loudon, *An Encyclopedia of Cottage, Farm and Villa Architecture and Furniture* (London: Longman, 1833), 276.

258c William T. Sugg, *The Domestic Uses of Coal Gas …* (London: W. King, 1884).

258b Eugene Clarence Gardner, *The House that Jill Built …* (Springfield, MA: Adams, 1882), 21.

259t J. Pickering Putnam, *The Open Fireplace in all Ages* (Boston, MA: Osgood, 1880).

259bl *Cabinet Maker*, Oct. 1882, 70.

259br By Charles M. Burns, jun.; *American Architect and Building News*, 3 Sept. 1881.

260t *American Architect and Building News*, 11 Aug. 1877.

260b 'For Mr. A. Besant', *Architect*, 23 June 1877.

261t *Country Life*, vol. 150, 30 Aug. 1973, 554–57.

261b Richardson Studio, Brookline, Boston, MA, in *American Architect and Building News*, 27 Dec. 1884.

262b *Moniteur des Architectes* (1885), pl. 26.

262t *Gewerbehalle* (1879), 33.

263tl *The British Architect and Northern Engineer*, 16 Jan. 1885.

263tr *Cabinet Maker*, Aug. 1886, 41.

263b E. Keary with J. G. Sowerby and T. Crane, *At Home Again* (London: Marcus Ward, 1886).

264 Eugen Napoleon Neureuther, *Baierische Gebirgslieder* (Tübingen: Cotta, 1831; here 1834 edn).

265tl Architect M. A. Gruska; *Revue Générale de l'Architecture et des Travaux Publics* (1869), pl. 14.

265tr From A. Rosenberg, *Defregger* (Bielefeld: Velhagen & Klasing, 1897), 56.

265b *Gewerbehalle* (1864), 31.

266 Georg Hirth, *Das deutsche Zimmer der Renaissance* (Munich: Hirth, 1879–80), 5.

267 Ludwig II Museum, Chiemsee-Herrenchiemsee/Wittelsbacher Ausgleichsfonds, Munich.

268 *Zeitschrift des Kunstgewerbevereins in München* (1878).

271t Room no. 86. Photo Munich Stadtmuseum.

271b Villa Schön, Worms (destr.); *Zeitschrift des Bayerischen Kunstgewerbevereins zu München* (1886), pls 35–36.

272 'Skizze zu einem Wirtschaftszimmer', Georg Hirth, *Das deutsche Zimmer der Renaissance* (Munich: Hirth, 1879–80), 29.

275 'Jagdzimmer', *Illustrierte Frauenzeitung*, 11 Dec. 1887.

276t *Architektonische Rundschau* (1886), pl. 76.

276b *Illustrierte Frauenzeitung*, 15 Nov. 1896, 88.

278t Bibliothèque-Musée de la Comédie-Française, Paris. Photo Patrick Lorette.

278b Present whereabouts unknown; reproduced in J. Bourne and V. Brett, *Lighting in the Domestic Interior* (London: Sotheby's, 1991).

279l & r P. Lacroix, *XVIII siècle: Lettres, sciences et arts, France 1700–1789* (Paris: Firmin Didot, 1878), 243.

281 T. Child, 'An Artist's House', *Decorator and Furnisher*, vol. 4, June 1884, 99.

282 A. Simoneton, *La Décoration intérieure* (Paris: Aulainier, 1893–95), 150.

283 *Album Général d'Ameublement Parisien* (Paris: Camis, n.d [after 1890])

284t Henry Havard, *Dictionnaire de l'ameublement* (Paris: Quantin, 1887–89), vol. 1, pl. 5; signed 'Mangonnot del.'

284bl *Album Général d'Ameublement Parisien* (Paris: Camis, n.d [after 1890]).

284br *Revue Générale de l'Architecture et des Travaux Publics* (1889), 41–44, pl. 21.

287 'Gravure van Smeeton Tilly', S. O. Roosjen et al., *Merkwaardigheden von Hindeloopen* (Lleuwarden, 1855).

288t C. von Lützow, *Kunst und Kunstgewerbe auf der Wiener Weltausstelung 1873* (Leipzig: Seemann, 1875), 459.

288b R. Mejborg, *Gamle danske Hjem i det 16de, 17de og 18de Århundrede* (Copenhagen: Roms, 1888).

289 P. Naumann, *Möbel und Zimmer auf der deutsch-nationalen Kunstgewerbeausstellung München 1888* (Dresden: Gilbers, 1889), 119. Photo in Städtisches Museum Flensburg.

290 C. Nyrop, *Fra den Kunstindustrielle Udstilling* (Copenhagen: Schubothes, 1879).

291t & b Photos courtesy Muzeum Tatrzańskie, Zakopane. I am much indebted to its director, Teresa Jabłońska.

292 S. Witkiewicz, *Tygodnik Illustrowany*, vol. 12 (new series): 29 Dec. 1888, 404 and 26 Jan. 1889, 69.

293 Photograph by Johannes Jaeger, late 19th century.

294 Photo Eric Olsen, *c.* 1900. With thanks to I. J. G. Røkke, Billedsamlingen, Universitetsbiblioteket i Trondheim.

295 R. T. Pritchett, *Art Journal* (1877), 34.

297 Fru Emma Gad (ed.), *Vort Hjem* (Copenhagen: Nordiske Forlag, 1903), vol. 3, 148.

298 C. and K. Larsson, *Ett Hem* (Stockholm: Bonnier, 1899).

299 Photo courtesy Skagens Museum.

300 Eugène-Emmanuel Viollet-le-Duc, *Histoire d'une maison* (Paris: Bibliothèque d'Éducation, n.d. [1874]).

302 Historisches Museum der Stadt Wien, Vienna.

303 After Carl Bennewitz von Loefen, jr.; *Illustrierte Frauenzeitung*, 1 Jan. 1895, 84. bpk/Kunstbibliothek der Staatliche Museen zu Berlin.

304 *Die Gartenlaube* (1888), 821.

305l *Die Gartenlaube* (1888), 661.

305r *Die Gartenlaube* (1887), 247.

307 Architect Julius Faulwasser; 'Neuere Hamburger Küchen-Einrichtungen und Anlagen', *Innendekoration* (1893), 145–48.

308t F. Kiefhaber, *Moderne Möbel* (1894; no title page), Kunstbibliothek Berlin.

308b F. Luthmer, 'Schmucke Küchen', *Innendekoration* (1893), 153–57.

309 Georg Hirth, *Das deutsche Zimmer der Renaissance* (Munich: Hirth, 1879–80), 121.

312l W. H. Loftie, *A Plea for Art in the House* (London: Macmillan, 1876).

312r 'Painting by E .L. Henry', Clarence Cook, *The House Beautiful* (New York: Scribner, 1877), 256.

313 Georg Hirth, *Das deutsche Zimmer der Renaissance* (Munich: Hirth, 1879–80), 21.

315t Apartments in Prenzlauer Berg, Berlin. Photo: author.

315b W. Claude Frederic, architect, *American Architect and Building News*, 2 Aug. 1884.

Index